MW01174775

Bridging the European Divide

November 2007

Dear Shirley,

Thank you for your wonderful support over my short time at this dynamic college. Your advocacy for international issues inspired me to do my utmost here at FSC. I'm grateful for your efforts. With great appreciation, Josh Spero

Bridging the European Divide

Middle Power Politics and Regional Security Dilemmas

JOSHUA B. SPERO

ROWMAN & LITTLEFIELD PUBLISHERS, INC.
Lanham • Boulder • New York • Toronto • Oxford

ROWMAN & LITTLEFIELD PUBLISHERS, INC.

Published in the United States of America
by Rowman & Littlefield Publishers, Inc.
A wholly owned subsidiary of The Rowman & Littlefield Publishing Group, Inc.
4501 Forbes Boulevard, Suite 200, Lanham, MD 20706
www.rowmanlittlefield.com

P.O. Box 317, Oxford OX2 9RU, UK

British Library Cataloguing in Publication Information Available

Library of Congress Cataloging-in-Publication Data

Spero, Joshua B.
  Bridging the European divide : middle power politics and regional security dilemmas /
Joshua B. Spero.
    p.   cm.
  Includes bibliographical references and index.
  ISBN 0-7425-3553-3 (cloth : alk. paper)
  1. Poland—Foreign relations—1989– 2. Geopolitics—Poland. 3. Europe,
Central—Politics and government—20th century. I. Title.
  DK4450.S68   2004
  327.4'009'049—dc22

                                                    2004002715
Printed in the United States of America

♾™ The paper used in this publication meets the minimum requirements of American
National Standard for Information Sciences—Permanence of Paper for Printed Library
Materials, ANSI/NISO Z39.48-1992.

For Ellen, my wife, in honor of our long Polish heritages

Contents

Abbreviations

CFE	Conventional Forces in Europe
CMEA	Council for Mutual Economic Assistance
CSCE	Conference on Security and Cooperation in Europe
CSFR	Czech and Slovak Federative Republic
EC	European Community
EEU	East European Report
EU	European Union
FBIS	Foreign Broadcast Information Service
FRG	Federal Republic of Germany
GDR	German Democratic Republic
JPRS	Joint Publications Research Service
MSZ	*Ministerstwo Spraw Zagranicznych* (Ministry of Foreign Affairs)
NATO	North Atlantic Treaty Organization
PfP	Partnership for Peace
PPN	*Polskie Porozumienie Niepodleglosciowe* (Polish Alliance for Independence)
SOV	Soviet Union Report
ULB	Ukraine–Lithuania–Belorussia
UN	United Nations
USSR	Union of Soviet Socialist Republics
WEU	West European Report

Acknowledgments

Anyone who begins the long journey to write a dissertation and then refine, craft, and even restructure it into a book never quite knows the depth and challenge of completing that quest until that volume reaches the final print.

From my dissertation advisors, Bruce Parrott, Ilya Prizel, and Arthur Rachwald, I learned that focus, determination, and clarity pay off when the doctoral student reaches critical turning points. Their patience and vision gave me the direction I needed both when I undertook this great dissertation task and when I actually completed the dissertation. Their advice and steadfastness for the dissertation and for my transition into academe to become a professor of international relations and comparative politics made the years 1999 and 2000 particularly rewarding. In the end, the dissertation became a much better product because of their direction, and the sole responsibility for its content rests with me.

Undoubtedly, this book could never have evolved if it hadn't been for my dissertation committee of Bruce Parrott, Ilya Prizel, Arthur Rachwald, Stephen Szabo, and Jeffrey Simon, who pushed me to new heights and made my work much better as a result of their incisive questions and insightful recommendations. Their advice had a significant impact on expanding my research and writing. They have been wonderful colleagues with whom I've worked for many years.

Today, this book can see the light of day with the essential efforts, valuable reinforcement, and consistent reassurance from the excellent managerial and editorial staff at Rowman & Littlefield, Susan McEachern, Matthew Hammon, April Leo, and Jeska Horgan-Kobelski.

To the outstanding faculties, staff, and administrators with whom I've had the pleasure to work—the Department of Government at Dartmouth College, the Department of Political Science at Merrimack College, and, since 2002, in the

Department of Social Sciences at Fitchburg State College, I give my humble thanks for their advocacy and collegiality. To the Chairman of the Fitchburg State College Social Sciences Department, Michael Turk, and my exceptional colleagues in the Departments of Political Science, History, and Economics, I am especially grateful for their support and advice in helping me to see this book completed.

To those other mentors and colleagues who brought me along during the 1980s, who encouraged and supported me as I started my doctorate in the early 1990s, and who helped me reach the end of dissertation journey and complete this book, I owe a great debt of gratitude. They not only served as mentors with whom I have worked professionally inside and out of the U.S. government for many innovative years, but have also been valuable colleagues and friends. Although the list is long, there are countless others who have given their time and support, and their impact on me and on so many others is tremendously felt. They provided the reassurance and guidance necessary to see me through many challenges, especially those no longer with us: Sean Kay, Robert Pape, Andrew Michta, Jeffrey Taliaferro, Steven Burg, Roy Macridis, Stephen Burant, Phillip Petersen, Jacob Kipp, Graham Turbiville, David Glantz, Christopher Donnelly, Daniel Nelson, Ronald Linden, Thomas Szayna, Frank Umbach, Martin Sletzinger, Alan Stolberg, Gale Mattox, Eliot Cohen, William Wohlforth, Steven Brooks, Christianne Wohlforth, David Kang, Galia Bar-Nathan, Daryl Press, Angelia Means, John Shalikashvili, Wesley Clark, John Abizaid, Henry Shelton, Daniel Christman, Richard Myers, Dennis Blair, Stephen Rippe, David Petraeus, Joseph Collins, Keith Dayton, Andrew Berdy, Thomas Bowden, Michael Lohr, Paul Ryan, Mark Brzezinski, Ian Brzezinski, Catherine Kelleher, David Fontanella, Christine Krithades, Ronald Bachman, Barry Zulauf, Peter Zwack, Ralph Peters, Jennifer D. P. Moroney, James Townsend, Victor Papacosma, Ronald Asmus, Stephen Blank, Michael Szporer, Stephen Larrabee, Theresa Hitchens, Stuart Johnson, Hans Binnendijk, Andrew Bair, Bogdan Kipling, Walter Christman, Anne Bader, Peter Podbielski, Robert Stockwell, James Hendricks, Maxwell Alston, Michael Brown, Michael Chapman, Kori Schake, Mats Berdal, John Kidder, Gregory Hoffman, Reka Szemerkenyi, Thomas Culora, Ronald Bonesteel, Raymond Zickel, James Vorhees, Stephen Guenther, Daniel Whiteneck, Dennis Quinn, Timothy Thomas, Pamela Sloan, William Mendel, Harold Orenstein, Lester Grau, Timothy Sanz, Wlodomir Miszalski, Ferenc Kalmar, Rudolf Tokes, Janusz Radvani, Alice Mink, Florence Rotz, Patricia Carly, Christine Wormuth, Jeremy Strozer, Adam Domanski, Steven Burgess, and Steele Means.

All of the people I interviewed over the years, particularly in Central and Eastern Europe, played a fundamental role in shaping and aiding the development of the dissertation and this book, too. To them, I am eternally grateful, especially to those with whom I also worked very closely to help Poland reintegrate into Europe via our respective official governmental capacities during the 1990s. Without their knowledge and rich, diverse opinions, I couldn't have written with the understanding I did. I acknowledge their fortitude and contribution to European security, particularly, as above, those who have passed away. Their names are listed in the bibliography.

My experiences as both U.S. government researcher and policymaker on European and NATO security issues from 1988 to 2000 provided a distinct vantage point to investigate how and why post-Communist, middle power Poland tried to overcome the historic security dilemmas facing it. Whether Poland could overcome such historic dilemmas and could serve as a model for middle power politics became the basis of this book. Membership in the policy-making community provided a heightened appreciation of the integral connection between government policy and research on post-Communist Europe and NATO, and enabled more clearly an application of the theories of middle power formation, national security decision-making, and alignment strategy toward larger, traditionally hegemonic states.

In writing a dissertation, transforming it into a book, working full time to help shape American foreign policy and military strategy, raising a family, and supporting my spouse in her pursuit of the ministry, I came to understand not only some of life's biggest challenges, but also its most wonderful realities. Family is my bedrock and friends have been crucial in unfailing support.

Too often, family takes a back seat to these other life challenges. There were certainly moments when I wished the sacrifices such as my required time away or contemplation alone hadn't taken so much energy, separate from my family. Yet, through all the years, my loving, steadfast wife, Ellen, now an ordained and practicing minister, and our energetic, unflappable sons, Samuel and Henry, never stopped supporting me—they are my foundation. My parents, Robert and Janet Spero; my brother, Jeremy Spero, and his family; my sister, Jessica Spero; my late grandmother, Lillian Spero; my uncle Richard and aunt Irene Spero and their sons; and my uncle James and aunt Barbara Nathenson and their family; my parents-in-law, John and Marisha Rowse; sister-in-law, Katharine Haberle and her family; and Aunt Katharine Rowse listened to me without fail and gave me whatever help they possibly could to see me through this journey.

Family and friends provided those important doses of reality that we all understand let us see what's important in life. They crystalized many things for me. This is why I dedicate this book to Ellen and our long Polish heritages that have taken and will continue to take us down long paths with so many good people.

Introduction

The European Divide Bridged

Do middle powers matter for great powers geopolitically in confronting the unconventional threats from twenty-first-century nation-states or nonstate actors? By studying certain middle power politics, foreign policy strategies, and important historical junctures, we can better grasp the impact such middle powers have today in the tragic aftermath of the September 11, 2001, terrorist attacks. In exploring the early 1990s evolution of how key regional middle powers perceived and advocated political power options, this book tells the largely untold story behind the motives of significant middle power decisions and repercussions. This analytical story examines whether or not effective new alternatives existed for middle powers' interactions with great powers, particularly regional security alignments. Such regional alignment decisions stemmed from ideas, opportunities, and realities necessary to transform nation-states amid acute regional uncertainty, global upheaval, and international systemic change. The foreign policy decisions, then, determined within an early anarchical and volatile post–Cold War international system, continue to affect security dilemmas in the post-9/11 era.[1] As a result, by better understanding how to bridge the gap between changes in material incentives and the role of ideas, we may become more aware of how much the anarchical system and its unitary state actors attempt to reduce great power security dilemmas. This knowledge might enable us to analyze more effectively how the "material setting" weighs on the "basic causal mechanisms" of decision making and how much the uncertainty involved affects development of ideas and evolution of choices.[2] Therefore, this book aims to fill a significant gap in the literature to elucidate different types of power politics and ways of assessing security dilemmas and foreign policy decisions. Regardless of whether the attendant middle power alignments increase or reduce regional stability, this book argues that middle powers and their geopolitical roles matter primarily to great powers.

Unlike great powers, analysis of middle powers centers mainly on their attempts to survive under great power dominance or their relatively weak global influence. Middle powers survive most often by trying to play great powers against one another, avoiding them, or restricting their intent through subordination. Clearly, middle powers cannot act effectively alone and must defend against great power alignments for a very long time, given their frequent geographical predicaments, limited resources, or modest power projection capabilities.[3] In today's globalized world, however, states, organizations, corporations, and nonstate actors increasingly interconnect.[4] As a result, more analysis remains necessary to explore the impact certain middle powers have on regional security dilemmas. This book thus focuses on the regional strategies that specific middle powers formulate and implement against great powers to grapple with globalization's security dilemmas. The volume necessarily remains limited, however, when assessing in depth such security dilemmas as terrorism, weapons of mass destruction proliferation, ethnonational and resource conflict, immigration upheaval, financial meltdown, narcotics or human trafficking, or environmental degradation. Rather, this book's thesis considers how a significant European middle power like the early post–Cold War Republic of Poland attempted to survive global anarchy and tried differently to overcome its centuries-old regional security dilemmas. Why that strategy mattered or not for the seemingly perennial, hostile, and regional, great power system in which Poland constantly strove to survive provides the foundation for this book.

Since the unipolar system, especially after 9/11, continues to rely upon America, we witness the United States designating weak or failed states as threats to global stability.[5] The question arises: Do certain middle powers regionally affect great power security dilemmas differently and do they play specialized and regional middle power roles? In viewing a critical historical juncture like the end of the Cold War and examining theoretically and empirically how certain middle powers affected traditionally volatile regional security dilemmas—ones resulting in seemingly incessant conflicts and wars—a particular "hot spot" stands out. Early post-Communist Poland's regional middle power alignment strategy and imprint on great power security dilemmas characterized a different type of middle power role at the end of the Cold War. Poland's early post–Cold War strategy then arguably transformed its middle power into one of the most prominent post-9/11 "geopolitical pivots."[6] Therefore, by examining this important and relatively unexplored pivotal Central-East European "heartland" state, the following extends both theoretical and case study analyses, and may provide a baseline to study other middle powers more in-depth and related to historic, geopolitical security dilemmas.

Whereas security dilemmas frequently resulted from decisions leading to regional or world wars, this book reveals why we should pinpoint Poland's early post–Cold War strategy, theoretically and empirically. To wit, by assessing Poland's influence during a historical juncture like the early 1990s, we can better explain its post-9/11 geopolitical odyssey and why that remains significant today. Subsequently, this book discerns how this pivotal middle power wrestled with limited and effective alternatives for regional and international security to change its role and place in Europe. Yet, the early post–Cold War story looks at how Poland still dealt with its perennial insecurity, ultimately reducing security dilemmas within the emerging and unpredictable pan-European security architecture. In analyzing the foreign policy alignments and theoretical directions Poland took toward its neighbors in the early 1990s, we might better delineate a middle power model to explain the uncertain pan-European security architecture's metamorphosis. We might also apply a middle power politics interpretation to examine how powers in the twenty-first century confront hostile post-9/11 nation-states and even nonstate actors more efficiently. Possible models might in turn aid researchers and strategists to investigate if middle power politics matters to counter traditional nation-state confrontations or even transnational threats by building effective coalitions with great and smaller powers alike.

Consequently, this study looks at whether an emerging sovereign and regionally pivotal country like Poland provides a new understanding of middle power politics based on its early post–Cold War foreign policy strategy.[7] The study demonstrates how historically, insecure states survived the early global post–Cold War anarchy which will enable a better means to explain how they counter more effectively the threats posed in the chaotic post-9/11 era. As America and other great powers attempt to combat threats from hostile nation-states or non-state actors, middle power enhancement of historically unstable regions becomes ever more important. An effective post-9/11 global coalition against terrorism or other world threats, for example, could stem from multilateral cooperation among great and smaller powers. Such cooperation may better be advanced if great powers depend on stable middle powers that contribute regionally and internationally. Such cooperation might then greatly reduce security dilemmas. Hence, by examining if democratized middle powers like post-Communist Poland represent an example for how other middle powers might decrease historically destabilizing threats between and among great powers, this book traces how these objectives might be achieved.

Theoretically, this study should reveal whether middle powers seek security by "bridging" with other middle or great powers. This relatively unexplored type of alignment differs from the conventional wisdom focused on unipolar, bipolar, or multipolar "balancing" against or "bandwagoning" with specific states, or aggressive alignments to aggrandize territory or to dominate regionally. Bridging represents alignment by middle powers with all neighbors to lessen historic security dilemmas, rather than playing countries off of one another, or hiding behind neutrality or nonalignment. Thus, theoretically charged debates in international relations provide the foundation to build upon the arguments this book raises for a middle power politics model and regional security dilemmas.[8]

To illustrate, the geopolitical regional impact of a middle power like Poland stems from its geographical definition and location. Polish territory comprises 120,725 square miles with a population of 38.6 million people. These geopolitical parameters remain somewhat small, but, when coupled with ties toward neighboring Germany, Ukraine, and Russia, the geostrategic picture changes dramatically, especially if cooperative, nonhostile alignments develop.[9] For instance, Zbigniew Brzezinski argues that the "critical core of Europe's security," particularly its impact on America, emanates from linkages of the Franco–German–Polish relationship and the "special geopolitical interest of Germany and Poland in Ukraine's independence." He asserts that, if Ukrainian independence prevails over traditional Russian neoimperialism, Ukraine "will gradually be drawn into the special Franco–German–Polish relationship." He also sees Ukraine, like Indonesia, South Korea, Turkey, and Iran, as a state critical to "geostrategic players," in particular Germany, Russia, France, China, and India, because the latter define "the capacity and the national will to exercise power or influence beyond their borders" to influence America geopolitically.[10] By assessing whether Central-East European middle powers like Poland not only reinforced security, but also decreased their own regional security dilemmas among great powers, this book argues for a cooperative middle power politics model.[11]

International anarchy, however, affects middle powers differently than great powers because it leads not to the conventionally held notion of a "self-help" world in which powers struggle to craft their own security destinies, often against other powers, but to an "other-help" set of circumstances. In an other-help world, middle powers don't have a choice about the kind of international anarchical system in which they try to survive, as self-help states do. Middle powers cannot exist in a self-help world on their own because great powers frequently ignore, manipulate, or even destroy them. In this study, middle power politics rests on different assumptions for new types of anarchical alignment such that states seek other help, not the typical self help, to persist, let alone survive.[12] This study discloses new archival materials, divulges unexplored insights, and extends self-help theory to demonstrate possible new models to consider.

By applying international relations theory to test empirical and policy implications, this book assesses middle power politics in terms of regional security cooperation versus conflict. Few works compare post–Cold War Polish–German ties in the early 1990s with Polish–Ukrainian ties and their impact on Russia, or the Russian impact on them.[13] Little analysis exists about the groundwork laid for the extensive post–Cold War civil-military cooperation on German, Polish and Ukrainian territory via the North Atlantic Treaty Organization's (NATO) nonmember outreach and enlargement.[14] Few analyses exist about the extent of the early post–Cold War Polish middle power model regarding the impact it made for twenty-first century transnational security challenges and coalition building, including Polish–U.S. relations.[15] Given Soviet collapse and Balkan instability in the early 1990s, Poland's middle power case study and model tests the merits and pitfalls of cooperation and conflict within the construct of bridging alignment. Polish post–Cold War political–military successes like its NATO integration in 1999 also resulted in post-9/11 economic expansion as evinced by its methodical path toward European Union (EU) membership. Early post–Cold War Poland, therefore, provides a middle power model for how a state reduced its security dilemma by implementing a security strategy between great and middle powers. Whether the Polish middle power model withstands the pressures from great powers in these first years of the twenty-first century will depend on the extent to which the relationships it created in the early 1990s remain resilient, flexible, pragmatic, and intact.[16]

The Heart of the European Crossroads

At the end of Cold War in the late 1980s, many Central European leaders and their populations, particularly those of Poland, believed that the future held more of the same difficulties and dilemmas they had experienced over several centuries.[17] The dramatic structural transformation of German unification and Soviet disintegration at the end of the 1980s and the beginning of the 1990s influenced Poland's regionally integrative security policies in ways not anticipated by many scholars or policymakers. Poland's post-Communist leaders, who emerged from the Polish Solidarity (*Solidarnosc*) underground activist movement, personified the first and leading democratic model for nonadvanced democracies in the crumbling Soviet Bloc to promote pluralism, free markets, and cooperative security. Polish underground activists—often anti-Communist scholars during the 1970s and 1980s—incorporated such ideas into new foreign policies after joining the first post-Communist Polish government and parliament in August 1989 (before the Berlin Wall fell). By showing how these activists devised and implemented various alignment strategies, this book imparts an extension of theory and sheds light on different policy practice. It explains how such a middle power strategy contributed to the demise of the Soviet Bloc, Warsaw Pact, and, with economic decline and centrifugal enthnonationalism, the USSR. Today, Poland stands alongside Great Britain as one of the strongest advocates of U.S. international interests, even under strong criticism from European powers such as Germany, France, and Russia. In turn, Washington recognizes Poland as a "close friend," demonstrating that middle power state strategies matter greatly in the post-9/11 era.[18] How enduring Polish–European as well as Polish–American ties remain, given transatlantic tensions plaguing the great power allies inclusive of Central-East Europe, will measure the abilities of practical middle power facilitation rather than disruption.

Since Polish decision making constitutes the basis for this empirical analysis, the book examines the critical period from 1989 to 1993, focusing on the first four non-Communist led governments under Foreign Minister Krzysztof Skubiszewski, the only minister to maintain his portfolio.[19] The Skubiszewski "era" gives a consistent baseline for analysis. His period in office and the foreign policies he promulgated enable this study to answer whether Poland believed it retained options as a middle power between two larger, more powerful neighboring states to deal effectively and constructively with its historic security dilemma. Whether Poland needed to find a means to promulgate its middle power policies differently by determining other-help strategies underlines the key theoretical thesis of this book. Furthermore, the book investigates if Skubiszewski's Ministry of Foreign Affairs (*Ministerstwo Spraw Zagranicznych*, hereafter *MSZ*) thought it could make post-Communist foreign policy from a "clean slate," particularly vis-à-vis the government and the president to promote and enact a sovereign post-Communist Polish foreign policy. Like prominent studies conducted about how and why a state's political elite organizes, formulates, and implements foreign policy decisions toward the international system, this book explores Skubiszewski's rationale toward Poland's neighbors and the uncertain, early post–Cold War pan-European security architecture.[20] In his own words:

> We have a vision of peace and freedom in a region that, in contemporary history, has too often been an arena of conflict, division, and domination. If Poland is free and democratic . . . so that foreign policy may be firmly based on the fundamental of external sovereignty and internal independence . . . its geopolitical and geo-strategic importance can and should be turned into an asset that supports peace and fosters freedom.[21]

Three case studies depict how bargaining and negotiation of the day-to-day decision-making processes resulted in Poland's post–Cold War European reintegration. These case studies examine how Polish post-Communist policymakers developed and actualized the foreign ministry's overall course. Demonstrations of diplomacy involve in-depth assessment of how Poland closed the post–World War II rift and established a new relationship with unified Germany. Furthermore, investigation shows how Poland created ties with the central Soviet authorities in Moscow, while simultaneously establishing linkages to the emerging, bordering, and great power Russian, and middle or smaller power, non-Russian newly independent states, Ukraine, Belarus, and Lithuania. Finally, promotion of security initiatives within the cooperative Visegrad Central European Triangle[22]—the former Czech and Slovak Federative Republic (CSFR) and Hungary—demonstrates how middle power Poland perfected strategy to disband the Warsaw Pact with these two smaller Central European Triangle states and start the membership drive toward NATO and the EU. Within each chapter, the book considers the kind of geopolitical behavior Poland exhibited and whether Warsaw acted to bridge in maneuvering toward its neighbors and the rapidly evolving European security structures. Therefore, the book evaluates the historic opportunities Polish foreign policy–makers felt existed for their Central-East European security role and how this middle power linchpin set the stage to become part of NATO and the EU. As importantly, the book elaborates why middle power politics should matter in the post–Cold War era and how such a power like Poland affects smaller and larger power strategies for coalition-building challenges of the twenty-first century.

The literature about the 1989 Central and Eastern European revolutions predominantly centers around the impact of Soviet foreign policy on the Eastern Bloc's dramatic changes.[23] Certainly, the peaceful 1989 drama of the Communist–*Solidarnosc* roundtable negotiations and, subsequently, the first post-Communist government freely elected in the Eastern Bloc caught the world's attention.[24] Many analyses of the historic 1989 revolutions credit or blame the last Soviet leader, Mikhail Gorbachev, with allowing the Soviet-dominated Eastern Bloc to democratize—even if such policies backfired on Moscow's Communist-based strategy and eventually resulted in the Bloc's dissolution. In the turmoil of the collapse of the Cold War bipolar system, the independently transitioning Central European states moved well beyond Gorbachev's Communist vision of reform.[25]

Other works depict the revolutions as originating from the loss of Soviet influence, whether managed by Moscow or not, and the discrediting and implosion of the Central and Eastern European Communist regimes.[26] Furthermore, some analyses portray the Central and East European transitions in terms of some Polish or Central-East European political, economic, military, or sociocultural perspectives.[27]

Important studies do focus on Polish foreign policy and its bearing on the 1989 revolutions. These significant works contribute to an understanding of the history-making events in the aftermath of 1989 and provide a broad overview of the development of Polish foreign policy.[28]

Yet, an in-depth analysis of Polish post-Communist foreign policy and middle power politics, based on the accounts of those *Solidarnosc*-era activists and post-Communist foreign policy–makers from 1989 to 1993, enriches understanding about the Skubiszewski era.[29] By using research comprising several dozen interviews during the past decade with Polish underground activists–cum post–Communist foreign policy–makers and previously unused archival documentation from Warsaw colleagues, this book captures viewpoints rare to research on post-Communist European states. This research about Warsaw's early post-Communist strategy from 1989 to 1993 enriches understanding of Poland's integration into NATO in March 1999 and its likely gain of EU membership in 2004. Additionally, the empirical case studies contain insights for comparative post–Communist political theory in such areas as democratization and regional interstate cooperation during a critical period of upheaval in European security. To guard against the selective memory of those interviewed, however, the book compares and contrasts interview material with Polish archival and public documentation from 1989 to 1993.

To build upon these firsthand accounts and the secondary Western literature elaborated above, the book also incorporates incisive and, oftentimes, controversial pre-Skubiszewski-era assessments about Poland's geopolitical difficulties between Germany and Russia.[30] These analyses show how the state handled its foreign-imposed or self-inflicted adversities. Coupled with interviews and historical appraisals, key Polish opposition and émigré publications from the 1960s to the 1980s buttress the book's examination of post-Communist foreign policy.[31]

Although some assessment of the story behind Poland's independent foreign policy from 1989 to 1993 exists in the literature, this book discloses new approaches about the beginning of Poland's post–Cold War strategy. Most studies on Polish post–Cold War foreign policy include some analysis on the transition from the fall of the Berlin Wall to the emergence of newly independent states of the former USSR.[32] All of the works referenced disclose important insights or detail inside accounts about the *MSZ*'s debates over foreign policy. These analyses contribute to knowledge about Warsaw's quest for integration into Western European political, economic, and security institutions. They also emphasize how Poland shaped its foreign and defense policies to contend with Germany and the USSR, before the latter collapsed, and toward the emerging post-Soviet states. Additionally, they credit post-Communist Poland with attempting to overcome some of its security concerns or security dilemmas. Clearly, though, new research that tests the kind of state alignment Poland demonstrated toward Germany and Russia can divulge new notions, possibly including new ways to assess Poland's regional security role in Central Europe and the roles of other middle powers globally. By applying the international relations theories above and analyzing post-Communist Poland's contributions to post–Cold War Europe, this book benefits scholars and policymakers by providing a different understanding of Poland's political relationships and its middle power model in rapidly transforming Europe. As Europe dramatically expands and tries to unify Western, Central, Eastern, and Southeastern Europe in the early years of the twenty-first century, this book leaves the reader to determine if the early post–Cold War Polish middle power politics model remains suitable to tackle the coming challenges.[33]

Notes

1. "Security dilemmas" define how states perceive themselves and how they initiate actions toward or respond to the actions of other states that frequently lessen security. See, especially, John H. Herz, *Political Realism and Political Idealism: A Study in Theories and Realities* (Chicago: University of Chicago Press, 1959), 4; Robert Jervis, *Perception and Misperception in International Politics* (Princeton, N.J.: Princeton University Press, 1976), 66; Charles L. Glaser, "The Security Dilemma Revisited," *World Politics*, vol. 50, no. 1 (October 1997): 191, 197; Charles L. Glaser, "Correspondence: Current Gains and Future Outcomes," *International Security*, vol. 21, no. 4 (spring 1997), 192–193; and John C. Matthews, III, "Correspondence: Current Gains and Future Outcomes," *International Security*, vol. 21, no. 4 (spring 1997): 193–197.

2. For linkage of material setting, new ideas, and foreign policy within the context of the Cold War's decline, see Stephen G. Brooks and William C. Wohlforth, "Power, Globalization, and the End of the Cold War: Reevaluating a Landmark Case for Ideas," *International Security*, vol. 25, no. 3 (winter 2000/2001): 6–7, 10–12.

3. Annette Baker Fox, *The Power of Small States: Diplomacy in World War II* (Chicago: University of Chicago Press, 1959); Robert L. Rothstein, *Alliances and Small Powers* (New York: Columbia University Press, 1968); David Vital, *The Survival of Small States: Studies in Small Power/Great Power Conflict* (London: Oxford University Press, 1971); Trygve Mathisen, *The Functions of Small States in the Strategies of the Great Powers* (Oslo: Bergen Tromso, 1971); R. P. Barston, ed., *The Other Powers: Studies in the Foreign Policies of Small States* (London: Allen & Unwin, 1973); Annette Baker Fox, *The Politics of Attraction: Four Middle Powers and the United States* (New York: Columbia University Press, 1977); Robert L. Rothstein, *The Weak in the World of the Strong* (New York: Columbia University Press, 1977); Peter J. Katzenstein, *Small States in World Markets* (Ithaca, N.Y.: Cornell University Press, 1985); Efraim Karsh, *Neutrality and Small States* (London: Routledge, 1988); Michael I. Handel, *Weak States in the International System*, 2nd ed., (London: Cass, 1990); Laurent Goetschel, ed., *Small States inside and outside the European Union: Interests and Policies* (Dordrecht, Netherlands: Kluwer Academic Press, 1998); Robert Chase, Emily Hill, and Paul Kennedy, *The Pivotal States: A New Framework for U.S. Policy in the Developing World* (New York: Norton, 1999); and Jeanne A. K. Hey, ed., *Small States in World Politics: Explaining Foreign Policy Behavior* (Boulder, Colo.: Reinner, 2003).

4. Thomas L. Friedman, *The Lexus and the Olive Tree: Understanding Globalization* (New York: Anchor, 2000); Brooks and Wohlforth, "Power, Globalization, and the End of the Cold War"; and Joseph S. Nye, *The Paradox of American Power: Why the World's Only Superpower Can't Go It Alone* (London: Oxford University Press, 2002).

5. *The National Security Strategy of the United States of America* (Washington, D.C.: U.S. Government Printing Office, 2002), 4 (preface).

6. Halford J. Mackinder, "The Geographical Pivot of History," *Geographical Journal*, vol. 23. (1904): 421–444; and Halford J. Mackinder, *Democratic Ideals and Reality* (Westport, Conn.: Greenwood, 1962). Many prominent works built on Mackinder, and some international relations theorists subsequently assessed small and middle power politics and their regional impact, depicting geopolitical "pivots" globally on every continent.

7. "Sovereign" foreign policy depicts an "independent" and "sovereign" state, as Hans Morgenthau underlined, to denote the ability "of a centralized power [to] exercise its lawmaking and law-enforcing authority within a certain territory. . . . The statement that the [state] is the supreme authority—that is, sovereign within a certain territory—logically implies that it is independent and that there is no authority above it." Hans J. Morgenthau and Kenneth W. Thompson, *Politics among Nations: The Struggle for Power and Peace*, 6th ed. (New York: Knopf, 1985), 328, 331. Additionally, Kenneth Waltz states that the independent and sovereign state "decide[s] for itself how it will cope with its internal and external problems, including whether or not to seek assistance from others and in doing so to limit its freedom by making commitments to them. States develop their own strategies, chart their own courses, make their own decisions about how to meet whatever needs they experience and whatever desires they develop." See Kenneth N. Waltz, *Theory of International Politics* (Reading, Mass.: Addison-Wesley, 1979), 95–96.

8. This middle power politics paradigm draws particularly on some of the broader arguments focused on great powers in Waltz, *Theory of International Politics*; Steven M. Walt, *The Origin of Alliances* (Ithaca, N.Y.: Cornell University Press, 1987); Jack Snyder, *Myths of Empire: Domestic Politics and International Ambition* (Ithaca, N.Y.: Cornell University Press, 1991); Paul Schroeder, "Historical Reality vs. Neo-realist Theory,"

International Security, vol. 19, no. 1 (summer 1994): 108–148; Jonathan Mercer, "Anarchy and Identity," *International Organization*, vol. 49, no. 2 (spring 1995): 229–252; and Randall L. Schweller, *Deadly Imbalances: Tripolarity and Hitler's Strategy of World Conquest* (New York: Columbia University Press, 1998).

9. Germany (landmass 137,821 square miles, population 82.8 million), Ukraine (landmass 233,090 square miles, population 49.8 million), and Russia (landmass 6.5 million square miles, population 147.5 million). "Geographical Locations, Background Notes," www.state.gov/www/backgroundnotes/eurbgnhhtml (20 January 2001). See also Jeffrey S. Kopstein and David A. Reilly, "Geographic Diffusion and the Transformation of the Postcommunist World," *World Politics*, vol. 53, no. 1 (October 2000): 1–37.

10. Zbigniew Brzezinski, *The Grand Chessboard: American Primacy and Its Geostrategic Imperatives* (New York: Basic, 1997), 40–41, 84–86.

11. On cooperative security: Ashton B. Carter, William J. Perry, and John D. Steinbruner, *A New Concept of Cooperative Security* (Washington, D.C.: Brookings Institution Press, 1992); and Janne E. Nolan, ed., *Global Engagement: Cooperation and Security in the 21st Century* (Washington, D.C.: Brookings Institution Press, 1994).

12. For some of the prominent explanations and debates concerning self-help and other-help, see the following: Waltz, *Theory of International Politics*; Schroeder, "Historical Reality vs. Neo-realist Theory"; Charles L. Glaser, "Realists as Optimists: Cooperation as Self-help," in *Realism: Restatements and Renewal,* ed. Benjamin Frankel, (London: Cass, 1996): 122–163; Mercer, "Anarchy and Identity"; Colin Elman and Miriam Fendius Elman, "Correspondence—History vs. Neo-realism: A Second Look," *International Security*, vol. 20, no. 1 (summer 1995): 182–193; Paul Schroeder, "Correspondence—History vs. Neo-realism: A Second Look," *International Security*, vol. 20, no. 1 (summer 1995): 193–195; Schweller, *Deadly Imbalances*; and Alexander Wendt, *Social Theory of International Politics* (Cambridge: Cambridge University Press, 1999).

13. Sherman W. Garnett, *Keystone in the Arch: Ukraine in the Emerging Security Environment of Central and Eastern Europe* (Washington, D.C.: Carnegie Endowment Press, 1995); Ilya Prizel and Andrew Michta, eds., *Polish Foreign Policy Reconsidered: Challenges of Independence* (London: Macmillan, 1995); Ilya Prizel, *National Identity and Foreign Policy: Nationalism and Leadership in Poland, Russia, and Ukraine* (Cambridge: Cambridge University Press, 1998); Lubomyr A. Hajda, ed., *Ukraine in the World: Studies in the International and Security Structure of a Newly Independent State* (Cambridge, Mass.: Harvard University Press, 1998).

14. Ethan B. Kapstein and Michael Mastanduno, eds., *Unipolar Politics: Realism and State Strategies after the Cold War* (New York: Columbia University Press, 1999); Jennifer D. P. Moroney and Taras Kuzio, eds., *Ukraine's Foreign and Security Policy: Theoretical and Comparative Perspectives* (Westport, Conn.: Greenwood/Praeger, 2002); James Sperling, Sean Kay, and S. Victor Papacosma, eds., *Limiting Institutions: The Challenge of Eurasian Security* (Manchester, U.K.: Manchester University Press, 2003).

15. Adrian Hyde-Price, *The International Politics of East Central Europe* (Manchester, U.K.: Manchester University Press, 1996): Zbigniew Brzezinski, *The Grand Chessboard*; Andrew A. Michta, ed., *America's New Allies: Poland, Hungary, and the Czech Republic in NATO* (Seattle: University of Washington Press, 1999).

16. "Charlemagne: Those Pesky Poles—In Which Old Members Offer New Ones Some Lessons in Negotiation," *The Economist*, November 29, 2003, 49.

17. Poland suffered the loss of its statehood when Russia, Prussia, and Austria promulgated three partitions of Poland during the late 1700s, in 1773, 1793, and 1795, see, especially, "Agonia: The End of the Russian Protectorate (1764–1795)" in Norman

Davies, *God's Playground: A History of Poland*, vol. 1 (New York: Columbia University Press, 1982), 511–546. Not until 1918 did Poland regain its independence, soon after it endured its fourth partition as a result of the signing of the Soviet–Nazi Molotov–Ribbentrop Pact on 23 August 1939.

18. George W. Bush, "Remarks by the President to the People of Poland," Office of the Press Secretary, 31 May 2003, www.whitehouse.gov/news/releases/2003/05/20030531-3.html (accessed 31 May 2003).

19. For important assessments on theories and practices of foreign policy decision making, see the special issue of *International Studies Review: Leaders, Groups, and Coalitions: Understanding the People and Processes in Foreign Policymaking*, edited by Margaret G. Hermann (Malden, Mass.: Blackwell Publishers, 2001).

20. From among many analyses, the following studies focus on both the Soviet and Eastern European, and emerging post-Soviet and post–Cold War Central European foreign policy establishments and how they constructed respective foreign policies based, in part, on the international system and the international system's impact on their respective state's behavior. See William Zimmerman, *Soviet Perspectives on International Relations, 1956–1967* (Princeton, N.J.: Princeton University Press, 1973), especially 3–24; Bruce Parrott, *Politics and Technology in the Soviet Union* (Cambridge, Mass.: MIT Press, 1983), principally 231–293; Jeffrey Simon, *Cohesion and Dissension in Eastern Europe: Six Crises* (New York: Praeger, 1983), particularly 1–11; Arthur R. Rachwald, *In Search of Poland: The Superpowers' Response to Solidarity, 1980–1989* (Stanford, Calif.: Hoover Institution Press, 1990), specifically, 108–127; Stephen F. Szabo, *The Diplomacy of German Unification* (New York: St. Martin's, 1992), primarily 17–52; and Ilya Prizel, *National Identity and Foreign Policy*, 12–37.

21. "Przemowienie ministra spraw zagranicznych prof. Krzysztofa Skubiszewskiego na XLIV sesji Zgromadzenie Ogolnego NZ" [Statement by the Polish Minister of Foreign Affairs, Prof. Krzysztof Skubiszewski at the 44th Session of the UN General Assembly], New York, September 25, 1989, in *Zbior Dokumentow* (Warsaw), no. 3 (1990): 150.

22. Leaders from Poland, the CSFR, and Hungary met in Visegrad, Hungary, from 13 to 15 February 1991 and "Visegrad" quickly became the nickname for the process of the Polish–CSFR–Hungarian regional cooperation, well into the late 1990s, as all three states advanced to NATO membership in 1999 and forged closer links to the European Community (EC) then, and EU today.

23. William E. Griffith, ed., *Central and Eastern Europe: The Opening Curtain?* (Boulder, Colo.: Westview, 1989); Karen Dawisha, *Eastern Europe, Gorbachev and Reform: The Great Challenge*, 2nd ed. (Cambridge: Cambridge University Press, 1990); Jerry Hough, *Russia and the West: Gorbachev and the Politics of Reform*, 2nd ed. (New York: Touchstone, 1990); Michael J. Sodaro, *Moscow, Germany, and the West from Khrushchev to Gorbachev* (Ithaca, N.Y.: Cornell University Press, 1990); and Michael McGwire, *Perestroika and Soviet National Security Policy* (Washington, D.C.: Brookings Institution, 1991).

24. It should be noted that the first free elections in the former Soviet-dominated Eastern Bloc in Poland (June 1989) were not entirely democratic. Based on one of the agreements from the Roundtable negotiations throughout 1989 between Lech Walesa's *Solidarnosc* and President Wojciech Jaruzelski's Communists, the Sejm (Parliament) only allowed one third of its seats to be contested. However, a Senate was also established and *Solidarnosc* candidates won ninety-nine of its hundred seats. The process of Poland regaining true sovereignty only occurred with the December 1990 presidential elections, which Walesa won, and the fully free October 1991 parliamentary elections.

25. Ernest W. Lefever and Robert D. Vander Lugt, eds., *Perestroika: How New Is Gorbachev's New Thinking?* (Washington, D.C.: Ethics and Public and Policy Center, 1989); Martin Malia, "To the Stalin Mausoleum," in *Eastern Europe . . . Central Europe . . . Europe*, ed. Stephen R. Graubard (Boulder, Colo.: Westview, 1991), 283–339; Phillip A. Petersen, "The Challenge to Soviet Strategic Deployment: An Emerging Vision of European Security," in *Jane's NATO Handbook, 1990–1991*, ed. Bruce George (Coulsdon, U.K.: Jane's Information Group, 1990): 323–334; Rey Koslowski and Friedrich V. Kratochwil, "Understanding Change in International Politics: The Soviet Empire's Demise and the International System," *International Organization*, vol. 48, no. 2 (spring 1994): 215–247; and Stephen G. Brooks and William C. Wohlforth, "Power, Globalization, and the End of the Cold War."

26. Valerie Bunce, "The Empire Strikes Back: The Transformation of the Eastern Bloc from a Soviet Asset to a Soviet Liability," *International Organization*, vol. 39, no. 1 (winter 1985): 1–46; Zbigniew Brzezinski, *The Grand Failure: The Birth and Death of Communism in the Twentieth Century* (New York: Collier, 1989); Charles Gati, *The Bloc That Failed: Soviet–East European Relations in Transition* (Bloomington: Indiana University Press, 1990); Jeffrey Simon, ed., *European Security Policy after the Revolutions of 1989* (Washington, D.C.: The National Defense University Press, 1991); J. F. Brown, *Surge to Freedom: The End of Communist Rule in Eastern Europe* (Durham, N.C.: Duke University Press, 1991); Voytek Zubek, "Walesa's Leadership and Poland's Transition," *Problems of Communism*, nos. 1–2 (January–April 1991): 69–83; Piotr Wandycz, *The Price of Freedom: A History of East Central Europe from the Middle Ages to the Present* (London: Routledge, 1992); Thomas W. Simons, Jr., *Eastern Europe in the Postwar World*, 2nd ed. (New York: St. Martin's, 1993); Gale Stokes, *The Walls Came Tumbling Down: The Collapse of Communism in Eastern Europe* (New York: Oxford University Press, 1993); Andrew Michta and Ilya Prizel, eds., *Post-Communist Europe: Crisis and Adjustment* (New York: St. Martin's, 1993); and Renée De Nevers, *Comrades No More: The Seeds of Change in Eastern Europe* (Cambridge, Mass.: MIT Press, 2003).

27. Timothy Garton Ash, *The Magic Lantern: The Revolution of '89 Witnessed in Warsaw, Budapest, Berlin and Prague* (New York: Random House, 1990); Ralf Dahrendorf, *Reflections on the Revolution in Europe: In a Letter Intended to Have Been Sent to a Gentleman in Warsaw* (New York: Times Books, 1990); Stanislaw Baranczak, *Breathing under Water and Other East European Essays* (Cambridge, Mass.: Harvard University Press, 1990); Misha Glenny, *The Rebirth of History: Eastern Europe in the Age of Democracy* (London: Penguin, 1990); Bartlomiej Kaminski, *The Collapse of State Socialism: The Case of Poland* (Princeton, N.J.: Princeton University Press, 1991); Jeffrey C. Goldfarb, *After the Fall: The Pursuit of Democracy in Central Europe* (New York: Basic Books, 1992); Andrew Nagorski, *The Birth of Freedom: Shaping Lives and Societies in the New Eastern Europe* (New York: Simon & Schuster, 1993); Timothy Garten Ash, *In Europe's Name: Germany and the Divided Continent* (New York: Random House, 1993); Regina Cowen Karp, ed., *Central and Eastern Europe: The Challenge of Transition* (Oxford: Oxford University Press, 1993); Marek Matraszek, *Poland: The Politics of Restoration* (London: Alliance, 1994); Leszek Balcerowicz, *Socialism, Capitalism, Transformation* (Budapest: Central European University Press, 1995); Juan J. Linz and Alfred Stepan, *Problems of Democratic Transition and Consolidation: Southern Europe, South America, and Post-Communist Europe* (Baltimore, Md.: Johns Hopkins University Press, 1996); Karen Dawisha and Bruce Parrott, eds., *The Consolidation of Democracy in East-Central Europe: Authoritarianism and Democratization in Postcommunist Societies* (Cambridge: Cambridge University Press, 1997); and Ilya Prizel, "The

First Decade After the Collapse of Communism: Why Did Some Nations Succeed in their Political and Economic Transformations While Others Failed?" *SAIS Review*, vol. 19, no. 2 (summer–fall 1999): 1–15.

28. Rudolf L. Tokes, "From Visegrad to Krakow: Cooperation, Competition, and Coexistence in Central Europe," *Problems of Communism* 40/6 (November–December 1991): 100–114; Ronald D. Asmus and Thomas S. Szayna, with Barbara Kliszewski, *Polish National Security Thinking in a Changing Europe: A Conference Report* (Santa Monica, Calif.: RAND/UCLA Center for Soviet Studies, 1991); Andrew Michta, *East Central Europe after the Warsaw Pact: Security Dilemmas in the 1990s* (New York: Greenwood, 1992); Joshua Spero, "The Budapest-Prague-Warsaw Triangle: Central European Security after the Visegrad Summit," *European Security*, vol. 1, no. 1 (spring 1992): 58–83; Stephen J. Flanagan, "NATO and Central and Eastern Europe: From Liaison to Security Partnership," *Washington Quarterly* (spring 1992): 141–151; F. Stephen Larrabee, *East European Security after the Cold War* (Santa Monica, Calif.: RAND National Defense Research Institute, 1993); Paul Latawski, "The Polish Road to NATO: Problems and Prospects," *Polish Quarterly of International Affairs*, no. 3 (summer 1993): 69–88; Jeffrey Simon, "Does Eastern Europe Belong in NATO?" *Orbis* (winter 1993): 21–35; Alfred A. Reisch, "Central and Eastern Europe's Quest for NATO Membership," *RL/RFE Weekly Report*, 9 July 1993: 33–47; Paul Latawski, *The Security Road to Europe: The Visegrad Four* (London: Royal United Services for Defence Studies, 1994); John R. Lampe and Daniel N. Nelson, eds., in collaboration with Roland Schonfeld, *East European Security Reconsidered* (Washington: Wilson Center Press, 1993); Theo van den Doel, *Central Europe: The New Allies?: The Road from Visegrad to Brussels* (Boulder, Colo.: Westview, 1994); Andrzej Korbonski, "The Security of East Central Europe and the Visegrad Triangle," in *The Legacy of the Soviet Bloc*, eds. Jane Shapiro Zacek and Ilpyong J. Kim (Gainesville: University Press of Florida, 1997), 159–177; and Matthew Rhodes, "The Idea of Central Europe and Visegrad Cooperation," *International Politics*, vol. 35, no. 2 (June 1998): 165–186.

29. Interviews I have conducted since 1989 demonstrate the unique insights about Polish foreign policy that are provided by firsthand accounts of those who formulated and implemented the independent and increasingly sovereign Polish state's policies. The following people were interviewed and are detailed in the bibliography (interviewee position, date and location of the interview): Andrzej Ananicz, Ivan Baba, Tadeusz Chabiera, Jacek Czaputowicz, Kazimierz Dziewanowski, Konstanty Gebert, Artur Hajnicz, Mariusz Handzlik, Lech Kaczynski, Andrzej Kaminski, Andrzej Karkoszka, Grzegorz Kostrzewa-Zorbas, Stanislaw Koziej, Michal Kurkiewicz, Roman Kuzniar, Eligiusz Lasota, Jerzy Makarczyk, Jerzy Milewski, Zdzislaw Najder, Jerzy Marek Nowakowski, Janusz Onyszkiewicz, Jan Parys, Jan Maria Rokita, Radek Sikorski, Zygmunt Skorzynski, Pawel Soloch, Hanna Suchocka, Petr Szczepanski, Henryk Szlajfer, Andrzej Towpik, Grzegorz Winid, Grzegorz Wisniewski, Michal Wyganowski, and Krzysztof Zielke.

30. Roman Dmowski, *Niemcy, Rosja i kwestja polska* [Germany, Russia and the Polish Question], (Warsaw: Instytut Wydawniczy PAX, 1991); Adolf Bochenski, *Miedzy Niemcami a Rosja* [Between Germany and Russia] (Warsaw: Polityka, 1937); Hugh Seton-Watson, *Eastern Europe between the Wars, 1918–1941* (Cambridge: Cambridge University Press, 1946); Flora Lewis, *A Case History of Hope: The Story of Poland's Peaceful Revolution* (New York: Doubleday, 1958); Josef Korbel, *Poland between East and West: Soviet and German Diplomacy toward Poland, 1919–1933* (Princeton, N.J.: Princeton University Press, 1963); Norman J. G. Pounds, *Poland between East and West* (Princeton, N.J.: D. Van Nostrand, 1964); Hansjakob Stehle, *The Independent Satellite*

(London: Praeger, 1965); Adam Bromke, *Poland's Politics: Idealism vs. Realism* (Cambridge, Mass.: Harvard University Press, 1967); Piotr Wandycz, *Soviet-Polish Relations, 1917–1921* (Cambridge, Mass.: Harvard University Press, 1969); M. K. Dziewanowski, *Joseph Pilsudski: A European Federalist, 1918–1922* (Stanford, Calif.: Hoover Institution Press, 1969); Juliusz Mieroszewski, *Materialy do Refleksji i Zadumy* [Materials for Reflection and Musing] (Paris: Instytut Literacki, 1976); Zbigniew K. Brzezinski, *The Soviet Bloc: Unity and Conflict*, rev. and enl. ed. (Cambridge, Mass.: Harvard University Press, 1976); M. K. Dziewanowski, *Poland in the Twentieth Century* (New York: Columbia University Press, 1977); Piotr Wandycz, *The Lands of Partitioned Poland, 1795–1918*, vol. 7 (Seattle: University of Washington Press, 1974); Joseph Rothschild, *East Central Europe between the Two World Wars*, vol. 9 (Seattle: University of Washington Press, 1974); Norman Davies, *God's Playground: A History of Poland*, 2 vols. (New York: Columbia University Press, 1982); Jakub Karpinski, *Countdown: The Polish Upheavals of 1956, 1968, 1970, 1976, 1980...* (New York: Karz-Cohl, 1982); Sarah M. Terry, *Poland's Place in Europe: General Sikorski and the Origin of the Oder-Neisse Line, 1939–1943* (Princeton, N.J.: Princeton University Press, 1983); Norman Davies, *Heart of Europe: A Short History of Poland*, 2nd ed. (Oxford: Oxford University Press, 1986); Ray Taras, *Poland: Socialist State, Rebellious Nation* (Boulder, Colo.: Westview Press, 1986); Teresa Toranska, *"THEM": Stalin's Polish Puppets* (New York: Harper & Row, 1987); Adam Michnik, *Letters from Prison and Other Essays* (Berkeley: University of California Press, 1987); Piotr Wandycz, "Poland's Place in Europe in the Concepts of Pilsudski and Dmowski," *East European Politics and Societies* (fall 1990); Paul Latawski, ed., *The Reconstruction of Poland, 1914–23* (New York: St. Martin's, 1992); and Timothy Snyder, *The Reconstruction of Nations: Poland, Ukraine, Lithuania, Belarus, 1569–1999* (New Haven, Conn.: Yale University Press, 2003).

31. Among the most important opposition journals over the Solidarity era that included analyses on Polish foreign policy were *Kontakt, Krytyka, Kultura, Nowa Koalicja*, and *Oboz*. See also the following important works: Krzysztof Skubiszewski, *Zachodnia Granica Polski [Poland's Western Border]* [Gdansk, Poland: Wydawnictwo Morskie—Instytut Baltycki w Gdansku, 1969); *PPN: Polskie Porozumienie Niepodleglosciowe* [PPN: Alliance for Polish Independence], sponsors, Gustaw Herling-Grudzinski, Leszek Kolakowski, and Jerzy Lerski (Paris: Instytut Literacki, 1978); Zdzislaw Najder, ed., *Polskie Porozumienie Niepodleglosciowe: Wybor Tekstow* [Alliance for Polish Independence: Electoral Text] (London: Polonia, 1989); Leopold Tyrmand, ed., *Kultura Essays* (New York: Free Press, 1970); Robert Kostrzewa, ed, *Between East and West: Writings from Kultura* (New York: Hill & Wang, 1990); and Michael Bernhard and Henryk Szlajfer, eds., *From the Polish Underground: Selections from Krytyka, 1978–1993* (University Park, Pa.: The University of Pennsylvania Press, 1995).

32. Notable analyses include Thomas Szayna, *Polish Foreign Policy under a Non-Communist Government: Prospects and Problems* (Santa Monica, Calif.: RAND, 1990); Krzysztof Zielke, "Polityka Wschodnia Rzeczypospolitej Polskiej na Progu Lat Dziewiedziesiatych" [Poland's Eastern Policy on the Threshold of the 1990s], in *Polityka Rzeczypospolitej Polskiej na Progu Lat Dziewiedziesiatych*, ed. Jadwiga Staniszkis (Warsaw: Instytut Studiow Politycznych Polskiej Akademii Nauk, 1991); Stephen R. Burant, "Polish-Lithuanian Relations," *Problems of Communism* (May–June 1991): 67–84; Waldemar Kuczynski, *Zwierzenia Zausznika* [Confidence of a Confidante] (Warsaw: Polska Oficyna Wydawnicza, 1992); Grzegorz Kostrzewa-Zorbas, "Imperium kontratakuje" ["The Empire Strikes Back"] in *Lewy Czerwcowy* [Blow from the Left], eds. Jacek Kurski and Piotr Semka (Warsaw: Editions Spotkania, 1992): 147–188; Krzysztof Gor-

ski, *Dwutorowosc Polskiej Polityki Wschodniej w latach 1989–1991* [Polish Two-Track Eastern Policy, 1989–1991] (master's thesis: Uniwersytet Warszawski, 1992); Jan B. de Weydenthal, "Poland Supports the Triangle as a Means to Reach Other Goals," *RL/RFE Weekly Report*, vol. 1, no. 23 (5 June 1992): 2; Jan Zielonka, "Security in Central Europe: Sources of Instability in Hungary, Poland and the Czech and Slovak Republics with Recommendations for Western Policy," *Adelphi Paper* 272 (autumn 1992): 41–53; Henryk Szlajfer and Janusz Prystrom, eds., *Report on the State of National Security: External Aspects* (Warsaw: Polish Institute of International Affairs, 1993); Stephen R. Burant and Voytek Zubek, "Eastern Europe's Old Memories and New Realities: Resurrecting the Polish–Lithuanian Union," *East European Politics and Societies,* vol. 7, no. 2 (spring 1993): 370–393; Grzegorz Kostrzewa-Zorbas, "The Russian Troop Withdrawal from Poland," in *The Diplomatic Record, 1992–1993*, ed. Allan E. Goodman (Boulder, Colo.: Westview, 1995), 113–138; Jaroslaw Kurski, *Lech Walesa: Democrat or Dictator?* (Boulder, Colo.: Westview, 1993); Stephen R. Burant, "International Relations in a Regional Context: Poland and Its Eastern Neighbors—Lithuania, Belarus, Ukraine," in *Europe-Asia Studies*, vol. 45, no. 3 (1993): 395–418; Jacob Kipp, ed., *Central European Security Concerns: Bridge, Buffer or Barrier?* (London: Cass, 1993); Zdzislaw Najder, *Jaka Polska: Co i Komu Doradzalem* [What Kind of Poland: What and to Whom I Advised] (Warsaw: Editions Spotkania, 1994); Czeslaw Mojsiewicz, *Polska i jej nowi sasiedzi (1989–1993)* [Poland and her new neighbors (1989–1993)] (Torun, Poland: Wydawnictwo Adam Marszalek, 1994); Ilya Prizel and Andrew Michta, eds., *Polish Foreign Policy Reconsidered: Challenges of Independence* (London: Macmillan, 1995); Teresa Toranska, *My* [Us] (Warsaw: Oficyna Wydawnicza MOST, 1994); Andrew Cottey, *East-Central Europe after the Cold War: Poland, the Czech Republic, Slovakia and Hungary in Search of Security* (Houndmills, U.K.: Macmillan, 1995); Kazimierz Dziewanowski, *Polityka w Sercu Europy* [Politics in the Heart of Europe] (Warsaw: Oficyna Wydawnicza, 1995); Jeffrey Simon, *NATO Enlargement and Central Europe: A Study in Civil-Military Relations* (Washington, D.C.: National Defense University Press, 1996); Adrian Hyde-Price, *The International Politics of East Central Europe* (Manchester, U.K.: Manchester University Press, 1996); Ilya Prizel, *National Identity and Foreign Policy*; and Elizabeth Pond, *The Rebirth of Europe* (Washington, D.C.: Brookings Institution Press, 1999).

33. Mark Landler, "Poland Takes Pride in Assertive Stance toward Neighbors," *New York Times*, December 19, 2003, 1, A10 and "After Backing U.S. in Iraq, Poland Waits Expectantly for Economic Payback," *New York Times*, December 21, 2003, A16.

1

Putting Middle Power Politics
Theory into Practice

In an international system that increasingly connects individuals, countries, and markets, states are still key actors in international politics and define their stake in the system by their power or security. Rational decision making generally accounts for how leaders determine options, alternatives, and subsequent decisions for countries and companies to take in the international system or global marketplace. However, the particular and often flawed nature of decision makers plays a crucial role in how they utilize the different political, economic, military, and sociocultural capabilities under their state's possession, how they define their respective national interests, and how they struggle for power (seen mostly as military power) with or against each other. This struggle for power frequently leads decision makers to seek more power, influence, prestige, and security as their primary objectives, more often than not resulting in aggression rather than cooperation within the anarchical international security system. The struggle for power then remains the principal consideration in crafting international politics. Consequently, the international system's anarchical structure pushes state leaders to strengthen themselves by alignment with or against other states.[1]

Given these traditional nation-state definitions, how do middle powers attempt to survive in global anarchy, particularly when facing great power security dilemmas? The answer lies in an extension of the self-help theory that calls attention to how certain middle powers regionally affect great power security dilemmas. To understand better how middle powers survive in global anarchy via the alignments they promulgate with great powers, middle power politics theory necessitates explanation by extending important alignment strategies not confined to great power self-help frameworks. A theory of middle power politics, then, delineates new theoretical and alignment assumptions beyond great power self help to survive in global anarchy.

The conventional wisdom in international relations theory rests predominantly on great power politics and the concomitant concept of self-help.[2] In self-help anarchy, great powers choose how to ensure their power or security—often, their very survival—because they have choices about whether to cooperate with or oppose others to affect the international security system. The means to undergird power or security and assure survival involve myriad alignment strategies such as diplomacy, neutrality, appeasement, collective security, arms building, and alliance formation. This great power self-help conventional contention emanates from unipolar, bipolar, or multipolar anarchy. Most often this results from alliance formation emanating from balancing or bandwagoning behavior for materialist, threat-based, norm-focused, or identity-driven reasons. Yet, an alternative hypothesis exists to explore middle power behavior and its consequential alignment strategies. If middle powers cannot exist in a self-help world because great powers frequently ignore, manipulate, or even destroy them—because they often view middle powers as "buffer states"—then we could expect anarchy to lead to alternative alignment explanations for middle power survival.[3]

The theoretical analysis below sets the baseline for historically understanding how Poland arguably became a pivotal middle power in the twenty-first century. On the one hand, to build upon the important works on middle power politics, this analysis first addresses whether such a middle power strategy typically portrayed resorts to a self-help strategy to survive global anarchy. On the other hand, in exploring middle power alignments and seeking to extend international relations theory, this analysis also views whether it matters if the origins of early post–Cold War Poland affected historically great power regional security dilemmas differently. Secondly, the historical assessment that follows the theoretical sections underlines the traditional security dilemmas facing Poland and often consuming it. Thus, this analysis expands upon the few works done recently on middle power politics, international relations theory, and pivotal Central–East European heartland security dilemmas.[4] These theoretical and historical analyses show not only how the Polish geopolitical pivot determined its alignment strategy differently when faced with the same seemingly perennial security dilemmas at the end of the Cold War, but also offers a basis for more research on pivotal middle powers.

This chapter employs some of the main arguments in international relations theory to extend important alignment approaches, building upon underutilized theoretical explanations for arrangements states muster to survive global anarchy. In trying to extend traditional alignment theories to explain middle power politics differently from great power frameworks, this chapter aims to enrich understanding of possible new alignment patterns from relatively unexamined case studies. Granted, a theoretical extension in international relations necessarily remains limited and certainly not all-encompassing for middle powers. Indeed, the analysis below offers a means of examining particular nation-states, their foreign policy strategies, and specific geographical regions within distinctive security systems and at historically critical junctures.[5] The purpose of pin-pointing pivotal middle power politics and disaggregating what new and significant alignment strategies may have emerged tries to reveal theoretical implications for other pivotal middle powers. By arguing that middle powers make a difference regionally, this unpacking of theory and practice covers different angles than great power frameworks. Hence, middle power politics theory explains how such pivotal states as early post-Communist Poland sought to strengthen themselves, not just historically and traditionally balance against or bandwagon with certain states. Further, a theory of middle power politics also builds on alignment that enable states to "transcend," "bind," or "engage," to effect change, or merely to survive.[6] Arguments concern why this theoretical extension differs from traditional self-help in international relations and how historical frameworks elucidate arduous middle power actualities.

The following analysis demonstrates, then, the significance of a middle power politics theory and some of the significant historical foundations as a means to extend regional alignment models. First, the chapter reviews some of the main arguments in international relations theory concerning great power alignment. Secondly, this provides the baseline to extend alignment theory and develop a middle power politics alternative from great power constructs that give middle powers short shrift. This analysis develops recent middle power assessments, particularly toward Central and Eastern Europe, and extends their argumentation beyond the description of middle powers and traditional alliance theory within great power politics frameworks. Thirdly, the chapter focuses on the emerging European post–Cold War framework in the early 1990s to explain the potential for increased security dilemmas, and investigates why they did not in fact materialize. Fourthly, an assessment of Poland's historic security dilemmas explains the reasoning behind Central-East Europe's instabilities and reinforces the importance of middle power alignment promoted by post–Cold War Poland. Hence, chapter 1 sets the foundation for the remaining chapters that focus on case studies to test whether middle power politics theory discloses an extension of middle power alignment beyond self-help and explains reduction of regional security dilemmas. Such security dilemmas revolve around how much the impact of post-Communist Poland affected unified Germany, the post-Soviet successor states, and the smaller Central European neighbors.

International Relations Theory as We Know It

The conventional wisdom of the anarchical self-help world centers almost solely on how great powers exist and survive by balancing and bandwagoning. Arguments by Kenneth Waltz and Stephen Walt dominate the field to explain the self–help anarchical world of great power politics and subsequent state alignment choices.[7] According to Waltz, balancing and bandwagoning, and the distribution or redistribution of power within the systemic balance of great powers, leads to weaker state alignment with the strongest state. He views bandwagoning as the opposite of balancing alignment with periodic "balancing of would-be leaders" among states.[8] Walt varies from Waltz by regarding balance of threat as more important than balance of power. For Walt, states measure the merits of bandwagoning with or balancing against other states by determining not only which state or coalition appear strongest, but also which state or states seem most threatening. Therefore, if serious threats appear, Walt claims a state's leaders need to consider risks, decide how to respond, and calculate alignment toward the threatening state, even if weaker states capitulate to stronger, more threatening ones.[9]

Based on these systemic models, the upheaval resulting from the Cold War's end presumably would have seen great power states allying to balance more than to bandwagon to protect themselves in a self-help world from either the strongest or most threatening state.[10] Both Waltz and Walt reason that most states would resort to balancing, either to gain more power against other states or threats. In a self-help system, both authors believe states, either to preserve themselves or maximize power or security, would balance rather than bandwagon with the stronger or more threatening power.[11] The end of the Cold War, however, provoked numerous debates on systemic and state preservation, different alignments, and nonstate actors influencing state alignments more seriously.[12]

Significant alternative alignment strategies that stem from the underutilized framework of Paul Schroeder, for example, posit important variants from the traditional balancing and bandwagoning of Waltz and Walt. For Schroeder, "self-help means, at least generally and primarily, the potential or actual use of a state's own power along with that of other units for the purposes of compellence, deterrence, and other modes of controlling the actions of one's opponents." Yet, in differing from Waltz and Walt, Schroeder counters that self-help remains "relatively rare" and even defines a "fallback policy or last resort," not "balancing against an actual or potential hegemon." As a result, he presents four alignment categories to which states turn, sometimes in combination, that include designating self-help as its own alignment category. He contends that, given the period from the emergence of Westphalian states in 1648 to the beginning of the post–World War II era in 1945, "most unit actors within that system [should have] responded to crucial threats to their security and independence by resorting to self-help." Instead, great and small powers attempted, per their capabilities, "to protect their vital interests" in alternative ways. Notably, these European states faced prohibitively costly odds that negated their resort to long-term self-help strategies. To protect themselves, these states more often than not developed armed forces, forged temporary alliances, or initiated diplomacy that Schroeder identifies differently than simply self-help strategies. Important alignment measures taken included "hiding" from threats, broadening what Jack Snyder and Thomas Christensen called "buckpassing," by "ignoring or declaring neutrality" toward one or even both sides during crises. The objective focused on gaining or increasing security without initiating formal alliances, and attempting defensively to avoid the "storm" of conflict or war in isolation. Or, if such options evaporated and states still tried to avert allied commitments or resorting to force, they intended to "hide" from others by seeking security trade-offs via "diplomatic services, friendship, or non-military support."[13]

In introducing other viable alternative alignment strategies without resorting to self-help, Schroeder introduces "transcending," examines bandwagoning differently, and outlines "specializing" as important means toward achieving outcomes without turning to self-help. "Transcending" refers to states trying to grapple with international anarchy and its concomitant "conflictual politics" by resolving problems, stopping threats, or thwarting repetitive threats. To achieve this transcending strategy, an "institutional arrangement" needs to exist based on "international consensus or formal agreement on norms, rules, and procedures." This also develops some of the arguments that Glen Snyder elaborated to advance third-party ties without necessarily generating alliances between or among those states against immediate threats, or extant or emerging regional power(s), or conciliatory (cooperation) or compromise (appeasement) strategies with domineering or threatening states. Given the concepts of transcending and hiding, Schroeder further claims, in contrast to Waltz and Walt, that bandwagoning merits a more distinctive category of alignment. Unlike Waltz and Walt, who argue that alliances dominate and bandwagoning occurs less than balancing and more often signifies insecurity and even loss of independence in the trade-off for security, Schroeder maintains that bandwagoning happens more than balancing. He asserts that "throughout the Westphalian era states both great and small, aware of their vulnerability and threats, sought survival in the international arena not only by means of strategies other than balancing (by bandwagoning, hiding, and transcending) but also, precisely, by specializing." As Schroeder argues, what "specializing" signifies for middle power politics arises from the capabilities "to perform certain important international functions or fill particular vital roles within the system that no other unit could do or do as well." Consequently, Schroeder expects middle powers that specialize to propound options entailing "support of assistance" for other powers to promote middle power "leadership on these functional grounds." Nation-state survival might then stem from such specialized functions and roles, even as such states might not possess the outright abilities to defend their state's integrity. Yet, their specialization within the regional or international system created the path toward survival from Westphalia to World War II, even resulting in longevity and prosperity. As Schroeder states quite frequently, such "functions and roles modified the behavior of states, including great powers, and significantly changed their purposes and methods in using power."[14]

To a certain degree, Randall Schweller expands some of the arguments above and offers differing depictions of configurations for either alliances or "alternative" state alignments in terms of revisionist or status quo great powers. For Schweller, "bandwagoning" signifies alignment with a stronger state or coalition, and is not opposite to balancing. A state often bandwagons not only to increase power, but also to gain a reward and profit by responding to an opportunity, not just a threat. Similar to Schroeder's "transcending," Schweller's "binding" behavior with rivals in bilateral relationships restrains or controls alliance members instead of allying them against other threatening states. When such arrangements or even alliances form multilaterally, especially in collective security terms, weaker and stronger states try to attract, even integrate rising (revisionist) powers institutionally within a "new international order." They attempt to enable greater "voice" within the alliance, promote cooperation and consensus, or entangle and prevent systemic disruption. Beyond bandwagoning and binding alignment, balancing results when a state attempts to ally with a weaker state or coalition against a revisionist stronger state. Yet, balancing more often maintains or even increases tensions that usually result in aggression, an alignment separate from balancing or bandwagoning. Such political, economic, military, sociocultural aggression, or a combination of these, may descend into global tensions. These great power tensions epitomized the past century's world wars and Cold War. Consequently, "aggression" implies threatening or warlike behavior and delimits the opposite of bandwagoning, balancing, or binding, where the latter three alignments are not necessarily mutually exclusive and sometimes are even overlapping.[15] Here, he provides a framework beyond balancing, bandwagoning, and binding behaviors to form alliances, and offers alignment alternatives of "distancing" and "engagement." In distancing, or as Schroeder labels it "hiding," status quo states strive to avoid diplomatic or military coordination with greater revisionist-state threats, endeavoring to shun any alignment, if possible, except when contiguity makes this impossible. The opposite of distancing, though, concerns engagement. Importantly, engagement involves behavior characteristic of balancing, but also a strategy combining concessions and threats toward rising powers by state(s) resolved to "minimize conflict and avoid war without compromising the integrity of the international order." Consequently, Schweller's self-help strategy, encompassing his state descriptors above, differs from those of previous authors by focusing on less costly, possibly profitable alignment where great powers determine balances of interests in habitually unfavorable systemic orders.[16]

Charting New Theoretical Territory

If pivotal middle powers like post-Communist Poland represent an alignment that potentially extends the theory of self-help to explain influences on great power security dilemmas, then we might expect certain theoretical assumptions to explicate such behavior. Recent analysis shows the importance of extending the concept of traditional self-help alignment to explain the peaceful and cooperative reduction of historic and regional security dilemmas.[17] Consequently, if global anarchy affects middle powers differently than great powers, leading not just to the traditional, great power self-help world, then we could expect anarchy to lead to an alternative alignment strategy. This strategy might demonstrate a pivotal middle power "other-help" set of circumstances. In an other-help world, pivotal middle powers don't have a choice about the kind of international anarchical system in which they try to survive. They depend on other powers, whether great powers or not, for their survival, let alone their well-being, since their well-being relies on the "well-being of others" to achieve security most effectively.[18] They remain pivotal because they do affect regional security dilemmas and can influence how great powers might choose to transform the anarchical international system. But, as the literature contends, pivotal middle powers function and survive within a great power–dominant system, including the current unipolar American-dominated global order. They face the regional and international security systems based on great power calculating. Such pivotal middle powers would need to determine not only what kind of alignment ensures their survival, but also whether certain foreign policy strategies enable them to take a role, at a minimum, within their respective regional, middle power security systems. Unlike great power frameworks, middle power analysis demonstrates how other-help strategies can create options amid anarchy. These options potentially avoid self-help's all-too-often compromising or sacrificing of middle power sovereignty over its foreign policy. On the one hand, whether promoting hostile or cooperative alignment, traditional self-help definitions portray either alliance or non alliance options. An other-help framework for pivotal middle powers, on the other hand, designates the often stark realities of regional antagonism without choices for the kind of system in which to function and to be dependent on others. Therefore, such antagonism frequently forces these middle powers into very narrow regional alignment and possibly alliance paths, but not necessarily always resulting in establishing alliances to survive.

That is why this book focuses on whether a pivotal middle power like Poland needed to establish alliances immediately in the post–Cold War world through traditional alliance behavior. Regional, other-help realities may be the basis for determining whether it was early post-Communist Poland's foreign policy that projected a new kind of alignment called "bridging," an alignment pattern that necessarily did not spur tradition and immediate alliance building. In bridging, the strategy to align with all neighbors cooperatively to reduce regional security dilemmas reveals a means to avoid allying with states simply to oppose others or actually to confine potential allies. Bridging devises another means to change security dynamics for all regional powers favorably, and is not necessarily dependent on forming traditional alliances.[19] If this alignment illustrates an extension for pivotal middle power politics to affect regional security dilemmas differently, then it might provide an impetus for reassessing how pivotal middle powers formulate their regional behaviors, toward greater and smaller powers alike. Bridging might provide a baseline not only for how other regionally geopolitical middle power pivots may form alliances, but also, perhaps more importantly, for how they begin to overcome historical security dilemmas without necessarily resorting to traditional alliance behavior.

Bridging alignment builds on, but differs from, traditional alignment or collective security alliance options that had been expected to emerge in the early post–Cold War era. Bridging explains a new form of alignment particularly where pivotal middle powers aid great powers differently, not necessarily by focusing solely on alliance formation. In Poland's case, NATO membership by the late 1990s, significant influence in the Organization for Security and Cooperation in Europe, and impact on the Council of Europe, European Union, and UN over the past fifteen years rendered notable institutional developments for these cooperative or collective security arrangements.[20] But, these institutional linkages based on democratic norms, values, and standards stemmed mainly from the essential and pivotal bilateral and trilateral ties Poland initially established with its great power neighbors. The preinstitutional bridge-building alignment toward all great, middle, and smaller power neighbors explains Poland's rapid evolution. In just a few years, Poland transformed from Soviet satellite to sovereign middle power, to initiate a strategy within an international system it could not redefine as great powers can in self-help anarchy. At least in Poland's case, as a pivotal middle power, this analysis argues that Warsaw needed to rely on other-help to formulate its early post–Cold War means toward any kind of favorable geopolitical ends. This alignment went beyond simply diplomacy to survive in global anarchy. Such alignment rendered by a pivotal middle power entailed functioning without choices for changing the international security system in which that power maneuvered. Great powers might seek to bridge like middle powers, but great powers have choices in self-help anarchy to affect international security dynamics. Pivotal middle powers seek security and try to project power regionally, knowing that great powers, and especially unipolar America, guide where the international system moves. Where did pivotal middle power alignment emerge, though, and why wouldn't it necessarily just have been a subset of a self-help strategy, or bridging alignment simply a means to put together a collective security system?

This book argues that Poland experienced collective security systems that historically resulted in its isolation, subservience, and even demise prior to the international systemic changes at the end of the Cold War. By pursuing a cooperative security alignment strategy in the early 1990s, a middle power such as Poland arguably found its pivotal and regional role that enabled it to survive and contribute to international security in the twenty-first century. Since middle power Poland proved itself a consistently reliable regional security contributor during the 1990s, Warsaw's strategists envisioned wider roles with other middle and great powers—and smaller powers—in the international security system, even through its limited means. Thus, early post–Cold War Poland's strategy became important for great power neighbors and unipolar America to utilize for its middle power resources and assets in "heartland" Europe, and elsewhere like the Balkans, Afghanistan, and Iraq. Great powers did not ignore Warsaw or try to manipulate its middle power role only to serve subserviently.[21]

Pivotal middle power roles in the late 1990s and now in the post-9/11 era stem from important roots. Like post–World War II Franco–German great power cooperation and reconciliation in anarchy, post-Communist Poland implemented nonconfrontational external alignment, built a capitalist-oriented economy, and decoupled from Soviet economic backwardness.[22] Given the rapidly changing Cold War structure of global production toward capitalism and away from Soviet Communism,[23] Poland prospered by enacting the first successful and truly post-Communist Soviet Bloc free market reforms.[24] The early post–Cold War decade also witnessed Poland aligning with traditionally hegemonic great powers Germany and Russia, and antagonistic middle power Ukraine, differently than Cold War "satellite" or interwar balancer.[25] By logrolling to form an antiexpansionist domestic consensus on foreign policy,[26] as the Soviet Bloc disintegrated, post-Communist Poland utilized the post–Cold War redistribution of material capabilities for cooperative reintegration—and overcame the Soviet satellite legacy.[27] By examining why post-Communist Poland pivotally affected great and other powers regionally, this book examines what different alignment strategy evolved and explains an alternative to traditional self-help theory. Hence, the case study analyses in the subsequent chapters use pivotal middle power alignment to argue for an extension of self-help through other-help and offer insights for middle powers, struggling with regional security dilemmas.

Beyond Conventional Wisdom

Contrary to variations of great power politics theory, important contributions about middle powers focus attention on why these smaller states mattered in the early 1990s and why they remain important in the twenty-first century. Clearly, as argued above, middle powers by themselves cannot confront great powers for any great duration. By extending Schroeder's concept of specializing, utilizing some of the arguments that Schweller formulates on engaging, bridging explains a new type of alignment beyond self-help and argues for an other-help framework. Analysis extends alignment theory of geopolitically pivotal middle powers like post–Cold War Poland, its survival, and its new form of bridging behavior. Such alignment enabled Warsaw's policymakers to promote crucial regional cooperation in the early post–Cold War years between historically antagonistic Germany and Russia. Without the ability to form the pivotal bilateral and trilateral linkages—security alignment not defined as alliances—Poland would very likely not have later integrated into NATO and the EU by the late 1990s and early twenty-first century, respectively.[28] This other-help alignment to bridge between and among contiguous or regional great powers not only engaged nations differently—cooperatively—but also afforded Poland the means to play its pivotal middle power role between great powers.

Poland survived in the post–Cold War anarchy dominated by great powers because it dealt with realities differently than it had in the interwar era of fateful balancing and alliances, or the Cold War period of compromised, subservient diplomacy that lead to Soviet satellitedom. Polish foreign policy–makers understood the limitations of trying to form alliances bilaterally or trilaterally based on their pitfalls of lost statehood or compromised sovereignty in foreign policy. They appreciated how nonpredatory bandwagoning regionally might reduce some great power tensions, but likely generate other possible security concerns. Given the twentieth century's constant state of conflict or war, Poland couldn't necessarily expect its neighbors to cooperate and support Warsaw's sovereignty in foreign policy–making. Nor could Poland depend on a type of collective security system to evolve from the post–Cold War upheaval to protect its domestic, peaceful post-Communist democratic revolution to lead Central-East Europe in 1989. Yet, they faced the post–Cold War reality without options like great powers, but created a specialized role via other help as the great powers rapidly changed the international security system. That middle power specialization within the heart of Europe provided a multifold bridge for regional great powers. Since the great powers called the shots, particularly over the collapse of the Cold War security framework, Poland specialized regionally to regain its sovereignty over foreign policy and contributed differently in Europe's heartland.

The concept of middle power bridging that Poland illustrated contributes to regional and international security and stability nonaggressively and extends traditional international relations alignment theories. Bridging represents alignment by middle powers with all neighbors to lessen historic security dilemmas. In an other-help world, middle powers shun playing states against one another. They align with more than the one or two other neighbors, often the greater contiguous powers. Middle power bridging builds upon the notion that "under a wide range of conditions, adversaries can best achieve their security goals through cooperative policies, not competitive ones, and should, therefore, choose cooperation when these conditions prevail."[29] Bridging between and among neighboring states defines how middle powers build the ties that bind so that regional stability-enhancing alliances might simply emerge, let alone expand peacefully. That argument forms the basis for analyzing the origins of middle power security alignment not through alliance theory, but through the critically important baseline to explain nonalliance alignment that enhances regional stability differently.

The case studies in the subsequent chapters provide the context for better understanding how such pivotal middle powers as Poland dealt with Germany, Russia, Ukraine, Lithuania, Belarus, the Czech and Slovak Republics, and Hungary. Indeed, these case studies demonstrate how Poland first needed to establish and expand its bilateral and trilateral state-to-state relationships before Warsaw could integrate into such alliances as NATO, rather than assessing everything in terms of alliance theory or collective security alignment. There's a significant history behind how Poland reintegrated into Europe and why alliance theory cannot fully explain such variables as regional security alignment. Not every pivotal middle power joins regional alliances or possesses institutional alliance options regionally. But bridging alignment broadens explanation about pivotal middle power behavior. As some collective security norms, rules, and procedures did evolve pragmatically by the twentieth century's end in Europe, Poland's early post–Cold War alignment strategy placed it to contribute to the emerging post-9/11 international security framework.[30]

By assessing great powers, post–Cold War theoretical and empirical analyses aptly illustrate causes of aggression and war, or cooperation, mainly by great power balancing or bandwagoning.[31] None links such international relations theory and foreign policy processes to middle power politics, however, as a way of showing the peaceful impact on great powers.[32] Contrary to conventional wisdom, alterations in aggregate power distribution resulting from the Communist Bloc's collapse by the early 1990s did not necessarily increase security competition or conflict across all regions.[33] This analysis develops a middle power politics theory by explaining post–Cold War cooperative changes for historically antagonistic middle and great power relations. It argues that Polish–German relations followed aspects of Franco–German post–World War II reconciliation, while Poland promoted regional cooperation toward Ukraine and Russia, as well as smaller regional neighboring states.[34] By assessing if Central-East European middle powers not only reinforced their security, but also reduced tensions and decreased security dilemmas among great powers, this analysis extends middle power explanations by assessing other-help decision-making.

The subsequent case study chapters, however, also consider how bridging in an other-help anarchical world compares to balancing and bandwagoning in self-help's global anarchy. Contentions over whether Poland's middle power politics depicted bandwagoning with Germany or balancing with NATO against Russia raise important issues regarding the merits of bridging. Did residual Soviet military power in post-Soviet Russia truly threaten Poland or NATO for that matter? Did Poland really portray post–World War II Franco–German rapprochement as an allusion for Poland to support unified Germany's NATO when NATO's changing post–Cold War role still opposed Soviet power? Did Poland's goal of maintaining American military presence in Europe mainly signify the hope to counterbalance residual Soviet military capabilities? These questions remain critical to analysis about Polish bridging alignment strategy and whether balancing, bandwagoning, or bridging reveals the best analytical framework for middle power politics. Such issues enable greater theoretical and empirical explanation about whether Poland represented a middle power role regionally or tried to become a greater power over the less capable powers emerging independently on its borders.

In bridging great power change and middle power politics theory, this book explains the merits and pitfalls of middle powers seeking security.[35] What explains, then, how key middle powers reassured and enhanced great powers, even America the unipolar power, particularly after the Cold War's collapse?[36] For example, the anticipated post–Cold War great power balance again endangered Central and Eastern Europe middle powers. Aggressive or submissive middle power alignments should have arisen. Central-East Europe could have been expected to react to the changing material incentives of European great powers, like the interwar or Soviet eras, by playing neighboring great powers against each other; resorting to an outside power, such as Britain, France, or America, to align against Germany and/or the USSR; balancing unified Germany and post-Soviet Russia, and even post-Soviet Ukraine, against one another, or band-wagoning with some of them against others; attempting to dominate smaller Central or Eastern European nations; or trying to remain nonaligned, or possibly neutral. In post–Cold War Poland, post-Communist leaders should have aggressively aligned against neighbors, the ones seen most threatening, simply to survive. Yet, such developments didn't occur to any significant extent.

Instead, after destructive world wars and damaging Cold War repression, post-Communist Poland promulgated new alignment with larger, uncertain neighbors. As the Cold War framework disintegrated, no European leader adopted Otto Von Bismarck's 1860s strategy. Bismarck's German "hub and spokes" linked most European states to the new German "center" to "remain both tied down and beholden to Berlin."[37] Unlike in the 1860s, in the 1990s a binding of states like unified Germany and post-Communist Russia to one state "hub" didn't materialize. Rather, a multipolar European security system emerged, shaped by great powers, including the influence by America, the super power. Germany's late twentieth-century unifier, Helmut Kohl, did achieve German unification within EU and NATO structures, extending German-U.S. ties in the U.S.-dominated international system.[38] No single state, however, attracted West, Central, and East Europe into one dominant system. Hence, post-Communist Poland aligned with larger neighbors differently—initiating a new, nonconfrontational stance. Certainly, democratizing, activist-cum-post-Communist policymakers wanted to avoid Poland's historic partitions and satellite-dom.[39]

The vast systemic transformation crucially altered how much post-Communist middle power alignment mattered for regional cooperative security. By attempting to avert its historic pitfalls, would Poland's external alignment, promulgated regionally during the early 1990s, have arisen without America's influence? Arguably, without strengthened American–German ties, regional tensions would not have lessened and aggression in Central-Southeastern Europe might have increased.[40] Such developments would greatly have hindered Poland's European reintegration. Moreover, America's strategic partnership with Russia and Ukraine played an essential role in allowing middle powers like Poland to regain sovereignty over their respective foreign policy directions and stabilize after decades of dominance or uncertainty vis-à-vis neighbors. This new U.S.–European security "umbrella" via its cooperative engagement and enlargement strategy enabled Poland to move away from the Soviet orbit and elude potential Russian neoimperial resurgence.[41] Importantly, Poland promoted a new brand of regional security cooperation among great powers that played a specialized regional role in pushing the great powers to reevaluate the transatlantic relationship between America and NATO. Unquestionably, Poland hedged against Russian neoimperialism by advocating America's long-term European role, NATO's institutional structures to retain German integration, and post-Soviet states' independence. Yet, without the historic Soviet Bloc's crumbling, Poland's post-Communist bridging alignment would likely not have unfolded.[42] Consequently, when faced with enormous systemic changes, Polish foreign policy–makers defined an other-help world existence. Contrary to the typically self-help world in which Polish balancing or bandwagoning succumbed to earlier ill-fated twentieth-century pursuits, Poland attempted neither to hide in neutrality nor hide its post–Cold War ambitions. Poland built bridges to all regional powers. Warsaw took advantage of international upheaval, finding a specialized place in other-help anarchy as a middle power to survive. Once Poland created the new, early post–Cold War security relationships with its great power neighbors Warsaw solidified the linkages to enable it to reintegrate into Europe. If it had played neighboring states off of one another, or sided with one neighbor against another, Poland might not have solidified peaceful, nonconfrontational alignment bilaterally and trilaterally that could then result in the sort of institutional integration developments that followed suit in the late 1990s and early twenty-first century. As a result, Poland demonstrated at the outset of the post–Cold War era its import to the great regional powers in "the center of Europe"—for Poland to be seen as a pivotal post–Cold War "bridge" for West and East.[43]

Understanding Poland's Middle Power Politics and Strategy

The history behind Poland's post–Cold War alignment strategy discloses important roots for how Poland's first post-Communist foreign minister designed and promoted different and significant middle power alignment. Krzysztof Skubiszewski faced the challenges to formulate and implement a foreign policy representative of Poland's newly elected post-Communist government and responsive to Central-East Europe's upheaval. From the moment he arrived, Skubiszewski became enmeshed in historical turning points. He navigated a new foreign policy strategy as part of Central-East Europe's first post-Communist government in the spring of 1989. As he tried to promote a much different alignment direction for the Polish middle power, the *Solidarnosc* movement led the largely peaceful revolutions from Poland to sweep across the heart of Europe by late that summer. The nonpartisan foreign minister understood the precarious geopolitical location in which Poland found itself once again amid great international upheaval. In those early weeks and months, and, during the four successive governments in which he served from 1989 to 1993, Skubiszewski methodically considered options to take his country beyond its "disadvantaged situation" geopolitically. He tried to transform it through new relationships with both a unifying Germany and a disintegrating USSR as the Cold War framework in Central-East Europe collapsed. Whereas the foreign minister described Poland's geopolitical reality between these two great powers as "a curse for us, we have been gripped in a vice, and the two powers have exercised pressure on us," he emphasized pan-European cooperation via sovereign Polish foreign policy.[44] What follows provides the historical picture that characterized Skubiszewski's terms during these four tumultuous and painstaking years for building democracy at home and constructing new foreign policy alignment.

Does one come away from the following historical overview, seeing Poland as a model of pragmatism for middle power politics, or as a democratizing nation-state that acted rashly and disruptively? To discern more clearly the notion of security dilemmas between larger unified Germany and post-Soviet Russia through Skubiszewski's lengthy tenure, Skubiszewski's goals must be weighed against whether he chose options that solidified Poland abroad and developed foreign policy consensus at home. One of the best ways to grasp Poland's middle power regional role and determine whether pragmatism won out over rashness is to understand Poland's vision of *racja stanu—raison d'état* or "interest of the state." This explains why Skubiszewski and his efforts to convince other key players to believe in *racja stanu* truly distinguished his motives as Poland searched for full sovereignty over its foreign policy. Critical junctures focus on the uncertainty over German unification, multifaceted planks toward Soviet disintegration and the emerging post-USSR states, development of a cooperative Visegrad Central European Triangle and initiation of links to NATO and a baseline to the EU. The ofttimes political acrimony, however, that existed among top government leaders and elected politicians constantly threatened to derail Poland's overarching goal of regaining sovereignty over its foreign policy to chart new courses. Throughout Skubiszewski's years we observe key building blocks promulgating the fundamental tenets of *racja stanu*, even as domestic debates endangered misgauging Europe's historic opportunities for changes.

To answer the question of whether Skubiszewski and his *MSZ* team formulated and implemented a pragmatic policy—i.e., whether it turned out to project a new bridging other-help strategy—Warsaw's security dilemma between Bonn and Moscow must also be seen beyond contemporary middle power alignment. Some of Poland's post–World War II foreign policies and pivotal émigré and underground notions helped Skubiszewski design his post-Communist strategy. Analysis about Poland's Communist-era lessons of semisovereign foreign policy, particularly during the leadership of Wladislaw Gomulka from 1956 to 1970, and incisive émigré and underground ideas from the mid-1960s to late 1980s, illustrates antecedents of Skubiszewski's post-Communist vision for Poland's security dilemma between Germany and Russia. Thus, an overall appraisal of Skubiszewski's regional alignment sets the baseline for subsequent chapters on Poland's middle power strategy toward great, middle, and smaller power neighbors within a rapidly changing regional and international system.

Poland's Semisovereignty during the Communist Era

Characterized by Polish and non-Polish analyses as caught "between East and West," Poland sees itself as a state constantly striving not only to maintain its independence and sovereignty between Germany and Russia, but also at times, to fight for its very survival.[45] This depiction of Poland trapped in a security dilemma between Germany and Russia embodies Poland's struggle for the freedom to exist and to rule over its own destiny, especially since the three partitions in the late 1700s by Russia, Prussia, and Austria. Yet, as one notable Polish political historian commented, Poland experienced a "fourth" type of foreign partition with the 1939 Nazi–Soviet Pact because Poland's "independent existence depended entirely on German–Russian relations, over which we [Poland] had no influence."[46] Consequently, Poland endured a legacy of limited sovereignty with the decisions made by the great powers at the 1943–1945 Allied Conferences in Tehran, Yalta, and Potsdam. Ultimately, backed by Soviet leader Josef Stalin, the Polish Communists consolidated their rule by the late 1940s and prevented any free and democratic elections in Poland for nearly forty years.

Though Poland's democratic bid to regain full sovereignty reached a dramatic crossroads during 1989 with the *Solidarnosc*–Communist Roundtable and partially free elections, Warsaw's Communist-era semisovereignty remained, particularly in Gomulka's policies toward Bonn and Moscow. The de-Stalinization policies of Soviet leader Nikita Khrushchev during the early 1950s served as the turning point for allowing Poland's limited sovereign foreign policy making to develop. Khrushchev's secret speech denouncing Stalin's terror at the 1956 Soviet Communist Party's Twentieth Congress released Polish frustrations against the tenets of Soviet Marxist domination. Poland's Communist elite and a large majority of the population demanded greater sovereignty over its policies.[47] Given this restlessness, Gomulka realized that, to maintain power and demonstrate enough loyalty to Moscow, he needed to find a compromise within Polish society. As he solidified power during the fall of 1956 and throughout 1957, Gomulka explained that the "Polish way to socialism" signified that "every country should possess full independence and the right of every nation to sovereignty in an independent country should be fully respected." Moreover, he argued "the specific feature of the Polish nation determined by its history is the unique sensitivity to its independence. This is the result of the partitions, the centuries of oppression of the nation whose tradition is a millennium long."[48] Gomulka not only upheld Poland's national interests to keep control of Poland's Communist Party and the state itself, but he also ensured his fealty to Moscow remained unwavering.[49] By using such a rationale, Gomulka's leadership promulgated foreign policies on regional security issues like the Rapacki Plan and the Oder–Neisse Polish–German border to demonstrate Warsaw's limited sovereignty over its foreign policy.

Even if Gomulka's leadership initiated policies toward Bonn with the tacit approval of Moscow, Poland still displayed an ability to conduct its limited sovereign policymaking toward the Federal Republic of Germany (FRG) and the West. The first effort focused on the 1957–1958 regional denuclearization plan for Central Europe launched by Polish foreign minister Adam Rapacki. Rapacki stated that the removal of Soviet nuclear forces from Poland, Czechoslovakia, and the German Democratic Republic (GDR) and the removal of American nuclear weapons from the FRG conceivably enabled these four states to forgo any future manufacturing or stockpiling. Warsaw regarded its foreign policy initiative as important not only for addressing these states directly, but also for declaring its position on a key European security issue—arms control—reserved for both superpowers. More importantly, the Rapacki Plan attempted to deter the West Germans from obtaining nuclear weapons. This Polish (and Soviet) concern underlined Warsaw's great fear of a militarily more powerful Germany, particularly given that the FRG started to rearm conventionally when it decided to join NATO in 1955. However, underlying these aspects of the Rapacki Plan, Gomulka's leadership implicitly upheld the continued role of the United States to determine the major issues of European security as the other superpower, an unstated Polish objective in the Rapacki Plan that masked differences between Warsaw and Moscow. By portraying the Rapacki Plan in terms of restraining West German nationalism, Gomulka tried to deny Moscow its dominance in Central Europe and stem the Soviet desire for more power in Europe. Furthermore, the Rapacki Plan also envisioned a partial withdrawal of Soviet forces from Poland. Though Gomulka acquiesced under the threat of force by Khrushchev and allowed Soviet troops to remain in Poland in 1956, his advocacy of the Rapacki Plan less than two years later again raised Polish national interests at variance with those of the USSR. Given these implied Polish objectives within the plan's overall stated goal of a denuclearized and potentially neutral Germany, Warsaw aspired to a more equitable relationship with Moscow.[50]

The Western powers rejected this lofty, but unrealistic Polish diplomacy, arguing that Rapacki's denuclearization proposal nullified the Western nuclear deterrent in Europe and detrimentally affected the global superpower balance of power. First of all, NATO remained dependent on nuclear retaliation against the larger Warsaw Pact conventional military threat. To yield their nuclear deterrent in the FRG would severely limit West European nuclear resolve. Moreover, FRG leaders strongly favored reunification with the GDR and rejected the Polish contention, like the Soviet argument, that German neutrality increased European security. Contrary to Bonn's position, Poland desired to maintain the post–World War II status quo by strengthening the GDR's status, by forcing the FRG to renounce any territorial demands, and by obtaining Bonn's pledge to uphold the Oder–Neisse border. However, West European fears that neutralization of Germany would result in an American military withdrawal from Europe prevented any consideration of the Rapacki Plan. Simply put, the U.S. and NATO strategy relied on the FRG's firm commitment to the alliance and its nuclear deterrent. The FRG's obligation to stand as the bulwark against the superior

Warsaw Pact conventional military threat precluded a lesser power like Poland from proposing arms control initiatives which upset the global superpower balance of forces. In the end, the Rapacki Plan's failure stemmed from Poland's unrealistic strategy to advance its interests.[51]

Poland did demonstrate its semisovereign foreign policy, however, by promoting the Rapacki Plan with its implicit, different national interests from the USSR's, even if it failed internationally. Yet, in the Rapacki regional security initiative, Poland's leaders continually felt enormous uncertainty over the FRG's refusal to confirm the Oder–Neisse line. Ever since the Yalta and Potsdam decisions, the status of Poland's contested western border with what became the GDR remained unresolved, pending a future peace conference to propound a formal treaty.[52] At those summits, the Western powers, particularly the FRG and America, played into Stalin's hands and increased Warsaw's fears by not recognizing the Oder–Neisse border. For Poles, whether Stalin-controlled Lublin Communists or independent London nationalists, the indefinite border created tensions until the 1991 Polish–German State Treaty resolved all territorial disputes.[53] Over several decades, Poland endured the Stalinist and subsequent Cold War legacy of geopolitical dependency on Moscow to maintain the security of Poland's western border. When the FRG elections in 1969 brought a new government to power that promised both to promote a new eastern policy and to establish some type of Polish–German modus vivendi, however, Gomulka sought to begin dialogue with Bonn.[54]

Even though Poland's misgivings about the Oder–Neisse line allowed Gomulka to unite most of the population around an anti-German stance in the years before newly elected FRG chancellor Willy Brandt took office, unofficial Polish efforts to reconcile Poles and Germans occurred several years prior to the official Polish–German rapprochement. The Polish Church, long known for its ability to maneuver between the Communist and non-Communist parts of Polish society, provided the impetus toward Polish–German reconciliation when its controversial and unsanctioned pastoral letters to German bishops in the mid-1960s sparked disputes with Gomulka's leadership and throughout the Communist Party. By offering forgiveness to the West German bishops concerning the atrocities of World War II, the Polish bishops provoked Gomulka's regime, mainly because the Communist authorities feared the Church's political role and refused to allow it to represent foreign policy interests.[55] Gomulka's fear mongering, however, drew upon the historic Polish anxiety toward German might.[56] The Polish leadership stressed to the population the dire implications of continual German revanchism toward the Polish western border. Additionally, this territory contained about a quarter of Poland's population and almost a third of its industrial production. Hence, the specter of losing one of the few tangible gains from the war played upon Polish nationalist sentiment.[57]

Warsaw's recognition of Soviet dominance over its security in Europe won Poland limited latitude on foreign policy, the result of Gomulka's loyalty for the 1968 Warsaw Pact invasion of Czechoslovakia, and facilitated Gomulka's reconciliation with the FRG. With Brandt's victory, Bonn tried to mend relations with Poland as the FRG also attempted to achieve its larger goal of establishing a better FRG–USSR relationship. Once Brandt's government reversed the long-standing post–World War II sequence of unification, elections, and that territorial negotiations to demonstrate he first wanted to talk about the political and territorial issues such as the border, Gomulka reversed his anti-German rhetoric. The Polish leader then began planning the first official Polish–German talks since the 1934 Non-Aggression Pact. Yet, even if Gomulka attempted to exert his own foreign policy, it took the August 1970 USSR–FRG Treaty to usher in Polish–German normalization and eventually the Polish–FRG treaty that December. By following Moscow's policies toward Bonn, the Poles avoided the sensitivity of the FRG's objection over recognizing the GDR and negotiated directly with Brandt's government. Though the Polish–FRG treaty failed to mention the "final border recognition" clause Gomulka adamantly wanted, the Polish leader still achieved a milestone. That achievement focused on the Polish–German bilateral treaty to increase regional security, even if the Bonn government seemed more intent on forging links to Moscow than to Warsaw. In fact, both Polish and Soviet treaties signified political, albeit not legal, steps with the renunciation of territorial claims and endorsement for the integrity of the Polish–German border. Subsequently, the internationally recognized Polish–FRG treaty of 1970 also advanced European security and defined a breakthrough for Polish foreign policy from which Skubiszewski determined, twenty years later, to build a post-Communist foreign strategy.[58]

Foreign Policy Tenets:
Émigré and Underground Perspectives

The roots of Skubiszewski's post-Communist foreign policy also stem from the tenets of some of the key Polish non-Communist émigré and underground notions about policy toward Germany and Russia. From the late-1940s until the late 1980s, the premier Polish émigré journal, the Paris-based *Kultura*, provided penetrating analyses of Poland's geopolitical status between Germany and Russia. The Polish diaspora's ability to obtain articles from the Polish underground and other prominent European intellectuals, publish them together with works from the Polish émigré community, and smuggle *Kultura* consistently into Poland promoted a broad debate about Poland's historic security dilemma between Germany and Russia.

From the outset, *Kultura*'s editorial staff, including its prominent London-based Polish political publicist and historical commentator, Juliusz Mieroszewski, became one of the most iconoclastic Polish intellectual journals within the Polish émigré community and throughout the Polish underground. Often taking positions that resulted in heated debates about such important geopolitical issues as Poland's "historical claim" to rule over Ukraine, Lithuania, and Belorussia, what Mieroszewski termed the "ULB," *Kultura*'s articles raised difficult questions and regularly published contrary opinions vis-à-vis the Polish diaspora, Polish underground, and Communist leaders. Above all, during the 1960s and 1970s, Mieroszewski, the most renowned *Kultura* editorial writer and contributor offered Poles inside Poland and abroad unabashed criticism of Poland's foreign policy in the twentieth century. Such criticism angered the Communist authorities and they tried to suppress his analysis, often infuriating Communist and non-Communist Poles alike, who refused to repudiate historical Polish territorial aggrandizement.[59]

Mieroszewski formulated a clear and enduring vision for Poland to overcome its historic security dilemma between Germany and Russia. His thesis rested on the geopolitical reality that "we can demand that the Russians renounce imperialism on the condition that we, too, once and for all give up our traditional historical imperialism in all its forms and manifestations."[60] His critique also posed a stark reality with which Polish leaders needed to grapple seriously if they wanted to achieve long-term peaceful relations with their two larger neighbors.[61]

Further, Mieroszewski argued that Poland needed to forswear the imperialist policies no longer relevant for the predominantly Polish unitary post–World War II middle power state. Instead, Poland needed to act as a bridge for Russia to the West. This "bridge," Mieroszewski felt, would enable Warsaw to "Europeanize" Russia.[62] Such a Polish geopolitical "evolution," Mieroszewski posited, would allow Poland to avoid its seemingly perennial quandary as either a Russian "satellite" or a German–Russian "pawn," particularly the repetition of the German–Soviet Treaty of Rapallo.[63] To normalize Polish–Russian relations in the Cold War, Mieroszewski asserted that Poles needed to move beyond their military legend of the 1920 "Miracle on the Vistula" against Russia and their unrealistic centuries-old "battle" to control the *Kresy*—Poland's so-called ULB territories.[64] Moreover, Mieroszewski predicted that when the Cold War ended and the USSR faced "decolonization"—quite a radical thought for its time (1966)—Poland and even Russia held the possibility for rejoining the European community of nations. Thus, Mieroszewski enunciated his concept for a new Poland, a future sovereign, free state that would forsake any domination of the ULB.[65]

Mieroszewski's rebuke of both Polish and Russian imperialism equally as a "barbarian anachronism" toward the ULB also provided a compelling notion for both states to consider that self-determination rightfully belonged to the ULB. Whether under a Pilsudskiite "Eastern program" based on the "lofty Jagiellonian idea"[66] or a repressive tsarist and subsequent Communist "Great Russian Program," Mieroszewski argued "the ULB issue determined Polish–Russian relations and condemned us [Poles] to either imperialism or to satellitedom." If competition over domination of the ULB continued between Poland and Russia, Mieroszewski contended that Polish independence would remain fleeting. Therefore, only true independence for each of the ULB states founded upon "good-neighborly relations" with Warsaw and Moscow would reduce and likely eliminate Russian and Polish imperialism in the *Kresy*.[67]

For Mieroszewski, Jozef Pilsudski's Eastern policy initially demonstrated pragmatism because it "aimed at leading Poland out of the German–Russian vicious circle." Had Pilsudski achieved the federated alliance he sought with the ULB, particularly an independent Ukraine and some form of "democratic," non-Bolshevik Russia, Mieroszewski surmised that Polish independence could have succeeded without dominance from either Moscow or Berlin. However, Roman Dmowski's domestic-led nationalistic opposition toward anti-Russian and Polish–ULB federated policies, resistance from the ULB, and antagonism toward Poland from the weakening Russian White Armies defeated Pilsudski's vision for an Eastern federation. Post-Pilsudski Poland faced even more dire consequences with the Ribbentrop–Molotov Pact and the Yalta agreement. But, for all his criticism of Pilsudski, Mieroszewski stated, "Pilsudski was right in appreciating that only a world power could endure between Russia and Germany, not a middle-size state." Poles, Mieroszewski stated, endured the demise of their state between Germany and Russia, and he discerned that "no one will make the Poles into an imperialist nation. We already have our imperialistic great-power phase behind us."[68] Although Mieroszewski remained concerned about possible German revanchism, he stressed that an FRG contained within the European Cold War framework gave Poland an opportunity to serve as "Russia's major partner" in Central-East Europe.[69] Furthermore, he felt that the German threat to Poland remained outdated regarding the historic German *Drang nach Osten* (March to the East). To eliminate German irredentism, he argued Germans must finally recognize the Oder–Neisse border and renounce territorial aspirations for Ukraine. By acknowledging Central-East Europe's territorial integrity, he believed the FRG would increase its chances for German unification and reconciliation with Russia.[70]

In an important set of arguments, Mieroszewski also devised a different Polish security role with Poland acting as a "bridge" for Russia to Europe. Warsaw stayed dependent on Moscow, but avoided another fateful security dilemma ending in partition or destruction between powerful neighbors, primarily because U.S. troops remained stationed in the FRG.[71] Mieroszewski asserted, however, that Poles needed to think beyond their "us or them mentality" toward the Russians. Accordingly, he said "we must seek contact and an understanding with those Russians who are prepared to recognize the full right to self-determination of the ULB." Similarly, "we must forever renounce our right to Wilno and Lwow. . . . We must also give up all designs that would, when the opportunity arises, aim to establish our predominance in the East at the expense of those three nations."[72] Even if Mieroszewski neglected to recognize that Russian dissidents might some day help liberalize policies toward the ULB, his important recommendations set a strong foundation for some of the Polish dissidents who were to comprise *Solidarnosc*. With Poland's *Solidarnosc* and compatriot Central and Eastern European dissidents, including those from the Soviet Republics, cooperation began across the East Bloc.[73] His sagacity presaged lessons applied by Skubiszewski's *MSZ* to develop postimperial policies toward Germany and Russia. It also elucidated how post-Communist Poland could reintegrate into Europe by "creat[ing] a Polish–Hungarian–Czech grouping [to] strengthen the position of cooperating partners vis-à-vis Moscow."[74]

Mieroszewski's death in 1976 marked the rise of some important Polish underground publications that greatly affected Skubiszewski's post-Communist strategy. Influenced by Mieroszewski's writings, several pivotal Polish underground foreign policy thinkers in May 1976 published a document titled *Polskie Porozumienie Niepodleglosciowe* (PPN: Polish Alliance for Independence) and smuggled it abroad. Its release occurred just before the 1976 food price riots and the creation of the Worker's Self-Defense Committee, a prelude to *Solidarnosc's* creation. The PPN document's authors, a prescient group of intellectuals led by Zdzislaw Najder and Jan Olszewski, who became key post-Communist foreign policy–makers, introduced a significant program of assumptions and goals which underlay many of the policies Skubiszewski later promoted. The PPN document elaborated its foreign policy priorities by stressing "the sovereignty of the nation [is] understood as an inalienable right of a national collective to decide its own fate." Furthermore, Polish–German relations required "full information and free exchange of people and ideas [that] constitute the only manner of solving age-old quarrels." In the PPN document, Russia, as opposed to the USSR, "constitutes the most crucial aspect of Polish foreign policy." Their statement that "real sovereign equality precluded an authentic friendship between the Polish and Russian nations" went beyond Mieroszewski's stance. For Ukraine, Lithuania, and Belorussia, the PPN document proclaimed, like Mieroszewski, that Poland must not aspire to any territory. Yet, the PPN document demanded from those of the ULB region the "guarantee to the Poles living in those territories equal rights and the free preservation of the Polish language and the national culture."[75] Such powerful declarations concerning how Poland needed to change its foreign policy reverberated throughout the underground and émigré communities.

The coalescence of *Solidarnosc* after Pope John Paul II's visit to Poland in 1978 and the labor unrest in 1979–1980 allowed these émigré and underground writings to emerge as planks in the ten-million-strong movement. Under labor leader Lech Walesa's leadership, one of the significant statements by *Solidarnosc* resounded inside and outside Poland in the form of the "Message to the Working People of Eastern Europe." Focused on the plight of trade unions throughout the East Bloc, the "message" echoed sentiments about freedom and independence, and encouraged common action. It read, "delegates of the First Congress of Independent Trade Union *Solidarnosc* sends the workers of Albania, Bulgaria, Czechoslovakia, East Germany, Romania, Hungary, and all peoples of the Soviet Union their greetings and words of respect. . . . We want to express our deep feelings of our common destiny. . . . In spite of lies spread in your countries, we are a free and genuine union. . . . We will support all of you who enter the difficult road leading to the creation of free trade unions."[76]

Shortly after this bold "message" reached millions of workers and intellectuals around Central and Eastern Europe, Poland's Communist authorities imposed martial law and imprisoned leaders such as Walesa. Even though they tried to intimidate the *Solidarnosc* movement by incarcerating its leadership during the 1980s and suppressing underground publications, the Communist regime failed to stem the underground's determination to publish analyses on Polish Western and Eastern policies which built upon Mieroszewski's arguments and continued to present important non-Communist alternatives. For instance, during Easter 1984, Warsaw activists formed the Congress of National *Solidarnosc* and actually advocated German reunification to redress the Yalta accord, but also demanded a guarantee of the inviolability of Poland's western border.[77] Later that November another underground group comprising the political organizations the *WSN* (Liberty–Justice–Independence), the Political Movement, Liberation, and the Liberal–Democratic Party "Independence," used Poland's November Day of Independence to disseminate a statement about cooperation to support Soviet Bloc states. Their statement underscored that "the road to freedom lies in cooperation with our brothers from behind the Sudeten and Carpathian Mountains and from the other bank of the River Bug."[78] Furthermore, on Yalta's fortieth anniversary, this same WSN, Liberation, and Independence group released another, more passionate declaration on Polish Eastern policy, calling for common ground among ULB dissidents to unite against Communist repression, recognize Poland's eastern frontiers, and uphold the ULB's independence. That declaration underlined "the necessity of common agreement in the future regarding the contemporary eastern frontier of Poland, although it was forced upon us by alien forces," a frontier that needed to remain intact and comprise free and independent states.[79]

Two young underground thinkers, Aleksander Hall and Grzegorz Kostrzewa-Zorbas, who later figured prominently as foreign policy advisors, also authored incisive pieces in the mid-1980s. From Hall, who had belonged to several opposition groups in Gdansk since the late 1960s and became one of the first advisors to join Tadeusz Mazowiecki's cabinet in September 1989, came a profound statement on Polish–Russian relations. He wrote that "in the present order of things neither Poland's independence nor genuine understanding between Poles and Russians is possible. But it is possible to make preparations for both and we should undertake them now."[80] For Kostrzewa-Zorbas, the underground served as a laboratory for testing foreign policy ideas, particularly through his important underground foreign policy journal, *Nowa Koalicja*, dedicated to opposing Communism regionally in Central-East Europe. To hide his identity, he edited and published under the pseudonym Marcin Mieguszowiecki, and also played an active role in the WSN group. In one of *Nowa Koalicja*'s first issues, he wrote about the "need for a coalition of Eastern European countries." This concept became the underpinning of some of Skubiszewski's key foreign policy tenets five years later, when Kostrzewa-Zorbas took over as the deputy director of the Department of Europe, one of only a handful of non-Communists to join the *MSZ* after Skubiszewski.[81]

Such declarations and statements reflected the fundamental philosophies by the foreign policy thinkers in *Solidarnosc*. As Konstanty Gebert, a famous journalist in both the *Solidarnosc* and post-Communist eras, and well known by the underground pseudonym Dawid Warszawski, reminisced about foreign policy issues raised by *Solidarnosc* during the underground period:

> Quite a number of prominent people involved in *Solidarnosc*'s thinking were simply quite well versed in the different traditions of Russian culture as well as Ukrainian history. This prevented them from having a simplistic view of what was happening out there. Russia, Ukraine, Lithuania, Belorussia were real entities with real histories, with real cultures. We identified the issues at stake in the region as political issues vs. national issues. It was not a clash of Pole vs. Russian; it was a clash of freedom movements against oppressive regimes. And, this was language in which we could make ourselves understood to Russians, Ukrainians, Lithuanians.[82]

Taken together, the semisovereign moves by Gomulka and the notions espoused by the Polish émigré community toward Germany and Russia inspired the *Solidarnosc* underground activists and provided a foundation for the future post-Communist foreign policy. Given the upheaval unleashed throughout Poland in the late 1980s by Soviet leader Gorbachev's "new thinking" in foreign policy, many of the fundamental changes demanded by the Polish underground became possible. Moreover, Gorbachev's flexibility toward Soviet Bloc reform not only transformed Polish–Soviet relations, but also challenged the fundamental principles on which the Polish Communist leadership based its survival. One of those transforming events centered on Gorbachev's Polish visit in July 1988. In their joint statement, leaders Wojciech Jaruzelski and Gorbachev endorsed the "full respect for the independence of all parties and sovereign equality of socialist states, [including] the approach to resolving problems." This marked an important step for Polish–Soviet relations as Moscow signaled its intention to allow Warsaw greater leeway in its foreign policy.[83]

Within a month of Gorbachev's visit, workers' strikes erupted in Poland and opposition leaders met with Czech counterparts on the Polish–Czechoslovak border. Only Walesa could peacefully quell the youthful strikers, after much negotiation, and rekindled momentum in the *Solidarnosc* movement. The August 1988 joint statement by Polish opposition activists such as Adam Michnik and Czech playwright Vaclav Havel denounced the Warsaw Pact on the twentieth anniversary of the Soviet invasion of Czechoslovakia. Among other things, the statement dared Communist authority to revise the Warsaw Pact by yielding sovereignty to the pact's individual states.[84] It quickly became apparent that Gorbachev's foreign policy flexibility served much more than just as a catalyst to reform the pact's internal systems. All told, the Polish–Soviet statements and the Polish–Czech opposition declarations underscored the decay of the Polish Communist system.

Gorbachev's commitment not to interfere in the internal affairs of Warsaw Pact states nullified the "Brezhnev Doctrine," the Soviet foreign policy based on the 1968 Warsaw Pact invasion of Czechoslovakia meant to ensure Warsaw Pact state "loyalty" by military intervention. Gorbachev's Moscow maintained that Polish reform remained an internal affair and did not necessitate Warsaw Pact intervention, however, as long as the Poles upheld the Warsaw Pact's integrity. As in Khrushchev's agreement with Gomulka before him, Gorbachev permitted Jaruzelski the latitude to experiment with domestic reform in an attempt to strengthen the socialist system. Unlike Khrushchev, however, Gorbachev's liberalization in the Soviet Bloc and Jaruzelski's reforms uprooted the Polish Communist system. During 1989 political events in Poland overtook any Communist ability to control democratic protest, led to the *Solidarnosc*–Communist Roundtable negotiations, and, ultimately, resulted in power sharing with *Solidarnosc* after its overwhelming victory in the June elections. Moscow did not intervene politically or militarily, and by August 1989, the first post-Communist coalition government in the Soviet Bloc since World War II began forming in Warsaw.[85]

Poland's Democratic Transition:
Free and Popular Elections

In order to examine the phases of the Skubiszewski era and how the foreign minister began to reshape the *MSZ*, the democratic context for Poland's nascent foreign policy needs a brief overview. Although foreign policy played a relatively small role in the historic Roundtable talks from 6 February to 5 April 1989 between Walesa's moderate *Solidarnosc* team and Jaruzelski's reformed Communists, important statements appeared in the documents published. First of all, both sides agreed that politically the "common goal" focused on "an independent, sovereign, democratic, and economically strong Poland whose security rests on alliances in which she is an equal partner." Second, after the elections mandated by the Roundtable, the government approved by the Polish parliament (Sejm) should proceed in an "evolutionary" manner with the "indispensable [political, economic, and social] reforms," which remain "consonant with the nation's *raison d'état*." By underscoring that "radical" or "conservative" opposition to such reforms might endanger such an "evolutionary approach," the Roundtable Agreement cautioned against extreme changes to the state's foreign policy.[86] In the aftermath of the agreement, Walesa declared that "We can as a nation peacefully build an independent, sovereign, secure Poland with equal alliances, but the roundtable has not fulfilled all expectations. I stress, however, that for the first time we talked to each other using force of argument, not arguments of force."[87] Yet, the Roundtable's evolutionary, self-limiting text aroused consternation among the *Solidarnosc* factions. Disputes soon emerged and proved disruptive for the *Solidarnosc* governments, making a fully sovereign foreign policy difficult.[88]

With the Roundtable Agreement in April 1989, Poland descended into a frenzied democratic election campaign that culminated only two months later. The surprising election defeat of so many of the Communist candidates suddenly placed *Solidarnosc*'s leadership and its many victorious candidates in the unfamiliar position to forge Central and Eastern Europe's first government under a non-Communist prime minister. No politician or political commentator anticipated the *Solidarnosc* win or the Communist failure to form a government. Despite a majority of Communists in uncontested seats in the newly elected Sejm, Jaruzelski's hand-picked Communist prime minister, Czeslaw Kiszczak, the former interior minister from the martial law era, faltered in his attempt to build support for a Communist-led government. Even as they observed the remarkably large fissures in the Polish Communist Party and understood their lack of a parliamentary majority, the moderate *Solidarnosc* leaders maintained calm amid the rapid political upheaval. At the same time that the Communists failed to form a popularly elected government, the new Sejm demonstrated its pragmatism by saving Jaruzelski's presidency. Only through the efforts of the moderate *Solidarnosc* parliamentarians did Sejm manage by one vote to elect Jaruzelski and show that Poland remained sensitive to the other Warsaw Pact states closely watching Poland's historic democratic experiment. Thus, Walesa, the *Solidarnosc* king maker, turned to one of his closest advisors, Mazowiecki, a devout Catholic opposition journalist and key *Solidarnosc* leader, to construct Poland's first post-Communist government.[89]

Given the overwhelming popular mandate, Poland's new government strove in September to implement a different set of policies from those of its Communist predecessors. The new prime minister and his advisors believed they needed to wrest some control away from the Communists on foreign policy. While *Solidarnosc*'s intent centered on reversing the state's economic crisis, Mazowiecki strove to formulate a sovereign foreign policy to advance Poland's democratic cause. Hard bargaining between Mazowiecki and the Communists resulted in the securing by the *Solidarnosc*-led government of the *MSZ*'s top position, the only one of the three ministries related to foreign policy and national security that they controlled from the outset. The other two ministries, national defense and internal affairs, remained under Communist military leadership for some time. He quickly chose the politically independent, *Solidarnosc*-oriented, Skubiszewski to head the *MSZ*. However, the prime minister and his advisors, though strongly favoring a fully sovereign foreign policy, believed they needed to create it in an evolutionary manner, even if events quickly overtook the Roundtable Agreement.[90] In presenting his vision to Parliament, Mazowiecki declared an abiding commitment to continue Poland's alliance commitments, but also to change policy in accordance with democratic principles:

> Our openness to the whole of Europe does not mean repudiation of our previous ties and obligations. Our reiteration that the new government will honor Poland's alliance obligations is not a tactical placatory expedient. This stems from our understanding of Poland's *raison d'état* and analysis of the international situation. . . . Our foreign policy has to be credible and open, reacting to changes taking place in the world from the point of view of our national interests.[91]

The prime minister's speech defined the Polish middle power state's beginnings for developing a sovereign foreign policy. The sensitivity toward which these first democratically elected post-Communist Central-East European leaders displayed offers a very measured and practical foreign policy approach. By indicating that Poland would work within limited regional means, that its foreign policy choices remained dependent on its great power neighbors, foremost its Soviet dominator and alliance structure, the new non-Communist premier understood that Poland needed to carve out a new alignment strategy. Therefore, the "Skubiszewski era" started with an independent Poland facing the challenge over how rapidly to introduce a sovereign foreign policy, one on which the foreign minister quickly sought to place his mark.

The Strategy of *Racja Stanu*

Gomulka's semisovereign foreign policies and the underground and émigré arguments served as a strong foundation for many of the principles Skubiszewski brought to the *MSZ* in mid-September 1989. It remains important first to ask, however, why Mazowiecki chose Krzysztof Skubiszewski as Poland's first post-Communist foreign minister. The sixty-two-year-old Skubiszewski brought a scholarly, legal, and non–partisan background to the *MSZ*'s top post. With more than four decades as a professionally trained lawyer and international law professor at the Adam Mickiewicz University of Poznan, with a Ph.D. in International Law from Harvard University, Skubiszewski built an international academic reputation as a researcher, teacher, and guest lecturer. During the 1960s and 1970s, he found positions at Columbia University, the University of Geneva, and Oxford University. As professor at the prestigious Institute of State and Law of the Polish Academy of Sciences since 1973, he frequently published works about the practical and international legal norms that he felt must guide Poland. Skubiszewski's approach to democratic tenets and international legal principles defined his views on foreign policy and derived from the political bridge building he pursued before his *MSZ* years. He personified this diversity of political interests best throughout the 1980s when he not only joined *Solidarnosc*'s Trade Union Congress of Delegates, the Wielkopolska Political Club "Lad I Wolnosc" (Order and Freedom), and the Primate's Social Council, but also Jaruzelski's Consultative Council.[92]

By upholding nonpartisan views based on internationally recognized legal norms throughout his life, Skubiszewski portrayed himself as a pragmatist who forged consensus and compromise with people from different political backgrounds. Over many years, he projected a public persona by espousing his beliefs in Polish publications, ranging from books to journals. Such issues focused on the international legal importance of Polish–German relations by maintaining the Oder–Neisse border, the necessity of repealing the 1982 Polish law that dissolved *Solidarnosc*—a violation, he felt, of the international labor conventions approved by Poland—and the repatriation of Poles whom Stalin forcibly exiled to Siberia and Kazakhstan during World War II.[93] To appear credible with both the *Solidarnosc* opposition and the Communist leadership, Skubiszewski established visibly close ties with the church and the government. He first participated on the Primate's Social Council from 1981 to 1984, an effort demonstrably to support the Vatican's views during the martial law era. When he agreed to join Jaruzelski's Consultative Council from 1986 to 1989, he offered advice by pressing *Solidarnosc*'s concerns with the government publicly in the council's uncensored journal. Even if some in *Solidarnosc* viewed Jaruzelski's Consultative Council suspiciously because they saw the Council's non-Communist members as "pawns" used only to serve Communist purposes, the *Solidarnosc* leadership saw Skubiszewski as "ours," not "theirs."[94]

Arguably, the Consultative Council acted as a forerunner for the Roundtable talks, given that the Communists needed to gain legitimacy as the economy faltered and *Solidarnosc* regained momentum. During his years on the council, Skubiszewski clearly articulated some of the tenets he later brought to the *MSZ*, namely that every Pole remained entitled to his legal rights and Poland needed to abide by international law. Hence, he exemplified an informed and internationally recognized scholar and also the bridge builder Mazowiecki wanted to lead the foreign ministry.[95]

Skubiszewski's selection to become the first post-Communist foreign minister allowed several important trends to unfold in Polish–German and Polish–Soviet relations. As Mazowiecki's sole non-Communist governmental "power" minister, Skubiszewski immediately occupied the spotlight in Poland and abroad. Within weeks, he acted not only to broaden significantly Poland's relationship with the FRG, employing his German expertise and respect for the Polish–German treaties his Communist predecessors had enacted, but also to initiate different relations with the USSR, based on *Solidarnosc* underground and Polish émigré convictions. Skubiszewski's foreign policy tenets concentrated on three main areas. First, Poland must secure and strengthen its independence. Second, Warsaw required an improved, if not entirely new, set of good-neighborly relations with all its bordering states, relations founded on equal partnership, international law, and territorial inviolability. Finally, the independent Polish nation-state needed to reintegrate into Europe. For Skubiszewski, the two most important state-to-state relationships Warsaw wanted to change were with Bonn and Moscow.[96]

From the outset, Skubiszewski underscored publicly Poland's foreign policy principles and its *racja stanu*. At his confirmation hearings before the Sejm's Committee on Foreign Affairs, he stated that Poland's foreign policy "must be based on the principle of independence and sovereignty of the state. It requires normalization, i.e., getting rid of ideological premises, and the dependence of the ministry [*MSZ*] on one political party must be eliminated." Moreover, he said that changes to *MSZ* personnel would be based on "competence and loyalty to the government." He also argued that "foreign policy is first of all to serve all interests of the state and the dictate of this or that ideology must be ruled out."

Regarding Polish–German relations, he emphasized that "the most important thing for these relations is the conglomerate of matters pertaining to the Polish western border. In this matter we have to stand on the legal grounds as provided by the treaty of 1970." Furthermore, he stressed that the issue of Germany's potential unification "concerned the relations between two German states and the stance of four superpowers . . . and should be adjusted to the European security requirement, i.e., be in line with the all-European trend for disarmament and reduction of armaments." He stressed the importance of guaranteeing that a future united Germany not threaten "the European order." Should such a development occur, Skubiszewski argued that Poland wanted "to eliminate any signs of questioning Poland's western border."[97]

In another public statement during which Mazowiecki's new ministers gave a press conference, Skubiszewski elaborated first on Poland's *racja stanu* and then on its specific priorities. The Polish foreign minister stressed that "Polish foreign policy will be geared to the state's political independence in external and internal affairs: ensuring the external calm that is essential in order to implement the [internal] reforms." Next, he emphasized that "what is happening in Poland is a normal process that does not clash with our international commitments. Relations with the Warsaw Pact countries are based and will be based on a respect for these commitments." Moreover, he believed that "the task of Polish foreign policy will be to reform the Council on Mutual Economic Assistance [CMEA]. We must also open ourselves widely to the West, the next step being an agreement with the European Economic Community [EC]."[98] Lastly, at a meeting of new ministers with Jaruzelski, Skubiszewski discussed the challenges of formulating a sovereign post-Communist foreign policy. First, he declared "a coalition-type cabinet should pose no difficulties in concrete situations, though in practical situations it is often difficult to say exactly what the [Polish] *raison d'état* is." His goals for a strong, independent, and sovereign foreign policy rested on "a policy backed by a strong state, and that is the chief link between economic and foreign policy." Secondly, for Skubiszewski, "a proper coordination of cooperation between all political and constitutional forces may also have a major effect on foreign policy." Above all, the foreign minister felt that a "major responsibility rests on the president and on Sejm and Senate" for Poland to develop its regional foreign policy role.[99]

By employing the new post-Communist government to build a fully sovereign Polish foreign policy, Skubiszewski understood that he cautiously needed to navigate between Warsaw's rapidly transforming western and eastern neighbors. As he took over the helm of the *MSZ*, Skubiszewski faced a myriad of challenges, both within the ministry and throughout the government, given his self-proclaimed mission to make the state truly independent and sovereign, based on legal and democratic principles. In his first broad foreign policy address to Sejm, he stated that "since the first days of its existence the [post-Communist] government has been doing everything to restore full independence of the state. . . . The foundation of the foreign policy of our state is the national interest and the Polish *racja stanu* implemented with respect for dictates of morality and for international law."[100] During his four years as foreign minister, Skubiszewski shaped Polish foreign policy in his own mold and brought very dynamic *Solidarnosc* thinkers to the *MSZ* to develop and implement some key underground and émigré notions into post-Communist policy, particularly regarding Polish relations with Germany, the USSR, and the Western European security institutions. As his foreign policy became evident, Skubiszewski stated that "Poland's foreign policy priority is to include our country into European cooperation on different planes. This is inextricably associated with the settlement of relations with the Germans and the Soviet Union. In order to operate in Europe well, we must have good relations with both Germany and Moscow."[101]

To institute these foreign policy priorities, Skubiszewski focused on methodically building new relations with all of Poland's neighbors. His first priority concentrated on developing a new relationship with Germany that drew upon the inroads made by the exchange of letters in the mid-1960s taken by the Polish and German bishops, and by the positive steps taken officially between both states in the Gomulka–Brandt treaty. At the same time, albeit more cautiously than in his push toward Bonn, Skubiszewski redefined Poland's links with the USSR, including the beginning of painstaking negotiations with obstinate Soviet officials over Soviet force withdrawals from Poland. Within one year, he would also define separate links from Soviet Moscow with the evolving Republic leaderships bordering Poland, including Russia. Furthermore, Skubiszewski created a trusted relationship with his Central European counterparts to form the regional cooperative Visegrad Triangle, an attempt to formulate coordinated strategy toward Moscow and Brussels. For the former, Poland and the Visegrad states focused on synchronizing the negotiations of their new bilateral security treaties with the USSR. For the latter, Warsaw, Prague, and Budapest eventually determined to align their positions toward NATO, with Poland providing a security integration strategy as early as spring 1990, to increase their chances for future membership. Even though the surprise victory by the former Communists in the fall 1993 elections ended Skubiszewski's era and the string of four *Solidarnosc* governments, Skubiszewski had transformed post-Communist Polish foreign policy.[102]

Although he left the *MSZ* in late 1993, Skubiszewski made an indelible impact on Polish foreign policy and his legacy promised to influence subsequent Polish foreign ministers, as attested to by the tribute paid to him by President Walesa. Walesa's words resonated when he proclaimed that "future students of Polish foreign policy will doubtless refer to the 'Skubiszewski era'—an era of assiduous effort to win Poland its worthy and rightful place on the international and European political scene."[103]

Middle Power Politics Emergent

Poland rapidly transformed ideas into policies as non-Communist underground activists came to power democratically. After the Communist Bloc's first partially free and democratic election since the late 1940s in June 1989, the newly elected Polish government quickly integrated Western notions into foreign policy. Foreign Minister Skubiszewski forged pragmatic and cooperative policies toward a unifying Germany and a disintegrating USSR. This strategy reconstructed Poland's external alignment.[104] Skubiszewski focused on European reintegration as the Soviet Bloc collapsed. By incorporating underground intellectual arguments and various Western notions into strategy, Skubiszewski and the government instituted an other-help policy.[105]

Poland's impact on post–Cold War great power security reveals its middle power role. This marked a significant break with Poland's security dilemma between Germany and Russia from its Cold War frontline battleground.[106] By examining how concerns in the former Soviet Bloc led to the demise of politically bankrupt and economically backward Communist regimes, we observe Poland's regional role emerge.[107] Highly controversial Polish foreign policy debates appeared in Cold War–era clandestine and émigré literature[108] such as the scholarly notion that each satellite nation "has the irrefutable right of independence . . . self-determination automatically abolishes all alliances of states that have not obtained an unquestionable and unanimous agreement of all participants."[109] Ultimately, these scholars incorporated such ideas into new foreign policies after joining the first post-Communist Polish government and parliament in August 1989. This strategy, inter alia, contributed to the demise of the Soviet Bloc, the Warsaw Pact, and, with economic decline and centrifugal enthnonationalism, the USSR.[110]

Poland, therefore, illustrates how a state reduced its security dilemma by implementing a cooperative security policy and forging a pragmatic bridge between democratic and nondemocratic, or slowly democratizing, great powers.[111] The dramatic structural transformation of German unification and Soviet disintegration influenced Poland's regionally integrative policies.[112] Poland characterized its democratic model for nonadvanced democracies in the crumbling Soviet Bloc to promote pluralism, free markets, and cooperative security.[113] Few analyses exist about how much Poland's post–Cold War impact relates to security challenges in the twenty-first century, including coalition building.[114] Given Soviet breakdown and Balkan instability in Europe during the last decade, middle powers like Poland test the merits and pitfalls of cooperation and conflict in a region historically challenged by regional security dilemmas.

Notes

1. For these state definitional dimensions, see Nicholas J. Spykman, *America's Strategy in World Politics* (New York: Harcourt Brace Jovanovich, 1942), 7; Klaus Knorr, *The War Potential of Nations* (Princeton, N.J.: Princeton University Press, 1956), 35–36; Raymond Aron, *The Century of Total War* (Garden City, N.Y.: Doubleday, 1954), 195–208; Frederick L. Schuman, *International Politics: The Destiny of the Western State System* (New York: McGraw-Hill, 1969), 271; and Hans J. Morgenthau and Kenneth W. Thompson, *Politics among Nations: The Struggle for Power and Peace*, 6th ed. (New York: Knopf, 1985), 4–14. For important works that analyze anarchy in the international system, see Hedley Bull, *The Anarchical Society* (New York: Columbia University Press, 1977), and Martin Wight, *Systems of States* (Leicester: Leicester University Press, 1977). For important collections on the late Cold War and post–Cold War eras, see, among others: William C. Wohlforth, *The Elusive Balance: Power and Perception* (Ithaca, N.Y.: Cornell University Press, 1993); Michael E. Brown, Sean M. Lynn-Jones, and Steven E. Miller, eds., *The Perils of Anarchy: Contemporary Realism and International Security* (Cambridge, Mass.: MIT Press, 1995); Sean M. Lynn-Jones and Steven E. Miller, eds., *The Cold War and After: Prospects for Peace*, exp. ed. (Cambridge, Mass.: MIT Press, 1997).

2. Kenneth N. Waltz, *Theory of International Politics* (Reading, Mass.: Addison-Wesley, 1979); Steven M. Walt, *The Origin of Alliances* (Ithaca, N.Y.: Cornell University Press, 1987; Jack Snyder, *Myths of Empire: Domestic Politics and International Ambition* (Ithaca, N.Y.: Cornell University Press, 1991); David A. Baldwin, ed., *Neorealism and Neoliberalism: The Contemporary Debate* (New York: St. Martin's, 1993); and Randall L. Schweller, *Deadly Imbalances: Tripolarity and Hitler's Strategy of World Conquest* (New York: Columbia University Press, 1998).

3. "Buffer-state diplomacy" can be seen in terms of the variables affecting states such as geography, capability distribution, and foreign policy orientations, and the attendant behavioral consequences, which illustrate key parameters for this book's analysis of Warsaw's foreign policy. They will be examined below to show how Poland challenged its status as a "buffer state." Michael Greenfield Partem, "The Buffer System in International Relations," *Journal of Conflict Resolution*, vol. 27, no. 1 (March 1983), 4, 25. For approaches taken by "buffer states" and others toward them, see also John Chay and Thomas E. Ross, eds., *Buffer States in World Politics* (Boulder, Colo.: Westview, 1986).

4. Karl Mueller, "Patterns of Alliance: Alignment Balancing and Stability in Eastern Europe," *Security Studies*, vol. 5, no. 1 (autumn 1995): 38–76; Wener Bauwens, Armand Clesse, and Olav F. Knudsen, eds., *Small States and the Security Challenge in the New Europe* (London: Brassey's, 1996); Miriam Fendius Elman, "The Foreign Policies of Small States: Challenging Neorealism in Its Own Backyard," *British Journal of Political Science*, vol. 29, no. 2 (April 1995): 171–217; Mark Kramer, "Neorealism, Nuclear Proliferation, and East-Central European Strategies," in *Unipolar Politics: Realism and State Strategies after the Cold War*, eds. Ethan B. Kapstein and Michael Mastanduno (New York: Columbia University Press, 1999), 385–463.

5. Colin Elman and Miriam Fendius Elman, eds., *Bridges and Boundaries: Historians, Political Scientists, and the Study of International Relations* (Cambridge, Mass.: MIT Press, 2001).

6. These alignment concepts come primarily from Paul Schroeder, "Historical Reality vs. Neo-realist Theory," *International Security*, vol. 19, no. 1 (summer 1994): 108–148; and Schweller, *Deadly Imbalances*.

7. For seminal works, see Kenneth N. Waltz, *Theory of International Politics* (Reading, Mass.: Addison-Wesley, 1979), and Steven M. Walt, *The Origin of Alliances* (Ithaca, N.Y.: Cornell University Press, 1987).

8. Waltz, *Theory of International Politics*, 126.

9. Walt, *The Origin of Alliances*, 28–33, and "Alliance Formation in Southwest Asia," in Robert Jervis and Jack Snyder, eds., *Dominoes and Bandwagons: Strategic Beliefs and Great Power Competition in the Eurasian Rimland* (Oxford: Oxford University Press, 1991), 52–53.

10. Great debate still exists about balancing and Bandwagoning. In addition to those works mentioned above, see Glenn H. Snyder, *Alliance Politics* (Ithaca, N.Y.: Cornell University Press, 1997).

11. Waltz, *Theory of International Politics*, 105–107, 111–112, 117–126; Walt, *The Origins of Alliances*, 263–266 and "Alliances, Threats, and U.S. Grand Strategy: A Reply to Kauman and Labs," *Security Studies*, vol. 1, no. 3 (spring 1992): 450–451.

12. Judith Goldstein and Robert O. Keohane, eds., *Ideas and Foreign Policy: Beliefs, Institutions, and Political Change* (Ithaca, N.Y.: Cornell University Press, 1993); Richard Ned Lebow and Thomas Risse-Kappen, eds., *International Relations Theory and the End of the Cold War* (New York: Columbia University Press, 1995); Peter J. Katzenstein, ed., *The Culture of National Security: Norms and Identity in World Politics* (New York: Columbia University Press, 1996); William C. Wohlforth, "Reality Check: Revising Theories of International Politics in Response to the End of the Cold War," *World Politics*, vol. 50, no. 4 (July 1998): 650–680; Alexander Wendt, *Social Theory of International Politics* (Cambridge: Cambridge University Press, 1999); and Kenneth N. Waltz, "Structural Realism after the Cold War," *International Security*, vol. 25, no. 1 (summer 2000): 5–41.

13. Schroeder, "Historical Reality vs. Neo-realist Theory," 116–117; and Thomas J. Christensen and Jack Snyder, "Chain Gangs and Passed Bucks: Predicting Alliance Patterns in Multipolarity," *International Organization*, vol. 44, no. 2 (spring 1990): 137–139, 167–168. See also Paul W. Schroeder, *The Transformation of European Politics, 1763–1848* (Oxford: Clarendon Press, 1994).

14. Schroeder, "Historical Reality vs. Neo-realist Theory," 117–118, 125–127; and Glen H. Snyder, "Alliances, Balance, and Stability," *International Organization*, vol. 45, no. 1 (winter 1991): 128–131.

15. Schweller, *Deadly Imbalances*, 65–71, 191–192.

16. Schweller, *Deadly Imbalances*, 71–77, 83–91. In addition to the authors cited, for antagonistic or aggressive versus cooperative or conciliatory alignments, see, inter alia: Robert Axelrod, *The Complexity of Cooperation: Agent-Based Models of Competition and Collaboration* (Princeton, N.J.: Princeton University Press, 1997); Stephen Van Evera, *Causes of War: Power and the Roots of Conflict* (Ithaca, N.Y.: Cornell University Press, 1999); and John J. Mearsheimer, *The Tragedy of Great Power Politics* (New York: Norton, 2001).

17. Charles L. Glaser, "Realists as Optimists: Cooperation as Self-Help," in Benjamin Frankel, ed., *Realism: Restatements and Renewal* (London: Cass, 1996): 122–163.

18. Jonathan Mercer, "Anarchy and Identity," *International Organization*, vol. 49, no. 2 (spring 1995): 233–236; and Colin Elman and Miriam Fendius Elman, "Correspondence—History vs. Neo-realism: A Second Look," *International Security*, vol. 20, no. 1 (summer 1995): 182–195, especially 188. For different views on "other-help" frameworks, see Paul Schroeder, "Correspondence—History vs. Neo-realism: A Second Look," *International Security*, vol. 20, no. 1 (summer 1995): 194; Schweller, *Deadly*

Imbalances; and Alexander Wendt, *Social Theory of International Politics*, 238–242, 275–278, 291, 350–352.

19. "Problemy polityki zagranicznej u progu roku 1991—Wystapienie ministra spraw zagranicznych RP Krzysztofa Skubiszewskiego w Sejmie" [Foreign Policy of the Republic of Poland in 1991—Address by the Polish Foreign Minister Krzysztof Skubiszewski in the Sejm] (Warsaw, 14 February 1991), *Zbior Dokumentow*, no. 1 (1992): 34. "Remarks by President to Faculty and Students of Warsaw University," Poland, 15 June 2001, www.whitehouse.gov/news/releases/2001/06/20010615-1.html (accessed 1 August 2001).

20. Ashton B. Carter, William J. Perry, and John D. Steinbruner, *A New Concept of Cooperative Security* (Washington, D.C.: Brookings Institution Press, 1992), and Daniel C. Thomas, *The Helsinki Effect: International Norms, Human Rights, and the Demise of Communism* (Princeton, N.J.: Princeton University Press, 2001).

21. Joshua B. Spero, "Looking beyond NATO and EU Enlargement: Northeastern Europe and Russian Security Dynamics," in *The Transatlantic Relationship: Problems and Prospects*, ed. Sabina A.-M. Auger (Washington: Woodrow Wilson International Center for Scholars, 2003), 104–114.

22. Michael Loriaux, "Realism and Reconciliation: France, Germany, and the European Union," in *Unipolar Politics: Realism and State Strategies after the Cold War*, ed. Ethan B. Kapstein and Michael Mastanduno (New York: Columbia University Press, 1999), 378; and Jeffrey W. Taliaferro, "Security Seeking under Anarchy: Defensive Realism Revisited," *International Security*, vol. 25, no. 3 (winter 2000/2001): 1–59.

23. Brooks and Wohlforth, "Power, Globalization, and the End of the Cold War," 7–10.

24. Bartlomiej Kaminski, *The Collapse of State Socialism: The Case of Poland* (Princeton, N.J.: Princeton University Press, 1991); Leszek Balcerowicz, *Socialism, Capitalism, Transformation* (Budapest: Central European University Press, 1995), and "Limping towards Normality: A Survey of Poland," *The Economist*, October 27, 2001: 3–16.

25. Juliusz Mieroszewski, *Materials for Reflection and Musing* (Paris: Instytut Literacki, 1976), Piotr Wandycz, *The Price of Freedom: A History of East Central Europe from the Middle Ages to the Present* (London: Routledge, 1992), and Krzysztof Skubiszewski, *Polityka zagraniczna i odzyskanie niepodleglosci: Przemówienia, oswiadczenia, wywiady 1989–1993* [Foreign Policy and Regaining Independence: Addresses, Declaration, Interviews, 1989–1993] (Warsaw: Wydawa Interpress, 1997).

26. Jack Snyder, *From Voting to Violence: Democratization and Nationalist Conflict* (New York: Norton, 2000), 72, 252–253, 259, 309; Marjorie Castle and Ray Taras, *Democracy in Poland*, 2nd edition (Boulder, Colo.: Westview, 2002).

27. Jeffrey Simon, ed., *European Security Policy after the Revolutions of 1989* (Washington: National Defense University Press, 1991); Andrew Michta, *East Central Europe after the Warsaw Pact Security Dilemmas in the 1990s* (New York: Greenwood, 1992); Gale Stokes, *The Walls Came Tumbling Down: The Collapse of Communism in Eastern Europe* (New York: Oxford University Press, 1993); Ilya Prizel, *National Identity and Foreign Policy: Nationalism and Leadership in Poland, Russia, and Ukraine* (Cambridge: Cambridge University Press, 1998); and Roman Kuzniar, ed., *Poland's Security Policy, 1989–2000* (Warsaw: Scholar Publishing House, 2001).

28. "Poland and the EU," *The Economist*, August 28, 2003, www.economist.com/displaystory.cfm?story_id=2020783 (accessed September 20, 2003).

29. Glaser, "Realists as Optimists," 123.

30. Brian Frederking, "Constructing Post–Cold War Collective Security," *American Political Science Review*, vol. 97, no. 3 (August 2003): 363–378.

31. Arthur A. Stein, *Why Nations Cooperate: Circumstance and Choice in International Relations* (Ithaca, N.Y.: Cornell University Press, 1990); Stephen M. Walt, *Revolution and War* (Ithaca, N.Y.: Cornell University Press, 1996); and Randall L. Schweller and William C. Wohlforth, "Power Test: Evaluating Realism in Response to the End of the Cold War," *Security Studies*, vol. 9, no. 3 (spring 2000): 60–107.

32. Some important studies do focus on middle power alignment and impact regionally, such as Kramer, "Neorealism, Nuclear Proliferation, and East-Central European Strategies," 437–438, 462; and Chase, Hill, and Kennedy, *The Pivotal States*.

33. Zbigniew Brzezinski, *The Grand Failure: The Birth and Death of Communism in the Twentieth Century* (New York: Collier, 1989); Philip Zelikow and Condoleezza Rice, *Germany Unified and Europe Transformed: A Study in Statecraft* (Cambridge, Mass.: Harvard University Press, 1998); Lubomyr A. Hajda, ed., *Ukraine in the World: Studies in the International and Security Structure of a Newly Independent State* (Cambridge, Mass.: Harvard University Press, 1998); Ilya Prizel, *National Identity and Foreign Policy: Nationalism and Leadership in Poland, Russia, and Ukraine* (Cambridge: Cambridge University Press, 1998); Angela Stent, *Russia and Germany Reborn: Unification, the Soviet Collapse, and the New Europe* (Princeton, N.J.: Princeton University Press, 1999); and Celeste A. Wallander, *Mortal Friends, Best Enemies: German-Russian Cooperation after the Cold War* (Ithaca, N.Y.: Cornell University Press, 1999).

34. Janusz Reiter "New Map of World: Does Russia's Return to Europe Bode Ill for Poland?" *Rzeczpospolita*, January 31, 2002, www.rp.pl/gazeta/wydanie_020131/publicystyka/publicystyka_a_1.html (accessed February 8, 2002).

35. Andrew Kydd, "Sheep in Sheep's Clothing: Why Security Seekers Do Not Fight Each Other," *Security Studies*, vol. 7, no. 1 (autumn 1997): 114–154.

36. Paul M. Kennedy, *The Rise and Fall of the Great Powers: Economic Change and Military Conflict from 1500 to 2000* (New York: Random House, 1987); and Sean M. Lynn-Jones and Steven E. Miller, eds., *The Cold War and After: Prospects for Peace* (Cambridge, Mass.: MIT Press, 1993).

37. Henry Kissinger, *Diplomacy* (New York: Simon & Schuster, 1994), 134–135; Christensen and Snyder, "Chain Gangs and Passed Bucks," 137–139, 167–168; and Josef Joffee, "Bismarck or Britain? Toward an American Grand Strategy after Bipolarity," in *American Foreign Policy: Theoretical Essays*, 3rd ed., ed. G. John Ikenberry (New York: Addison Wesley Longman, 1999), 605–609.

38. John S. Duffield, "Political Culture and State Behavior: Why Germany Confounds Neorealism," *International Organization*, vol. 53, no. 4 (autumn 1999): 765–803.

39. Zbigniew K. Brzezinski, *The Soviet Bloc: Unity and Conflict*, rev. and enl. ed. (Cambridge, Mass.: Harvard University Press, 1976); and Arthur R. Rachwald, *Poland between the Superpowers: Security vs. Economic Recovery* (Boulder, Colo.: Westview, 1983).

40. John J. Mearsheimer, "Back to the Future: Instability in Europe after the Cold War," in *The Cold War and After: Prospects for Peace*, exp. ed., eds. Sean M. Lynn-Jones and Steven E. Miller (Cambridge, Mass.: MIT Press, 1997), 141–192; Ronald D. Asmus, Richard L. Kugler, and F. Stephen Larrabee, "Building a New NATO," *Foreign Affairs*, no. 4 (September/October 1993): 28–40; and Joshua B. Spero and Frank Umbach, "NATO's Security Challenge to the East and the American-German Geo-Strategic Partnership in Europe," *Occasional Papers* (Cologne, 1994).

41. Prizel, *National Identity and Foreign Policy*; and Andrew A. Michta, ed., *America's New Allies: Poland, Hungary, and the Czech Republic in NATO* (Seattle: University of Washington Press, 1999).

42. Gideon Rose, "Neoclassical Realism and Theories of Foreign Policy," *World Politics* 51 (October 1998): 155–156.

43. "Remarks by President to Faculty and Students of Warsaw University," Poland, 15 June 2001, www.whitehouse.gov/news/releases/2001/06/20010615-1.html (accessed August a, 2001); and Aleksander Kwasniewski, "Poland's Solidarity with America," *New York Times*, July 17 2002, A23.

44. Miklos Ritecz, "Wedged between Two Powers: Interview with Foreign Minister Krzysztof Skubiszewski," *Nepszabadsag* (Budapest), 6 June 1991, *Foreign Broadcast Information Service–Eastern Europe* (hereafter, *FBIS–EEU*), 11 June 1991, 31.

45. For the well-known literature that examines this historical security dilemma, see, inter alia, Roman Dmowski, *Niemcy, Rosja i kwestja polska* [Germany, Russia and the Polish Question] (Warsaw: Instytut Wydawniczy PAX, 1991); Viscount d'Abernon, *The Eighteenth Decisive Battle of the World: Warsaw, 1920* (London: Hodder and Stoughton, 1931); Adolf Bochenski, *Miedzy Niemcami a Rosja* [Between Germany and Russia] (Warsaw: Polityka, 1937); Josef Korbel, *Poland between East and West: Soviet and German Diplomacy toward Poland, 1919–1933* (Princeton, N.J.: Princeton University Press, 1963); Norman J. G. Pounds, *Poland between East and West* (Princeton, N.J.: D. Van Nostrand, 1964); Adam Bromke, *Poland's Politics: Idealism vs. Realism* (Cambridge, Mass.: Harvard University Press, 1967); M. K. Dziewanowski, *Joseph Pilsudski: A European Federalist, 1918–1922* (Stanford, Calif.: Hoover Institution Press, 1969); Piotr Wandycz, *The Lands of Partitioned Poland, 1795–1918*, vol. 7 (Seattle: University of Washington Press, 1974); Joseph Rothschild, *East Central Europe between the Two World Wars*, vol. 9 (Seattle: University of Washington Press, 1974); Juliusz Mieroszewski, *Materialy do Refleksji i Zadumy* [Materials for Reflection and Musing] (Paris: Instytut Literacki, 1976); Zbigniew K. Brzezinski, *The Soviet Bloc: Unity and Conflict*, rev. and enl. ed. (Cambridge, Mass.: Harvard University Press, 1976); Norman Davies, *God's Playground: A History of Poland*, 2 vols. (New York: Columbia University Press, 1982); Arthur R. Rachwald, *Poland between the Superpowers: Security vs. Economic Recovery* (Boulder, Colo.: Westview, 1983); Sarah M. Terry, *Poland's Place in Europe: General Sikorski and the Origin of the Oder-Neisse Line, 1939-1943* (Princeton, N.J.: Princeton University Press, 1983); Ray Taras, *Poland: Socialist State, Rebellious Nation* (Boulder, Colo.: Westview Press, 1986); Adam Michnik, *Letters from Prison and Other Essays* (Berkeley, Calif.: University of California Press, 1987); Ilya Prizel and Andrew A. Michta, eds., *Polish Foreign Policy Reconsidered: Challenges of Independence* (Houndmills: Macmillan, 1995); and Ilya Prizel, *National Identity and Foreign Policy: Nationalism and Leadership in Poland, Russia, and Ukraine* (Cambridge: Cambridge University Press, 1998).

46. Juliusz Mieroszewski, "The Political Thought of *Kultura*," in *Kultura Essays*, ed. Leopold Tyrmand (New York: Free Press, 1970), 291.

47. This book focuses on Polish foreign policy and will not examine at length the turmoil which occurred during the early to mid-1950s, particularly the "Polish October," concerning the Polish Communist elite, the intellectuals, and the labor movement. See important analyses in the literature: Flora Lewis, *A Case History of Hope: The Story of Poland's Peaceful Revolution* (New York: Doubleday, 1958); Richard F. Staar, *Poland 1944-1962: The Sovietization of a Captive People* (New Orleans: Louisiana State University Press, 1962); Hansjakob Stehle, *The Independent Satellite* (London: Praeger,

1965); Adam Bromke, *Poland's Politics*; Brzezinski, *The Soviet Bloc*; Peter Raina, *Political Opposition in Poland, 1954–1977* (London: Poets and Painters, 1978); Jakub Karpinski, *Countdown: The Polish Upheavals of 1956, 1968, 1970, 1976, 1980...* (New York: Karz-Cohl, 1982); and Teresa Toranska, *"THEM": Stalin's Polish Puppets* (New York: Harper & Row, 1987).

48. Wladyslaw Gomulka, *Przemowienia* [Speeches] (Warsaw, 1956–1957), 40, 268–269, as cited in Bromke, *Poland's Politics*, 113, 118; and Brzezinski, *The Soviet Bloc*, 343.

49. Brzezinski, *The Soviet Bloc*, 244, 264, 294; and Ryszard J. Kuklinski, "Wojna z narodem widziana od srodka" [The War Against the Nation Seen From the Inside], *Kultura*, no. 4/475 (1987): 20. Former Polish Colonel Kuklinski provided important political and military insights in his article about the Soviet and Warsaw Pact planning for conventional war in Europe, starting in the late 1950s.

50. Rachwald, *Poland between the Superpowers*, 19–21; "The Polish Government Memorandum Concerning the Creation of an Atom-Free Zone in Central Europe" in *Polish Viewpoint, Disarmament, Denuclearization, European Security Documents, Declarations, Statements*, ed. Jozef Winiewicz (Warsaw: Polonia, 1967), 4; Bromke, *Poland's Politics*, 129–131; Andrew A. Michta, *Red Eagle: The Army in Polish Politics, 1944–1988* (Stanford, Calif.: Hoover Institution Press, 1990), 50–52; and Prizel, *National Identity and Foreign Policy*, 87–88.

51. Taras, *Poland: Socialist State, Rebellious Nation*, 82; Rachwald, *Poland between the Superpowers*, 21–24, 28–29; and Stehle, *The Independent Satellite*, 222, 249–250.

52. *Foreign Relations of the United States: Diplomatic Papers: The Conferences at Malta and Yalta, 1945* (Washington, D.C.: U.S. Government Printing Office, 1955), 973–974; "Protocol of the Proceedings of the Berlin (Potsdam) Conference," *Documents on Germany, 1944-1985* (Washington, D.C.: Department of State, 1985), 63; and "Report of the Crimea Conference (Yalta)," in *From Stalinism to Pluralism: A Documentary History of Eastern Europe since 1945*, ed. Gale Stokes (New York: Oxford University Press, 1991), 16–17.

53. The London-based Poles comprised the government-in-exile and lost to the Stalinist-backed Communists in the post–World War II battle to control Poland. The Polish–German State Treaty of 1991 is examined later in this chapter and in greater detail in chapter 2.

54. Sarah M. Terry, *Poland's Place in Europe: General Sikorski and the Origin of the Oder-Neisse Line, 1939–1943* (Princeton, N.J.: Princeton University Press, 1983), 356; Rachwald, *Poland between the Superpowers*, 9; Brzezinski, *The Soviet Bloc*, 348; Bromke, *Poland's Politics*, 101.

55. For background, see, among others, Adam Michnik, *The Church and the Left*, translated by David Ost (Chicago: University of Chicago Press, 1993), 84–94; Rachwald, *Poland between the Superpowers*, 63; and Prizel, *National Identity and Foreign Policy*, 87–88, 113–114.

56. Gomulka, *Przemowienia*, 200; and Bromke, *Poland's Politics*, 110.

57. Bromke, *Poland's Politics*, 100.

58. Zdzislaw M. Rurarz, "The Polish-German Border Question," *Global Affairs* (fall 1990): 60–73; and Rachwald, *Poland between the Superpowers*, 54–71.

59. For background and analysis on Mieroszewski's influence and *Kultura*'s impact, see Robert Kostrzewa, "Preface," in *Between East and West: Writings from Kultura*, ed. Robert Kostrzewa (New York: Hill & Wang, 1990), ix-xii; and Konstanty A. Jelenski,

"Introduction," in *Between East and West: Writings from Kultura*, ed. Robert Kostrzewa (New York: Hill & Wang, 1990), 4–8, 18–19.

60. Juliusz Mieroszewski, "Imperialism: Theirs and Ours," in *Between East and West: Writings from Kultura*, ed. Robert Kostrzewa (New York: Hill & Wang, 1990), 43. Mieroszewski continuously reasoned that Poles must remember Poland's history, that Poland's period as a great power over the East had passed since the late 1600s, and that Poles should remember that Russia after the sixteenth century would always assert its great power European status. He used two factual points of departure. First, the 30 January 1667 Truce of Andruszow, in which Poland transferred rule over Smolensk, Czernichow, Siewierszczyzna, Siebiez, and Kiev to Moscow, effectively partitioned Ukraine between Poland and Russia. Second, the 1 May 1686 Polish–Russian Gryzmultow Eternal Peace Treaty, signed in Moscow, defined the historical crossroads in the Polish–Russian relationship—the foundation for Poland's eventual reliance on Russia. See Mieroszewski, "The Political Thought of *Kultura*," 262, as well as Mieroszewski, *Materialy do Refleksji i Zadumy*, particularly "Polska 'Ostpolitik," [Poland's *Ostpolitik*], 110–122; Mieroszewski, *Imperialism: Theirs and Ours*, 48. See also Jerzy Iranek-Osmecki, "Geopolityczne warunki dla realizacji suwerennosci narodow Europy wschodniej," [Geopolitical Conditions for the People of Eastern Europe to Obtain Sovereignty], *Oboz* (November 1987): 47–56; Ilya Prizel, "Warsaw's *Ostpolitik*," in *Polish Foreign Policy Reconsidered: Challenges of Independence*, eds. Ilya Prizel and Andrew A. Michta (London: Macmillan, 1995), 95–128, especially 96–97; Prizel, *National Identity and Foreign Policy*, especially 94–102.

61. For examples of how Mieroszewski's arguments found adherents, but also sparked debates among the Polish diaspora, Polish underground, and Polish Communist leadership, see, inter alia, the important underground journal, *Nowa Koalicja*, one of the most forthright publications from 1985 to 1989 that focused specifically on freedom and independence for the Central and East European states, including the ULB and Baltic republics; Ilya Prizel, *National Identity and Foreign Policy*, especially 94–102; Raina, *Political Opposition in Poland*, 177–179; Michnik, *Letters from Prison*, 201-222; Adam Bromke, "Polski 'Ost-Zachod Politik,'" [The Polish East-West Politics], *Kultura* (November 1973): 52–55; Juliusz Mieroszewski, "Ksiegi ugody i diaspory Adama Bromke" [Books of Conciliation and the Diaspora of Adam Bromke], *Kultura* (November 1974): 10–13; "Co Robic?: Perspektywy Polskie" [What is to be Done?: Polish Perspectives], *Kultura*, (September 1975): 35–43.

62. It must be remembered that after World War II Poland was no longer a multinational state threatened internally by multinational strife, but nearly an ethnically homogeneous one because of the mass relocation and expulsion of its former German and Ukrainian citizens, and the Nazi-run Holocaust—the methodical annihilation of European Jewry and other nationalities, with many of the extermination concentration camps located in Polish areas incorporated into the Third Reich. See Andrew A. Michta, "Democratic Consolidation in Poland after 1989," in *The Consolidation of Democracy in East-Central Europe*, ed. Karen Dawisha and Bruce Parrott (Cambridge: Cambridge University Press, 1997), 71.

63. Mieroszewski, "The Political Thought of Kultura," 267; Mieroszewski, "Imperialism: Theirs and Ours," 44; and Mieroszewski, *Ewolucjonizm* [Evolutionism] (Paris: Instytut Literacki, 1964). The 16 April 1922 Treaty of Rapallo between the Soviet Union and Germany broke Moscow's isolation in Europe, created political, economic, and military ties between Moscow and Berlin, and laid the foundation for the tragic 1939

Molotov–Ribbentrop Pact. Nicholas V. Riasanovsky, _A History of Russia_, 3rd ed. (New York: Oxford University Press, 1977), 567.

64. For background on the Polish victory recounted as the "Miracle on the Vistula" in the 1920 Polish–Soviet War, see, among others, Viscount d'Abernon, _The Eighteenth Decisive Battle of the World: Warsaw, 1920_ (London: Hodder and Stoughton, 1931), 11–12; Norman Davies, _White Eagle, Red Star: The Polish Soviet War, 1919–1920_ (New York: St. Martin's, 1972), 22; and Korbel, _Poland between East and West_, 58–60.

65. Mieroszewski, "Rosyjski 'kompleks polski' i ULB" [Russia, Poland's Complex, and the ULB], in _Materialy do Refleksji i Zadumy_; Mieroszewski, "The Political Thought of _Kultura_," 267, 290–291; Mieroszewski, "Imperialism: Theirs and Ours," 49.

66. Davies explains that the "Jagiellonian idea" evolved from the strong Polish "Romantic" tradition of inclusiveness and democracy during the Polish–Lithuanian Commonwealth. Examples included the Act of Horodlo in 1413 and the testament of Sigismund-August in 1572, that focused on "'love, harmony, and unity' of the different communities of the realm." The so-called Ukrainian Cossack prophet, Wenyhora, supposedly called on all the peoples of the region, mainly Poles, Ukrainians, and Jews, to stop fighting and learn to live and respect each other. For the Polish Romantics, this philosophy meant that Poland should become the leader of many nationalities under one peaceful commonwealth. Norman Davies, _Heart of Europe: A Short History of Poland_ (Oxford: Oxford University Press, 1986), 322–323.

Wandycz and Bromke also provide some essential background for understanding Polish Marshal Jozef Pilsudski's motives behind pursuing a "national mission" coupled with the "Jagiellonian idea," or the vision for "restoring Poland's pre-1772 border with Russia and reviving the ancient federation of Poland, Lithuania, and the Ukraine." Both historians draw from Pilsudski, himself, _Pisma wybrane_, vol. 1, 111, 196, in describing the years 1918–1921, but also from Witold Kamieniecki, _Ponad zgielkiem walk narodowosciowych. Idea jagiellonska_ [Above the Noise of the Nationality Struggles: The Jagiellonian Idea] (Warsaw, 1929) and Oskar Halecki, in his "Idea jagiellonska" [Jagiellonian Idea], _Kwartalnik historyczny_, vol. 51 (1937), that underscored the idea to mean "the spread of Latin civilization, peace policies, and the attraction of a regime based on freedom." See Piotr Wandycz, "Poland's Place in Europe in the Concepts of Pilsudski and Dmowski," _East European Politics and Societies_ (fall 1990): 460–461; Bromke, _Poland's Politics_, 39; and Prizel, _National Identity and Foreign Policy_, 68–72, 94–99.

67. Mieroszewski, "Rosyjski 'kompleks polski' i ULB"; Mieroszewski, "The Political Thought of _Kultura_," 263, 273; Mieroszewski, "Imperialism: Theirs and Ours," 43–44.

68. Mieroszewski, "The Political Thought of _Kultura_," 290, 292. D'Abernon, _The Eighteenth Decisive Battle of the World_, 11–12, provides some important background to the Polish great power phase.

69. Mieroszewski, "The Political Thought of _Kultura_," 297. Mieroszewski failed to acknowledge NATO's and the EU's critical, stabilizing roles contributing to the FRG's security and post–World War II peaceful reemergence, an important dimension of European security that chapter 5 addresses in detail in the context of post-Communist Polish–German relations.

70. Mieroszewski, "The Political Thought of _Kultura_," 256–258. See also Ilya Prizel, "Russia and Germany: The Case for a Special Relationship," in _Post-Communist Europe: Crisis and Adjustment_, ed. Andrew Michta and Ilya Prizel (New York: St. Martin's, 1993), 25–27.

71. Mieroszewski, "The Political Thought of _Kultura_," 293, 297.

72. Mieroszewski, "Imperialism: Theirs and Ours," 49.

73. Mieroszewski, "The Political Thought of *Kultura*," 265.

74. On Mieroszewski's thesis that Polish–Hungarian–Czechoslovak cooperation should be encouraged to foster a "cooperative" policy for Poland toward Moscow, chapter 5 examines such cooperative security in more detail. Mieroszewski, "The Political Thought of *Kultura*," 269, 273.

75. "Program Polskiego Porozumienia Niepodleglosciowego w Kraju," [Program of the Alliance for Polish Independence], in *PPN: Polskie Porozumienie Niepodleglosciowe* [PPN: Alliance for Polish Independence], eds. Gustaw Herling-Grudzinski, Leszek Kolakowski, and Jerzy Lerski (Paris: Instytut Literacki, 1978), 7–26; Andrzej Albert, "Wschodnie granice Polski," [Poland's Eastern Border], in *Polskie Porozumienie Niepodleglosciowe: Wybor Tekstow* [Alliance for Polish Independence: Electoral Text], ed. Zdzislaw Najder (London: Polonia, 1989), 288–325; Zbigniew Wegrzynski, "O programie i roli PPN" [The PPN's Program and Role], *Kultura* (April 1977): 87–90; Zdzislaw Najder, *Jaka Polska: Co i Komu Doradzalem* [What Kind of Poland: What and To Whom I Advised] (Warsaw: Editions Spotkania, 1994), 9–29; Karpinski, *Countdown*, 182–183; Jaroslaw Kurski, *Lech Walesa: Democrat or Dictator?* (Boulder, Colo.: Westview, 1993), 32–33; Leszek Kolakowski, "The Intelligentsia," in *Poland: Genesis of a Revolution*, ed. Abraham Brumberg (New York: Vintage Books, 1983), 65; Jan Maria Rokita, "Prawo-Ustroj-Suwerennosc" [Law, Structure, Sovereignty], *Ruch "Wolnosci i Pokoj": Czas Przyszly* [Movement of "Freedom and Peace": Future Time], no. 3/4 (fall 1988–winter 1989): 33–35; Jacek Czaputowicz, "Kilka uwag o wojsku," [Some Observations on the Military], *Ruch "Wolnosci i Pokoj": Czas Przyszly*, no. 3/4 (fall 1988–winter 1989): 46–47; and "Zey" [Krzysztof Wolicki], "About the Future," in *From the Polish Underground: Selections from Krytyka, 1978–1993*, ed. Michael Bernhard and Henryk Szlajfer (University Park: The University of Pennsylvania Press, 1995), 69–92.

76. "Uchwala nr 17/81, przyjeta przez Krajowy Zjazd Delegatow NSZZ 'Solidarnosc' 8 wrzesnia 1981 roku" [Resolution No 17/81 of the First Congress of Delegates of Trade Union Solidarity, September 8, 1981], excerpted from "Polska: Wybor z Najnowszych Dokumentow" [Poland: Excerpts from Recent Documents], *Nowa Koalicja*, no. 1 (1985): 55.

77. "Biuletyn Informacyjny Solidarnosci," no. 89, 6 June 1984, in Information Centre for Polish Affairs—*Studium Spraw Polskich*, (5 July 1984): 24.

78. "Fragmenty Deklaracji Politycznej WSN—Wolnosc, Sprawiedliwosc, Niepodleglosc" [Fragments of the Political Declaration of WSN—Liberty, Justice, Independence], excerpted from "Polska: Wybor z Najnowszych Dokumentow" (Poland: Excerpts from Recent Documents"), *Nowa Koalicja*, no. 1 (1985): 64–65.

79. "Fragmenty Deklaracji Politycznej WSN—Wolnosc, Sprawiedliwosc, Niepodleglosc" [Fragments of the Political Declaration of WSN—Liberty, Justice, Independence], excerpted from "Polska: Wybor z Najnowszych Dokumentow" (Poland: Excerpts from Recent Documents"), *Nowa Koalicja*, no. 1 (1985): 63.

80. Aleksander Hall, excerpted from *Polityka Polska*, no. 2/3, *Stadium Spraw Polskich*, (5 July 1984): 25.

81. As elaborated, the concept entailed that "each nation has the irrefutable right of preserving her identity, as well as political freedom . . . She can freely choose partners in each situation to cooperate in the field of politics and economy, to choose military alliances . . . Each nation has the irrefutable right of independence. . . . The right [to] self-determination automatically abolishes all alliances of nations and states which have not obtained an unquestionable and unanimous agreement of all participants. No country has

the right, under any circumstances and in the name of any cause, to infringe upon the rights and interests of any other country, especially in imposing her language, culture, creed, ideology, cooperation and agreements, or any other national union." See Marcin Mieguszowiecki and Adam Realista (WSN), "Razem jestesmy silniejsi: O potrzebie koalicji narodow Europy Srodkowo-Wschodniej" [Together We Are Stronger: The Need for a Coalition of Eastern European Countries], *Nowa Koalicja*, no. 1 (1985): 66–72.

82. Interview conducted by the author with Konstanty Gebert in Warsaw on June 6, 1994. See also Wieslaw Szukalski, "Geopolityczne warunki dla realizacji suwerennosci narodow Europy Wschodniej" [The Geopolitical Stipulation for the Realization of Sovereignty of the Eastern European Nations], *Oboz* (November 1987): 47–54.

83. "Wspolne oswiadczenie Polsko-Radzieckie" [Joint Polish-Soviet Statement, Warsaw, 14 July 1988], *Zbior Dokumentow*, no. 3 (1989): 76; and Krzysztof Gorski, "Dwutorowosc Polskiej Polityki Wschodniej w latach 1989–1991" [Polish Two-Track Eastern Policy from 1989–1991] (Master's Thesis, Uniwersytet Warszawski, 1992), 31–33.

84. See Zbigniew Brzezinski, *The Grand Failure: The Birth and Death of Communism in the Twentieth Century* (New York: Collier, 1989), 131; "'Orange Alternative' Marks 1968 Intervention," DPA, 1141 GMT, 20 August 1988, *FBIS-EEU*, 22 August 1988, 33; and "Charter 77 Statement on the Occasion of 21 August, Published in Prague: Without the Truth Nothing Can Improve," *Frankfurter Allgemeine*, 18 August 1988, *FBIS-EEU*, 18 August 1988, 6–7.

85. See, inter alia, Brzezinski, *The Grand Failure*, 117–130; Adam Michnik, "Revolt of the Radiators," in *Perestroika: How New Is Gorbachev's New Thinking?* ed. Ernest W. Lefever and Robert D. Vander Lugt (Washington, D.C.: Ethics and Public and Policy Center, 1989), 199–205; Z [Martin Malia], "To the Stalin Mausoleum," in *Eastern Europe . . . Central Europe . . . Europe*, ed. Stephen R. Graubard (Boulder, Colo.: Westview, 1991), 283–339; Arthur R. Rachwald, *In Search of Poland: The Superpowers' Response to Solidarity, 1980–1989* (Stanford, Calif.: Hoover Institution Press, 1990), 108–127; Charles Gati, *The Bloc that Failed: Soviet–East European Relations in Transition* (Bloomington: Indiana University Press, 1990), 167–170; Karen Dawisha, *Eastern Europe, Gorbachev and Reform: The Great Challenge*, 2nd ed. (Cambridge: Cambridge University Press, 1990), 218–224; and William E. Griffith, ed., *Central and Eastern Europe: The Opening Curtain?* (Boulder, Colo.: Westview, 1989).

86. "Roundtable Agreements," *Trybuna Ludu*, 7 April 1989, *FBIS-EEU*, 5 May 1989, 19–20.

87. Speech by *Solidarnosc* leader Lech Walesa at the final meeting of the Roundtable talks at the Palace of the Council of Ministers in Warsaw, Warsaw TV Service, 1540 GMT, 5 April 1989, *FBIS-EEU*, 6 April 1989, 32–33.

88. For analysis of the Roundtable Agreement and its implications for foreign policy, see, among others, Thomas S. Szayna, *Polish Foreign Policy under a Non-Communist Government: Prospects and Problems* (Santa Monica, Calif.: RAND, 1990), 10–13; Louisa Vinton, "Domestic Politics and Foreign Policy, 1989–1993," in *Polish Foreign Policy Reconsidered: Challenges of Independence*, eds. Ilya Prizel and Andrew A. Michta (Houndmills: Macmillan, 1995), 28–33; and Lucja Swiatkowski Cannon, "Polish Transition Strategy: Successes and Failures," in *The Legacy of the Soviet Bloc*, eds. Jane Shapiro Zacek and Ilpyong J. Kim (Gainesville: University Press of Florida, 1997), 143–144.

89. Vojtek Zubek, "Walesa's Leadership and Poland's Transition," *Problems of Communism*, no. 1–2 (January–April 1991): 72–73.

90. Waldemar Kuczynski, *Zwierzenia Zausznika* [Confidence of a Confidante] (Warsaw: Polska Oficyna Wydawnicza "BGW," 1992), 47. Kuczynski became Mazowiecki's closest advisor during the forming of the first *Solidarnosc*-led government and later took over as the privatization minister. See also Vinton, "Domestic Politics and Foreign Policy," 31–32.

91. "Expose sejmowe premiera PRL Tadeusza Mazowieckiego, fragmenty dotyczace pomocy zagranicznej i stosunkow miedzynarodowych" [Sejm Exposé by the Polish Prime Minister Tadeusz Mazowiecki/Excerpts Concerning Foreign Aid and International Relations, Warsaw, 12 September 1989], *Zbior Dokumentow*, no. 3 (1990): 24–25.

92. "PAP Profiles New Government Members," (Polish Press Agency) 13 September 1989, *FBIS-EEU*, 14 September 1989, 48.

93. See Krzysztof Skubiszewski, *Zachodnia Granica Polski* [Poland's Western Border] (Gdansk: Wydawnictwo Morskie, 1969); "Inauguracyjne posiedzenie Rady Konsultacyjnej przy Przewodniczacym Rady Panstwa" [Inaugural Meeting of the Consultative Council by the Presiding State Council] *Rada Naradowa* (21 March 1987): 2–3; and "Problemy polskiej emigracji" [Problems of Polish Emigration], *Rada Naradowa* (2 July 1988): 4–5.

94. Kuczynski, *Zwierzenia Zausznika*, 47.

95. Gorski, *Dwutorowosc Polskiej Polityki Wschodniej*, 35–36; and Vinton, "Domestic Politics and Foreign Policy," 32.

96. Szayna, "Polish Foreign Policy Under a Non-Communist Government," 14; Vinton, "Domestic Politics and Foreign Policy," 24–25; and Prizel, "Warsaw's Ostpolitik," 98.

97. "Sejm Committees Interview Ministers," PAP, 1804 GMT, 8 September 1989, *FBIS-EEU*, 11 September 1989, 36. It should be noted briefly that Skubiszewski well understood the significance and difficult history of the twentieth century regarding the Polish–German border. In his 1969 book, *Poland's Western Border*, Skubiszewski examined the Oder–Neisse border's controversial evolution and the international negotiations involved in its post–World War II demarcation. It is important to remember that he published this account as a Poznan University professor of international law and, at that time, did not have any affiliation with the Polish government. Even if his work was published just as the important thaw in Polish–German relations began and a year before Gomulka and Brandt signed the normalization treaty, Skubiszewski, in support of the Polish Government's position, elaborated Poland's priorities to secure a final and permanent Polish–German border. He argued that the border necessitated international resolution through a treaty negotiated by the four Allied Powers, the two Germanys, and, importantly, Poland. See Skubiszewski, *Zachodnia Granica Polski*, especially 560–562, in which he also cites Juliusz Mieroszewski, *Kehrt Deutschland in den Osten zuruck? Polen-Deutschland-Europa* [The German Turn-About in Eastern Restraint? Poland–Germany–Europe], (Berlin: 1961).

98. "We Present the Members of the New Government," *Rzeczpospolita*, 13 September 1989, *FBIS-EEU*, 18 September 1989, 42.

99. "New Ministers Meet with Jaruzelski," *Trybuna Ludu*, 14 September 1989, *FBIS-EEU*, 20 September 1989, 36.

100. "Sejmowe Expose Ministra Spraw Zagranicznych RP Krzysztofa Skubiszewskiego" [Sejm Expose by Minister of Foreign Affairs of the Republic of Poland, Krzysztof Skubiszewski], Warsaw, 26 April 1990, *Zbior Dokumentow*, no. 2 (1991): 8.

101. "Skubiszewski Comments on German Talks," PAP, 1256 GMT, 10 May 1990, *FBIS-EEU*, 14 May 1990, 47.

102. Roman Kuzniar, "Polish Foreign Policy: An Attempt at an Overview," in *Yearbook of Polish Foreign Policy, 1993/1994*, ed. Barbara Wizimirska (Warsaw: Polish Institute of International Affairs, 1994), 17–20.

103. "Epilog: Przemowienie Prezydenta Rzeczypospolitej Polskiej," [Speech by the Polish President] in Krzysztof Skubiszewski, *Polityka Zagraniczna i Odzyskanie Niepodleglosci: Przemowienie, Oswiadczenia, Wywiady 1989-1993* [Foreign Policy and Independence Regained: Speeches, Declarations, Interviews] (Warsaw: Interpress, 1997), 397.

104. Joshua B. Spero, "Poland's Perennial Crossroads: Between East and West?" in *The Future of East-Central Europe*, eds. Andrzej Dumala and Ziemowit Pietras (Lublin: Curie University Press, 1996), 273–292.

105. See, inter alia, Krzysztof Skubiszewski, *Poland's Western Border* (Gdansk: Instytut Baltycki, 1969); and "Statement by Polish Minister of Foreign Affairs at 44th Session of UN General Assembly," *Zbior Dokumentow*, no. 3 (1990): 150.

106. Christensen and Snyder, "Chain Gangs and Passed Bucks," 167; and Mueller, "Patterns of Alliance," 50–53.

107. Walt, *Revolution and War*, 345.

108. Wieslaw Szukalski, "The Geo-political Stipulation for the Realization of Sovereignty of the Eastern European Nations," *Oboz* (November 1987): 47–54; and Zdzislaw Najder, ed., *Alliance for Polish Independence: Electoral Text* (London: Polonia, 1989), 288–325.

109. Marcin Mieguszowiecki and Adam Realista, "Together We Are Stronger: The Need for a Coalition of Eastern European Countries," *Nowa Koalicja*, no. 1 (1985): 66–72.

110. For example, Z [Martin Malia], "To the Stalin Mausoleum"; Phillip A. Petersen, "The Challenge to Soviet Strategic Deployment: An Emerging Vision of European Security," in *Jane's NATO Handbook, 1990–1991*, ed., Bruce George (Coulsdon, U.K.: Jane's Information Group, 1990): 323–334; Rey Koslowski and Friedrich V. Kratochwil, "Understanding Change in International Politics: The Soviet Empire's Demise and the International System," *International Organization*, vol. 48, no. 2 (spring 1994): 215–247; and Brooks and Wohlforth, "Power, Globalization, and the End of the Cold War."

111. Taliaferro, "Security Seeking Under Anarchy," 150–152.

112. Edward D. Mansfield and Jack Snyder, "Democratization and the Danger of War," *International Security*, vol. 20, no. 1 (summer 1995): 5–38; and Michal Ksiezarczyk, "Openness Toward the East," *Zycie Warszawy*, 18–19 August 1990, 1, 4.

113. Samuel P. Huntington, *The Third Wave: Democratization in the Late Twentieth Century* (Norman: University of Oklahoma Press, 1991); Juan J. Linz and Alfred Stepan, *Problems of Democratic Transition and Consolidation: Southern Europe, South America, and Post-Communist Europe* (Baltimore, Md.: Johns Hopkins University Press, 1996); and Jack Snyder, *From Voting to Violence: Democratization and Nationalist Conflict* (New York: Norton, 2000).

114. Joshua B. Spero, "The International Coalition against Terrorism," *Insight Magazine* (3 December 2001): 41–43.

2

Understanding Poland's
Middle Power Politics and Strategy

By analyzing the five distinct phases of Polish foreign minister Krzysztof Skubiszewski's tenure, the following provides an integral overview to demonstrate the key facets of each post-Communist government's important political challenges and broad strategy from 1989 to 1993. Given the theoretical and historical context from the previous chapter as the baseline, this analysis illustrates how Skubiszewski guided and oversaw the alignment strategy he helped create for Polish foreign policy and how he survived four successive governments. Like the historical overview and basic post–Cold War context for how Poland became the first post-Communist Central-East European nation-state, this chapter assesses if the five phases broadly reviewed depict middle power Poland as a model of pragmatism. Inherent in Skubiszewski's strategy lie Poland's vision of *racja stanu* and how it applied to the critical junctures Poland faced during these four tumultuous years. The sense of great uncertainty over German unification, Soviet disintegration, and Visegrad Central European Triangle initiation enable us to render better judgment of the case study chapters that follow this overview chapter.

Defining the Stakes: The First
Mazowiecki Phase, Fall 1989-Fall 1990

When Skubiszewski became foreign minister, the FRG and USSR still existed. Within several months, the Berlin Wall fell and the Cold War framework collapsed. Even with the unexpected denouement of a divided Cold War Europe, Skubiszewski defined Poland's *racja stanu* at the beginning of his leadership and readily promulgated new policies toward Poland's neighbors. Skubiszewski, having already stated in his confirmation hearings that Warsaw anticipated the likelihood of German unification, viewed the geopolitical upheaval of an undivided Europe as an opportunity to achieve his goals of securing Poland's independence, strengthening its sovereignty over foreign policy, and reintegrating the state into Europe. Indeed, in his first interview to the Polish press, just before his first trip abroad, he explained Polish foreign policy objectives toward Germany and the USSR. On German unification, he said, "there is no doubt that this is a matter, firstly, for the Germans themselves. They have a right to decide their own fate, including their state's fate. But there are other levels." He considered that because the four powers still occupied Germany they needed to determine the FRG's future "as a united state." Finally, the unification process required all of Germany's neighbors, the two German states, and the four allied powers to conduct negotiations at the "all-European level." On Soviet "Finlandization," denoting the subservience by Poland to decisions by Moscow, he rationalized that "the sovereignty of the Polish state externally, and full independence as far as our internal affairs is concerned, are the principles of our foreign policy." Regarding the concept of "Finlandization," Skubiszewski asserted that "I would have various doubts which are, after all, shared by the Finnish people. Poland will arrange its foreign relations in such a way that it becomes a fully sovereign country."[1] Clearly, Skubiszewski respected Finland's early post–Cold War strategy to institute full sovereignty in foreign policy from the USSR, as he also wanted for Poland.

All of these goals remained consistent with the foreign minister's strategy of developing a new, circumspect, and judicious foreign policy toward Bonn and Moscow. The foundation for these policies stemmed from the *Solidarnosc* era's underground tenets and the Polish émigré community's writings, especially from Mieroszewski and particularly based on the PPN declaration's recommendations. Skubiszewski echoed some of these recommendations almost immediately in his first major foreign policy address by stressing the need to establish relations with Poland's western and eastern neighbors by focusing on equal partnership, international law, and territorial inviolability.[2] In this speech, given on 25 September 1989 at the United Nations General Assembly's Forty-Fourth Session, Skubiszewski described the tenets that became the fundamental principles for the period he served as foreign minister. For Skubiszewski, "Poland has a geostrategic location that makes her position militarily significant. This has a bearing on the whole region." What Poland needed to do focused on shaping "Polish foreign policy firmly to implement the fundamentals of external sovereignty and internal independence. Poland will do her best to maintain peace, freedom, and good-neighborly cooperation in Europe." What Skubiszewski wanted the international community to understand stemmed from the fact that "if Poland is free and democratic, then her geopolitical and geostrategic importance could and should be turned into an asset that supports peace and fosters freedom."[3]

In the speech, Skubiszewski also articulated a cautious vision about Polish policy toward the FRG, the USSR, and Western institutions. Although not mentioning the FRG by name, he signaled his intent toward Bonn for months to come regarding the Polish–German Oder–Neisse border, as stipulated by the 1970 Polish–German treaty. He stated that "today much emphasis must be put on the duty of all states not to question the frontiers and on the obligation to treat frontiers as inviolable." Within this international legal context, he linked Polish political strategy to the USSR by stressing that "we shall respect existing treaties and we firmly believe in mutual respect for national interests. Yet, such respect does not impose any limitations regarding the choice and change of the systems of government." For Skubiszewski, his new, democratically elected government remained indicative of a Poland bent on promoting its "vital interests" which, he underscored, did not "conflict with the interests of others," including Warsaw's right to "contribute to the re-creation of a united Europe in which Poland should have her place."[4] Such a statement allowed Skubiszewski to consider any number of options, including exploring links to Western European institutions hitherto prohibited by Moscow and the Warsaw Pact, for example, NATO and the EC.

At that UN session, Skubiszewski also met with his FRG, GDR, and USSR counterparts for the first time and discussed ways to build relations, particularly by planning ministerial visits. After his talks, Skubiszewski briefed the press about Poland's objectives for new relationships with Germany and the USSR. With respect to the FRG and GDR, Skubiszewski commented that Poland foresaw Polish–German links developing within the framework for European security and based on how the United States, USSR, United Kingdom, and France consented to the likelihood of German unification. Specifically, he reiterated his formula for German unification: "Of course the German nation which is divided today and lives in two states can organize its life in the way it wants to do it but one has to remember that this does not exhaust the problem." To unite, the FRG needed to abide by four-power "consent" within the European context because unification reconfigured European geopolitics, especially for all of Germany's contiguous states.[5] With regard to the Polish–Soviet relationship, Skubiszewski believed mutual areas for agreement needed to evolve on such bilateral issues as the format for political consultations, the unresolved issues from World War II, and the status of the Warsaw Pact.[6] From the fall to the winter, Skubiszewski laid the foundation for the Polish–German and Polish–Soviet relationships, meeting several times with his counterparts and establishing the initial negotiating terms of reference.

Several weeks after the UN General Assembly session, Skubiszewski hosted Soviet foreign minister Eduard Shevardnadze and began to redefine the Polish-Soviet allegiance beyond the Communist era's status of "independent satellite" toward a relationship of equal partnership. Shevardnadze came to Warsaw on 24

October to assess whether Poland, as the first state to elect a non-Communist-led government from the Warsaw Pact, remained a committed Eastern Bloc member. However, just before his visit, Skubiszewski gave a very candid interview in which he foresaw the "reshaping of a national strategy" toward the USSR. He argued that since post–Communist Poland strongly rejected the "Yalta accords as a dialogue between superpowers at the expense of medium and small countries, or as a dictate toward those countries," Poland refused to adhere to a "concert orchestrated by the superpowers." For the newly democratizing post–Communist middle power, "membership in the Warsaw Pact, as in all the other accords we have with the USSR, requires taking the interests of all the partners into consideration." Moreover, he declared that "using our army for offensive purposes is really unthinkable, if only because the Warsaw Pact, as it is formulated, is essentially a defense pact." Consequently, Poland no longer functioned under "the so-called Brezhnev doctrine." Skubiszewski pronounced that "Mazowiecki's government advocates sovereignty outwardly and internally. This stand will directly affect the nature of relations with our big neighbor."[7] Clearly, the foreign minister intended to change the way Poland operated within the Warsaw Pact.

Bearing this emerging Polish foreign policy in mind, Skubiszewski welcomed Shevardnadze for consultations. During several hours of discussions, much of which included Prime Minister Mazowiecki, Skubiszewski emphasized that "relations with the Soviet Union, Poland's most important partner, must change in order to correspond to the socio-political processes taking place in the two countries." Such a statement revealed Poland's determination to broaden its allegiances and put Moscow on notice that, although Warsaw upheld its commitment to the Warsaw Pact, Skubiszewski already believed the Polish–Soviet relationship resolutely had been transformed with his ascension as Polish foreign minister. Furthermore, he raised the issue of "moral recompense for the Poles who were victims of the Stalinist repression in the Soviet Union" and received a promise from Shevardnadze that the USSR intended to compensate for the World War II wrongs to the greatest extent possible.[8] In the end, both states signed a joint communiqué that underlined "further development and strengthening of good-neighborly cooperation and mutual observance of alliance commitments to serve vital interests of the two states and peoples and meet the needs of security and stability on the European continent. . . . Bilateral links in all the areas will be continued in accordance with . . . respect for sovereignty, equal rights, noninterference in internal affairs."[9] Even if Skubiszewski promoted a foreign policy based on the mutual respect for the geopolitical location of both states, he also needed to determine how long Soviet troops should remain stationed on Polish territory. Soviet troop deployments and the difficult troop withdrawal negotiations Skubiszewski's *MSZ* foresaw presented one of the most complicated dimensions for Poland's unfolding foreign policy. Yet, he argued early in his tenure that Poland must increasingly free itself both from the Cold

War's Polish–Soviet ideological platitudes and from unnecessarily limiting treaty commitments.

After Shevardnadze's first and most important visit in Warsaw, Skubiszewski moved rapidly to build the Polish–German relationship. He understood that the fall 1989 deterioration in the GDR had not only already created a new geopolitical crossroads in European security, but also upheld the *Solidarnosc* tenet that even if "a unified Germany remained within the realm of the possible, the Polish–German border issue must be resolved."[10] While focused on changing the Polish–Soviet relationship, Skubiszewski quickly realized that the pace of change throughout the GDR dominated Bonn's agenda and that the *MSZ* needed to concentrate its efforts to improve Polish–German relations, if Warsaw wanted to attain FRG chancellor Helmut Kohl's border guarantee. By building on the thirty-year-old Polish-German Church linkages and increasing the mutual trust beyond the 1970 Gomulka–Brandt Treaty, Skubiszewski believed the chances increased for obtaining Bonn's affirmation of the Polish–German border.

Chancellor Kohl's historic visit to Poland took an even more dramatic turn within twenty-four hours of his arrival on 9 November 1989 when the Berlin Wall fell. Although Kohl left Poland after the first day to address the rapid changes in both the GDR and FRG, he returned the next day. The break in the chancellor's Polish visit, however, didn't disrupt its anticipated symbolism for Polish–German post-World War II healing, still in its nascent stages since Chancellor Brandt's 1970 trip to Warsaw, and even added more drama with the acceleration of German unification. During the talks, Kohl underscored that "the success of the Polish road towards democracy will be the success for the entire Europe." In his turn, Premier Mazowiecki asserted that "we are well aware of the burden of history on our relations. But our talk also concerned the future and economic issues."[11] Both Mazowiecki and Kohl described deep anxieties their respective states held toward each other, but challenged Polish–German animosities dividing their peoples by looking to better relations based on post–World War II Western European model of cooperation.

The dinner toasts revealed the deep sense of reconciliation both leaders wanted to instill with the chancellor's visit. For the Polish premier, those who made the achievement of the 1970 Polish–German treaty possible already demonstrated an important dimension for the new Polish foreign policy. To overcome the tragedy of World War II, in which both sides suffered enormously, Mazowiecki pointed to the beginning of Polish–German reconciliation in the mid-1960s. "It is hard," Mazowiecki said, "not to appreciate the role which the message of Polish bishops to German bishops played in removing these animosities." The post-Communist Polish premier saw a natural progression from the religious reconciliation and the subsequent Polish–German treaty breakthrough to the resolution of "the political divisions as it concerns the most fundamental national interest: the right to life within safe borders, not questioned by anybody. He who understands and respects this, can count on understanding also in Poland." Fundamentally, the question that remained was the issue of the Polish–German border along the Oder and Neisse rivers. That determined the Polish–German relationship as Germany unified and post-Communist Poland continued to democratize.[12] For his part, the German chancellor attempted to finish what his predecessor Brandt had started, the German post–World War apology to Poland and its people, saying "the Germans and the Poles—neighbors in the heart of Europe—have spent most of their history living in peace, a fact not sufficiently known." According to Kohl, it remained necessary to establish a new relationship, now that Bonn saw a leader in Warsaw who believed in the same post–World War II democratic values. In order "to break the vicious circle of hatred and coercion, lawlessness and expulsion, and build new bridgeheads of accord, reconciliation, good-neighborly relations, and cooperation," the West German leader, like Konrad Adenauer in the earlier reconciliation with France and Israel, determined "to produce a lasting reconciliation between the German and Polish peoples." Kohl declared that "it is the task of European dimensions that is comparable with the German–French reconciliation, without which the process leading to the unification of our part of Europe would not exist."[13] Hence, if toasts captured the spirit of the potential turning point in Polish–German ties, the future appeared quite optimistic. The actual step-by-step development of relations, however, portended a great many hurdles to overcome.

Given the accelerated developments in both the GDR and FRG, the Polish leadership also strove to improve relations with the Soviet Union, with Mazowiecki visiting Moscow twice within two weeks in late November and early December. The prime minister's first trip focused on not only meeting his counterpart in Moscow, but also visiting Leningrad and Katyn. The purpose of his Leningrad visit was to demonstrate Poland's attempt to build relationships with Russian leaders outside of Moscow, while the purpose of his Katyn visit was to pay respect to Polish World War II officers who had been murdered by the KGB. Though Skubiszewski did not travel on this first USSR trip, his secretary of state, Boleslaw Kulski, represented the *MSZ* and Aleksander Hall, Mazowiecki's minister without portfolio in the Council of Ministers and a *Solidarnosc* advocate of greater ties to non-Soviet Russia, guided the visit by the first non-Communist leader from the Warsaw Pact. During the trip, Mazowiecki ensured that his Soviet hosts understood Poland's new policies, explaining that the Polish–Soviet relationship needed to "develop on the basis of sovereignty, good neighborly relations and mutual respect." Moreover, Polish–Soviet relations remained important, but "irrespective of Poland's adherence to the Warsaw Pact. The entire Warsaw Pact is ever more speaking of and moving toward an ever greater emphasis on its political and not its military character."[14] In the end, both sides officially committed to the new tenets Poland's post-Communist government wanted to foster as a matter for establishing a different relationship. Their "alliance relations" stemmed from "the principles of mutual confidence, respect for the freedom of choice of the path of sociopolitical development, full equality of rights and noninterference in internal affairs."[15] At least for Mazowiecki and the Polish leadership, the development of the Polish–Soviet relationship portended a concerted, practical, and nonconfrontational strategy to redefine how the first post-Communist state in the Warsaw Pact would attempt to align with its larger eastern and western neighbors in order to reintegrate into Europe.

A week later, Prime Minister Mazowiecki, accompanied by his foreign minister, President Jaruzelski, and Communist Party First Secretary Mieczyslaw Rakowski, again traveled to Moscow, this time for the meeting of Warsaw Pact political leaders. Even in December 1989, the Polish delegation remained the only leadership comprised of non-Communists. Although the formal communiqué failed to reveal any significant results, both Mazowiecki and Skubiszewski held press conferences that elaborated on important issues they had raised with their Communist counterparts.[16] In commenting on how Poland saw its links to Moscow and the other Warsaw Pact members, the prime minister stated that "we now need a relationship that would be acceptable to Polish society, and not a relationship that is imposed from above." Moreover, Skubiszewski disclosed that the Warsaw Pact leaders adopted a resolution "acknowledging the intervention in Czechoslovakia in 1968 as an illegal act and political, harmful mistake." Additionally, he stressed that the Polish delegation initiated and gained acceptance of a Warsaw Pact consensus that "the Warsaw Treaty is no grounds for any intervention in the internal affairs of states."[17] With these efforts, the Polish leadership moved closer to its objective for removing the ideological and politico-military limitations the Soviet-imposed Warsaw Pact had placed on Poland since its 1955 creation.

As 1989 came to a close, events affecting Central European security continued unabated. The GDR's swift collapse and the FRG leadership's hesitation regarding recognition of the Polish–German border emboldened Skubiszewski to press harder for international acknowledgment of Poland's national interest. In a speech focused on German unification before the Polish Parliament that December, the foreign minister reiterated Poland's critical issues for relations with the FRG, particularly in the wake of Chancellor Kohl's ten-point German unification plan which neglected the integrity of the Polish–German border. In focusing on Kohl's late-November speech to the German Parliament, Skubiszewski addressed Poland's lawmakers in terms of the German chancellor's key point about which the "unlimited respect for sovereignty and safety of each state," cited both German states but not Poland. "Sovereignty," Skubiszewski declared, "also means territorial sovereignty, it is obvious." For the Polish foreign minister, "the so-called legal pronouncements of the FRG, its court verdicts, and administrative acts do not dissociate themselves from the borders of 1937. Thus, the question arises: How does the chancellor's plan treat the sovereignty of Poland's territory in its current shape?" He answered his question by proclaiming that "our state interests and our *racja stanu* associate with the European attitude. We support the ideas of a united Europe and the implementation of this idea through cooperation and integration of European states." As a result, he asserted that "the changing relations between the German states should be part of the unification of

Europe and achievements in this area on the scale of the entire continent." The
bottom line remained that, in order for German unification to succeed, "European unification should always be paramount."[18]

Even though Skubiszewski maintained a public strategy to achieve "Polish–
German reconciliation" by placing the onus for its success on Bonn's "recognition of Poland's western border without understatements," he also realized that a
political balance remained necessary given the FRG's domestic politics.
Skubiszewski understood that Poland needed to maintain patience as Kohl's
Christian Democratic Union Party (CDU) faced the predicament of fragile political alliances with its far-right parties in upcoming FRG elections; it was the
far-right parties, who most vociferously questioned the Polish–German border.
More importantly, however, as a trained international lawyer, Skubiszewski
knew that, though the Kohl leadership wanted a Polish–German border accord, it
would take time to change some of the FRG's laws. Unlike the *MSZ*'s practical,
legal approach to German unification, alarmist Communist views in Poland led
by the former prime minister, Rakowski, focused only on the Polish Communists' traditionally defined views of the threat of German nationalism and inherent opposition toward improving Polish–German relations.[19] Despite these Polish Communist opinions, Skubiszewski's *MSZ* built upon the slow, but steadily
improving Polish–German relationship, moving beyond Communist rhetoric that
the *MSZ* viewed as unhelpful and gaining significant momentum from the 14
November 1989 joint Polish–German statement. In attempting to conclude some
kind of final, legal post–World War II understanding between their sovereign
states, Skubiszewski determined that Poland's foreign policy strategy toward
German unification necessitated a balancing of legal realities for both countries.
The noted foreign policy columnist Konstanty Gebert later commented to me in
Warsaw about what he perceived as the foundation for successful post-
Communist relations with the FRG:

> There is a common Christian democratic philosophy of history between *Soli-
> darnosc* and the CDU. Kohl had a very good internal, legal German argument
> that he could not make any guarantees in the name of future, united Germany.
> We Poles needed to be less paranoid, but even if the Americans believed Kohl,
> the French and British didn't and many in Poland failed to understand the
> FRG's constitutional debates. Remember we must have perspective in Poland
> when we talk about a *Solidarnosc* movement that refused to respect the im-
> posed legal order from the Communist martial law era.[20]

These policies sought first to promote the basis for long-term linkages between Warsaw with Bonn and Moscow to establish Skubiszewski's vision of
sovereign, middle power Poland's permanent foundation with both larger
neighboring states. Even with the momentous events in Germany and their impact on Central Europe, Skubiszewski remained undeterred in his strategy of
engagement with both the FRG and USSR leaderships. He believed in a me-

thodical, painstaking series of steps to create the basis for defining Poland's practical post-Communist foreign policy framework with Bonn and Moscow. The goal focused not only on upholding Warsaw's priorities for independence, but also on enabling Poland freely to reintegrate into Europe and shed the stigma of a "satellite" state. During 1990, Skubiszewski and some recognized *Solidarnosc* foreign policy experts he would bring to the *MSZ* constructed an innovative diplomacy that promoted a careful balance of interests between two precipitously changing neighbors. As Warsaw's confidence grew from the *Solidarnosc* experiments in political and economic reforms, Skubiszewski not only tried to devise relations he believed to maximize Poland's security with its stronger neighboring states, but also began to create the partnerships as a regional facilitator. As he articulated in September 1989, Skubiszewski wanted to develop a fully sovereign Polish foreign policy to sustain the state's values based on pluralistic development, greater security, and decreased threats. His main objective concentrated on projecting Poland's status as a "security-maximizer" and "cooperative other-helper," not promoting Poland as the kind of "power-maximizer" or "aggressive competitor" of the 1930s that attempted to play Germany and the USSR against each other.[21] Given the initial successes with both Germany and the USSR in the first six months of his *MSZ* leadership, Skubiszewski became more active in the second half of Mazowiecki's premiership toward the European democratic institutions and value systems the new Warsaw coveted to join. Such institutions as NATO and the EC, constituting foundations for political, economic, and military security, established and preserved stability in Western Europe during the Cold War. Skubiszewski respected how European and American policymakers depended for nearly fifty years on their multilateral ties, which institutionalized their relationships, rather than the hostile bilateral alliances which formed in the 1930s and led to World War II.

Innovative Diplomacy via Subtle Strategy: The Second Phase, Winter–Fall 1990

Poland's experiment as the first post-Communist democratic state and the Berlin Wall's collapse sounded the death knell for Central and Eastern European Communist leaderships. By the winter of 1990, Skubiszewski believed the top priorities of Polish foreign policy involved resolving uncertainty over German unification, recognizing changes required in policies toward Soviet disintegration and the emerging post-USSR states, developing the cooperative Visegrad Central European Triangle, and establishing more serious links to NATO. Furthermore, Skubiszewski tried to gain rewards for Poland by aligning with neighboring states, as he guided Poland within the upheaval created by Central Europe's democratic revolutions and the bipolar European security system's collapse. By promoting nonthreatening behavior and democratic values, Skubiszewski's foreign policy focused on achieving accommodation with Poland's stronger neighbors. Moreover, in attempting to project a nonthreatening stance, Warsaw strove to bridge with the states in the European security structure to which it desired to belong, namely NATO. Therefore, Poland sought to advance regionally via linkages to all neighbors, not with any one neighbor to the detriment of others, before European reintegration became possible.

In several broad foreign policy speeches during the first months of 1990, Skubiszewski laid out the aims of Polish foreign policy, specifically within the context of "Poland's dilemma between the Soviet Union and Germany" and the need "closely to coexist with our mighty neighbors." He described the necessity to develop long-lasting relationships built on "an appropriate shaping of common interests, good-neighborly cooperation and partnership based on equal rights, mutual respect for interests and for agreements made." Independent Poland required a foreign policy free of the "tremendous ideological burden[s], of multifarious dependence and satellite-like relations" during the Communist era. Poland wanted to have cooperative relations with all of its neighbors, confirmation regarding its borders, reorganization of the Warsaw Pact, and outreach to all regional organizations and alliances, including NATO, to promote practical cooperation and to demonstrate a greater seriousness about joining some day. Moreover, Skubiszewski wanted to change Poland's relations with outdated structures such as the Warsaw Pact because Warsaw no longer saw the pact as a military requirement. Coupled with a willingness to heal the post–World War II rift with a rapidly unifying Germany, Warsaw determined to establish a new Eastern policy comprising dual relations between Poland and the USSR and between Poland and the emerging neighboring republics, including Russia. Furthermore, Skubiszewski raised the possible connection between "the temporary stationing" of Soviet troops on Polish territory and "the evolution of the German problem," primarily the Oder–Neisse border, but declared that "the government considers the withdrawal of the troops a foregone conclusion." Finally, similarly to the like-minded Czechoslovaks and Hungarians, Skubiszewski felt that regional cooperation aided all three states to coordinate more effectively toward the East as they attempted to integrate into Western institutions.[22]

From the winter to the spring of 1990, the *MSZ* concentrated on developing both a different regional and Eastern strategy. At the year's outset, a debate arose in Poland about a possible Polish–Czechoslovak "confederation" since several prominent Czech underground leaders rose to power in late 1989 on the shoulders of their most famous dissident, internationally renowned playwright Vaclav Havel. A call by Polish-American geostrategist Zbigniew Brzezinski for the revival of the World War II confederative concept that had never materialized during the 1940s caused a stir in Warsaw and Prague and influenced debate.[23] In addition to the debate over Central European cooperation, heated arguments appeared in Polish foreign policy journals between government officials and nongovernmental advisors over Poland's role in Central European security. Sparked in part by an American Department of Defense official, Phillip Petersen, who published an unclassified assessment on Central European security from the Soviet standpoint, Polish policymakers and experts became dismayed over how Petersen's analysis depicted Poland outside emerging or proposed European security structures.[24] Such public debate in Warsaw appeared to affect the *MSZ* as Skubiszewski increased his statements on the need to work more closely with Poland's neighbors.[25] In fact, the first visits by the Czech foreign minister and president to Warsaw strengthened the rationale to form a regional cooperative effort, especially with President Havel's well-received speech to the Polish parliament. Within weeks, Polish, CSFR, and Hungarian foreign ministry officials coordinated the first summit for that spring in Bratislava.

During that winter, Skubiszewski also took his first trip to Bonn, to regularize foreign ministerial counterpart consultations and to articulate the Polish position on a future unified Germany in Europe. He not only wanted to strengthen commitments from the FRG leadership on the border, but also believed that the accelerating pace of German unification necessitated Warsaw's advocacy for Germany's stabilizing European role. Given that Skubiszewski became alarmed over calls by GDR and Soviet leaders for future German neutrality after unification, he determined, as the first top European foreign policymaker to enunciate this belief publicly, that a unified Germany belonged in Europe's current security system, and specifically in NATO.[26] He stated that Germans deserved their right to self-determination over their future status regionally and continentally, and he feared that German neutrality signified future regional destabilization if united Germany remained outside European security structures.[27] Though the Germans hesitated to support Poland on the border, they soon agreed to Warsaw's participation in the "2 Plus 4" unification talks that spring and remained grateful for Skubiszewski's commitment to having a future united Germany in NATO.[28]

By the spring, Skubiszewski's foreign policy began to change seriously, particularly when he fulfilled the promise he had made at his confirmation hearings to hire personnel who upheld democratic and post-Communist principles, much to the consternation of the *MSZ*'s Communist apparat. Specifically, underground *Solidarnosc*-era activists such as Vice Minister Jerzy Makarczyk, an international law professor, and European Deputy Director Grzegorz Kostrzewa-Zorbas, one of the last political prisoners freed in 1989, began to steer the *MSZ* in new directions. In Makarczyk, Skubiszewski found an alter ego in his international law colleague from the Poznan University days and a second in command who often represented the foreign minister abroad, especially in the tough negotiations over the coming years with Moscow. By bringing Kostrzewa-Zorbas to the *MSZ*, Skubiszewski sought to channel the same creativity exhibited by the underground foreign policy editor and fiery dissident into innovative post–Communist foreign policy recommendations. In fact, what first attracted Skubiszewski to Kostrzewa-Zorbas had been the latter's recommendations in private memoranda to restructure the *MSZ*'s Section of Soviet Relations and establish a new Eastern policy, formulated while working in late 1989 at the Senate's newly created Center of International Studies.[29]

Given Lithuania's declaration of independence in March 1990, the disintegration of the USSR accelerated, Skubiszewski wanted the *MSZ* to tackle the pressing daily issues regarding the shaping of Eastern policy differently and innovatively. Soon after hiring Kostrzewa-Zorbas, Skubiszewski agreed to implement his proposals and supported the formation of territorial sections dealing with Russia, Ukraine, Belorussia, the Baltic republics, the Transcaucasus, and Central Asia.[30] This new and consolidated structure entailed a wholesale personnel turnover; Kostrzewa-Zorbas was delegated the authority by Skubiszewski to recruit whomever he deemed necessary to oversee these country desk responsibilities. Compared with other Central European and even Western European states, the *MSZ*'s restructuring appeared revolutionary, as the ministry positioned itself to deal with the consequences of the disintegration of the USSR in spring 1990, well before the August 1991 Soviet *coup d'état*.[31] Moreover, Kostrzewa-Zorbas filled these consolidated and new positions with *Solidarnosc* allies and scholars trained in Soviet nationality policy from Warsaw University and specialists with connections to the Soviet republics. As a result, 100 percent turnover occurred in the consolidated slots, making them the only *MSZ* section to achieve such a feat in Skubiszewski's *MSZ* tenure.[32]

Predominantly in their twenties and early thirties, these new personnel quickly developed an Eastern policy during the spring and summer of 1990 that defined a two-track approach toward the Soviet "center" in Moscow and the non-Soviet leaderships emerging in Russia and the other republics bordering Poland. From the outset, Kostrzewa-Zorbas clearly articulated Skubiszewski's new, dual Eastern orientation by stating that Polish–Soviet relations first needed to be founded upon an equal partnership. This partnership gained its legitimacy, he argued, because "the more our sovereignty and equality are implemented, the better our relations with the Soviet Union." According to Kostrzewa-Zorbas, Warsaw's promotion of a second track within the Eastern policy stemmed from the fact that "Poland cannot be a party to any internal alliances between components of the USSR, which does not mean we should be deaf and blind to the changes occurring there." He argued that "we should maintain relations on two levels—with the confederation as a whole—the USSR is aiming toward a confederation—and with this a confederation's component members," that is, the increasingly important constituent republics. Furthermore, he posited that the new political, economic, and security environment in Central and East Europe demanded the creation of new legal systems and a new security relationship with the USSR, not a text based on the Friendship and Cooperation Agreement from 1965, let alone clauses from 1945. Moreover, he foresaw that "Poland, anxious to be an integral part of the West, wants to be open to the East at the same time." Lastly, as a "bridgehead" to the West, Kostrzewa-Zorbas believed that Poland provided the historic opportunity for both its state and its eastern neighbors to integrate into the European community of nations.[33]

The spring to summer of 1990 also witnessed a number of important multilateral meetings that influenced European security and at which Skubiszewski played a key role for Poland. On 9 April, the Bratislava Summit initiated by President Havel focused on the first formal, post–Cold War regional cooperative effort among the leaders from the Central and Southeastern European states.[34] According to Skubiszewski, the summit reviewed "common problems" such as the dramatic political, economic, and social reforms experienced by the newly emerging democracies and how they believed they needed to work together to solve them. However, he felt the necessity "to bring about systematic and well-prepared work on the assumptions, essence and form of cooperation," particularly among the three historically most cooperative Central European states.[35] As the Polish press emphasized, this first summit allowed Central Europeans "to believe that our countries may return to Europe through the road used by Spain, Portugal or Greece, from dictatorship to democracy, from poverty to wealth."[36]

With the evolution of a new Eastern policy and the development of a Central European regional cooperative strategy, Skubiszewski's *MSZ* also looked toward an endgame on German unification. The complexities of the "2 Plus 4" negotiations, however, presented Skubiszewski with the dilemma linked to the Warsaw Pact's continued existence, the pending Conventional Forces in Europe (CFE) arms control agreement, and the Soviet troops stationed in both the GDR and Poland. Given its opposition to Soviet control of the Warsaw Pact, Poland determined to try to liquidate the internal Warsaw Pact military mechanisms, particularly building on Hungary's first democratic election that brought non-Communist Jozef Antall to power as prime minister in May.

Because the *MSZ* saw that the CFE treaty negotiations yielded only an agreement that formalized the military status of the Warsaw Pact and bloc-to-bloc system that ignored the newly independent Central European states and preserved what Poland considered the Pact's old structures and system, Skubiszewski needed to implement his strategy quickly. He wanted to abolish the Pact's military structures and try to reorganize its political mechanisms to reflect democratic functions by breaking the Soviet political monopoly in the Pact. Although he sought both Hungary's and the CSFR's support, the new Budapest leadership indicated its desire to withdraw immediately from the Pact and the Prague leadership remained focused only on Soviet force withdrawals from its territory. Skubiszewski and the Polish government believed that the non-Soviet Pact members needed to coordinate the demise of the Pact, or else risk Soviet exploitation of their differences. Warsaw governmental leaders felt that, without military structures, the Pact held no meaning. Therefore, Poland attempted to convince Hungary and the CSFR to coordinate strategy against Moscow, not to depart from the Pact unilaterally, but to kill the Pact formally.[37]

Other regionally important and related issues to the Polish strategy to disband the Warsaw Pact's military structures also arose as the Pact's June Political Consultative meeting in Moscow approached. Ironically, during the prelude to the Warsaw Pact's meeting and before the "2 Plus 4" talks reached their final stages in Paris and Moscow that summer and fall, the Poles continued to hesitate to initiate negotiations on Soviet force withdrawal with Moscow. Even with presidential aspirant Walesa's declaration that all Soviet troops in Poland must withdraw by the end of 1990, the Polish government remained cautious. The leadership felt that it needed to take certain diplomatic tracks sequentially to obtain the Oder–Neisse border confirmation and to pressure Moscow on the Warsaw Pact's military structures, not yet bargain on Soviet troop withdrawals from Poland.[38] On the one hand, the German leadership focused solely on the "2 Plus 4" talks and wanted unification agreed to before their November national elections. On the other hand, the Polish government, still uncertain about the true commitment of the FRG government concerning the integrity of the Polish–German border, desired to exert whatever pressure on Bonn as necessary to obtain a formal agreement. But Poland lost what some analysts believed was the crucial time to negotiate with a weakened Moscow.[39] Nevertheless, as the "2 Plus 4" talks began, Skubiszewski's confidence grew, particularly after FRG President Richard von Weizsaecker's visit to Warsaw. The Polish foreign minister stated both sides believed that the basis for a future border treaty appeared possible. In Skubiszewski's words, "The unfortunate frontier debate on the Oder-Neisse line is over. Now I am optimistic for relations between the two countries, as they have a new foundation with this visit."[40]

Within several months, Skubiszewski achieved Poland's objectives at the "2 Plus 4" talks[41] and on 12 September the treaty on German unification came into force, delineating "confirmation of the definitive nature of the borders of the united Germany" and "binding it under international law."[42] The treaty culminated a significant series of steps to create a Polish–German formula for common interests in which Poland believed it played a constructive role in European security, and through which Poland's integration into Europe would increase.

Skubiszewski's Central European strategy toward the progressive dismantling of the Warsaw Pact took a new turn just before Mikhail Gorbachev hosted the Pact's 7 June Political Consultative meeting. In anticipation of the meeting, the Polish prime minister, president, and foreign minister met with President Havel to discuss how to coordinate Central European strategy toward Moscow. After this strategy session, Mazowiecki gave a press conference at which he stated, "I think that the Warsaw Treaty should be essentially reformed on the principle of full equal rights of its participants in all areas, both political and military ones. One should at the same time think about a new European security system already today."[43]

According to an account of the subsequent late-night meetings on that first day of the Warsaw Pact meeting in Moscow, one of the Polish delegates depicted President Havel's exciting, lastminute initiative as a "total surprise."[44] Apparently, late in the day before leaders convened, Havel sent messages to Warsaw and Budapest, signaling his intention to propose the Pact's dismantling. In Moscow the following day, Havel then argued publicly for a "fundamental transformation of the whole Warsaw Pact and its function."[45] Such calls to change the Pact came on the heels of the new democratically elected Hungarian government's statement about potential Hungarian withdrawal from the pact,[46] accelerating events that Skubiszewski thought rash, given the delicate balance he felt was required to negotiate future security issues with Bonn and Moscow. This chain of events certainly hastened Skubiszewski's plan for disbanding the pact's military structures, going beyond the Polish scheme for effectively "hollowing out" the pact. For Skubiszewski and the Polish delegation, Havel's message clearly enunciated Prague's determination to manipulate Moscow "to launch the process of dismantlement by drafting a declaration" among the Central European delegations to present to the Soviet leader.[47] Yet, Hungary and Poland joined the CSFR in forging a consensus over the several days in Moscow, with Hungarian prime minister Antall publicly stating at the close of the summit that Budapest would soon withdraw from the Warsaw Pact's unified military command structure.[48] In effect, Warsaw achieved its goals by convincing its Central European colleagues to compromise by not withdrawing from the pact entirely, but agreed to pressure Moscow concertedly to disband the Pact in the coming months on Central European terms. Above all, Poland emerged energized from the Moscow Pact meeting, solidified its triangular relationship, and deemed the time right for both a more assertive Eastern and NATO policy.

By the fall, as Polish–NATO relations progressed Skubiszewski's new *MSZ* team redefined its Eastern strategy. The *MSZ*'s Eastern policy not only took more shape as Skubiszewski planned his first visit to the USSR in October, but also gained more attention publicly when the Senate invited the foreign minister to speak on the subject. Appearing before many of his old scholarly colleagues, now senators, Skubiszewski meticulously described the *MSZ*'s "long-range, energetic, and careful" Eastern strategy toward the Soviet leadership, or Soviet "center," and the evolving non-Soviet leaders in the Russian, Ukrainian, Lithuanian, and Belorussian republics. Both foreign minister and senators found common ground in recognizing that Poland's neighboring republics, entities which all agreed had already begun proving they could begin to separate themselves from Moscow's Soviet grip, needed Poland's support for their "self-determination" through formalized cooperation. Clearly, though, both the Polish government and parliament concurred that the Soviet reforms and upheaval in the USSR did not necessitate any changes to the Soviet republic's borders. To uphold his rationale for developing a new Eastern policy during the past several months, however, Skubiszewski declared, "our openness to the East is total. We belong to Europe, to Western European culture; we need to cultivate and expand ties with the East. . . . The idea of a 'bridge' contains many elements which are of concern to us and which I am carrying forward." For Skubiszewski, "our situation, which was once our curse, must today become our blessing, but that depends on us." To aid the East, he elaborated that because "Poles are understood in the East [due to] centuries of interflow of values," Warsaw planned to establish new ties to its eastern neighbors. Poland needed to move beyond the past conflicts and Communist-era rhetoric and wrongful actions toward the state's neighboring peoples and their cultures.[49]

With this Eastern strategy in mind, the government and Parliament proceeded to forge an approach toward both the Soviet central and non-Soviet republic leaderships. In October 1990 Poland began to apply concrete steps to its "two-track" Eastern strategy of relations with the central government in Moscow and the emerging independent republic leaderships in Russia, Ukraine, and Belorussia. Skubiszewski actually traveled to Moscow twice, while also going to Kiev and Minsk in order to create closer ties with the Russian, Ukrainian, and Belorussian leaderships. On the whole, Skubiszewski's first visit to introduce his new Eastern policy achieved significant results in Kiev and Moscow, the latter with Russian republican leaders. Additionally, his counterpart talks continued with the Soviet leadership in Moscow, including the first important face-to-face salvo on the status of Soviet troops in Poland. His discussions in Minsk, however, failed to accomplish the objective of establishing initial ties, but did gain a commitment to continue dialogue. However, the fact that Poland became the first country to conclude accords with Ukraine and Russia, respectively, underlined what many of the underground and émigré publications advocated during the Cold War. Moreover, the two declarations established an important foundation from which Poland constructed the important future treaties with independent Ukrainian and Russian leaderships in the post–Soviet era, making the results of Skubiszewski's trip unique compared to those of any other European foreign minister. No other European leadership saw the coming downfall of the USSR and acted with foreign policies to formalize relationships before Warsaw in October 1990.[50]

While Polish foreign policy–makers expanded relations to the Soviet republic leaderships, they continued to improve their relationship with Germany, especially in the wake of Chancellor Kohl's solid victory in the December German national elections. After great negotiation and delay, but shortly after the German elections, Skubiszewski and his German counterpart met in Warsaw on 14 November 1990 to sign the historic "Treaty on the Confirmation of the Polish–German Border." This document finally upheld Poland's Western border along the Oder and Neisse Rivers, concluding a process begun almost exactly twenty years earlier when Gomulka and Brandt reached the initial Polish–German accord. It defined a historic moment in the post–World War II era of mending relations between the two states and established a model along the lines of the post–World War II Franco–German reconciliation. Both Hans-Dietrich Genscher, the German foreign minister, and German chancellor Kohl, also on hand for the ceremony, echoed optimistic sentiment when they stated that not only did the treaty play an important role in Germany's unification, but also it united instead of divided a border to reinforce Europe's unification.[51]

Although parallels existed between Poland's fragile security in the 1930s and its status in the early 1990s, the emerging post–Cold War Warsaw policy-makers attempted to reintegrate into Europe, not as belligerents, but as facilitators, both for Poland's sake and for the benefit of their neighbors. To its east, Poland lay between the evolving Soviet republics of Lithuania, Ukraine, Belarus, and Russia, including Kaliningrad, an area that potentially cut a small part of Russia off from the Soviet Union. To its west, Poland faced an economically formidable, yet possibly overextended, unifying Germany. Facing different geographical concerns than in either 1918 or 1945, however, Polish foreign policy–makers concentrated on eastern policy without continual concern over their western border. Warsaw's confidence increased because the FRG stayed firmly embedded in NATO and the EC during the Cold War and its geopolitical status remained intact after German unification.

Such a critical moment in history gave Poland the daunting responsibility of helping to create a stable security environment that once again promised to affect Central Europe. At such a historic moment, as indicated by Skubiszewski's emerging Western and Eastern policy during 1990, Poland appeared to choose integration into Europe over playing Moscow and Bonn against each other, of not "aggressively balancing" between them, as in the 1930s. Skubiszewski recognized that Western European security institutions such as NATO prevented war within their region and ideally should more effectively decrease future tensions before they became conflicts such as the tensions beginning to boil in Yugoslavia. Therefore, Skubiszewski and his *MSZ* team negotiated as equal partners with their stronger western and eastern neighbors via a bridging strategy, to build the case for Poland's integration into Europe's multilateral institutions—institutions which had preserved peace for almost fifty years by forging universally–accepted guidelines for behavior and cooperation.[52]

Polish Presidential Politics, Soviet Backlash, Domestic Balancing: Winter–Fall 1991

Even as Poland's foreign policy developed into a comprehensive strategy for integration into the West and redefined outreach toward the East, the winter of 1991 witnessed the emergence of Soviet hard-line forces in Moscow and of a new and different Polish president. With the abrupt resignation of Soviet foreign minister Shevardnadze, Skubiszewski saw the end temporarily to any progress in Soviet force withdrawal talks he initiated with Soviet leaders in Moscow during his October 1990 trip.[53] Skubiszewski's negotiating team believed they needed to counter Moscow's resistance by trying to strike a deal with Bonn regarding the FRG's troop withdrawal strategy toward the USSR. Yet, Shevardnadze's resignation, coupled with the Soviet military's growing influence demonstrated subsequently by their January 1991 attack in Vilnius, greatly concerned Warsaw.[54] Moreover, Poland's December elections culminated in Walesa's resounding presidential victory over Mazowiecki and Poland's second post-Communist government transition among new players and *Solidarnosc* factions. Through all of this domestic change, Skubiszewski survived as minister, but some Polish conservative parties charged him with moving too slowly in developing relations with post-Soviet states. He endured criticism during the presidential campaign, particularly from some analysts who soon joined Walesa's cabinet, because they felt he pursued too methodical a foreign policy toward Germany and the USSR, while enacting too restrained a strategy toward the post-Soviet states. By his adherence to the self-limiting principles from the 1989 Roundtable Agreement, Skubiszewski enlarged the task of making foreign policy under Poland's first post-Communist, dynamic, and domineering President.[55]

The December 1990 presidential victory catapulted Walesa from his renowned *Solidarnosc* Labor Union leadership to the highest politically elected post in Poland. By harshly criticizing Mazowiecki and, by extension, Skubiszewski, on Soviet troop withdrawals, one of the few foreign policy issues he raised during the electoral campaign, Walesa now faced the reality of overseeing Poland's foreign policy after having broken ranks with many in *Solidarnosc*. Shortly before the presidential elections, the new government formed under Jan Krzysztof Bielecki kept Skubiszewski at the helm of the *MSZ* because of his political neutrality and foreign policy experience. It soon became clear, however, that Walesa wanted to assume the mantle of foreign policy head as president, a situation different from his predecessor and one that ultimately put him at odds on a number of important foreign policy decisions with the government.[56] Furthermore, though Walesa used the issue of Soviet force withdrawals to apply campaign pressure against Mazowiecki, whom many viewed as too hesitant toward Moscow, Walesa failed to elaborate on any larger Eastern policy or comment on the implications of the German factor for Polish–Soviet force withdrawal negotiations. For Mazowiecki's *MSZ* negotiating team, the rationale for Soviet force withdrawals initially focused on German unification and German guarantees of the Oder–Neisse border. Once the Polish–German treaty came into force in November 1990, the *MSZ* negotiating team on troop withdrawals concentrated more on how to deal with the Soviet–German negotiations over Soviet troop withdrawals from Germany that excluded Poland. This exclusion proved particularly frustrating to the *MSZ* since Soviet troops needed primarily, among other things, to transit sovereign Polish territory, Polish negotiators argued, to return to the USSR. Yet, with the election behind him, President Walesa determined to take charge of foreign policy, directing the *MSZ* rather than delegating to Skubiszewski the making of foreign policy, especially Eastern policy. At the same time, Moscow's conservative backlash stalled troop withdrawal talks as Walesa and his new presidential team started to give mixed signals on Eastern policy.[57]

Differences particularly over Eastern and NATO policy soon emerged publicly between Walesa's presidential advisors, divided into those who supported the proindependence movements in the USSR and those who favored the Soviet conservative line, particularly the hard-line Soviet military stance. The former comprised such long-time underground leaders as Jaroslaw and Lech Kaczynski, respectively chief of staff and minister of state for national security, and Zdzislaw Najder, *Solidarnosc* Citizen Committee chairman. The latter coterie consisted of Walesa's chauffeur, chief of cabinet, eventually presidential chancellery secretary of state, and closest confidante, Mieczyslaw Wachowski, Vice Admiral and Minister of Defense Piotr Kolodziejczyk, and chief of the national security bureau Jerzy Milewski, who oversaw a small staff in support of but separate from Walesa's cabinet. The more moderate Skubiszewski and his *MSZ* staff found themselves limited in the range of options from which they could choose, particularly how quickly to press Moscow to withdraw its forces from Poland, how closely to develop relations with the post-Soviet successor states, and how strongly to promote Polish–NATO ties.[58]

Amid the domestic upheaval, Skubiszewski continued to expand the series of relationships with Poland's neighbors that upheld territorial integrity, non-confrontational military doctrine, and regional security cooperation.[59] The first major test between Skubiszewski's *MSZ* and Walesa's team stemmed from the next Central European summit, this time slated for Visegrad, Hungary. According to accounts from both his advisors and *MSZ* officials, Walesa tried to delay and even cancel the Visegrad Summit because he believed the Polish president's international stature was above that of Central European leaders, Havel and Antall. Some policymakers also believed Walesa wanted to kow tow to Moscow and not upset the Kremlin by advocating a more concerted Central European move toward NATO as the Warsaw Pact crumbled.[60] Even though the Polish leadership postponed the summit for several weeks, Walesa finally agreed to the mid-February date that marked the first Central European–focused summit, an event that occurred during the turmoil from the growing disintegration in the USSR. At Visegrad, for the first time democratically elected leaders from what became known as the Visegrad Triangle convened to sign a declaration on political, economic, and security cooperation. They promised to undertake concerted efforts to integrate their region into the new Europe and to collaborate on security policies, including coordination on military issues.[61]

After the Visegrad Summit, Polish foreign policy–makers quickly assessed the impact for Poland's policies and the impact throughout Central Europe. Skubiszewski attempted to explain that the Triangle would not become a "military alliance," but would be a mechanism for "loose cooperation."[62] To reduce concerns in Moscow, Skubiszewski stated that the Triangle wanted to strengthen "stability" and "security" in Central Europe. He stressed that triangular security coordination primarily meant closely consulting on the dissolution of the Warsaw Pact and the CMEA and on the friendship and cooperation treaties being renegotiated with Moscow and between it and Warsaw, Prague, and Budapest, respectively. At the same time, he stressed that Poland, the CSFR, and Hungary did not need to render any "immediate assistance" to each other to meet an impending threat, albeit he did underscore that the three states intended to enact bilateral military agreements.[63] Within this regional cooperative context, however, Skubiszewski foresaw "more intensive cooperation with security organizations such as NATO," particularly as the Polish-German relationship expanded. The *MSZ* prepared Walesa for the president's first trip to NATO headquarters and the *MSZ*'s European Department strongly recommended a concerted, step-by-step NATO membership strategy—well before NATO stated its readiness to accept new members.[64]

In the early stages of Walesa's presidency, Polish policy toward Germany remained relatively consistent, with the *MSZ* still leading under Bielecki's Government to complete important agreements after the border treaty from November 1990. Polish–German relations significantly improved with the signing of their "Treaty on Good Neighborliness, Friendship and Cooperation" on 17 June 1991.[65] The treaty underlined the guarantee of territorial integrity, border inviolability, political independence, economic development—particularly vis-à-vis the EC—and equal minority rights for citizens living in each other's states. As Skubiszewski testified "there is not European unity and European order without a good accord and solid Polish–German cooperation and joint activity." To build on European unity and order, the Polish foreign minister elaborated that "the Germans support our strategic aim of entry into the European Community. . . . It points to relations of European dimensions, it stresses the direction of joint activities for a pan-European security system." For Skubiszewski, the treaty signified that Poland overcame its "fears" of the larger German neighbor, that words finally transformed the relationship into deeds.[66]

The treaty symbolized a new era in Polish–German relations. In contrast to the Polish–German 1934 Non-Aggression Treaty, both states pledged to reject territorial claims, reaffirmed their post–World War II borders, and upheld minority rights in both states. One other important difference also existed. Unlike the collective security system in the 1930s that deteriorated when, among other things, Germany withdrew from the League of Nations, the Polish–German State Treaty of 1991 witnessed Germany pulling Poland into a pan-European security system.

Soon after Bielecki's signing of the Polish–German treaty in Germany, Walesa and his advisors traveled to NATO headquarters in Brussels, marking the first time a Polish head of state had ever visited. The NATO visit, however, had resulted in some controversy among Walesa's advisors, as Wachowski evidently crossed out an important segment from the draft of Walesa's speech to the North Atlantic Council, over the protest of Lech Kaczynski and Skubiszewski. Given the sensitivity in Warsaw about instability in the East, Wachowski may have believed it unwise to permit the language in the foreign ministry's first version of the speech. The incident also demonstrated his ability to overrule the key foreign policy–makers in Walesa's circle and in the government on Polish–NATO and Polish–Soviet relations. The segment was the following:

We cannot, however, hide the truth [about Polish-Soviet relations]. There are problems that cast a shadow over our cooperation. Even though we have tried to be flexible in the negotiations, there still is no movement on the withdrawal of the Soviet troops stationed in Poland. The USSR has proposed dates that fall far in the future and an extremely slow tempo for the withdrawal of these units.

Such policy toward a sovereign Poland is not tolerable. We are waiting for a positive breakthrough that will improve the atmosphere for peace on the entire continent.[67]

Furthermore, Walesa gave mixed signals about the extent he envisaged for Poland's relationship to NATO, particularly given the growing instability in the Soviet Union. During his press conference at NATO, he stated that "we cannot allow a vacuum to develop in our part of Europe after the collapse of the Warsaw Treaty Organization and Council for Mutual Economic Assistance. Europe has to help us in our efforts to manage this region."[68] While declaring that Poland's intention remains "to advocate a united Europe, which includes the Soviet Union without giving . . . the USSR the impression that we are doing something against its interests," Walesa underlined that, at that time, Poland would not immediately seek to join NATO.[69] Moreover, Skubiszewski contended publicly after the NATO talks that disagreements with Moscow over Soviet troop withdrawal negotiations continued to slow Polish–NATO relations.[70]

Unlike Walesa and more akin to Skubiszewski, Lech Kaczynski proposed a third policy option. He said that Poland must not again, as during the 1930s, become overly "dependent" on Moscow for its security just because both states remain "fated to be allies to each other." Kaczynski emphasized that Poland sought "various forms of rapprochement with NATO" and also needed to secure ties with all of Europe's security institutions. He understood that unilaterally safeguarding its security remained unrealistic. But Kaczynski remained skeptical about NATO statutes that failed to envision "more relaxed associate membership" for Poland.[71] Moreover, he underscored that "the problem of security guarantees exists. In the long run, Poland views NATO as the single most important security structure in Europe. It intends, however, to participate in what it considers to be the 'soft structures,' namely the Conference on Security and Cooperation in Europe (CSCE) and the Council of Europe—structures it maintains are cooperative bodies, not institutions."[72] Hence, Walesa's *Solidarnosc* advisors, including Skubiszewski, desired increased NATO links leading to serious Western ties, while his pro-Soviet advisors seemed to gain the upper hand by keeping NATO at arm's length.[73]

Such divisiveness among Walesa's advisors continued during the failed Soviet coup d'état from 19 to 21 August 1991, as Walesa wavered between siding with Soviet hard-liners and Russian reformers. During the drama in Moscow, Walesa, his national security team, and the government appeared at odds over the gravity of the situation in Moscow. No Polish cabinet meetings occurred and, though Lech Kaczynski requested the National Defense Committee convening, a body designed specifically for top officials to confer on potential threats to Poland, President Walesa refused the plea. Apparently, only Wachowski and Kolodziejczyk gave official advice to Walesa in the crisis. During the coup, Walesa appeared to side with the Soviet Emergency Committee in the initial stages of the crisis. Rather than supporting Gorbachev or Boris El'tsin, Walesa first called former Communist generals Jaruzelski and Kiszczak for help, then thought about sending a letter of support to coup leader Gennadii Yanaev and only as the coup collapsed, decided to speak to Russian anti-coup leader El'tsin. According to Milewski, Walesa's reasoning stemmed most likely from his concern over control of the 45,000 Soviet forces still stationed in Poland, the president's view that Gorbachev had abdicated his Soviet leadership, and Walesa's belief about El'tsin's likely defeat. Some in Poland credit Prime Minister Bielecki with preventing Walesa from sending the letter of support to Yanaev. Moreover, the prime minister's supporters praised his attempt to address the Polish public on the state of the crisis, especially since Bielecki created a special ministerial-level crisis staff that included Skubiszewski and wanted to report its conclusions. Walesa, however, stopped Bielecki from going on national television. In all, the president's seemingly erratic behavior wrecked any remnants of unity among his advisors. The final straw came when both Kaczynski brothers and several other top Walesa advisors decided to resign during the coup, but waited until the fall, after the coup's fallout became clear. Walesa's uncertain behavior set the tone for the coming months, as those advisors who stayed in his cabinet and those who left to join opposition parties debated whether the president had tried to "Finlandize" Poland, to the detriment of a sovereign foreign policy, in deference to Moscow dictates.[74]

Political Turmoil and National Security Consolidation: Winter 1991–Summer 1992

With the dissolution of both Yugoslavia and the USSR, and the first full Polish parliamentary elections at the end of 1991, democratic Poland tried to define a national security policy focused on rapid integration into Europe. For Polish foreign policy–makers, particularly under the new conservative government of Jan Olszewski, the implications of several new countries emerging to Poland's east posed both security concerns and challenges. Poland's new government came to power very apprehensive about Eastern instability and Russian military resurgence, vowing to "decommunize" the ministries Olszewski's government controlled. In Skubiszewski's case, only after Walesa convinced him did the very reluctant foreign minister serve his third successive prime minister, but he came to regret his decision as the political power battles soon started between Walesa and Olszewski. With its accession Olszewski's government declared that, by virtue of its geopolitical location in the heart of a new Europe, Poland promoted European integration for Central Europe as a bridge between East and West Europe, since Warsaw no longer feared a unified Germany. Given Poland's stated foreign policy aims, however, some of the new players in the Olszewski government believed that the breakup of the USSR portended dangers and risks, even if it resulted in a smaller national security threat. They stressed that the uncertainty of Ukrainian sovereignty, regional tensions between Kiev and Moscow over nuclear weapons control, and Russia's revived "neoimperial" policies toward the former non-Russian republics of the USSR impelled Warsaw to find ways to defuse the potential for increased instability.

As a result, Skubiszewski found himself involved in a debate over Eastern policy and NATO membership. Skubiszewski faced the new premier, Jan Olszewski, who took charge in late 1991 and surrounded himself with anti-Moscow and pro–NATO advisors such as the first civilian defense minister, Jan Parys, Najder, and the Kaczynski brothers. On the pro-Moscow side, the foreign minister needed to balance the interests of Walesa's advisers such as Wachowski and Milewski, both of whom advocated yielding to Moscow's wishes and holding NATO at arm's length.[75] For Skubiszewski, the six months of Olszewski's leadership witnessed serious policy disputes between the president and premier over support for or opposition to NATO's membership, Russian intentions, and Ukrainian independence. Throughout this stormy political period, the foreign minister constantly counseled moderation and compromise to avoid alienating leaders of NATO, Russia, and Ukraine.

All of these Polish policymakers not only confronted the serious problem of integrating Poland into regional security structures such as NATO, but also wanted to build relations with unpredictable Russia and to help struggling new states such as Ukraine. One plank of Skubiszewski's foreign policy that Olszewski's government upheld centered on the Visegrad Triangle and its European integration strategy toward NATO.[76] In the wake of the disintegration stemming from the failed Soviet August coup d'état during late fall and early winter 1991, the Triangle formed regular consultative groups to expedite "full integration" into European political and economic structures and promote "equal security."[77] With the formal dissolution of the USSR on 25 December 1991, the Triangle leaders sought stronger assurances from Western institutions for their security. Their efforts met with some success as U.S. secretary of state James Baker and German foreign minister Genscher's jointly proposed in early October to implement a "Euro-Atlantic pact from Vladivostok to Vancouver."[78] Encouraged by the American–German statement, the Triangle leaders declared in their 6 October 1991 Krakow Declaration, as a follow-up to the Visegrad Summit, the need to extend relations with both the EC as associate members and with NATO beyond their "diplomatic liaison" status.[79] The NATO Rome Declaration on Peace and Cooperation, the basis for creating the North Atlantic Cooperation Council that NATO heads of state and government announced in November 1991, also signaled the alliance's commitment to significant outreach toward Central and East Europe.[80] Such steps by NATO met some of Poland's concerns, but failed to fulfill a key objective of the *MSZ* and Olszewski's advisors regarding a clearer path to NATO membership. Though Skubiszewski continued to pursue NATO linkages through the "Visegrad" regional cooperation, some of Olszewski's advisors and other ministers tried to pressure Walesa on NATO membership via other strategies.

During the early months of 1992, Polish foreign policy–makers debated Poland's geographical location between an economically tested Germany and an uncertain Russia. Walesa's maneuvers initiated a strange series of foreign policy changes in opposition to Skubiszewski and Olszewski. Despite the government's consistent policy toward building NATO ties and increasing the possibility of membership, Walesa tried to devise alternatives to NATO because he believed NATO hesitated to integrate Warsaw into the Western community of states. The president's Bureau of National Security portrayed a narrower option than even the president, however, particularly influenced by the Russian military. Walesa's advisors argued that Poland should not join NATO because NATO opposed Russia. These contrasting views within the Polish leadership set the stage for Walesa's fleeting and contradictory policy notions toward NATO and the East.[81]

In March 1992 one of the ways Walesa dealt with the uncertainty surrounding the instability arising from the collapse of Yugoslavia and the USSR concerned his initiative for the short-lived idea of a security alternative to NATO. Much to the chagrin of a surprised Olszewski government and presidential advisors Wachowski and Milewski, Walesa envisioned former Warsaw Pact countries forming a group to counter Western hesitation to integrate them into NATO and the EU. The concepts of NATO-II or "NATO-Bis" created much confusion and skepticism, both inside Poland and in the West, since Walesa described the concept as both an alternative to NATO membership and as a preparatory grouping of states from the Baltic Sea to the Black Sea until NATO offered membership. The problem with this concept stemmed from its exclusion of Russia and disagreement from some former Warsaw Pact and from former Soviet states regarding their desire to join NATO. During Walesa's first visit to Germany in March 1992, he raised the idea of NATO-Bis without prior coordination with his foreign or defense ministers,[82] confounding the Polish government, the Germans, and other countries. The notion resulted in quite negative press.[83] Until Olszewski's government fell in the summer of 1992, the prime minister remained at odds with the president, calling for quick NATO membership and raising the merits of NATO much more seriously than Walesa as an issue for national debate. Though Skubiszewski advocated closer Polish links to NATO, he demurred throughout the winter and spring of 1992 publicly to Olszewski's advisors, especially the defense minister, to speak more strongly in favor of Poland's membership in NATO. Olszewski's challenge over NATO membership arose from the larger battle for control of foreign policy and proved quite divisive leading into the summer of 1992.[84]

The tension between premier and president over NATO membership also involved Poland's Eastern policy, particularly Olszewski's contention that Walesa, and by extension Skubiszewski, sacrificed Polish sovereignty to cooperate with Russia on force withdrawals from Poland. Seen as "Finlandizing" Polish foreign policy, Olszewski's government argued that the Polish–Ukraine relationship needed equal weight with the Polish–Russian relationship.[85] Certainly, Poland's foreign policy continued to account for the significant role post-Soviet

Russia played in Polish security. Yet, Olszewski and Walesa remained divided over how much to yield to Moscow to obtain a new bilateral treaty. Simultaneously, Skubiszewski deferred to the president on concessions to Russian hard-liners and the *MSZ*'s Russian Section believed El'tsin more amenable than the Russian military to the Polish national interest and Poland's quest for a sovereign foreign policy.[86] Ultimately, both treaties Warsaw signed in May with Kiev and Moscow, respectively, not only proved Skubiszewski's foreign policy succeeded in overcoming some aspects of Poland's historical security predicament, but also entailed serious controversy until the actual Polish–Russian ceremony.[87]

After Walesa's summits with Ukrainian and Russian leaders, he battled with the Olszewski government, coming to a standoff that resulted in the third *Solidarnosc* government's fall. The chaotic domestic political spring of 1992 temporarily sidetracked Skubiszewski's foreign policy tactics, but failed to prevent the foreign minister's strategic aims of methodical Western integration and careful Eastern cooperation. Even though the Polish rightists criticized Skubiszewski for failing to uphold Poland's sovereignty in the face of Walesa's perceived acquiescence to Moscow hard-liners on Russian force withdrawals, the foreign minister insisted that domestic politics remain separate from foreign policy. Furthermore, under political attack as a Communist agent from leaked interior ministry documents, Skubiszewski did his utmost to distance himself from the accusations, whether true or false.[88] Such domestic upheaval exacerbated when Olszewski's government broke the final political straw by condemning Walesa publicly, not only resulted in the government's downfall but also proved very troubling for Walesa's leadership in 1992. Not until a new government formed under Hanna Suchocka, with Skubiszewski maintaining Walesa's confidence and remaining for his fourth and final term, did the president unquestionably shape foreign policy.[89]

Consolidation of Objectives toward West and East: Summer 1992–Fall 1993

When Walesa brokered the selection of Peasant Party leader Waldemar Pawlak as prime minister in the immediate aftermath of the Olszewski upheaval, he confidently demonstrated his presidential ability. When Pawlak failed to muster a stable coalition after several weeks, the president picked Suchocka to form the fourth post-Communist *Solidarnosc* government. The Suchocka administration consolidated Poland's Western integration policies and attempted to attain as many agreements and treaties with bordering post-Soviet states as possible. With the new prime minister beholden to the president, particularly given that she needed to hold a large, fractious multiparty coalition together, Walesa and Skubiszewski remained relatively free to direct foreign policy. Given that Prime Minister Suchocka's government worked more effectively with Walesa, consen-

sus emerged on foreign and defense policy. Walesa formally established Poland's first post-Communist national security strategy on 2 November 1992
when he approved the "Tenets of the Security Policy and Defense Strategy of the
Republic of Poland." Approval came during a meeting of the National Defense
Committee, chaired by the president and composed of the senior national security, military, and legislative officials in the government and parliament. This
process concluded nearly two years of efforts by intergovernmental task forces
and working groups to formulate the strategy's final policies.

In the document, the Polish leadership clearly articulated its strategic goal to
reintegrate into Europe by joining the Western European security system. To
achieve this strategic goal, Warsaw challenged the European institutions it believed most viable to guarantee Polish and Central European security—NATO
and the EU—to admit Poland. Warsaw promoted European security further east,
but not to the detriment of Eastern Europe. This strategy focused on solidifying
the new and historically important ties with NATO's allies, particularly Germany. Obviously, Poland desired to prevent the repetition of a security vacuum,
gray sphere, or buffer zone regionally in Central Europe, to overcome both security dilemmas Warsaw endured during the interwar and Yalta eras. Implicitly,
however, Polish foreign policy–makers understood the necessity to guarantee
their security in multilateral institutions that connect the United States with
Europe, provide a nuclear umbrella, and reduce instability for Warsaw and its
other regional and young democratic societies.[90] Hence, this national security
strategy provided the basis from which Suchocka's government promulgated its
policies during the year she held her government together. It provided
Skubiszewski with his presidential blueprint to oversee final developments of
foreign policy, unobstructed from domestic political turmoil.

During the Suchocka government's transition and early rule, Skubiszewski
articulated his overarching view regarding the requirements for stability and consistency in Polish foreign policy, attacking indirectly those politicians he felt
negatively affected Poland's Western integration strategy during 1992. While
many of Olszewski's top advisors argued during and especially after Olszewski's
premiership that the Olszewski government truly brought Poland closer to the
West and NATO rather than the overly cautious *MSZ*, Skubiszewski refused to
take any blame for his gradualist strategy. He stated that "our foreign policy has
become our only stabilizing factor, for it shows our partners, including those in
NATO, that not everything in Poland has succumbed to political turmoil."
Moreover, he criticized the "irresponsibility" of some Polish politicians who, he
felt, "brought us dangerously close to the limit that must not be crossed." For
Skubiszewski "the *raison d'état* and the interests of a law-governed state should
remain the highest priority." With these priorities, he asserted that "it is necessary to establish in Europe the kind of stabilizing infrastructure that would eliminate such dangers quickly and efficiently. This is what places Europe under an
obligation to form a uniform system of European security." Therefore, he foresaw that NATO served now primarily to "realize that the security of the coun-

tries of Central and Eastern Europe is inseparably linked to the security of the sixteen NATO countries themselves. Poland's foreign policy has been a major factor in making NATO realize this connection." Such a Polish policy went back to 1990, when Skubiszewski and his *MSZ* team began preparing the foundation for closer NATO ties and future membership.[91]

Given this clear statement as the *MSZ*'s baseline, Skubiszewski proceeded, under Walesa's authority, to work with the Suchocka government to make deliberate and progressive foreign policy toward West and East. It also remains important to realize that Suchocka believed from the outset that only Skubiszewski could act to find common ground between the president and the new premier. Only the cooperative Skubiszewski, Suchocka argued, when he believed consensus achievable on Western and Eastern policy issues, provided the bridge for the government and the state.[92]

Almost immediately, Skubiszewski and Suchocka traveled to Vienna to discuss important security issues. In meetings with Central and Southeastern European NATO and non-NATO leaders, including leaders from the Visegrad Triangle, Suchocka and Skubiszewski discussed the ongoing concerns over the war in former Yugoslavia and the merits of a free trade zone. Such a zone began within the Visegrad member states and extended to Austria, Italy, Slovenia, Croatia, and Bosnia-Herzegovina. The Skubiszewski and Suchocka intent concentrated on making Poland and Central Europe as politically and economically attractive as possible to the West, especially since Poland just started to demonstrate signs of some economic success in its 1989–1990 economic reform programs.[93] This meeting also marked the first formal occasion when it became apparent that the growing strains within the CSFR might conceivably lead to its dissolution. In the coming weeks and months, Skubiszewski strongly advised the CSFR government led by Vaclav Klaus not to dissolve the CSFR union, but, if the dissolution became inevitable, at least to preserve the Visegrad process, however possible.[94]

Throughout the fall and into the early winter of 1993, Skubiszewski and Suchocka pursued a Western integrationist line and expanded links to the post-Soviet states bordering Poland. The prime minister's first major foreign policy address delivered at the Lublin Catholic University reflected Skubiszewski's thinking by underlining the importance of Poland's objectives for NATO and EU membership, Polish–German, and Polish–Russian relations.[95] Specifically, she stated that "each country participating in the process of integration stabilizes its international position and consolidates its real sovereignty and [Germany] is today our liaison in contacts with the EC and NATO, at the same time the German road to the east leads through Poland." She foresaw, however, that Russia remained a "great country" and Warsaw expected Moscow to "co-shape with Germany the situation in our region."[96] As a result, over her first months in office, Skubiszewski prepared Suchocka to meet with German, Russian, Belarusian, Lithuanian, and Ukrainian counterparts. On the whole, these visits proved successful, both in Warsaw and in the respective countries, setting the stage for bilateral relations to expand and for Poland to negotiate final terms in additional bilateral agreements—including final withdrawals of all Russian forces from Polish territory by November 1993.

One of Skubiszewski's priorities for 1993 centered on building a much stronger relationship with Ukraine in order to overcome some of the difficult Polish–Ukrainian history and to reduce regional tensions, particularly since the Russian–Ukrainian relationship had deteriorated during the Suchocka period. During the late fall and into the early winter, Skubiszewski made several important statements on Poland's Eastern policy, especially the importance of Ukraine, and asserted that "our policy of building up security in Europe in all external directions coincides with the policy which Ukraine pursues."[97] At the same time, Skubiszewski maintained his pragmatic approach for Poland by developing relations equally with both Ukraine and Russia to avoid misperceptions by either Kiev or Moscow leaders that Poland wanted to play its neighbors against one another.[98] In late December 1992, Skubiszewski traveled to Kiev and met with the Ukrainian president, prime minister, and foreign minister in order to confer on the next steps in Polish–Ukrainian relations and to arrange Suchocka's final plans before her first visit to Ukraine as prime minister. After his meetings, he described Polish–Ukrainian cooperation as strategically "decisive as far as European security is concerned."[99]

As Suchocka and Skubiszewski expanded relations both east and west to the extent possible in the winter and spring, both focused more intently on advancing links to NATO, especially after Suchocka's initial, short trip to Brussels in October 1992.[100] Importantly, during that October, Walesa admitted for the first time publicly that Skubiszewski disagreed with the president's early 1992 surprise idea for a NATO-Bis, stating that, with Suchocka's new government, a "high convergence" existed on foreign policy between the president and prime minister.[101] By late January, for example, during Suchocka's trip to the annual World Economic Forum in Davos, Switzerland, she met with several NATO member counterparts, held talks with the Russian and Ukrainian premiers, and gained more public commitments for Polish membership in NATO from NATO secretary general Manfred Woerner. Both she and Woerner told the press that the secretary general envisioned Poland as the first state from the Visegrad Triangle to join NATO. For NATO, Woerner saw Poland as the first initiator of democratic reforms in Central and Eastern Europe and, one that continued to uphold its prominent stabilizing role regionally.[102] By February, the Polish government announced that the Polish navy would participate in NATO's June maneuver exercise designated "Baltops 1993." This marked the first time a former Warsaw Pact state would be allowed to maneuver with NATO states and was an indicator that NATO had already begun its earnest attempt to cooperate more closely with states such as Poland.[103]

At the same time, Walesa's national security advisor Milewski finally admitted publicly that the NATO-Bis idea was "suspended in a conceptual void." His rationale relied on the fact that "if the NATO-2 concept is to be realized, Western states must first acknowledge it as interesting enough and significant enough from their own viewpoint. There is no such interest on the part of the West so far, and this is why the concept remains in the sphere of ideas and has not been transformed into a concrete proposal."[104] In the spring, Skubiszewski returned to NATO headquarters and told reporters that Poland's links to NATO were "very good" and claimed that his "step-by-step" NATO membership strategy remained the best approach.

During that trip Skubiszewski defined Poland's place within the larger context for European security. In commenting on the fighting in former Yugoslavia, he stated that "in this kind of war there is the opportunity for NATO to act together with other partners, also with our participation."[105] For his part, NATO Secretary General Woerner declared "the minister [Skubiszewski] and I have become friends. We discussed relationships between Poland and NATO." The secretary general concluded that "I think he and I both agree as to the path that has been chosen. . . . It seems obvious that if NATO does decide to accept new members, Poland will be one of the first candidates."[106] Overall, though NATO seemed not yet ready to enlarge, relations with Poland progressed seriously, as Skubiszewski's NATO integration strategy, albeit painstaking, won support from an increasing number of senior leaders from NATO nations to support Poland's efforts.[107]

During the spring and summer of 1993, Russia and Ukraine became especially worrisome as Russia increasingly pressured Ukraine politically, economically, and militarily, and as hard-line Russians became more influential. These developments placed President Walesa and Skubiszewski in a bind. They needed to guide their state carefully between Moscow and Kiev, while maintaining good relations with Western Europe in order to integrate Warsaw into Western security and economic structures rapidly. Furthermore, Polish–Ukrainian ties became problematic after Kiev proposed another type of security structure, not only to decrease anxiety, but also to pressure Moscow. At an April 1993 CSCE meeting in Prague, Ukraine announced its notion for a collective security zone. By Ukrainian minister of foreign affairs Anatolii Zlenko's definition, this "zone of stability" or "tool of preventive diplomacy" encompassed a sphere from the Baltic to the Black Sea without Russia.[108] Although Warsaw advocated Ukrainian independence before any other country and recognized better than many states Ukraine's sense of insecurity regarding Russia, Walesa ironically found Zlenko's alternative security option impractical, even given the Polish president's earlier security thinking.[109] Paradoxically, Walesa deemed this Ukrainian attempt as self-isolating, even though he also realized it countered Russian efforts to consolidate the Commonwealth of Independent States, which many Ukrainians viewed as Russian moves to resurrect its former USSR empire. Polish leaders found especially disturbing the public statements by Ukrainian politicians that linked the nuclear weapons on Ukrainian territory to security guarantees in such a "zone of stability."[110] Moreover, even though Skubiszewski and the Polish leadership found NATO's hesitancy to integrate Poland and other Central European states frustrating, they understood that if Poland supported the Ukrainian security proposal such backing spelled a likely rejection for Poland's Western efforts and only raised Russian concerns of an anti-Russian security zone. Without any firm Western commitment to ensure security, Polish leaders desired to placate both the Ukrainian and the Russian governments. Instead of supporting the Ukrainian security plan Warsaw advised Kiev's leadership during the latter part of 1993 to work as a stable bilateral partner, both with Warsaw and Moscow.[111]

Although Poland rejected Ukrainian initiatives to strike a regional security arrangement against Russia, the Poles still faced the geopolitical reality of a splintered or even divided Ukraine, that is, eastern Ukraine leaning toward Moscow and western Ukraine centered more on Western ties. Russia's attempt to reassert its defined "sphere of influence" throughout the former USSR and "protect" the Russian minorities in the "near abroad" compelled Warsaw to play several policies simultaneously. The May 1992 Polish–Russian Treaty on Friendship and Cooperation, similar to the treaty signed with Germany in 1991, acknowledged that independent Poland and democratic Russia held many common interests and in it both agreed to overcome their past. Tensions lessened to the point that both presidents met again in late August 1993, when El'tsin signaled his willingness to allow Poland to join NATO at some future date.[112] Both sides, however, quickly interpreted this major statement differently, with the Poles believing Polish integration into NATO met with Russia's approval and the Russians thinking such a move too hasty. Hence, the Poles again found themselves frustrated in attempting to work constructively with an Eastern partner and integrate into Western security structures.

After the failed October 1993 Russian coup d'état, a series of events occurred which only spelled the continuation of tense relations between Poland and Russia. First, the infamous "El'tsin Letter," sent to German, French, British, and American leaders, pronounced that Russia refused to accept Central European NATO membership as it would isolate Russia and damage Russian national interests.[113] Second, with the December 1993 Russian parliamentary elections, the nationalist forces under Liberal Democratic Party leader Vladimir Zhirinovskii increased regional tensions for states such as Poland as Russian opposition to Polish membership in NATO grew.[114] By the end of 1993, not only did Polish–Russian relations appear headed for continued difficulties, but the string of four Polish post-Communist *Solidarnosc* governments also ended, when Suchocka's government fell and Polish "reformed Communists" won a majority in parliament and government. The passing of the *Solidarnosc* governments also saw the close of the Skubiszewski era, but his legacy certainly lived on in subsequent Polish foreign policy strategy and regional security cooperation.

Providing the Regional Middle Power Legacy

The rebirth of Polish independence in 1989 enabled Poland's first post-Communist foreign minister in Central and Eastern Europe's first post-Communist government to formulate and implement a remarkably pragmatic and steady foreign policy. This policy proved particularly adept with the regional turmoil of the Cold War's collapse. During four years as foreign minister, Skubiszewski withstood four changes of government, never veered far from his original objectives of making Poland's foreign policy fully sovereign, and created new cooperative relationships with all of Poland's neighboring states. Given the drama of East and West Germany's integration and the USSR's disintegration, Skubiszewski methodically and nonthreateningly guided the Polish middle power to deal with its security dilemma between larger, historically hegemonic Germany and Russia. Skubiszewski's *MSZ* faced a state to its west that became larger within the first year of Poland's post-Communist independence and a state to its east which disintegrated into four new entities on Poland's border toward the end of Warsaw's third post-Communist year. By late 1990, Poland devised a foreign policy concentrated both on promotion of stability-enhancing measures with the bordering, independent Eastern states and on integration into Western Europe's security structures. By late 1992 this foreign policy blueprint enshrined Poland's first post-Communist national security strategy. By expanding the Communist-era inroads toward the FRG and applying in practice some of the theoretical tenets of the émigré and underground writings toward Russia, Skubiszewski enacted predominantly bridging regional policies. Cooperation with all neighboring states rather than playing them off of each other or shunning vital linkages underlined what Poland believed necessary to reintegrate into Europe.

Warsaw feared the type of early post–Cold War animosities that erupted into regional wars in the Balkans and former USSR because they seemed similar to the regional hostilities that led to World War II. The war that destroyed the former Yugoslavia and threatened most of the Balkans, and the instability caused by the dissolution of the USSR, contributed to the desire of Poland to prevent its larger neighbors from viewing it as a buffer state lying in a no-man's-land or security vacuum. Under Skubiszewski's moderate and consistent foreign policy leadership, democratic Poland projected a policy that contributed to post–Cold War European security and stability. Undoubtedly, Poland was determined to avoid the historic pitfalls that so frequently ended in war and the subsequent destruction in Poland. Since the former underground movements attained power democratically in Central Europe, with Poland leading these emerging democracies, the elected Warsaw leadership recognized that Poland remained pivotal to Central European stability.[115] Such a situation impelled these foreign policy-makers, some of them underground dissidents who became policymakers almost overnight, to cooperate closely among themselves and with other European states to preclude a recurrence of Poland's entrapment and isolation between stronger, potentially hostile Germany and Russia.

This chapter analyzed Skubiszewski's rationale for challenging Poland's "buffer state" status to prevent repeating the loss of its statehood, to avoid a fifth partition in three hundred years. Through his consistent advocacy of foreign policy based on international law, Skubiszewski designed a foreign strategy founded upon state-to-state agreements. He consistently prevailed in the Polish policy battles with a moderate and methodical set of policies toward West and East that avoided pitting neighboring states against Poland or against each other. Such interstate relationships resulted in closing the post–World War II rift with unifying Germany, engaging the USSR before it disintegrated, establishing direct links to the post-Soviet successor states, and developing a regional cooperative framework with Budapest and Prague. As the creation of the Visegrad Triangle, the demise of the Warsaw Pact, new relations with Moscow, and outreach to NATO and the EU demonstrate, Poland bridged with its neighbors and the transforming European security institutions. Thus, this chapter's broad assessment of post-Communist Polish foreign policy provides the baseline for examining in the following three case studies how Skubiszewski's strategy specifically established new relationships with Germany, the USSR and post-Soviet successor states, and the Visegrad Triangle, the latter in connection with Poland's strategy toward Moscow and NATO. By demonstrating that Poland devised and implemented a policy based on bridging rather than balancing or bandwagoning, the three case studies in the chapters that follow prove that Skubiszewski's geopolitical alignment created an entirely new set of productive relations with the larger and stronger German and Russian states.

Notes

1. Barbara Grad, Warsaw Television Service, 1730 GMT, 22 September 1989, *FBIS-EEU*, 25 September 1989, 36.

2. Skubiszewski, *Zachodnia Granica Polska*, 561–567. Two of Skubiszewski's nongovernmental advisors from his earliest days, Artur Hajnicz and Wojciech Lamentowicz, some of the foremost Polish scholars on Germany and the USSR during both the *Solidarnosc* era and in the post-Communist period, played important roles in helping to draft the foreign minister's speeches. In discussions with me in Warsaw on 9 June 1991 and 10 June 1994, Hajnicz said that he often based his analyses on the debates in and recommendations from *Kultura*, particularly those written by Mieroszewski. Furthermore, he explained that he gleaned many insights from his scholarly underground colleagues, many of whom became the first members of the Polish senate's newly created Center of International Studies in September 1989, namely, Tadeusz Chabiera, Jacek Czaputowicz, Kazimierz Dziewanowski, Antoni Kaminski, Grzegorz Kostrzewa-Zorbas, Eligiusz Lasota, Jerzy Marek Nowakowski, Zygmunt Skorzynski, and Henryk Szlajfer. See also Artur Hajnicz and Zygmunt Skorzynski shortly after the June 1989 Polish elections in Henryk Wozniakowski, "Central Europe: Illusion or Opportunity? (Krakow-

Tyniec, 22–25 June 1989)," *Tygodnik Powszechny* (Krakow), no. 30, 23 July 1989, (Joint Publications Research Service, hereafter, *JPRS-EER*), 29 August 1989, 1–3.

3. "Przemowienie ministra spraw zagranicznych prof. Krzysztofa Skubiszewskiego na XLIV sesji Zgromadzeaie Ogolnego NZ" [Statement by the Polish Minister of Foreign Affairs, Professor Krzysztof Skubiszewski at the 44th Session of the UN General Assembly] (New York, 25 September 1989), *Zbior Dokumentow,* no. 3 (1990): 142.

4. "Przemowienie ministra spraw zagranicznych prof. Krzysztofa Skubiszewskiego na XLIV sesji Zgromadzenie Ogolnego NZ," 136, 143.

5. "[Skubiszewski] Interviewed on Meetings," PAP, 2334 GMT, 1 October 1989, *FBIS-EEU*, 2 October 1989, 48–49.

6. "Foreign Affairs Minister's UN Talks Continue: Meets Shevardnadze in New York," Warsaw Domestic Service, 0800 GMT, 1 October 1989, *FBIS-EEU*, 2 October 1989, 48; "[Skubiszewski] Holds Meetings With Counterparts," PAP, 0003 GMT, 2 October 1989, *FBIS-EEU*, 2 October 1989, 49.

7. Roman Prister, "Exclusive Interview with Polish Foreign Minister Professor Krzysztof Skubiszewski: Without a Trace of Dependence," *Ha'aretz* (Tel Aviv), 19 October 1989, *FBIS-EEU*, 26 October 1989, 57. See also Szayna, *Polish Foreign Policy,* 23.

8. "Meeting With Leaders Held," Warsaw Television Service, 1830 GMT, 24 October 1989, *FBIS-EEU*, 25 October 1989, 62; "PAP Gives Roundup of Meetings," PAP, 2240 GMT, 24 October 1989, *FBIS-EEU*, 25 October 1989, 62–63; "[Skubiszewski] Interviewed by Warsaw TV," Warsaw Television Service, 1900 GMT, 25 October 1989, *FBIS-EEU*, 26 October 1989, 53–55.

9. "Wspolny komunikat o wizycie czlonka Biura Politycznego KC KPZR, ministra spraw zagranicznych ZSRR, Eduarda Szewardnadze w Polsce" [Joint Communiqué on the Visit of a Member of the Political Bureau of the CPSU CC, Minister for Foreign Affairs of the USSR, Eduard Shevardnadze in Poland] (25 October 1989), *Zbior Dokumentow,* no. 4 (1990): 36.

10. Hajnicz provided in interview with me in Warsaw on 10 June 1994. See also Szayna, *Polish Foreign Policy,* 18–19, and Artur Hajnicz, "Poland Within Its Geopolitical Triangle," *Aussenpolitik,* no. 1 (1989): 30–40.

11. "PAP First Day Roundup," 10 November 1989, *FBIS-EEU*, 13 November 1989, 68.

12. "Mazowiecki Dinner Speech," PAP, 9 November 1989, *FBIS-EEU*, 13 November 1989, 67.

13. "Dinner Speech by Federal Republic of Germany Chancellor Helmut Kohl, Honoring Recently and Democratically Elected, Polish Prime Minister, Tadeusz Mazowiecki," *Rzeczpospolita,* 10–12 November 1989, 2, *FBIS-EEU*, 14 November 1989, 51–54.

14. "Mazowiecki Travels to USSR for Talks," PAP, 0125 GMT, 24 November 1989, *FBIS-EEU*, 27 November 1989, 73; "Mazowiecki Assesses Talks," Warsaw Domestic Service, 2216 GMT, 24 November 1989, *FBIS-EEU*, 27 November 1989, 75; "Mazowiecki News Conference," Warsaw Domestic Service, 1414 GMT, 25 November 1989, *FBIS-EEU*, 27 November 1989, 77.

15. "Komunikat Polsko-Radziecki o wizycie Premiera PRL, Tadeusza Mazowieckiego w ZSRR" [Polish-Soviet Communiqué on the Visit of the Polish Prime Minister Tadeusz Mazowiecki in the USSR] (Moscow, 27 November 1989), *Zbior Dokumentow,* no. 4 (1990): 43.

16. "Komunikat prasowy o spotkaniu przywodcow panstw-stron Ukladu War-szawskiego" (Press Communiqué Following the Moscow Meeting of Leaders of the States-Parties to the Warsaw Pact), Moscow, 4 December 1989, *Zbior Dokumentow*, no. 4 (1990): 254–256.

17. Leon Bojko, "Interview with Premier Tadeusz Mazowiecki: It is Possible to Change Geopolitics," *Gazeta Wyborcza* (Warsaw), 29 November 1989, *FBIS-EEU*, 5 December 1989, 61; "Skubiszewski, Mazowiecki Remarks," PAP, 2233 GMT, 4 December 1989, *FBIS-EEU*, 5 December 1989, 61; "Poland's Mazowiecki," PAP, 2139 GMT, 4 December 1989, *FBIS-EEU*, 7 December 1989, 6.

18. "Oswiadczenie Ministra Spraw Zagranicznych PRL Krzysztofa Skubiszewskiego" [Statement by the Polish Minister of Foreign Affairs Krzysztof Skubiszewski] (Warsaw, 7 December 1989), *Zbior Dokumentow*, no. 4 (1990): 7–10.

19. Andrea Tarquini, "Interview with Mieczyslaw Rakowski, Polish United Workers Party First Secretary," *La Repubblica* (Rome), 15 December 1989, *FBIS-EEU*, 20 December 1989, 58.

20. I conducted this interview with Gebert in Warsaw on 6 June 1994.

21. See chapter 1.

22. Katarzyna Kolodziejczyk, "Three Directions: Skubiszewski Outlines Foreign Policy Goals," *Rzeczpospolita*, 10–11 February 1990, *FBIS-EEU*, 13 February 1990, 50; and "Sejmowe exposé Ministra Spraw Zagranicznych RP Krzysztofa Skubiszewskiego" [Sejm Exposé by Minister of Foreign Affairs of the Republic of Poland, Krzysztof Skubiszewski] (Warsaw, 26 April 1990), *Zbior Dokumentow*, no. 2 (1991): 11–18.

23. "A Long Way Off: Deputies' and Senators' Statements to PAP," *Sztandar Mlodych*, 4 January 1990, *FBIS-EEU*, 10 January 1990, 67.

24. It remains important to understand that few analysts had identified the implications for how the dramatic changes in Europe quickly affected European security. Phillip Petersen, the assistant for Europe and the USSR in the Office of the Under Secretary of Defense for Policy, remained one of the few Western analysts who grasped the significance of the dynamics before and immediately after the collapse of the Berlin Wall, the dissonance of Soviet European security policy, and the reactive American policy toward Europe, especially Central and Eastern Europe. I worked as Petersen's deputy. That analysis caused a major debate in Poland primarily because Petersen underscored that the Soviets portrayed Poland as being neutral and outside the emerging European security system, even as the Soviets knew they couldn't prevent Germany's unification and its inevitable integration into NATO. See Phillip A. Petersen, "The Challenge to Soviet Strategic Deployment: An Emerging Vision of European Security," in *Jane's NATO Handbook, 1990–1991*, ed. Bruce George (Coulsdon, U.K.: Jane's Information Group, 1990): 323–334; Ryszard Bobrowski, "Europa bez Polski" [Europe Without Poland], *Tygodnik Solidarnosc*, no. 16, vol. 83 (20 April 1990): 6; and Ryszard Bobrowski, "Polska Poza Europa?" *Polska w Europie: ZSSR 1990* (Warsaw), May 1990, 35–39; Michael R. Gordon, "Aide Differs with Cheney on the Soviet Threat," *New York Times*, 13 March 1990, A15; and Peter Almond, "Soviet Empire Will Fall, Pentagon Expert Predicts," *Washington Times*, 12 March 1990, A6.

25. Grzegorz Kostrzewa-Zorbas confirmed the impact of the Petersen analysis in discussions in the Pentagon with Petersen and me in March 1990.

26. Krystyna Koziol, "Skubiszewski News Conference on Soviet Ties, Reunification," Warsaw Domestic Service, 1736 GMT, 9 February 1990, *FBIS-EEU*, 12 February 1990, 48.

27. Eugeniusz Guz, "Communiqué Issued on Talks," PAP, 2305 GMT, 6 February 1990, *FBIS-EEU*, 7 February 1990, 53–54.

28. In the "2 Plus 4" negotiations, the United States, Great Britain, France, the USSR, the FRG, the GDR, and Poland participated. "Skubiszewski Addresses 'Open Skies' Forum," PAP, 2044 GMT, 12 February 1990, *FBIS-EEU*, 14 February 1990, 50.

29. Kostrzewa-Zorbas devised his "two-track" Eastern policy, before he was recruited to the *MSZ*. He shared his views with Skubiszewski, Mazowiecki, and Aleksander Hall the prime minister's advisor, as well as *Solidarnosc* leader Walesa and his advisor, Jaroslaw Kaczynski, in a 22 March 1990 private memorandum entitled, "Tezy do Polskiej Polityki Wschodniej u Progu Lat Dziewiedziesiaytch" [Theses on Polish Policies Toward the East on the Threshold of the 1990s].

30. Krzysztof Skubiszewski, "Polska wobec wschod—wystapienie ministra spraw zagranicznych RP Krzysztofa Skubiszewskiego w Senacie" [Poland and the East—Statement by the Polish Foreign Minister Krzysztof Skubiszewski in the Senate, Warsaw, 7 September 1990], *Zbior Dokumentow*, no. 3 (1990): 20.

31. Only after the failed August 1991 Soviet coup d'état, in some cases, several years later, did American and European governments divide their agencies or departments responsible for formulating and implementing policy toward the USSR into any kind of country desk configurations defined by the individual Soviet republics.

32. Grzegorz Kostrzewa-Zorbas, "Imperium kontratakuje" [The Empire Strikes Back] in *Lewy Czerwcowy* [Blow from the Left], eds. Jacek Kurski and Piotr Semka (Warsaw: Editions Spotkania, 1992), 150–151.

33. Michal Ksiezarczyk, "Otwartosc wobec wschodu" [Openness Toward the East—interview with Grzegorz Kostrzewa-Zorbas], *Zycie Warszawy*, 18–19 August 1990, 1.

34. The April 1990 Bratislava Summit brought together regional leaders not seen in the capital of Slovakia since the Napoleonic 1806 Bratislava Pressburg Peace Treaty meeting. The states included Poland, the CSFR, Hungary, Italy, Yugoslavia, and Austria. See "Slovak Prime Minister Milan Cic's toast at the Bratislava Castle, Prague Domestic Service, 9 April 1990, *FBIS-EEU*, 10 April 1990, 4; and "Bratislava Summit News Conference," Prague Domestic Service, 9 April 1990, *FBIS-EEU*, 12 April 1990, 8–11.

35. "Sejmowe expose Ministra Spraw Zagranicznych RP Krzysztofa Skubiszewskiego" [Sejm Exposé by Minister of Foreign Affairs of the Republic of Poland, Krzysztof Skubiszewski] (Warsaw, 26 April 1990), *Zbior Dokumentow*, no. 2 (1991): 24.

36. Adam Michnik, PAP, 9 April 1990, *FBIS-EEU*, 12 April 1990, 48.

37. "Sejmowe expose Ministra Spraw Zagranicznych RP Krzysztofa Skubiszewskiego" [Sejm Expose by Minister of Foreign Affairs of the Republic of Poland, Krzysztof Skubiszewski], *Zbior Dokumentow*, no. 2 (1991): 23.

38. "Walesa Demands Soviet Troop Withdrawal," PAP, 2135 GMT, 18 January 1990, *FBIS-EEU*, 19 January 1990, 60. Even before officially declaring himself a presidential candidate that spring, Walesa actually raised the questions on the status of Soviet troops on Polish territory as one of the few foreign policy issues he subsequently employed in the fall presidential campaign. Walesa attacked Mazowiecki for his hesitant position on starting Soviet force withdrawal talks with Moscow. Even if Walesa's attacks only played into Moscow's tactics for stalling troop withdrawal talks, the tension between Walesa and Mazowiecki extant since Mazowiecki had assumed the premiership, was only exacerbated as both started competing for the presidency and sowed the seeds for a vindictive campaign that tore apart the *Solidarnosc* movement by late 1990.

39. Grzegorz Kostrzewa-Zorbas, "The Russian Troop Withdrawal from Poland," in *The Diplomatic Record, 1992–1993*, ed. Allan E. Goodman (Boulder, Colo.: Westview, 1995), 118. See also Vinton, "Domestic Politics and Foreign Policy," 37–43.

40. "Skubiszewski Praises Visit," DPA (Hamburg), 5 May 1990, *FBIS-EEU*, 7 May 1990, 45.

41. "Przemowienie ministra spraw zagranicznych RP Krzysztofa Skubiszewskiego na spotkaniu ministerialnym konferencji '2 Plus 4'" [Statement by the Polish Foreign Minister Krzysztof Skubiszewski at the Ministerial Meeting of the '2 Plus 4' Conference] (Paris, 17 July 1990), *Zbior Dokumentow*, no. 3 (1991): 46–64.

42. *Traktat o ostatecznej regulacji w odniesieniu do Niemiec* [Treaty on the Final Settlement with Respect to Germany], (Moscow, 12 September 1990), *Zbior Dokumentow*, no. 3 (1991): 69.

43. Jerzy Malczyk, "Mazowiecki Meets Jaruzelski, Havel," PAP, 1325 GMT, 7 June 1990, *FBIS-EEU*, 8 June 1990, 7.

44. Kostrzewa-Zorbas, who, at the time, had just been appointed deputy director of the Polish *MSZ*'s Department of Europe, provided this inside view. He was sent to Moscow by Foreign Minister Skubiszewski shortly after his appointment to help negotiate Poland's position on the possibility of dissolving the Warsaw Pact's military structures. I interviewed Kostrzewa-Zorbas in Washington, D.C., on 25 March 1993.

45. "CSFR Brings 'Draft' Declaration," CTK, 1201 GMT, 7 June 1990, *FBIS-EEU*, 8 June 1990, 7.

46. "[Hungarian Minister of Foreign Affairs Geza Jeszenszky] to Discuss Withdrawal in Moscow," Budapest Domestic Service, May 28, 1990, *FBIS-EEU*, May 31, 1990, 32.

47. "Deklaracja panstw-stron ukladu Warszawskiego przyjeta na naradzie doradczego komitetu politycznego" [Declaration of the States-Parties to the Warsaw Treaty Adopted at the Session of the Political Consultative Committee] (Moscow, 7 June 1990), *Zbior Dokumentow*, no. 2 (1991): 136–139.

48. "Hungary Not to Participate in Pact Exercises," MTI, June 8, 1990, *FBIS-EEU*, June 8, 1990, 53.

49. Krzysztof Skubiszewski, "Polska wobec wschodu—wystapienie ministra spraw zagranicznych RP Krzysztofa Skubiszewskiego w Senacie" [Poland and the East—Statement by the Polish Foreign Minister Krzysztof Skubiszewski in the Senate, Warsaw, 7 September 1990], *Zbior Dokumentow*, no. 3 (1990): 15–17; "Uchwala Senatu Rzeczypospolitej Polskiej w sprawie polityki wschodniej Rzeczypospolitej Polskiej" Resolution of the Senate of the Polish Republic on the Eastern Policy of the Polish Republic] (7 September 1990), *Polska w Europie* (January 1991): 55–56. See also Prizel, "Warsaw's Ostpolitik," 100–101.

50. Kostrzewa-Zorbas, "Imperium kontratakuje," 156–157; Michta, *East-Central Europe after the Warsaw Pact*, 73–76.

51. "Traktat miedzy Rzeczapospolita Polska a Republika Federalna Niemiec o potwierdzeniu istniejacej miedzy nimi granicy" [Treaty Between the Polish Republic and the Federal Republic of Germany on the Confirmation of the Border Between Both States] (14 November 1990), in Jan Barcz and Mieczyslaw Tomal, *Polska-Niemcy: Dobre sasiedztwo i przyjazna wspolpraca* (Warsaw: Polski Instytut Spraw Miedzynarodowych, 1992), 19–24.

52. "Polska a bezpieczenstwo europejskie—przemowienie Ministra Spraw Zagranicznych RP Krzysztofa Skubiszewskiego, do Zgromadzenia Polnocnoatlantyckiego"

[Poland and European Security—Address by the Polish Foreign Minister Krzysztof Skubiszewski to the North Atlantic Assembly] (London, 29 November 1990), *Zbior Dokumentow*, no. 4 (1991): 10–12.

53. "Oswiadczenie Ministra Spraw Zagranicznych RP Krzysztofa Skubiszewskiego w Zwiazku z rezygnacja Eduarda Szewardnadze ze stanowiska Ministra Spraw Zagranicznych ZSRR,' [Statement by the Polish Foreign Minister Krzysztof Skubiszewski in Connection with the Resignation of Eduard Shevardnadze from His Post of the Minister for Foreign Affairs of the USSR] 20 December 1990, *Zbior Dokumentow*, no. 4 (1991): 18–19. See also Zubek, "Walesa's Leadership," 77.

54. "Foreign Ministry Makes Statement," PAP, 1242 GMT, 11 January 1991, *FBIS-EEU*, 14 January 1991, 34.

55. Vinton, "Domestic Politics and Foreign Policy," 36–44; Prizel, "Warsaw's Ostpolitik," 98–104; Kostrzewa-Zorbas, "Imperium kontratakuje," 155–164; and Michta, *East-Central Europe after the Warsaw Pact*, 87–90.

56. Zubek, "Walesa's Leadership," 83; and Kostrzewa-Zorbas, "Imperium kontratakuje," 167–169.

57. Kostrzewa-Zorbas, "Imperium kontratakuje," 164–165; Kurski, *Lech Walesa*, 105–111; Zubek, "Walesa's Leadership," 77; Kostrzewa-Zorbas, "The Russian Troop Withdrawal from Poland," 119–120; Lech Walesa, *The Struggle and the Triumph: An Autobiography* (New York: Arcade, 1991), 254–255; Vinton, "Domestic Politics and Foreign Policy," 34–36; and Prizel, "Warsaw's Ostpolitik," 101–102.

58. Kostrzewa-Zorbas, "Imperium kontratakuje," 164–180; Najder, *Jaka Polska*, 172–277; Michal Bichniewicz and Piotr Rudnicki, *Czas na Zmiany: Z Jaroslawem Kaczynskim rozmawiaja* [Time for Change: Conversations with Jaroslaw Kaczynski] (Warsaw: Editions Spotkania, 1994), 57–104; Kurski, *Lech Walesa*, 105–120; and Teresa Toranska, *My* [Us] (Warsaw: Oficyna Wydawnicza MOST, 1994), especially the interviews from the chapters on Jaroslaw Kaczynski, Jan Krzysztof Bielecki, and Jacek Merkel.

59. For important assessments of Polish military doctrine and role in Central Europe, see Stanislaw Koziej, "Military Doctrine: A Non-Confrontational Model of Military Doctrine in the Future European Security System," *Journal of Slavic Military Studies*, no. 4 (December 1993): 515–540; Andrzej Karkoszka and Pawel Wieczorek, "The New Challenges Facing Poland's Armed Forces," in *Report on the State of National Security: External Aspects*, ed. Henryk Szlajfer and Janusz Prystrom (Warsaw: Polish Institute of International Affairs, 1993): 93–130; and Andrew A. Michta, "Safeguarding the Third Republic: Security Policy and Military Reform," in *Polish Foreign Policy Reconsidered: Challenges of Independence*, eds. Ilya Prizel and Andrew A. Michta (London: Macmillan, 1995), 73–94.

60. Kurski, *Lech Walesa*, 14–17, 120; Kostrzewa-Zorbas, "Imperium Kontratakuje," 178–179.

61. See "Deklaracja o wspolpracy Rzeczypospolitej Polskiej Czeskiej i Slowackiej Republiki Federacyjne i Republiki Wegierskiej w dazeniu do integracji Europejskiej" [Declaration of the Republic of Poland, the Czech and Slovak Federal Republic and the Republic of Hungary on Cooperation in Pursuit of European Integration] (Visegrad, 15 February 1991), *Zbior Dokumentow*, no. 1 (1992): 236–237. Nearly seven centuries earlier, the Polish, Bohemian, and Hungarian kings met at Visegrad and similarly agreed to cooperate to reduce tension throughout this region and overcome historical animosities. Though this Visegrad Summit (1335) failed to ensure long-term peace in the region, it

embodied an effort by Central European leaders to set aside their age-old rivalries, solidify cultural bonds among their peoples, and negotiate agreements to strengthen their governments and countries. For good overviews of the 1991 Visegrad Summit and the Visegrad Triangle, see, inter alia, Jan B. de Weydenthal, "The Visegrad Summit," *Report on Eastern Europe* (1 March 1991): 28; Rudolf L. Tokes, "From Visegrad to Krakow: Cooperation, Competition, and Coexistence in Central Europe," *Problems of Communism*, no. 40, vol. 6 (November–December 1991): 100–114; Joshua B. Spero, "Central European Security," *Problems of Communism*, vol. 40, no. 6 (November–December 1991): 141–151; Andrew A. Michta, *East Central Europe after the Warsaw Pact*; Grzegorz Kostrzewa-Zorbas, "Security for the East Europeans," *Problems of Communism*, vol. xli, nos. 1–2 (January 1992): 148–149; Andrew A. Michta, "Poland, Czechoslovakia, and Hungary: The Triangle in Search of Europe," in *Post-Communist Eastern Europe: Crisis and Reform*, ed. Andrew A. Michta and Ilya Prizel (New York: St. Martin's, 1992), 53–83; Jan Zielonka, "Security in Central Europe: Sources of Instability in Hungary, Poland and the Czech and Slovak Republics with Recommendations for Western Policy," *Adelphi Paper* 272 (autumn 1992), 41–53; David Shumaker, "The Origins and Development of Cooperation in Central Europe," *East European Quarterly* (fall 1993): 351–373; Christoph Royen, "The Visegrad Triangle and the Western CIS: Potential Conflict Constellations," in *East European Security Reconsidered*, ed. John R. Lampe and Daniel N. Nelson, in collaboration with Roland Schonfeld (Washington, D.C.: The Wilson Center Press, 1993), 75–92; Franciszek Golembski, Andrzej Kupich, Jozef Wiejacz, "Polska w ugrupowaniach regionalnych," [Poland in Regional Groupings] in *Rocznik Polskiej Polityki Zagranicznej, 1992* [Yearbook in Polish Foreign Policy, 1992] ed. Barbara Wizimirska (Warsaw: Polish Institute of International Affairs, 1994), 83–89; Paul Latawski, *The Security Route to Europe: The Visegrad Four* (London: Royal United Services Institute for Defence Studies, 1994), 14–32; Andrew Cottey, *East-Central Europe after the Cold War: Poland, the Czech Republic, Slovakia and Hungary in Search of Security* (Houndmills, U.K.: Macmillan, 1995), 126–135; Adrian Hyde-Price, *The International Politics of East Central Europe* (Manchester, U.K.: Manchester University Press, 1996), 223–269; Andrzej Korbonski, "The Security of East Central Europe and the Visegrad Triangle," in *The Legacy of the Soviet Bloc*, ed. Jane Shapiro Zacek and Ilpyong J. Kim (Gainesville: University Press of Florida, 1997), 159–177; and Matthew Rhodes, "The Idea of Central Europe and Visegrad Cooperation," *International Politics*, no. 2, vol. 35 (June 1998): 165–186.

　　62. See "Skubiszewski on Cooperation with Hungary, CSFR," PAP, 17 April 1991, *FBIS-EEU*, 18 April 1991, 29; and "Skubiszewski on Cooperation with Prague, Budapest," *Rzeczpospolita*, 18 April 1991, *FBIS-EEU*, 23 April 1991, 32.

　　63. "Polityka Zagraniczna Rzeczypospolitej Polskiej w roku 1991—expose Sejmowe Ministra Spraw Zagranicznych RP Krzysztofa Skubiszewskiego" [The Foreign Policy of the Republic of Poland in 1991—Sejm Exposé of the Polish Foreign Minister Krzysztof Skubiszewski] (Warsaw, 27 June 1991), *Zbior Dokumentow*, no. 1 (1992): 53, 58.

　　64. "Foreign Policy Outlined Further," PAP, 2045 GMT, 12 March 1991, *FBIS-EEU*, 13 March 1991, 38. See Grzegorz Kostrzewa-Zorbas, "System Bezpieczenstwa Miedzynarodowego: Dla Polski i Europy Srodkowej na lata dziewiecdziesiate," [The International Security System: For Poland and Central Europe in the 1990s] (Warsaw, 16 March 1991), policy memorandum provided to me.

65. See *Traktat: Miedzy Rzeczapospolita Polska a Republika Federalna Niemiec o dobrym sasiedstwie i przjaznej wspolpracy* [Treaty: Between the Republic of Poland and the Federal Republic of Germany on Good-Neighborliness, Friendship and Cooperation], 17 June 1991.

66. Krzysztof Skubiszewski, "The Treaty is Aimed at a Unified Europe," *Die Welt*, 17 June 1991, *FBIS-EEU*, 18 June 1991, 19; and "Interview with Foreign Minister Krzysztof Skubiszewski," Warsaw TVP Television Network, 1750 GMT, 16 June 1991, *FBIS-EEU*, 18 June 1991, 19–20.

67. I obtained both the original *MSZ* version of the speech, which contains significant revisions from the Department of Europe and the version from which Wachowski supposedly removed this segment for Walesa to present at NATO headquarters. For a description of this interesting chain of events regarding Polish–NATO and Polish–Soviet relations, see Kurski, *Lech Walesa*, 128.

68. Report by "P.A.D.," *Zycie Warszawy*, 3 July 1991, *FBIS-EEU*, 10 July 1991, 30.

69. Valerii Peresada, "Dogonit li Pol'sha 'Briussel'skii Ekspress?'" [Will Poland Catch Up with the 'Brussels Express?], *Pravda*, 8 July 1991, 3.

70. "Poland's Walesa Speaks at NATO Headquarters: Alters Speech on USSR," PAP, 2152 GMT, 3 July 1991, *FBIS-West European* (hereafter, *WEU*), 5 July 1991, 2.

71. Zbigniew Lentowicz, "An Emergence from 'No Man's Land' into the West," *Rzeczpospolita*, 23 May 1991, *FBIS-EEU*, 30 May 1991, 16.

72. Interview I conducted with Lech Kaczynski and Grzegorz Kostrzewa-Zorbas in Warsaw on 11 June 1991.

73. Krzysztof Skubiszewski, "Future Architecture of European Security," in *Jane's NATO Handbook, 1991–1992*, ed. Bruce George (Coulsdon, U.K.: Jane's Information Group, 1991), 391–393.

74. Kurski, *Lech Walesa*, 122–127; Kostrzewa-Zorbas, "Imperium kontratakuje," 175–180; Najder, *Jaka Polska*, 258–277; Toranska, *My*, 137–139; Bichniewicz and Rudnicki, *Czas na Zmiany*, 90–91; Zarembski, "Reportage on Response to Gorbachev Dismissal: Government Issues Statement," Warsaw Radio Warszawa Network, 1700 GMT, 19 August 1991, *FBIS-EEU*, 20 August 1991, 26; and Jaroslaw Kaczynski, "Gdzie tkwil blad?" [Where the Cowards Stood Out], in *Lewy Czerwcowy*, ed. Jacek Kurski and Piotr Semka (Warsaw: Editions Spotkania 1993), 44–46.

75. For example, Address by Polish Foreign Minister Krzysztof Skubiszewski at Sejm Session," Warsaw TVP Television Second Program Network, 0733 GMT, 8 May 1992, *FBIS-EEU*, 12 May 1992, 15–22; Krzysztof Skubiszewski, "Racja stanu z perspektywy polskiej" [Raison d'état from the Polish Perspective], in *Rocznik Polskiej Polityki Zagranicznej, 1992*, ed. Barbara Wizimirska (Warsaw: Polski Instytut Spraw Miedzynarodowych, 1994), 35–44; Vinton, "Domestic Politics and Foreign Policy," 54–56; and Jan B. de Weydenthal, "Political Problems Affect Security Work in Poland," *RFE/RL Research Report*, no. 16 (17 April 1992).

76. Petr Janyska, "We Have to Keep Together: Interview with Foreign Minister Krzysztof Skubiszewski," *Respekt* (Prague), no. 5, 3–9 February 1992, *FBIS-EEU*, 7 February 1992, 17–19; Lech Lewandowski, "Reforms and the Interests of a Law-Governed State: Interview with Foreign Minister Krzysztof Skubiszewski," *Polska Zbrojna*, 19–21 June 1992, *FBIS-EEU*, 30 June 1992, 24.

77. For example, see descriptions of the Triangle's emergency meeting in Warsaw on 20 August 1991 to assess the Soviet coup, discuss secret mobilization of Triangle armed forces, and strengthen their coordinated approach toward the EC: "Polish, Hungar-

ian, and Czech Ministers Meet," *DPA Communiqué* (Warsaw), 20 August 1991; and Peter Michielsen, "Interview with Polish Foreign Minister Krzysztof Skubiszewski," *NRC Handelsblad*, 4 September 1991, *FBIS-EEU*, 11 September 1991, 21.

78. Joint statement by Secretary of State James A. Baker III and Hans-Dietrich Genscher, minister of foreign affairs for the Federal Republic of Germany, U.S. Department of State, Washington, D.C., 2 October 1991.

79. "The Krakow Declaration," 6 October 1991, Krakow, Section II, 1; "Tripartite Summit Issues Declaration," PAP, 6 October 1991; and "Krakow Talks Ministers Welcome Euro-Atlantic Pact Idea," *Ceskoslovensky Rozhlas* (Prague), 6 October 1991, 6.

80. North Atlantic Council, "The Rome Declaration on Peace and Cooperation," 7–8 November 1991, NATO Press Service.

81. Interview I conducted with Lech Kaczynski in Warsaw on 11 June 1991 and with Zdzislaw Najder in Warsaw on 12 June 1991. See also Anita Gargas and Piotr Gerczuk, "Wachowski and Others: Interview with Lech Kaczynski," *Nowy Swiat*, 16 April 1992, *FBIS-EEU*, 28 April 1992, 19–20; Vinton, "Domestic Politics and Foreign Policy," 50–60; Najder, *Jaka Polska*, 278–368; and Bichniewicz and Rudnicki, *Czas na Zmiany*, 105–158.

82. Karol Sawicki, "Further on Visit by Poland's Lech Walesa: Meets with Stoltenberg," *Frankfurter Rundschaft*, 30 March 1992, *FBIS-WEU*, 31 March 1992, 6–7 and "Walesa Discusses EC, NATO, Government Reform," Warsaw TVP Television Network, 1730 GMT, 9 April 1992, *FBIS-EEU*, 10 April 1992, 19. See also Bichniewicz and Rudnicki, *Czas na Zmiany*, 74–75; and Jan Parys, "Bitwa o wojsko" [The Battle for the Army], in *Lewy Czerwcowy*, ed. Jacek Kurski and Piotr Semka (Warsaw: Editions Spotkania, 1992), 71–74.

83. Krzysztof Kolodziejczyk, "Nowe konceptcje dla Europy Srodkowo-Wschodniej" [New Concept for Central-East Europe], *Rzeczpospolita*, 31 March 1992, 1; and Karol Groblewski, "NATO-bis sliczne jak pani [NATO-Bis Is as Lovely as You, Madam], *Rzeczpospolita*, 14 October 1992, 2.

84. Stanislaw Lukaszewski, "We Cannot Alter the Defense System on Our Own: Interview with Defense Minister Jan Parys," *Polska Zbrojna*, 3–5 April 1992, *FBIS-EEU*, 8 April 1992, 15; A. Andrzejewski, "Leopards on the Vistula: Interview with Polish Foreign Minister Krzysztof Skubiszewski," *Wprost* (Poznan), 8 March 1992, *FBIS-EEU*, 17 March 1992, 11; "[Olszewski] Comments on Martial Law 'Plan of Action," Warsaw TVP Television Network, 1730 GMT, 10 April 1992, *FBIS-EEU*, 13 April 1992, 16; "Center Alliance Leader Voices Support for Parys," PAP, 1438 GMT, 10 April 1992, *FBIS-EEU*, 13 April 1992, 16; "Milewski Denies Claims of Plans for Martial Law," PAP, 1738 GMT, 11 April 1992, *FBIS-EEU*, 13 April 1992, 16–17; Vinton, "Domestic Politics and Foreign Policy," 50–60; Kostrzewa-Zorbas, "Imperium kontratakuje," 164–180; Radek Sikorski, "Poles Apart," *The Spectator*, 27 June 1992, 9–12; and Prizel, "Poland's Ostpolitik," 102.

85. Kostrzewa-Zorbas, "The Russian Troop Withdrawal from Poland," 120; and interviews by me with Kostrzewa-Zorbas in Washington, D.C., on 15 October 1993 and with Radek Sikorski, former vice minister of defense under Jan Parys, in Washington, D.C., on 5 November 1993. For a description about how Finland rejected any clauses limiting an independent Finnish foreign policy after the dissolution of the USSR by brokering the new Finnish–Russian treaty in January 1992 see John Lukacs, "Finland Vindicated," *Foreign Affairs*, vol. 71, no. 4 (fall 1992), 50.

86. Interviews I conducted with Parys and Kostrzewa-Zorbas in Washington on 28 August 1992.

87. "Walesa, Ukraine's Kravchuk Sign Cooperation Treaty; Praise 'Friendly' Relations," Radio Warszawa Network, 1400 GMT, 18 May 1992, *FBIS-EEU*, 19 May 1992, 8. See also Prizel, "Warsaw's Ostpolitik," 109–111.

88. "Lista Konfidentow" [List of Confidantes], *Gazeta Polska*, 4 June 1993, 3.

89. Vinton, "Domestic Politics and Foreign Policy," 50–60; Najder, *Jaka Polska*, 278–368; Bichniewicz and Rudnicki, *Czas na Zmiany*, 105–158; Toranska, *My*, 129–150; and Kostrzewa-Zorbas, "Imperium kontratakuje," 164–180.

90. For the entire text of the document see *European Security*, no. 2 (summer 1993): 320–340.

91. Lewandowski, "Reforms and the Interests of a Law-Governed State," 24–26. See also "New Ministers Outline Goals," PAP, 2131 GMT, 13 July 1992, *FBIS-EEU*, 14 July 1992, 23.

92. My interview with Hanna Suchocka, in Warsaw on 9 June 1994.

93. "Suchocka Returns from European Summit, Comments," PAP, 2007 GMT, 18 July 1992, *FBIS-EEU*, 20 July 1992, 33; and "Suchocka, EC Representatives Discuss Membership," PAP, 1625 GMT, 22 July 1992, *FBIS-EEU*, 23 July 1992, 17.

94. "Czech Prime Minister Holds Talks with Suchocka; Suchocka 'Very Pleased,'" Warsaw TVP Television First Program Network, 1730 GMT, 13 September 1992, *FBIS-EEU*, 14 September 1992, 14; "Suchocka Returns from Budapest; Agreements Signed," Warsaw TVP Television First Program Network, 1730 GMT, 24 September 1992, *FBIS-EEU*, 25 September 1992, 13; and "Antall, Skubiszewski Discuss Foreign Policy," MTI, 1631 GMT, 13 October 1992, *FBIS-EEU*, 15 October 1992, 17.

95. KUL is the famous university where Pope John Paul II once taught, and it became an important independent academic bastion and outlet from Communist censorship and academic persecutionduring marial law. Suchocka chose KUL as the site for her first major foreign policy address because she, too, taught there and because her chancellery advisors, Jan Maria Rokita and Mariusz Handzlik, both graduated from KUL and played a large role during Martial Law as students in many foreign policy–related activities. I interviewed Suchocka and Rokita in Warsaw on 10 June 1994, and also Handzlik from 12–15 June 1994 in Warsaw and Lublin, and in Washington, D.C. during the 1990s.

96. "Wystapienie premiera RP Hanny Suchockiej na inauguracji roku akademickiego KUL, Lublin" [Appearance of Premier of the Republic of Poland Hanna Suchocka at the Beginning of the Academic Year at KUL], 18 October 1992, in *Rocznik Polskiej Polityki Zagranicznej, 1992*, ed. Barbara Wizimirska (Warsaw: Polski Instytut Spraw Miedzynarodowych, 1994), 18–19; Prizel, "Warsaw's Ostpolitik," 105; and "Suchocka: Policy Oriented toward NATO, EC," PAP, 1449 GMT, 18 October 1992, *FBIS-EEU*, 19 October 1992, 20–21.

97. Volodymyr Savtsov, "Let Us Lean on What Brings Us Closer Rather Than on What Separates Us," *Holos Ukrayiny* (Kiev), 24 October 1992, *FBIS-Union of Soviet Socialist Republics Report* (hereafter *USR*), 15 November 1992, 80–81; "Skubiszewski Briefs Sejm on Eastern Policy," PAP, 2323 GMT, 18 November 1992, *FBIS-EEU*, 24 November 1992, 23.

98. Prizel, "Warsaw's Ostpolitik," 113–114; and Jan B. de Weydenthal, "Poland on Its Own: The Conduct of Foreign Policy," *RL/RFE Research Report*, vol. 2, no. 2 (January 1993): 4.

99. "Polish Foreign Minister Meets Kravchuk, Kuchma," *Ukrayinske Telebachennya* Television Network, 1700 GMT, 30 December 1992, *FBIS-SOV*, 31 December 1992, 46–47; and "Skubiszewski Visits Kiev, Discusses Relations," Warsaw TVP Television Second Program, 0700 GMT, 31 December 1992, *FBIS-EEU*, 4 January 1993, 47.

100. "Suchocka Addresses Businessmen in Brussels," PAP, 2131 GMT, 7 October 1992, *FBIS-EEU*, 9 October 1992, 12.

101. "Walesa Satisfied with Suchocka Cabinet," PAP, 1724 GMT, 8 October 1992, *FBIS-EEU*, 13 October 1992, 16.

102. "Poland's Suchocka Meets Counterparts," PAP, 1928 GMT, 30 January 1993, *FBIS-WEU*, 1 February 1993, 3–4.

103. "Navy to Participate in NATO Exercise," PAP, 1921 GMT, 5 February 1993, *FBIS-EEU*, 8 February 1993, 31–32.

104. "Security Chief Interviewed on NATO-2 Concept," *Gazeta Krakowska*, 25 February 1993, *FBIS-EEU*, 9 March 1993, 24. See also Maria Wagrowska, "Uczmy sie angielskiego, ale nie zapominajmy o rosyskim [Let Us Learn English, but We Had Better Not Forget Our Russian] (Interview with National Security Advisor, Jerzy Milewski), *Rzeczpospolita*, 8 September 1992, 3.

105. "Skubiszewski, NATO Secretary-General Meet," PAP, 1447 GMT, 9 March 1993, *FBIS-EEU*, 10 March 1993, 32.

106. Malgorzata Alterman, "On the Threshold of the Pact: Interview with NATO Secretary General Manfred Woerner," *Gazeta Wyborcza*, 17 March 1993, *FBIS-EEU*, 24 March 1993, 27.

107. See Jan B. de Weydenthal, "Poland's Security Policy," *RL/RFE Research Report*, vol. 2, no. 14 (2 April 1993); and Arthur Rachwald, "Poland Looks West," in *Post-1989 Poland: Challenges of Independence*, ed., Andrew Michta and Ilya Prizel (New York: St. Martin's, 1995), 129–155.

108. For the proposal's text, see *Gazeta Wyborcza*, 24 May 1993, *FBIS-Soviet Union* (hereafter *SOV*), 27 May 1993, 46–47. See "Zlenko on European Security Alliance," Mayak Radio Network (Moscow), 12 October 1993, *FBIS-SOV*, 12 October 1993, 86–87.

109. Andrzej Lomanowski, "Walesa, Kravchuk, and the Abandoned Zone," *Gazeta Wyborcza*, 26 May 1993, *FBIS-SOV*, 27 May 1993, 47.

110. Ryszhard Koval, "Contemporary Geopolitical Doctrines," *Vecherniy Kiev*, 12 November 1992, *FBIS-USR*, 5 December 1992, 34.

111. Andrzej Prusinowski, "Lech Walesa in Ukraine: Partners, Not Allies," *Polityka*, 5 June 1993, *JPRS-East Europe Report* (hereafter *EER*), 2 July 1993, 11.

112. Joint Polish-Russian Declaration, 26 August 1993, Polish Embassy, Washington, D.C.

113. "El'tsin's Secret Letter on NATO Expansion," *Mlada Fronta Dnes* (Prague), 2 December 1993, *FBIS-SOV*, 3 December 1993, 6; Prochazkova and J. Stetina, "Interview with El'tsin Foreign Policy Advisor, Dmitrii Rurikov: You No Longer Need to be Afraid of US," *Lidove Noviny* (Prague), 15 December 1993, *FBIS-SOV*, 20 December 1993, 49.

114. "Interview with Vladimir Zhirinovskii: If NATO is enlarged, This Will Not Contribute to Peace," *Kurier* (Vienna), 1 February 1994, *FBIS-SOV*, 1 February 1994, 21–22.

115. See Jerzy Marek Nowakowski, "Polska pomiedzy wschodem a zachodem: Szansa 'Pomostu' czy historyczne fatum" [Poland between East and West: A Chance of 'Bridge Building' or Historical Fate], in *Polska w Europie* (April 1993): 5–20.

3

From German Unification
to European Integration

From the outset of his terms as foreign minister, Krzysztof Skubiszewski strove to resolve the uncertainty over Poland's western border and to develop a new relationship with the FRG. By using his formative academic expertise in Polish–German relations, Skubiszewski moved quickly to plan a comprehensive strategy as the former repressive government in Poland gave way to post-Communist democratization, several months before the shattering impact of the Berlin Wall's fall.

The key to understanding the pragmatic Polish foreign minister focuses on the rationale behind the attempt to heal the post–World War II Polish–German rift, particularly how German unification influenced Skubiszewski. By analyzing how Skubiszewski sought to achieve Poland's national security goals and what foreign policy alignment it demonstrated toward Germany, we better grasp the five critical political problems Skubiszewski faced. The first issue with which Skubiszewski grappled concerned how to obtain recognition of Poland as an independent actor in Central European security. Within that context, Polish foreign policy then needed to respond to German unification and determine whether to promote four-power control of the unification process or not. Thirdly, by ensuring that Bonn unequivocally accepted Poland's western border, even if that meant delaying Soviet force withdrawal talks with Moscow, Skubiszewski sought to reduce and hopefully eliminate one of Poland's greatest worries. Next, he wanted to participate in the "2 Plus 4" talks on German unification to demonstrate how Poland regionally played a crucial role in European security and stability as a facilitator, not antagonist. Lastly, Skubiszewski believed that, in ultimately overseeing the withdrawal of Soviet troops from Poland, in coordination with the reluctant FRG he enabled Bonn to realize Warsaw's objectives of European reintegration in Polish–German partnership. Whether this alignment signified an other-help or a self-help strategy amid regional and international anarchy explains Poland's middle power politics and its impact regionally.

The Path to Cooperative State Alignment:
Solidarnosc Roots and Transition

Artur Hajnicz, one of the leading Polish *Solidarnosc* experts on Germany and a post-Communist foreign policy advisor to Skubiszewski, provided a strategic framework publicly in January 1989 for a new Polish–German relationship.[1] Hajnicz's rationale for reorienting foreign policy stemmed from redefining the Polish *raison d'état*.[2] He suggested that Poland emphasize the state's "nonpartisan interests" in formulating a foreign policy based on "reconciliation" and "normalization of relations" toward a future unified Germany. As argued in chapter 2, this strategy buttressed Poland's limited development of relations with Bonn, based on the 1970 Polish–German treaty. Hajnicz, however, went much further by recognizing Germany's potential for unification.

Hajnicz also wrote that Poland no longer needed to resort to its "flight to the [Soviet] protectorate" as a means to avoid residual Polish concerns over German irredentism. He argued that during the closing stages of World War II, Stalin manufactured Warsaw's dependency on Moscow to define Poland's "Yalta state" and "illegitimately" provide the rationale for "Soviet armored divisions between the Elbe and Oder." Furthermore, the FRG's rejection of Berlin's legitimacy under the Hallstein Doctrine left Poland in a "paradox" geopolitically.[3] On the one hand, the USSR "guaranteed" Poland's western border, but only through the large number of its military forces in the GDR. On the other hand, the anti-Communist FRG leadership refused to recognize the early post–World War II territorial changes by the American–British–Soviet–French agreement to expand Poland two hundred kilometers westward, primarily due to the expulsion of millions of Germans from those territories.[4] As explained in chapter 2, without a post–World War II peace treaty to decide the fate of the Polish–German region and without agreement by the FRG to recognize the Polish–German border legally unless Germany unified, Warsaw's leadership remained beholden to Moscow. In all, Hajnicz saw that the Yalta agreement's geopolitical reality resulted in a seemingly permanent Polish Communist compromise to maintain limited sovereignty in exchange for political legitimacy from Moscow.

Unlike the Communist leadership, however, Hajnicz believed that Polish society, particularly some in the Polish underground, foresaw that Mikhail Gorbachev's "new thinking" in Soviet foreign policy offered the possibility for Poland to establish a different relationship to the FRG. Moreover, Hajnicz asserted that to establish a new Polish–German relationship Poland needed to refute the notion of the "protection" by Soviet troops in both Poland and the GDR, the latter an artificial state. Hence, Hajnicz believed that since some in *Solidarnosc* favored improving Polish–German ties, a future democratic Poland with *Solidarnosc* as part of the state's leadership must necessarily recognize the FRG's legal right to unify with the GDR.[5]

For Hajnicz the prospect for improved Polish–German relations, even under the Polish Communist leadership of General Wojciech Jaruzelski, started with FRG foreign minister Hans-Dietrich Genscher's visit to Warsaw in January 1988. During his trip, Genscher signaled the FRG's intention to uphold the Oder–Neisse border and to work with Jaruzelski. Genscher's visit proved significant because he met with bishops, cultural figures, and, most importantly, Lech Walesa and *Solidarnosc*'s leadership. For the *Solidarnosc* leadership, such a gesture signified a break in the FRG's policy during the 1980s, when Bonn focused mainly on relations to the superpowers and the GDR, supported Jaruzelski's martial law, and kept the *Solidarnosc* movement at a distance.[6] Yet, Genscher's January 1988 Warsaw trip allowed *Solidarnosc*'s leaders to think more seriously about mobilizing public opinion against Jaruzelski's Communists, especially when the workers and students struck in April and May 1988 to protest the deteriorating Polish economy and brought the state to the brink of collapse. Finally, Genscher's important sojourn enabled German experts such as Hajnicz to forecast a departure from the "Soviet protectorate," if Poland's underground movement as well as official government improved its relations with the FRG.[7]

Moreover, Hajnicz's article argued that Gorbachev's foreign policies not only allowed Poland to benefit by interacting with the FRG, but also revealed the disconnect between the Soviet leader's vision of a "common European home" and Poland's post–World War II geopolitical status. By the time of the Polish 1988 strikes, Gorbachev's concept of European security, in which states such as Poland instituted their own reforms but remained within the Soviet-dominated security system, created a groundswell for Warsaw's government and *Solidarnosc* to forge a compromise not fully dependent on Moscow.[8]

According to Hajnicz, it became "impossible to have a European house without tearing down the satellite-fences, gates, and walls surrounding the Central European apartment." He believed that as Western Europe attempted to unify politically and economically, Poland and "the people of Central Europe want to create for themselves a cozy nook in which to live in human dignity and thus feel at home in old Europe." To achieve a geopolitical status that removed the onus of Poland's precarious interwar-era balancing of Germany and Russia against each other, Hajnicz argued for a third option. He stated that Poland's Communists needed to design a "with-with" strategy to promote a sovereign Polish foreign policy based on accommodating geopolitical behavior toward both the FRG and USSR. Unexpectedly, after *Solidarnosc*'s stunning electoral victory in June 1989, Hajnicz found himself in a formal advisory position to shape Poland's German policy. As events unfolded rapidly in Central Europe during the fall of 1989, the FRG increased its rapprochement with Moscow and

Warsaw, Gorbachev discarded the hard-line GDR leadership, and *Solidarnosc* began the first serious improvement in Polish–German relations since the signing of the 1970 Polish–German treaty.[9]

Trying to Heal the Post–World War II
Polish–German Rift

Before the Mazowiecki government formed, the newly elected Polish Parliament passed two important declarations related to Polish–German relations. One of the first acts of the Parliament centered on reexamination of important anniversaries, such as that of the 1939 Nazi–Soviet Agreement. On 23 August 1989, the fiftieth anniversary of the Molotov–Ribbentrop Pact, the Sejm declared that the pact contradicted "the fundamental principles of international law" and underscored a discredited example of reprehensibly "imperial," "secretive," and "predatory" thinking "from the very beginning."[10] Likewise, the 30 August 1989 Senate declaration emphasized the need to maintain the territorial status quo, particularly to preserve "the peaceful contemporary European order" and, in connection with the mid-1960s exchanges of letters between Polish and German bishops, to expand "genuine and lasting reconciliation" between both states.[11] Therefore, with history playing a prominent role in their early legislative pronouncements, the elected *Solidarnosc* parliamentarians and even a majority of Communist legislators determined to establish new Polish–German relations.

The parliamentary declarations recognized both the historical wrongs committed by Nazi Germany and Stalinist Russia against Poland and presaged Skubiszewski's policy of linking the Polish–German religious reconciliation of the 1960s to contemporary Polish–German diplomatic relations. Skubiszewski attested to this aim when he stated that the healing between Poland and the FRG arose not only from many personal contacts across borders by the underground and the post–World War II German generations, but also from "bold initiatives of the Church . . . the stand of the Polish bishops in 1965." He emphasized that the bishops held a special place within *Solidarnosc* and the post-Communist Polish government when "their words about mutual forgiveness being deeply Christian, belong to the treasury of the public life in today's Poland." During the mid-1960s, Skubiszewski declared, "the nation did not wield power in the state, so the bishops spoke for the nation and, being so heavily tried by the war, we understand the suffering of those Germans who were deprived of their native land and homes, who experienced wrongs and injustice."[12]

The new foreign minister's statement resonated because of his own wartime experiences of displacement in western Poland, his expertise on Germany, and his writings on Polish–German relations. Skubiszewski's early scholarly research on the history of the Oder–Neisse border and analysis of the Polish Catholic Church and its Western links provide much insight for his later policymaking.[13] It is important to recall that during the Communist era, just as Polish–

German relations began to improve under Gomulka in 1969 and the *Ostpolitik* of FRG chancellor Willy Brandt, Poznan University professor Skubiszewski argued for international resolution of Poland's western border:

> The territory beyond the Oder and Neisse line stopped being a bargaining chip that any German government could either offer Poland or take away. . . . It is important to recognize that Bonn doesn't lose anything by recognizing the Oder–Neisse border, but gains a better position for the FRG in trying to attain unification. . . . European states would rather live with a divided Germany than consent to a hegemonic, unified Germany. . . . Relations between German and Polish politicians depend upon the question of the border.[14]

By upholding these arguments after becoming foreign minister, Skubiszewski's overriding foreign policy objective focused on improving the Polish–German relationship quickly in order to reintegrate Poland into Europe via Bonn.[15] He believed Poland needed to move beyond the 1970 Polish–German Treaty to obtain Bonn's affirmation of the Polish–German border. In developing his German strategy, Skubiszewski took his lead from Prime Minister Mazowiecki, who laid the foundation for Polish–German relations on 12 September 1989. Speaking before the Sejm, Mazowiecki said "we desire to open Poland to Europe and the world." Mazowiecki believed that Poland required a "breakthrough" with Bonn in order to cooperate with EC states. In calling for "genuine reconciliation" with the FRG, Mazowiecki hoped for Polish–German ties "commensurate with that achieved between the Germans and French."[16]

Such a statement marked a major departure not articulated since the 1970 Polish–German treaty. The Polish prime minister sought to enunciate Poland's independent Western reintegration strategy, the first time in the post–World War II era that a non-Communist government elected in Central or Eastern Europe promulgated such a policy. After Mazowiecki's speech, Skubiszewski described how he wanted the *MSZ*'s German policy to develop. By using the international legal norms about which he wrote in his academic career, Skubiszewski defended Poland's emerging democratic foreign policy. During his first international trip as foreign minister to participate at the late September UN General Assembly session, Skubiszewski discussed German unification with journalists. Possible German unification, Skubiszewski stated, remained not only an issue for the Germans, but also for the United States, United Kingdom, France, and USSR—the four great powers in Germany. For these powers and for all of Europe, he argued, German unification required a formal peace treaty, as stipulated by the 1945 Potsdam Conference, to uphold the German post–World War II state borders. This stipulation also reinforced "the sovereignty of the Polish state externally, the full independence as far as our internal affairs are concerned [and] the principles of our foreign policy."[17]

Upon his return to Warsaw, Skubiszewski reiterated Poland's legally focused treaty formula for German unification that involved the four powers, the two Germanys, and Poland. He stressed four key points all linked to the states involved in the questions of German unification and the Oder–Neisse border. His first point emphasized unification as "the Germans' business; it is a matter of self-determination." At the same time, however, Skubiszewski's second point highlighted the role of the four powers in unification and underlined that "without their agreement, the situation of the Germans cannot be changed." Next, the foreign minister contended that because "German unification is a European matter in my view, the discussion [of the Oder–Neisse border] is unnecessary. It interferes with our [Polish–German] relations." For Skubiszewski and Poland, "the treaty on normalization of Polish-German relations of 1970 is entirely clear." Moreover, "we have the statement made by Foreign Minister Genscher [accepting inviolability of the border] at the UN that was an important statement for us." The last point for Skubiszewski concerned not just "the border issue, but the discussion of it." Thus, he revealed that "an alternative channel for discussion in these matters [exists], not just [between] the two foreign ministries, but also special plenipotentiaries of the federal chancellor and our premier."[18]

As the situation rapidly deteriorated in the GDR with the East German exodus through Hungary, Austria, and Czechoslovakia into the FRG during that August and September, the Polish government tried to accelerate the slow-moving Polish–FRG special plenipotentiary talks. The talks actually began by Jaruzelski as a prelude to the projected Polish visit in 1988 of FRG chancellor Helmut Kohl. Both governments increased the tempo of their plenipotentiary talks immediately after Mazowiecki took over in mid-September. Just after Skubiszewski became foreign minister, Mieczyslaw Pszon, Prime Minister Mazowiecki's special representative, and Horst Teltschik, Chancellor Kohl's special envoy and national security advisor, met on 14 September for the first time to prepare for the first real chance for Chancellor Kohl to visit Poland.

Teltschik's meetings with Mazowiecki and Skubiszewski in Warsaw solidified the Polish–German linkage. The resulting statement a few weeks later announced Kohl's 9–14 November visit, the first one by the chancellor to a post-Communist Warsaw Pact state. Expectations rose when Pszon declared in early October the intention to discuss economic assistance, in an attempt to reschedule Poland's huge debt to the West, issue a joint statement on the bilateral relationship, including the sensitive question of the Polish–German border, and visit several historically significant sites. Both sides agreed on visits to the German Krzyzowa Castle in Polish Lower Silesia and the nationally important Polish shrines at Czestochowa, the Pope's Catholic University in Lublin, and the infamous Oswiecim (Auschwitz) concentration camp. It was at Krzyzowa, or Kreisau as the Germans referred to it before it became Polish territory after World War II, that the German opposition to Hitler convened in 1944 to plot against the Third Reich. Both Poland and the FRG saw the site as an important demonstration of Polish–German reconciliation and opposition to historical extremism and tyranny.[19] More importantly, both sides agreed to meet at Krzyzowa instead of Annaberg, the latter a controversial location originally demanded by the German associations of expellees as the place to hold mass rallies because of its large number of German minorities. The compromise to meet at Krzyzowa to revive its stature of German antitotalitarian protest and birthplace to some of the early Christian Democratic Union party leaders went a long way to defuse ethnic minority tensions.[20]

In the weeks prior to Chancellor Kohl's Polish visit, Skubiszewski expanded on a number of issues concerning Polish–German relations in various European interviews. With regard to German unification, the foreign minister said that all Europeans, including Poles, believed that both the FRG and GDR must work within the European legal framework if their countries determined to unify. "We are against a destabilization in Europe," he said. Moreover, Skubiszewski emphasized that "we are for the current order in Europe, because only within the framework of this order can our reforms be implemented."[21] When pressed on the issue of the affirmation of the Polish–German border, particularly whether the post–World War II Franco–German relationship illustrated a model for the future Polish–German association, Skubiszewski replied that "the border is a legal fact and the Oder–Neisse border cannot be changed. I think that the statement by FRG Foreign Minister Genscher at the United Nations [September 1989] was very important: the minister said that Poland will have secure borders in the future." Moreover, Skubiszewski stated that the Franco–German rapprochement defined the border settlement. As a result, no disputes arise today over that border, he asserted. Consequently, Skubiszewski maintained that, as a "jurist," he believed "pacta sunt servanda (treaties must be observed). I only hope that the FRG Chancellor will go further in interpreting the Warsaw Treaty [1970 Gomulka–Brandt treaty], wherever there are differences."[22]

When asked to comment on the issue of the German minority in Poland, the minister responded that, even before he became foreign minister, he had recommended to then Polish leader General Jaruzelski, through the general's Consultative Council, that Poland "introduce the criteria of language and nationality in a census." That way, Skubiszewski asserted, Poland would know just "how many people in Poland consider themselves Germans." The issue for Skubiszewski came down to the fact that "In Poland there are people who are 100 percent Polish, but their ancestors were German citizens, and, therefore, they say that they are Germans themselves. But there is a difference between citizenship and ethnic origin."[23] As the new popularly elected Polish government grappled with German unification, the German "minority" issue in Poland remained problematic for the Polish–German relationship. The *MSZ* found it needed to factor the German minorities into many of the bilateral agreements Warsaw hoped to achieve with Bonn in the coming months.

In preparation for the German chancellor's first visit to Poland, Skubiszewski looked to some of the foremost *Solidarnosc* experts on Germany to help him formulate Poland's strategy toward Bonn. Such specialists as Hajnicz and Wojciech Lamentowicz heavily influenced Skubiszewski's vision for Poland's FRG policies, as was evident when they traveled with the foreign minister, along with *MSZ* officials and parliamentarians, on 7 November to Vienna. In Austria, Skubiszewski and his Viennese counterpart, Alois Mock, cosponsored, with their respective ministry institutes, a Polish–Austrian conference focused on Poland's democratization process. During the discussions, Skubiszewski underlined that Poland needed to eradicate its Soviet "protectorate" status, as Hajnicz termed it, to create new links to the FRG to benefit Warsaw's policies toward both Bonn and Moscow. To emphasize this, Skubiszewski stated that "our foreign policy should be dominated by public interest rather than the interest of the ruling party. . . . Relations with the USSR must be stripped of all residual traces of past history." By beginning to break Moscow's hold over Polish foreign policy, Skubiszewski foresaw the possibility for Warsaw to help "eliminate . . . the division of Europe." He underlined that "no other country is in any way threatened by what is happening in Poland." With this constructive approach, the Polish foreign minister said, in relation to the interwar period that "Germany's failure to realize the advantage to Europe of a strong Poland flanked by Germany and Russia resulted in disastrous consequences."[24] Poland's post-Communist democratic path, Skubiszewski implied, symbolized democratization regionally, particularly for the USSR. Hence, Skubiszewski argued that the opportunity by democratic West Germany to cooperate with democratizing Poland should not be missed, especially to create more stability regionally without threatening neighboring states. This speech set the stage for Kohl's historic visit.

November 1989 Crossroads:
Chancellor Kohl Visits Poland

Given the difficult Polish–German history, the Polish foreign minister believed that reconciliation between some post–World War II Poles and Germans provided a good example for how official Polish-German ties in 1989 could evolve into "agreements between states." Skubiszewski declared that Chancellor Kohl's pending trip to Poland "can help the situation," especially in addressing German minority rights in Poland that Polish Communist governments "regrettably" avoided. Furthermore, he stressed that "it was not Poland that wanted to change borders in 1939—it was Hitler's Third Reich. . . . The redrawing of Polish borders after the war was decided not by Poland but by the four allied powers." Yet it remained crucial to the foreign minister that, "if the two parts of Germany wanted to become unified, they would have to do it within the confines of their present borders. . . . This must be stated with utmost clarity, and it would be a good thing if all competent politicians were to understand it." Personally, he also attested to the historical hardship that "it was those same powers which also decided on the expulsion of the German population from Poland's Western territories. . . . These people, too, became victims of the war. I myself was displaced during World War II, so I understand the tragic fate of all displaced persons.[25] On the latter point of Poland's western territories, however, it bears remembering that Skubiszewski viewed as Polish territory the post–World War II geographical area Poland gained from Germany that extended Poland's western border nearly two hundred kilometers. The post–World War II Polish leaderships wanted to secure the western territory Poland absorbed from Germany, mainly to gain land where many Poles lived, as well as Germans, and to obtain as much territory from a defeated Germany as possible. Thus, Skubiszewski believed that Chancellor Kohl's impending visit confronted post-Communist Poland with the difficult problem of German minority rights and post–World War II restitution.[26]

The Polish–German summit gave hope to both Bonn and Warsaw about a post–World War II healing between Germans and Poles, particularly through the anticipated signing of a Polish–German declaration. Just before his departure Kohl commented that he intended to open "a new chapter in the history of our relations. . . . The 1,000-year-old history of Polish–German relations, really, was shaped by very long periods by friendship. . . . They have lived in peace for the greater part of their history. Unfortunately, this is something that many people have forgotten." Furthermore, he explained that both Poles and Germans "experienced indescribable suffering," given the Nazi horrors of war and the Holocaust, and the Germans killed or expelled from Poland after World War II. The German chancellor underscored, however, that Poland's peaceful 1989 revolution provided a historical moment "to produce a lasting reconciliation between the German and Polish peoples." Like previous German chancellor Konrad Adenauer, Kohl thought his visit "a task of European dimensions that is comparable with the German–French reconciliation, without which the process leading to the unification of our part of Europe would not exist." Lastly and even more importantly for the Polish national interest, Kohl "respected" and did not intend to "question" the fact that "the territories situated inside Poland's western border are now inhabited by Polish families and these areas have become their home for over two generations."[27]

Prime Minister Mazowiecki remained more cautious than the German chancellor. Just before Kohl's arrival, he stated that "the attitude of the two peoples toward each other is primarily a question of generations. Older people still have fresh memories of the war. . . . The desire for closer relations with the FRG is very strong among the young." Moreover, Mazowiecki indicated that these important talks certainly involved the Polish–German "border" as much as "reconciliation." For Mazowiecki, "the Oder–Neisse border is not up for discussion. . . . [A] satisfactory solution can only be found in a European state of peace, in which the inviolability of borders is generally recognized." Finally, as a priority, Mazowiecki stressed that "the separation of Europe can only be eliminated . . . [if] a process of growing economic and cultural cooperation" occurs.[28] For Polish commentators such as editor Michnik, the chancellor's visit culminated the conciliation first begun between Polish and German bishops in their exchange of letters in the mid-1960s. This "historical watershed broke the psychological barrier and introduced new perspectives of thought about Polish–German relations." The ceremony both leaders scheduled at Krzyzowa, commented Michnik, offered "the best of all possible symbols, namely, that the Germans associated with the Kreisau Group lay down their lives in a struggle for a political order to be based on democratic and Christian values." As a caveat to all Poles and advice for Mazowiecki and Kohl, however, Michnik wrote "the matter of the German minority in Poland should not be made out to be the 'blank spot,'" as the Polish Communist leaders had propagandized since World War II. He underlined that all Polish citizens deserved the same rights in a democracy, but that past Polish and German governments contributed to tensions between Poles and Germans by manipulating the minority populations in each state. For Michnik, minority issues no longer served as "the subject of bargaining between governments."[29] Thus, with these interviews and commentary as a prelude to the historic visit, the next steps in the Polish–German relationship commenced.

It became clear shortly after Chancellor Kohl's arrival in Poland on 9 November that the GDR's upheaval, particularly the Berlin Wall's fall, overshadowed the visit. Yet, before the Berlin Wall fell and at the end of the first day's official talks, Kohl said "I think about reconciliation and our common history . . . . Unfortunately, this century, and especially the time from 1933, contains dreadful chapters. Our goal is to correct these errors keeping in mind the generation of our children." In his turn, Mazowiecki provided an overview of what lay in store for the rest of the visit, when he commented that "[we] reviewed the Polish-German issues from the historical point of view for it is not possible to break away from history in Polish–German talks. After all, neither the chancellor nor myself have such an intention. For we are well aware of the burden of history on our relations."[30] The previous evening's formal dinner, however, witnessed revealing speeches by both leaders.

Mazowiecki and Kohl described deep anxieties their states held toward each other, but declared the need to overcome the historic Polish–German animosities that divided their peoples. By looking to a better relationship based on the post–World War II West European cooperative model, both leaders sought to move beyond historic aggression and apprehension. In his toast, the Polish premier declared the Polish and German bishops and the Polish–German treaty of 1970 provided both states the foundation for overcoming these "difficulties." For Poland, "reconciliation" with the FRG remained necessary, but "determination [must] make up for negligence with regard to access to the German language and culture for those who identify with this tradition."[31] For his part, the German chancellor went a long way to complete the German post–World War II apology to Poland and its people. He expounded that "several months ago, I recalled the boundless suffering inflicted on Poland as a result of World War II . . . by the hands of Germany."[32] Yet, he reminded the political leadership that over two million innocent Germans lost their lives in the post–World War II expulsions. With this statement, Kohl then turned to his future hopes for a new German–Polish relationship, asserting that "we encourage you to persist in following the road you have chosen, for Europe needs a free and stable Poland!" Without advocating a definitive guarantee of the Polish–German border, the chancellor underscored that "we will adhere to the well-known provisions of our German and Eastern policy, based on national and international law, which also means that we adhere to all parts of the 1970 treaty."[33]

Although Chancellor Kohl interrupted his visit to Poland by traveling to the FRG and GDR to celebrate the Berlin Wall's collapse, he returned to Poland to pay homage at several historic sites. By paying tribute to the millions of people who died at Auschwitz, by underscoring at the Jasna Gora Monastery that Polish–German reconciliation, was an example for Europe to emulate, and by asking forgiveness in a Polish and German language ceremony at Krzyzowa Castle, Mazowiecki and Kohl tried to define a new Polish–German relationship.

Just like Kohl's embrace of French president François Mitterand at Verdun several years earlier, his reconciliation with Mazowiecki at a mass in Krzyzowa on the former estate of Count Helmuth James von Moltke, an opponent of Hitler, marked a new start in Polish–German ties. Their embrace and statements after the service showed how far both states had come in just a few days: "this is an important moment in the life of our nations. It was there—on this very spot at the center of Europe after a period of 24 years, we—both we on the banks of the Vistula and they on the banks of the Rhine—are surely able to understand the wisdom of what was said by Polish Cardinal Jozef Wyszynski: "We forgive and we ask for forgiveness. . . . Let us depart into a good and peaceful future." In response, Mazowiecki said, "we attended this mass with seriousness and in the spirit of brotherhood. We are bound to this brotherhood and obliged to those who used to gather in Krzyzowa."[34]

After these emotional events Mazowiecki and Kohl signed a joint statement on 14 November that stipulated some very far-reaching agreements and compromises.[35] As a result of this historic trip, Poland and the FRG agreed to cooperate economically and politically, including billions of deutsche marks debt assistance and relief, respect for the territorial integrity and sovereignty of all European states within current borders, and protection of the rights of Poles and Germans living in each other's states. Importantly, this last area focused on upholding the teaching of both languages in each state's schools, publications in both languages freely imported and distributed, cultural institutes and libraries established in both states, war memorials preserved and protected, and more effective application processing for the resettling of minorities in both countries.[36] Such agreements marked a serious improvement in Polish–German relations. Yet, during and immediately after Kohl's visit questions again arose over the uncertainty of Poland's western border, about which no concrete agreement occurred beyond the German statement of intent to guarantee of the border.

After Kohl's trip, both sides remained frustrated because Kohl, according to Polish *MSZ* advisors such as Hajnicz, expected clear support from Mazowiecki as the Berlin Wall collapsed. Rather, Mazowiecki, consumed with concerns about Poland's ties to the USSR and the Warsaw Pact, focused more on the uncertainty over Kohl's policies toward the Polish–German border, not wholehearted public support for German unification. Furthermore, even after the fall of the Berlin Wall, Chancellor Kohl stated that he remained bound by the German Constitution regarding confirmation of the Polish–German border and that only a unified German parliament could approve the conformation of the Polish–German border. More importantly, the unexpected fall of the Berlin Wall forced Kohl to focus on the larger issues of the likely collapse of the GDR and the decision to consider unifying both German states. Given that the GDR still existed, Kohl needed to contend not only with a separate East German leadership in disarray, but also his own parliament and right-wing nationalists, some of whom vocally clamored for former German territory in Poland.[37]

To voice some of his dissatisfaction about the Oder–Neisse border issue, Foreign Minister Skubiszewski took issue with Kohl while the chancellor was still traveling around Poland. The Polish foreign minister argued, "we respect the Germans' right to self-determination, but within the framework of the existing borders, which are part of the European order." Once again, he returned to the international legal formula he employed upon becoming foreign minister, not only to define a new Polish–German relationship, but also to delineate the broad thrust of Poland's foreign policy. By contending that "the unification of Germany is a European question now. . . . Whether a new big power develops in the heart of Europe—because a reunited Germany is a big power—is a question for all of Europe and, in particular, for Germany's neighbors." It remained critical to understand, Skubiszewski emphasized, that "the situation that developed after the war cannot be changed now under any circumstances. . . . There are [German] politicians who say that there is still the problem of the peace treaty and there is still the problem of the borders of 1937. . . . We should forget 1937 now."[38] Even with the great likelihood of German unification, the Polish foreign minister maintained Poland's top priority for the confirmation of the current Polish–German border. By using the December 1970 Polish–German treaty as his foundation and advancing its principles in the November 1989 Polish–German joint statement, the Polish foreign minister certainly wanted to support the healing between the two former adversaries. Skubiszewski's larger objective, however, remained to solidify the Polish–German relationship by obtaining the international legal document to confirm the border once and for all. That way, Skubiszewski hoped to build a true Polish–German partnership in order to reintegrate into Europe.

The Oder–Neisse Border Uncertainty and German Unification

Before Skubiszewski developed the Polish–German partnership, he confronted the German chancellor's politically ambiguous ten-point German unification plan, which failed to mention the integrity of the Oder–Neisse border. The failure by Kohl in his surprise 28 November Bundestag speech to uphold Bonn's intent from the joint Polish–German statement two weeks earlier caused more consternation for Warsaw. Skubiszewski wanted to finish the momentous year by obtaining Bonn's definitive commitment to draft a final border agreement according to a concerted timetable.

Given the chancellor's ten-point plan, Skubiszewski now faced a number of German political uncertainties. Increasingly, the Kohl government concentrated on its reelection strategy for the fall 1990 German elections, particularly regarding the problem of the far-right German Republican Party, which challenged the Polish–German border's integrity. Secondly, Skubiszewski confronted Poland's left- and right-wing political parties, primarily Communists and nationalists, who traditionally agitated against perceived German revanchism, even if Bonn's official policy rejected German right-wing fanaticism. Some left- and right-wing Polish criticism of the Mazowiecki government centered on the Polish leader's reluctance to castigate Kohl publicly. They pressured Mazowiecki's government to condemn the German chancellor's failure to recognize his own Bundestag's 8 November declaration never to question Poland's border.[39] Finally, Skubiszewski understood that German unification entailed changes in German law in order for Bonn to recognize the Oder–Neisse border. Because of his international legal expertise, the Polish foreign minister knew that acknowledgment of the Oder–Neisse border by a unified Germany entailed a slow, step-by-step process. Nevertheless, all of these drawbacks failed to deter Skubiszewski from trying to gain German and international acceptance of Poland's post-Communist European reintegration. Ultimately, Skubiszewski's underlying criterion for creating a Polish–German relationship stemmed from finding common ground to integration, not further Central European upheaval.[40]

When Skubiszewski delivered his lengthy response in the Polish parliament on Kohl's ten-point unification plan, he elaborated the comprehensive international legal requirements to confirm Poland's post–World War II western border.[41] Undoubtedly, he underlined Poland's intent when he stated "the recognition of Poland's western border without understatements, as we have always emphasized, is a fundamental premise of Polish–German reconciliation." Moreover, he underscored that the German chancellor's plan "assumed a significant change in the existing political, military, and territorial system in the heart of Europe." The German unification plan, Skubiszewski argued, should account for the new situation it created in Europe because it affected not only all unified Germany's neighbors, but also all of the four powers. For Poland, a "new power" in the heart of Europe defined "a great problem of world politics." That made all the more disturbing the "ambiguity" over the "real legal position" of Bonn's plan.[42]

In this parliamentary speech, the Polish foreign minister also stressed that the German chancellor and foreign minister assured Polish interlocutors in Warsaw that "any change regarding the two German states would not violate anybody's security, and in particular would not violate the security of the Germans' neighbors." Such a commitment satisfied Poland but, given the rapid acceleration of events from the Berlin Wall's collapse to Kohl's ten-point plan, Skubiszewski declared that "we must demand a clear and unconditional stand in the matter of borders. . . . The FRG gave its consent to the Oder–Neisse line as the western border of Poland, in the normalization treaty of 1970." Moreover, he asserted "the border on the Oder–Neisse is part of the European order." To pursue European unification, not only in Bonn, Skubiszewski stated Poland upheld the tenet that the emerging post–Cold War European states must "unite within established borders and without territorial disputes; Poland has no such disputes with anyone."[43] Yet, Skubiszewski still signaled his flexibility concerning German unification in his parliamentary speech.

By boldly articulating his unification vision to the Polish parliament, Skubiszewski first called attention to unified German membership in NATO. He stated that "history does not know cases of confederations, not to mention federations, where the members are part of different alliances and different military organizations."[44] This path-breaking statement acknowledged support for and acceptance of a future unified Germany in NATO, a position at variance with that of the USSR and delineated before in statements by the United States, Great Britain, and France; the latter two states were opposed to unification. Importantly, first-hand U.S. policy-making accounts of German unification divulge that only in late January 1990 did talk initially begin publicly on unified Germany in NATO by the key states involved.[45] Though Skubiszewski's speech received little international attention, he clearly enunciated Poland's priorities toward unification for the coming months: convince the four powers involved of the pragmatic role Poland sought to play in negotiations; gain confirmation of the Oder–Neisse border by consistently lobbying Bonn, NATO, and Warsaw Pact capitals, even as Poland developed a strategy to distance itself from the Pact's military structures; and build support for unified Germany in NATO.

As the turbulent year came to a close, Skubiszewski gave another revealing interview about the Oder–Neisse border that expanded on some of the points he raised to the Polish parliament. First, he explained Poland's rationale for separating the issues of the integrity of the Oder–Neisse border from German unification, citing the idea that if two bordering states determine to unite, they unite "within their existing borders." The German unification process within the framework of "international law and in light of European politics," as he described it, remained separate from the issue of affirming the Polish–German border. Furthermore, regarding post–World War II Franco–German cooperation as a model for Polish–German reconciliation, Skubiszewski stressed that such cooperation grew from the strong basis of the Franco–German border agreement. Similarly, he contended that Warsaw and Bonn needed to negotiate a border treaty before Polish–German reconciliation could truly develop. Second, Skubiszewski asked rhetorically why the Germans agreed that the future status of Berlin's division remained an issue for the allied powers to decide when Bonn rejected four-power involvement in German unification. He declared that "involvement of the great powers has remained as a relic of the war, just as Berlin has remained a relic of the war." Third, unlike European counterparts, Skubiszewski felt compelled to distinguish between German "unification" and the misinterpreted "reunification." By not using "reunification," he underlined that Poland avoided misunderstanding about "something that was a fact in the past. True, in the past the old 'German Reich' was a fact, but a unification of the two Germanys would be something new." Finally, he portrayed the eastern territory Poland lost compared to the western lands it gained at the end of World War II,[46] stressing "Poland was not at the negotiating table when the decisions were made at Yalta. Almost half of Poland went to the Soviet Union. That is why the great powers decided to give the German areas east of the Oder and the Neisse to Poland." He concluded, "people also seem to forget that at that time the supreme authority in Germany belonged to the armies of occupation. . . . Regardless of what form it takes, a possible German unification must be seen as a European question."[47]

As Poland moved away from its Communist "satellite" status, Skubiszewski tried to engage Bonn in negotiations on several issues and attempted to steer a cautious course toward Moscow, since Soviet Warsaw Pact troops remained stationed on Polish territory. In effect, Skubiszewski intended to establish a bridge with Germany in order to reintegrate into Europe. Yet, Warsaw remained sensitive to the changes in Central Europe confronting the USSR and the integrity of the Soviet Bloc. Skubiszewski's foreign policy vision concentrated on fostering, sustaining, and preserving his middle power's evolving democratic values based on pluralistic development, greater security, and decreased threats. He wanted to broaden the nascent partnership with Bonn by projecting an image as a regional facilitator. By bridging and cooperating constructively with the stronger FRG, Skubiszewski wanted to remove the onus of international isolation, given Poland's harsh martial law era and the battles it periodically lost against its more powerful neighboring states. Unlike Warsaw's aggressive, balancing, and disastrous policies between Nazi Germany and Stalinist Russia during the 1930s, for example, resulting in Poland's isolation and ending in the consequences of World War II, Skubiszewski's *MSZ* resolved to maximize Poland's post-Communist security peacefully and constructively.[48]

Trade-Offs on Alignment Strategies toward the Oder–Neisse Border

By maintaining his nonthreatening stance on European borders and international legal arbitration regarding German unification, Skubiszewski demonstrated the beginnings of Warsaw's bridging strategy. Such a long-term state-to-state vision supported principles enshrined in multilateral forums like NATO, the EC, the CSCE, and the Council of Europe. However, the *MSZ* needed to evaluate its options to designate a specialized middle power role within its larger European integration strategy. This meant using incentives, in some cases deciding to employ a carrot-and-stick policy, to gain FRG verification of the all-important Oder–Neisse border.

The winter–spring in 1990 signified a period of rapid development in Polish foreign policy. Skubiszewski altered his stance several times vis-à-vis Bonn to try to obtain concessions on the Oder–Neisse border, benefiting by employing some tactics, but missing opportunities with other alignment maneuvering. The first major test of 1990 occurred during Skubiszewski's early February trip to Bonn to discuss the quickening pace of German unification and Bonn's increasing role in European security. Initially he wanted to reiterate privately Poland's desire for a greater German public commitment to the Oder–Neisse border. Secondly, Skubiszewski remained determined to demonstrate Poland's commitment to a stable German unification process to increase European stability, not decrease it. Third, the foreign minister underscored Poland's support for the future united Germany's full NATO integration. Skubiszewski believed that Warsaw's commitment to this goal showed Poland's practical and bold concept for European security. At that time, he remained the only European foreign minister publicly to support the FRG's commitment to a future unified Germany in NATO.[49] It appeared that he thought Poland's advocacy on such an important issue held the carrot out to Bonn in exchange for confirmation of the Oder–Neisse border. However, Poland increasingly saw that the German leadership's predilection for the geopolitical status quo toward the East too often delayed fundamental changes in European security and defense policy. An example that soon created tension between Bonn and Warsaw focused on the FRG's belief that Soviet troops need not necessarily withdraw from Poland.[50] This German predilection soon resulted in serious frustrations that easily might have been avoided, Warsaw argued in hindsight, if both states had communicated better and agreed earlier than in late 1991 on force withdrawals.[51]

Although Skubiszewski's trip marked an improvement in Polish–German relations, he still came away empty-handed on further clarification of the Polish–German border. The main reason he determined to bolster Chancellor Kohl's unification plan stemmed from his fear that Soviet and East German calls for a unified neutral Germany defined an "unclear, impractical, and maybe dangerous [status] for the future."[52] Skubiszewski also well understood Poland's limited role in influencing the German–Soviet talks about unification and believed Poland should support Kohl's strategy toward Moscow to facilitate Poland's western border guarantee. Given that Kohl expected to travel to the USSR to meet Gorbachev a few days after Skubiszewski departed Bonn, the foreign minister stated that "we are neighbors situated in a geo-strategic region in Europe. . . . We naturally have common interests and must develop these interests." To place Poland's two powerful neighbors in a broader context, he said "the existence of a German–Polish community of interests and a Polish–Soviet community of interests, is in the interest of Europe." However, the foreign minister added, "I am afraid of a single and completely independent German path. The Germanys should be incorporated into various European structures. . . . We must be thinking today—and in the long-term—about new European structures and about a new European security system, before unification can safely take place." Skubiszewski then delineated the key Polish foreign policy priorities. By declaring that "[Bonn] will explain certain circumstances which will provide the USSR with some guarantees and assurances, and they will show a path along which one should proceed, assuming that a united Germany can remain in NATO."[53] Hence, the foreign minister claimed Poland's stake, albeit limited, in the emerging European security structure.

Yet, the foreign minister still found himself in an awkward position when asked his views in a press conference with the German foreign minister about Poland's stance toward NATO forces in unified Germany. In trying to portray a conciliatory response regarding Moscow's almost certain opposition to the inclusion of a unified Germany in NATO, Skubiszewski equivocated by saying he "could not yet get friendly with such a thought in the current conditions in Europe. We would like to avoid a move of NATO troops to the East." Instead of staving off debate, Skubiszewski then created more problems for himself in Poland's future negotiating position toward Moscow, when he stated that "other practical solutions in case of unification must be sought here. . . . One must not forget that Soviet troops, however reduced, will remain on GDR territory."[54] This conviction later hindered his efforts to negotiate Soviet force withdrawals from Polish territory, as Poland delayed starting withdrawal negotiations with Moscow. By focusing too much on Polish–German issues and believing Moscow remained flexible for the foreseeable future, Skubiszewski deemed he first needed to handle specific issues such as the uncertainty over the Oder–Neisse border before commencing force withdrawal talks with the USSR.

Moreover, the Polish focus on German–NATO issues unexpectedly detracted from Skubiszewski's objective on the Polish–German border question. Compounded by Kohl's continual preoccupation with his reelection campaign until the early fall of 1990, the foreign minister received only a verbal German commitment in Bonn on the Oder–Neisse border.[55] Skubiszewski put the best spin on the German response by declaring that Germany would "join together, which means the FRG, the GDR, and Berlin: nothing more, nothing less. The border remains."[56] Thus, Skubiszewski left Bonn without any stronger German border commitment beyond the 14 November 1989 joint Polish–German statement and faced a series of conflicting policy decisions in the coming weeks.

Given Poland's commitment for unified Germany's NATO integration, Skubiszewski believed such an issue as Soviet force withdrawals from Poland remained secondary. However, he still needed to contend with the surprise assertion in mid-January by Polish presidential aspirant Lech Walesa that Soviet forces must withdraw from Poland. Subsequently, Skubiszewski also confronted Walesa's denunciation that "stationing them [Soviet troops in Poland] is a waste of money."[57] Therefore, Skubiszewski and the Polish government found themselves in a bind. Increasingly, the conservative advisors around Walesa decried Poland's hesitancy to initiate force withdrawal talks as an affront to Polish sovereignty, particularly when they claimed the Polish government appeared overly cautious toward a weak USSR. Additionally, though Walesa's inner circle remained supportive of Skubiszewski's overall German strategy, they criticized him for separating German and Eastern policies—specifically, force withdrawal negotiations—and rejected the foreign minister's methodical course between both neighboring states. At the same time, these radical arguments resonated publicly in Warsaw because Prague and Budapest brokered force withdrawal agreements with Moscow on their own timetables. Such negotiating by smaller states irked Poland's conservatives. They disagreed that Skubiszewski needed to delay negotiations with Moscow, criticizing his seemingly sole focus on German policy without significant changes to Poland's Eastern policy.[58]

Such criticism of the government actually triggered one unusual and short-lived balancing maneuver by Skubiszewski and Mazowiecki between Bonn and Moscow as another way to win concessions from Germany on the Oder–Neisse border. Just after returning from Bonn, Skubiszewski broke with the moderated approach he held toward the unifying FRG and, attempting to counter German hesitation on the border issue, claimed that now "Poland attaches the same importance to its relations with the USSR," as with the FRG.[59] Mazowiecki soon followed with a more revealing statement that sparked a lot of controversy. On 22 February the Polish premier declared, "like every nation we must also look at our security realistically, from the perspective of the balance of forces, from the perspective of alliances, and we must assess from that perspective the continued presence of the [Soviet] forces."[60] The premier's declaration suggested that Soviet forces should remain stationed in Poland and opposed Walesa's statements. Moreover, Mazowiecki now ran the risk of erroneously trying to balance Moscow against Bonn by threatening to keep Soviet troops on Polish territory in order to get Bonn to concede on Poland's western border.[61] Yet, on 10 February 1990 in Moscow, Kohl's efforts proved remarkably successful when Gorbachev agreed, not only to German unification, but also to a unified Germany in NATO. Even though they pressured Bonn about Soviet forces, Mazowiecki and Skubiszewski soon recognized that, if Poland wanted to participate in the emerging "2 Plus 4" talks on German unification, Warsaw needed Bonn's approval to join the four powers. Since the FRG leadership wanted to achieve Germany's economic and security unification within the coming months, Kohl concentrated on negotiating Soviet troop withdrawals from East German territory without focusing on Soviet withdrawals from Poland.[62]

By the spring the Polish government conceded its threats to Bonn over Soviet troop deployments had failed to capture Bonn's attention and Skubiszewski determined to succeed in gaining Poland's participation in the emerging "2 Plus 4" talks. Though reluctant to accede to Warsaw's request for "2 Plus 4" participation, especially given Poland's hedge against the FRG on Soviet troops, Bonn agreed to include the Poles, but only at the urging of Moscow and Washington.[63] As the "seventh" member of German unification negotiations in July 1990, Skubiszewski won a diplomatic victory, but suffered a setback in negotiations on withdrawals in late 1990 and 1991, a setback having significant repercussions during the next year for Warsaw.[64]

Although the Polish leadership admitted its failure to affect Kohl's German unification policies, Warsaw still upheld unified Germany's right to join NATO. In his April speech to the Polish parliament, his first comprehensive public review of foreign policy, Skubiszewski gave several reasons for why Poland had changed its strategy toward the FRG. First, he only termed as "a hypothetical question" the "extent" of a connection to the "temporary stationing" of Soviet troops on Polish territory. Secondly, he declared Soviet force withdrawals as a "foregone conclusion." Finally, he stated that Warsaw now believed "the evolution of the German problem" allowed Poland enough bargaining room with Bonn to find a solution to the border issue. Skubiszewski also revealed his gratitude for the recent resolutions of the FRG and newly elected GDR parliaments, which favored the current Polish–German border, while he admitted Poland's limited role in obtaining Kohl's formal border commitment. Significantly, the foreign minister said that "there can be no European unity with a divided Germany and all of us desire European unity."[65] Therefore, Poland's carrot-and-stick policy toward Bonn, a strategy focused on alignment with an uncertain USSR against an increasingly confident FRG, failed to convince the Kohl government to affirm the post–World War II Polish-German border before the December 1990 all-German elections.

Given Bonn's priority to unify economically and secure Moscow's commitment for admitting united Germany to NATO in the early spring, Skubiszewski dropped the balancing strategy and now focused entirely on a bandwagoning policy to demonstrate to the FRG Poland's beneficial role in the "2 Plus 4" talks. On 30 April 1990, he sent his U.S., French, and U.K. counterparts a diplomatic note to underscore Poland's commitment to participate "constructively" and "contribute" to an "early and successful conclusion." To illustrated Poland's positive role, Skubiszewski compromised by promising to "reaffirm" the current Polish–German border at the "outset" of German unification rather than before unification.[66] This compromise marked a departure from Skubiszewski's stand and aided ties to Bonn.

On 2 May, another development favoring Polish foreign policy transpired when FRG president Richard von Weizsaecker and foreign minister Genscher came to Warsaw and delivered the most reassuring public statements on the Polish–German border. During his presidential dinner, von Weizsaecker paid tribute to Poland's "pioneering role" and its "courageous," "peaceful," and "inspiring example" for its neighbors and for transforming Europe. The German president, albeit a ceremonial figure, remained revered domestically and internationally for his moral standing and integrity. His declaration to the Polish leadership that night, therefore, played an enormous role in allaying apprehension over the border. The president assured his audience that "Poland can without reservation trust that the border questions between us are, in their substance, irrevocably clarified and that in the process of German unification that is coming about they will receive the necessary internationally binding treaty." Not only did the German president proclaim that Poland's border remained inviolable, but he also reassured Central Europeans when he stated that "we respect it [Polish–German border] and do not have now or in the future any territorial claims against Poland or any other neighbor."[67]

For his part, Skubiszewski viewed the FRG president's visit as a tremendous success and believed that both states crossed a certain threshold in improving their relations. The Polish foreign minister praised the FRG president, summarizing the visit in the German press as "of historic importance" and saying "there is the fact that for me and us Poles it is a source of satisfaction that a statesman of this federal president's stature comes to us with such moving words. Now reconciliation between the two peoples has to a great extent become a reality."[68] By the time of von Weizsaecker's departure, Prime Minister Mazowiecki illustrated the turnaround in Polish foreign policy by indicating that Poland no longer required that the FRG sign a border treaty before unification.[69]

Such a decision by the Polish government marked another turning point in Polish–German relations. Both sides, now more confident than at any other time in the post–Cold War era, trusted verbal commitments as a prelude to a border treaty. Skubiszewski and the Polish government felt more secure after von Weizsaecker's critical trip and believed that Kohl's December reelection appeared likely, with Bonn's tacit commitment to agree to the border treaty. For Poland, the overriding concern about its border subsided with Warsaw's inclusion in the penultimate round of the "2 Plus 4" talks. Unlike during the Yalta and Potsdam summits at the close of World War II, the great powers included Poland in deciding this crucial Central European security question because the Mazowiecki government showed cooperative behavior for the stronger "2 Plus 4" participating states and for expediting unification. Though Polish–German ties improved with the discussion of the Polish–German border during the preparation for the 17 July participation of Skubiszewski at the "2 Plus 4" talks, the FRG and USSR also met secretly. They negotiated on 16 July 1990, with implications for Soviet force withdrawals from Germany and without the involvement of Poland or any other of the four powers.

Unbeknownst to Skubiszewski as he traveled to Paris on 17 July to meet with his counterparts for the first time at the "2 Plus 4" talks, the Kohl–Gorbachev talks in the North Caucasian mountain retreat of Arkhyz resulted in the surprise Zheleznovodsk Accord. First, Kohl decisively moved to fix German monetary, economic, and social union on 1 July 1990 to stem the tide of even greater upheaval in both the FRG and GDR, particularly to prevent thousands more East German citizens seeking refuge in the more stable FRG. By making a one-to-one exchange rate between the deutsche mark and ost mark, Kohl also sought to gain the critical East German votes he needed to win the December election. Secondly, after the conciliatory and reassuring visit of his president and foreign minister to Poland in May, the German Chancellor believed he now could seal with Gorbachev the final agreement to have unified Germany in NATO and to obtain a commitment for Soviet forces to withdraw from East German territory by 1994. At their press conference in Zheleznovodsk the German and Soviet leaders agreed on German unification and Soviet troop withdrawals from the GDR. Though the Zheleznovodsk Accord symbolized Germany's European-focused role and the USSR's acquiescence, both of which served Polish interests, Warsaw's exclusion from the German–Soviet negotiations only compounded Poland's miscalculated, self-imposed delays on its own Soviet force withdrawal talks.[70]

The Paris and Moscow foreign ministerial meetings among the "2 Plus 4" states, however, represented a significant achievement for Skubiszewski's German policy as they enshrined his tenets in the final documentation. The international legal formula Skubiszewski steadfastly expounded, both as Poland's first post-Communist foreign minister and as a respected international law professor, soon became part of the "2 Plus 4" treaty. Skubiszewski's Paris participation allowed the foreign minister to highlight the legal inviolability of Poland's western border and to exhibit Warsaw's contribution to European security in support for German unification and greater European integration from late 1989. It also placed the Polish foreign minister on the world stage as part of the new, post–Cold War Europe.[71] Just before the conclusion of the treaty, Skubiszewski gave a radio interview on the fifty-first anniversary of the outbreak of World War II. In this important interview he declared that the Germans "ought to perceive and ought to see in their policy the great advantage resulting from the fact that they have no joint border with Russia." It remained important, Skubiszewski underlined, that "the Polish state, a strong, rich one with a democratic system, functioning well, being a stabilizing factor in a rich Europe, is situated between themselves and Russia." More importantly, he told his listeners "such a Poland need not fear its German and Russian neighbors." Unlike the Poland of the interwar era, he stressed, "which aimed to keep an equal distance from Moscow and Berlin, we make it our aim to have very good and close cooperation with both Moscow and Bonn."[72] His speech served as a prelude to the final "2 Plus 4" ceremony two weeks later.

The "Treaty on the Final Settlement with Respect to Germany" on 12 September in Moscow concluded the penultimate step in Skubiszewski's strategy for creating a new and better post–World War II Polish–German relationship. The Moscow document stood for the principles Skubiszewski promoted from his first days as foreign minister. It stipulated that both unified Germany and post-Communist Poland "shall confirm the existing border between them in a treaty that is binding under international law. The united Germany has no territorial claims whatsoever against other states and shall not assert any in the future." Only the Polish–German Oder–Neisse border treaty remained for Skubiszewski and Poland to sign.[73]

With the treaty on Germany's post–World War II settlement signed, Germany formally unified in October, opening the way for final agreement on the Oder–Neisse treaty. On 14 November 1990, exactly one year after both states signed their joint statement in Warsaw, both foreign ministers again met in Warsaw to conclude the historic "Treaty on the Confirmation of the Polish–German Border." The signing ceremony occurred several weeks before Chancellor Kohl easily won reelection, proving Bonn's verbal commitment to Warsaw after the political balancing Kohl felt he needed to use against his domestic right-wing opposition. As Kohl and Mazowiecki watched, the two foreign ministers finally closed this harsh and difficult historical chapter. Skubiszewski took great pride in shaping and implementing the Polish–German model of reconciliation along the same parameters as the Franco–German post–World War II relationship with its internationally defined legal framework for ties.[74] After the ceremony, the Polish foreign minister said, "the Polish–German border treaty is not only a Polish matter but also a German one. The treaty is proof of all-German consent to the border. . . . Germany signed it of its own free will."[75] For Skubiszewski, Poland achieved four of its five post-Communist foreign policy objectives toward the FRG. First, Bonn recognized Poland as an independent international actor. Secondly, the four powers played key roles in German unification. Third, the four powers included Poland on issues critical to Warsaw's national security. Finally, Germany now guaranteed formally the Polish–German border. As the press commentary concluded, "in the 1950s, when the FRG and France embarked on the task of building a European Community, the border along the Oder–Neisse became the actual line that divided us from Europe. . . . Now, the Yalta border mechanism is dismantled. For both states, the border treaty is one of the most significant events in their post-war policy."[76]

Poland's geostrategic circumstances from 1989 to 1990 differed from both its interwar-era policy of balancing Germany against Russia and its semi-sovereign Yalta status during the Cold War. From the outset of his terms as foreign minister, Skubiszewski focused on obtaining the objective of a Polish–German border treaty. Overall, Skubiszewski intended to work within the international legal framework with the four powers to confirm Poland's western border and to uphold, as much as possible, the strategy to bandwagon with Germany in favor of both Germany's unification and Poland's European reintegration. Despite Kohl's vacillation on the Polish–German border and Poland's attendant inconsistent, albeit short-lived and aggressively balancing, policy of Moscow against Bonn, Warsaw's confidence grew because the FRG remained politically, militarily, and economically integrated in NATO and the EC. Skubiszewski thus avowed the necessity of facilitating German unification in order to reintegrate into Europe.

After achieving his objective to reduce Poland's historic security dilemma between Germany and Russia with the November 1990 Polish–German border treaty, Skubiszewski envisioned Warsaw serving as a "bridge," not a "buffer zone," between West and East. Poland understood that its reintegration into Europe depended on a European Germany. Poland recognized from the beginning of its post–Communist democratic path that it needed to tie its Western integration strategy to the stronger Germany, overcoming great historical animosities against Germany and the German people. Certainly, the road toward reintegration presaged rough times politically, economically, and militarily as Polish society continued to undergo serious democratization and domestic reform. In assessing Skubiszewski's foreign policy strategy toward German unification in the period before the Polish–German border treaty, however, we can see that the *MSZ* mistakenly attempted tactical maneuvers by trying to balance the continued stationing of Soviet forces on Polish territory against the FRG.

Upon recognition of its balancing policy failure, Skubiszewski shifted more concertedly toward a bridging strategy to reduce any continuing post–Cold War perceptions of Germany's historically threatening posture. On the one hand, the

Polish Government's balancing tactic against the FRG failed to convince the Kohl leadership on the Polish–German border question. On the other hand, the temporary Polish balancing alignment succeeded partially with Soviet support for Poland's "2 Plus 4" participation. Once Skubiszewski and Mazowiecki realized that Moscow's support for Poland's participation in the "2 Plus 4" talks leveraged Kohl diplomatically, Warsaw concentrated on a nonthreatening policy toward the FRG. Ultimately, by remaining sensitive to its limited impact between these two larger states and to its role as the first Warsaw Pact or Western state to support membership of unified Germany in NATO, Skubiszewski needed the trade-off of Poland's aggressive stance. Poland's challenging both the legitimacy of the Warsaw Pact and Soviet troops stationed in Poland brought the emerging democratized Warsaw Pact member too far ahead of even the rapid chain of events in Central-East Europe. This recognition provided Skubiszewski the perspective to develop a moderated, cooperative bridging policy by spring 1990, a policy that avoided any further competitive maneuvers perceived as playing states off one another, whether aggressively balancing or bandwagoning against the FRG. As a result, Polish foreign policy–makers gained the benefit of German respect and signed a historic border treaty that formed the basis for Warsaw's European reintegration.

The Polish–German model exemplified how states, formerly enemies, aligned to promote regional stability without long-term recourse to a threat-based strategy. Furthermore, this cooperative model enabled both states to forge more effective policies, respectively, with an unstable Moscow. Both states felt more secure with their domestic reforms. Yet, the USSR's growing internal instability and disintegration over the next year tested the new Polish–German cooperation and challenged Warsaw and Bonn over Soviet force withdrawals.

Managing Strains: Bridging between Unification and Disintegration

Though 1991 started auspiciously for Polish–German relations with the completion of the border treaty and the beginning of negotiations on a comprehensive state treaty, the increasing Soviet conservative backlash negatively affected the negotiation over the transit of Soviet troop withdrawals from both Germany and Poland. As Poland tried to begin troop withdrawal talks formally with Moscow in September 1990, Skubiszewski also attempted to enlist Bonn's support against Soviet obstinacy on withdrawal negotiations.[77] At the beginning of the year, the Polish foreign minister depicted the growing Warsaw–Bonn friendship as one that in 1989 and 1990 "produced a desirable breakthrough that lays open the way for the establishment of the Polish–German community of interests." Poland foresaw the possibility of resolving some of the outstanding issues focused on minorities in both states and post–World War II compensation for Nazi harm done to Poles and for Germans expelled by Poles.[78] Furthermore,

Skubiszewski believed that "Poles and Germans could make an essential contribution to the unification of our continent and to a common collective security system," particularly as other Western European states began to see Poland contributing to stability and security in Central Europe.[79]

The first round of Polish–Soviet force withdrawal talks actually began in November 1990 and Warsaw's negotiating strategy focused on the important dimension of Soviet transit from Germany via Poland. From the outset the Polish strategy, drafted in the summer of 1990 by the head of the Polish negotiating team, Grzegorz Kostrzewa-Zorbas, one of the few *Solidarnosc* activists to join the *MSZ* after the foreign minister, underscored that "the Soviet Army must withdraw from Poland much sooner than from Germany." His reasoned that "the withdrawal from Poland cannot be dependent legally, or in any other way, on the withdrawal from Germany." This argument stemmed from the *MSZ*'s view that, contrary to the Zheleznovodsk Accord, "Poland must remain a fully independent strategic entity, not a middle ground between big players. German-Soviet agreements must not determine Polish policy," unless negotiated with Poland, just as Czechoslovakia and Hungary independently negotiated force withdrawal arrangements.[80] Given the major steps Poland and Germany took during the preceding year, Bonn's hesitation to start state treaty talks and its silence regarding Polish positions on force withdrawal transit from Germany during the initial months of 1991 frustrated Warsaw.

The Polish foreign minister indicated that he realized the electoral changes in unified Germany, including new personnel on German negotiating delegations, temporarily delayed movement toward final state treaty drafting. However, he expressed greater concern over the lack of response from Bonn to the larger issues of Soviet force withdrawals and the timing and legality of the transits from both states. In a major foreign policy speech to Parliament in February 1991, Skubiszewski argued "the agreement on the termination of the stationing of troops here should be concluded at the same time as that on the transit of troops." To underscore his concern, Skubiszewski declared that "the legal basis of the transit, however, has serious gaps and imprecision. That is why it is necessary to negotiate a detailed agreement which will provide a precise and safe regulation to all kinds of transit." As his rationale for a legal document, he tried to gain support from both Bonn and Moscow. He maintained that Poland constantly supported German unification by its "constructive approach to the consequences of this unity as a European event." Moreover, he believed that Warsaw's intent to negotiate force withdrawals with Bonn and Moscow demonstrated an important effort to reduce regional tensions and still adhere to principles of sovereignty. Yet, the Polish foreign minister remained adamant that "there can be no chaos and no forced transports without consulting us. . . . The fact that we are on stand by to allow transits from Germany is proof of our support for the unification of Germany."[81] Even though Skubiszewski's arguments appeared logical, Bonn negotiators focused on German–Soviet withdrawal talks to Poland's detriment.

Despite Skubiszewski's clear appeal and intent toward Bonn and Moscow, the FRG remained distant about its strategy toward Soviet force withdrawals, indicating its desire to see an orderly withdrawal of Soviet troops from its territory, no matter the situation in Poland. Like the German–Soviet negotiations on German unification, which basically excluded Poland, Bonn assumed Poland needed to accommodate Moscow by maintaining Soviet forces on Polish territory. According to Kostrzewa-Zorbas, Bonn's reluctance to show leadership in Central Europe underscored that "no German position developed, not to mention any active policy, even though Germany benefited the most when Russian troops moved more than six hundred kilometers eastward."[82] Like Chancellor Kohl's vague stance toward the Polish–German border until just before his re-election, Bonn again displayed erratic and, in Warsaw's view, unhelpful behavior as Poland tried to negotiate with the USSR.[83] Granted, Bonn may still have smarted from Warsaw's unsuccessful and fleeting tactics against the FRG on Soviet troops stationed in Poland before unification. Additionally, Bonn may have found itself daunted by unification's requirements. Moreover, Bonn saw Moscow as more important to its security than Warsaw, believing that it had already resolved the outstanding geopolitical problems in the Polish-German relationship with the border treaty's signing. Clearly, Kohl staunchly defended Gorbachev as the Soviet leader lost a growing number of political battles to hard-liners.

Paradoxically, Germany's relentless defense of Gorbachev contrasted sharply with Soviet actions in the Baltic nations that January. The harsh images of Soviet military assaults against Lithuanians and Latvians coincided with the Soviet military's pressuring of Poland, when Soviet trains from Germany attempted to transit Poland. In response, the Polish border authorities prevented trains carrying weaponry from transiting Polish territory, though not Soviet trains carrying military personnel and dependents.[84] Indeed, Bonn's close relationship to Gorbachev, its intent to have Soviet forces withdraw from German territory by 1994, and its unyielding belief that Gorbachev's USSR needed to remain intact put Kohl's government in the awkward position. Kohl continued to defend Gorbachev as the USSR rapidly deteriorated, even as leading Russian reformists such as Boris El'tsin challenged the weakened Soviet leader. Nevertheless, developments in the USSR failed to move Bonn to discuss Polish initiatives regarding coordination of Polish and German positions on Soviet force withdrawals.[85]

As a result, the *MSZ* believed Germany lost valuable time to resolve a critical regional security issue. The chief Polish negotiator on Soviet force withdrawals revealed several important insights about Bonn's diplomacy since he also dealt with Bonn on European reintegration. First, Polish reintegration strategies into Europe caused tension when the Germans candidly told Polish force withdrawal negotiators in late 1990 that "Poland should neither join any Western organization [implying NATO and the EC] nor establish any entity that excluded the USSR" because of Gorbachev's instability. Kohl believed it owed Gorbachev much for the Soviet leader's courageous support of both German unification and unified German NATO membership. According to the *MSZ*, Bonn policymakers failed to see the benefits in late 1990 of Central European regional cooperation among Poles, Czechoslovaks, and Hungarians, fearing that cooperation mistakenly disrupted Soviet policy in Europe. The Germans worried about coordination by the three Central European states on security issues. After a number of Polish–German consultations in the spring of 1991, the Poles defused German concerns about Central Europe's regional security cooperation and Poland's European reintegration strategies.[86] Secondly, Warsaw worked closely with its Visegrad ministry counterparts to maintain "solidarity despite financial losses suffered by Prague and Budapest when they ignored a lucrative offer from Bonn to open substitute transit routes." Thirdly, as Germany negotiated timetables with Moscow, Bonn failed to provide Warsaw any details of its negotiations.[87] Thus, though Warsaw convinced Bonn of Central Europe's positive intent to reintegrate into Europe, Poland still faced German reluctance to coordinate on Soviet troop withdrawals.

Without Soviet compliance to basic Polish negotiating terms in late 1990 and throughout 1991, Polish negotiators also experienced setbacks to their diplomatic overtures to the FRG. The *MSZ* team declared that "as long as you [Soviets] neither accept our proposal of the final date of your troop withdrawal from our soil nor give us a reasonable counter proposal [Poland originally proposed the end of 1991], we cannot admit your transit trains, planes, and trucks. The issues of your withdrawal from Germany and from our country are of equal weight and none of them should be left unsolved." Further complications arose when the Poles found out in the spring of 1991 that the Soviets had persuaded the Germans to accept transit terms through Poland without consultation with Warsaw.[88] For Warsaw this directly infringed on Poland's sovereignty. The chief Polish force withdrawal negotiator again divulged that "the Soviets had told them [Bonn] a year earlier [spring 1990] that they had guaranteed transit via Poland," without negotiating with Warsaw and months before Warsaw initiated talks with Moscow. The Poles reacted angrily to German officials in the German Embassy in Warsaw and in talks in Bonn, with the question: "Why did they [Germans] assume that Poland was still a Soviet dependency?" In effect, *MSZ* officials argued that both Bonn and Moscow had consulted over Warsaw's head. In hindsight, *MSZ* officials contended that, without consulting the Poles, the Germans had set Polish–Soviet negotiations back by nearly two years.[89]

By the summer of 1991, both the Polish and German negotiators found more common ground in their strategies toward Moscow, even as instability increased in the USSR and culminated in the failed Soviet coup d'état that August. One Polish argument that resonated with German negotiators, even as the German leadership continued to uphold the precarious Gorbachev leadership, focused on rapid withdrawal of Soviet troops from Poland. German negotiators began to understand Soviet intentions better when the Polish interlocutors argued that Poland wanted to "deprive the much larger Soviet army remaining in Germany of significant military capability and effectiveness as a strategic asset or political leverage of the aggressive Moscow conservatives." Even so, Kostrzewa-Zorbas concluded that Poland's often awkward relationship with Bonn on Soviet troop withdrawals characterized a problem with the German mindset. In a way, he underlined that "Germans, psychologically used to living in a front-line state, responded that a foreign army in Poland was not their concern, only a Polish and Soviet concern."[90]

Even with the tensions between Warsaw and Bonn over Soviet troop withdrawals, Skubiszewski never lost sight that Poland needed Germany to reintegrate into Europe. Though tensions existed in the first half of 1991, the foreign minister still pursued his integrationist strategy via the FRG, by concluding incrementally new agreements and treaties. Warsaw discerned that no other state than Germany could assist its European reintegration as effectively. This explains why Skubiszewski strove to build what might initially be designated a nonpredatory bandwagoning policy with Bonn. By bandwagoning nonthreateningly with Germany, Poland gained the benefits of the stability the Kohl government wanted to promote to its east. Then, Poland could seek to build a larger bridge between Germany and Poland that extended to the USSR to unify as much of Europe as possible. Both Poland and Germany appreciated the post–Cold War objective of reducing animosity against each other and attempted to create a Polish–German model of reconciliation and cooperation akin to the Franco–German relationship. Simultaneous to the slow progress in their respective force withdrawal negotiations with Moscow, communication channels improved between Warsaw and Bonn so that, by June 1991, they finally agreed to the principles of their state treaty.[91]

German Advocacy of Poland's European Re-integration

The momentous treaty fulfilled a series of practical steps Skubiszewski had vowed to implement since 1989. That he succeeded with his German counterparts in less than two years remains remarkable. As he said during German press interviews the day of the treaty's Bonn signing, "democratic Poland and a united Germany are the expression of the great changes in Europe. From the Polish point of view, this logical consequence in Europeanization of foreign policy aims to link Poland closely to the West." Furthermore, he proclaimed that the treaty "creates the legal and political foundations for the community of interests of Poles and Germans."[92] Moreover, much of Skubiszewski's success resulted from the avid support of his German counterpart.

From the outset of Skubiszewski's appointment, Genscher rarely hesitated to lend whatever support was feasible, though his support sometimes clashed with positions taken by Kohl, particularly on the Polish–German border. Shortly before the treaty ceremony, Genscher first appealed to the EC directly in a public letter stating that though its "negotiations with Poland . . . are only making slow progress . . . the relaxation of trade restrictions and EC admission could be fulfilled as soon as possible."[93] The German foreign minister's commitment underscored some of the consequential portions agreed to by both states in the treaty, focusing on a united and free Europe based on minority rights, rule of law, sovereignty, territorial integrity, border inviolability, and regional security coordination.[94]

In contrast to their hostile history for most of the twentieth century, Poland and Germany now undertook to build a new and practical relationship. As Skubiszewski stated to the Polish Parliament, "the signing of the Treaty on Good-Neighborliness and Friendly Cooperation brings to an end the laying of the legal and political foundations of a Polish–German community of interests. . . . For, it is a reflection of the European option in Poland's foreign policy." At the ceremony, Skubiszewski noted that compensating the inmates of the concentration camps and forced laborers the Reich remained unresolved. But he announced the creation of the Polish–German Reconciliation Foundation to function with German funds to start once the respective parliaments ratified the treaty. Thus, Polish and German governments finally resolved to deal with this problem.[95] Despite this unresolved issue, the crowning post–Cold War achievement lay in the powerful German commitment to reintegrate the weaker Polish state into Europe politically, economically, and militarily.

Even as the USSR disintegrated in the aftermath of the unsuccessful August 1991 coup, Poland continued to expand links with Bonn. One significant development resulted from the first joint meeting of the Polish, German, and French foreign ministers in Weimar, Germany. Meeting just one week after the coup, the ministers agreed to cooperate on security predicaments confronting Europe, such as the threat of mass migration due to conditions in the crumbling USSR. Discussion of assistance to the post-Soviet successor states with Poland seen to play a role along with its important West European partners also demonstrated how the Polish–German relationship already helped promote Poland's continental reputation. For Skubiszewski, "France, Germany, and Poland will in the future have a great role to play in European cooperation. The good relations existing hitherto between Germany and France can now include Poland."[96] Collaboration also improved when, during the next visit of Genscher to Poland, both sides agreed to increase border cooperation and border crossings to promote cultural exchange and commerce. Furthermore, both ministers worked more closely on the emerging regional initiatives with the newly independent Baltics. Finally, Genscher repeated Germany's commitment to assist Poland with EC membership. Indeed, both ministers emphasized that "Poland could also become a bridge for closer links between its eastern neighbors and the EC."[97]

From 1992 to 1993, Skubiszewski also maintained his strategy to increase Polish–German ties, particularly economic links based on Poland's EC associate membership agreement in December 1991. Even as long-time foreign minister Genscher retired and Polish government transitions occurred amid almost annual domestic political turmoil between the president and his opponents, Skubiszewski consistently championed expanded Warsaw–Bonn ties as a means to increase Poland's European reintegration. Though Skubiszewski raised some concern in Parliament about the perceptions of German economic domination over Central Europe, he urged parliamentarians and the public to implement the many regional political and economic integration initiatives arising from the commitments in Polish–German state treaty. The foreign minister underscored the potential for Polish–German tension if Poland exaggerated claims that Germany wanted to control Poland economically, particularly from the more nationalistic Polish representatives from the Confederation for Independent Poland and the Christian–National Union. Skubiszewski recognized the need to gain political support to pass the pending EC associate membership legislation and pressed for greater parliamentary backing for Germany because of Bonn's key role in European reintegration.[98]

Confidence in German intentions grew when the new German foreign minister, Klaus Kinkel, made his first trip in Central and East European trip to Poland. During his visit, Kinkel declared that "on the way to Europe, Poland can build upon our support and solidarity. . . . Poland has already taken important steps on the path toward Europe." Skubiszewski responded by stating "we are definitely counting on Germany's support." He added, moreover, that Warsaw understood Kinkel's advice to revamp seriously Poland's legal system in order to meet EC requirements. In 1992, these statements formed the basis for continued development in Polish–German relations with progress on border and customs processing agreements, projects to link autobahns, military training, and interior ministry coordination, especially on counternarcotics cooperation. As the foreign ministers noted in late July, "both sides are implementing and putting into practice what has been legally agreed between us."[99]

Over what amounted to his final year as foreign minister, from fall 1992 to fall 1993, Skubiszewski harnessed the stronger public support by Germany for Polish European Union (EU)—the EC having transitioned and broadened to form the EU at the Maastricht Summit—and NATO membership. The German statements illustrated the success of Poland's strategy to reintegrate into Europe. After the short-lived and tumultuous domestic period under Prime Minister Jan Olszewski, during which Poland's German policy slowly but continually improved, Skubiszewski consolidated his reintegration strategy without domestic distractions within the more amenable government of Hanna Suchocka. During Suchocka's first key foreign policy address, Skubiszewski's impact resounded when Suchocka declared that "Poland does not make any territorial claims in relation to her neighbors, neither do any our neighbors question our borders." Moreover, she underscored that "Poland can promptly ensure its membership in NATO herself if she can guarantee its security by herself and, owing to friendly relations with neighbors, becomes a stabilizing factor in the region." Suchocka clearly tried to advance Warsaw–Bonn ties when she advocated strongly backing the FRG's "liaison" role to the EU and NATO for Poland. Finally, she upheld not only Germany's support for Poland's European reintegration, but also Bonn's need to build ties with the East "through Poland."[100]

Chapter 3

Several meetings with Chancellor Kohl and Foreign Minister Kinkel in late 1992 and 1993 provided the basis for consolidating Skubiszewski's German strategy. During the months before *Solidarnosc*'s first electoral loss in September 1993, Skubiszewski and the Suchocka government obtained the commitment from Chancellor Kohl that Skubiszewski carefully pursued over his nearly four years in office. In November, Kohl asserted Polish–German relations as "vital for Europe" and exclaimed that "our common goal is and should be the creation of neighborly relations as good as those between France and Germany. . . . Past misunderstandings cannot divert us from our goals." For Germany and Europe, the German chancellor said "we want a reformed Poland to find its place in the future European Union . . . [Poland] should know that Germany wants it to become part of the EU." For Suchocka and her delegation, the meeting with Kohl "is another step forward in European integration."[101] The meetings in September went even further, when Kohl affirmed that NATO leaders would consider Poland's determination to join the institution at the NATO summit in January 1994. Moreover, he told the press that "Poland has been an important part of the whole Europe and that is why it is normal for it to follow the road towards the community."[102] Given the Polish expectations for NATO membership, an objective Skubiszewski began to articulate in summer 1990 as he solidified bilateral neighborly ties, German support for Poland culminated an unprecedented, rapid implementation of Skubiszewski's strategy to redefine Polish–German relations. By guiding the *MSZ* for four years toward Poland's post–Communist objectives and transforming most of the goals into pragmatic and internationally respected policies, Skubiszewski attained German commitment for Poland's European reintegration.

Conclusion: Building Bridges
toward Germany and Beyond

From September 1989 until September 1993, Skubiszewski crafted a dynamic German policy that remained relatively consistent, having achieved the majority of the goals he defined for Poland, but with some temporary setbacks. For Skubiszewski the relationship with Germany, particularly during the stages of German unification, focused on obtaining the following four objectives in order to begin Poland's European reintegration. First, Poland required that Bonn unambiguously agree to Poland's western border in a treaty to conclude peacefully the outstanding uncertainty from the post–World War II territorial settlements. Second, to achieve this critical objective, Skubiszewski believed Poland also needed to gain Bonn's support for Poland as an independent actor in Central European security, primarily in the unification process. Furthermore, he recognized that Germany's rapid unification necessitated four-power control of the unification process, a crucial tenet he advocated throughout his forty-year academic career at Poznan University—well before he became Polish foreign minister. Lastly, the Polish foreign minister and his *MSZ* team believed strongly in trying to coordinate with unified Germany the orderly withdrawal of Soviet troops from both Poland and Germany, a national security objective that proved quite difficult to accomplish.

Skubiszewski's strategy stemmed primarily from his seminal notions about Polish–German relations. Poland's "nonpartisan interests" in foreign policy formulation arose from "reconciliation" and advancing "normalization of relations" toward a future unified Germany. This 1989 strategy buttressed Poland's development of relations with Bonn, but went much further than that of any Polish Communist leadership by recognizing German potential for unification. Poland no longer needed to resort to its "flight to the [Soviet] protectorate" to avoid residual Polish concerns over German irredentism. These ideas, emanating from the underground "Poland in Europe" seminars in the 1980s, immediately became Skubiszewski's post-Communist policy.[103] In early fall 1989, before any other member of the Warsaw Pact elected a post-Communist government, Poland signaled the need for four-power control of likely political and legal German unification. Skubiszewski convinced all states involved in German unification to consider Poland's legitimate security dilemma concerning the post–World War II integrity of the Oder–Neisse border. Though West Germany and the other great powers mostly ignored Poland in the early unification stages, all eventually heeded Skubiszewski's caveats during the four-power process in 1990.[104]

As the Polish government logrolled domestically to form a post-Communist Polish consensus on a new German policy, Skubiszewski aligned middle power Poland with an uncertain, great power West Germany to support its future unification in NATO. Such bandwagoning surprised not only Bonn, but also Moscow. Given Poland's nominal Warsaw Pact commitment, Skubiszewski gauged that endorsement of unified Germany in NATO would mitigate Polish–German border tensions and bilaterally build a regional trilateral bridge between Bonn and Moscow. In contrast to the USSR, Poland feared potentially neutral Germany. If Poland hid behind conceivable neutrality to avoid possible German unification, Warsaw's foreign policy–makers risked worsening historic security dilemmas between Bonn and Moscow. Even though Soviet troops remained stationed on Polish territory, Skubiszewski advocated unified Germany in NATO to promote nonthreatening European alignment and to secure an other-help means of regional stability without feasible alternatives.[105]

Despite this bridging strategy, Poland found itself in a strategic quandary. While Poland cautiously adhered to Soviet commitments, Warsaw and Bonn misperceived intentions as Poland modified regional security objectives. Warsaw indicated to the West a new alignment favoring democratization, free market reform, and, most importantly, temperate foreign and military policy. In early 1990, however, Warsaw's support for a future unified Germany in NATO failed to persuade Bonn to confirm the Polish–German border.[106] By temporarily revising its bridging policy Poland tried to balance Moscow and Bonn by hiding between them. Warsaw at first indicated that Soviet troops would not withdraw from Poland to hedge against German obstinacy on the Oder–Neisse border. Poland tried fleetingly to maintain a buffer zone between West and East. Though such a strategy might delineate Polish balancing against Germany, Bonn ignored Poland's ploy. Warsaw then refined its bridge building by deeming participation in unification talks more important than Soviet troop withdrawal tactics. Warsaw needed Bonn's support and soon gained German approval to participate in the final unification phases, reinforced by Washington and Moscow. Since late 1989, Poland had never hesitated to uphold German unification on four-power terms, unified German membership in NATO, and Polish–German border resolution.

After the completion of German unification in 1990 and border treaties in 1991, Poland achieved several critical foreign policy goals with Germany to solidify European security. First, Warsaw and Bonn agreed to a historic interstate treaty. The treaty not only signified an end to their antagonistic post–Cold War political history, but also formalized security coordination and European reintegration. Next, Poland strove to coordinate the complex Soviet force withdrawals with Germany. Although Polish–German tensions existed, especially on troop transit of Polish territory, Warsaw kept Bonn informed about withdrawal negotiations with Moscow as Soviet hard-liners consolidated power. By the failed 19–21 August 1991 Soviet coup d'état, Bonn finally supported transit terms agreed between Warsaw and Moscow. Subsequently, Warsaw persuaded Bonn to reverse its neglect of Russian president Boris El'tsin as the USSR collapsed.[107]

Shortly after the failed Soviet coup, Bonn upheld stability-enhancing policies more actively to bring Poland closer to NATO and the EU, while both nations calculated the impact of post-Soviet Russian security on regional stability. By December 1991, Russia superseded the USSR and force withdrawal negotiations accelerated. Bonn recognized that Warsaw's important October 1990 accord with the Russian foreign ministry, the first international agreement Russia signed, aided Bonn's negotiations with Moscow because of withdrawal advice Warsaw provided.[108] Although Germany finally accepted Poland's initiative to coordinate Russian troop withdrawals in late 1991, Bonn missed opportunities to collaborate with Warsaw during 1990–1991. Germany wanted only to negotiate with the USSR, seeing it as a great power. Bonn refused to coordinate transparently with Poland on Soviet troop transit across sovereign Polish territory, even as middle power Warsaw tried to pursue its specialized role in bridging between Bonn and Moscow.[109] In fact, Bonn agreed to most Soviet hard-liner terms to influence Soviet force withdrawals from eastern Germany, but didn't attempt to secure legal and financial requirements to transit Poland. If Poland were a great power, conceivably Germany might have viewed early Polish–German troop withdrawal negotiations differently since Poland might have leveraged more by pressuring, blustering, or bluffing during negotiations.

Yet, it took middle power Poland's preventing certain Soviet transits to put Bonn and Moscow on notice, by declaring breaches of sovereignty by Bonn and Moscow. Germany and the USSR regarded Poland's middle power maneuvering as aggressively balancing Bonn and Moscow against one another. Poland countered that only by disrupting unscheduled Soviet troop travel, often by unmarked rail cars and involving nonnegotiated hazardous materials, could Warsaw protect its safety and sovereignty, and bring great powers to the negotiating table to form bridges rather than the barriers they projected.[110] Both great power neighbors ultimately recognized Poland's right to uphold its sovereignty and security as a bridge between Germany and Russia, but all three nations lost valuable time and financing.[111] Hence, Polish–German ties, including Soviet troop withdrawals, reveal how formerly hostile states reduced security dilemmas, ultimately cooperating through bridging to reach historic agreements. In seeking security[112] to foster democratization, reduce regional threats to survive, and prosper,[113] Poland attracted critical foreign direct investment, increased regional stability supportive of sovereignty and cooperative security, and encouraged Russian reformers.[114] Polish–German post–Cold War relations paralleled Franco–German post–World War II reconciliation[115] and signified an important model for transitioning middle powers seeking to decrease the "severity" of security dilemmas.[116] Whether Poland balanced, bandwagoned, or bridged, seeking other-help or self-help in its middle power strategies toward its eastern neighbors such as great power Russia, middle power Ukraine, and smaller powers, Lithuania and Belarus, demonstrates different middle power alignment in the next chapter.

Notes

1. Hajnicz played a prominent role as one of founders of the "Poland in Europe" seminar series that started as an underground movement in 1986. The series brought together several dozen political scientists, historians, economists, lawyers, sociologists, and journalists at the Holy Trinity Church in Warsaw. The gatherings provided the crucial avenue to publish the discussions and debates over Poland's potential contribution to Europe. Some of their notions particularly influenced Skubiszewski's development of Polish post-Communist foreign policy, as will be demonstrated, because of the underground movement's innovative ideas about Poland's historical security dilemma between Germany and Russia. Such celebrated participants included future post-Communist prime ministers Tadeusz Mazowiecki and Jan Olszewski, parliamentarian and later foreign minister Bronislaw Geremek, and post-Communist ambassador to the United States Kazimierz Dziewanowski. The arguments from these unofficial, anti-Communist seminars culminated in a four-day international conference entitled "Central Europe—Illusion or Opportunity?" at the Benedictine Abbey in Tyniec, close to Krakow. Sponsored in June 1989 with the editor of the Catholic monthly *Znak*, the conference organizers, led by Hajnicz, predicted accurately many of the subsequent revolutionary events that occurred that fall throughout Central Europe. Shortly after the Polish senate convened for the first time in August 1989, many of the "Poland in Europe" coterie, including Hajnicz, transitioned into the Senate's new Center for International Studies and officially began to publish the *Poland in Europe* journal. See Zygmunt Skorzynski, "Konwersatorium i Fundacja 'Polska w Europie'" [The Seminar and Foundation 'Poland in Europe'] in *Polska w Europie* [Poland in Europe] (May 1990): 98–100. I also interviewed Hajnicz at length in Warsaw on 9 June 1991 about the movement's history.

2. Note that Hajnicz published his analysis and recommendations about Polish–German relations in a West German journal several months before the *Solidarnosc*-Communist Roundtable dialogue began in April 1989. See Artur Hajnicz, "Poland within Its Geopolitical Triangle," *Aussenpolitik*, no. 1 (1989): 30–40.

3. Note that the Hallstein Doctrine remained in effect toward all Communist states, except the USSR, until the FRG's establishment of diplomatic relations with Romania in 1967, just before the West German–inspired Ostpolitik (Eastern) policy began. This policy upheld the division of Europe even as it extended new West German links to the east.

4. Note that France only recognized de jure the Oder–Neisse border in 1960 and, subsequently, the United States and Great Britain only until the Polish–German Treaty of 1970.

5. Hajnicz, "Poland within Its Geopolitical Triangle," 31–34; and Ronald D. Asmus and Thomas S. Szayna, with Barbara Kliszewski, *Polish National Security Thinking in a Changing Europe* (Santa Monica, Calif.: Center for Soviet Studies, 1991), 13. Hajnicz and other colleagues such as Tadeusz Chabiera, Jacek Czaputowicz, Grzegorz Kostrzewa-Zorbas, Eligiusz Lasota, Jerzy Marek Nowakowski, and Zygmunt Skorzynski, also elaborated these arguments during interviews as a group with me in Warsaw on 9 June 1991 and 10 June 1994 at the Senate's Center of International Studies. Czaputowicz, in particular, told me in a separate interview on 8 June 1994 in Warsaw that, as a student leader in the underground and just before the momentous Polish June 1989 elections, he traveled to Berlin, as a member of the "Poland in Europe" movement to demonstrate support for the East German opposition leaders. He went in the spring of 1989, at a time when the East German dissidents still endured persecution by the GDR's Communist government. Czaputowicz, who assumed duties in the post-Communist Polish foreign ministry in the Department of Europe and, then on Policy Planning Staff in the early 1990s, became instrumental in the summer of 1989 in arranging an important meeting of East German opposition leaders with *Solidarnosc* chairman Lech Walesa in Gdansk. At Walesa's meeting, the GDR oppositionists relayed insights such as the serious growing opposition to the GDR's Communists, later used by the Polish Senate Center's analysis as background for newly inaugurated parliamentarians in August 1989. See also Thomas S. Szayna, *Polish Foreign Policy under a Non-Communist Government: Prospects and Problems* (Santa Monica, Calif.: RAND, 1990), 15–19. It should be noted that, although *Solidarnosc* recognized the need to help the FRG to absorb the GDR, the Polish underground remained antagonistic to German leaders, who refused to recognize human rights abuses in Central and Eastern Europe during the 1980s. In the late 1980s, Helmut Kohl and Polish Communist leader General Wojciech Jaruzelski also remained concerned about offending Gorbachev, as the Soviet leader tried slowly to reform Central Europe and pressure the GDR leader, hard-liner Erich Honecker.

6. Ilya Prizel, *National Identity and Foreign Policy: Nationalism and Leadership in Poland, Russia, and Ukraine* (Cambridge: Cambridge University Press, 1998), 114–115. See also Timothy Garton Ash, *In Europe's Name: Germany and the Divided Continent* (New York: Random House, 1993).

7. Hajnicz, "Poland within Its Geopolitical Triangle," 36–37. In the wake of the 1988 worker–student strikes and failed governmental economic reform half-measures, Jaruzelski yielded to *Solidarnosc*'s calls for political dialogue and the eventual *Solidarnosc*-Communist Roundtable.

8. See, inter alia, Mikhail Gorbachev, *Perestroika: New Thinking for Our Country and the World* (New York: Harper & Row, 1987), 190–205; Sarah M. Terry, "The Future of Poland: Perestroika or Perpetual Crisis?" in *Central and Eastern Europe: The Opening*

Curtain, ed. William E. Griffith (Boulder, Colo.: Westview, 1989), 178–217; Arthur R. Rachwald, *In Search of Poland: The Superpowers' Response to Solidarity, 1980–1989* (Stanford, Calif.: Hoover Institution Press, 1990), 121–127; and Prizel, *National Identity and Foreign Policy*, 112–118.

9. Hajnicz, "Poland within Its Geopolitical Triangle," 40. For analysis on West German views toward the East, some incorporating views toward Poland at the end of the Cold War and the early phase of the post–Cold War period, see Stephen F. Szabo, "The New Germany and Central European Security," in *East European Security Reconsidered*, ed. John R. Lampe and Daniel N. Nelson (Washington, D.C.: Woodrow Wilson Center Press, 1993), 37–38; F. Stephen Larrabee, ed., *The Two German States and European Security* (New York: St. Martin's, 1989); Ulrich Weisser, *Toward a New Security Structure in and for Europe: A German Perspective* (Santa Monica, Calif.: RAND, 1990); Ronald D. Asmus, *Germany in Transition: National Self-Confidence and International Reticence* (Santa Monica, Calif.: RAND, 1992); Stephen F. Szabo, *The Diplomacy of German Unification* (New York: St. Martin's, 1992), 72–76; Philip Zelikow and Condoleezza Rice, *Germany Unified and Europe Transformed: A Study in Statecraft* (Cambridge, Mass.: Harvard University Press, 1997), 207–208, 218–222; George Bush and Brent Scowcroft, *A World Transformed* (New York: Vintage, 1998), 247–248, 250–251, 260–262; and Angela Stent, *Russia and Germany Reborn: Unification, the Soviet Collapse, and the New Europe* (Princeton, N.J.: Princeton University Press, 1999), 118–119.

10. "Oswiadczenie sejmu PRL w zwiazku z 50 rocznica umow Niemiecko-Radzieckich" [Declaration of the Sejm of the PPR on the 50th Anniversary of the German-Soviet Agreement], Warsaw, 23 August 1989, *Zbior Dokumentow*, no. 1 (1990): 16.

11. "Oswiadczenie senatu PRL w zwiazku z 50 rocznica wybuchu II wojny swiatowej" [Declaration of the Senate of the PPR on the 50th Anniversary of the Outbreak of the Second World War] (Warsaw, 30 August 1989), *Zbior Dokumentow*, no. 1 (1990): 19–20; Adam Michnik, *The Church and the Left*, translated by David Ost (Chicago: University of Chicago Press, 1993), 84–94; Prizel, *National Identity and Foreign Policy*, 87–88, 113–114; Arthur Rachwald, *Poland between the Superpowers: Security vs. Economic Recovery* (Boulder, Colo.: Westview, 1983), 63; and *German–Polish Dialogue: Letters of the Polish and German Bishops and International Statements* (New York: Atlantic Forum, 1966).

12. "Sejmowe expose Ministra Spraw Zagranicznych RP Krzysztofa Skubiszewskiego" [Sejm Exposé by Minister of Foreign Affairs of the Republic of Poland, Krzysztof Skubiszewski] (Warsaw, 26 April 1990), *Zbior Dokumentow*, no. 1 (1991): 20.

13. Marian Turski, "To Invest in Democracy: Dispatch from Vienna," *Polityka* (Warsaw), 18 November 1989, *FBIS-EEU*, 5 December 1989, 70; and Krzysztof Skubiszewski, *Zachodnia Granica Polski* [Poland's Western Border] (Gdansk: Wydawnictwo Morskie—Instytut Baltycki w Gdansku, 1969), 460–466.

14. Skubiszewski, *Zachodnia Granica Polski*, 1969, 555, 556–567.

15. See chapter 2 for analysis of the Rapacki Plan and the 1970 Polish–German treaty; for the ways the Rapacki Plan tried to engage the FRG to reduce nuclear weapons on its territory and Gomulka's initiatives employed to normalize relations with the FRG, see Skubiszewski, *Zachodnia Granica Polski*, 557–561.

16. "Expose sejmowe premiera PRL Tadeusza Mazowieckiego/fragmenty dotyczace pomocy zagranicznej i stosunkow miedzynarodowych" [Sejm Exposé by the Polish Prime Minister Tadeusz Mazowiecki/Excerpts Concerning Foreign Aid and International Relations] (Warsaw, 12 September 1989), *Zbior Dokumentow*, no. 1 (1990): 26.

17. Barbara Grad, "Foreign Minister Skubiszewski Interviewed at the UN General Assembly, Discusses 'Finlandization,' United Germany," Warsaw Television Service, 1730 GMT, 22 September 1989, *FBIS-EEU*, 25 September 1989, 36.

18. Karl-Ludwig Guensche, "Unification—the Germans' Business: Interview with Polish Foreign Minister Krzysztof Skubiszewski," BILD (Hamburg), 2 October 1989, *FBIS-EEU*, 4 October 1989, 40; and "Skubiszewski's UN Visit to New York End; TV Interview on Visit," Warsaw Television Service, 2125 GMT, 2 October 1989, *FBIS-EEU*, 4 October 1989, 39.

19. "Talks Begin Eighth Round," PAP, 1816 GMT, 14 September 1989, *FBIS-EEU*, 15 September 1989, 41; "Meets Mazowiecki; Sees 'Progress' in Negotiations," PAP, 2221 GMT, 15 September 1989, *FBIS-EEU*, 18 September 1989, 39; "Official Previews Upcoming Kohl Visit," PAP, 1845 GMT, 10 October 1989, *FBIS-EEU*, 17 October 1989, 64–65.

20. For important reasoning by Kohl and his staff in planning to visit historically sensitive sites in Poland, particularly in grappling with the demands by the German expellee associations, who refused to recognize the Oder–Neisse border and advocated Poland return territory to Germany, see, among others, Gunter Muchler and Klaus Hofmann, *Helmut Kohl: Chancellor of German Unity, A Biography* (Bonn: Press and Information Office of the Federal Government, 1992), 172–173; "Interview with FRG Chancellor Helmut Kohl," Warsaw Television Service, 1900 GMT, 8 November 1989, *FBIS-EEU*, 9 November 1989, 55–57; and Prizel, *National Identity and Foreign Policy*, 116.

21. Geri Nasarski, "Interview with Polish Foreign Minister Krzysztof Skubiszewski," ZDF Television Network (Mainz), 1800 GMT, 26 October 1989, *FBIS-EEU*, 27 October 1989, 49.

22. Nasarski, "Interview with Polish Foreign Minister Krzysztof Skubiszewski," 49–50; Ulricha Schmidla, "Reunification Acceptable Only within Existing Borders: Interview with Polish Foreign Minister Krzysztof Skubiszewski," *Die Welt* (Hamburg), 13 November 1989, *FBIS-EEU*, 14 November 1989, 60; and Lucian O. Meysels, "We Were Also Divided: Interview with Polish Foreign Minister Krzysztof Skubiszewski," *Wochenpresse* (Vienna), 10 November 1989, *FBIS-EEU*, 14 November 1989, 61.

23. Nasarski, "Interview with Polish Foreign Minister Krzysztof Skubiszewski," 50. See Skubiszewski, quoted in "Inauguracyjne posiedzenie Rady Konsultacyjnej przy Przewodniczacym Rady Panstwa" [Inaugural Meeting of the Consultative Council by the Presiding State Council], *Rada Naradowa*, 21 March 1987, 2–3.

24. Turski, "To Invest in Democracy: Dispatch from Vienna," 69.

25. Turski, "To Invest in Democracy: Dispatch from Vienna," 69–70.

26. Prizel, *National Identity and Foreign Policy*, 73–79, 118–120.

27. "Interview with FRG Chancellor Helmut Kohl," 9 November 1989, 55, and Janusz Reiter, "Without German-Polish Understanding There Can Be No Prospect of a Europe without Hatred and Hostility," *Gazeta Wyborcza*, 9 November 1989, *FBIS-EEU*, 14 November 1989, 54–55. Note that Reiter, a *Solidarnosc* expert on Germany and a journalist on Adam Michnik's staff after the June 1989 elections, eventually became Poland's ambassador in Bonn.

28. Stefan Dietrich, "Caution Required When Using the Word Reconciliation: Interview with Polish Prime Minister Mazowiecki," *Frankfurter Allgemeine* (Frankfurt Am Main), 8 November 1989, *FBIS-EEU*, 9 November 1989, 58.

29. Adam Michnik, "It Is Not a Case of Aid for Poland," *Gazeta Wyborcza*, 8 November 1989, *FBIS-EEU*, 13 November 1989, 77–78.

30. "PAP First Day Roundup," 10 November 1989, *FBIS-EEU*, 13 November 1989, 68.

31. "Mazowiecki Dinner Speech," PAP, 9 November 1989, *FBIS-EEU*, 13 November 1989, 67 and "Speech by Premier Tadeusz Mazowiecki at a Dinner in Honor of FRG Chancellor Helmut Kohl in Warsaw on 9 November," *Rzeczpospolita*, 10–12 November 1989, *FBIS-EEU*, 14 November 1989, 53–54.

32. For Kohl's July 1989 statement, see "Oswiadczenie Kanclerza RFN Helmuta Kohla w sprawie granicy Polsko–Niemieckiej" [Statement by Chancellor of the Federal Republic of Germany Helmut Kohl on the Issue of the Polish–German Border] (Bonn, 11 July 1989), *Zbior Dokumentow*, no. 3 (1990): 113–115.

33. "Dinner Speech by Federal Republic of Germany Chancellor Helmut Kohl, honoring recently and democratically elected, Polish Prime Minister, Tadeusz Mazowiecki," *Rzeczpospolita*, 10–12 November 1989, *FBIS-EEU*, 14 November 1989, 51–53. It is also important to note that Kohl stated on several occasions to the Bundestag in 1985 and 1986 the importance of the inviolability of borders of all European states and the rejection of territorial claims, specifically citing the 1970 Polish–German treaty. Helmut Kohl, "State of the Nation in Divided Germany," speech to the Bundestag, 27 February 1985, *Statements & Speeches* (Bonn: German Information Center, 1985), 4–6; and, as referenced by Gebhard Schweigler, "German Questions or the Shrinking of Germany," in *The Two German States and European Security*, ed. F. Stephen Larrabee (New York: St. Martin's, 1989), 84.

34. It should be noted that nearly 7,000 people from both Poland and Germany attended the emotional outdoor mass in Krzyzowa, including some protesting from the German expellee associations and some from Silesia and parts of northeastern Poland. The protesters demanded that the German language be spoken in Polish schools and church services. Hitherto, since the Polish Communists had outlawed such demonstrations, the fact that the post-Communist government allowed the Germans to demonstrate peacefully marked a turning point in the freedom of expression throughout Poland in the early months after the June 1989 elections. "[Kohl] Speaks at Jasna Gora Monastery," Warsaw Domestic Service, 1800 GMT, 12 November 1989, *FBIS-EEU*, 13 November 1989, 73; "Hamburg DPA Account," 1309 GMT, 12 November 1989, *FBIS-EEU*, 13 November 1989, 72; C.Z.E., "More Than a Symbol," *Sztandar Mlodych*, 13 November 1989, *FBIS-EEU*, 15 November 1989, 61; and "Kohl Pays Homage at Auschwitz," PAP, 1122 GMT, 14 November 1989, *FBIS-EEU*, 15 November 1989, 60.

35. Note that despite all of the agreements, both sides failed to sign an overall "Polish–German declaration," as planned, because of the continuing controversy over the Oder–Neisse border. Instead, Mazowiecki and Kohl decided at the end of the visit to compromise and save face by signing their joint statement.

36. "Wspolne Oswiadczenie Premiera PRL Tadeusza Mazowieckiego i Kanclerza RFN Helmuta Kohla" [Joint Statement of Polish Premier Tadeusz Mazowiecki and FRG Chancellor Helmut Kohl] (14 November 1989), *Zbior Dokumentow*, no. 4 (1990): 157–171; and Muchler and Hofmann, *Helmut Kohl*, 177–179.

37. According to Hajnicz and his colleague Tadeusz Chabiera, in an interview with me in Warsaw on 10 June 1994, both Mazowiecki and Kohl misunderstood each other during their first meetings. According to Hajnicz and Chabiera, only after unification could questions over the Polish–German border be resolved. Hence, both states agreed that only a "joint statement" could be signed.

38. Schmidla, "Reunification Acceptable Only within Existing Borders," 59–60.

39. For examples of alarmist left- and right-wing Polish views on the tension over the uncertainty of the Polish–German border, interpretations about how many Germans the Polish post–World War II state expelled, and the problems caused by the German minority in Poland, see Zbigniew Niemcewicz, "The Infantile Right-Wing Disorder," *Dziennik Baltycki*, 15 November 1989, *FBIS-EEU*, 15 December 1989, 68–69; Ryszard Marek Gronski, "The Infantile Right-Wing Disorder," *Polityka*, 18 November 1989, *FBIS-EEU*, 15 December 1989, 66–68; Jerzy Urban, "The Sting That Follows the Kisses," *Trybuna Ludu*, 22 November 1989, *FBIS-EEU*, 29 November 1989, 81–84; Andrea Tarquini, "Interview with Mieczyslaw Rakowski, Polish United Workers Party First Secretary," *La Repubblica* (Rome), 15 December 1989, *FBIS-EEU*, 20 December 1989, 58; and Prizel, *National Identity and Foreign Policy*, 114–115.

40. Hajnicz and Chabiera related Skubiszewski's German strategy, parts of which they helped to formulate, in interviews with me in Warsaw on 9 June 1991 and 10 June 1994.

41. Note that on the day Skubiszewski delivered his Polish parliamentary speech, Kohl stated in Strasbourg at an EC summit that he accepted Poland's western border, the first time he stated so publicly since the Berlin Wall's fall. Most likely, his statement was in response to the German parliament's criticism of his ambiguous stance. "Kohl Accepts Poland's Western Border," PAP, 1815 GMT, 8 December 1989, *FBIS-EEU*, 11 December 1989, 76; and "Genscher, Ruehe Defend Kohl on Border Question," DPA (Hamburg), 1219 GMT, 17 December 1989, *FBIS-WEU*, 18 December 1989, 5.

42. "Oswiadczenie Ministra Spraw Zagranicznych PRL Krzysztofa Skubiszewskiego" [Statement by the Polish Minister of Foreign Affairs Krzysztof Skubiszewski] (Warsaw, 7 December 1989), *Zbior Dokumentow*, no. 4 (1990): 7–10; and "Speech by Foreign Minister Krzysztof Skubiszewski at Sejm meeting in Warsaw on 7 December," *Rzeczpospolita*, 8 December 1989, *FBIS-EEU*, 14 December 1989, 69–71.

43. "Oswiadczenie Ministra Spraw Zagranicznych PRL Krzysztofa Skubiszewskiego," 8–9.

44. "Oswiadczenie Ministra Spraw Zagranicznych PRL Krzysztofa Skubiszewskiego," 10. Insights into Poland's German strategy also come from interviews I conducted with Hajnicz and Chabiera in Warsaw on 9 June 1991 and 10 June 1994.

45. See Bush and Scowcroft, *A World Transformed*, 234–236; and Zelikow and Rice, *Germany Unified and Europe Transformed*, 208–216.

46. It is important, however, to reiterate some historical context, given Skubiszewski's argument about other powers determining Poland's post–World War II western territory. It must be noted that General Wladyslaw Sikorski, the prime minister of Poland's World War II London government-in-exile apparently related to Soviet leader Josef Stalin in 1941 that "it is not the Ukrainians [in formerly eastern Poland] who matter to me, but the territory in which the Polish element is dominant," that is, much of the pre–World War II German territory Poland gained in the postwar settlements. Thus, this World War II historical context must be borne in mind when analyzing Skubiszewski's unswerving stance regarding the territorial integrity of post-Communist Poland as one of the main planks of his foreign policy. See Sarah M. Terry, *Poland's Place in Europe: General Sikorski and the Origin of the Oder-Neisse Line, 1939-1943* (Princeton, N.J.: Princeton University Press, 1983), 130; and Prizel, *National Identity and Foreign Policy*, 68, 73–79.

47. Piet de Moor, "For Us the Border Question No Longer Exists," *De Volkskrant* (Amsterdam), 9 December 1989, *FBIS-EEU*, 20 December 1989, 55–57. For a good analysis of the overall questions of Polish–German relations from a German perspective

and a useful interview with Skubiszewski based mainly on the Polish foreign minister's December 1989 speech to the Polish parliament, see Hansjakob Stehle, "Western Border a Sore Point—Foreign Minister Krzysztof Skubiszewski Does Not Understand Bonn's Hesitation," *Die Zeit* (Hamburg), 22 December 1989, *FBIS-EEU*, 7 February 1990, 25–26.

48. Schweller, "Bandwagoning for Profit," 74–75, 83, 88–89, 93, 99, 101, 105–107; Glaser, "Realists as Optimists," 124–126; Deborah Welch Larson, "Bandwagon Images in American Foreign Policy: Myth or Reality?" in *Dominoes and Bandwagons: Strategic Beliefs and Great Power Competition in the Eurasian Rimland*, ed. Robert Jervis and Jack Snyder (Oxford: Oxford University Press, 1991), 85–87, 102–103; and Andrew A. Michta, *East Central Europe after the Warsaw Pact: Security Dilemmas in the 1990s* (New York: Greenwood, 1992), 74–78.

49. Krystyna Koziol, "Skubiszewski News Conference on Soviet Ties, Reunification," Warsaw Domestic Service, 1736 GMT, 9 February 1990, *FBIS-EEU*, 12 February 1990, 48.

50. This chapter examines Polish–German tensions over Soviet troop withdrawals from Germany and Poland in more detail below. Chapter 4 examines the controversial Polish-Soviet force withdrawal negotiations in greater depth.

51. On the historical rationale for German views on security and stability, particularly in connection to its emerging post–Cold War bilateral relationship with the USSR and later Russia, see, among others, Walter Laqueur, *Russia and Germany: A Century of Conflict* (New Brunswick, N.J.: Transaction, 1990); Josef Joffe, "'The Revisionists': Germany and Russia in a Post–Bipolar World," in *New Thinking and Old Realities: America, Europe, and Russia*, ed. Michael T. Clark and Simon Serfaty (Washington, D.C.: Seven Locks, 1991), 113–115; Ilya Prizel, "Russia and Germany: The Case for a Special Relationship," in *Post–Communist Eastern Europe: Crisis and Reform*, ed. Andrew A. Michta and Ilya Prizel (New York: St. Martin's, 1992), 21–52; Szabo, *The Diplomacy of German Unification*, 31–52; and Stent, *Russia and Germany Reborn*, 97–114.

52. Berndt Conrad, "Poland and Germany Must Develop a Community of Interests: Interview with Foreign Minister Krzysztof Skubiszewski," *Die Welt* (Hamburg), 8 February 1990, *FBIS-EEU*, 8 February 1990, 52.

53. Koziol, "Skubiszewski News Conference on Soviet Ties, Reunification," 48; and Conrad, "Poland and Germany Must Develop a Community of Interests," 52.

54. Eugeniusz Guz, "Meets Kohl; Communique Issued," PAP, 2316 GMT, 7 February 1990, *FBIS-EEU*, 8 February 1990, 51.

55. It remains important for historical context to understand that Kohl revealed to U.S. president George Bush at Camp David on 24 February 1990 that "the Polish-German question is not serious." He rationalized to the president that "in the FRG today, eighty-five to ninety percent of the population is in favor of the Oder-Neisse border." The German chancellor felt the Poles needed to understand that only an all-German parliament could ratify a border treaty. What remained disturbing for the United States and, by extension, the Poles, stemmed from Kohl's refusal to include the Poles in the upcoming "2 Plus 4" talks. Instead, Kohl preferred the United States to mediate between the Germans and Poles because he believed that "Gorbachev is not interested in the Oder-Neisse border. There are old Polish cities in the USSR." See Bush and Scowcroft, *A World Transformed*, 251–252.

56. Koziol, "Skubiszewski News Conference on Soviet Ties, Reunification," 48.

57. See "Walesa Invited to Visit Soviet Union," PAP, 1529 GMT, 18 January 1990, *FBIS-EEU*, 19 January 1990, 59–60; "Walesa Demands Soviet Troop Withdrawal," PAP,

2135 GMT, 18 January 1990, *FBIS-EEU*, 19 January 1990, 60; and "Walesa Views Soviet Troop Pullout, Other Issues," PAP, 2200 GMT, 8 February 1990, *FBIS-EEU*, 9 February 190, 63.

58. Grzegorz Kostrzewa-Zorbas, "The Russian Troop Withdrawal from Poland," 130; Asmus and Szayna, *Polish National Security Thinking in a Changing Europe*, 18–21; Vinton, "Domestic Politics and Foreign Policy, 1989–1993" 38–39; Zdzislaw Najder, *Jaka Polska: Co i komu doradzalem* [How I Saw Poland: Who I Advised] (Warsaw: Editions Spotkania, 1993), 151–153; and Ilya Prizel, "Warsaw's Ostpolitik: A New Encounter with Positivism," in *Polish Foreign Policy Reconsidered: Challenges of Independence*, ed. Ilya Prizel and Andrew A. Michta (London: Macmillan, 1995), 110.

59. Katarzyna Kolodziejczyk, "Three Directions: Skubiszewski Outlines Foreign Policy Goals," *Rzeczpospolita*, 10–11 February 1990, *FBIS-EEU*, 13 February 1990, 50.

60. "Mazowiecki: bez dwuznacznosci w sprawie granic" [Mazowiecki: Unequivocal on the Border Issue], *Gazeta Wyborcza*, 22 February 1990, 1; and Vinton, "Domestic Politics and Foreign Policy," 40.

61. Janusz Reiter, "Po co the wojska" [Why Those Troops], *Gazeta Wyborcza*, 14 February 1990, 1; "Daily Opposes 'Early' Soviet Troop Withdrawal," PAP, 1920 GMT, 7 February 1990, *FBIS-EEU*, 8 February 1990, 50; and "Demonstrators Demand Soviet Withdrawal," Warsaw Domestic Service, 1800 GMT, 7 February 1990, *FBIS-EEU*, 8 February 1990, 50. For good overviews of Poland's maneuvering on Soviet force withdrawals, see Richard Weitz, "Pursuing Military Security in Eastern Europe," in *After the Cold War: International Institutions and State Strategies in Europe, 1989–1991*, eds. Robert O. Keohane, Joseph S. Nye, and Stanley Hoffmann (Cambridge, Mass.: Harvard University Press, 1993), 355–359; and Mark Kramer, "Neorealism, Nuclear Proliferation, and East-Central European Strategies," in *Unipolar Politics: Realism and State Strategies after the Cold War*, ed. Ethan B. Kapstein and Michael Mastanduno (New York: Columbia University Press, 1999), 388–393.

62. See Muchler and Hofmann, *Helmut Kohl*, 185–187; Szabo, "The New Germany and Central European Security," 38; Gerhard Wettig, "Moscow's Acceptance of NATO: the Catalytic Role of German Unification," *Europe-Asia Studies*, vol. 45, no. 6 (1993): 953–972; and Prizel, *National Identity and Foreign Policy*, 117.

63. For Polish and Soviet arguments, see "Skubiszewski Addresses 'Open Skies' Forum," PAP, 2044 GMT, 12 February 1990, *FBIS-EEU*, 14 February 1990, 50; Adolf Reut, "Skubiszewski on German Unification," PAP, 2355 GMT, 14 February 1990, *FBIS-EEU*, 16 February 1990, 48–49; "Skubiszewski Addresses Sixth Polish–FRG Forum," Warsaw Television Service, 1830 GMT, 23 February 1990, *FBIS-EEU*, 26 February 1990, 57–58. Though Kohl opposed the U.S. position that favored appropriate Polish "2 Plus 4" participation, he and Bush needed to respond to Moscow's strong support for Poland's participation. Kohl finally decided in late February at the end of the Camp David visit to support Polish participation. It also remains important to realize that Bush attempted to mediate between Kohl and Mazowiecki on the German guarantee of the Polish–German border. According to Bush's account, he first conferred with Kohl telephonically on 20 March 1990, a day before Mazowiecki's White House meeting. Bush and Kohl agreed on the strategy for the U.S. president to "assure" Mazowiecki that Kohl firmly believed that "the current GDR–Polish border should be the permanent German-Polish border." During the meeting at the White House with Bush on 21 March, Mazowiecki stated, "the Polish people are paranoid about agreements being made over their heads. It is crucial to us to ensure that our Western territories are not just a gift from Stalin—that they are guaranteed by all the powers, not just a unilateral act by one." Bush

then recommended that Mazowiecki consider the possibility that, with Washington's push, Kohl might "agree" to draft border treaty language with the Polish premier before unification. See Bush and Scowcroft, *A World Transformed*, 252, 260–262; and Zelikow and Rice, *Germany Unified and Europe Transformed*, 219–222.

64. Moscow pressed for Poland's inclusion in the "2 Plus 4" talks to gain whatever leverage possible against the West on unification and also conceivably to delay force withdrawal negotiations with Warsaw, both because of the major policy battles among Gorbachev's advisors over German unification (February to June 1990) and the increasing strength of Soviet military hard-liners. See Stent, *Russia and Germany Reborn*, 119–124. A notable argument related to me in Warsaw on 10 June 1994 by parliamentarian Janusz Onyszkiewicz, the vice minister of defense during the German unification process, concentrated on the fact that Poland needed to secure its borders through treaty guarantees from Germany and adapt to policies at that time which would be considered within the "2 Plus 4" negotiations. He said "it was of utmost importance for us to win a consensus from the four big powers and not antagonize the USSR." However, he underlined that "the Western powers were cautious and noncommittal, while we convinced the USSR to play a supportive role. This was helped because we knew not to raise the issue of Soviet troop withdrawals from Poland."

65. "Sejmowe expose Ministra Spraw Zagranicznych RP Krzysztofa Skubiszewskiego" [Sejm Exposé by Minister of Foreign Affairs of the Republic of Poland, Krzysztof Skubiszewski] (Warsaw, 26 April 1990), *Zbior Dokumentow*, no. 2 (1991): 16–18.

66. "Nota Ministra Spraw Zagranicznych RP Krzysztofa Skubiszewskiego do Sekretarza Stanu USA oraz Ministrow Spraw Zagranicznych Francji, ZSRR i Wielki Brytanii w sprawie traktatu RP z Niemcami" [Note by the Polish Foreign Minister, Krzysztof Skubiszewski, to the U.S. Secretary of State and the Ministers for Foreign Affairs of France, the USSR and Great Britain concerning a Polish–German Treaty] (Warsaw, 30 April 1990), *Zbior Dokumentow*, no. 2 (1991): 33.

67. "von Weizsaecker Dinner Speech," DPA (Hamburg), 1047 GMT, 2 May 1990, *FBIS-EEU*, 3 May 1990, 38.

68. "Skubiszewski Praises Visit," DPA (Hamburg), 5 May 1990, *FBIS-EEU*, 7 May 1990, 45.

69. "Mazowiecki: Border Treaty after German Unity," Paris Domestic Service, 1700 GMT, 6 May 1990, *FBIS-EEU*, 7 May 1990, 45. See also Kazimierz Woycicki, "Poland and Germany—A Community of Interests," *Rzeczpospolita*, 2-3 May 1990, *FBIS-EEU*, 8 May 1990, 28–29; and Janusz Reiter, "This German Builds Confidence: FRG President in Poland," *Gazeta Wyborcza*, 2–3 May 1990, *FBIS-EEU*, 13 June 1990, 9–10.

70. See Muchler and Hofmann, *Helmut Kohl*, 194–202; "M.S. Gorbachev and H. Kohl News Conference," *Pravda* (Moscow), 18 July 1990, *FBIS-SOV*, 19 July 1990, 22–30; Szabo, "The New Germany and Central European Security,"; 37–39; Prizel, "Russia and Germany: The Case for a Special Relationship," 30–34; Stephen F. Szabo, "Federal Republic of Germany: The Bundeswehr," *European Security Policy after the Revolutions in 1989*, ed. Jeffrey Simon (Washington, D.C.: National Defense University Press, 1991), 191; Szabo, *The Diplomacy of German Unification*, 95–108; and Stent, *Russia and Germany Reborn*, 131–142.

71. "Przemowienie ministra spraw zagranicznych RP Krzysztofa Skubiszewskiego na spotkaniu ministerialnum konferencji '2 Plus 4'" [Statement by the Polish Foreign Minister Krzysztof Skubiszewski at the Ministerial Meeting of the '2 Plus 4' Conference] (Paris, 17 July 1990), *Zbior Dokumentow*, no. 3 (1991): 46–64.

72. "Skubiszewski Reviews Polish Foreign Policy," Warsaw Domestic Service, 2100 GMT, 1 September 1990, *FBIS-EEU*, 4 September 1990, 30.

73. "Traktat o ostatecznej regulacji w odniesieniu do Niemiec [Treaty on the Final Settlement with Respect to Germany] (Moscow, 12 September 1990), *Zbior Dokumentow*, no. 3 (1991): 69, 73. See also Jan Barcz, *Udzial Polski w konferencji "2 + 4": Aspekty prawne i proceduralne* [Polish Participation in the "2 + 4" Conference: Legal and Procedural Aspects] (Warszawa: Polski Instytut Spraw Miedzynarodowych, 1994). Note that the treaty included the following: "The right of the united Germany to belong to alliances, with all the rights and responsibilities arising therefrom, shall not be affected by the present treaty." This represented a small victory for Skubiszewski, who never disputed Germany's right to be part of NATO, but only questioned temporary status of NATO and Soviet troops on German territory.

74. "Traktat miedzy Rzeczapospolita Polska a Republika Federalna Niemiec o potwierdzeniu istniejacej miedzy nimi granicy" [Treaty between the Polish Republic and the Federal Republic of Germany on the Confirmation of the Border Between Both States] (14 November 1990,) in Jan Barcz and Mieczyslaw Tomal, *Polska-Niemcy: dobre sasiedztwo i przyjazna wspolpraca* (Warszawa: Polski Instytut Spraw Miedzynarodowych, 1992), 19–24. "Historic Border Treaty with FRG Signed 14 November; Genscher Arrives to Sign Treaty," DPA (Hamburg), 14 November 1990, *FBIS-EEU*, 14 November 1990, 34 and "Spokeswoman Comments on event," PAP, 12 November 1990, *FBIS-EEU*, 14 November 1990, 34.

75. "Skubiszewski Notes Importance of Border Treaty," PAP, 1036 GMT, 16 November 1990, *FBIS-EEU*, 19 November 1990, 57.

76. Karol Zbikowski, "The Treaty Has Been Signed," *Gazeta Wyborcza*, 15 November 1990, *FBIS-EEU*, 20 November 1990, 38.

77. Chapter 4 analyzes Polish–Soviet and Polish–Russian troop withdrawals.

78. "Problemy polityki zagranicznej u progu roku 1991—Wystapienie ministra spraw zagranicznych RP Krzysztofa Skubiszewskiego w Sejmie" [Foreign Policy Issues at the Start of 1991—Address by the Polish Foreign Minister Krzysztof Skubiszewski in the Sejm] (14 February 1991), *Zbior Dokumentow*, no. 1 (1992): 37–39.

79. "Poland's Solidarity Paved the Way for Changes in Europe: Interview with Foreign Minister Krzysztof Skubiszewski," *Der Morgen* (Berlin), 4 February 1991, *FBIS-EEU*, 8 February 1991, 35. See also Arthur Rachwald, "Looking West," in *Polish Foreign Policy Reconsidered: Challenges of Independence*, ed. Ilya Prizel and Andrew A. Michta (London: Macmillan, 1995), 132–135.

80. Kostrzewa-Zorbas, "The Russian Troop Withdrawal from Poland," 120. See also Vladimir Kondrastyev, "Interview with German Foreign Minister Hans-Dietrich Genscher," Moscow Television Service, 1800 GMT, 12 October 1990, *FBIS-SOV*, 15 October 1990, 21–22.

81. Skubiszewski, "Problemy polityki zagranicznej u progu roku 1991," 36–38; Klaus Frankel, "Skubiszewski Interviewed on Relations with FRG," Berlin Radio Aktwell Network, 2100 GMT, 4 March 1991, *FBIS-EEU*, 5 March 1991, 29.

82. Kostrzewa-Zorbas, "The Russian Troop Withdrawal from Poland," 130. Kostrzewa-Zorbas also confirmed this view of "the paradox of German inaction" during interviews with me on 6 February 1991 in Oslo, on 13 January 1992 in Warsaw, and on 25 March 1993 in Washington.

83. Klaus Franke, "No Border between Prosperity and Poverty: Interview with Foreign Minister Krzysztof Skubiszewski," *Berliner Zeitung* (Berlin), 5 March 1991, *FBIS-*

EEU, 12 March 1991, 27–28; and "Country 'Technically' Ready for Troop Withdrawal," PAP, 1459 GMT, 11 March 1991, *FBIS-EEU*, 12 March 1991, 27.

84. Kostrzewa-Zorbas, "The Russian Troop Withdrawal from Poland," 128.

85. See Prizel, "Russia and Germany: The Case for a Special Relationship," 32–33; Angela Stent, *The Soviet Union, Eastern and Western Europe before and after German Unification*, National Council for Soviet and East European Research (October 1990); and Gerhard Wettig, "German Unification and European Security," *Aussenpolitik*, no. 1 (1991): 13–19.

86. Kostrzewa-Zorbas, "The Russian Troop Withdrawal from Poland," 130.

87. Kostrzewa-Zorbas, "The Russian Troop Withdrawal from Poland," 128. Hungarian and Czechoslovak foreign ministry officials also confirmed this German political and financial maneuvering on Soviet troop transit with their respective states during interviews I conducted in Oslo on 6 February 1991 at a NATO-Central European security-defense forum and in Budapest on 13 June 1991.

88. Kostrzewa-Zorbas, "The Russian Troop Withdrawal from Poland," 125–126.

89. Kostrzewa-Zorbas, "The Russian Troop Withdrawal from Poland," 120, 126, 130–131. Both Kostrzewa-Zorbas and Lech Kaczynski, then Polish minister of state for national security, discussed the same concerns with me in Warsaw on 11 June 1991. They elaborated on both the German and Soviet policies toward Poland on Soviet force withdrawals from both Polish and German territory. See also "Soviets Said to Stall Troop Withdrawal Talks," AFP (Agence France Press), 1748 GMT, 27 May 1991, *FBIS-EEU*, 28 May 1991, 13.

90. Kostrzewa-Zorbas, "The Russian Troop Withdrawal from Poland," 131. See also "No Barriers to Start of Soviet Troop Transit," Radio Warszawa Network, 1800 GMT, 6 June 1991, *FBIS-EEU*, 7 June 1991, 16.

91. "Traktat: Miedzy Rzeczapospolita Polska a Republika Federalna Niemiec o dobrym sasiedstwie i przjaznej wspolpracy" [Treaty: Between the Republic of Poland and the Federal Republic of Germany on Good-Neighborliness, Friendship and Cooperation], 17 June 1991, Bonn, Germany.

92. Krzysztof Skubiszewski, "The Treaty Is Aimed at a Unified Europe," *Die Welt*, 17 June 1991, *FBIS-EEU*, 18 June 1991, 19.

93. "Genscher: EC Should Admit East European Nations," ADN, 0735 GMT, 5 June 1991, *FBIS-WEU*, 5 June 1991, 14.

94. "Traktat: Miedzy Rzeczapospolita Polska a Republika Federalna Niemiec," 1–7, 10–11.

95. "Polityka zagraniczna Rzeczypospolitej Polskiej w roku 1991—Expose sejmowe ministra spraw zagranicznych RP, Krzysztofa Skubiszewskiego" [Foreign Policy of the Republic of Poland in 1991—Sejm Exposé by the Polish Foreign Minister Krzysztof Skubiszewski] (27 June 1991), *Zbior Dokumentow*, no. 1 (1992): 52–54.

96. "Genscher, Polish Counterpart view Bilateral Ties," DPA, 1709 GMT, 28 August 1991, *FBIS-WEU*, 29 August 1991, 5.

97. "[Genscher] Meets with Skubiszewski, DPA, 0801 GMT, 4 February 1992, *FBIS-EEU*, 4 February 1992, 22; "Further on Skubiszewski Meeting," and 1156 GMT, 4 February 1992, *FBIS-EEU*, 4 February 1992, 22–23; Boleslaw Wdowczak, "Joint News Conference by German Foreign Minister Hans-Dietrich Genscher and Polish Foreign Minister Krzysztof Skubiszewski," Radio Warszawa Network, 1800 GMT, 4 February 1992, *FBIS-EEU*, 5 February 1992, 18.

98. BAN Report, "Poland Only Has a Chance Together with the EC," *Zycie Warszawy*, 18 March 1992, *FBIS-EEU*, 24 March 1992, 28; and "Polityka zagraniczna pan-

stwa: trwalosc i zadan w zmiennych okolicznosciach" [Foreign Policy of the State: The Durability of Goals and Tasks in Changing Circumstances], in Kryzsztof Skubiszewski, *Polityka zagraniczna i odzyskanie niepodlegnosci: przemówienia, oswiadczenia, wywiady 1989–1993* [Foreign Policy and Regaining Independence: Addresses, Declaration, Interviews, 1989–1993] (Warsaw: Wydawa Interpress, 1997); Prizel, *National Identity and Foreign Policy*, 116–123; and Vinton, "Domestic Politics and Foreign Policy," 60–61.

99. "[Kinkel] Meets with Skubiszewski," DPA, 1038 GMT, 29 July 1992, *FBIS-EEU*, 29 July 1992, 10; "Skubiszewski, Kinkel Hail Border Cooperation," PAP, 1544 GMT, 29 July 1992, *FBIS-EEU*, 30 July 1992, 17; "Suchocka, Kinkel Discuss Socioeconomic Situation," PAP 1726 GMT, 29 July 1992, *FBIS-EEU*, 31 July 1992, 17; "Cooperation Discussed with Luftwaffe Commander," PAP, 1159 GMT, 30 July 1992, *FBIS-EEU*, 31 July 1992, 17; and C.G., "Kinkel Agrees on Border Traffic Facilitation with Poland—Three Agreements Signed," *Frankfurter Allgemeine* (Frankfurt), 30 July 1992, *FBIS-WEU*, 13 August 1992, 7–8.

100. "Wystapienie premier RP Hanny Suchockiej na inauguracji roku akademickiego KUL, Lublin" [Appearance of Premier of the Republic of Poland Hanna Suchocka at the Beginning of the Academic Year at KUL] (18 October 1992), in *Rocznik Polskiej Polityki Zagranicznej, 1992* [Yearbook of Polish Foreign Policy, 1992], ed. Barbara Wizimirska (Warsaw: Polski Instytut Spraw Miedzynarodowych, 1994), 18–19; Prizel, "Warsaw's Ostpolitik," 105; Rachwald, "Looking West," 136-138; "Suchocka: Policy Oriented Toward NATO, EC," PAP, 1449 GMT, 18 October 1992, *FBIS-EEU*, 19 October 1992, 20–21.

101. "Suchocka Comments on Visit to Germany," Radio Warszawa Network, 1510 GMT, 6 November 1992, *FBIS-EEU*, 9 November 1992, 26–27; "Suchocka Reports 'Amazing Understanding' with Kohl," PAP, 1629 GMT, 5 November 1992, *FBIS-EEU*, 12 November 1992, 19; "Kohl: Relations 'Vital for Europe,'" DDP (Berlin), 1319 GMT, 5 November 1992, *FBIS-EEU*, 12 November 1992, 19; and C.G. and K.B., "Kohl Wants to Help Poland into the EC," *Frankfurter Allgemeine*, 6 November 1992, *FBIS-EEU*, 12 November 1992, 19.

102. Tadeusz Olszanski, "Suchocka Meets with Kohl in Budapest," Radio Warszawa Network, 1005 GMT, 2 September 1993, *FBIS-EEU*, 2 September 1993, 23; and "NATO Membership to Be Discussed at January Summit," PAP, 2021 GMT, 2 September 1993, *FBIS-EEU*, 3 September 1993, 14.

103. Skubiszewski, *Poland's Western Border*, 460–466; Hajnicz, "Poland within Its Geopolitical Triangle," 30–40; and Skorzynski, "The Seminar and Foundation 'Poland in Europe,'" 98–100.

104. Szabo, *The Diplomacy of German Unification*, 72–76; Zelikow and Rice, *Germany Unified and Europe Transformed*, 207–208, 218–222; and Stent, *Russia and Germany Reborn*, 118–119.

105. "Statement by Polish Minister of Foreign Affairs Krzysztof Skubiszewski" (7 December 1989), *Zbior Dokumentow*, no. 4 (1990): 7–10. See also Schweller, "Bandwagoning for Profit," 78–79, 88–89, 104–107; and on logrolling, see Jack Snyder, *Myths of Empire: Domestic Politics and International Ambition* (Ithaca, N.Y.: Cornell University Press, 1991).

106. Stehle, "Western Border a Sore Point—Foreign Minister Krzysztof Skubiszewski Does Not Understand Bonn's Hesitation," 25–26.

107. Kostrzewa-Zorbas, "The Russian Troop Withdrawal from Poland," 113–138; and Louisa Vinton, "Domestic Politics and Foreign Policy," 37–38.

108. Private memorandum given to me, Grzegorz Kostrzewa-Zorbas, "Theses on Polish Policies toward the East on the Threshold of the 1990s," 22 March 1990. Chapter 4 examines how the *MSZ* prepared for the collapse of the USSR, particularly Warsaw's diplomatic relations with El'tsin's Russian foreign ministry.

109. Paul Schroeder, "Historical Reality vs. Neo-realist Theory," *International Security*, vol. 19, no. 1 (summer 1994): 108–148.

110. Kostrzewa-Zorbas, "The Russian Troop Withdrawal from Poland," 118; and Zdzislaw Najder, *How I Saw Poland: How and to Whom I Advised*, 151–153.

111. More analysis on Soviet troop withdrawals follows in chapter 4. See also Andrew Kydd, "Trust, Reassurance, and Cooperation," *International Organization*, vol. 54, no. 2 (spring 2000): 352–353; and James D. Fearon, "Bargaining, Enforcement, and International Cooperation," *International Organization*, vol. 52, no. 2 (spring 1998): 296. Though closely focused on Soviet/Russian–German troop withdrawal negotiations, Celeste Wallander's sparing analysis only states how Poland "undermined Russia's ability to fulfill its commitments," not the intricate tactics Soviet military hard-liners used against Polish negotiators and German rejections of Poland's initiatives. Celeste A. Wallander, *Mortal Friends, Best Enemies: German–Russian Cooperation after the Cold War* (Ithaca, N.Y.: Cornell University Press, 1999), 75–76.

112. Glaser, "Realists as Optimists," 25–26, 161–163; Andrew Kydd, "Sheep in Sheep's Clothing: Why Security Seekers Do Not Fight Each Other," *Security Studies*, vol. 7, no. 1 (autumn 1997): 152–154; and Taliaferro, "Seeking Security under Anarchy," 136–140, 159.

113. Witold Beres, Krzysztof Burnetinski, and Andrzej Romanowski, "Building the Foundation for Poland's Foreign Policy: Interview with Professor Krzysztof Skubiszewski," *Tygodnik Powszechny*, November 1, 1994, 1, 4, 8.

114. Anne Applebaum, "The Polish Model," *Wall Street Journal*, 14 June 2001, available from Johnson's Russia List, #5300, (15 June 2001).

115. Loriaux, "Realism and Reconciliation: France, Germany, and the European Union," 378–379; Philip H. Gordon, *France, Germany and the Western Alliance* (Boulder, Colo.: Westview, 1995).

116. John Reed, "Rebirth of a Nation," *Financial Times*, 10–11 August 2002, 1; Glaser, "Realists as Optimists," 25–26, 161–163; and Taliaferro, "Seeking Security under Anarchy," 159.

4

From Soviet Disintegration to Post-Soviet Neighboring Links

The challenges of the Soviet empire's collapse and the rapid disintegration of the Soviet Communist power base confronted Poland not only with the emergence of four independent nations on its eastern border, but also potentially different possibilities for a new era in Eastern strategy. As important, this extraordinary Eastern upheaval embroiled Skubiszewski in foreign and domestic policy disputes concerning the twin challenges of a powerful, domineering, post-Communist Polish president and several post-Communist premiers. Why the foreign ministry established a two-track policy with the Soviet "center" and emerging non-Soviet neighboring Lithuanian, Russian, Ukrainian, and Belorussian republics forms the basis for understanding how Skubiszewski maneuvered between domestic political battlegrounds and foreign security dilemmas. Traditionally, Eastern policy debates caused Poland no end of controversy and frequently became the difference between stable and unstable governments, let alone regional tensions leading to war.

How did these traditional Eastern policy disputes enter into the designs of post-Communist foreign policy–makers as they sought to craft a middle power role between its perennial great power antagonists? To determine what kind of alignment strategy Skubiszewski and his *MSZ* team employed, analysis needs to account for how Poland grappled with the following four key problems. First, the rationale behind how Poland gained the USSR's acceptance of Poland's post-Communist independent middle power role in Central–East European security needs explanation. This provides better understanding of both reactions and initiatives regarding the USSR's disintegration and Poland's alignment toward the emerging post-Soviet leaderships. For Poland, this signified a tremendous leap in foreign policy, as Warsaw's policymakers struggled to solidify linkages with four new neighboring non-Soviet republics. In the process, a key issue revolved around how Poland and its eastern neighbors could overcome historic difficulties with the *Kresy*—the oft disputed eastern borderlands between Poland and Russia. While those two challenges didn't consume Skubiszewski's tenure, the reactions and initiatives over hard-nosed negotiations concerning Soviet troop withdrawals from Poland did, as did dealing with two failed Moscow coups d'état in August 1991 and October 1993. What became most telling for Skubiszewski and Poland's Eastern policy–makers stemmed from their keen appreciation "as an immediate [western] neighbor, we could become the first victims of more serious conflicts there [the East]. That is why the bridge that we are building to the East must be supported by very strong Western pillars."[1] Therefore, in assessing the impact regionally of the collapse of one of the last international empires, this chapter revolves around Poland's middle power role, examining whether it became more than a middle power in and of itself regionally, and whether it reduced regional security dilemmas.

During his four years in office, Skubiszewski faced domestic political and bureaucratic struggles to influence Poland's foreign policy, some of which stemmed from historic ethnonationalist territorial claims. These difficulties arose from some of Poland's nascent political parties, who made claims on the *Kresy* and from the emerging post-Communist neighboring states against Poland. For Skubiszewski, some of the *Solidarnosc* underground's ideas and the Polish émigré community's analyses affected post-Communist policymaking options, particularly how to defuse and possibly overcome the tensions of ethnonational territorial demands. To counter the potentially destabilizing impact of ethnonational differences, not only on Polish domestic politics, but also in response to Poland's neighbors against Polish minorities abroad, Skubiszewski argued for reconciliation and cooperation with all of Poland's eastern neighbors.[2] Some of the key Eastern policy–makers Skubiszewski brought to the *MSZ* came from the small Polish foreign policy community of young, underground experts. Former underground journal editors Grzegorz Kostrzewa-Zorbas and Andrzej Ananicz formed the nucleus of the *MSZ*'s Eastern policy team in the early 1990s.[3] Their foreign policy journals contributed to the weakening of the Polish Communist system. Their non-Communist views also prepared the way for a new policy once they joined the *MSZ* in 1990.[4] Accordingly, noted *Solidarnosc* journalist Konstanty Gebert, the legacy of underground principles provided post-Communist policymakers the basis for understanding the political psychology of Polish–Russian relations:

> It is sometimes surprising to discover that Poles—supposedly the Russian-haters—were much more willing to include Russia in Europe than other Central European states, supposedly Russophiles. Since we are stuck in this together, we must get to know each other, get to know our good sides. Noble figures like Sakharov morally challenged us. If people like him were able to grapple with the wrongs of Russian imperialism, assume the burden of responsibility, we better do it, too.[5]

Creating a Post-Communist Eastern Policy

Skubiszewski came to his new position with a practical understanding of the Polish–Soviet relationship. During the late Communist era as a professor at Poznan University, Skubiszewski participated in Wojciech Jaruzelski's Consultative Council, a short-lived advisory group under the Polish Communist leader, and wrote an article on the need for a series of steps to repatriate Poles forced to live in Kazakhstan and Siberia.[6] This analysis of the Stalinist forced migrations signified Skubiszewski's early effort to pose a sensitive issue publicly, but in such a way as to offer options that both the Polish Communist regime and the USSR might accept.[7] Such notions of compromise quickly became Skubiszewski's trademark as foreign minister.

He prided himself on policies that reflected internationally recognized legal norms for foreign policy behavior. By basing his decisions on internationally accepted documents from the United Nations, The Hague, the CSCE, and NATO, Skubiszewski employed sanctioned Western principles and standards. During his confirmation hearings before the newly elected Parliament, Skubiszewski stated that "loyalty" to the popularly elected government, not to the Communist Party, dictated the change from the *MSZ*'s ideologically based procedures to promote a sovereign foreign policy.[8] However, the foreign minister remained cautious, even at the cost, for example, of not quickly appointing more *Solidarnosc* personnel and demoting Communist holdovers. It appeared that Skubiszewski, though he advocated a break with past personnel policy, remained beholden to the limitations of the April 1989 *Solidarnosc*–Communist Roundtable Agreement.[9] Thus, shortly after assuming office, Skubiszewski and Premier Tadeusz Mazowiecki acquiesced to Communist pressure by appointing the long-serving foreign ministry apparatchik Boleslaw Kulski as *MSZ* vice minister responsible for Eastern policy and Soviet Bloc affairs.[10]

Although Kulski's continued responsibilities delayed serious change in Skubiszewski's Eastern policy, his first speech abroad contradicted the Communist appointment. By stating that Poland intended to "change our system of government," Skubiszewski underscored that the new government "acts in such a way that the promotion of our vital interests is in no conflict with the interests of others."[11] Evidently, Skubiszewski envisioned shaping and implementing a new Eastern strategy differently from *MSZ* personnel encountered upon becoming foreign minister. Most likely, his initial strategy stemmed from sensitivity toward the nearly 60,000 Soviet troops stationed on Polish territory as part of the Warsaw Pact.[12]

Though cautious about appointing non-Communist personnel to the *MSZ* at the outset, Skubiszewski raised sensitive issues during his early encounters with his Soviet counterpart at the UN and in Warsaw only a few weeks after becoming minister. In his first meeting with Soviet foreign minister Eduard Shevardnadze, the Polish foreign minister underlined that Poland intended to pursue reforms as an independent and nonthreatening post-Communist actor. They agreed to discuss such issues as reform of the Warsaw Pact and the CMEA, with Skubiszewski saying publicly, "I feel that it [CMEA] plays a very weak, if indeed any, role in economic development." Given the sweeping post–Communist political changes in Poland, both ministers agreed that their alliance relationship needed revision.[13]

Shevardnadze's visit to Poland on 24 October gave Skubiszewski the opportunity to begin transforming the Polish–Soviet relationship. Shevardnadze intended this first official meeting with the first post-Communist Warsaw Pact foreign minister to support Gorbachev's "new thinking" and to demonstrate Poland's continued adherence to the Soviet Bloc. However, just before Shevardnadze's arrival, Skubiszewski stated that Poland resolved to build a sovereign foreign policy separate from, but sensitive toward, the USSR. He viewed Moscow's several-year-old reform policies as innovative, but not necessarily consistent with Poland's new leadership. According to Skubiszewski, Poland's Communist-era "satellite" relationship to the USSR no longer defined the means by which both states needed to work together. He told a foreign reporter that "ties relying even on the tiniest form of dependence are inconceivable." Though Skubiszewski expected to change Poland's Soviet policy "gingerly and gradually," he vowed to accelerate "changes in our foreign policy toward West Europe and on issues stemming from traditional partition of the continent."[14] Even this small departure from traditional post–World War II Polish–Soviet ties put Moscow on notice.

Even as the sole non-Communist in the *MSZ*, Skubiszewski remained determined to project Poland as an independent actor in Central European security. Over a series of meetings, the Polish leadership and Soviet foreign minister discussed political and economic relations. Shevardnadze stated that Moscow envisioned prioritizing political over military relations in the Warsaw Pact. He underscored that Poland's new political leadership remained a committed ally, even as Warsaw introduced political and economic reforms different from those of the USSR. Skubiszewski pressed the Soviet foreign minister to recognize that Poland's economic reform symbolized a true break with the Communist economic system, deeming it a requirement to "give up the formula of coordinating economic plans." In response, Shevardnadze said, "we are vitally interested in Poland overcoming the crisis. . . . I know the Polish government devotes much attention to economic relations with the West. This is the right thing to do." Furthermore, though reluctant to provide specifics for how the USSR anticipated rehabilitating the Polish victims of Stalinist repression, Shevardnadze pronounced Moscow ready to examine this controversial issue.[15] Above all, the joint communiqué pledged to respect Poland's national interests, as both states worked toward "mutual benefit" and respect for all "interests."[16] As one prominent Polish journalist commented, successful Eastern policy remained dependent on Soviet "reformists." Yet, Poland needed not only to expand relations with reformers in Moscow, but also "with respect to the Lithuanians and the Ukrainians . . . in Vilnius and in Kiev."[17]

Prime Minister Mazowiecki also strove to improve relations by visiting the USSR in late November to gain Soviet acceptance of Poland as an independent actor. Before Mazowiecki's departure, however, Polish leaders set the stage for the premier's trip. To demonstrate solidarity with the democratization movements in the USSR, prominent Polish and Lithuanian politicians and intellectuals, primarily from *Solidarnosc* and its incipient Lithuanian counterpart, *Sajudis*, exchanged letters publicly. The letters underlined each side's intent not to claim territory, particularly the historically controversial areas in and around Lithuanian Vilnius, and sought to bolster cooperation by respecting the rights and cultural autonomy of the respective minority populations living in each country.[18] Though these letters marked the beginning of the often times strained Polish–Lithuanian relationship, post–Communist Warsaw and Vilnius leaders recognized the importance of mobilizing their respective populations to signal resolve to Soviet leaders.[19]

Two significant interviews also marked the tone for Mazowiecki's trip. First, Skubiszewski reiterated the challenge of designing a fully sovereign foreign policy when he said "there was a lack of independence about the policy, and the ministry [*MSZ*] itself and its personnel were an appendage of one political party." Even if Poland defined its own path, he also argued that "we can learn quite a number of things from states such as Finland, [but] I avoid the term ["Finlandization"] because there is something pejorative about it."[20] Secondly, prior to his departure, the Polish premier stated that Poland "respected allied treaties," but "a feeling of freedom of choice accompanies this, and not a feeling of subordinating oneself to someone's commands." Poland viewed the USSR as a "partner" in security and economic affairs, but he stressed that "a strong and democratic Poland" remains necessary for the USSR to have a stable western border. Therefore, Mazowiecki expected the trip to achieve "equivalent cooperation . . . stamping out the so-called blank spots, giving moral satisfaction to victims of Stalinist terror."[21]

The objectives of this first trip focused on overcoming Polish–Soviet tensions and building new relationships to Russian politicians and intellectuals. Instead of traveling with the Polish delegation, Skubiszewski decided to send his vice minister Kulski to represent the *MSZ* and stayed in Warsaw to testify at a Sejm hearing on the sensitive issue of Poles living in the USSR. He laid out the case for what Poland wanted from the Soviet leadership for the Polish minorities in the USSR by arguing that all Poles needed to "cultivate their Polishness and the decision whether to emigrate or stay . . . should belong to these people alone."[22] This statement provided the premier's delegation with an important policy, particularly for Aleksander Hall, a Russian specialist and advisor to Mazowiecki.

By employing the same arguments from his days as a young *Solidarnosc* leader, Hall used this historic trip to seek greater ties to Russia. Hall initiated with the Moscow and Leningrad regional officials Polish language and educational programs via Poland's efforts to supply teachers, even Polish priests, to spend extended periods in Russia, broadcast Polish television programs to all

Soviet republics bordering Poland, and reestablish Polish–Russian linkages, implicitly to forge post-Communist links. In principle, Soviet leaders agreed to Hall's initiatives, as he met with Communist officials in Moscow, Poles living in the USSR, and non-Communist Russian intellectuals.[23] As a result, the final communiqué underscored "the development of national identity among the people of the Polish nationality in the USSR and ethnic groups of the USSR nations living in Poland."[24]

Mazowiecki asserted that democratic principles needed to undergird Polish–Soviet ties, too. Such principles delineated "equal rights, mutual benefit, and democratization among states in accordance with the right of states and peoples to self-determination." Though cautious about raising the issue of Soviet forces stationed in Poland, Mazowiecki revealed that Poland expected the Warsaw Pact to evolve into a more politically focused organization, implying less need for military structures, including Soviet troops stationed outside the USSR. Such questions played a critical role when Polish–Soviet withdrawal negotiations began within the next year.[25] However, the most significant development occurred when Mazowiecki addressed representatives of the USSR's Polish community and met separately with Russian intellectuals in both Moscow and Leningrad.

During his speech to the Polish community, the premier described the outline of a new Eastern policy toward the Soviet and non-Soviet republic leaderships. For Poles in the USSR, Mazowiecki underlined that they "can play an important role as a natural bridge between Poland and the Soviet Union, as well as between the Polish and Russian, Lithuanian, Belorussian, and Ukrainian peoples." Cautiously, he advised that building these bridges "requires understanding for the aspirations of these peoples and the cultivation of attitudes of mutual respect and tolerance." Therefore, he determined "to ensure that appropriate conditions exist in Poland for the cultural development of ethnic minorities, including Lithuanian, Belorussian, and Ukrainian minorities."[26]

His meetings with Russian intellectuals also highlighted Poland's enormous changes. He said, "we need success from your transformation and you need success from our transformation." According to Mazowiecki, Poland's reforms represented the bellwether for some democratic and pluralistic solutions which "do not threaten European stability."[27] As testimony to the support Mazowiecki received from the Russian intellectual community, Andrei Sakharov declared that "throughout my whole life the problems of the Poles were equally close to me as the problems of my own country. The road she has chosen does not only determine the fate of Poland, but also has its repercussions for the whole camp of socialist countries."[28] After the trip, Polish commentators observed the new Polish leadership demonstrated a different Eastern approach—one representing the majority of the Polish people, not the Communist Party.[29]

The New Eastern Policy Takes Shape

Mazowiecki's trip provided a crucial foundation for determining Poland's new Eastern policy. Not only did the prime minister signal Poland's firm resolve to initiate a more equitable and pragmatic state-to-state relationship with the USSR, given the Soviet political flexibility to broaden ties. Warsaw also became more convinced that to regain sovereignty over foreign policy required a new set of relationships with the bordering Soviet republics, as Moscow loosened its grip on those regions and as they consolidated independence. The premier's trip and its repercussions also enabled Poland to develop its other-help role regionally on eastern policy—to survive and to try to prosper between Eastern and Western great powers by linking great, middle, and small powers.

Some of the first thoughts from post–Communist Polish experts on how Poland needed to change its Eastern policy came from an internal memorandum written by Kostrzewa-Zorbas, who traveled to Lithuania from 7 to 14 October 1989. His observations underscored important dimensions of Eastern policy and reached the leadership via Hall, one of Kostrzewa-Zorbas' Gdansk underground era colleagues. It remains one of the first post-Communist documents to detail not only the crucial problems Warsaw faced in the coming years, specifically with Lithuania, but also general implications for other Soviet republics. The memorandum analyzed in great detail the *Sajudis* strategy for making Lithuania independent and foretold that its leadership under Vytautas Landsbergis already "prepared for the practical aspects of government . . . after the elections [February 1990] and total independence." The memorandum cautioned, however, that Lithuania's "relationship with the rest of the USSR is not yet worked out." Furthermore, Kostrzewa-Zorbas warned "it would be impossible for Poland politically to establish good relations with Lithuania by using the Warsaw-Moscow axis." This particularly raises angst given "the rise of Polish autonomy that not only puts up a barrier between the Polish minority in Lithuania and Lithuanians, but also between Poland and the emerging Lithuanian state." Kostrzewa-Zorbas believed Soviet pressure to hold the USSR together increasingly jeopardized Lithuania's independence. Polish and Russian minority tensions in Lithuania also compelled Warsaw to work harder "to gain understanding on all fronts with Lithuania." Given these admonitions, he recommended ways to diffuse tensions.[30]

The most important way to solve these ethnonational tensions, Kostrzewa-Zorbas argued, stemmed from the desire for peaceful change by the newly elected democratic Polish leadership. To start a practical and potentially productive working relationship with *Sajudis*, something Kostrzewa-Zorbas didn't believe possible with Moscow or Lithuanian Communist politicians, the Mazowiecki leadership needed to "steer the Polish minority in Lithuania to maintain its ties to Poland," not to Soviet Moscow. The rationale focused on separating the Lithuanian Communist leaders from those already emerging as post-Communist pragmatists, such as Czeslaw Okinczyc. Kostrzewa-Zorbas also argued that "Polish autonomy in several Polish majority areas in and around Vilnius undercut the building of a Baltic multiethnic region. It also undercut the democratization of the USSR. It might spread to Belorussia, Ukraine, and other multi-ethnic republics which could start ethnic unrest, the consequences of which are hard to foresee." Worse, he stated that such autonomous movements as that of the Polish minority in Lithuania "might pave the way for demands of Lithuanians, Ukrainians, and Belorussians in Poland." As a result, this development "might even cause a re-opening of questions of autonomy for Silesia, and other parts of Western and Northern Poland by those calling themselves authentic or cultural Germans." To counter potential instability, he recommended Poland and Lithuania seek compromise, especially after the February 1990 elections. He predicted *Sajudis* would capture a considerable majority and "bilaterally guarantee the present state borders, confirm human rights for all minorities in both states, and eliminate fear of historic Polish intervention into Lithuania."[31] These statements underscore the strategy Kostrzewa-Zorbas soon used toward the Soviet republics, after joined the *MSZ* in June 1990.[32]

The close of the momentous year of Central and East European revolutions in 1989 presented Skubiszewski with the question of how fast to proceed on Eastern and Western policies. Unlike the other Central European Communist leaderships, however, Poland remained essentially alone in its post-Communist quest to develop and implement a sovereign foreign policy separate from the USSR. Only in early 1990 did other Central European states consolidate their post–Communist political gains, as the USSR disintegrated. His quandary also involved the issue of the Soviet troops stationed in Poland and Poland's economic dependence on the USSR for raw materials. As chapter 2 demonstrated, Skubiszewski's positive options remained virtually nonexistent on Soviet troop withdrawal negotiations and he faced the reality of employing those troops in Poland to bargain for the confirmation of the Polish–German border.[33] Intent on forging a practical and nonthreatening middle power alignment policy toward Poland's great power neighbors, Skubiszewski tried to reconcile the extension of Poland's democratic-based foreign policy with its accommodation toward the FRG and USSR. Theoretically, Skubiszewski attempted to align Poland with democratizing states (USSR) and firmly democratic states (FRG) by bridging and upholding the sanctity of state borders and the making of sovereign foreign policy. To reintegrate into Europe and its security structure without threatening the USSR, Skubiszewski needed to navigate between rapidly changing and potentially threatening Moscow and Bonn. Swift geopolitical changes in the dissolution of the USSR and the unification of Germany at the beginning of 1990 tested Skubiszewski's bridging strategy. Skubiszewski sought to work closely with both neighbors, establishing close ties with Bonn and redefining relations with Moscow—difficult, at best, given Warsaw's attempt to shed delicately its Soviet satellite status.

As 1990 began, Skubiszewski also became enmeshed in a protracted domestic political struggle over Soviet force withdrawals between Mazowiecki and *Solidarnosc* labor leader Lech Walesa, both of whom started vying for the first post-Communist presidency. Skubiszewski doubted the United States conceived of withdrawing its troops from Europe and he expected USSR troops to remain in some parts of Central and Eastern Europe. He reasoned that "people so often forget this when they speak of doing away with the military blocs." Furthermore, he stated that "the Americans are guests in Europe, not the Russians. The latter will stay along the Bug River and that is not so far from Berlin and Vienna." Unlike any other Warsaw Pact state, he implied that post-Communist Poland's present security remained dependent on American troops staying in Europe, perhaps to hedge against resurgent Soviet power, and the reality, at the end of 1989, that Soviet forces intended to stay in Europe, too. Moreover, he wanted his rhetoric to reach Bonn to underscore Poland's border concerns.[34] However, presidential candidate Walesa, who prided himself on trying to manage many of the government's policies from behind the scenes, held a surprise meeting with the Soviet ambassador to Poland. That furtive tête-à-tête in Gdansk on 18 January 1990 sparked a national debate over force withdrawals and put Mazowiecki's government on the defensive.[35]

Walesa's surreptitious meeting with Soviet ambassador Vladimir Brovikov created a domestic political frenzy that shook Mazowiecki's government and challenged Skubiszewski's policy. First of all, Walesa called for Soviet forces to withdraw much earlier than the government was demanding. In fact, Walesa's press spokesman revealed that Walesa declared that all forces needed to withdraw by the end of 1990.[36] Secondly, a stunned Mazowiecki learned about the meeting from the Polish press. For Polish rightist parties and for those demonstrating against Soviet forces in Poland, Walesa's brash behavior toward the Soviet ambassador brought a welcome change from the methodical governmental policies.[37] In response to Walesa's surprise announcement, the government countered by impulsively asserting that "we are not opening the issue of the stationing of Soviet troops in Poland. . . . We believe that Walesa indeed will do everything he can to bring about the withdrawal of forces."[38] Publicly mocking Walesa's abilities to deal with the Soviets, the government failed to anticipate Walesa's impending presidential bid. For Skubiszewski, Walesa's pronouncement directly questioned the *MSZ*'s methodical Eastern policy and complicated already strained dealings with Bonn. Strangely, Walesa then remained relatively silent on troop withdrawals, except when he criticized the government for avoiding the issue, rather than actually defining a game plan for Polish–Soviet negotiations.[39] The premier soon realized the political implications of Walesa's attacks, particularly for the upcoming presidential campaign, and by the summer of 1990 approved Skubiszewski's plan to initiate withdrawal talks.

As analyzed in chapter 2, Skubiszewski won praise from the German leadership for his public stand on unified Germany in NATO by the winter of 1990, contrary to Moscow's position, but failed to secure the German chancellor's commitment to the Polish–German border. For Skubiszewski, the dilemma between Soviet force withdrawals and German unification stemmed from his belief that a neutral unified Germany signified a dangerous Germany. If a unified Germany became neutral he believed that "after a few years a politician will come and say we must change this, we need a large army to support our policy. Today a neutralization is not possible."[40] Skubiszewski departed Bonn, disappointed over the German failure to commit to Poland's western border and uncertain if his strategy to support membership for unified Germany in NATO improved Polish–German relations.

Yet, Skubiszewski compounded his difficulties by reiterating that Soviet forces need not necessarily withdraw from East Germany.[41] Such a declaration opposed the intentions of his German hosts, who desired Gorbachev's approval for unification and wanted united Germany in NATO with Soviet troops withdrawn. On the one hand, Polish protests against Soviet troops grew, including statements even by Communist president Jaruzelski and, following his 18 January declaration, by Walesa, in which the *Solidarnosc* leader stated that "stationing them [Soviet troops in Poland] is a waste of money."[42] On the other hand, some in the Polish press argued that potential German neutrality and traditional "drifting towards the East and Russia" required Warsaw to play one of the few international security "trump cards" it possessed. That maneuvering entailed that "a new game will soon begin in European security. . . . Europe is interested in its [Soviet troops] remaining on our territory till a new security system is created." Moreover, the editorial admonished, "it is worth realizing how much this card is worth. If we give it away right now, making Russians withdraw, we will not get a penny for it." Finally, the editorial underlined that Poland's good international reputation stemmed from Skubiszewski's pragmatism and caution, a policy that depended on the difficult "test" of whether to request Soviet troops withdraw from Poland to reach a German border accord.[43]

The failure to reach a German accord placed Warsaw in an awkward position. By trying to play the presence of Soviet troops in Poland against Germany, Skubiszewski thought that he would force Bonn to reconsider. He tried to reinforce this position by saying Soviet troops should remain in East Germany. Such tactical maneuvers, however, failed to convince Bonn. Instead, Polish foreign policy–makers imposed limits on themselves. Ultimately, this balancing or even detrimental bandwagoning against Bonn potentially cost Warsaw leverage against a weakened Moscow in subsequent withdrawal talks.[44] Moreover, Walesa's conservative advisors attacked the government for sacrificing Poland's sovereignty.[45] Though Skubiszewski and Mazowiecki finally gained the support of America, France, and the United Kingdom for Polish participation in the "2 Plus 4" talks by the spring, the government believed Moscow remained the key to changing Kohl's mind during the negotiations.[46]

Even if Poland lost negotiating leverage to Moscow on troop withdrawal talks later in 1990 and 1991, some Polish experts contend the leadership fell into a catch-22 situation. As elaborated in chapters 1 and 2, Poland required the USSR's clout to participate in the "2 Plus 4" talks and to pressure Bonn on the Polish–German border. Yet, Warsaw also realized that, to plan secretly to disband the Warsaw Pact, Skubiszewski needed time to convince his post-Communist Hungarian and Czech counterparts to work in tandem with Poland, not to act alone to disband the Pact.[47] Although Warsaw remained virtually consumed with German unification in the winter of 1990, Skubiszewski tried to develop a more robust Eastern policy. Soon to be a facilitator within limited geopolitical means and, arguably, a "specializer" between great powers, middle power Poland next redefined Eastern policy as Skubiszewski restructured the *MSZ*.[48]

Eastern Policy's New Dynamic: The *MSZ* "Young Turks" Take Charge

After five months in office, Skubiszewski began to reorganize the *MSZ*. He wanted to change the *MSZ*'s Communist personnel policy and infuse the ministry with new thinking not dependent on party affiliation. He announced in mid-January, with the approval of the premier, the removal of several nominations of general officers slated to become the consuls general in Moscow, Minsk, Kiev, and Lvov. These military officers did not represent the Foreign Service and belonged to the old regime.[49] In February, Skubiszewski reasoned, "I have eliminated the Communist Party positions associated with diplomatic posts. I have prevented certain nominations left over from the previous government." Yet, he faced difficulty hiring non-Communist personnel with adequate diplomatic training. Thus, he recruited the younger generation, many out of universities, but this proved a lengthy process.[50]

When he did decide to start replacing *MSZ* apparatchiks, Skubiszewski attempted to bring new people into the higher ranks. By that winter he identified some of the key personnel to enact a new Eastern policy. He turned to one of his old international law colleagues, Jerzy Makarczyk, and convinced him to become the first non-Communist vice minister, charged with reorganizing the *MSZ* administratively and with actually running the *MSZ*, when Skubiszewski traveled, or with leading specific negotiations abroad. The foreign minister felt very comfortable having Makarczyk as his second-in-command, considering the vice minister's wealth of experience as an international law specialist since 1962, extensive lecturing in the United States, FRG, Japan, and Great Britain, and his presidency of the Association for International Law in 1988.[51] Next, the foreign minister decided, after reading another important private memorandum by Kostrzewa-Zorbas, that he wanted the *Solidarnosc* activist to become the *MSZ*'s new European deputy director, responsible, inter alia, for the USSR Section. As it turned out, this memorandum determined the *MSZ*'s links to the emerging non-Soviet republic leaders.

Written by Kostrzewa-Zorbas in the spring, the memorandum recounted his recent month-long travel to Moscow, Kiev, Lvov, Minsk, Vilnius, and Kaunas and detailed meetings with senior members of the USSR government, Russian Inter-Regional Deputies Group, and leading Ukrainian, Belorussian, and Lithuanian activists.[52] The memorandum again reached the leadership, as well as Walesa and his key advisor, Senator Jaroslaw Kaczynski, whom Kostrzewa-Zorbas also knew very well from Gdansk. The analysis marked a turning point for the *MSZ*'s Eastern approach, as Kostrzewa-Zorbas argued for "Poland to adopt a new multi-phased Eastern policy," given the increasing democratization that "hastens the disintegration of the Soviet Union both on national and societal levels." Because the USSR's disintegration weakened the foundation for the Polish–Soviet relationship, Kostrzewa-Zorbas underscored that "to fill the void, one should establish immediate contacts with the new Republic authorities, especially those in Russia." He cautioned, however, that "we must not add to the disintegration of the USSR, but we must not ignore the realities and develop relations with our emerging neighbors, because Moscow's imperial Soviet guarantee of the status quo is no longer realistic." For Kostrzewa-Zorbas, "Poland could, by reaching out to meaningful powers and promoting compromise, add stability to this process of change." Consequently, he defined the concept of a "two-track" Eastern policy. Its political objective focused on "gradually building a complex system of relations between Poland and each concrete Soviet Republic," including possible cross-border legal and customs agreements beyond extant cultural and educational linkages.[53]

Kostrzewa-Zorbas also raised the important issue of Poland's eastern border. He likened this sensitive question to Poland's concern over its western border and argued that some misunderstanding arose within the leaderships of the growing independence movements in Ukraine, Belorussia, and Lithuania. He asserted that the post–World War II "legal," "psychological," and "propagandistic" Soviet legacy of border redrawing resulted in unnecessary and damaging perceptions between Poland and each Soviet republic bordering Poland. Poland needed to conclude "mutual agreements," he assessed, with each bordering republic "to establish the firm, unmovable borders which would put to rest any unrealistic dreams." To achieve this goal, Poland required formal "relationships through regular consultations as soon as the new republics elect their parliaments and presidents, and establish independent foreign ministries." Such foreign policy initiatives posited a historic breakthrough for Poland, Kostrzewa-Zorbas argued, and Poland need not wait for final elections "to expand the network of Polish consulates to prepare to elevate the relations between Poland and each Soviet republic to that of state-to-state status." These changes to Eastern policy "cannot be underestimated," he avowed. A large "psychological effect" would help the emerging democratization movements in the Soviet Republics if Poland granted "national recognition," he claimed. By "building a base for diplomatic relations with these emerging nations," Kostrzewa-Zorbas believed Poland not only "enhanced cooperation, but minimized disagreements." The bottom line remained that "today Poland is in the attractive position to be a political force for the improvement of relations with all of these Republics, especially Russia." He concluded "such a turning point in improving Poland's national security can also start by encouraging these Republics to open consulates in Warsaw, an effort that would do much to cure the ignorance and phobias about and by these nations."[54]

The memorandum proposals proved very timely as Lithuania declared its independence in March 1990 and the devolution of power from the Soviet "center" in Moscow accelerated. In response to the 12 March 1990 Lithuanian independence declaration, the Polish foreign minister underlined that "what happens in Lithuania is relevant to us. . . . We have historic relations with Lithuania. We have a long past. This is not insignificant."[55] Such a statement partially addressed the pressing concerns Skubiszewski felt about the ominous developments in Lithuania, given the Soviet regime's political condemnation of Lithuanian independence, its economic blockade against the Baltic state, and its military maneuvers in and around Vilnius. The Polish government's sensitivity about recognizing Lithuania's aspirations and not antagonizing Moscow failed to prevent Polish and Lithuanian parliamentary delegation visits to each capital to support Lithuanian independence. Even though the Polish government understood the potential to antagonize Moscow, soon after the March independence declaration Mazowiecki aided the Landsbergis government economically and even offered to arbitrate between Vilnius and Moscow, a bold step to take when the USSR warned that Lithuanian independence remained an internal Soviet issue.[56]

Skubiszewski's public statements began to reflect the impact of the Kostrzewa-Zorbas analysis as the foreign minister started to put his *MSZ* team together that summer in order to formulate a new and specific Eastern policy. That spring he described generally Poland's Eastern policy, stating that "the development of separate relations with the [Soviet] republics [remain] separate from those with the USSR as a whole." He focused on "the republics which voluntarily remain within the USSR. The case of secession from the Soviet Union is another category." This meant he cautiously tread between the formal relationship Poland developed with the USSR and the bordering Soviet republics, some of which wanted independence (e.g., Lithuania), and some of which endeavored to obtain greater freedom from Soviet Moscow (e.g., Ukraine and Russia). Skubiszewski maintained that "the concept of these relations, especially in light of the fact that the republics are winning independence in certain matters, needs to be worked out."[57] Moreover, important April and May 1990 visits by Lithuanian foreign minister Algirdas Saudargas gave Skubiszewski the chance to welcome Saudargas to Warsaw officially, an important gesture of support for Lithuanian independence. Additionally, Skubiszewski said that, as "Poland was the first country to have published a declaration on the Lithuanian question, friendly to Lithuania, our view is that talks should be held between Moscow and Vilnius. Without talks, without finding some arrangements, the Lithuanian situation cannot be solved." He also revealed that, given the increased potential for Russia and Ukraine to proclaim independence, "as far as I know these nations that are our neighbors do not have any genuine claims concerning the border, and if there were such claims, they would be completely out of the question."[58]

Yet, presidential candidate Walesa again challenged the government. In a provocative statement about Lithuanian independence, Walesa declared that "the only solution is to dissolve the Soviet Union." He continued with the sweeping statement that "you can establish ties founded on completely different principles—free will, freedom. You cannot try to prevent an unavoidable trend by force because this dissolution must come."[59] However, just before Skubiszewski's participation in an important Warsaw Pact Moscow summit to determine the fate of the Pact's military structure, Walesa contested the government's policies and increased tension vis-à-vis Soviet Moscow. The Polish government found itself in a bind as it tried to design a more specific Eastern policy while also cautiously attempting to disband the Pact.[60] Given these security dilemmas, the arrival of Kostrzewa-Zorbas at the *MSZ* on 1 June gave Skubiszewski and Vice Minister Makarczyk the opportunity to shape an Eastern implementation strategy.

As Kostrzewa-Zorbas started his duties, the *MSZ* underwent a significant restructuring after Skubiszewski delegated to Makarczyk the task of reorganizing key departments. Makarczyk envisioned enacting such changes "particularly [to] affect those departments that specialize in European affairs and stem from the new priorities of Polish foreign policy." Specifically, he consolidated into a single department all responsibilities for Europe, including the Soviet Union. To attempt to change the structure, Makarczyk explained that "the ministry will still rely on its present employees who have shown and will show loyalty, professionalism, and hard work. The remainder will be released in a way so as not to feel any resentment or with any feeling of being wronged." The objective for minister and vice minister remained to remove, replace, or shuffle department directors and deputy directors.[61]

Given this *MSZ* vision, Kostrzewa-Zorbas rapidly moved to remove personnel and create a new Eastern policy. He realized quickly the need to combat entrenched bureaucratic opposition by the Communist apparatchiks, who occupied every policy-making or policy-influencing position in the *MSZ* except for Minister Skubiszewski and Vice Minister Makarczyk. Skubiszewski gave Kostrzewa-Zorbas responsibility for building an Eastern policy and linking it to Western European strategy. Even though his deputy directorship appeared junior within the hierarchy, Kostrzewa-Zorbas actually took responsibility for Eastern policy from Vice Minister Kulski, maintained direct access to Skubiszewski, and possessed free reign to change the personnel in the Soviet Affairs Section.[62]

One of the first revelations from Kostrzewa-Zorbas about the apparatchiks around him came when he reviewed the May 1990 report on Polish policy toward the USSR. That report, given to him by the European director, specified that "the Soviet Union is the guarantor of Polish sovereignty." He immediately deleted that sentence and demanded that his staff reformulate the report. The staff's reaction verged on incredulity; at the staff level such change remained alien to policymaking. If Kostrzewa-Zorbas intended to restructure the *MSZ*'s Soviet Section upon assuming his job, he soon realized the need to hire loyal personnel. He later wrote that "they [old staff] understood when Skubiszewski gave me a free hand in changing 100 percent of the section's staff because literally 100 percent were graduates of Moscow's diplomatic schools. . . . I wasn't sure who had or had not had any connections harmful to our national security." As a result, he replaced everyone.[63]

His vision for the USSR Section focused on dividing it into country desks and functional responsibilities, a visionary means for dealing with the USSR's disintegration. In an August 1990 memo to the new *MSZ* director of the Personnel Department, Iwo Byczewski, another *Solidarnosc* activist Skubiszewski had hired, Kostrzewa-Zorbas proposed a radical new "Eastern structure." He proposed creating, inter alia, desks for the Russian Federation, Ukraine, Belorussia, the Baltic states, the Transcaucasus, and Central Asia, in addition to Soviet foreign and domestic policy, economic issues, and cultural, religious, and human rights.[64] The vice minister accepted his proposal and Kostrzewa-Zorbas then started to recruit colleagues and others recommended to him primarily from Warsaw University, many of whom had participated as young activists in *Solidarnosc*, not affiliated with the Communist Party. He wanted to find people who believed in overcoming the "marginalization of Poland as belonging to a permanent Soviet zone of security." Kostrzewa-Zorbas wanted *Solidarnosc* allies with diverse academic backgrounds and who were trained in Soviet affairs and European security issues. He desired to hire those who saw democratized Poland as a regional stabilizer, facilitator, and bridge builder, particularly toward European integration with NATO and the EC.[65]

Over the coming months, he built his Soviet Section with scholars in their twenties and early thirties to infuse a dynamism and creativity in devising Eastern policy. These scholars epitomized Poland's post–Communist foreign policy–makers with, in many cases, their Western education in the United States, Great Britain, and France from 1989 to 1990, their preparation in Western policymaking methods, and, frequently, their background in Soviet nationality policy. Such important *Solidarnosc* activists as his colleagues Andrzej Ananicz and Jacek Czaputowicz, the latter founder of the antimilitary "Wolnosc i Pokoj" (Freedom and Peace) movement, joined Kostrzewa-Zorbas, Ananicz as his deputy director and Czaputowicz as his consular affairs/Polonia outreach/Baltic expert. Other important experts such as Jerzy Stankiewicz, Michal Kurkiewicz, Krzysztof Jachowicz, Joanna Strzelczyk, Jakub Wolasiewicz, Tat'iana Lewicka, and Tomasz Leoniuk, covered Belorussia, Russia, and Ukraine, with Leoniuk starting in the new embassy in Kiev from 1990 and later becoming its consul general.[66] Under the direction of Kostrzewa-Zorbas, these staffers conceived eastern policy and constituted the only post–Communist *MSZ* section that had a 100 percent turnover by the end of 1991.

As Kostrzewa-Zorbas quickly assembled a new team, he devised and implemented a creative Eastern policy. Kostrzewa-Zorbas stated that "thanks to our independent politics, the border of the Western world will move closer to the Soviet Union. That is an example of the advantages to be gained from Poland's role as a bridgehead between civilizations." He elaborated that "Poland, with its definitely pro-Western orientation, has no intention of building a 'Berlin Wall' along the Bug River." For Kostrzewa-Zorbas equality of relations underlined the basis for productive Polish–Soviet relations. At the same time, the best outcome in the USSR for Poland arose, he explained, from the evolving confederation within the Soviet Union and the respective relationships Poland pursued with the "confederation's component parts." To provide the context for changing Eastern policy, he described the credo he still upheld to the underground journal *Nowa Koalicja*. The credo advocated cooperation between democratic forces throughout the Communist Bloc, not the frequently misperceived notion of a Central European federation.

In fact, the actual objective of Kostrzewa-Zorbas, both from his underground journal and, in 1990, for his *MSZ* policy, focused on regional cooperation to liberate Communist Bloc populations from oppression. According to Kostrzewa-Zorbas, "just as we must abandon bloc thinking, so too must we abandon thinking according to the Pilsudski and Roman Dmowski stereotypes." He meant old doctrines from the debates over Eastern policy between Pilsudski and Dmowski at the outset of the Second Republic's era after 1918 failed to address contemporary reality and, if implemented, portended untold harm regionally. For example, Pilsudski wanted a Polish–Ukrainian alliance against Bolshevik Russia, while Dmowski desired a Polish–Russian alliance against both Ukraine and Germany. Given the importance of the democratically inspired independence movements in the bordering Soviet republics, Kostrzewa-Zorbas argued that Poland needed to overcome Pilsudskiite and Dmowskiite stereotypes. It remained important to build relationships with the popular dissident movements in Lithuania, Ukraine, and Belorussia and develop the first true international linkages to Russian democratic reformers such as Boris El'tsin, Anatolii Sobchak, Gavril Popov, and Mikhail Bocharov of the Russian Interregional Deputies Group. These Russian deputies comprised a growing and popular anti-Soviet group of politicians, academicians, and even dissidents like Sakharov with whom the *MSZ* wanted to work.[67] The option, he believed, lay in pursuing a two-track policy of relations, one with Soviet Moscow under Gorbachev and the other with emerging non-Soviet leaderships in the Republics, without resorting to form "internal alliances" with any of them and avoiding playing them off one another. Yet, he warned that anti-Gorbachev elements continued to threaten "a comeback in the Soviet Union" that imperils "our security and we cannot rule out such an eventuality."[68]

The questions thus arise: Would Poland become a great power in Central-East Europe in its attempt to influence and possibly dominate the emerging, weaker, and smaller post-Soviet powers to its east? How would such a development affect Poland's bridging role between stronger, more threatening Russia and Germany? Or, would Poland avoid this potential new security dilemma by rejecting the historical missteps it took during the interwar period when it balanced powers against each other through competing alliances? This next section centers on what Poland did to grapple with these questions concerning important regional security dilemmas.

Poland's Two-Track Policy to Overcome
the Kresy as "the Polish Borderlands"

On the fifty-first anniversary of the start of World War II, Skubiszewski reviewed foreign policy in a significant interview. Taking the position that Poland provided a "very important factor in European stability," the foreign minister expounded that "the Polish state, a strong, rich one with a democratic system, functions well as a stabilizing factor in a rich Europe." He continued, "such a Poland need not fear its German and Russian neighbors." Contrasted with the interwar policy, Skubiszewski exclaimed that Pilsudski and Jozef Beck "aimed to keep an equal distance from Moscow and Berlin." Post-Communist Poland, he asserted, "aims to have very good and close cooperation with both Moscow and Bonn." In analyzing the complex series of Soviet events, however, he no longer saw the USSR as a "monolith," existing with non-Soviet Lithuania, Belorussia, Ukraine, and Russia, including Kaliningrad. Given that Belorussia and Ukraine had declared their sovereignty, with Russia prepared to break with the Moscow Soviet "center," and Lithuania still clinging to independence, Skubiszewski foresaw that these entities would "become our partners," not subjugated under another dominant regional power. The new Eastern policy, he argued, defined "dualism; on the one hand, relations with the Soviet federation, the USSR, and on the other, relations with our immediate neighbors, who will choose whether to stay in the Soviet federation, or confederation, or whether perhaps they leave it, as Lithuania is leaving." Yet, Poland already realized that these Soviet republics "all will be fully independent states. . . . Here I do not see any danger for Poland if we keep pace with the international political reality being created, [over] which we have a certain influence, but, of course, much does not depend on us." Hence, he remained "optimistic" and determined for Poland to avoid "isolation" by monitoring the changes on its eastern borders.[69] Moreover, he rejected great power status, which he could have chosen to guide a Polish survivalist strategy against Moscow and Bonn, one based only on threats rather than one developed more via cooperation. For Skubiszewski and Polish foreign policy, this stability-enhancing strategy illustrated Poland's potential for specialization as a middle power supporter to smaller powers. By promoting democratization and, therefore, enabling great powers to transform the regional security system more peacefully, Poland determined to build linkages to survive the regional and international anarchy stemming from the USSR's disintegration.

Since Poland relied upon the great powers to determine the larger European system's changes, Skubiszewski carved out a middle power niche for Poland to specialize in bridging differences, not creating upheaval. By recognizing that Poland existed as a historically lesser power without options to overtake its neighbors aggressively, Skubiszewski sought to build an other-help strategy to redefine Poland's role in the regional anarchy overtaking European security. This recognition marked more than simply a new diplomacy; the other-help strategy underlined an attempt to survive by reducing historic security dilemmas and serving as a bilateral partner differently between East and West. In his first comprehensive speech on Eastern policy, given in response to the Senate's request in September 1990 that the minister respond to specific questions, Skubiszewski marked a turning point in Poland's strategy.[70] Skubiszewski described how Kostrzewa-Zorbas, as his European Department deputy director, had already begun thoroughly to restructure functional areas and hire new personnel in "the extremely important" Soviet Affairs Section. By establishing responsibilities for individual republics, which had never before existed, the *MSZ*'s "wholly new" Soviet Section undertook to develop a plan to expand Polish consulates in Moscow, Leningrad, Minsk, Kiev, and Lvov, while trying to open one in Riga that combined responsibilities for Estonia and Alma-Ata. He stated that Poland's changed Eastern policy "will not interfere directly in the evolution of new relations between the USSR's components and nations, including the nations which wish to leave the USSR, but this does not mean that we cannot react to the fact of such changes." More importantly, he declared that "the level of pluralization of our relations with the USSR must be accommodated to the level of the internal pluralization of our neighbor taken as a whole." For Skubiszewski, Eastern relations equated with policies toward "fully independent and sovereign states," excluding military issues. He maintained that Poland's relations with Russia, which he did not identify as the USSR because of its growing independence movement, required "regularization." Therefore, he argued that Russia "determines the pace of change in the USSR," even if progress on democratization remained slow.

The Polish foreign minister also noted that Lithuania remained a "separate case," given its need to improve the rights of the Polish community living there. Skubiszewski reiterated that "Poland has no territorial claims against Lithuania" and no reason "to change the present borders with Lithuania, Belorussia, Ukraine—and the Soviet Union, too." Moreover, he stressed that once Lithuanian declared its independence, "that afternoon I presented a meeting of the government with a proposal—that was my idea—that we must move very fast and be very specific." The government, Skubiszewski argued, quickly accepted the declaration that stayed "in line with Lithuanian interests as well as the vital interests of Polish policy," one "absolutely sympathetic to Lithuania's economic and other requests." However, this "realistic policy treats all the issues integrally," that is, the Soviet authorities need to play a role in a "certain triangle," based on issues affecting the Polish–Lithuanian border. Lastly, the improvement of the Polish minority population, especially in educational and cultural areas, requires both states, which desire intently to cooperate, to work together on sensitive issue of ethnic minority rights.[71]

The Polish foreign minister then prepared for his first USSR trip, a multipurpose visit that symbolized a crucial juncture in Poland's relationship toward the USSR, but more importantly, toward Soviet republics planning independence.[72] As Kostrzewa-Zorbas described, Poland planned to seek ties with the republics, particularly the Russian Federation, because "an increasingly explicit stabilizing factor is the stance taken by El'tsin, who has, on Russia's behalf, succeeded in reaching an agreement even with the radical Lithuanians."[73] Before his departure, Skubiszewski defined his objectives, saying that Shevardnadze's invitation to visit centered around "European matters and bilateral issues," while the trip to Moscow, Kiev, and Minsk focused on "establishing relations on a wider basis. Various relations have existed although they have been firmly subordinated to the center."[74] One incisive Polish assessment also underscored that "Poland in the role of a bridge [provides] a transmission belt between a USSR that is becoming democratic and Europe."[75] Finally, the Soviet press noted before Skubiszewski arrived for meetings with the Soviet leadership, as well as the Russian Federation prime minister Ivan Silaev and newly appointed foreign minister Andrei Kozyrev that "Poland has become a sovereign country, carrying out an independent foreign policy determining its own internal political structure and future. Undoubtedly these changes benefit Poland, but we are having to learn how to be independent when the country is burdened with the difficult legacy of the past."[76]

By meeting with Soviet and Russian leaders, non-Russian republic leaders, and non-Communist activists, Skubiszewski strove to promote his new Eastern democratization strategy.[77] In his first meetings on 10–11 October, Skubiszewski concentrated on expanding the Polish–Soviet relationship. During the discussions with Gorbachev and Shevardnadze, the Soviet leader stated that "irrespective of what is taking place both in our country and in yours, I hope that we will be able to gain control over the situation. . . . I have complete trust in the Polish nation."[78] Debate revolved around how to draft a new Polish–Soviet treaty and begin Soviet troop withdrawal negotiations. The foreign ministers agreed in principle to terms for initiating both processes, while Skubiszewski described the Polish "two-track" Eastern policy as nonthreatening. Warsaw wanted Soviet Moscow to understand that the Polish experiment in democratization and economic reform provided a model. Poland also needed to ensure the continuation of Soviet oil and natural gas in exchange for foodstuffs. Additionally, Warsaw tried to gain more information about Polish officers killed during World War II, not only in Katyn, but also in Ostaszkow, Kozielsk, and Starobielsk, to eliminate the age-old "blank spots."[79]

Another important issue related to Poland's initiative to open consulates in the USSR. The Soviet foreign minister accepted consulates slated for Riga, Alma-Ata, and Vilnius. The talks, however, hit a snag regarding the status of Kaliningrad and the 1939 Molotov–Ribbentrop Pact. Without denying that the USSR might transform the "Kaliningrad Oblast into a German autonomous republic," Shevardnadze "emphasized that this oblast continues to be closed to any discussion." On the 1939 pact, Shevardnadze told Skubiszewski that "Moscow also did not agree to recognize the whole of the Molotov–Ribbentrop Pact as invalid."[80] Though both sides disagreed on these points, they signed a progressive communiqué on 16 October.

Skubiszewski's team intended to conclude the historic visit with a Polish–Soviet ceremony to show respect for the preeminent Soviet role in all of

Skubiszewski's discussions. Both sides expressed satisfaction with the communiqué that centered on developments in European security, especially German unification, the "2 Plus 4" treaty, and the November CSCE summit, including the CFE Treaty.[81] During his press conference, Skubiszewski also raised an important dimension of his two-track policy by explaining that "despite the declaration on Lithuania's separate statehood, some concrete moves in Polish-Lithuanian relations need preparations which must be made by Lithuania, since these matters are controlled by Soviet institutions."[82] Given the tightrope he walked between Soviet Moscow and the non-Soviet leaderships, Skubiszewski clearly sought to demonstrate a practical Eastern approach with good intentions.

In between two visits to Moscow, Skubiszewski went to Kiev on 12 October to demonstrate Poland's support for Ukraine's sovereignty declaration, establishing formal ties with the non-Soviet Ukrainian foreign ministry. The foreign minister's strategy rested upon the reestablishment of close historical and cultural ties between Poles and Ukrainians. Given the new great power configurations emerging in Russia and Germany, the Polish and Ukrainian sides understood the implications of their middle power roles. Consequently, the strategy acknowledged the difficult periods after Soviet consolidation in the early 1920s, forced resettlements in the late 1940s, and democratization initiated by the loose Ukrainian opposition movement, Rukh.[83] By signing a declaration, Skubiszewski and his Ukrainian counterpart, Anatolii Zlenko, determined to use the historic visit to distance Kiev from Moscow's political grip, to buttress Ukrainian independence, and to begin to put the onerous Polish–Ukrainian history behind them. Within this path-breaking document, both sides upheld the significance of sovereignty. The declaration underscored regional cooperation, with Poland pledging to support Ukraine's "Europeanization," and focused on Ukraine's participation in pan-European and international security organizations to reduce international problems of mutual interest. Both states asserted their mutual aim to strengthen democratization and forge common foreign policy objectives by promoting the precepts of border inviolability, territorial integrity, noninterference in domestic policies, and peaceful resolutions to disagreements. To avoid territorial disputes, both ministers affirmed the permanent border agreement signed on 15 February 1951. To facilitate cross-border information and increase communication, they also stipulated the opening of consular offices in Kiev and Warsaw, particularly to reduce problems concerning respective minorities, foster equal rights, preserve culture, religion, and language, and improve education to overcome ethnic tension.[84] Upon departing, Skubiszewski stressed that "the point is to have relations not only with Moscow but with the nations and republics bordering us as well, and Ukraine ranks prominently in this respect." Furthermore, he stressed that "the talks have confirmed our policy toward the east, so important for us, is systematic and develops well."[85] Therefore, he believed the two-track strategy achieved key objectives in Ukraine.

What Skubiszewski's delegation encountered in Minsk stood in marked contrast to what they had found in Kiev. Immediately, the dynamics changed. Whereas the Ukrainian foreign ministry displayed the Polish, Ukrainian, and

Soviet flags during the Kiev visit, the Belorussians placed only the Polish and Soviet flags on their official cars, an action indicative of an uncertain state still subservient to Soviet Moscow. Though Belorussia had declared sovereignty on 27 July 1990, the leadership maintained close ties to an increasingly conservative Soviet leadership. More importantly, after many years of Communist rule that intentionally instilled fear about Polish irredentism against post–World War II Belorussian territory, Belorussian leaders wanted to proceed cautiously with Skubiszewski's delegation. Furthermore, the Belorussian Popular Front leadership, the only semblance of a democratizing force in Belorussia, remained too weak to mobilize opposition members in Parliament. In fact, Skubiszewski confronted a Belorussian leadership that initially declared the Polish Bialystok region as Belorussian territory because more ethnic Belorussians inhabited the area than Poles. To make matters worse, the Polish delegation found Belorussians not only deferred mostly to Soviet Moscow, but years of Soviet Communism had blunted much of a Belorussian identity, both in the leadership and society. Indeed, even Belorussian Popular Front chairman Zenon Poznyak, an anti-Communist advocate for independence, expressed the historic fear about "the stronger and more attractive character of Polish culture . . . about the purely Belorussian identity of Bialystok and the anti-Belorussian attitude of the Polish church." Such views clouded the significant recognition Poland offered Belorussia to support its sovereignty. As a result, Warsaw became more sensitized to Poland's Belorussian minority and did not assume they sought to reunite with Poles.[86]

Unlike the Ukrainian and Russian leaderships, the Belorussian Communist loyalty to Soviet Moscow and the Belorussian opposition's fear about perceived Polish imperialist tendencies prevented the Minsk leadership from signing a declaration. Yet, Skubiszewski's pragmatic strategy yielded a statement that neither state maintained any "territorial claims" against each other. In the end, he said that the initiation of Polish–Belorussian relations was "just the beginning" and "we have returned with a communiqué about further talks that do not, however, include the borders."[87]

After the difficult trip to Belorussia, Skubiszewski returned to Russia to sign another declaration, this time with his newly appointed Russian counterpart. By taking advantage of fortuitous developments, the Polish delegation established close relations with the Russian government, an objective promoted by the new *MSZ* Soviet Section. Certainly, the Russian leadership understood Skubiszewski's seriousness about establishing formal relations with the non-Soviet republics, given the tangible results in Polish–Ukrainian ties. It dawned on Premier Silaev and Foreign Minister Kozyrev that a Polish–Russian agreement had strengthened Russia's newly declared sovereignty on 12 June 1990. For his part, Skubiszewski saw Russia both as an important entity and a regional contributor, particularly to Baltic cooperation. Citing important links from Russian Kaliningrad with the Baltic Sea states, Skubiszewski praised Russia's "emergence onto the broad international arena."[88] Subsequently, the momentum between the Polish and Russian leadership enabled the signing of Russia's first international document, underscoring ties based on "international law, sovereignty, and territorial integrity" to achieve mutually advantageous cooperation.[89]

On 16 October 1990, Skubiszewski returned to Moscow ostensibly because the recently appointed Russian foreign minister needed several days to get organized and President El'tsin wanted the Russian parliament to approve the document. The Russians, however, also requested that the Polish delegation return to Moscow, so as not to have the Ukrainians outdo the Russians.[90] The end result proved important since the declaration addressed the same significant aims as the one with Ukraine. Not only did the foreign ministers renounce any territorial claims against each other, but they also reiterated their affirmation for the Polish–Soviet state border demarcation next to the Baltic Sea, as originally agreed on 5 March 1957. Furthermore, the declaration directed both states to "exchange diplomatic and consular missions with each other." At the signing ceremony, the Russian premier concluded that such a "significant event" commits Russia to the "friendly relations" it desires to create "again in all areas with the Republic of Poland."[91]

After the Polish delegation departed Russia, both sides commented favorably on the talks. Kozyrev stated that he "favored the comprehensive development of traditional ties with neighboring states with the aim of bringing them into line with natural interests and potential."[92] Kostrzewa-Zorbas proclaimed that "the Russian side underlined the importance that the first international document to be signed by the first Russian Foreign Minister since the declaration of Russian sovereignty is a declaration of friendship and good-neighborly cooperation with Poland." He added, "Poland is the first country to have recognized Russia's sovereignty. Anyone with even scant knowledge of European history realizes the importance of this act." For the *MSZ*, the Polish–Russian declaration resulted in the commitment for "constant political consultations." Kostrzewa-Zorbas concluded that, though "the only missing element is the military sphere and that is being settled between Poland and the USSR. . . . Polish-Russian cooperation contributes to international security, especially European security."[93]

After this historic trip, Skubiszewski focused primarily on Lithuania. When questioned by the media about whether Poland "no longer considered Lithuania part of the USSR," the foreign minister declared, "that is not how I would view the issue, because in many respects Lithuania is linked to the USSR, despite the declaration of independence." He explained, "we do not want to interfere in the internal affairs of the USSR, to aid the dismantling of the USSR or prevent that from happening." Skubiszewski then divulged, however, that when telephoning Shevardnadze after Lithuania had declared its independence, he asserted that "Lithuania is our neighbor, we have certain ties with it, and that is why we have and will have a position on this issue." In response, Shevardnadze said, "we understand Poland's position." Crucial to Polish–Lithuanian ties remained the reality that, without independence, Lithuania continued as a "transitional state." Skubiszewski argued that Poland stood ready to establish formal relations only when "the independence question assumes a more concrete form" by dealing with Soviet control of the border. Finally, without formal ties, Skubiszewski remained angry over the delay of Warsaw's plan to open a consulate in Vilnius.[94]

By December, Polish–Lithuanian relations improved with Lithuanian Supreme Council president Landsbergis's unofficial meeting with Skubiszewski in Warsaw. After the talks, the Polish foreign minister praised the spectrum of ties and Lithuania's independence drive. However, he cautioned that Poland still upheld Lithuania's goals, but that "we are not able to do for Lithuania all that depends on Lithuanian–Soviet relations." Although he mentioned that the talks included the rights of the Polish minority in Lithuania, Skubiszewski highlighted that "Poland supports aspirations of the Baltic Republics to have their representation at international conferences, [especially] their participation in CSCE." Such advocacy indicated a turning point in Warsaw–Vilnius relations and demonstrated Poland's attempt to increase regional backing for its foreign policy. As a result, the *MSZ* expected Soviet experts to begin expert-level talks "striving to solve . . . economic, transport and multi-lateral policy issues."[95]

By late December 1990, several events dramatically affected Polish Eastern policy. First, Soviet hard-liners consolidated power to force Shevardnadze's 20 December resignation. The day of the resignation Skubiszewski declared that Shevardnadze's diplomacy recognized Poland's "multidimensional character of our present Eastern policy."[96] Secondly, Walesa won the presidency, ending both the slow, step-by-step post–Communist policy and initiating a different Eastern strategy. The *MSZ*'s main focus relied less on Western uncertainty, with the November 1990 German border treaty, and more on Eastern instability.[97] Yet, confusion erupted in Warsaw and Moscow with Walesa's 22 December 1990 inauguration speech, at which he sent seemingly contradictory signals to Moscow and then reversed himself several days later.

In his speech Walesa maintained that Eastern policy focused on Russia, Ukraine, Belorussia, and Lithuania, without mentioning the USSR.[98] This statement set off a torrent of criticism from Moscow and a flurry of maneuvers within the *MSZ*.[99] As assessed in chapter 1, Walesa's anti-Soviet advisors temporarily held the upper hand in drafting the inaugural speech, particularly Krzysztof Wyszkowski and Jacek Masiarski, who had been writing editorials in *Tygodnik Solidarnosc* prior to the presidential election. Yet, Walesa quickly pushed them aside and turned toward his more pro-Soviet advisor, Mieczyslaw Wachowski. When confronted by the press after the speech and taken to task over whether his implication was that "Poland no longer borders the USSR," Walesa's spokesman tried to rescind the glaring omission by responding that "Walesa was thinking of the USSR when he said 'Russia,' because the shortened form is often used by U.S. Presidents." According to Kostrzewa-Zorbas, Walesa's pro-Soviet advisors pressured the *MSZ* to release a similar statement, but the *MSZ* foiled it arguing that "it could really have worsened our relations with the pro-independence [Russian] elite in the USSR."[100]

To understand the reasoning behind the president's views toward Moscow, primarily the result of his pro-Soviet advisors, one must analyze the decisions

Walesa made in late December regarding ambassadorial appointments and in January concerning the Soviet crackdown in Lithuania. Without Skubiszewski or any other *MSZ* officials present, Walesa met with Soviet ambassador Iurii Kashlev on 28 December 1990 and soon after with the hard-line Polish ambassador to Moscow, Stanislaw Ciosek, whom Skubiszewski wanted to remove. After these meetings, Walesa extended Ciosek's term, a decision that haunted policymakers during the failed Soviet coup d'état, in August 1991, as the Ambassador had held close ties with coup plotters, not El'tsin's coterie.[101]

When the Soviet military repression occurred in Vilnius on 13 January 1991, Walesa again confounded *MSZ* officials and, this time, the Polish people when he reacted very cautiously and failed to offer public support to Landsbergis.[102] Just two days before the Soviet assault, Lithuanian parliamentarian Czeslaw Okinczyc implored the Polish parliament to recognize Lithuania formally, anticipating the ensuing Soviet violence. Okinczyc's plea reverberated particularly because of his ethnic Polish background and, though the Parliament failed to recognize Lithuania formally, Sejm declared its readiness to provide humanitarian assistance.[103] The *MSZ* also sought to bolster Lithuania, stating that, though "Poland does not influence issues which belong to internal competencies of whatever country, including Lithuania . . . the Government has rendered its support for justified aspirations of the Lithuanian nation . . . [and] remains highly interested in preserving peace and tolerance in our region."[104]

During the crisis, Skubiszewski and the foreign ministry increased their public pronouncements. The *MSZ* summoned the Soviet charge d'affaires to account for the increasing tensions in Lithuania. He responded that Soviet "military units have been directed only to Lithuania . . . in keeping with the law . . . [on] military conscription. . . . If the population of the [Lithuanian] Republic expresses through a referendum a will to secede from the Soviet Union, then of course this will be respected."[105] Furthermore, as the violence commenced in Vilnius with Soviet troops killing fifteen and wounding scores more, Lithuanian foreign minister Saudargas joined Okinczyc on 13 January in a surprise visit to plead with the Polish leadership and Poles across Poland to support Lithuania. Even though they stressed that Lithuania would not create a government-in-exile, the foreign minister emphasized that "the drama shows Stalinism is still alive and it shows the world that unpunished crimes can revive. Nobody is protected from this, including Western countries."[106] Skubiszewski then held a news conference at which he underlined the extent of Poland's stand against the violence in Vilnius. The Polish foreign minister clearly supported "Lithuanian aspirations," but reiterated that problems needed resolution by "discussion and negotiation," before diplomatic recognition and formal relations proceeded. He stated that "we already have had a great deal of cooperation with Lithuania, only it was hampered by the fact that Lithuania did not control her borders." Yet, Skubiszewski remained pragmatic and underscored the importance of Lithuanian independence by counseling that in "our experience we can say that the path to independence is a very long path."[107]

Given the conservative backlash in Moscow, the violence in Vilnius, the resignation of his Moscow counterpart, and the election of an unpredictable Polish president, the Polish foreign minister foresaw eastern policy options becoming more limited. Therefore, during the early months of 1991, Skubiszewski and his European Department worked progressively to complete several other important policy objectives, namely to liquidate successively the military and political structures of the Warsaw Pact and to expand the Visegrad Central European regional cooperation with Prague and Budapest.[108] It also needs recalling that the Persian Gulf War, especially its major fighting phases from January to March 1991, overshadowed many European security issues, including the USSR's disintegration. As a result, the conservative forces grew in strength because the Western coalition nations fought in the Gulf region and focused much less on strained relations between Warsaw and Moscow, and Moscow and other capitals.[109] While Skubiszewski promoted the two-track policy before Soviet hard-liners attempted to overthrow Gorbachev, Eastern policy took shape slowly, reaching fruition only in late 1991 after the USSR collapsed.

An important example stemmed from Skubiszewski's annual parliamentary presentation. Arguably, during his mid-February 1991 parliamentary speech, Skubiszewski characterized Poland's evolutionary Eastern policy as one that bandwagoned with rather than balanced against Germany and the USSR. He stated that "the essential dilemma of our policy is Poland's position between Germany and the USSR. Germany is an economic giant. . . . The USSR, suffering from the economic collapse, remains a military power and its huge military arsenal may be a source of various complications depending on how the internal situation evolves." The Polish strategy focused on "pursuing a policy of close and intensive contacts with our powerful neighbors." According to Skubiszewski, the most important objective remained to "reject prejudices and distancing ourselves, [because] we have also finished with the legacy of . . . satellite dependence on the USSR at the expense of sovereignty." To underline his pragmatic approach, he argued that "we are giving concrete effect to the postulate of close links with one and the other neighbor; there is no balancing the intensiveness of relationships." Finally, to demonstrate concrete goals, he elaborated that "our relations with Germany may and probably will be developing in a special way in view of our aspiration to join the EC through our ties with the West." In this way, Skubiszewski felt "we should pursue our Eastern policies to become an attractive partner for the East; acting with caution and moderation . . . . our Eastern policy has not caused trouble so far."[110]

Instead of extending comprehensively the web of Eastern linkages the *MSZ* desired as part of its two-track policy, however, Walesa and his staff curtailed policy options. Some in the *MSZ* detected a much more complicated reasoning for the lack of significant progress in the two-track policy as the USSR disintegrated. The unrelenting delays and obstructive tactics of the Soviet withdrawal negotiations created such problems for Warsaw. Rather than continue to respond strongly to the Soviets at the negotiating table, the president's National Security Bureau issued a report on the need to make "concessions regarding the withdrawal of the Soviet forces." Chief negotiator Kostrzewa-Zorbas said that "the Belweder [president's chancellery] intervened when we were at our peak when the minister of foreign affairs came up with the idea of making Polish efforts more dynamic." The result for the *MSZ* appeared bleak for the negotiations, as "the back of the active Polish politics toward the East had been broken." According to top *MSZ* officials, the president's decisions sounded the death knell for an expansion of the two-track policy. At least until after the failed Soviet August coup, some of Walesa's anti-Soviet advisors and some in the *MSZ*'s European Directorate argued that Walesa had presided over the "Finlandization" of Polish Eastern policy.[111]

The Tortuous Twists and Turns
of Soviet Troop Withdrawals

Given the Polish leadership's delays in starting force withdrawal negotiations with Moscow, the *MSZ* faced great uncertainty when talks finally began in November 1990. Chapter 3 detailed Skubiszewski's German strategy as a result of the complex issues involved with withdrawals from the FRG and Poland. Skubiszewski's team prepared to deal with Shevardnadze by determining priorities for negotiations in the summer of 1990. Kostrzewa-Zorbas defined the key points regarding Soviet troops still stationed on Poland's territory. In a nutshell, these priorities focused on overcoming "Poland's isolation as the last nation in Europe that had not reached agreement on a withdrawal of Soviet troops stationed on its soil." Given this problem, Poland needed to overcome the "Continuation of Follow-On Forces Attack, NATO's operational plan for pre-emptive strikes against Soviet troops and installations in Central Europe, both nuclear as well as conventional." Because Soviet troops signified an infringement on Poland's sovereignty and prevented "security ties with NATO, the West European Union, bilateral ties with the United States or other Western European nations . . . . Warsaw would have an assured place on a NATO list of targets." Not only did this paradox create a security dilemma for Warsaw, but it also inhibited "foreign investment because of uncertain security and the unclear international status of Poland." Taken together, the prognosis of the security threats Kostrzewa-Zorbas delineated for Skubiszewski and the *MSZ* leadership appeared quite worrisome.[112]

Government consensus emerged by fall 1990 that any "residual Soviet forces would fulfill a significant mission in Poland, even in a post-Cold War environment." Coupled with the *MSZ* analysis, the premier realized that he needed to counter Walesa's harsh criticism on force withdrawals. The Polish leadership also understood that the Soviet forces served in "the role of an imperial anchor to keep Warsaw close to Moscow," instead of the old rationale to provide "an effective military instrument of conquest in Western Europe." Either way, the *MSZ* concluded Soviet troops must withdraw, and Skubiszewski requested Shevardnadze heed the Polish requirement for full withdrawal by the end of 1991. When Skubiszewski delivered the diplomatic note in September 1990, Warsaw underlined that the 1956 agreement and the 1957 accord on the "temporary stationing of these troops in Poland" required immediate revision. Moreover, "an agreement on reparations payable by the USSR to Poland for damages and losses sustained by Poland as a result of the said stationing" seriously required negotiation.[113]

The Polish negotiating team contended with numerous Soviet arguments over nearly two years and seventeen rounds of Polish–Soviet negotiations. Warsaw argued publicly that "Poland based its position entirely on international law and tried to marginalize other aspects, including those that were political and economic." The Soviets and, after the disbandment of the USSR, the Russians, refused to uphold "legal argumentation." Instead, the Moscow negotiators stuck primarily to "many historic, symbolic, political, and economic reasons for an indefinite, or at least much prolonged, Soviet army presence in Poland." To buttress their legal rationale, the Poles played a tough line, too, defending their "sovereign rights of a nation-state [to] demand a prompt withdrawal of unwanted foreign military forces, unless the host nation had specific legal obligations stipulated by valid treaties." These Polish arguments fell mostly on the deaf ears of the Soviet military, which controlled most of the negotiations. Until the Poles implemented stern measures such as blocking unauthorized Soviet transits from East Germany via Poland, the Soviets never yielded. Unlike any other Central European state, Poland argued that no treaties, including the 1955 Warsaw Treaty, provided "valid" post–Cold War stipulations to base Russian troops in Poland.[114]

After his departure from government, the chief *MSZ* negotiator revealed the difficulty the Polish side faced throughout the talks, particularly when defending the legal rights of a sovereign state. According to Kostrzewa-Zorbas, "when they studied the bizarre heritage of Communist foreign policy, the Polish officers found several minor (but classified) Polish–Soviet executive agreements establishing financial and technical regulations of troop stationing, as if *the fact of stationing* [original emphasis] was rooted enough in the natural or customary law." For the Polish team this argument remained illegitimate. Indeed, the Polish–Soviet archival documentation revealed that "the oldest relevant agreement was signed in December 1956, despite the previous stationing of troops for more than a decade."[115] However, Moscow adamantly employed such agreements to legitimize Russian forces in Poland in the early 1990s.

Myriad disputes nearly derailed the talks at several junctures. According to accounts by several negotiators, Soviet arguments included such "historic" reasoning as "the Soviet Union having acquired rights and properties (military bases) in the post–Third Reich parts of western Poland through a war victory." To counter this particular argument, the Polish delegation asserted that without legal justification, especially after the final agreement to confirm the Polish–German border, Poland merited "unrestricted rights on its whole territories regained in the aftermath of World War II." Though the Soviet delegation dropped this rationale after several negotiation rounds, they continued to raise "symbolic" and "political" issues.[116]

The Soviet side depicted these issues as vital "extraterritorial strategic interests at stake." These strategic interests focused on how "the Soviet army had a legitimate right to maintain 'the strategic continuity' from the USSR through Poland to the bulk of its forward deployed forces still occupying the former GDR." Hence, the Soviet side claimed, "smaller nations had to obey agreements made by other (larger) nations, for example, the USSR and Germany." Above all, Moscow stated that "instead of being an international troublemaker, Poland must fulfill the Soviet–German (bilateral) agreement, signed in the summer of 1990 on transit through the Polish territory." In response, the Polish team persuaded the Soviet side to retract this reasoning after several more rounds by summer 1991, particularly because the Germans refused to uphold this Soviet argument and because the Poles believed this reasoning conceivably created the basis for "igniting Polish memories of the 1939 Soviet–German agreement." Yet, another dispute arose on economic aspects the Soviets maintained required funding to construct Soviet-based housing for troops.[117]

For the Polish negotiators the Soviet economic rationale proved very misleading. Given that Moscow continued its strategic ballistic missile modernization and German withdrawal negotiators revealed to the Poles that Bonn "gave the USSR all the necessary money in advance" for transit and relocation requirements, the Polish negotiators saw through Soviet tactics. Furthermore, the Poles proposed to pay each Soviet soldier an incentive to withdraw smoothly, or that both sides waive "financial claims related to the troop stationing," including the Polish proposition to forgive "environmental damages that for more than forty-five years had exceeded any capacity of assessment." Over time, the Soviets rebuffed these options, preferring not to discuss environmental damage and, despite the refusal of Polish negotiators, requesting that any Polish funding go to the Soviet military leadership for distribution to the troops. Such Polish proposals proved too cumbersome because both sides resisted compromise. Throughout the negotiating the Polish side pushed to obtain the time frame, the tacit acceptance of which Warsaw understood it had received from Shevardnadze in October. The timetable, though, evaporated amid the Moscow December 1990 hard-liner backlash. Therefore, Polish negotiators believed they needed to establish a quid pro quo as a bargaining chip, to link the requirement for a withdrawal timeline to "Polish permission for transit via railroads, highways and airspace for Soviet units leaving the GDR."[118]

The Polish negotiating team also encountered additional obstacles that stemmed from the Soviet military leadership's tactical maneuvering and from the Polish presidential staff. The Soviet military killings in Vilnius, juxtaposed with Moscow's order for unmarked military trains to transit Polish territory without Polish agreement, challenged Poland's political will. The Soviet military provocation resulted in a Polish blockade at the Polish–German border because the Polish authorities protested that, without agreement, Polish law prohibited train transit that carried military equipment across Polish territory.[119] In a test of political will, Polish negotiators also withstood Soviet military bluster by the Northern Group of Forces commander, Viktor Dubynin, when he declared, both at the negotiations and publicly:

> We will return home—there is no alternative here. But we will leave with our heads held high, with unfurled military banners, with a feeling of satisfaction from the international duty we have fulfilled, and with dignity and honor. If the Polish side does not agree with the Soviet protocol on settling legal, property, and financial questions and does not display goodwill, then the Soviet forces will return to the territory of the great Soviet power in accordance with our plans and along the routes planned by us. In that event, however, we will bear all responsibility only for the life and health of Soviet people and we will shed responsibility for the Polish side.[120]

Remarkably, after Dubynin's statement, the chief of the Soviet negotiating team, Ambassador Valentin Koptieltsev, disavowed the Soviet commander's remarks, but the Soviet general again antagonized the negotiations. By indicating that "there shall be no talk about withdrawing our army from Poland before the Western Group of Soviet Forces completes its withdrawal from Eastern Germany," General Dubynin continued his adversarial approach. In response, Skubiszewski publicly admonished the Soviets, arguing that "the attitude that Soviet troops will leave Poland only after they are gone from Germany is unacceptable to us. Poland's relations with Europe also call for their withdrawal."[121] Moreover, the Polish foreign minister underscored that Poland's lengthy history of Soviet military transit between the GDR and USSR underscored the hypocrisy of Soviet complaints.[122]

To call Dubynin to task for his statement, the *MSZ* drafted a recommendation to declare the Soviet general persona non grata, but the Polish presidential chancellery rejected it. The chancellery's rejection signaled that Walesa's staff viewed Soviet pressures differently from the *MSZ* negotiating team. For the *MSZ* negotiators, the president's inclination to favor a lessening of Poland's tough responses came at a crucial moment and at a high cost, since Ambassador Koptieltsev agreed for the first time in the negotiations to consider withdrawing Soviet forces on a specific timetable.[123] To worsen matters for the negotiations, Skubiszewski appeared to succumb to Soviet pressures and heed the Polish chancellery's directives. He divulged that "the Soviet side has not agreed to our suggestion of completing the withdrawal of the Soviet forces by the end of 1991 . . . . Was it possible to bring about an earlier withdrawal of the Soviet forces? No . . . it was out of the question. . . . The presence of two divisions in Poland is of no military significance."[124] In mid-February, Walesa and his advisors determined at the inaugural meeting of the National Security Council that Poland must yield to Moscow's wishes for a timetable on Soviet force withdrawals.[125]

Walesa and some of his staff then challenged the *MSZ* negotiating position by announcing that Poland had unilaterally acceded to Soviet troop withdrawal demands.[126] Janusz Ziolkowski, formerly a distinguished post-Communist senator and one of Skubiszewski's old Poznan University colleagues released the presidential statement.[127] Walesa talked in terms of ridding Poland of Soviet bases, but raised publicly the year 1994 as a concrete date for the first time. Contrary to the Polish negotiating team's position, the president's statement allowed Moscow to hold Poland to a position later than Warsaw's original stance of the end of 1991.[128] While Walesa's representative, Ziolkowski, announced that Warsaw no longer required such a time frame for force withdrawals, other advisors seemed divided over force withdrawals and Eastern policy. These disputes now became very controversial, with Polish foreign policy splintered over whether to balance against Moscow, bridge between Moscow and Bonn, or "Finlandize"—hide in neutrality—by yielding to Moscow demands. The split boiled down to quarrels between those of Walesa's advisors who supported the USSR's hard-liner position and those who opposed Moscow's heavy-handed tactics. Evidently, the pro-Moscow faction of Wachowski, Piotr Kolodziejczyk, the defense minister, and Jerzy Milewski, a key National Security Bureau aide all within Walesa's innter circle, defeated the anti-Moscow group of advisors. Walesa's advisors who lost this debate mainly comprised Jaroslaw Kaczynski, Lech Kaczynski, and Zdzislaw Najder. Directing the *MSZ* in late February to end the Polish blockade of the unauthorized transit of Soviet troops from Germany, Walesa declared that Poland yielded to Moscow's demands.[129] Above all, the controversy witnessed Skubiszewski backing away from the foreign ministry's bridging strategy, upholding the presidential decision and conceding to Soviet negotiators.[130]

Though the Polish negotiators seemed hamstrung by the continual Soviet military's political maneuvering, some in the Polish leadership believed self-imposed constraints ended any Polish bargaining ability. In effect, those believing that Soviet negotiators wanted to neutralize any Polish counterproposals toward Moscow now thought most of Warsaw's key cabinet-level officials had neutralized themselves. Those arguing against Moscow's strategy asserted that only the political will of the new premier, Jan Krzysztof Bielecki, deflected the Soviet military's belligerent negotiating tactics, balancing the splintering within the Polish government. Apparently, Skubiszewski took what Moscow proposed when he met with Soviet chief of the general staff Mikhail Moiseev, who came to Warsaw in mid-March 1991 and stated, as Moscow's senior negotiator, that Soviet forces intended to withdraw at the end of 1993. Without reaching any agreement on paper, Moiseev simply issued his statement and Warsaw acquiesced. After the meeting, Skubiszewski related that "flexibility requires that some moves be taken right now, but they are limited to some extent. . . . Should large Soviet units begin to leave Poland, it is possible that some transit [from the FRG] could start. Its extent will be determined, which does not mean any change in our position that it is necessary to conclude agreements on withdrawal." Additionally, he attempted to divert domestic criticism by stating "we want to avoid the problem of internationalization, but as we know other states, including some superpowers, call attention to the fact that Poland is a country which has failed to solve the question of pullout of Soviet troops till now." Believing an agreement imminent, Skubiszewski waited for Moscow's draft.[131]

When Bielecki and vice foreign minister Makarczyk traveled to Moscow in early April, ostensibly seeking to obtain an intergovernmental agreement on troop withdrawals, they believed Moscow had verbally committed to signing it. Yet, the Soviet side raised the issue of transforming Soviet military bases into Polish–Soviet joint ventures, as part of a troop withdrawal agreement, once Soviet forces withdrew. Further, Polish ambassador Ciosek impressed upon Premier Bielecki the business appeal of future Polish–Soviet companies on abandoned bases.[132] Given the Polish suspicion raised by such an initiative, Bielecki returned to Poland and requested that Makarczyk's staff assess the Soviet proposal and draft negotiation particulars. The *MSZ* recommended that Bielecki reject such joint ventures because they entailed a Soviet attempt to conduct future intelligence operations out of these supposed unused bases, an assessment that later proved helpful when the Russians again raised it in spring 1992. Bielecki accepted the recommendation and held firmly against Soviet pressures, but not before Dubynin suddenly announced that some Soviet units intended to withdraw without specifying how to use the unoccupied military bases. Dubynin arranged the action with Soviet commanders in Poland, without notifying the Polish military, and simply ordered Soviet troops to withdraw.[133]

Interestingly, during a state visit to Brussels just a day before Bielecki's Moscow trip, Walesa revealed his notion about Soviet troop withdrawal negotiations. For the Polish president, "it is not a question of us chasing them out, nor slighting the honor of the Soviet Army. Today the Soviet Army has absolutely no interest, be it economic or political, in maintaining a presence in Poland." In fact, Walesa divulged his rationale when he stated that "it will be much easier to reach a compromise on an eventual deadline for completing the pull-out. I am pleased that Moscow has brought forward this deadline by a year."[134] Clearly, Walesa wanted the troops to leave Poland, but yielded to timetables the Soviet military pressed rather than what his *MSZ* recommended.[135]

Such a statement disclosed that the President acceded both to his pro-Soviet advisers and to Soviet hard-liner tactics. He willingly sacrificed some of the original *MSZ* positions, discrediting much of what Skubiszewski tried to negotiate in those difficult months during late 1990 and throughout 1991. Because the Polish president and the premier remained at odds over Soviet force withdrawal positions at times, Polish–Soviet strains continued and Moscow leveraged Warsaw consistently at the negotiating table. Kostrzewa-Zorbas resigned in July and Soviet delays lasted until the August 1991 aborted Soviet coup. Only in the fall of 1991 did initialing of an agreement finally occur.[136]

The Failed Soviet Coup d'État
and Polish Eastern Policy

The Soviet coup d'état from 19 to 21 August 1991 marked yet another dramatic turning point in Eastern policy. Such upheaval caused by Poland's great power neighbor to the East again significantly affected Warsaw's alignment strategy, creating divisiveness among top Polish foreign policy–makers. The initial gambits of the Soviet coup d'état cast Walesa as siding with the Soviet plotters, while Poland's government differed on actions toward the rapidly emerging post–Soviet independent states. Like the confusion among presidential advisors and between the president's chancellery and premier's staff during Soviet force withdrawal negotiations, the early phase of the Soviet leadership overthrow testified to the same divisiveness. Though he remained primarily behind the scenes, Skubiszewski and the *MSZ* acted immediately, calling Soviet ambassador Kashlev for urgent consultations, confirming the status of Polish–Soviet troop talks, and mobilizing Czech and Hungarian foreign and defense officials to confer in Warsaw.[137] Publicly, Bielecki's spokesman also announced on 19 August that the government was closely watching the serious developments via the intergovernmental crisis team on which Skubiszewski participated, condemned the use of force, and would ensure Poland's security.[138] Inexplicably, the president remained silent during the first two days, rejecting proposals to speak to the Polish people, rebuffing the premier's request to address the nation, and spurning the pleas for closer contacts with NATO by the minister of state for national security. Yet, he did speak to some of his national security advisors and also sought advice from former Communist leader Jaruzelski and former interior minister Czeslaw Kiszczak.[139] No meetings of the National Defense Committee convened, in contradiction to the February restructuring of the committee for such emergencies. Only on 20 August did Walesa's spokesman provide any update on the coup to the public, speaking about the president's decision not to convene emergency meetings and about the world leaders with whom Walesa had spoken.[140]

Eventually, by the afternoon of 21 August, when El'tsin's prodemocratic forces prevailed peacefully over the Soviet hard-liner revolt, Walesa decided to appear on Polish television. The public observed, however, only Walesa's conversation with the Russian president. During the brief talk Walesa demonstrated Poland's "concern" about Gorbachev's captivity in the Crimea and about the situation in Moscow. Without committing to Polish–Russian ties beyond "friendship," the Polish president wanted "to be careful so that no one can accuse us of interfering in your [El'tsin's] internal affairs." Despite El'tsin's clear desire to enhance firm relations and consistent presidential contacts, Walesa ignored him and simply wished El'tsin well.[141]

Given these events, incidents during the failed Soviet hard-liner uprising revealed a Polish president on the defensive from his critics for behavior during Poland's most serious post-Communist crisis. Various Polish sources revealed that the president mainly communicated with his pro-Soviet advisors and former Polish Communist leaders, and even intended to contact the head of the Soviet mutiny, Gennadii Yanaev.[142] For instance, in his hasty postcoup press conference, Walesa divulged, "I decided in the conversation to present the situation and to request from him [Jaruzelski], where he has influence, to appeal or to cooperate." He elaborated that "this time Poles would take a joint approach to this difficult subject so that there would be no kind of division." Arguing that, as "a democratically elected president," he remained charged with "consulting to a maximum," Walesa stated that he needed "to choose the best solutions and not make mistakes. . . . I needed the views of Jaruzelski and Mr. Kisczak."[143] To his anti-Soviet, pro-El'tsin advisers, such reaction from the former *Solidarnosc* leader manifested the worst intentions. Even more disturbing, the Polish president sided neither with Gorbachev nor El'tsin at the beginning of the coup. Instead, under his direction, some from Walesa's staff apparently tried unsuccessfully to call Yanaev and also prepared a letter never sent to the instigator of the Soviet uprising.

According to sources privy to the draft, the letter supposedly declared Walesa's acceptance of Yanaev's scheme. In the words of Walesa's first minister of state for national security, Jacek Merkel, whom the president unexplainably fired several months before Moscow's August actions, "he [Walesa] would have sent it, but it was heroically blocked at the last moment by Prime Minister Bielecki. Had the letter gone out, Walesa would have joined the likes of Muammar Qaddafi, Saddam Hussein, and Stanislaw Tyminski," the latter of whom was the nationalistic and antidemocratic politician who challenged Walesa for the presidency in the runoff round.[144] Notwithstanding this harsh rhetoric, Walesa never publicly denied that he and his staff had composed such a letter nor, if so, that he had intended to send it to Yanaev. Indeed, the defeat of the Soviet plot demonstrated that Walesa still instinctively clung to the Soviet regime over the emerging Russian leadership. The Polish president continued to try to appease the implacable Soviet troop withdrawal demands, demonstrating his commitment to Gorbachev, who soon faltered, and disdaining deeply the loyal colleagues Walesa often abandoned in the heat of the moment.[145]

As the Soviet insurrection dissipated and El'tsin's Russian Republic consolidated power, Walesa again committed Poland to what some of his advisors criticized as a continued "Finlandization" of Eastern policy. Given Walesa's indecisiveness, the Kaczynski brothers prepared to resign and given Moscow's political transition, other anti-Soviet presidential advisors such as Najder, Jan Parys, and Jan Olszewski pressed for a return to a more forceful Eastern policy. All of these advisors believed the long-delayed and fully free parliamentary elections in October promised a possible change to a stronger government. At the same time, Skubiszewski tried to revitalize the *MSZ*'s strategy on Soviet troop withdrawals. In a statement released on 22 August, he underscored that the postcoup atmosphere provided the "solution" required for settling outstanding negotiation problems. By delaying the treaty, Skubiszewski argued that Soviet negotiators went against "the requirements of our good relations and [such actions] do not lie in the broader interest of peaceful development in Europe."[146] Within days, Walesa phoned Gorbachev after the latter's release from the Crimea and capitulated to the demands of the irreparably weakened Soviet leader.

On 28 August the Polish–Soviet presidential talks, broadcast on Polish television, witnessed a docile Walesa seemingly giving up any force withdrawal position Poland still held. Walesa declared that he "wished greater cooperation in every sphere" and that both the Soviet force withdrawal negotiation and economic cooperation, including large Soviet debt to Poland, necessitated quick resolution. In response, Gorbachev appealed to Poland to recognize that "we do want to withdraw the forces as quickly as possible. . . . I ask for understanding, assuring that we will do everything as quickly as possible." That point caused the Polish president to interrupt:

> I hope that this does not look as if Poland wants to exploit the difficulties of the Soviet Union at this moment. We do not want to humiliate the Soviet Army. All countries are condemned to cooperation. We want to tell the Soviet nations that you are so economically linked that you are fated to each other, fated to cooperation, naturally under new conditions.[147]

Hence, Walesa determined Poland should yield to Soviet force withdrawal terms, retreating from the Polish timeline requirements and scuttling Skubiszewski's team. More importantly, Walesa admitted publicly his disagreement with Skubiszewski's two-track Eastern policy.[148]

A flurry of *MSZ* activity also occurred just before the Walesa–Gorbachev discussion. On 26 August, Skubiszewski announced that Poland finally stood ready to establish diplomatic relations and advance cooperation with its eastern neighbors given the cascade of their independence declarations. By this time, however, a number of nations around the world already declared their support for the emerging post-Soviet states. Poland retained a different status compared to most of the international community, which had only begun to recognize the existence of these evolving post–Soviet states. For the steady and methodical Skubiszewski the basis of the two-track policy remained intact, even if Walesa would disagree publicly several days later in his televised talk with Gorbachev. To initiate concrete steps toward the Baltic states, Skubiszewski sent Kostrzewa-Zorbas to deliver letters of intent to each of the Baltic foreign ministries personally and, within days, each Baltic capital agreed to restore interstate relations— relations involuntarily severed since the 1940 Soviet annexation.[149] Despite these diplomatic successes, Skubiszewski needed to defend his eastern policy after harsh attacks by anti-Soviet Presidential Advisory Committee members Najder, Parys, and Olszewski.

These conservative leaders, who comprised some of Walesa's advisors, formally broke with their *Solidarnosc* colleagues Walesa and Skubiszewski for the first time publicly, and attacked Eastern policy at a public forum with Walesa and in the press for its "caution," "ambiguity," "subservience," and "indecisiveness" toward Soviet Moscow. All three advisors agreed that Poland had missed an extremely important opportunity to rid the state of Soviet troops, particularly to seal a deal on a timeline in early 1991. Parys suggested "Poland might agree to the last Soviet soldier leaving this country no sooner than 1994. Instead of compromise, we are unilaterally conceding."[150] Olszewski added that the missed chance occurred "not because we failed to appreciate the problem, but because we were entirely mistaken in looking for guarantees to safeguard our security against non-existent threats from the West." He continued by saying that Poland had focused mistakenly on German relations since 1989 and "neglected" the "more important area" of Eastern policy with "our major partners and our predominant interests of the moment in Moscow and Kiev." To underscore, he chastised the leadership because "whereas until December 1990 we still attempted to propose some new initiatives, since January this year our behavior on this front has been entirely passive." In Olszewski's mind, "we failed to realize the idea—promoted by Warsaw from the very beginning—of a parallel foreign diplomacy line to be pursued on two levels: that of the republics and that of the central administration." His reproach focused not on the fact that the two-track policy began as a serious policy, but that Warsaw postponed "taking advantage of its position as a state to promote the autonomy of the Baltic Republics, [and that] Poland displayed a total lack of interest in the matter."[151] Najder left little room for interpretation:

> The unsuccessful putsch exposed an absence of ideas in our eastern policy on how to behave toward the USSR and how to react to its disintegration, decommunization, and the appearance of independent republics. We have been very late in reacting and our reaction uncoordinated.[152]

Furthermore, Najder believed that Belorussia, Ukraine, and Lithuania needed Poland and since "Poland is virtually nonexistent east of the Bug River," the foreign ministry and the Polish leadership must regain what initiative they employed during the fall of 1990.

The post-Soviet era, the advisors argued, demanded bold thinking. Such policy should focus especially on Belorussia because Poland remained "the only window to Europe, and if we do not help the Belorussians find a place for themselves in the new world situation, who will?"[153] Najder warned that "the moment of danger has passed, but we do not know what comes next." Like Najder, Olszewski concluded that "it would be inappropriate for us to try to undergo a Finlandization exercise, even though our opposition [*Solidarnosc*] for years regarded such a situation as an ideal solution for Poland." He expounded, "the idea of Finlandization has always been a mistaken notion in our case and neutrality is most definitely not a viable proposition in our part of Europe." With regard to the crumbling USSR, he expounded that "we can only play one of two roles in relation to the Soviet Union (as until now) or to Russia (as of now): either as a partner or as a satellite." In order to overcome Poland's difficult past, Olszewski considered "the interwar concept of an 'equidistance' in our mutual relations a makeshift attempt to reach a middle-course solution. . . . Poland is too weak for such a solution [interwar option]. We must define our position in no uncertain terms, on the basis of our overriding interests." For the future prime minister, "the question of securing care and assistance for Polish ethnic minorities abroad, [is] particularly acute in Lithuania, and tomorrow it will probably become apparent in Ukraine [and] Belorussia" and also necessitated greater attention.[154] Thus, Walesa's advisors launched major criticism against their president and *Solidarnosc* colleague, breaking with him publicly and forcing both president and foreign minister to counter the charges.

Walesa and Skubiszewski responded quickly and forcefully by defending Poland's Eastern policy, albeit differently. Inherent to their defense of Poland's Eastern strategy was an emphasis on the limitations of eastern policymaking. The Polish president's simple rejoinder placed politics above substance as he rationalized that "our desires and our possibilities are two entirely different matters." Putting Najder on the spot in front of the press, Walesa retorted "Perhaps Mr. Najder could do things better, but I am president, and I do what is possible." Finally, in words that seemingly fell on deaf ears, the president urged, "let us not use this meeting as an opportunity for accusations, but as one to examine what is happening in the world."[155] Skubiszewski rebutted the conservative accusations by stating that his Eastern policy "was being pursued intensively for months, that is, from the time when some of the Soviet Republics declared their sovereignty last year." Moreover, the foreign minister countered that "we opened ourselves to contacts, we showed a far-reaching initiative as part of our entire Eastern policy months ago. The republics did not always take advantage of that and this stemmed from the limitations they faced: till the coup their situation was very difficult." He credited the two-track policy as "an act of looking ahead and proof of our vision." Not only did "we not [want] to embarrass the republics with our initiatives," Skubiszewski remonstrated, but Poland also understood that "a policy of lively contacts with the republics had to be characterized by a certain amount of finesse." To reinforce his concern about Lithuanian obstinacy over the ethnic Polish minority problems, particularly its suspension of Polish Communist coup supporters in the Salcininkai and Vilnius districts, Skubiszewski reiterated that his visit to Vilnius depended on a Lithuanian resolution to minority problems, "about which I cannot forget."[156]

During his trip to The Hague in early September, Skubiszewski also rebutted his critics, castigating not just Polish conservatives but also the West, over ignorance about the Soviet collapse. Skubiszewski declared, "the West has always looked to Gorbachev and had kept the Baltic peoples, the Russians, and [the] Ukrainians at a distance." According to Skubiszewski, "we saw the centrifugal forces. . . . Now, everything is collapsing, but this collapse has already started last year. That is why we were able to respond then to the modest start which the republics were then making." Given the previous uncertainty over the future of the USSR and its new Union Treaty, he pronounced, "I am happy that we thought last year about agreements with the republics. The Soviet Union, we concluded, must be approached on two levels. The West was unwilling to understand that." Certainly, Poland wanted to extend its initial linkages, but "the problem was that the republics did not know where their powers lay and what was still decided by the center." Now, Skubiszewski maintained, "areas of competence in the trading field have been clarified, that will be a gain in itself." Yet, to demonstrate his sensitivity to Western concerns, he did emphasize that "we are concerned about the question of who has control over the arms in the Soviet Union, about the Soviet Union's commitments with regard to conventional arms in Europe," about troop withdrawals, and about the Soviet debt to Poland.[157] Soon after his trip to The Hague, Skubiszewski traveled to Moscow.

While in Moscow briefly on a 10–12 September trip for a CSCE meeting, Skubiszewski further lambasted his critics. He argued that "relations with Russia have been maintained, but in view of the position of the Russian Government and President El'tsin the pace of these relations had to be adjusted to the pace of internal changes and to the wishes of Russia." Regarding Lithuania, he elaborated by saying that "Lithuanian authorities thus deprived them of the opportunity to express their interests and made Poles defenseless." He believed that, after meeting with his Lithuanian counterpart in Moscow, a formal Lithuanian motion to reverse the suspension remained expeditious and, as both states started expert-level drafting of a cooperation declaration, Skubiszewski now considered seriously taking his long-delayed Vilnius trip.[158]

Even with the *MSZ*'s efforts to expand bilateral relationships with eastern neighbors, the political winds appeared set to change rapidly in the fall of 1991. After the October elections resulted in an unwieldy legislature comprising twenty-nine different political parties, the potential for further political dispute increased. Worse for Skubiszewski, Olszewski became the new premier, after wrangling with Walesa to form a new government, and the assertive prime minister brought with him advisors such as Najder and, in a daring move, named Parys to head the defense ministry as the first civilian. As the tension mounted from the outset, this government politically confronted the president's chancellery, particularly over Eastern policy in 1992.

New Eastern Ties after Soviet Demise

Skubiszewski's two-track policy allowed Warsaw to expand the initial links to the nascent post-Soviet leaderships in the former Soviet republics bordering Poland. The foreign minister spent the next two years methodically expanding Warsaw's ties to Moscow, Kiev, Vilnius, and Minsk until he left office. His priority remained signing multiple agreements with each Soviet successor state, always aiming to achieve state-to-state relations in the way he had accomplished with Germany. The multitude of foreign ministerial meetings and high-level exchanges that occurred from the fall of 1991 culminated in several presidential and prime ministerial visits by the end of 1993. Interestingly, Skubiszewski found that relations accelerated with Ukraine and Belarus, while Polish–Russian ties slowly improved and Polish–Lithuanian linkages experienced consistent difficulties. Above all, Skubiszewski understood that, though Poland needed to continue to work with Gorbachev, Polish Eastern policy required an accelerated engagement with post–Soviet republic leaderships. When Russia, Ukraine, and Belarus established the Commonwealth of Independent States (CIS), the *MSZ* declared that "the policy of successive development of contacts with the three republics helps promptly to shape mutual relations." On 8 December 1991, with the CIS's formation, the *MSZ* emphasized that "the developments in the Soviet Union confirm the rightness of Poland's Eastern policy," that is, providing a middle power bridge to great powers and emerging middle and small powers.[159]

Relations developed swiftly with Ukraine and Belarus in the fall of 1991. Within two weeks of the Moscow insurrection's collapse, Ukrainian foreign minister Zlenko made his first trip to Warsaw and signaled with Skubiszewski some major developments in their relations. Both sides agreed to establish diplomatic ties, exchange special government emissaries to each capital, and make consular arrangements, in addition to arranging final details of their long-delayed economic cooperation. At the press conference, Skubiszewski stated that "Ukraine, which we look upon as a sovereign state, is entering the European political scene." He also said Poland intended to promote Ukraine at the upcoming CSCE conference to demonstrate Ukraine's role in European security. For his part, Zlenko responded that "Ukrainian-Polish cooperation can play a strategic role in solving problems presently facing a uniting Europe. . . . It is no accident that the first official visit after the declaration of independence in Ukraine is to Poland." Furthermore, with the long Ukrainian–Polish history, he believed relations now developed from the "principles of equality and partnership."[160] By October the Ukrainian prime minister, Vitold Fokin, arrived in Warsaw to sign the economic agreement and underscored that "as neighboring countries, Poland and Ukraine have common traditions and a common history. Therefore, they should find a common path and help each other."[161] By the 1 December 1991 Ukrainian referendum on independence, Poland became the first state formally to recognize Ukraine.

Skubiszewski's statement on Ukrainian independence sounded a note of satisfaction over the culmination of the *MSZ*'s efforts to forge Polish–Ukrainian ties. For him, "since the beginning of the transformations in the USSR, and especially since the beginning of the emancipation of the republics within the borders of the USSR, Poland pursued a clear and consistent eastern policy." Such "a policy of establishing and expanding relations with the peoples who border us in the East" substantiated Skubiszewski's design based on bridging states amid the regional anarchy stemming from the USSR's collapse.[162] This strategy enabled Poland to demonstrate its unique and specialized middle power role not just between Germany and Russia, but among great, middle, and small powers, reducing potential threats by bilaterally linking to all of its neighbors. Poland became a gateway for the emerging post-Soviet states to orient Westward. Choosing to disrupt and survive without regard to the states emerging to its east would likely have upended Poland's stability-enhancing relationship established with Germany to its west. To reduce tensions from the USSR's collapse that easily could have destabilized the region, Poland sought to allay concerns by reaching out to all of its new neighbors cooperatively. Rather than resort to self-help simply to survive, Poland developed its other-help strategy that pinpointed very meticulous ways to initiate bilateral linkages to its east that built upon and solidified the ties to its west.

Given the Ukrainian independence referendum, Skubiszewski foresaw that, "within the inviolable present borders, we welcome this independence. Our eastern history had been long, hard, and frequently tragic. Today we extend our hand of friendship to the Ukrainian people." In a direct reference to future relations based on a protection of minority rights in both Ukraine and Poland, the foreign minister also envisioned "full and unrestricted opportunities for Poles in Ukraine. For our part, we guarantee Ukrainians in Poland similar opportunities."[163] In response to Poland's support, particularly as the tumultuous year of 1991 closed, Ukrainian president Leonid Kravchuk assessed in an interview that "any complications in the Polish-Ukrainian past can be easily overcome today by way of friendly agreements." Kravchuk believed common national interests and contiguity allowed Ukraine to follow Poland's admirable reform example.[164]

Poland's ties to Belarus dramatically improved during the fall, too. Though minority problems and territorial issues continued to plague both sides, Belarusian foreign minister Petr Kravchenko stated that "a kind of gentleman's agreement exists between me and Mr. Skubiszewski. . . . If we are to pursue universal values . . . we must resolve all nationality issues on a practical and political level." The minister indicated that progress continued, as foreign ministerial expert delegations worked closely together during the late summer and early fall to draft a declaration.[165] Faster than expected, Warsaw and Minsk reached accord when Belarusian prime minister Vyacheslav Kebich came to Warsaw and signed the good-neighborly declaration in early October. Importantly, the declaration confirmed the Polish–Belarusian border and obligated both states to protect the ethnic, cultural, and linguistic identity of the respective minorities in both countries. Furthermore, both sides pledged to uphold "the principles of equality, respect for sovereignty and territorial integrity of the two states, and non-interference in internal affairs." Both sides also agreed to open diplomatic and consular relations and to discuss bilateral relations within the context of international security. The talks between the Belarusian prime minister and Polish leadership marked significant progress in Polish–Belarusian ties, as Skubiszewski elaborated that both sides sought to discuss in greater detail over the coming months "security questions and border traffic." In a sign of concrete cooperation, Kebich declared that his state intended to open two new border crossings. Walesa exclaimed that the closeness of Poland and Belarus boded "ethnically and historically . . . a beneficial common future."[166]

In yet other developments, Vice Minister Makarczyk and his Soviet counterpart met several times during the fall to initial the withdrawal treaty terms. For the first time, dates appeared publicly on specific force withdrawals. Moscow agreed to withdraw all combat troops by 15 November 1992 and committed itself, in principle, to a final withdrawal of its six thousand remaining communications, logistics, and intelligence troops by the end of 1993. Makarczyk reasoned that "the acceptance of the dates fixed for the pullout was a sovereign decision of the Polish Government that should be assessed in the European context." To place the troop withdrawals in the larger European security framework, Makarczyk also explained that "we are regularly in touch with European organizations and remember that Soviet troops stationed in Germany find themselves on the territory of the EC and NATO." Given expanded ties between Poland and both the EC and NATO, Makarczyk believed it remained necessary "to facilitate the realization of the German-Soviet treaty."[167] He conceded, however, that "had it not been for the coup we would not have reached as far as we did."[168] As he elaborated on the treaty's final terms in December 1991, "we have totally eliminated the road transit because of the danger of accidents, because of the environment, as well as possible desertions." Hence, the *MSZ* went into the next year expecting to complete a withdrawal treaty with Russia in place of the USSR.[169]

After the Soviet collapse, Polish–Lithuanian relations accelerated, but not without strains. Both sides required compromise over the minority issues and over the difficult interwar history. By maintaining that only acceptable European standards allowed Poland to sign agreements with Lithuania, Skubiszewski and his *MSZ* team, particularly Jacek Czaputowicz, persevered and even withstood public criticism by Lithuanian president Landsbergis.[170] In November, the situation worsened when a short-lived controversy arose with Lithuanian defense minister Audrius Butkevicius, who claimed that "there is a threat to the republic not only from the east—a USSR that is in the process of disintegrating—and from the west, that is, from Poland."[171] Such rhetoric hindered Polish–Lithuanian ties, but Skubiszewski's early January visit reduced tension.

The Polish foreign minister finally traveled to Vilnius and stated on the eve of his departure that "my visit is not a beginning of the relations, it is just a new stage in their development. I believe we will be able to sort out some difficulties the Polish population encounters in Lithuania . . . to re-instate self-rule in the Vilnius and Salcininkai districts."[172] His counterpart, Saudargas, previewed the visit by saying that "common-sense [was] taking the upper hand and it was symbolic that the Polish-Lithuanian Declaration would be signed on such a sad day as January 13," the first-year anniversary of the Soviet massacre in Vilnius.[173]

With the signing of the declaration both states overcame a lengthy period of mutual recriminations. Both ministers agreed to a "mutual recognition of state independence, observance of international law, respect for sovereignty and territorial integrity, principles of equality, respect for human rights and fundamental freedoms." Both states promised noninterference in each other's internal affairs and renounced any territorial claims. The declaration mainly concentrated on the national minorities in both states. The declaration stated that each state would "be guided by European standards provided for in appropriate documents of the CSCE," such as fulfillment of "opportunities to fully meet their linguistic, cultural, religious and educational needs . . . and to create guarantees of their non-discrimination in political and economic life." Significantly, both ministers declared that consistent consultations had focused on "cooperation in the international arena and international issues subject to the interest of both sides," such as the recently created Baltic Council. All of these commitments laid the groundwork for a state treaty both men believed possible during the coming year.[174]

Both ministers also praised resolution to problems that had prevented the visit for nearly twenty-one months. Skubiszewski stressed that "Poland's desire is to maintain the best and the most wide-ranging relations with the Lithuanian state and government." In answering a question about the small Lithuanian protests regarding the difficult interwar history, Skubiszewski counseled calmness, saying "I can assure Lithuania and Lithuanians that there will not be a second General Zeligowski." This implied that Poland held no territorial claims against Lithuania (Polish general Zeligowski took Vilnius by force in 1920). For his part, Saudargas emphasized that "this is the start of cooperation between the states of Lithuania and Poland under new conditions both in our states and in international politics." He did explain, however, that "the work on this declaration did not include the problem of assessment of the entire historical context."[175] Yet, Skubiszewski summed up the trip by declaring that "the Poles [living in Lithuania] could see that establishing relations with Lithuania gathers momentum." His satisfaction appeared evident when he described his Lithuanian interlocutors who "meet all the significant demands and solve the question of local self-governments [in Lithuanian districts inhabited by Poles]." Finally, Skubiszewski simply declared that when "extremists on both sides do not like some actions it means that we follow the right track. It is necessary that local residents reach agreement with local authorities. Poland cannot do everything for the Poles [in Lithuania]."[176]

Skubiszewski's pragmatic strategy for expanding bilateral linkages with each new neighboring state remained consistent, particularly as the new Olszewski government vowed rapid acceleration of Eastern ties. Leading governmental voices such as Najder and Parys advocated swift simultaneous movement toward institutions such as NATO. As a result, Walesa and Olszewski battled to dominate eastern policy, having divided the president's former chancellery staff into diametrically opposing camps. The first camp still comprised the pro-Soviet presidential staff of Wachowski, Milewski, and Tadeusz Wilecki, the latter named general staff chief over Defense Minister Parys's veto.[177] On Olszewski's side stood Najder, Parys, the Kaczynski brothers, and Kostrzewa-Zorbas, who moved to the defense ministry in early 1992 to form the first civilian defense policy department, a radical decision by Parys and his twenty-nine-year-old vice minister, Radek Sikorski.[178] In the middle of these policy battle lines Skubiszewski remained foreign minister, persuaded by Walesa to keep running the *MSZ*, but concerned about the increasing bitterness between the president and prime minister.

After the initial weeks of Olszewski's government, an unsettled calm in eastern policy existed.[179] Skubiszewski spent the first weeks of the new government trying to invigorate the linkages with Belarus and Russia, specifically by signing declarations, as ties with Ukraine and Lithuania progressed to reach agreements in early 1992.[180] The Polish foreign minister finally crowned the Polish-Belarusian relationship in late April with a treaty, a key objective for all of Poland's top national security officials. After several prime ministerial and foreign ministerial trips between Minsk and Warsaw from February to March,

Polish and Belarusian officials reached a new stage in relations. The 23–24 April prime ministerial meeting in Warsaw marked a high point for both states as they upheld principles on "cross-border cooperation, trade, rights and obligations of ethnic minorities, protection of authors' rights and patents." Both foreign ministers committed themselves to "all-round development" of their cooperation, including political dialogue that aimed to enhance communication as Belarus built its independent and denuclearized army from Russia. Both Olszewski and Kebich "consider[ed] the possibility of opening a Belarusian [commercial] consulate in the northern Polish port city of Gdynia." Given the border disputes that marred Skubiszewski's visit in October 1990, Polish–Belarusian ties had now improved significantly, with commitments to open consular and trade delegations in both states.[181]

Eastern policy, however, took a different turn in the spring, as regional tensions mounted between Russia and Ukraine over control of nuclear weapons, the Black Sea Fleet, and Crimea, just as the Polish leadership completed final planning for top-level meetings with both states. The consensus goal in the *MSZ* remained to reduce tension between Moscow and Kiev, but also between those capitals and Warsaw. Skubiszewski strove to steer foreign policy equally toward both Moscow and Kiev so as not to play them against each other. In contrast, Parys and others tried to strengthen Ukrainian links to increase Ukrainian sovereignty and push Russia on force withdrawals and encourage Moscow on Polish NATO membership.[182]

A sign of limited improvement occurred when Russian defense minister Pavel Grachev, now El'tsin's chief representative, met with the Polish leadership to complete final details on the withdrawal treaty. After meeting with Grachev, Skubiszewski and Milewski revealed that by "striving to end talks on issues" which now concerned seven outstanding financial points, El'tsin's leadership finally "made it possible to make progress on the issue that has been lasting too long." In order to accommodate Moscow, however, Warsaw compromised. Skubiszewski reconsidered Grachev's revival of the "joint Polish – Russian ventures [that] will be set up using some former facilities of the Soviet Army." Even though Skubiszewski criticized Russian tactics, arguing that "ecological damage remained to be solved as General Dubynin refused to let Polish experts into Russian military units," the tension remained palpable between Olszewski's defense ministry and the *MSZ* over the joint ventures.[183]

The tension over the Russian "joint ventures" within the Polish government and between the Polish premier and president also contributed to the suspension of defense minister Parys by Walesa, pending a parliamentary hearing over the minister's harsh public criticism of Walesa's secret military dealmaking. The few defense civilians who opposed the *MSZ* and president's chancellery, led by Kostrzewa-Zorbas and his deputy, Krzysztof Zielke, instigated a major internal governmental dispute over presidential willingness to yield to the Russian joint venture demands.[184] Furthermore, Vice Defense Minister Sikorski also voiced publicly, following on the heels of the Parys suspension, that Polish–Ukrainian ties should balance Polish–Russian relations.[185] Consequently, the tension between Olszewski and Walesa increased, as Eastern policy moved, in fits and starts, toward final treaty planning with Kiev and Moscow.[186]

The first presidential visit between Walesa and Kravchuk occurred in Warsaw on 18 May and culminated Skubiszewski's two-year campaign to build relations. These discussions entailed extensive explanation about Ukraine's plan to uphold nonproliferation of weapons, especially nuclear weapons, to continue its denuclearization process, and to weigh options about linkages to NATO. To Skubiszewski, the strengthening of Polish–Ukrainian security relations enhanced European security and stability. Kravchuk clearly expounded that "Ukraine pledges to pursue the target policy of neutrality, but that does not prevent it from cooperation with those structures in case of major unrest in Europe."[187] Both presidents signed not only the state treaty, but also numerous agreements that included formal border crossings. Overall, the treaty guaranteed border inviolability, rejected territorial demands, and renounced aggression. Though Walesa underlined the difficult history between the two states, he declared their post–Cold War ties now focused on "creating a new order in this part of the world. . . . Poland and Ukraine originate from the same Slavonic roots. . . . We shape our mutual relations on completely new principles, consciously, and independently."[188]

Kravchuk praised his host's commitment to an independent Ukraine and stressed that Kiev held Warsaw in high esteem, particularly since Poland had been the first state to recognize the results of Ukraine's independence referendum. He viewed the relationship as one founded on "warm feelings toward our people, faith in the actions of Ukraine's government, and trust in the highly promising future of our ties."[189] The Ukrainian president elaborated that "our nations, which are again independent, should form a new deal in Europe." He rationalized that "Ukraine, while moving toward democratic Europe, will respect the CSCE acts, and has also decided to rid itself of its nuclear arms so as to create the basis for a new Europe without borders."[190]

Though he desired better ties with Warsaw than Walesa wanted to offer, Kravchuk nevertheless declared that Ukraine's relations with Warsaw was "greater" than with any other state in the former USSR. He pronounced "Poland an equal partner for us, whereas Russia is trying to speak to us from the position of 'elder brother' and is proceeding from imperial positions."[191] Kravchuk aimed these remarks at Moscow because Russia pressured Ukraine over control of the Black Sea Fleet and he looked to Poland to balance against Moscow. Walesa did not respond publicly. Generally, however, positive assessments resulted from all of the Ukrainian meetings, including those with embattled premier Olszewski. Both states began to reconcile and enact practical interstate ties. Therefore, the trip signaled both a new beginning for Warsaw–Kiev relations and for Walesa's long-delayed Russian trip.

Notably, an atmosphere of mutual respect and tough-mindedness toward the negotiations within the overall cooperation treaty marked the prelude to the Russian visit. For the Polish president, "the opening of a new stage in relations" focused on tackling the "problems on which we will be able to reach agreement." Walesa desired what he portrayed as a Polish–Russian leadership role in post–Communist Europe, but quickly elaborated that this "realization of his idea depended primarily on how well the two countries were to fulfill their commitments under international law." Significantly, he added that Polish–Ukrainian relations began from "scratch without looking back." This rationale underscored why ties with Russia appeared more problematic. For Walesa, it took "two to tango" in Polish–Russian relations. To put this into perspective, he said that "if we succeed in striking up—and most important of all, implementing—an honest relationship with Russia, the interests of other states will be borne in mind as our cooperation materializes."[192]

For his part, the Russian president described meetings with Walesa as "between two tough guys, who know how to defend the interests of their nations and who have realized that they have to go hand in hand toward building new relations between Russia and Poland." At a dinner he hosted for Walesa, El'tsin said that "now that we are making most painful and difficult economic reforms, your experience helps us see more clearly the light at the end of the tunnel and gives us more strength and assurance." He continued, "our approaches to major international issues are close or coincide." On this last note, El'tsin declared his intention to "solve uneasy questions on the Russian troop withdrawal from Polish territory. The [potential] compromise," he revealed, "equally corresponds to the interests of both peoples."[193] Thus, the signing of a troop withdrawal treaty promised to challenge both sides.

The last minute maneuvering, however, between Olszewski, his experts in Warsaw, and Walesa, with his pro-Soviet advisors, at the Moscow summit involved a game of brinkmanship in which Olszewski prevailed at high cost. Separate from the two presidents, Skubiszewski and Grachev, not Kozyrev, negotiated the final political and financial details of the controversial withdrawal agreement. After great wrangling, Skubiszewski and Grachev reached a stalemate, actually forwarding the final negotiation to both presidents. As Polish radio reported, "the issue concerned the deployment of Russian communications battalions, to ensure communication links between Moscow and units of the Russian armed forces stationed on the territory of the former GDR."[194] This partially accounted for the problem, with the public dispute deadlocked over the stationing of the final six thousand troops. The internal problem, however, really stemmed from the Russian reactivation of the Soviet treaty clause that called for transforming military bases into commercial ventures under Russian control after all forces departed.[195] As word reached Warsaw that Skubiszewski and Walesa might yield on the issue of permanent "commercial joint ventures" near the Polish–German border and, implicitly, allow former Soviet bases to operate conceivably as intelligence outlets, Olszewski intervened via cable directly to Walesa. He pleaded for Walesa to persuade El'tsin to drop the "Finlandizing" clause. The Polish premier refused to relent over what he believed to be a vital issue of Polish sovereignty in the state's highest national interest.

Based on the critical analysis provided to Olszewski's advisers, from the defense ministry's defense policy staff, the premier understood that the Russian military ploy finally needed to end. In fact, Olszewski's cable bypassed Skubiszewski because of the premier's frustration over the foreign minister's failure to provide him a copy of the final withdrawal treaty draft. Certainly, Olszewski's cable elicited a heated reaction from Walesa, as the Polish president reluctantly agreed and pressed El'tsin at the late-night drafting session. At variance with his senior advisers, El'tsin boldly deleted the joint ventures text from the draft treaty.[196]

After the late-night negotiations, Skubiszewski put the best face on the withdrawal treaty. He stated that "we now have the issue of troop withdrawal from Poland fully agreed, something which we did not have so far. This is an important achievement, but a short-term issue, while what really matters is the beginning of a long-term policy of very good relations and cooperation." In defending his stance during the protracted talks, Skubiszewski declared that "negotiations with the Russian side . . . continued up to the last moment." Though he didn't reveal specific problems, he appeared "satisfied" over the treaty's signing, "an issue on which I have worked since my first months in office [that] is now settled." Skubiszewski remained more concerned that "Poland do all within her limited means to ensure stability and build cooperation . . . as the main aim of eastern policy." In the end, Olszewski won the battle over joint ventures, while Skubiszewski compromised, a reality the foreign minister acknowledged, but disputed the way the final series of events unfolded.[197]

What Walesa and Skubiszewski attained on the Russian trip beyond the withdrawal treaty also proved commendable. At Polish initiative, unplanned at the trip's outset, both sides formulated a joint statement that denounced "the Stalinist regime [that] caused enormous suffering and brought irreversible moral harm to Polish and Russian people."[198] Walesa proclaimed that "we achieved everything we wanted, in relation to the past history and the future prospects of Polish–Russian relations," a future in which "both states can support each other, strengthen cooperation and restore economic ties based on new principles and reciprocity." In response, El'tsin welcomed "relations built from the principles of true equality, respect for each other's sovereignty, and mutual advantage."[199] From their declaration of October 1990 to their treaty in May 1992, Poland and Russia overcame great obstacles to agree to new interstate ties.[200]

Although victorious on the Russian troop withdrawal treaty, Olszewski found himself embroiled in too many domestic political disputes with Walesa. Upon the Polish president's return from Moscow, the government soon collapsed. Just before the government's fall, however, Skubiszewski achieved one of the Olszewski government's foreign policy priorities. The late June visit by Belorussian president Stanislav Shushkevich symbolized the penultimate step in Skubiszewski's Eastern strategy. In their state treaty, both sides sought to enhance the protection of their respective minority populations, with Shushkevich stating that "the situation of the Belarusian minority in Poland had significantly improved in recent years, thanks to the understanding and peaceful policies of the Polish Government." Though Skubiszewski held that some outstanding issues concerning the Polish minority required attention by Minsk, particularly in regions part of Poland before World War II, he deemed the treaty's provisions very successful.[201]

Now, only a state treaty between Poland and Lithuania remained for Skubiszewski to obtain as part of his Eastern strategy. Yet another Polish government formation delayed the coordination of a Polish–Lithuanian treaty, this time under parliamentarian Hanna Suchocka, who, it turned out, represented the last prime minister for whom Skubiszewski worked. With Suchocka's ascendancy, Skubiszewski agreed to stay as foreign minister, taking himself out of contention for international appointments, because he wanted to achieve the final goals of his original foreign policy objectives. Clearly, Suchocka demonstrated that she intended to advance Skubiszewski's strategy as she quickly began meeting with many of her Eastern counterparts. Both premier and foreign minister strove to extend Poland's bilateral Eastern relationships rapidly and, in her first foreign policy speech, Suchocka underlined that "Poland does not make any territorial claims in relation to her neighbors, neither does any of our neighbors question our borders." Moreover, she stressed that "Poland's interest lies in the consolidation of the independence, also in economic terms, of her Eastern neighbors and in helping them embark upon a road to European integration." Like Skubiszewski, Suchocka emphasized that "we do not want them [the post-Soviet successor states] to turn away from Europe, although one cannot say that Europe has given them a friendly hand." In terms of Poles who lived abroad, the premier declared that Poland "expected those countries [the post-Soviet successor states] to observe the rights of Polish minorities. The Polish will aims to solve peacefully problems ensuing from the past which not only unites but also separates us." Finally, regarding Russia, Suchocka announced that "Poland wanted Russian respect for Polish national interests both in security and economic relations, including the necessity to solve the problem of financial debt and increase trade."[202] Thus, the Suchocka administration concentrated on invigorating economic relationships and reducing minority tensions to expand Eastern policy, objectives Skubiszewski attempted to implement in state treaties and agreements.

Within weeks of her appointment, Suchocka traveled to Minsk to sign agreements with Belarus and to speak with Polish minority groups in Grodno. She consolidated some of the initial economic cooperation from the previous year by signing financial, cultural, scientific, and educational agreements. Moreover, she exclaimed, "Poland is interested in Belarus being a fully independent state. We are also interested in assisting Belarus in her march towards Europe." She vowed that Poland intended to sign many more agreements with Belarus to provide the developing post–Soviet leadership more opportunities to orient itself toward Europe, via Poland. Yet, one of her advisors, the former parliamentarian and underground activist Jan Maria Rokita, stated that "Belarusian officials referred to very scant assistance their country was getting from the West. This made it necessary for Belarus to expand cooperation with Russia." Furthermore, Belarusian premier Kebich commented that Poland played a very important economic and political role for his young state and raised the possibility that both states expected to "reduce the concentration of military forces" on their border. Both premiers also discussed minority rights, particularly concerning those Poles and Belarussians living on the border and agreed to improve border crossings and allow easier access to both states. While in Grodno, Suchocka met with the Union of Poles in Belarus and declared that as "the Belarusian identity is reborn, so is the identity of Poles living here. These are parallel processes and the success of democratic reforms is a guarantee of their successful accomplishment." In her assurances to Polish audiences about minority rights in Belarus, she spoke about the importance of the rights of minorities in both states, the concerns raised with the Belarusian leadership, and how "Poland does not forget about the Poles living in Belarus and will render them any possible assistance."[203]

Within six months, the Polish president made his first trip to Belarus, culminating the slow, but steady bilateral relationship Skubiszewski built over two years. Upon his arrival, he said, "this treaty is being implemented very sluggishly. . . . We must open new customs control posts along our border to encourage economic and cultural relations between our peoples." When asked about President Shushkevich's recent statement that Belarus might not join the "CIS collective security bloc" initiated by Moscow, Walesa cautioned that such an issue remained an internal matter, but he thought Shushkevich "to be a shrewd politician working for the benefit of the Belarusian people."[204] After his counterpart meetings, Walesa reiterated that reduced tensions provided a historic opportunity for the two similar states and that "Poland will never see an enemy in Belarus. . . . We have had enough disrespect, foolishness, and grief in our past relations."[205] Both sides concurred in aiding border crossings to increase contacts between citizens and concluded "the West is not ready to provide its market either to Polish or Belarusian goods."[206] In his remarks to the Belarusian Supreme Soviet, Walesa underscored that both "Slavic peoples recovered their freedom and sovereignty, and can freely settle their problems and choose their way of life. Neighbors need no middlemen to reach a mutual understanding." Consequently, he declared that "Poland is watching the consolidation of the Belarusian state with sympathy and great interest. . . . When we work real hard, we will be able to maintain the sovereignty and build a good future for our peoples."[207] Above all, Walesa asserted that "I speak to Poles living in Belarus that, without fail, [they] need to love the land whose bread [they] are eating and don't do anything which might disunite us."[208]

Like Polish–Belarusian relations, Polish–Ukrainian relations developed expeditiously throughout 1993, as Skubiszewski, Suchocka, and Walesa all traveled to Kiev to reinforce Poland's commitment to Ukrainian democratization and improved bilateral ties. Skubiszewski provided important context for where he wanted to expand Polish–Ukrainian relations. The Polish–Ukrainian dialogue and cooperation in the UN, CSCE, and Council of Europe all provided mutually reinforcing multilateral arenas for Warsaw and Kiev to demonstrate the importance of the bilateral relationship. When it came to NATO, which unlike CSCE bound states institutionally together to reduce conflict, Skubiszewski underlined that "NATO is a real security factor which already exists at present .... I expect Poland to join NATO at a certain time, should this alliance wish to expand." However, by working within the framework of NATO's North Atlantic Cooperation Council, Skubiszewski believed both Warsaw and Kiev could exhibit solidarity in their quest to increase regional stability in Central and East Europe. At the same time, he explained that Ukraine's desire to join the Polish–Czechoslovak–Hungarian Visegrad Triangle, although admirable, "would be difficult." He continued, "the point is that the member states of the 'Visegrad Group' are closely tied not only to one another, but also to the EC, with which they have signed appropriate bilateral cooperation treaties. At present, I cannot imagine countries which do not have such agreements among 'Visegrad' members." To encourage Ukraine's aspirations, however, he said both states needed to "get the world interested in the democratic processes underway in our states, with a view to ensuring Western assistance to them, not assistance from time to time, as has been the case, but permanent and businesslike assistance."[209] Lastly, he emphasized to Kiev and Moscow that "for us, it is not a question of choosing between Russia and Ukraine. ... We have important dealings with both."[210]

Suchocka's January Ukrainian trip provided another opportunity to sign agreements, discuss with her counterpart the importance of expanding the Polish–Ukrainian relationship into new areas, and grapple with the very sensitive issue of ethnic minorities in both states. Her trip resulted in agreements with Premier Leonid Kuchma to extend trade, enhance border cooperation, and approve the concept for future presidential consultative committee formats to communicate more effectively.[211] Even if Suchocka failed to settle all of the problems concerning Polish minorities, she talked extensively with Kuchma about implementing economic reform and about Warsaw's priority for "the economic and political stabilization of Ukraine." In commenting on the first visit by a Polish premier to post-Soviet Ukraine, Kuchma declared that "Poland is a strategic partner for us. ... We reached full and mutual understanding on a wide range of issues. ... I appreciate the values of the Polish model of economic restructuring although at first I had been against the 'shock therapy' to the economy." They agreed to advance their relationship and speed the creation of the presidential advisory channel on security and defense issues.[212]

Suchocka then dealt with the difficulties some Polish political groups in Poland and some Ukrainian groups in Ukraine felt toward the respective ethnic minorities in both states and about historical wrongs by both states during and immediately after the World War II. The Polish delegation did its best to dampen concerns about minority problems and to make amends for historical conflicts, saying publicly that "ethnic Poles living in Ukraine must show that they are loyal citizens of the state in which they live. Poles more than any other nation must put their lives into the balance, to show that they are Poles." She asserted that it remained very important to agree "that all rulers treat national minorities with understanding if they are aware of their significance and if they are loyal citizens of the states where they happen to live."[213] In the end, Suchocka and her team failed to accomplish all the trip's objectives, including travel to Lvov, because ethnic minority problems generated more meetings in Kiev, but the results underlined Poland's efforts to broaden Central and Eastern European stability.[214]

Both states then spent the spring of 1993 paving the way for another presidential summit, this time in Ukraine that May. Russian–Ukrainian relations, however, continued to deteriorate. The increased tensions gave Warsaw great pause because Poland ostensibly upheld an equal, practical, and nonthreatening stance toward both Ukraine and Russia. As a result, Walesa declared in Lvov, his first visit before coming to Kiev, that "the Polish–Ukrainian dialogue has acquired a new meaning and new content over the past year, but it is not fully satisfactory. . . . The faster and better domestic matters are put right in each country, the faster we shall emerge side by side on the world scene." Yet, to maintain the solid relations developed since October 1990, Poland needed to tread lightly with Ukraine on security issues. Walesa and Skubiszewski recognized that Russia viewed the slightest sign of the development in Warsaw–Kiev security relations as an attempt to build a Polish–Ukrainian cordon sanitaire on Russia's western border. Hence, Walesa let Kravchuk know from Lvov that "the main thing now is to reach agreement on problems of political and economic security in the region which, in the long run, will become an influential factor in the all-European process." Ukrainian proposals from April 1993 about a collective security zone that excluded Russia, however, worried Walesa. Understandably, he cautioned that there remained "the need to determine its [the Ukrainian proposals] status and create a mechanism to guarantee its implementation. It must be formed on the basis of the inviolability of borders, irrespective of circumstances, and non-use of force to resolve inter-state disputes."[215]

Polish–Ukrainian security ties remained tense over Ukrainian foreign minister Zlenko's April 1993 CSCE initiative for an unwieldy "Baltic to the Black Sea security zone."[216] Warsaw not only found the Ukrainian security proposal awkward, given Poland's quest to join NATO and the EC, but also yielded to pressure from the U.S. and NATO headquarters to nullify independent Ukraine's security ambitions. National Security Advisor Milewski stated that "we perceive our security in the construction of a Euro-Atlantic system of security." Poland wanted clearly to ensure Ukraine understood that, in order to integrate into the Western community, denuclearization needed to occur and security zone proposals which excluded Russia held no place in Poland's European reintegration strategy. With this approach, Poland especially wanted to prevent Ukraine's international isolation.[217]

At the Kiev airport, Walesa cleared the air immediately about Ukraine's security zone concept. In response to media questions about the Kravchuk proposal, Walesa stated that "we must strive for our security and for the security of Europe in general; but it would not be a good thing if we were to set up new structures, proposing new solutions which would divide us. President Kravchuk is seeking security and that is very good. We will seek it together."[218] Despite this statement, the Polish and Ukrainian presidents reached several important agreements and met for the first time in their Consultative Committee format over the next two days.

Signed documents entailed further economic cooperation, legal assistance on civil and criminal cases, and notification mechanisms on nuclear accidents, as well as nuclear safety and radiation protection. For Walesa, "Ukrainian independence in 1991 was an act emanating from the Polish essence. We are in mutual need of one another. It is impossible to imagine Europe without a democratic and independent Ukraine. . . . We acknowledge that the stabilization of two of the biggest countries, and two of the largest states of this region will decide the future of our peoples and of the whole of Central and East Europe." Kravchuk responded that "the crucial geo-political changes that have been taking place in Europe witness Poland and Ukraine becoming important centers in Central and Eastern Europe in terms of supporting the general atmosphere of stability, security, and good relations." Furthermore, he believed that "today's harsh realities will help Ukraine and Poland build their relations as strategic partners." Both presidents concurred that the Consultative Committee, a Kravchuk initiative from December 1992, served as the main conduit for attaining closer links both states greatly wanted, even if Kravchuk remained silent about the security zone idea and deferred to Walesa's broad approach to security structures.[219] Skubiszewski described in the summit's aftermath by saying that "we think a single security system should be established in Europe and that there should not be various zones. Of course, we realize that present-day Europe has various levels of security—for example, NATO. For this reason, therefore, we are turning to the West because we also want to belong to this region." He added, "the West should come to us here. . . . I am generally in favor of forging the strongest possible links with NATO and the Western European Union."[220] Hence, with the Polish–Russian summit scheduled for August, Skubiszewski and the Polish leadership struggled to maintain pragmatic bilateral relationships vis-à-vis both Kiev and Moscow.

As analyzed in chapter 2, Polish–Russian relations also improved noticeably during El'tsin's early administration, mainly due to the Russian leader's respect for Poland's national interests and his willingness to compromise on such issues as the final Russian force withdrawals from Poland. During the early phases of El'tsin's leadership, reformers came to the fore and some hopeful signs occurred in Polish–Russian relations, particularly under Russian premier Egor Gaidar. Even as Russian–Ukrainian relations remained strained and began to worsen during 1993, Polish–Russian ties progressed. In October 1992, Gaidar met with Walesa and Suchocka in Warsaw. He discussed ways to alleviate the former Soviet debt to Poland, arranged for necessary Russian oil deliveries to Poland, and pledged to build a new oil pipeline between the states. Before his departure, Gaidar stated that "despite certain structural differences in the system of organizing the economy, the experience of the Polish reforms has a great significance for Russia since the problems, mistakes and contradictions are the same."[221]

Even with tensions mounting among opposing political forces in Moscow and between Moscow and post-Soviet successor states, El'tsin traveled to Warsaw. Upon his arrival, El'tsin stated that "Russia attaches prime importance to Poland amongst East European countries. . . . Poland has always played a big role in Eastern Europe." By demonstrating Russia's changed view since the disbandment of the USSR, the Russian leader underscored that "since 1992 Russian–Polish relations started to change for the better. We have been and will be friends with Poland, and we think this friendship is very important."[222] After El'tsin signed the trade and pipeline treaty,[223] he underscored Polish–Russian progress:

> There is no place in the new Russian-Polish relations for hegemonism or dictate, or for an older-younger brother mentality. The principles of our relations are: respect for sovereignty, equality and partnership. . . . What is at issue is a historic breakthrough between our two Slavonic countries since the last subunit of the Russian Army will withdraw from Poland, not as agreed on 31 December this year, but three months earlier. I hope this will be a farewell of friends.[224]

Yet, the night of 24 August and the early morning of the next day signified an important development. The Polish leader maneuvered El'tsin to concede on Polish requests to join NATO, in a small tête-à-tête over some very late-night drinking in the Warsaw outskirts.[225] Apparently, Walesa and El'tsin drank into the early morning hours of 25 August, just before they released the Joint Polish–Russian Declaration that announced:

> The presidents touched on the matter of Poland's intention to join NATO. President Walesa set forth Poland's well-known position, which met with understanding by President El'tsin. In the long term, such a decision taken by a sovereign Poland in the interests of overall European integration does not go against the interests of other states, including the interests of Russia.[226]

This statement immediately set off a flurry of reactions from both sides. Both presidents emerged from their all-night meeting for an early morning news conference at which El'tsin echoed the NATO clause and agreed, saying that "the leaders of the former USSR used to come here to give instructions. Times have changed. Now there are two sovereign states and one must respect their stands and the present talks consisted of a lively discussion, a conversation between two people who know life well." Walesa responded that "Russia has a great politician, decisive and cast in a mold worthy of the greatness of that country. He is very fond of arguments, but he also accepts them."[227] After he emerged later that day from his counterpart talks, Skubiszewski discussed Poland's determination to join NATO and declared that "it is a very essential step not only in the interests of Poland's security, but European security as well." He then stressed that "NATO must open itself to new members. . . . I appeal to NATO to do this quickly because it has been slow in its transformation; transformation means just that: accepting new members."[228]

Interestingly, about the same time as Skubiszewski made his statement on NATO, conflicting signals emerged from El'tsin's entourage. El'tsin's press secretary explained that "Russia regards Poland's desire to integrate into European institutions with respect, including into the military bloc NATO." Additionally, he believed that "Democratic Russia itself is participating in integration processes." To begin a strategy of backtracking from their president's commitment, however, the press secretary stressed that "assessing the evolution of European processes, one should realize that NATO is part of the bloc system of the past. Investing into the past is less expedient than investing into the future." To place the joint declaration into a larger Russian perspective, the press secretary concluded that "Russia takes into account Poland's desire to integrate into NATO, but Russia will assess this process exclusively from the interests of cooperation between the two countries, undoubtedly taking into account its own strategic interests."[229] Therefore, the Poles obtained an important objective with the NATO clause in the joint declaration, but other events in Russia quickly overtook the Russian commitments to the Poles.

After the summit, the uproar over El'tsin's concession to Walesa on NATO membership intensified, with a number of Russian statements and interviews in which El'tsin's senior advisors and cabinet members rejected the clause in the Joint Polish–Russian Declaration. Representative of these was a statement by the Russian ambassador to Poland justifying his president's actions as "oversimplified and misunderstood" by the media. Furthermore, the ambassador reiterated that, though Poland remained sovereign, Russia was concerned about Poland's determination to join NATO so quickly. He argued that "if the West finds that this process can be sped up, it is up to Poland and NATO, but I don't expect it will happen very soon."[230] Not only did the "El'tsin Letter" that September to Bonn, Paris, London, and Washington convince the West to postpone any invitations for NATO membership, but the El'tsin stalemate with the Russian parliament also erupted in violent confrontation that October. These events caused consternation in Western capitals such that the West hesitated to upset El'tsin's precarious leadership.[231] The backlash of another mutinous environment in Moscow also overshadowed El'tsin's flexibility toward Walesa, particularly in the aftermath of the Russian parliamentary elections and the rise of anti-El'tsin Communists and nationalists.[232] By fall 1993 the Polish elections also ushered in the end of the post-Communist *Solidarnosc*-led governments in Poland.

Before the end of the Skubiszewski era in Polish Eastern policy, however, the important Polish–Lithuanian relationship expanded, even though both sides failed to agree to the final interstate treaty during Skubiszewski's reign. One of the challenges for the Polish leadership resulted from the string of Lithuanian prime ministers they encountered in late 1992 and 1993. Though each Lithuanian counterpart appeared ready to conclude the final details of the interstate treaty, the Polish side had to wait for the Lithuanians to regroup and determine Vilnius's priorities with each new government. When the new Lithuanian prime minister, Aleksandras Abisala, visited Warsaw in September 1992, the Polish leadership believed both sides took a major step toward the formal treaty, this time by agreeing on investment, border service protection of trade, and interior ministry collaboration on combating crime. In his talks, Skubiszewski focused on cross-border traffic, security issues in the Baltic region, and protecting the cultural heritage in each state. The Polish foreign minister also stated that "Poland wished to enable Lithuania to find a place for herself in the international arena," and emphasized that "Poland needed a strong Lithuania, since this would be an important element in our security."[233]

By early 1993, Lithuania's new prime minister, Bronislovas Lubys, met with Suchocka in the Polish northeastern town of Suwalki to try to forge final treaty provisions and promote a free trade zone. In their joint communiqué, both states reiterated their desire to uphold Polish minority rights in Lithuania and Lithuanian minority rights in Poland, while also declaring that a joint economic commission would focus on establishing a free trade zone. The prime ministers stated they now wanted to start formal treaty drafting sessions and expected Suchocka to visit Vilnius by the summer.[234] After Skubiszewski conferred with his new counterpart, Povilos Gylys, in Warsaw that February, both prepared for Suchocka's trip to Vilnius.[235]

As it turned out, Suchocka met with her third Lithuanian prime minister within nine months, Adolfas Slezevicius, in late July. The prime ministerial meeting achieved the long overdue compromise both sides had struggled to find over the interpretation of Poland's hostile annexation of Vilnius in 1920. In her statement on Polish radio, Suchocka assessed the situation optimistically, proclaiming both sides stood on the verge of an interstate treaty by early September 1993. She underscored that "we have agreed with the prime minister that historical issues—issues which are our heaviest burden—should not present an obstacle for the development of our mutual relations, and we have agreed that these issues should be subject of a separate declaration, rather than being included in the Polish–Lithuanian Treaty."[236]

This statement helped both sides to refine the treaty drafting terms that summer. Some of Skubiszewski's most capable negotiators, the original old-hand activists whom he, Makarczyk, and Kostrzewa-Zorbas had hired, such as Byczewski, Ananicz, and Czaputowicz, played key roles in negotiating final treaty details. Yet, stumbling blocks continued and both sides failed to reach agreement on either the treaty or historic declaration before Moscow's October violence sidetracked their efforts.[237] Soon after the Russian parliamentary confrontation, the Suchocka government fell and parliamentary elections resulted in the first reformed Communist coalition government, led by a Peasant Party premier. Consequently, the end of the four post-Communist governments in which Skubiszewski served also delayed a Polish–Lithuanian treaty until 1994.

New Roles in Post–Cold War Central Europe:
Bridging Amid Anarchy

Foreign Minister Skubiszewski maneuvered between a powerful, domineering post-Communist president and several post-Communist premiers, each of whom held differing views on Eastern policy. Through these tumultuous domestic and international periods, Skubiszewski managed to maintain his overall bridging approach to the Soviet and post-Soviet leaderships, even if at times Polish relations with those leaders remained uncertain. What Skubiszewski and his dynamic *Solidarnosc* team tried to achieve with Poland's Eastern neighbors represented a step-by-step promotion for long-term linkages to bridge multiple relationships. This two-track Eastern approach geared Poland early on to look beyond the anticipated downfall of the USSR, well before many countries regionally detected such Soviet trends. This extended Eastern policy upheld Warsaw's priorities to conduct sovereign foreign policy by shedding the Communist-era "satellite" onus and reintegrating freely into Europe. Further, Skubiszewski wanted to craft relations to maximize Poland's security without threatening Poland's neighbors. By proving Poland's positive intentions, Skubiszewski continually renounced irredentism over the historic Polish eastern borderlands in order to convince NATO and EC member states of Poland's security-enhancing role in Central-East Europe.

Skubiszewski also desired to develop partnerships as a regional facilitator—as a middle power in a specialized role uniquely suited—by bridging with the post–Soviet successor states as early as he believed possible. Because Poland faced great powers without options to change a strategic landscape that Germany and emerging post-Soviet Russia primarily determined, Poland chose not to disrupt, but to seek "other-help" by reaching out to neighbors. This bridging strategy focused especially on middle power Ukraine in order to overcome historic pitfalls and to solidify relationships as two middle powers between their great and uncertain neighboring powers, Germany and Russia. For Skubiszewski the well-being and security of Ukraine enhanced Poland's security and he tried to aid Ukrainian independence to a great extent. This strategy aimed to convince Russia to move away from neoimperial tendencies and westward toward integrationist strategies. He thought this strategy strengthened the international view of Poland as a bridge-building role model to Europe for these newly democratizing states, one that great powers could ignore but at the risk of creating more upheaval in European security. Yet, if great powers simply discounted such middle power stability-enhancing steps, regional stability might worsen. Consequently, Skubiszewski argued that to sustain his state's pluralistic and peaceful values, Poland's Eastern policy should project nonthreatening and cooperative policies toward traditional adversaries, a strategy consistent with a "security-maximizing" state, but one intended to facilitate other-help world. This post-Communist foreign policy stood in marked contrast to that of the 1930s, when Poland had tried aggressively to balance Germany against the USSR, only to have Hitler and Stalin dismember Poland when no allies existed to prevent the inevitable invasions.[238]

To a certain degree a counterargument against bridging asserts that Poland balanced or bandwagoned against Russia, given the residual power Moscow authorities maintained, even after the USSR's collapse. This might explain Polish president Walesa's reluctance to pressure Moscow on force withdrawals or side with the new Russian leader Boris El'tsin in the early stages during and after the failed August 1991 Soviet coup. Furthermore, the argument that Poland bandwagoned with either Germany or Ukraine against Moscow, seeing Russia as threatening to Poland's democratization and stability, merits more analysis. The next chapter explores whether these rationales stemmed from Poland's Western security efforts to join NATO as a counterweight to Russia or Warsaw's strategy to maintain American troops as a trip wire against Russian neo-imperialism. Suffice it to say that Poland's Eastern policy demonstrated a new kind of alignment that carefully implemented step-by-step linkages bilaterally to solidify stability and security, not only for Poland's democratization, but also for the democratizing reformers emerging in Poland's great, middle, and smaller power neighbors. To the extent possible, Poland's foreign policy management of its own anarchical survival amid the extraordinary changes consuming the Central-East European region before, during, and after the USSR's demise, testifies to how it delicately strove to broaden links to each of its eastern neighbors.

Post–Cold War Europe portended many uncertainties in the early 1990s and post-Communist Poland made its way steadily and cautiously toward its eastern neighbors. In his determination to achieve key political objectives peacefully, Skubiszewski gained the acceptance of Poland, first by Soviet Moscow and then by post–Soviet Russia, as an independent actor in Central European security. The foreign minister attained this objective because he consistently tried to work with the changing Muscovite leaderships by forging political, economic, and security agreements that benefited both sides. To actualize such objectives, he constantly adhered to his initial arguments from September 1989 that interstate relationships necessitated incorporating international law and European standards of behavior, the tenets he advocated as fundamental to his two-track Eastern policy. If he needed to compromise in treaty negotiations by appeasing Soviet military obstinacy on troop withdrawals or delaying agreements with Lithuania over Polish minority disputes, Skubiszewski still obtained new state treaties with all of Poland's neighbors, except Lithuania. His persistence and patience toward Lithuania reaped the benefit of a state treaty shortly after he left office. Such achievements overcame the historical perception by Poland's eastern neighbors of an imperial Poland that appeared bent on recapturing the *Kresy*.

Though some conservative political voices in Poland criticized Skubiszewski for compromising too often, particularly on the protracted troop withdrawal negotiations, Skubiszewski contended that Poland required a larger vision for Eastern policy. He also understood that he remained beholden to Walesa and the president's advisors. He implemented the president's decisions as a loyal minister. Some found this service subservient and even categorized

Polish Eastern policy as "Finlandized," or neutralist and trying to hide from important decisions toward Moscow. Such criticism of Skubiszewski's strategy, among other issues, provoked a government crisis under Premier Olszewski. Yet, Skubiszewski's Eastern policy, founded upon methodical, sometimes slow progress in building interstate ties, left an important legacy as subsequent foreign ministers achieved stronger links to Russia, Ukraine, Lithuania, and Belarus. Even if some of the post-Soviet leaderships became more hostile toward the West and, by extension, Poland, Skubiszewski's successors utilized his Eastern agreements and treaties as their foundation to proceed. Skubiszewski's Eastern policy provided the baseline for Poland's post–Cold War Eastern policies well after he departed the diplomatic stage.

Notes

1. Katarzyna Nazarewicz, "Interview with Foreign Minister Krzysztof Skubiszewski: Politics Does Not Have to Clash with Morality," *Zycie Warszawy*, 15 June 1993, *FBIS-EEU*, 30 June 1993, 25.

2. Sejmowe Expose Ministra Spraw Zagranicznych RP Krzysztofa Skubiszewskiego [Sejm Exposé by Minister of Foreign Affairs of the Republic of Poland, Krzysztof Skubiszewski] (Warsaw, 26 April 1990), *Zbior Dokumentow*, no. 2 (1991): 8–29. For insightful analyses of the connection between nationalism and foreign policy, see Ilya Prizel, *National Identity and Foreign Policy: Nationalism and Leadership in Poland, Russia, and Ukraine* (Cambridge: Cambridge University Press, 1998); and Jack Snyder, *From Voting to Violence: Democratization and Nationalist Conflict* (New York: Norton, 2000), 72, 252–253, 259, 309.

3. Kostrzewa-Zorbas founded and edited the journal *Nowa Koalicja*, and Ananicz founded *Oboz*. These journals focused on liberating Central, Eastern, and Southeastern Europe from Communist oppression and raised sensitive issues in the Soviet Bloc, the USSR, and, to an extent, the West. Such issues centered on religion, economics, nationalities and émigré groups, and political history.

4. Background on *Nowa Koalicja* and *Oboz* come from interviews I conducted with Kostrzewa-Zorbas in Warsaw on 30 August 1990, shortly after he became the deputy director of the *MSZ*'s European Department and chief of its Soviet Affairs Section, and with Ananicz in Warsaw on 9 June 1991, when he worked as deputy chief of the *MSZ* Soviet Affairs Section, and on 10 June 1994, when he worked as the under secretary of state in the president's chancellery.

5. Interview I conducted with Konstanty Gebert, deputy editor-in-chief of *Gazeta wyborcza*, in Warsaw on 6 June 1994. Andrei Sakharov, one of the foremost among both Soviet nuclear physicists, and, later, Soviet dissidents and human rights advocates, symbolized for many in *Solidarnosc* how Russians needed to change their imperialist mentality.

6. Krzysztof Skubiszewski, "Problemy polskiej emigracji" [Problems of Polish Emigration], *Rada Naradowa*, 2 July 1988, 4–5.

7. Krzysztof Gorski, "Dwutorowosc Polskiej Polityki Wschodniej w latach 1989–1991" [Polish Two-Track Eastern Policy from 1989–1991] (Master's Thesis, Uniwersytet Warszawski, 1992), 35–36.

8. "Sejm Committees Interview Ministers," PAP, 1804 GMT, 8 September 1989, in *FBIS-EEU*, 11 September 1989, 36.

9. Chapter 1 analyzed the limits of the Roundtable Agreement.

10. Note that fifty-five-year-old Kulski started at the *MSZ* in 1967 and held positions as first and second secretary at the Polish Military Mission in West Berlin and then as counselor with plenipotentiary ministerial rank in Austria and the FRG. Before his appointment as vice minister, he had held the post of *MSZ* under secretary of state since 1988. See "Chronicle of Cadre Changes," *Trybuna Ludu*, 14 September 1989, *FBIS-EEU*, 20 September 1989, 39. Kostrzewa-Zorbas published a critical assessment of Kulski after both left government service, stating that Kulski "was supposed to guarantee the continuity of our politics toward the Soviet Union and the Warsaw Pact" on behalf of the Communists who still controlled the defense and interior ministries. See Grzegorz Kostrzewa-Zorbas, "Imperium kontratakuje" [The Empire Strikes Back] in *Lewy Czerwcowy* [Blow from the Left], ed. Jacek Kurski and Piotr Semka (Warsaw: Editions Spotkania, 1992), 149.

11. "Przemowienie ministra spraw zagranicznych prof. Krzysztofa Skubiszewskiego na XLIV sesji Zgromadzenie Ogolnego NZ" [Statement by the Polish Minister of Foreign Affairs, Professor Krzysztof Skubiszewski at the 44th Session of the UN General Assembly] (New York, 25 September 1989), *Zbior Dokumentow*, no. 3 (1990): 151.

12. Louisa Vinton, "Domestic Politics and Foreign Policy, 1989–1993," in *Polish Foreign Policy Reconsidered: Challenges of Independence*, eds. Ilya Prizel and Andrew A. Michta (London: Macmillan, 1995), 30–31; and Ronald D. Asmus and Thomas S. Szayna, with Barbara Kliszewski, *Polish National Security Thinking in a Changing Europe* (Santa Monica, Calif.: RAND, 1991), 18.

13. "Foreign Affairs Minister's UN Talks Continue: Meets Shevardnadze in New York," Warsaw Domestic Service, 0800 GMT, 1 October 1989, *FBIS-EEU*, 2 October 1989, 48.

14. Roman Prister, "Exclusive Interview with Polish Foreign Minister Professor Krzysztof Skubiszewski: Without a Trace of Dependence," *Ha'aretz* (Tel Aviv), 19 October 1989, *FBIS-EEU*, 26 October 1989, 57; and Thomas Szayna, *Polish Foreign Policy under a Non-Communist Government: Prospects and Problems* (Santa Monica, Calif.: RAND, 1990), 23.

15. "Meeting with Leaders Held," Warsaw Television Service, 1830 GMT, 24 October 1989, *FBIS-EEU*, 25 October 1989, 62; "[Shevardnadze] Interviewed by Warsaw TV," Warsaw Television Service, 1900 GMT, 25 October 1989, *FBIS-EEU*, 26 October 1989, 53–54.

16. "Wspolny komunikat o wizycie czlonka Biura Politycznego KC KPZR, ministra spraw zagranicznych ZSRR, Eduarda Szewardnadze w Polsce" [Joint Communiqué on the Visit of a Member of the Political Bureau of the CPSU CC, Minister for Foreign Affairs of the USSR, Eduard Shevardnadze in Poland] (25 October 1989), *Zbior Dokumentow*, no. 4 (1990): 36.

17. Adam Michnik, "Poland-USSR: Two Different Countries," *Gazeta Wyborcza*, 25 October 1989, *FBIS-EEU*, 30 October 1989, 46.

18. For the Polish letter, see "To Our Friends the Lithuanians," *Gazeta Wyborcza*, 16 November 1989, *FBIS-EEU*, 22 November 1989, 50. Among the prominent Poles who signed this letter were Bronislaw Geremek, Marek Karp, Adam Michnik, Jerzy Marek Nowakowski, and Henryk Wujec. For the Lithuanian response, see "To Our Friends the Poles," *Gazeta Wyborcza*, 16 November 1989, *FBIS-EEU*, 1 December 1989, 88. Among

the prominent Lithuanians who signed this letter were Virgilijus Cepaitis, Bronius Kuzmickas, and Vytautas Landsbergis.

19. See, among others, Grzegorz Kostrzewa-Zorbas, "Stosunki Polsko–Litewskie: Uwagi i Propozycje" [Polish–Lithuanian Relations: Observations and Propositions], Internal Memorandum to the Polish Senate Commission on Foreign Affairs and the Citizen's Parliamentary Club, 23 October 1989; Stephen R. Burant, "Polish-Lithuanian Relations: Past, Present, and Future," *Problems of Communism*, vol. 40 (May–June 1991), 67–84; Stephen R. Burant, "International Relations in a Regional Context: Poland and Its Eastern Neighbors—Lithuania, Belarus, Ukraine," *Europe-Asia Studies*, vol. 45, no. 3 (1993): 399–405; and Prizel, *National Identity and Foreign Policy*, 149–150.

20. Wojciech Zielinski, "Foreign Policy without Ideology: Interview with Krzysztof Skubiszewski, Polish Minister of Foreign Affairs," *Rzeczpospolita*, 16 November 1989, *FBIS-EEU*, 24 November 1989, 60–62.

21. "TASS Interviews Mazowiecki," PAP, 0204 GMT, 23 November 1989, *FBIS-EEU*, 24 November 1989, 54; and Malgorzata Trye-Ostrowska and Stanislaw Filipczak, "Government Spokeswoman's Remarks," PAP, 1737 GMT, 22 November 1989, *FBIS-EEU*, 24 November 1989, 52.

22. "Skubiszewski Discusses Poles in USSR," PAP, 1819 GMT, 24 November 1989, *FBIS-EEU*, 1 December 1989, 87.

23. "Mazowiecki News Conference," Warsaw Domestic Service, 1414 GMT, 25 November 1989, *FBIS-EEU*, 27 November 1989, 80. See also Aleksander Hall, *Zanim bedzie za pozno: przed wyborami prezydenckimi* [Before It's too Late: Before the Presidential Elections], (Gdansk, Poland: Info-Trade, 1994).

24. "Komunikat Polsko-Radziecki o wizycie Premiera PRL, Tadeusza Mazowieckiego w ZSRR" [Polish-Soviet Communiqué on the Visit of the Polish Prime Minister Tadeusz Mazowiecki in the USSR] (Moscow, 27 November 1989), *Zbior Dokumentow*, no. 4 (1990): 44.

25. "Mazowiecki News Conference," 78; and Gorski, *Dwutorowosc Polskiej Polityki Wschodniej*, 61–62.

26. "Speech by Premier Tadeusz Mazowiecki at a Meeting with Representatives of the Polish Community in the USSR Held at the Polish Embassy in Moscow on 25 November," *Rzeczpospolita*, 27 November 1989, *FBIS-EEU*, 30 November 1989, 75.

27. "Mazowiecki Addresses Leningrad Intelligentsia," PAP, 2024 GMT, 27 November 1989, *FBIS-EEU*, 30 November 1989, 76.

28. "Sakharov Says Poland Ahead of USSR's Changes," PAP, 1853 GMT, 20 November 1989, *FBIS-EEU*, 30 November 1989, 77.

29. Dariusz Fikus, "Without Embellishments," *Rzeczpospolita*, 29 November 1989, *FBIS-EEU*, 5 December 1989, 62; and Jacek Moskwa, *"Raison d'état* and the Lessons of the Past," *Rzeczpospolita*, 24 November 1989, *FBIS-EEU*, 28 November 1989, 76.

30. Background given to me by Kostrzewa-Zorbas in a Warsaw interview on 30 August 1990.

31. Kostrzewa-Zorbas, "Stosunki Polsko-Liteweskie," 23 October 1989, 1–11.

32. Note the historic tensions between Poland and Lithuania, particularly during the interwar era when Poland took territory in and around Vilnius, only for Lithuania to regain it when the USSR invaded Poland. See Burant, "Polish-Lithuanian Relations," 67–84; Burant, "International Relations in a Regional Context," 399–405; and Stephen R. Burant and Voytek Zubek, "Eastern Europe's Old Memories and New Realities," *East European Politics and Societies*, vol. 7, no. 2 (spring 1993): 370–393.

33. Chapter 2 underlined why Skubiszewski ultimately chose not to antagonize Moscow, given Poland's nascent post-Communist democratization, and tried to balance Moscow against Bonn unsuccessfully in February 1990. This section focuses on Skubiszewski's Eastern policy calculations during late 1989 and throughout 1990, including development of the two-track policy.

34. Hansjakob Stehle, "Western Border a Sore Point—Foreign Minister Krzysztof Skubiszewski Does Not Understand Bonn's Hesitation," *Die Zeit*, 22 December 1989, *JPRS*, 7 February 1990, 26.

35. Jaroslaw Kurski, *Lech Walesa: Democrat or Dictator* (Boulder, Colo.: Westview, 1993), 86–87; Kostrzewa-Zorbas, "Imperium kontratakuje," 157, 164; and *Czas na Zmiany: Z Jaroslawem Kaczynskim, rozmawiaja Michal Bichniewicz i Piotr M. Rudnicki* [Time for change: Talking with Jaroslaw Kaczynski, Michal Bichniewicz and Piotr Rudnicki] (Warsaw: Editions Spotkania, 1993), 62.

36. Kurski, *Lech Walesa*, 86; "Walesa Demands Soviet Troop Withdrawal," PAP, 2135 GMT, 18 January, 1989, *FBIS-EEU*, 19 January 1990, 60.

37. Kurski, *Lech Walesa*, 86; Kostrzewa-Zorbas, "Imperium kontratakuje," 164, and Tat'iana Zychlinska, "Anti-Soviet Demonstration Held in Legnica," Warsaw Domestic Service, 2200 GMT, 12 January 1990, *FBIS-EEU*, 16 January 1990, 79.

38. Leszek Kubiak and Jan Rozdzynski, "Government Spokeswoman on Soviet Troops, Reform," PAP, 1925 GMT, 19 January 1990, *FBIS-EEU*, 23 January 1990, 45; and Kostrzewa-Zorbas, "Imperium kontratakuje," 157.

39. Kurski, *Lech Walesa*, 87.

40. Berndt Conrad, "Poland and Germany Must Develop a Community of Interests: Interview with Foreign Minister Krzysztof Skubiszewski," *Die Welt*, 8 February 1990, *FBIS-EEU*, 8 February 1990, 52.

41. Eugeniusz Guz, "[Skubiszewski] Meets Kohl; Communiqué Issued," PAP, 2316 GMT, 7 February 1990, *FBIS-EEU*, 8 February 1990, 51.

42. "Demonstrators Demand Soviet Withdrawal," Warsaw Domestic Service, 1800 GMT, 7 February 1990, *FBIS-EEU*, 8 February 1990, 50; "Meeting Discusses Soviet Troops, Krakow Rallies," Warsaw Domestic Service, 2100 GMT, 12 February 1990, *FBIS-EEU*, 13 February 1990, 50; "Jaruzelski Supports Soviet Troop Withdrawal," Warsaw Domestic Service, 0600 GMT, 13 February 1990, *FBIS-EEU*, 13 February 1990, 50; and "Walesa Views Soviet Troop Pullout, Other Issues," PAP, 2200 GMT, 8 February 1990, *FBIS-EEU*, 9 February 190, 63.

43. "Presence of Soviet Troops May be 'Trump Card,'" *Gazeta Wyborcza*, as reprinted by PAP, 1205 GMT, 14 February 1990, *FBIS-EEU*, 15 February 1990, 45.

44. Randall L. Schweller, *Deadly Imbalances: Tripolarity and Hitler's Strategy of World Conquest* (New York: Columbia University Press, 1998), 65–71, 191–192; Richard Weitz, "Pursuing Military Security in Eastern Europe," in *After the Cold War: International Institutions and State Strategies in Europe, 1989–1991*, ed. Robert O. Keohane, Joseph S. Nye, and Stanley Hoffmann (Cambridge, Mass.: Harvard University Press, 1993), 355–359; and Joseph Grieco, "The Relative-Gains Problem for International Cooperation," *American Political Science Review*, vol. 87, no. 3 (September 1993): 742.

45. Grzegorz Kostrzewa-Zorbas, "The Russian Troop Withdrawal from Poland," in *The Diplomatic Record, 1992-1993*, ed. Allan E. Goodman (Boulder, Colo.: Westview, 1995), 130; Asmus and Szayna, *Polish National Security Thinking*, 18–21; Vinton, "Domestic Politics and Foreign Policy" 38–39; Najder, *Jaka Polska*, 151–153; and Ilya Prizel, "Warsaw's Ostpolitik: A New Encounter with Positivism," in *Polish Foreign*

Policy Reconsidered: Challenges of Independence, eds. Ilya Prizel and Andrew A. Michta (London: Macmillan, 1995), 110.

46. "Skubiszewski Addresses 'Open Skies' Forum," PAP, 2044 GMT, 12 February 1990, *FBIS-EEU*, 14 February 1990, 50; Janusz Reiter, "Po co te wojska," [Why Those Troops], *Gazeta Wyborcza*, 14 February 1990, 1; "Mazowiecki: bez dwuznacznosci w sprawie granic," [Mazowiecki: Unequivocal on the Border Issue], *Gazeta Wyborcza*, 22 February 1990, 1; and Vinton, "Domestic Politics and Foreign Policy," 40.

47. Interviews I conducted with Artur Hajnicz and parliamentarian Janusz Onyszkiewicz, former minister of defense, in Warsaw on 10 June 1994, corroborated Skubiszewski's pragmatic and complex strategy, involving not playing East against West. Chapter 5 analyzes Warsaw's strategy to dismantle the Warsaw Pact.

48. Paul Schroeder, "Historical Reality vs. Neo-realist Theory," *International Security*, vol. 19, no. 1 (summer 1994): 108–148.

49. "Party Posts Cease in Diplomatic Service," PAP, 2144 GMT, 11 January 1990, *FBIS-EEU*, 12 January 1990, 46; and "Skubiszewski Proposes Recalling Ambassadors, Others," PAP, 1542 GMT, 13 February 1990, *FBIS-EEU*, 14 February 1990, 51.

50. Barbara W. Olszewska, "Personnel Section: Movement in the Embassies," *Polityka*, no. 5, 3 February 1990, *JPRS-EER*, 27 March 1990, 15.

51. Olszewska, "Personnel Section: Movement in the Embassies," 14.

52. Grzegorz Kostrzewa-Zorbas, "Tezy do Polskiej Polityki Wschodniej u Progu Lat Dziewiecdziesiaytch" [Proposals for Polish Eastern Policy at the Threshold of the 1990s], private memorandum to senior polish officials, Warsaw, 22 March 1990.

53. Background provided to me by Kostrzewa-Zorbas in interview on 30 August 1990 in Warsaw.

54. Kostrzewa-Zorbas, "Tezy do Polskiej Polityki Wschodniej," 1–5.

55. "Skubiszewski Desires 'Good Relations,'" Warsaw Television Service, 13 March 1990, *FBIS-EEU*, 13 March 1990, 44. Burant and Zubek analyze in great depth the importance of the historic Polish–Lithuanian linkages, particularly during the period of the Kingdom of Poland and Grand Duchy of Lithuania. See Burant, "Polish-Lithuanian Relations," 68–69; and Burant and Zubek, "Eastern Europe's Old Memories and New Realities," 370–393. See also "Oswiadczenie Ministra Spraw Zagranicznych RP Krzysztofa Skubiszewskiego dotyczace stanowiska rzadu RP w sprawie Litwy" [Statement by the Polish Foreign Minister, Krzysztof Skubiszewski, Concerning the Position of the Polish Government on Lithuania] (Warsaw, 16 April 1990), *Zbior Dokumentow*, no. 2 (1991): 7.

56. See, inter alia, "Sejm Resolution on Lithuania," PAP, 22 March 1990, *FBIS-EEU*, 23 March 1990, 65; "Lithuanian delegation Arrives in Warsaw," PAP, 23 March 1990, *FBIS-EEU*, 26 March 1990, 39; "Mazowiecki Agrees to Mediate for Lithuania," Vilnius Domestic Service, 28 March 1990, *FBIS-SOV*, 28 March 1990, 78; "Lithuania to Import Goods from Poland," Vilnius International Service, 30 May 1990, *FBIS-EEU*, 31 May 1990, 71. See also Burant, "Polish-Lithuanian Relations," 71–74; Burant and Zubek, "Eastern Europe's Old Memories and New Realities," 379–380; Burant, "International Relations in a Regional Context," 400; and Prizel, *National Identity and Foreign Policy*, 149–150.

57. "Sejmowe expose Ministra Spraw Zagranicznych RP Krzysztofa Skubiszewskiego" [Sejm Expose by Minister of Foreign Affairs of the Republic of Poland, Krzysztof Skubiszewski] (Warsaw, 26 April 1990), *Zbior Dokumentow*, no. 2 (1991): 17.

58. "Skubiszewski Explains Lithuania Policy," PAP, 0754 GMT, 10 May 1990, *FBIS-EEU*, 10 May 1990, 44; Maria Skolarczyk, "Lack of a Security System: Interview with Foreign Minister Krzysztof Skubiszewski," *Rzeczpospolita*, 15 May 1990, *FBIS-EEU*, 22 May 1990, 33; and "Skubiszewski Meets Lithuania's Saudargas," PAP, 2230 GMT, 20 May 1990, *FBIS-EEU*, 22 May 1990, 35. See also "Ukrainian People's Movement Seeks Alliance," PAP, 1048 GMT, 16 May 1990, *FBIS-EEU*, 18 May 1990, 41; and Leon Bojko, "The First Act of a Sovereign Russia," *Gazeta Wyborcza*, 30 May 1990, *FBIS-EEU*, 4 June 1990, 49.

59. Michal Winiarski, "'Sweden Is Not Doing Enough for Poland: Interview with Solidarity Chairman Lech Walesa in Gdansk,'" *Dagens Nyheter* (Stockholm), 21 May 1990, *FBIS-EEU*, 25 May 1990 39.

60. "Skubiszewski: Pact in 'Crisis,'" Warsaw Television Service, 1730 GMT, 7 June 1990, *FBIS-EEU*, 8 June 1990, 37; and "Skubiszewski on Gorbachev Address," PAP, 1816 GMT, 7 June 1990, *FBIS-EEU*, 8 June 1990, 37.

61. Stanislaw Turnau, "A Revolution without Bitterness," *Gazeta Wyborcza*, 9–10 June 1990, *FBIS-EEU*, 19 June 1990, 45–46.

62. Kostrzewa-Zorbas described this strategy to me during an interview in Warsaw on 30 August 1990.

63. Kostrzewa-Zorbas, "Imperium kontratakuje," 150.

64. Grzegorz Kostrzewa-Zorbas, "W Gmachu" [In the Big Building], *MSZ memorandum*, Warsaw, 8 August 1990.

65. Kostrzewa-Zorbas, "The Russian Troop Withdrawal from Poland," 119.

66. I met these new Polish Eastern policymakers during my trip to Warsaw from 10–12 June 1991 and also hosted several of them in Washington in 1990–1992 during their various official trips or short-term education abroad.

67. At the time, I served as Fort Leavenworth, Kansas, U.S. Army Liaison and visiting fellow to the National Defense University in Washington. I worked with Russian national security officials, starting in early 1990, when few American or Western European officials even knew who comprised the Russian Interregional Deputies Group. I also coordinated certain European security issues with *MSZ* Soviet Affairs Section and European Directorate teams, and passed Polish insights on the emerging Russian leadership to senior U.S. government officials, some of whom followed up and some of whom ignored them.

68. Michal Ksiezarczyk, "Otwartosc wobec wschodu" [Openness Toward the East], *Zycie Warszawy*, 18–19 August 1990, 1, 4. For important background on the Russian Interregional Deputies Group, see *Informatsionnyi Biulleten': Izdanie Mezhregional'noi gruppyi narodnyikh deputatov SSSR* [Information Bulletin: Publication of the Inter-Regional Deputies Group of the USSR], ed. I. Kamanina (Moscow: V. Logunov, 13 September 1990).

69. "Excerpt of Interview with Foreign Affairs Minister Krzysztof Skubiszewski on the 51st Anniversary of the Outbreak of the Second World War," Warsaw Domestic Service, 2100 GMT, 1 September 1990, *FBIS-EEU*, 4 September 1990, 30.

70. "Senate Committee Discusses Eastern Policy," PAP, 1727 GMT, 5 September 1990, 7 September 1990, 43; "Uchwala Senatu Rzeczypospolitej Polskiej w sprawie polityki wschodniej Rzeczypospolitej Polskiej" [Resolution of the Senate of the Polish Republic on the Eastern Policy of the Polish Republic] (7 September 1990), in *Polska w Europie* (January 1991): 55–56. See also Prizel, "Warsaw's Ostpolitik," 100–101.

71. Krzysztof Skubiszewski, "Polska wobec wschodu—wystapienie ministra spraw zagranicznych RP Krzysztofa Skubiszewskiego w Senacie" [Poland and the East—

Statement by the Polish Foreign Minister Krzysztof Skubiszewski in the Senate] (Warsaw, 7 September 1990), *Zbior Dokumentow*, no. 3 (1990): 15, 19–23; Kostrzewa-Zorbas, "Imperium Kontratakuje," 157; and Gorski, *Dwutorowosc Polskiej Polityki Wschodniej*, 64–89.

72. Kostrzewa-Zorbas, "Imperium Kontratakuje," 157–158. Note that Skubiszewski briefly participated in two multilateral meetings in Moscow during the previous year as foreign minister, both concerning the Warsaw Pact at summits in November 1989 and June 1990.

73. Jerzy Rajch, "The Twilight of the Blocs: Interview with Grzegorz Kostrzewa-Zorbas, Deputy Director of the European Department, Ministry of Foreign Affairs," *Zolnierz Rzeczypospolitej* (Warsaw), 6 September 1990, *JPRS-EER*, 16 October 1990, 8.

74. "Statement by Foreign Minister Krzysztof Skubiszewski before His Flight to the Soviet Union," Warsaw Domestic Service, 1500 GMT, 10 October 1990, *FBIS-EEU*, 11 October 1990, 30. Accompanying Skubiszewski on this first critical bilateral trip to the USSR were Kostrzewa-Zorbas, Czaputowicz, and Kurkiewicz.

75. Jan Rygulowski, "Between Germany and Russia," *Tygodnik Solidarnosc* (Warsaw), 21 September 1990, *FBIS-EEU*, 2 October 1990, 27.

76. "Polish Foreign Minister's Visit Continues: Interview on Relations," TASS (Moscow), 2121 GMT, 10 October 1990, *FBIS-SOV*, 12 October 1990, 25.

77. Michta, *East-Central Europe after the Warsaw Pact*, 73–76.

78. Andrzej Siezieniewski, "Report on a News Conference with President Gorbachev, Prior to His Meeting with Visiting Polish Foreign Minister Krzysztof Skubiszewski," Warsaw Domestic Service, 1011 GMT, 12 October 1990, *FBIS-SOV*, 12 October 1990, 27.

79. See, among others, "Oswiadczenie TASS w sprawie zbrodni dokonanej na polskich oficerach w Katyniu" [TASS Statement Concerning the Crime Perpetrated on Polish Officers in Katyn] (Moscow, 13 April 1990), *Zbior Dokumentow*, no. 2 (1991): 48–49; "Oswiadczenie rzecznika rzadu RP w zwiazku z Oswiadczeniem TASS w sprawie zbrodni katynskiej," [Statement by the Polish Government Spokesman in Connection with the TASS Statement Concerning the Katyn Crime] (Moscow, 16 April 1990), *Zbior Dokumentow*, no. 2 (1991): 50–51; and Thomas S. Szayna, "Addressing 'Blank Spots' in Polish-Soviet Relations," *Problems of Communism*, vol. 37, no. 6 (November–December 1988), 37–61.

80. "Mutual Concerns Reaffirmed," Warsaw Television Service, 2155 GMT, 11 October 1990, *FBIS-SOV*, 12 October 1990, 27; "Skubiszewski, Shevardnadze Hold Talks," PAP, 2225 GMT, 11 October 1990, *FBIS-EEU*, 12 October 1990, 26; "Poland's Skubiszewski Continues Soviet Visit; Received by Gorbachev 12 October," Moscow Domestic Service, 1600 GMT, 12 October 1990, *FBIS-SOV*, 15 October 1990, 18.

81. "Joint Communiqué Concludes Skubiszewski Visit," TASS (Moscow), 1920 GMT, 16 October 1990, *FBIS-SOV*, 17 October 1990, 19–20.

82. "[Skubiszewski] Holds News Conference at Embassy," Moscow International Service, 1600 GMT, 13 October 1990, *FBIS-SOV*, 15 October 1990, 19.

83. Rukh, or Ukrainian Popular Front for Perestroika, coalesced thousands of people across Ukraine in the late 1980s and held its first congress from 7–10 September 1989, at which its delegates called for an end to the Communist monopoly on power and for greater freedom and democratization. For background, see M.T., "Kiev—Zero Hour," *Gazeta Wyborcza*, 8–10 September 1989, *FBIS-EEU*, 12 September 1989, 38; S.E., "Shcherbitskii Must Go," *Gazeta Wyborcza*, 11 September 1989, *FBIS-EEU*, 14 September 1989, 45; Jerzy Jachowicz, "Three Days of Freedom," *Gazeta Wyborcza*, 14 Septem-

ber 1989, *FBIS-EEU*, 21 September 1989, 31; Prizel, *National Identity and Foreign Policy*, 359–362; Burant, "International Relations in a Regional Context," 413; and Piotr Chmura, "Ukraina 1988: Poczatek drogi do niepodlegosci?" [Ukraine in 1988: Beginning the Road toward Independence?], *Nowa Koalicja*, no. 7 (1989): 12–18.

84. "Deklaracja o zasadach i podstawowych kierunkach rozwoju stosunkow Polsko-Ukrainskich" [Declaration on the Principles and Directions of Development of Polish-Ukrainian Relations] (Kiev, 13 October 1990), *Zbior Dokumentow*, no. 4 (1991): 25–30; Burant, "International Relations in a Regional Context," 409–411; Michta, *East-Central Europe after the Warsaw Pact*, 78–80; Ian Brzezinski, "Polish-Ukrainian Relations: The Geopolitical Dimension," *The National Interest*, no. 27 (spring 1992), 48–52; and Prizel, *National Identity and Foreign Policy*, 138–139, 360–361.

85. "Ukrainian, Polish Foreign Ministers Sign Protocol," PAP, 1950 GMT, 14 October 1990, *FBIS-SOV*, 15 October 1990, 81.

86. Agnieszka Magdziak-Miszewska, "Understanding Belorussia," *Zycie Warszawy*, 16 October 1990, *FBIS-EEU*, 23 October 1990, 42–43; Andrzej Siezieniewski, "'Impasse' Develops at Polish-Belorussian Talks," Warsaw Domestic Service, 1800 GMT, 15 October 1990, *FBIS-SOV*, 16 October 1990, 72; A. Maysen, "Poland's Skubiszewski Ends Belorussia Visit," Moscow Television Service, 1230 GMT, 16 October 1990, *FBIS-SOV*, 17 October 1990, 68; "Skubiszewski Statement on Belorussian Talks," Warsaw Domestic Service, 1900 GMT, 18 October 1990, *FBIS-EEU*, 19 October 1990, 35; and Burant, "International Relations in a Regional Context," 405–406.

87. Andrzej Siezieniewski, "Poland's Skubiszewski Visits Belorussia," Warsaw Domestic Service, 1500 GMT, 15 October 1990, *FBIS-SOV*, 16 October 1990, 72. Note that Czaputowicz revealed to me in Warsaw during an interview on 8 June 1994 that "we found that the Belorussians failed to conduct negotiations separately from Moscow. This image of the younger Slavic brother, though disputed by Ukrainians, was accepted by Belorussians. The Belorussians had simply failed to create their own identity independent from Moscow. This came through most clearly when the Soviet ambassador to Poland, Kashlev, traveled to Minsk with our delegation and persuaded the Belorussian foreign minister not to sign any kind of declaration with Poland. They really were diplomats from the same country. Though the Belorussian political opposition, led by Poznyak, held some promise, it couldn't mount any serious threat to the Belorussian satellite leadership." See also Maria Wagrowska, "Toward Europe without Being Weighed Down," *Rzeczpospolita*, 16 November 1990, *FBIS-EEU*, 27 November 1990, 46.

88. Leonid Timofeev, "Polish Foreign Minister Confers with Silaev," TASS, 1710 GMT, 12 October 1990, *FBIS-SOV*, 15 October 1990, 74; and "Vizit prodolzhaetsia" ("Visit Continues"), *Sovetskaya Rossiya*, 13 October 1990, 5.

89. "Official Contacts with Russia Restored," PAP, 2225 GMT, 12 October 1990, *FBIS-EEU*, 15. October 1990, 46.

90. Interviews I conducted with Kostrzewa-Zorbas and Kurkiewicz in Warsaw on 10 June 1991 and Czaputowicz in Warsaw on 8 June 1994.

91. "Deklaracja o przyjazni i dobrosasiedzkiej wspolpracy miedzy Rzeczapospolita Polska i Rosyjska Federacyjna Socjalistyczna Republika Radziecka" [Declaration on Friendship, Good-Neighborly Cooperation between the Republic of Poland and the Russian Soviet Federative Socialist Republic] (Moscow, 16 October 1990), *Zbior Dokumentow*, no. 4 (1991): 20–24.

92. Lev Aksenov and Boris Zverev, "Kozyrev Holds First News Conference," TASS, 1537 GMT, 18 October 1990, *FBIS-SOV*, 19 October 1990, 80.

93. Grzegorz Kostrzewa-Zorbas, "Foreign Ministry Official on Polish-Russian Pact," *Zycie Warszawy*, 17 October 1990, *FBIS-EEU*, 24 October 1990, 45–46.

94. Wojciech Gielzynski, "One Can Argue over the Degree of Success," *Tygodnik Solidarnosc*, 23 November 1990, *FBIS-EEU*, 4 December 1990, 26. See also Burant, "Polish-Lithuanian Relations," 74–75; and Kostrzewa-Zorbas, "Imperium kontratakuje," 156–157.

95. "Skubiszewski Receives Lithuania's Landsbergis," PAP, 1752 GMT, 5 December 1990, *FBIS-EEU*, 6 December 1990, 28.

96. "Oswiadczenie Ministra Spraw Zagranicznych RP Krzysztofa Skubiszewskiego w Zwiazku z rezygnacja Eduarda Szewardnadze ze stanowiska Ministra Spraw Zagranicznych ZSRR" [Statement by the Polish Foreign Minister Krzysztof Skubiszewski in Connection with the Resignation of Eduard Shevardnadze from His Post of the Minister for Foreign Affairs of the USSR] (Warsaw, 20 December 1990), *Zbior Dokumentow*, no. 4 (1991): 18–19.

97. Vinton, "Domestic Politics and Foreign Policy," 36–44; Prizel, "Warsaw's Ostpolitik," 98–104; Kostrzewa-Zorbas, "Imperium kontratakuje," 155–164; and Michta, *East-Central Europe after the Warsaw Pact*, 87–90.

98. "Walesa Delivers Inauguration Speech to Assembly," Warsaw Domestic Service, 1105 GMT, 22 December 1990, *FBIS-EEU*, 24 December 1990, 28; Lech Walesa, *The Struggle and the Triumph: An Autobiography* (New York: Arcade, 1991), 306–307; Burant, "Polish-Lithuanian Relations," 75; and Prizel, *National Identity and Foreign Policy*, 128.

99. Stanislav Kondrashov, "Coachman, Do Not Drive the Horses Too Fast," *Izvestiia* (Moscow), 3 January 1991, *FBIS-SOV*, 3 January 1991, 23.

100. Kostrzewa-Zorbas, "Imperium kontratakuje," 165; and Najder, *Jaka Polska*, 172–200.

101. Kostrzewa-Zorbas, "Imperium kontratakuje," 165–166.

102. Kostrzewa-Zorbas, "Imperium kontratakuje," 166; "Demonstration at USSR Embassy," PAP, 1410 GMT, 13 January 1991, *FBIS-EEU*, 14 January 1991, 37; and "Walesa, [Polish] Ambassador to USSR Discuss Lithuania," Warsaw Domestic Service, 1500 GMT, 14 January 1991, *FBIS-EEU*, 15 January 1991, 36.

103. "Lithuanian Deputy Asks Poles for Help," Warsaw TVP Television Network, 1830 GMT, 11 January 1991, *FBIS-EEU*, 14 January 1991, 37 and "Joint Sejm-Senate Statement," Warsaw Domestic Service, 11 January 1991, 1743 GMT, *FBIS-EEU*, 14 January 1991, 34. See Burant's overview of the events during the Soviet intervention, "Polish-Lithuanian Relations," 75–77.

104. "Foreign Ministry Makes Statement," PAP, 1242 GMT, 11 January 1991, *FBIS-EEU*, 14 January 1991, 34.

105. "Soviet Envoy 'Summoned' to Foreign Ministry," PAP, 2041 GMT, 11 January 1991, *FBIS-EEU*, 14 January 1991, 37.

106. "[Lithuanian Foreign Minister] Says Stalinism Still Alive," PAP, 1408 GMT, 13 January 1991, *FBIS-EEU*, 14 January 1991, 38.

107. "Skubiszewski: Lithuanian Aspirations Supported," Warsaw Domestic Service, 1800 GMT, 14 January 1991, *FBIS-EEU*, 15 January 1991, 36. See also "Skubiszewski on Relations with Lithuania," PAP, 1536 GMT, 16 January 1991, *FBIS-EEU*, 17 January 1991, 27.

108. Chapter 5 analyzes the Warsaw and Visegrad strategy toward Moscow to disband the Warsaw Pact and reject pressuring on new bilateral security clauses.

109. As an official in the Pentagon during the Gulf War, I observed daily the serious shift away from the important European security concerns for the United States, particularly toward the USSR's disintegration and Central Europe's struggle with Soviet hardliners, to political–military requirements of the Persian Gulf War.

110. "Problemy polityki zagranicznej u progu roku 1991—Wystapienie ministra spraw zagranicznych RP Krzysztofa Skubiszewskiego w Sejmie" [Foreign Policy Issues at the Start of 1991—Address by the Polish Foreign Minister Krzysztof Skubiszewski in the Sejm] (14 February 1991), *Zbior Dokumentow*, no. 1 (1992): 33. See also Warsaw's "Foreign Policy Outlined Further," PAP, 2045 GMT, 12 March 1991, *FBIS-EEU*, 13 March 1991, 38; Miklos Ritecz, "Wedged between Two Powers: Interview with Foreign Minister Krzysztof Skubiszewski," *Nepszabadsag* (Budapest), 6 June 1991, *FBIS-EEU*, 11 June 1991, 31; Ryszard Malik, "We Are Opening Up to the West, But Not Closing to the East: Interview with Foreign Minister Krzysztof Skubiszewski," *Rzeczpospolita*, 26 March 1991, *FBIS-EEU*, 3 April 1991, 26; and "Problemy polityki zagranicznej u progu roku 1991," *Zbior Dokumentow*, 35, 41.

111. Kostrzewa-Zorbas, "Imperium kontratakuje," 167, 170–171; Michal Bichniewicz and Piotr Rudnicki, *Czas na Zmiany: Z Jaroslawem Kaczynskim rozmawiaja* [Time for Change: Conversations with Jaroslaw Kaczynski] (Warsaw: Editions Spotkania, 1994), 46; and Najder, *Jaka Polska*, 208–212. In an interview with me in Washington, D.C., on 20 March 1991, both vice minister Jerzy Makarczyk and Kostrzewa-Zorbas described the plight of the *MSZ's* Eastern policy and the "air that had been taken out of the ministry's Eastern initiatives" in the early weeks of 1990 by some of the new team in the president's chancellery.

112. Kostrzewa-Zorbas, "The Russian Troop Withdrawal from Poland," 119.

113. Kostrzewa-Zorbas, "The Russian Troop Withdrawal from Poland," 122–123; Kostrzewa-Zorbas, "Imperium kontratakuje," 158–159; and "Nota Rzadu Rzechypospolitej Polskiej do Ministra Spraw Zagranicznych ZSRR Eduarda Szewardnadze dotyczaca rokowan w sprawie wycofania wojsk Radzieckich z Polski" [Note of the Government of the Republic of Poland to the USSR Foreign Minister Eduard Shevardnadze, Concerning Negotiations on the Withdrawal of Soviet Troops from Poland] (7 September 1990), *Zbior Dokumentow*, no. 3 (1991): 31–32. For a good overview of the troop withdrawal saga, see Vinton, "Domestic Politics and Foreign Policy," 36–44; for some historical background, see Janusz B. Grochowski, "Who Is to Defend the Security of the Country? Interview with Janusz Onyszkiewicz, Deputy Minister of Defense," *Zolnierz Rzeczypospolitej*, 9 May 1990, *JPRS-EER*, 8 June 1990, 14.

114. Kostrzewa-Zorbas, "The Russian Troop Withdrawal from Poland," 120. See also "Council of Ministers Informed on Soviet Withdrawal," PAP, 2334 GMT, 9 October 1990, *FBIS-EEU*, 10 October 1990, 30–31. Note, as Vinton describes, Polish general Zdzislaw Ostrowski, the Polish government's plenipotentiary for Soviet forces, criticized Kostrzewa-Zorbas for his brazenness toward Soviet troop withdrawal negotiators, arguing that the rationale for "Polish sovereignty" unnecessarily antagonized the Soviet side. See Vinton, "Domestic Politics and Foreign Policy," 67–68, in which she cites Zdzislaw Ostrowski, *Pozegnanie z Armia* [Farewell from the Army], (Warsaw: Czytelnik, 1992).

115. Kostrzewa-Zorbas, "The Russian Troop Withdrawal from Poland," 136–137. See also Jerzy Domanski, "Partners: Interview with Soviet Ambassador to Poland Iurii Kashlev," *Sztandar Mlodych*, 9–11 November 1990, *FBIS-EEU*, 19 November 1990, 55; "[MSZ] Spokesman Regrets Kashlev's Remarks," Warsaw Television Service, 1830 GMT, 16 November 1990, *FBIS-EEU*, 19 November 1990, 56; and "Ministry Denies Soviet Troop Transit Agreement," PAP, 1927 GMT, 22 November 1990, *FBIS-EEU*, 23

November 1990, 29. Note that the following article depicting Soviet troops in Poland from the December 1956 Polish–Soviet treaty states that "the temporary stationing of Soviet military units in Poland must not undermine the sovereignty of the Polish state and it must not lead to interference in the internal affairs of the Polish People's Republic." See Maria Wagrowska, "Soviet Troops in Poland—Facts and Questions," *Rzeczpospolita*, 8 May 1990, *FBIS-EEU*, 14 May 1990, 43.

116. Jan Parys, "Bitwo o wojsko" [The Battle over the Army], in *Lewy czerwcowy*, eds. Jacek Kurski and Piotr Semka (Warsaw: Editions Spotkania, 1993), 60–62; and Kostrzewa-Zorbas, "Imperium kontratakuje," 170–172.

117. In an interview with me on 10 June 1994 in Warsaw, Janusz Onyszkiewicz elaborated on how the Soviet military employed financial and economic arguments unsubstantiated by facts that the Polish delegation continually needed to discredit. Onyszkiewicz served as one of the first post-Communist civilians in the Polish Ministry of Defense, as vice minister, during much of the troop withdrawal negotiations. He related that "the Soviets often demonstrated they were not serious when, for example, Soviet chief of the general staff Moiseev visited Warsaw and protested that the USSR couldn't readily withdraw its forces from Poland as a result of the housing problem in the Soviet Union. This, we realized, certainly implied political pressure rather than economic constraints. When we stated that soldiers should first leave Poland and their families could follow, to reduce both the numbers of people returning to the USSR and the costs involved, General Moiseev refused to answer. He seemed at a loss for words."

118. Kostrzewa-Zorbas, "The Russian Troop Withdrawal from Poland," 124–127; Kostrzewa-Zorbas, "Imperium kontratakuje," 164–165; Kurski, *Lech Walesa*, 105–111; Walesa, *The Struggle and the Triumph*, 254–255; and Prizel, "Warsaw's Ostpolitik," 101–102. See also "Joint USSR Troop Talks Address Transit Issue," PAP, 2323 GMT, 12 December 1990, *FBIS-EEU*, 14 December 1990, 44; "No USSR Military Traffic Reportedly Authorized," Warsaw Domestic Service, 2200 GMT, 11 January 1991, *FBIS-EEU*, 14 January 1991, 39; V. Mostovoi, "Problems Beset Troop Withdrawals from East Europe," Moscow Central TV First Program Network, 1800 GMT, 15 January 1991, *FBIS-SOV*, 17 January 1991, 16.

119. See "Aid Convoy for USSR Turned Back to Germany," Warsaw TVP Television Network, 1830 GMT, 31 January 1991, *FBIS-EEU*, 1 February 1991, 28; "Ministry Statement on Soviet Convoy Crossing," PAP, 1856 GMT, 2 February 1991, *FBIS-EEU*, 4 February 1991, 34; "Ministry to Expedite Transfer of German Convoy," Warsaw Domestic Service, 1400 GMT, 6 February 1991, *FBIS-EEU*, 7 February 1991, 25; "[MSZ] Spokesman Comments on Convoy," *Polska Zbrojna*, 4 February 1991, *FBIS-EEU*, 7 February 1991, 25; "Who Wants to Misinform German Public Opinion?" *Polska Zbrojna*, 4 February 1991, *FBIS-EEU*, 7 February 1991, 25; and Kostrzewa-Zorbas, "The Russian Troop Withdrawal from Poland," 127–128.

120. Viktor Dubynin, "I Am Ashamed before Those Who Perished," *Sovetskaya Rossiya*, 24 January 1991, *FBIS-SOV*, 29 January 1991, 21–22; and "Soviet Army's Dubynin Cited on Troop Withdrawal," PAP, 1303 GMT, 16 January 1991, *FBIS-EEU*, 17 January 1991, 28. See also Witold Pawlowski, "Bugging Out Is My Specialty: Interview with Colonel General Viktor Dubynin, Commander of the Northern Group of the Soviet Armed Forces, Plenipotentiary of the USSR for Soviet Troops Stationed in Poland," *Polityka*, 13 April 1991, *JPRS-Union Military Affairs* (hereafer, *UMA*), 8 July 1991, 26–29.

121. "Skubiszewski Comments on Soviet Troops, Baltics," PAP, 0932 GMT, 24 January 1991, *FBIS-EEU*, 24 January 1991, 43. See also "C.O. Report: Transit of Soviets

May Become Disastrous; Poland: Withdrawal from Germany Is European Problem," *Die Welt*, 28 February 1991, *FBIS-WEU*, 1 March 1991, 14.

122. Kazimierz Woycicki, "The Continuity of Polish Efforts in a Turbulent World: Interview with Foreign Affairs Minister Krzysztof Skubiszewski," *Zycie Warszawy*, 17 January 1991, *FBIS-EEU*, 23 January 1991, 22.

123. "USSR Troop Withdrawal, Transit Talks Open," PAP, 2139 GMT, 11 February 1991, *FBIS-EEU*, 12 February 1991, 36; Kostrzewa-Zorbas, "The Russian Troop Withdrawal from Poland," 128; and Kostrzewa-Zorbas, "Imperium kontratakuje," 160–163.

124. Edward Krzemien and Marek Rapacki, "Nic o Polsce bez Polski" [Nothing about Poland Should Be Decided without Poland], *Gazeta Wyborcza*, 24 January 1991, in Krzysztof Skubiszewski, *Polityka Zagraniczna i Odzyskanie Niepodleglosci: Przemowienie, Oswiadczenia, Wywiady 1989–1993* [Foreign Policy and Independence Regained: Speeches, Declarations, Interviews] (Warsaw: Interpress, 1997), 110–111.

125. "Official [Merkel] on Soviet Withdrawal, Security Council," PAP, 2228 GMT, 14 February 1991, *FBIS-EEU*, 19 February 1991, 35; "Officials [Merkel and Milewski] Brief Press on New Security Departments," Warsaw TVP Television Network, 2133 GMT, 14 February 1991, *FBIS-EEU*, 19 February 1991, 37; Kostrzewa-Zorbas, "Imperium kontratakuje," 167.

126. Jozef Orzel, "Bezpieczenstwo panstwa to nie tylko sojusze: rozmowa z poslem Jackiem Szymanderskim, wiceprzewodniczacym Komisji Obrony Narodowej oraz z Grzegorzem Kostrzewa-Zorbasem, wicedyrektorem Departamentu Europy *MSZ*" [The Security of the State Is Not the Only Ally: Interview with Parliamentarian Jacek Szymanderski, Vice Chairman of the Committee on National Defense and with Grzegorz Kostrzewa-Zorbas, Vice Director of the Department of Europe at the *MSZ*], *Tygodnik Solidarnosc*, 19 April 1991, 12–13.

127. "[Ziolkowski] Briefs Press on Soviet Troop Withdrawal Talks," Warsaw TVP Television Network, 1830 GMT, 7 February 1991, *FBIS-EEU*, 8 February 1991, 34; Janusz Ziolkowski, "The Roots, Branches and Blossoms of *Solidarnosc*," in *Spring in Winter: The 1989 Revolutions*, ed. Gwyn Prins (Manchester: Manchester University Press, 1990), 47–48. See also Kostrzewa-Zorbas, "Imperium kontratakuje," 166–168.

128. "Walesa on Cooperation, Soviet Troop Withdrawal," MTI (Budapest), 13 February 1991, 1749 GMT, *FBIS-EEU*, 14 February 1991, 31.

129. Kazimierz Groblewski, "The Appointment Came as a Surprise: Interview with Lech Kaczynski, [newly appointed] Minister of State responsible for National Security," *Rzeczpospolita*, 9 April 1991, *FBIS-EEU*, 16 April 1991, 25; and Z.L., "The Belweder and the Army," *Rzeczpospolita*, 16 May 1991, *FBIS-EEU*, 23 May 1991, 15.

130. Kostrzewa-Zorbas, "Imperium kontratakuje," 164–180; Najder, *Jaka Polska*, 172–277; Bichniewicz and Rudnicki, *Czas na Zmiany: Z Jaroslawem Kaczynskim rozmawiaja*, 57–104; and Kurski, *Lech Walesa*, 105–120.

131. "Skubiszewski, Soviet General View Troop Pullout," PAP, 2140 GMT, 11 March 1991, *FBIS-EEU*, 12 March 1991, 27; "Interview with National Defense Minister Piotr Kolodziejczyk," Warsaw Domestic Service, 1500 GMT, 12 March 1991, *FBIS-EEU*, 13 March 1991, 36; Marek Majle, "We Are Not Out to Make a Quick Profit: Interview with Jan Parys, Head of Economic Group Negotiating the Soviet Army Transit Through Poland," *Rzeczpospolita*, 8 March 1991, *FBIS-EEU*, 13 March 1991, 36; and "USSR's Moiseev Comments on Talks," PAP, 1823 GMT, 12 March 1991, *FBIS-EEU*, 13 March 1991, 37.

132. "Official [Kostrzewa-Zorbas] on Walesa, Bielecki Visits to USSR," PAP, 1945 GMT, 29 March 1991, *FBIS-EEU*, 1 April 1991, 36; "Ostrowski Comments on Timetable," Warsaw TVP Television Network, 1730 GMT, 4 April 1991, *FBIS-EEU*, 5 April 1991, 28; Barbara Madajczyk-Krasowska, "Export, Import Settlement: Jan Krzysztof Bielecki on Economic Relations with USSR," 8 April 1991, *FBIS-EEU*, 19 April 1991, 15; and Maria Wagrowska, "Symbols and Facts," *Rzeczpospolita*, 11 April 1991, *FBIS-EEU*, 16 April 1991, 26.

133. "Dubynin Holds News Conference on Troop Withdrawal," PAP, 2039 GMT, 8 April 1991, *FBIS-EEU*, 9 April 1991, 25; Kostrzewa-Zorbas, "Imperium kontratakuje," 168–174; "Jan Krzysztof Bielecki: W swiecie podwyzszonej schizofrenii" [Jan Krzysztof Bielecki: A Glimmer Raised in Schizophrenia], in *My* [We], Teresa Toranska (Warsaw: MOST, 1994), 42–44; and Kostrzewa-Zorbas, "The Russian Troop Withdrawal from Poland," 126.

134. "PAD," "Walesa Interviewed on NATO, Soviet Relations," *Zycie Warszawy*, 3 April 1991, *FBIS-EEU*, 10 April 1991, 30.

135. Key Western analyses focus mainly on Soviet/Russian–German troop withdrawal negotiations, offering important insights from those standpoints, but neglecting to depict Polish negotiating strategy from the Polish perspective. Celeste A. Wallander, *Mortal Friends, Best Enemies: German-Russian Cooperation after the Cold War* (Ithaca, N.Y.: Cornell University Press, 1999), 75–76.

136. For examples of the strained Polish–Soviet ties and Poland's weakened troop withdrawal position, see, among others, "Soviets Said to Stall Troop Withdrawal Talks," AFP (Paris), 1748 GMT, 27 May 1991, *FBIS-EEU*, 28 May 1991, 13; "No Barriers to Start of Soviet Troop Transit," Warsaw Radio Warszawa Network, 1800 GMT, 6 June 1991, *FBIS-EEU*, 7 June 1991, 16; "Lack of Soviet Troop Withdrawal Accord Viewed," Warsaw TVP Television Network, 2030 GMT, 23 July 1991, *FBIS-EEU*, 24 July 1991, 18; A. Maksimchuk, "Light at the End of the Tunnel: Interview with V. Koptieltsev, Deputy Chief of USSR Foreign Ministry Administration," *Krasnaya Zvezda*, 26 July 1991, *FBIS-SOV*, 31 July 1991, 30–31; and "Troop Withdrawal Talks with USSR to Continue," PAP, 2116 GMT, 19 August 1991, *FBIS-EEU*, 20 August 1991, 28.

137. "Talks Commence 20 August," PAP, 1730 GMT, 19 August 1991, *FBIS-EEU*, 20 August 1991, 28. Chapter 5 analyzes the Central European activities during the failed Soviet uprising. Note that Lech Kaczynski revealed both he and his brother, Jaroslaw, "tried to pressure Walesa to put off the start of the next round of negotiations on the removal of the Soviet troops. One reason was that Ambassador Kashlev concluded that the new government [Moscow] should be treated as the permanent ruling body, while our own sources indicated that the coup was falling apart. The Russian side did not know whom it was representing. The *MSZ* wanted the talks to go ahead, and they did, yielding no progress." See Kaczynski's quote in Kurski, *Lech Walesa*, 124.

138. Andrzej Zarembski (government spokesman), "Reportage on Response to Gorbachev Dismissal; Government Issues Statement," Warsaw Radio Warszawa Network, 1700 GMT, 19 August 1991, *FBIS-EEU*, 20 August 1991, 26; "Government Monitoring Situation," PAP, 1959 GMT, 19 August 1991, *FBIS-EEU*, 20 August 1991, 26.

139. Former Communist interior minister Czeslaw Kiszczak also held the infamous title of imposer of martial law.

140. "No Official Reaction from Walesa," Warsaw Radio Warszawa Network, 0900 GMT, 19 August 1991, *FBIS-EEU*, 19 August 1991, 17; "Walesa Discusses Soviet Situation with World Leaders; Bush Calls Walesa," PAP, 0036 GMT, 20 August 1991, *FBIS-EEU*, 21 August 1991, 20; "Mitterrand, Delors Calls," PAP, 2102 GMT, 20 August 1991,

FBIS-EEU, 21 August 1991, 20; and "Walesa See No Need for Security Council Meeting," PAP, 1107 GMT, 20 August 1991, *FBIS-EEU*, 21 August 1991, 20.

141. "El'tsin, Poland's Walesa Discuss Events," Warsaw TVP Television Network, 1300 GMT, 21 August 1991, *FBIS-SOV*, 27 August 1991, 75–76. Importantly, Kostrzewa-Zorbas revealed that in the spring of 1991 the *MSZ* had drafted an invitation for El'tsin to visit Poland, proposed just before the Russian leader won the presidential elections. It had not been lost on the *MSZ*'s Soviet Section that El'tsin had already visited Prague and that he had now become the preeminent leader in Russia, with whom Poland needed to reckon as the USSR disintegrated. Once again, the president's staff rejected a request to improve Polish–Russian relations and Poland lost a valuable opportunity to make inroads with the increasingly significant Russian leadership. See Kostrzewa-Zorbas, "Imperium kontratakuje," 175. Note that Czech president Vaclav Havel sent the head of his office on 24 August to Moscow to offer El'tsin official congratulations on the "victory of democracy" and commitment to "the closest possible relations." See "El'tsin Meets CSFR Presidential Office Head," CTK (Prague), 1806 GMT, 24 August 1991, *FBIS-SOV*, 27 August 1991, 76.

142. This section comprises accounts from Toranska, *My*, 72–74, 137–139 (interviews with Bielecki and Jaroslaw Kaczynski, respectively); Bichniewicz and Rudnicki, *Czas na Zmiany*, 90–91; Kostrzewa-Zorbas, "Imperium kontratakuje," 175–180; Najder, *Jaka Polska*, 258–259; Kurski, *Lech Walesa*, 122–127; and Gorski, *Dwutorowosc Polskiej Polityki Wschodniej*, 111–114.

143. "News Conference with President Lech Walesa and Unidentified Reporters in Warsaw," TVP Television Network, 1515 GMT, 22 August 1991, *FBIS-EEU*, 26 August 1991, 23; and "Excerpts from a News Conference by President Lech Walesa at Belweder Garden," TVP Television Network, 1730 GMT, 22 August 1991, *FBIS-EEU*, 23 August 1991, 20.

144. Merkel, as quoted in Kurski, *Lech Walesa*, 127.

145. P.S., "Powers of Presidential Chancellery Chief Reduced," *Zycie Warszawy*, 12 September 1991, *FBIS-EEU*, 18 September 1991, 21; and "Center Accord Chief Proposes 'Shadow Cabinet,'" *Gazeta Wyborcza*, 23 September 1991, *FBIS-EEU*, 26 September 1991, 18-19.

146. "Skubiszewski on Soviet Troop Withdrawal Issue," PAP, 1517 GMT, 22 August 1991, *FBIS-EEU*, 23 August 1991, 22; "Soviet Army Withdrawal Talks Continue," PAP, 1635 GMT, 22 August 1991, *FBIS-EEU*, 23 August 1991, 22.

147. "Telephone Conversation between President Lech Walesa and USSR President Mikhail Gorbachev on 28 August," Warsaw TVP Television Network, 1759 GMT, 28 August 1991, *FBIS-EEU*, 30 August 1991, 26–27.

148. Kostrzewa-Zorbas, "Imperium kontratakuje," 176.

149. "Remarks by Skubiszewski at a News Conference in Warsaw on 26 August," Radio Warszawa Network, 1005 GMT, 26 August 1991, *FBIS-EEU*, 27 August 1991, 23; "[Polish] Official Goes to Baltics; Diplomatic Ties Sought," Warsaw TVP Television Network, 1515 GMT, 29 August 1991, *FBIS-EEU*, 30 August 1991, 25-26; "Diplomatic Ties with Latvia Restored," PAP, 1934 GMT, 2 September 1991, *FBIS-EEU*, 3 September 1991, 25; "Diplomatic Ties with Lithuania Reestablished," Warsaw TVP Television Network, 2057 GMT, 5 September 1991, *FBIS-EEU*, 6 September 1991, 22; and "Diplomatic Relations Reestablished with Estonia," PAP, 1546 GMT, 10 September 1991, *FBIS-EEU*, 11 September 1991, 20.

150. Parys, "Bitwo o wojsko," 59–62; and Wieslaw S. Debski, "Judgment on Eastern Policy," *Trybuna* 29 August 1991, *FBIS-EEU*, 5 September 1991, 19–20.

151. Danuta Jezowska, "Interview with Counselor Jan Olszewski, Adviser to President Walesa," *Glos Sz Czecinski* (Szczecin), 7–8 September 1991, *FBIS-EEU*, 19 September 1991, 24–25.

152. Stanislaw Grzymski, "Polish Conclusions from the USSR Crisis," *Rzeczpospolita*, 30 August 1991, *FBIS-EEU*, 5 September 1991, 20; Debski, "Judgment on Eastern Policy," 20.

153. Najder, *Jaka Polska*, 260–268; Grzymski, "Polish Conclusions from the USSR Crisis," 20. See also Krzysztof Zielke, "Polska w nowym ukladzie geopolitycznym—stan wyjatkowy w ZSRR a Polska racja stanu" [Poland in a New Geo-Political Arrangement—The State of Emergency in the USSR and Poland's *Raison d'État*], in *Polityka Wschodnia Rzeczypospolitej Polskiej na Progu Lat Dziewiedziesiatych* [Poland's Eastern Policy on the Threshold of the 1990s], ed. Jadwiga Staniszkis (Warsaw: Instytut Studiow Politycznych Polskiej Akademii Nauk, 1991), 15–17; and Burant, "International Relations in a Regional Context," 406.

154. Jezowska, "Interview with Counselor Jan Olszewski," 25–26.

155. Debski, "Judgment on Eastern Policy," 20; Vinton, "Domestic Politics," 43.

156. "Skubiszewski Discusses Soviet Treaty, CSFR," PAP, 1500 GMT, 5 September 1991, *FBIS-EEU*, 6 September 1991, 22; and Alina Kurkus, "Situation of Poles in Lithuania," PAP, 2203 GMT, 4 September 1991, *FBIS-EEU*, 10 September 1991, 7–8. For important analyses of the troubled Polish–Lithuanian relationship in the early 1990s, especially pre- and post-Soviet coup d'état problems between the Lithuanian post-Communist authorities and the Polish minority, pro- and anti-Lithuanian independence factions, and Warsaw support or disowning of Polish minority leaders in Lithuania, see Maja Narbutt, "Lithuania is Breaking Its Own Laws: Interview with Czeslaw Okinczyc," *Rzeczpospolita*, 12 September 1991, *FBIS-EEU*, 19 September 1991, 46; Burant, "International Relations in a Regional Context," 402–403; Burant and Zubek, "Eastern Europe's Old Memories and New Realities," 383–390; Burant, "Polish-Lithuanian Relations," 78–82; Prizel, "Warsaw's *Ostpolitik*," 122–123; and Prizel, *"National Identity and Foreign Policy,"* 148–151.

157. Peter Michielsen, "Interview with Foreign Minister Krzysztof Skubiszewski," *NRC Handelsblad* (Rotterdam), 4 September 1991, *FBIS-EEU*, 11 September 1991, 20.

158. "Skubiszewski Views Russian, Lithuanian Ties," PAP, 2207 GMT, 11 September 1991, *FBIS-EEU*, 12 September 1991, 23.

159. "Reaction to Belarus-Ukraine-Russia Commonwealth," PAP, 2151 GMT, 9 December 1991, *FBIS-EEU*, 10 December 1991, 23.

160. "Ukrainian Foreign Minister Visits Warsaw; Comments on Visit to Poland," Radio Warszawa Network, 1700 GMT, 7 September 1991, *FBIS-SOV*, 9 September 1991, 82–83; Krystyna Koziol, "Skubiszewski, Ukraine's Zlenko Assess Talks," Radio Warszawa Network, 1700 GMT, 8 September 1991, *FBIS-EEU*, 10 September 1991, 17; and M. Melnik, "Ukraine and Poland: Diplomatic Relations Will Be Established," *Pravda Ukrainy* (Kiev), 11 September 1991, *FBIS-USR*, 18 October 1991, 89.

161. Piotr Koscinski, "We Are Seeking a Common Path," *Rzeczpospolita*, 5–6 October 1991, *FBIS-EEU*, 10 October 1991, 17; E.W., "Polish-Ukrainian Economic Agreement," *Zycie Warszawy*, *FBIS-EEU*, 10 October 1991, 17; and "Foreign Minister on Ties with Ukraine," PAP, 26 November 1991, *FBIS-EEU*, 27 November 1991, 20.

162. "Statement by Foreign Minister Skubiszewski," *Rzeczpospolita*, 3 December 1991, *FBIS-EEU*, 6 December 1991, 27.

163. "Statement by Foreign Minister Skubiszewski," *Rzeczpospolita*, 27; "Walesa Cables Ukrainian Leader on Recognition," Radio Warszawa Network, 1900 GMT, 3

December 1991, *FBIS-EEU*, 4 December 1991, 26; and "Council of Ministers Statement Published," Radio Warszawa Network, 1700 GMT, 2 December 1991, *FBIS-EEU*, 3 December 1991, 18.

164. "Kravchuk Seeks 'Close Contacts' with Poland,'" PAP, 1934 GMT, 20 December 1991, *FBIS-SOV*, 23 December 1991, 63. See also Burant, "International Relations in a Regional Context," 410–411; and Prizel, *National Identity and Foreign Policy*, 139.

165. Dymitr Podbierezski, "Back to the Golden Age: Interview with Belorussian Foreign Minister Petr Kravchenko," *Rzeczpospolita*, 17 September 1991, *FBIS-SOV*, 25 September 1991, 56.

166. "Belarus's Kebich Visits; Agreements Signed," PAP, 1630 GMT, 10 October 1991, *FBIS-EEU*, 11 October 1991, 20; "'Abridged' form of 'Declaration on Good-Neighborly Relations, Mutual Understanding, and Cooperation between the Republic of Poland and the Republic of Belarus' Signed in Warsaw on 10 October," *Rzeczpospolita*, 11 October 1991, *FBIS-EEU*, 17 October 1991, 21; and Mikhail Malchum, "Prime Minister on Talks, with Poland's Walesa," TASS, 2205 GMT, 11 October 1991, *FBIS-SOV*, 17 October 1991, 76. See also Burant, "International Relations in a Regional Context," 406–407.

167. "Troop Withdrawal Treaty Signed with Poland," TASS, 1500 GMT, 26 October 1991, *FBIS-SOV*, 28 October 1991, 17–18; and Jerzy Malczyk, "Polish Vice Foreign Minister on Treaty," PAP, 1955 GMT, 26 October, 1991, *FBIS-SOV*, 28 October 1991, 18.

168. "Makarczyk: Soviet *Coup* Helped Troop Withdrawal," PAP, 0826 GMT, 27 October 1991, *FBIS-EEU*, 28 October 1991, 28.

169. Andrei Pershin, "Documents on Relations Initialed," TASS, 1432 GMT, 10 December 1991, *FBIS-SOV*, 11 December 1991, 9; and "Interview with Deputy Foreign Minister Jerzy Makarczyk," Radio Warszawa Network, 11 December 1991, *FBIS-EEU*, 12 December 1991, 23.

170. M.N., "Of Poland and Lithuania in Warsaw and Vilnius," *Rzeczpospolita*, 27 September 1991, *FBIS-EEU*, 3 October 1991, 18; "Interview with Foreign Minister Krzysztof Skubiszewski," Warsaw TVP Television Network, 1830 GMT, 3 October 1991, *FBIS-EEU*, 7 October 1991, 16–17; "Landsbergis 'Surprised' at Warsaw's Reaction," 2300 GMT, Radio Vilnius, 17 September 1991, *FBIS-SOV*, 19 September 1991, 45–46.

171. "A. Butkevicius Is Afraid of Poland," *Slowo Powszechne* (Warsaw), 22–24 November 1991, *FBIS-SOV*, 27 November 1991, 36.

172. "[Skubiszewski] Speaks on Eve of Visit," BALTFAX (Moscow), 1735 GMT, 12 January 1992, *FBIS-SOV*, 14 January 1992, 86.

173. "Saudargas Previews Visit," PAP, 1508 GMT, 10 January 1992, *FBIS-SOV*, 14 January 1992, 86.

174. "Further on [Polish–Lithuanian Ministerial] Meeting," Warsaw TVP Television Network, 1830 GMT, 12 January 1992, *FBIS-EEU*, 14 January 1992, 87; "[Skubiszewski] Meets Saudargas; Declaration Signed," Radio Vilnius, 0940 GMT, 13 January 1992, *FBIS-EEU*, 14 January 1992, 87.

175. V. Kanapienis, "News Conference Held After Signing," Radio Vilnius, 1700 GMT, 13 January 1992, *FBIS-EEU*, 14 January 1992, 88–89.

176. "Skubiszewski 'Optimistic' after Lithuania Visit," PAP, 1811 GMT, 14 January 1992, *FBIS-EEU*, 15 January 1992, 29–30; Burant, "International Relations in a Regional Context," 404–405; Prizel, "Warsaw's Ostpolitik," 122–123; Prizel, *National Identity and Foreign Policy*, 150–151.

218 Chapter 4

177. Juliusz Urbanowicz, "Showdown: Former Defense Minister Retired," *Warsaw Voice*, 12 January 1992, 3. See also Jeffrey Simon, *NATO Enlargement and Central Europe: A Study in Civil-Military Relations* (Washington, D.C.: National Defense University Press, 1996), 62–66.

178. For a unique conceptualization for the structure and activities of this pathbreaking, but short-lived civilian defense policy office from Grzegorz Kostrzewa-Zorbas, see "Sprawozdanie z dzialan Biura Ministra Obrony Narodowej d/s Polityki Obronnej w okresie wstepnym do 15 kwietnia 1992" [Report from the Scope of the Ministry of National Defense's Bureau of Defense Policy for the Period Starting from 15 April 1992], Internal Report, Warsaw, 17 April 1992.

179. "Ukraine's Defense Minister on Nuclear Weapons," PAP, 2047 GMT, 14 January 1992, *FBIS-EEU*, 15 January 1992, 29; "Talks on Troop Withdrawal, Russian Treaty Viewed," PAP, 2256 GMT, 23 January 1992, *FBIS-EEU*, 24 January 1992, 20; "[Ukraine] Talks with Poland on Treaty, Security Issues," PAP, 2210 GMT, 27 January 1992, *FBIS-EEU*, 28 January 1992, 59.

180. "Foreign Ministry Stresses Relations with East," PAP, 1935 GMT, 18 December 1991, *FBIS-EEU*, 19 December 1991, 22; Teresa Stylinska, "Polish-Russian Treaty Ready to Sign," *Rzeczpospolita*, 7–8 March 1992, *FBIS-EEU*, 12 March 1992, 19–20; Vladas Burbulis, "Polish Minister on Foreign Ties," ITAR-TASS (Moscow), 1957 GMT, 17 March 1992, *FBIS-EEU*, 18 March 1992, 20; and Roman Czejarek, "Skubiszewski on Talks with Lithuania's Saudargas," Radio Warszawa Network, 1510 GMT, 26 March 1992, *FBIS-EEU*, 27 March 1992, 26–27.

181. See "[Byczewski on] Treaty Initialed," PAP, 1408 GMT, 23 April 1992, *FBIS-EEU*, 24 April 1992, 15; Valentin Volkov and Vladas Burbulis, "Kebich Arrives in Poland, Signs Treaty," ITAR-TASS, 1736 GMT, 23 April 1992, *FBIS-SOV*, 27 April 1992, 54; Valentin Volkov and Vladas Burbulis, "[Kebich] Meets with Walesa," ITAR-TASS, 1224 GMT, 24 April 1992, *FBIS-SOV*, 27 April 1992, 54; and Burant, "International Relations in a Regional Context," 407–408.

182. Poland's detailed strategy toward NATO membership is the focus of chapter 5. See Jan B. de Weydenthal, "Polish-Ukrainian Rapprochement," *RFE/RL Research Report* (28 February 1992): 25–27; Vinton, "Domestic Politics and Foreign Policy," 54–56; Prizel, "Warsaw's Ostpolitik," 115–116; and Prizel, *National Identity and Foreign Policy*, 142–144, 375–377.

183. "Walesa, Russian Envoy [Grachev] Discuss Troop Withdrawal," PAP, 1404 GMT, 15 April 1992, *FBIS-EEU*, 16 April 1992, 17.

184. The thirty-year-old Zielke, a former National Security Bureau staffer under Jacek Merkel and Lech Kaczynski and then a colleague of Kostrzewa-Zorbas at the *MSZ*, left the foreign ministry with Kostrzewa-Zorbas to help form the new defense ministry's defense policy office. Trained at the University of California, Berkeley, from 1989 to 1990 under, among others, Czeslaw Milosz, Zielke specialized in geostrategy, international relations, and Soviet affairs, and started his doctorate under Jadwiga Staniszkis at the University of Warsaw; he completed it in 1999.

185. Kostrzewa-Zorbas, "The Russian Troop Withdrawal from Poland," 120; and interviews I had with Kostrzewa-Zorbas in Washington, D.C. on 15 October 1993 and with Radek Sikorski in Washington, D.C. on 5 November 1993. Parys, "Bitwo o wojsko," 67–75; and Najder, *Jaka Polska*, 343–356.

186. Interviews I had with Parys and Kostrzewa-Zorbas in Washington, D.C. on 28 August 1992. See also Najder, *Jaka Polska*, 334–342; Jan B. de Weydenthal, "Political Problems Affect Security Work in Poland," *RFE/RL Research Report*, no. 16 (17 April

1992); and "Address by Polish Foreign Minister Krzysztof Skubiszewski at Sejm Session," Warsaw TVP Television Second Program Network, 0733 GMT, 8 May 1992, *FBIS-EEU*, 12 May 1992, 16, 18–19.

187. "Skubiszewski Terms Kravchuk Visit 'Fruitful,'" PAP, 1545 GMT, 19 May 1992, *FBIS-EEU*, 20 May 1992, 12.

188. "Walesa, Ukraine's Kravchuk Sign Cooperation Treaty; Praise 'Friendly' Relations," Radio Warszawa Network, 1400 GMT, 18 May 1992, *FBIS-EEU*, 19 May 1992, 8; "Walesa Urges New Future," PAP, 2301 GMT, 18 May 1992, *FBIS-EEU*, 19 May 1992, 8; and Leonid Kornilov, "Poland Needs a Strong and Independent Ukraine," *Izvestiia*, 20 May 1992, *FBIS-SOV*, 22 May 1992, 42.

189. Leonid Kornilov, "Ukraine—A Partner with Prospects, Poland Believes," *Izvestiia*, 21 May 1992, *FBIS-SOV*, 22 May 1992, 42; and Viktor Demidenko, Valentin Volkov, and Vladas Burbulis, "[Kravchuk] Assesses Relations," ITAR-TASS, 0908 GMT, 19 May 1992, *FBIS-SOV*, 20 May 1992, 42.

190. "Walesa, Ukraine's Kravchuk Sign Cooperation Treaty; Praise 'Friendly' Relations," Radio Warszawa Network, 1400 GMT, 18 May 1992, *FBIS-EEU*, 19 May 1992, 8.

191. "Walesa, Kravchuk Sign Cooperation Treaty; Praise 'Friendly' Relations," Radio Warszawa Network, 1400 GMT, 18 May 1992, *FBIS-EEU*, 19 May 1992, 8. See also Prizel, "Warsaw's Ostpolitik," 109–111; Burant, "International Relations in a Regional Context," 411–412.

192. Sergei Postanogov and Sergei Ryabikin, "[Walesa] Views 'New Stage' in Relations," ITAR-TASS World Service, 1432 GMT, 22 May 1992, *FBIS-SOV*, 27 May 1992, 20; "Walesa Calls for Improved Ties With Russia," PAP, 2059 GMT, 22 May 1992, *FBIS-EEU*, 26 May 1992, 19; "[Walesa] Favors Warsaw-Moscow Axis," INTERFAX (Moscow), 1635 GMT, 22 May 1992, *FBIS-EEU*, 27 May 1992, 20; and "[Walesa] Interviewed on Ties," Russian Television Network, 1920 GMT, 22 May 1992, *FBIS-SOV*, 27 May 1992, 22.

193. Viktor Runov and Gennadii Talalaev, "El'tsin Hosts Dinner," ITAR-TASS, 1904 GMT, 22 May 1992, *FBIS-SOV*, 27 May 1992, 21; Gennadii Charodeev, "Discussion between Two Blunt Men Was How Boris El'tsin Described Nature of Talks in Kremlin with President of Poland," *Izvestiia*, 25 May 1992, *FBIS-SOV*, 27 May 1992, 20.

194. "Troop Withdrawal Treaty Signed," Radio Warszawa Network, 1140 GMT, 22 May 1992, *FBIS-SOV*, 22 May 1992, 14.

195. See, among others, Roman Przeciszewski, "Behind the Scenes of Negotiations: Interview with Witold Chodakiewicz, Vice Minister of Transportation and the Maritime Economy," *Polska Zbrojna*, 13 February 1992, *FBIS-EEU*, 20 February 1992, 7–9; and "Nigdy nie wyjda" [They will never go], *Nowy Swiat* (Warsaw), 21 April 1991, 1.

196. The background description of the events leading up to the compromise and final result stem from interviews with Parys and Kostrzewa-Zorbas in Washington, D.C., on 28 August 1992, and with Zielke in Washington, D.C., on 15 June 1993 and in Warsaw on 18 October 1993. See also Kostrzewa-Zorbas, "Imperium kontratakuje," 179–180; Najder, *Jaka Polska*, 348–362; Kostrzewa-Zorbas, "The Russian Troop Withdrawal from Poland," 129, 132; Vinton, "Domestic Politics and Foreign Policy," 57; Jaroslaw Kaczynski, "Gdzie tkwil blad?" [Where is the Error?], in *Lewy Czerwcowy*, ed. Jacek Kurski and Piotr Semka (Warsaw: Editions Spotkania 1993), 44–46; and Kurski, *Lech Walesa*, 122–127.

197. "Skubiszewski Summarizes Troop Talks with Russia," PAP, 2059 GMT, 23 May 1992, *FBIS-EEU*, 26 May 1992, 20; Vinton, "Domestic Politics and Foreign Pol-

icy," 54–57; and interview by the author with Kostrzewa-Zorbas in Washington, D.C. on 25 March 1997.

198. "Walesa, El'tsin Statement Condemns Stalinism," PAP, 2107 GMT, 22 May 1992, *FBIS-EEU*, 26 May 1992, 20.

199. See *Polska-Rosja: Traktat o Przyjaznej i Dobrosasiedzkiej Wspolpracy (podpisany przez prezydentow Lecha Walese i Borysa Jelcyna dnia 22 Maja 1992 w Moskwie oraz inne dokumenty)* [Poland–Russia: Treaty on Friendship and Good Neighborly Cooperation—Signed by Lech Walesa and Boris El'tsin on 22 May 1992 in Moscow Together with Other Documents], ed. Andrzej Zakrzewski (Warsaw: Polski Instytut Spraw Miedzynarodowych, 1992); and "Walesa Claims Visit to Russia Successful," PAP, 2248 GMT, 23 May 1992, *FBIS-EEU*, 26 May 1992, 20.

200. See Jan B. de Weydenthal, "Poland and Russia Open a New Chapter in Their Relations," *RFE/RL Research Report*, no. 25 (19 June 1992), 2–3.

201. "Walesa Signs Friendship Treaty with Belarus," PAP, 23 June 1992, *FBIS-EEU*, 23 June 1992, 18. See also Burant, "International Relations in a Regional Context," 407–408.

202. "Wystapienie premier RP Hanny Suchockiej na inauguracji roku akademickiego KUL, Lublin" [Appearance of Premier of the Republic of Poland Hanna Suchocka at the Beginning of the Academic Year at KUL] (18 October 1992), in *Rocznik Polskiej Polityki Zagranicznej, 1992* [Yearbook of Polish Foreign Policy, 1992], ed. Barbara Wizimirska (Warsaw: Polski Instytut Spraw Miedzynarodowych, 1994), 18–19; and Prizel, "Warsaw's Ostpolitik," 105.

203. "Suchocka Signs Economic Agreements with Belarus," PAP, 0008 GMT, 19 November 1992, *FBIS-EEU*, 19 November 1992, 16; "Kebich Satisfied With Polish Prime Minister's Visit," ITAR-TASS, 1352 GMT, 19 November 1992, *FBIS-SOV*, 23 November 1992, 55; and Konstantin Bolotevich, "Polish Premier Visits Grodno," ITAR-TASS, 1855 GMT, 18 November 1992, *FBIS-SOV*, 23 November 1992, 55.

204. "Lech Walesa Came to Belarus," Belinform Report (Minsk), 1525 GMT, 28 June 1993, *FBIS-SOV*, 29 June 1993, 61.

205. Mikhail Rudkovski, "[Walesa] Holds News Conference with Shushkevich," Radio Minsk Network, 1200 GMT, 28 June 1993, *FBIS-SOV*, 29 June 1993, 61.

206. "[Walesa] Meets with Kebich," ITAR-TASS, 2010 GMT, 28 June 1993, *FBIS-SOV*, 29 June 1993, 61–62.

207. "[Walesa] Addresses Supreme Soviet," PAP, 1040 GMT, 29 June 1993, *FBIS-EEU*, 29 June 1993, 62; and Mikhail Rudkovski, "Polish Leader Addresses Supreme Soviet," Radio Minsk Network, 1200 GMT, 29 June 1993, *FBIS-SOV*, 30 June 1993, 64.

208. "[Walesa] Says Poland Has 'No Territorial Claims' on Belarus," ITAR-TASS, 1917 GMT, 29 June 1993, *FBIS-SOV*, 30 June 1993, 64–65; "Walesa Factors No Border with Belarus by Year 2000," Radio Warszawa Network, 1600 GMT, 28 June 1993, *FBIS-EEU*, 29 June 1993, 32.

209. Volodymyr Savtsov, "Let Us Lean on What Brings Us Closer Rather Than on What Separates Us," *Holos Ukrayiny* (Kiev), 24 October 1992, *FBIS-USR*, 15 November 1992, 80–81; "Skubiszewski Briefs Sejm on Eastern Policy," PAP, 2323 GMT, 18 November 1992, *FBIS-EEU*, 24 November 1992, 23; and P.E.S., "Warning of New Insecurities," *Frankfurter Allgemeine*, 28 November 1992, *FBIS-EEU*, 2 December 1992, 19.

210. Prizel, "Warsaw's Ostpolitik," 113–114; and Jan B. de Weydenthal, "Poland on Its Own: The Conduct of Foreign Policy," *RL/RFE Research Report*, vol. 2, no. 2 (January 1993): 4.

211. "Polish Prime Minister Meets with Premier Kuchma," Kiev Radio Ukraine World Service, 1100 GMT, 12 January 1993, *FBIS-SOV*, 13 January 1993, 41; "[Suchocka–Kuchma] Sign Economic Agreements," INTERFAX (Moscow), 1812 GMT, 13 January 1993, *FBIS-SOV*, 14 January 1993, 41.

212. "Suchocka Assesses Outcome of Ukraine Visit," PAP, 1955 GMT, 13 January 1993, *FBIS-EEU*, 19 January 1993, 24–25; and "Roundup on Talk Results," Kiev Ukrayinske Telebachennya Television Network, 1700 GMT, 12 January 1993, *FBIS-SOV*, 13 January 1993, 4.

213. "Poland's Suchocka Urges Poles to Respect Statehood," PAP, 1203 GMT, 13 January 1993, *FBIS-SOV*, 14 January 1993, 41.

214. See Prizel, "Warsaw's Ostpolitik," 117–118; and Prizel, *National Identity and Foreign Policy*, 141–145. Suchocka and Rokita, and Mariusz Handzlik, advisor to Suchocka, gave this assessment on the first Kiev trip to me in interviews in Warsaw on 10 and 12 June 1994, respectively.

215. Galina Nekrasova, "Walesa Predicts No Major Boost in Ties," ITAR-TASS, 0726 GMT, 24 May 1993, *FBIS-SOV*, 24 May 1993, 56.

216. For the proposal's text, see *Gazeta Wyborcza*, 24 May 1993, *FBIS-SOV*, 27 May 1993, 46–47. See also "Zlenko on European Security Alliance," Mayak Radio Network (Moscow), 12 October 1993, *FBIS-SOV*, 86–87.

217. Andrzej Lomanowski, "Walesa, Kravchuk, and the Abandoned Zone," *Gazeta Wyborcza*, 26 May 1993, *FBIS-SOV*, 27 May 1993, 47; and Grzegorz Gorny, "Without Borders," *Zycie Warszawy*, 26 May 1993, *FBIS-SOV*, 27 May 1993, 47. See also Ryzhard Koval, "Contemporary Geopolitical Doctrines," *Vecherniy Kiev*, 12 November 1992, *FBIS-USR*, 5 December 1992, 34.

218. "Walesa Comments on Visit to Ukraine," Warsaw Third Program Radio Network, 1900 GMT, 26 May 1993, *FBIS-EEU*, 27 May 1993, 16.

219. "Agreements with Poland Signed in Kiev," INTERFAX (Moscow), 24 May 1993, *FBIS-SOV*, 25 May 1993, 7; Nadiia Derkach, "Lech Walesa: 'We Must Be Strong,'" *Za Vilnu Ukrayinu* (Lvov), 25 May 1993, *FBIS-USR*, 25 June 1993, 101–102; and "Communiqué Issued on Polish President's Visit," Radio Ukraine World Service (Kiev), 0500 GMT, 28 may 1993, *FBIS-SOV*, 28 May 1993, 46.

220. Pavol Minarik, "There Should Not Be Various Security Zones in Europe: Interview with Foreign Minister Krzysztof Skubiszewski," *Rude Pravo* (Prague), 9 June 1993, *FBIS-EEU*, 16 June 1993, 20–21. See also Andrzej Prusinowski, "Lech Walesa in Ukraine: Partners, Not Allies," *Polityka*, 5 June 1993, *JPRS-EER*, 2 July 1993, 11; "Skubiszewski Suggests Sevastopol Remain in Ukraine," PAP, 1458 GMT, 22 July 1993, *FBIS-EEU*, 23 July 1993, 27; Brzezinski, "Polish-Ukrainian Relations," 51–52; and Prizel, *National Identity and Foreign Policy*, 378–382.

221. "Gaydar, Walesa, Suchocka Meet, Discuss Finances," PAP, 2351 GMT, 3 October 1992, *FBIS-EEU*, 5 October 1992, 12; and "Russia to Provide Oil," PAP, 2036 GMT, 2 October 1992, *FBIS-EEU*, 5 October 1992, 13.

222. Aleksandr Potemkin, Iurii Sizov, Gennadii Talalaev, and Igor Shamshin, "El'tsin Declares Poland of 'Prime Importance,'" ITAR-TASS, 1801 GMT, 24 August 1993, *FBIS-SOV*, 25 August 1993, 4.

223. Vasilii Kononenko, "B. El'tsin's East European Tour: Rebuilding Burned Bridges," *Izvestiia*, 25 August 1993, *FBIS-SOV*, 25 August 1993, 5.

224. "President Boris El'tsin, Statement," Warsaw TVP Television First Program Network, 0850 GMT, 23 August 1993, *FBIS-EEU*, 25 August 1993, 23.

225. Interview I conducted in Warsaw on 15 June 1994 with a Polish television producer who had camped outside the countryside palace in the Helenuw locality near Warsaw, where both presidents negotiated the wording of the agreement. The producer obtained one of the first press scoops when both leaders emerged from their one-on-one drinking session to announce the news about Russia consenting to Poland's desires to join NATO.

226. "Joint Polish-Russian Declaration," 26 August 1993, Polish Embassy, Washington, D.C., 4; and "Joint Russian-Polish Declaration," ITAR-TASS, 1505 GMT, 25 August 1993, *FBIS-EEU*, 26 August 1993, 15.

227. "Walesa, El'tsin News Conference," Warsaw TVP Television First Program Network, 0901 GMT, 25 August 1993, *FBIS-EEU*, 26 August 1993, 12.

228. "Skubiszewski on Talks with Russian Foreign Minister," Radio Warszawa Network, 1700 GMT, 25 August 1993, *FBIS-EEU*, 26 August 1993, 13.

229. Aleksandr Potemkin, Iurii Sizov, Gennadii Talalaev, and Igor Shamshin, "Kostikov on Poland's NATO Aspirations,'" ITAR-TASS, 1707 GMT, 25 August 1993, *FBIS-SOV*, 26 August 1993, 13.

230. "[Russian] Envoy: Russian View of NATO Membership 'Misunderstood,'" PAP, 2027 GMT, 15 September 1993, *FBIS-EEU*, 16 September 1993, 20.

231. Among Russian policy statements concerning reassertion of Russia's "sphere of influence" over East-Central Europe, see "El'tsin's Secret Letter on NATO Expansion," *Mlada Fronta Dnes* (Prague), 2 December 1993, *FBIS-SOV*, 3 December 1993, 6; I. Prochazkova and J. Stetina, "Interview with El'tsin Foreign Policy Advisor, Dmitrii Rurikov: You No Longer Need to Be Afraid of US," *Lidove Noviny* (Prague), 15 December 1993, *FBIS-SOV*, 20 December 1993, 49.

232. "Zhirinovskii Cautions Neighbors on Joining NATO," RTP Internacional Television (Lisbon), 25 March 1994, *FBIS-SOV*, 28 March 1994, 8–9. For an important assessment on Zhirinovskii's views, see Jacob Kipp, *Vladimir Volfovich Zhirinovskii and the Liberal-Democratic Party: Statism, Nationalism and Imperialism*, Foreign Military Studies Office and Conflict Studies Research Centre, Royal Military Academy Monograph Series, January 1994.

233. "Walesa Receives Lithuanian Prime Minister," PAP, 1833 GMT , 28 September 1992, *FBIS-EEU*, 29 September 1992, 15; and "Agreements Signed," Radio Warszawa Network, 1200 GMT, 28 September 1992, *FBIS-EEU*, 29 September 1992, 15.

234. "Suchocka, Lubys Hold Talks," TVP Television First Program Network, 2145 GMT, 7 January 1993, *FBIS-EEU*, 8 January 1993, 19; and "Lubys, Polish Premier Sign Friendship Treaty," BNS (Tallinn), 1558 GMT, 8 January 1993, *FBIS-SOV*, 12 January 1993, 68.

235. "Lithuanian Foreign Minister Pays 'Fruitful' Visit," PAP, 1910 GMT, 19 February 1993, *FBIS-EEU*, 23 February 1993, 26.

236. "[Slezevicius] Agrees on Cooperation Document with Suchocka," Radio Vilnius Network, 0800 GMT, 27 July 1993, *FBIS-EEU*, 27 July 1993, 72; and "Suchocka on Talks with Lithuanian Leader," Radio Warszawa Network, 1400 GMT, 26 July 1993, *FBIS-EEU*, 27 July 1993, 15.

237. "Declaration on 'Interwar' Relations with Poland Drafted," PAP, 1803 GMT, 11 August 1993, *FBIS-SOV*, 12 August 1993, 72; and Jacek Fedor, "Still No Treaty," *Zycie Warszawy*, 19 August 1993, *FBIS-EEU*, 24 August 1993, 20.

238. Schroeder, "Historical Reality vs. Neo-realist Theory," 117–118, 125–127; Schweller, *Deadly Imbalances*, 71–77, 83–91; and Deborah Welch Larson, "Bandwagon Images in American Foreign Policy: Myth or Reality?" in *Dominoes and Bandwagons:*

Strategic Beliefs and Great Power Competition in the Eurasian Rimland, eds. Robert Jervis and Jack Snyder (Oxford: Oxford University Press, 1991), 85–87, 102–103.

5

Overcoming Regional
Security Dilemmas

The upheaval generated by the Berlin Wall's fall, Germany's unification, and the USSR's collapse threw the pan-European security system into such flux that post–Communist Poland struggled to survive amid unpredictable great power alignments and shaken multilateral institutions. Vigorous debates abounded about what kind of security architecture should emerge from such pan-European uncertainty. Consequently, Polish foreign policy–makers rationalized that the best regional security and integration strategy entailed solidifying Poland's Western orientation, bargaining with the USSR and post-Soviet states, and negotiating with European security institutions. By building on the integral bilateral relationships Warsaw believed essential with all its old and new neighbors alike, Foreign Minister Krzysztof Skubiszewski envisioned middle power Poland becoming regionally pivotal. In such great incertitude, Skubiszewski recognized that a political strategy to advance via "other help" depended on other nations and their support for Poland's long-term stability. Thus, he resolved that Poland avoid "schemes based on the idea of some sort of 'gray,' 'buffer,' or neutral zones," as once again "prone to the rivalry or the influence of powerful countries or great powers."[1]

These challenges required Skubiszewski and his *MSZ* staff to make historic decisions concerning the precarious pan-European security system. Such decisions laid the critical foundation for Poland's contributions to regional stability. Unlike its pitfalls during the interwar and Soviet eras, post–Cold War Poland's middle power security role between a unifying Germany and a disintegrating USSR marked an historical departure in the early 1990s. In many ways, the roots of Poland's regional strategy stemmed from creating the Central European Visegrad Triangle process with the Czech and Slovak Federative Republic

(CSFR)[2] and Hungary. By assessing what the early post-Communist Visegrad Triangle signified, this chapter determines if the Polish trilateral strategy helped synchronize and improve Central European security. Analysis of this trilateral security consultation process reveals whether Poland strengthened its bilateral negotiations with Moscow by coordinating regionally, before West Europe even focused on Central-East European regionalism. Notwithstanding Poland's European reintegration goal, the centrifugal tremors in the pan-European security flux greatly affected key alignment choices toward Russia and other emerging post-Soviet states. As in its post–Cold War reconciliation with Germany and bridge building to its eastern smaller, middle, and great power neighbors in the early 1990s, Poland tried to promote a specialized role for European reintegration.[3] Subsequently, Warsaw based its regional pivotal strategy not on provoking tensions or increasing regional security dilemmas, but on step-by-step integrative alignment.

Few studies analyze if Polish middle power politics affected a regional Warsaw–Prague–Budapest Visegrad Triangle security strategy to negotiate with Moscow and consolidate Polish sovereignty. Studies neglect to apply asymmetrical negotiation theory to test if connections existed between Polish–Soviet bilateral bargaining strategies and trilateral Visegrad positions.[4] Asymmetrical negotiation theory signifies that "real or perceived weakening of the strong state's aggregate structural power can alter the issue of power balance in the weak state's favor." Such recognition by the state deemed "weaker," i.e., a middle power that implements either a self-help or other-help strategy regionally to overcome an asymmetrical power imbalance, may reveal if the weaker state or states attain more "control" during negotiations. According to this theory, "the weak state fares better in negotiations in which it is defending against a perceived injustice by the strong state."[5] Assessments consider how Poland, together with its Visegrad counterparts, built on German unification, Soviet disintegration, and American–NATO relations to reinforce Poland's regional political strategy between great powers. Why Foreign Minister Skubiszewski initiated and fortified a formalized Visegrad process illustrates how Poland achieved otherwise unattainable regional security goals. Moreover, how Poland's trilateral alignment evolved sheds light on disbanding the Warsaw Pact, devising new security relationships with Moscow, and reintegrating into Europe through security structures like NATO and the EU. Accordingly, analysis illustrates the kinds of regional security options Poland weighed, especially if post–Cold War NATO didn't survive and America withdrew from Europe. Whether such middle power politics manifested an other-help stratagem, Poland needed to deal with its historic security dilemmas since Europe underwent dramatic upheaval, potentially resulting in myriad regional threats and internal alliance tensions.

One of the repercussions from the 1989 Central European revolutions gave Skubiszewski and his post-Communist *MSZ* team the opportunity to establish ties with Czechoslovak, and Hungarian counterpart reformists. The relationships developed among Polish, Czechoslovak, and Hungarian activists during the

Communist era yielded in late 1989 some important and closely coordinated policymaking within the Warsaw–Prague–Budapest regionally focused Triangle. These triangular links desired by post–Communist leaders stemmed from historic ties among the three states. Indeed, the underground activist movements in the 1970s and 1980s took many of their state-building tenets for freedom, independence, and sovereignty from the same beliefs of post–World War I leaders Tomas Masaryk of Czechoslovakia, Oscar Jaszi of Hungary, and Jozef Pilsudski of Poland. By consolidating these principles around dissident movements such as Czechoslovakia's Charter 77, Hungarian Istvan Bibo's *Festschrift*, and Poland's *Solidarnosc*, the three states moved toward their goals, enduring many tribulations up until 1989. With the rise and consolidation of post-Communist leaderships in the CSFR under Vaclav Havel, in Hungary under Josef Antall, and in Poland under Lech Walesa, underground activists became policymakers virtually overnight during the 1989–1990 period, implementing what they had espoused in the underground for many years.[6]

Such arguments need to prove what kind of pan-European security options Poland faced, what motives existed behind Polish domestic debates to result in the middle power options Poland ultimately chose, and what implications for Poland's future European reintegration these decisions intended. Important results arose from the Triangle leadership summits in Bratislava, Slovakia (April 1990), Visegrad, Hungary (February 1991), Krakow, Poland (October 1991), and Prague, CSFR (May 1992). Such efforts underlined a means for Poland and its Visegrad counterparts progressively to articulate their concerns and willingness to cooperate. During the Skubiszewski era, the Visegrad cooperation proved to Moscow the seriousness with which Poland and the Central Europeans calculated to negotiate and dismantle the Warsaw Pact, while bargaining for more equitable bilateral treaties. More importantly, the Visegrad cooperation exemplified regional efforts to begin a concerted European reintegration, particularly when serious debate erupted over the future survival of these European security institutions. Yet, Skubiszewski never planned this regional cooperation to signify a new alliance or bloc of states opposing an enemy. In fact, he emphasized continually that Visegrad cooperative initiatives with the emerging post-Soviet states helped reduce misperceptions by Moscow of a hostile alliance against the USSR. He underscored that the emerging post–Cold War European architecture required that sovereign states negotiate their future security since the end of the Cold War signified rapid change and potential new security dilemmas. Hence, the Visegrad cooperative vision denoted a regional process for reintegrating into Europe. In that regional process Skubiszewski saw an historic opportunity, albeit recognizing his middle power nation's limits, to change the shape of Poland and its role in great power pan-European security transformation.

Polish Goals behind Central European
Regional Cooperation

Reinvigorated regional cooperation among Polish, Czechoslovak, and Hungarian underground activists in the late 1980s allowed Poland's first post-Communist government significantly to alter the Warsaw–Prague–Budapest relationship. From the Communist system's collapse, activists favoring serious change in Central European foreign policy emerged. For the few, little known underground foreign policy scholars and journalists, the Polish underground journal *Nowa Koalicja* gave them an outlet in the mid-late 1980s to test the ideas they soon applied as key foreign ministry advisors. Such new foreign policy–makers comprised Grzegorz Kostrzewa-Zorbas and Andrzej Ananicz in Warsaw, Aleksandr Vondra in Prague, and Ivan Baba in Budapest.[7] The appeal in Central–East European states of *Nowa Koalicja* stemmed from the journal's ability to disseminate information and analysis throughout Europe, and its ardent effort to cover diverse topics concerning politics, economics, culture, nationalism, and security. Given that the journal reached readers in nearly fifteen Central and East European states, several Soviet republics, and some Western countries, *Nowa Koalicja*'s message played an invaluable role in connecting future Visegrad Triangle security policy–makers. The journal's credo for "Common Destinies and Goals" reverberated when many of its writers began working together in 1990.[8]

Ultimately, when Polish and Czech activists gathered furtively at the Polish–Czech border in late June 1989, just after Poland's parliamentary elections, the event reinforced *Solidarnosc*'s democratic message and supported Czechoslovakia's democratization. This meeting underlined the objectives of both opposition movements to "protest police harassment and legal action" against Czech dissidents, undertaken by the unreformed Czech regime to prevent their growing links with Polish underground leaders.[9] However, the Czech authorities failed to stop Czech oppositionists such as Jiri Dienstbier, the future post-Communist foreign minister, from publishing articles in new Polish publications like *Gazeta Wyborcza*, under the editorship of former dissident Adam Michnik.[10] When Tadeusz Mazowiecki formed a new, post-Communist government, one of his first duties resulted from an impassioned plea for action from Czech dissident Vaclav Havel. The Czech dissident, still fearing arrest by the Czech security apparatus himself, wrote to Mazowiecki and Hungarian reform Communist Imre Poszgay, a Politburo member, on behalf of Jan Carnogursky, a key Slovak dissident recently arrested for anti-Communist activities. In the letter Havel stated that "you both hold important positions in your respective countries; countries that are not only the closest neighbors of Czechoslovakia, but are tied to Czechoslovakia by numerous alliances." He continued, "were Czechoslovakia to embark on the road leading to reforms, one could not preclude the possibility that Carnogursky would receive a similar mission to the one that you have accepted." Moreover, the Czech dissident declared that "I am convinced that if both of you were to speak out publicly in defense of the arrested Slovak activists for democracy, who are threatened with absurdly high penalties, your calls would not remain without effect." In reply, Mazowiecki committed himself to seek Carnogursky's release, a gesture that initiated the Polish post-Communist policy to advance Central European cooperation.[11]

Within the first weeks of the inauguration of Warsaw's newly elected parliament and Skubiszewski's appointment as foreign minister, Poland's positions on the Warsaw Pact and regional relations changed markedly. Parliamentary and governmental statements defined the outlines of the new foreign policy. Given that Communist leaders remained in power in all other Central European countries, Warsaw's daring declarations on the need for Warsaw Pact member state sovereignty, in contrast to the outdated Pact tenets of socialist unity, and its formal apology for the 1968 Pact invasion of Czechoslovakia reverberated throughout Central Europe. For activists in Prague and Budapest, the Polish parliament's 17 August 1989 statement provided a watershed in Central European security. Post-Communist Poland's condemnation of military intervention and apology for Poland's participation as part of the Warsaw Pact invasion gave Hungarian and Czechoslovak activists hope for democratizing their states.[12]

Even as Warsaw cautiously measured the extent of its criticism of the Warsaw Pact, the new government clearly planned to change policy vis-à-vis the Pact and soon made its intentions known.[13] On the day he took office, Mazowiecki sent a strong message to Central Europeans, saying "we approach our neighbors, Czechoslovakia and other countries of our region, with a willingness to foster cooperation. We intend to free our relations of bureaucracy and base them on broader contacts, going beyond selected groups and political forces." In other words, Poland intended to gain full sovereignty by initiating post-Communist linkages to neighbors, unencumbered by Moscow's domination.[14]

Skubiszewski assumed his foreign ministerial responsibilities and, following Mazowiecki's speeches, gave a number of important interviews which focused on relations with the USSR, ties to rapidly changing Central Europe, and changes in the Warsaw Pact. By displaying a prudent approach from the outset regarding the speed with which Poland enacted change toward Moscow, Skubiszewski deliberately established a moderate, but lucid strategy. He moved toward Moscow cautiously and guided Poland toward the West in collaboration with Prague and Budapest. Before Shevardnadze's late October visit to Warsaw, Skubiszewski told a foreign interviewer that "there will be no choice but to make the Warsaw Pact the departure point for the future." He emphasized that "membership in the Warsaw Pact, as in all the other accords we have with the USSR, requires taking the interests of all the partners into consideration. . . . There is explicit political involvement in it."[15] While visiting Poland, Shevardnadze stated that "the two alliances [NATO and the Warsaw Pact] do exist and one should aim at their being gradually transformed into political-military organizations through developing civilian trends of their activity, with a simultaneous reduction of all military elements."[16] Furthermore, when asked in an interview by Michnik about denouncing the 1968 Czech invasion, Shevardnadze declined to apologize but did respond that "we have once and for all refuted the policy of imposing one's own opinion on others."[17]

Immediately following the bilateral meeting, both ministers participated in a Warsaw Pact gathering of foreign ministers that Skubiszewski hosted. No dramatic statements appeared in the final communiqué on 27 October, most likely because Skubiszewski personified the only post-Communist foreign minister from any of the Pact delegations. However, the ministerial communiqué underlined that the Pact members "respect the right of each nation independently to decide its own destiny, freely choose the road of social, political and economic development, without external interference [and] unconditional[ly] respect the inviolability of existing frontiers, territorial integrity, and sovereignty of states, [with] respect for the universally accepted principles and standards of international law."[18] This statement remained indicative of Skubiszewski's foreign policy tenets.

In the weeks after Shevardnadze's visit and the Warsaw Pact foreign ministerial meeting, Skubiszewski increased his criticism of the Warsaw Pact. He asserted that the Pact's qualitative character should change. Skubiszewski stated that "I regard the Warsaw Pact as nothing but an alliance, a defensive alliance, and not an instrument for intervening in other states, as happened in Hungary in 1956, and Czechoslovakia in 1968. In 1980/81 similar developments were in the air in Poland. Fortunately, these did not materialize."[19] On another occasion, he claimed that "the Warsaw Pact and its political and military organization must deal solely with external security, disarmament, and relations with NATO. The Warsaw Pact has nothing to do with our internal affairs. Today the reactions of our Warsaw Pact allies are not creating any problems for us."[20] These statements provided a prelude for the December Warsaw Pact summit in Moscow.

During the summit, both Skubiszewski and Mazowiecki advanced their views on changing the Pact and creating a strong foundation for relations with the post-Communist leaderships just emerging in Prague and Budapest at the end of that tumultuous fall. The premier and foreign minister still comprised the only two post-Communist leaders at the summit, and the Polish delegation included President Wojciech Jaruzelski and Communist Party First Secretary Mieczyslaw Rakowski. Even though the press communiqué stated only that summit leaders agreed with Gorbachev to forge "close collaboration and renewal in the contemporary conditions of the forms and methods of operation of the Warsaw Treaty," the Polish press conferences revealed more important details.[21] For the Polish leadership, the meeting's resolution, separate from the communiqué, finally rebuked the 1968 invasion of Czechoslovakia and marked a milestone in acknowledgment by the Pact of its historical mistake. Skubiszewski disclosed that Poland declared to the other Pact delegations that the 1968 intervention defined an "illegal act" and a "politically, harmful mistake." Furthermore, he divulged that the Polish delegation initiated and then built consensus to include the words in the resolution that "the Warsaw Treaty has no grounds for any intervention in the internal affairs of states."[22] Hence, the Pact's summit signified another step in the Polish strategy to change the Pact's role as much on Warsaw's terms as possible.

As the momentous fall revolutions culminated in nearly all of the Central and Eastern European states, Skubiszewski's public statements and several important articles by *Solidarnosc* foreign policy experts proclaimed Poland's intent to transform its Eastern Bloc relations and develop new Central European links. Skubiszewski described the impact of the emerging post–Communist leaderships in Czechoslovakia and Eastern Germany on the Warsaw Pact by stressing that such "favorable developments show that the internal affairs of the various individual members of the Warsaw Pact can be settled quite independently." Moreover, he asserted that "we accept the Warsaw Pact, although we do so with the accent on the total freedom of our legal and constitutional systems. That is something with which the Warsaw Pact must not concern itself, for it has no authority to do so." Finally, as became clear in Prague and Budapest in early 1990, Skubiszewski characterized the relationship inside the troubled Soviet-led alliance, "not [as] an international pact which monitors and oversees the common ideology of its member states, [but] exclusively a defensive alliance, nothing more."[23] His message explicitly articulated a Polish foreign policy designed to change the rules of international behavior within the crumbling Soviet Bloc, not by prompting unnecessary upheaval, but by promoting gradual change. Indeed, Skubiszewski wanted closer ties to Western institutions, particularly NATO, and intended to transform the Warsaw Pact.

After the Polish foreign minister's calls for change within the Warsaw Pact and sovereignty for its members, several prominent *Solidarnosc* experts, some parliamentarians and some nongovernmental analysts, published analyses about Poland's rapidly changing alliances.[24] These assessments called for Poland to disband the CMEA, convert the Warsaw Pact into a political organization, and create a Polish–Czechoslovak–Hungarian cooperative effort for more effective economic integration into Europe. Indeed, in the aftermath of the inconclusive early January meeting of CMEA prime ministers in Bulgaria, Poland and Czechoslovakia strongly denounced the CMEA for ruining their respective economies.[25] For these analyses, the Polish–Czechoslovak coordination on this issue revived the concept of the World War II federation championed by Polish leader Wladislaw Sikorski and Czechoslovak counterpart Eduard Benes against the Germans, but dropped by Benes in 1943 once Stalin accused both leaders of plotting against the USSR. Though the articles strongly promoted bilateral cooperation, including bilateral ties to Hungary, all of them rejected the Polish–Czech federation idea, a concept that Skubiszewski and his new post-Communist Czech counterpart, Dienstbier, also opposed. In response to the federation notion first rekindled by former U.S. national security adviser Zbigniew Brzezinski, via Polish Radio on 2 January, both foreign ministers stated publicly their concerns.[26]

Even though both ministers rejected the federation concept, they spoke very favorably about the impact of their new bilateral relationship on Central European stability amid the vast upheaval of German unification. In his statement, Skubiszewski said "a bilateral arrangement should initially concentrate on establishing a customs union, which should be followed by the establishment of an economic union. I have declared myself to be in favor of close ties with Czechoslovakia even before this debate [on federation] began, and consider such a development to be natural." In reply, Dienstbier proclaimed that "the future looks promising. I do not know of other circumstances where during the course of a month and from the formation of a new government, there has been such frequent bilateral contact between the representatives of our respective governments. . . . We agreed that Czechoslovak–Poland cooperation is extraordinarily important."[27] They soon expanded their linkages with prime ministerial and presidential visits to both states by the end of January. In fact, Mazowiecki revealed that he met with his Czechoslovak and Hungarian counterparts at the CMEA meeting. They discussed "fostering this cooperation," such that it "would not only mean economic rapprochement, but stems from the fact that these countries are our natural allies and that their own economies are being restructured into market economies."[28] As one incisive Polish analysis stressed, the trilateral meeting signified the potential for the formation of an "integrated economic group" to accelerate the process of market reform in all three states. If Poland faltered in advancing these opportunities, the analysis cautioned that Warsaw ran the risk of "damaging" its foreign policy.[29]

After these pieces appeared in the Polish press, the Polish–Czechoslovak relationship seriously advanced. Prime Minister Mazowiecki's visit to Prague and newly elected Czechoslovak president Havel's subsequent trip to Warsaw accelerated Central European regional cooperation, with Havel proposing important initiatives which the Polish leadership accepted. Just before Mazowiecki departed for Prague, he addressed the Polish parliament and declared "we want to make good use of the new opportunities in relations with Czechoslovakia. We are united not only by friendship, but also by joint interests." He claimed that "in close cooperation we may enjoy greater significance in Europe." Additionally, in a reference to Hungary, he stated, "we hope that we will share this point of view with our southern neighbors." Moreover, the premier proposed that Parliament and European governments consider "the creation of a pan-European political structure—a kind of permanent Council for European Cooperation to maintain permanent political dialogue among all participating CSCE states and, above all, to pave the way for pan-European forms of integration." Such a bold gesture demonstrated Poland's objective for proving its beneficial post–Communist strategy wherein "the military factor is clearly losing significance in the changing Europe and the future system of collective security will have to take this into clear account."[30]

During his brief visit to Prague on 22 January, Mazowiecki reiterated Warsaw's priority for regional cooperation. He said that both states were "capable of preparing a program convergent with the idea of European integration and that they would closely cooperate." Specifically, Mazowiecki felt that the bilateral relationship had already begun to overcome some of its historical strains when both sides agreed to improve local cross-border traffic and to eliminate wasteful enterprises that polluted both states along the Oder River.[31] Though such steps appeared small, Mazowiecki's meetings with the Czech leadership served to prepare for Havel's trip to Warsaw, especially talks on European reintegration strategies.

Havel's visit to Poland symbolized a major turning point in bilateral relations and reinforced Mazowiecki's European security initiative. After Mazowiecki and Skubiszewski met with Havel and his delegation, which included his advisor Aleksandr Vondra and First Deputy Prime Minister Jan Carnogursky, the Czech president gave one of the most significant speeches on Central European reconciliation and regional cooperation.[32] His speech recounted the close and cooperative history between Warsaw and Prague activists and the difficult history endured by anti-Communist freedom fighters in Poland, Czechoslovakia, and Hungary. As he declared, "Hungarians and Poles also bled for us and we know this very well and will not forget it. . . . We know well that without the many years of struggle by the Poles . . . we could hardly enjoy our newly won freedom today and the relatively smooth way in which everything happened." Furthermore, he paid tribute to Lech Walesa's peaceful resistance movement and to the post-Communist Polish Senate and Sejm for jointly denouncing the "shameful" 1968 Soviet invasion. With this stirring prelude, Havel turned to the solidarity he felt existed between both states for many decades. He then proposed that "from this really authentic friendship, based on a really good understanding of the fate which was enforced on us jointly, and the common lesson which we have learned from it, and mainly on the main ideals which connected us, a good coordination of our policy should ultimately grow, the process which you and we call the return to Europe." Such cooperation, Havel said, needed coordination with Hungary and he disclosed, "it is not by accident that I am going there tomorrow." To solidify such regional cooperation, the Czech president foresaw that "we should not fight to see who will get ahead of whom and who would fight his way through earlier to this or that European body. On the contrary, we should help each other in this effort in the spirit of the same solidarity with which in worse times you protested against our persecution and we against yours." Although he refused to predict how this "Central European coordination" needed to evolve institutionally, he recommended that Polish and Hungarian leaders, along with other Central European observers, come to Bratislava (Slovak capital of the CSFR) in the spring. Through the summit, he wanted to start formal cooperation so that "for the first time we have a realistic historical chance that we shall fill the huge political vacuum which came into being in Central Europe after the breakdown of the Hapsburg realm with something meaningful."

His proposition centered on taking advantage of "a chance to change Central Europe, a phenomenon which so far was only historical and spiritual, into a political phenomenon." For Havel, the Central European freedom movements required serious Western responses because "we have awoken and we have to wake up those in the West who slept through our awakening. This is a task which we shall carry out better the more united we are." Therefore, he underlined, "if we want to think about synchronizing or coordinating our steps on the path toward Europe, we must of course have a clear idea of what in fact should be at the end of this path—which Europe we are in fact approaching." That definition of Europe, Havel felt, necessitated one undivided, where borders such as the Oder–Neisse became "final and inviolable" and where the "formal attempt at friendship within the framework of the Warsaw Pact and CMEA, directed from above, disappears with the totalitarian systems." Finally, he saw the demise of totalitarianism removing "the inconspicuous, quiet, and malicious instigation of nationalist, selfish moods that were evoked according to the slogan of divide and rule."[33] Havel's speech immediately affected Poland's foreign policy, with the *MSZ* working to the best of its abilities to prepare for the Bratislava Central European meeting in the hope of spurring regional cooperation.

Central European Regional Cooperation: Toward the West and the USSR

From February to April 1990, under the compressed time constraints of the Bratislava Summit, Skubiszewski and his *MSZ* team formulated the best set of initiatives possible. After his first trip to Bonn in early February, where he supported a unified Germany in NATO, Skubiszewski gave a wide-ranging interview with the Polish press in which he spelled out his top foreign policy objectives. One of those priorities focused on Poland's European reintegration strategy, encompassing the twin policies of Polish–German reconciliation and USSR disintegration. Skubiszewski described one of his main directions "toward a Polish European policy reliant upon the possibilities of joining various European structures that already exist." He elaborated that Poland meant to take "the road to a new system of European security via integration with the European structures" as part of regional cooperative linkages.[34] It remains important to remember, however, that as Skubiszewski prepared for Bratislava, Prague policymakers delayed setting an agenda for the summit until just days before the summit convened. Finally, Skubiszewski decided that, given the forthcoming Bratislava Summit, Poland needed to extend a Central European cooperative strategy toward Western integration and USSR disintegration. This decision also resulted in a calculated trade-off between withdrawing Soviet forces from Polish territory and accelerating German unification talks.

Another important and pressing development related to, but separate from, the Bratislava preparation stemmed from the Warsaw Pact foreign ministerial meeting in Prague. After this mid-March Pact meeting, only Skubiszewski and Dienstbier gave a press conference. Significantly, both depicted the meeting as "businesslike and open." They focused on Shevardnadze's ostensible objections to including a unified Germany in NATO and some Central European delegation maneuvers to phase out quickly the Warsaw Pact's military structure. Both ministers demonstrated a unified front in support of Germany's NATO membership. They then began a strategy to discredit the military raison d'être of the Pact in favor of a purely political consultative role for its members.[35] Yet, even as Warsaw focused on senior-level meetings concerning German unification and the Warsaw Pact, the *MSZ* began to produce some of the first path-breaking analysis on key tenets that became the essence for Poland's fortification of Central European regional cooperation.

A key underpinning for instituting the Central European regional cooperation stemmed from the 31 March 1990 *MSZ* analysis on the positive and negative dimensions of a Central European confederation. This internal memorandum raised important issues for consideration, not only among Polish policymakers and experts, but also with their Central European counterparts at Bratislava. Skubiszewski turned to two *Solidarnosc* Central European scholars, Robert Mroziewicz and Henryk Szlajfer, to coordinate and write the analysis titled "Eastern European Research Establishment: Central European Confederation?" The significance centered not only on the issues the memo raised, but also on the contribution made to Central European policy coordination over the long term, particularly since Warsaw took the initiative to draft the analysis. For the first time, Poland officially demonstrated its two-pronged regional cooperative strategy. The Mroziewicz–Szlajfer analysis divided Poland's approach first into a strategy for how best to reintegrate into Europe and, next, how to deal with the USSR. It thus represented a specialization role Poland determined essential regionally to increase stability and security, while building bridges, consolidating disparate national strategies, and providing common ground trilaterally.

Regarding the West, the Polish memorandum simply stated that "the people of the land located between Germany and Russia desire integration with Western Europe" and the three Central European states specifically wanted full EC membership. To achieve this objective, both the industrialized West and its financial institutions should first aid the Central Europeans, but "reintegration requires that the Central European states embark on a path of development as was taken by Greece, Portugal, and Spain" in their early European integration. Secondly, by understanding that their reforms entailed great commitments and sacrifices, the memo held that competition among the three states should be avoided. Rather, "since we think that regional cooperation is a necessary stage on the road to integration into Western Europe, it is, therefore, necessary to do everything so as to minimize the negative aspects of this lack of mutual complementarity (and this does not only refer to the economic side)." Third, such regional cooperation necessitates that the Bratislava meeting find a "common definition for the Triangle," such that all three states understand "the position to which the Triangle aspires in Europe; the decisions to be made concerning the common desire to reach that position; and methods for realizing those desires." For these goals to come to fruition, Warsaw argued against the formation of a confederation, but accentuated that Poles, Czechs, Slovaks, and Hungarians needed to coordinate their policies around "the concept of European security," German unification, and the EC.

With regard to Eastern instability and Soviet disintegration, the memo also provided a rationale for Central European coordination. By underlining that "the highest political levels require coordination and decisions on the USSR, the Warsaw Pact, and the CMEA," Warsaw called for a joint strategy with Prague and Budapest to enhance their strategy toward Moscow. Such lofty designs demanded "an intergovernmental system" of groups of experts to meet and to coordinate positions in these areas in the coming months. Finally, the authors of the memorandum underscored that, though many historical tensions still threatened to derail their regional cooperation, "if there are burdens, then we all have them." For Warsaw, the imperative remained for "Czechoslovakia and Hungary to be aware that their prospects lie not only to the south, but also in cooperation with Poland and possibly Scandinavia," while not neglecting other states which might desire to join, such as Bulgaria and Romania.[36]

This preparation appeared to give the Poles what they wanted to advance the nascent stage of Central European regional cooperation concretely and pragmatically. Consequentially, Polish and Czech leaders used some of the points from the *MSZ*'s memorandum during the Bratislava Summit. Without anticipating its course, Polish representatives found the summit's spontaneous and often times free-flowing dialogue among leaders and foreign ministers to hinder final agreement on specifics for future coordination. Historic for the fact that President Havel brought leaders from Poland, Hungary, Italy, Austria, and former Yugoslavia together in Slovakia on 9–10 April, the Czech initiative suffered from too broad an agenda, organized among the participants at the last minute. The summit thus failed to gain consensus on specific objectives. Aside from the merits of forging Central European regional cooperation for the first time at such a high level and enlarging the recently created "Alpine-Adria" regional grouping to include not only Italy, Austria, Hungary, and Yugoslavia, but also the CSFR and possibly Poland, other factors sidetracked the Bratislava Summit.[37] Just the day before Bratislava, the Hungarian Communist leadership suffered a crushing electoral defeat to Antall's Hungarian Democratic Forum. Because the summit occurred before the new government formed, the Hungarian delegation represented lame duck, old-thinking leaders.[38] However the Polish leadership, represented at the summit by Jaruzelski, Mazowiecki, and Skubiszewski, wanted to build regional cooperation. They enunciated their concerns during the summit and worked behind the scenes to develop a regional cooperative effort, particularly to coordinate security issues.

For the Polish leadership, Bratislava provided a vantage point from which to gauge how best to shape regional cooperation. Rather than being a failure, the summit presented an opportunity to learn from mistakes and to prepare for coordinating more effectively and consistently. Yet, Warsaw quickly realized that the *MSZ* needed to take even more initiatives to transform ideas into actions, both to implement integration measures to move closer to Western Europe and to deal with the crumbling USSR more concertedly. At the summit itself Havel opened very ambitiously by promoting a wide-ranging plan for cooperation that encompassed ten general questions, but neglected to provide a means to achieve them. In fairness to Havel, his goals remained worthy. He stated that "the task facing Poles, Hungarians, Czechs and Slovaks today is a return to Europe. It must not be a Europe divided into two military blocs. To think about the return means to think about a Europe of the future and to work out a schedule for common actions on the principle of consensus."[39] Such commendable objectives rang true for the Polish delegation. The Czech president's key aims also elicited support from Warsaw's leadership, particularly the multilateral cooperation on European integration and the common strategies for dealing with the Warsaw Pact and CMEA. These aims reinforced overall common political, economic, security, sociocultural, and environmental approaches. Nonetheless, the Czech president only perfunctorily mentioned the ways to tackle these broad issues to the Central Europeans gathered. Separate presidential, prime ministerial, foreign ministerial, and staff-level working groups spent half a day discussing the means by which to resolve such questions. A short joint communiqué, in turn, disclosed only that "the exchange of views on the problem of European security, pan-European and regional cooperation proved fruitful to the participants [and] pointed to the emerging problem of national minorities and economic underdevelopment."[40] It is important to realize that this first post-Communist-initiated summit witnessed Communist-era activists struggling to put high-level politics into motion. The Polish post-Communist leadership comprehended enough of the potential for pitfalls to try to plan for a better set of coordinated linkages, both during and soon after the summit.

Although Mazowiecki felt the summit failed to forge a clear and practical program, he believed Havel's meeting laid the key groundwork for Central European regional cooperation. The Polish premier proclaimed that the most important Polish foreign policy objectives, in addition to "friendship with united Germany and the USSR," remained "exemplary cooperation between these three [Central European] countries, an exemplary situation which will influence the whole situation in Europe. We propose systematic consultations, especially between foreign ministers." Lastly, he emphasized that "we also spoke about our proposal for a Council for European Cooperation, about the Czechoslovak proposal for a Commission for European Security" to improve the CSCE. Furthermore, he underlined that "we agree that these are not rival proposals; that they can be integrated."[41] Hence, Mazowiecki looked to Skubiszewski to infuse the Central European regional cooperation with the necessary energy and methodically provide needed direction.

During the postsummit press conferences, Skubiszewski delineated his vision for regional cooperation. First, he asserted that Bratislava "strengthens the whole Helsinki process" and that the gathering "inaugurates the cooperation between the three states and begins their joint contributions to European unity." Next, he recognized that "the states have certain regional problems," but he argued that "our relations were, are, and will be close, although much still has to be adjusted within them." Third, he pronounced that "there is a need to reduce the role of the military in Europe, and the stand of these three states can be decisive for the Warsaw Pact." Furthermore, he felt that "in Polish foreign policy—and I believe not only Polish—in this area there is a binding principle of changes with stabilization.[42] This strategy articulated, Skubiszewski returned to Warsaw and prepared for the next steps in regional cooperation.

Poland's Strategy toward Europe and the Warsaw Pact

In the aftermath of Bratislava, Skubiszewski resolved to improve and to structure the Central European regional cooperation he believed necessary for coordinating key security issues. These focused on Soviet control over the Warsaw Pact and Western integration strategy. His first comprehensive foreign policy speech to the Polish parliament in April characterized important points of departure for Poland on regional cooperation, NATO, and the Warsaw Pact. With regard to regional cooperation, the Polish foreign minister stated that, unlike "existing links" of the Pact and CMEA, Poland desired the development of "the new future link [of] the integration of the Czecho–Slovak–Poland–Hungarian Triangle" into Europe. Triangle cooperation, he argued, defined Poland's "new regional links." The Bratislava Summit signified "the first contact in this team and a review of some common problems." Yet, it remains "necessary to bring about systematic and well-prepared work on the assumptions, essence, and form of cooperation between the three states which have so much in common." As his gauge for envisioning post–Cold War European security, Skubiszewski outlined that as "the German question finds its proper position in the European answer, so does the position of Poland become safe in the European peace order having a high degree of links and cooperation between states." In comparing post-Communist Poland with the interwar Second Polish Republic, Skubiszewski highlighted that during the 1930s, "politicians had to think in the categories of alliances, changing patterns of forces, existence or nonexistence of balance." In the post–Cold War era, he wanted to see "the all-European cooperation [that] constitutes a different world, eliminating or reducing antagonisms . . . without preparation for aggression and annexation." For Skubiszewski, this security concept did not represent a "utopia but a real chance of the present day. It is up to us, Europeans, whether and how much we use it. Poland's role will be important in this respect." He depicted a Europe in which "the role of alliances is changing" and elaborated on the future of NATO and the Warsaw Pact.[43]

Strikingly, Skubiszewski clearly articulated his vision for Europe with NATO as the preeminent European security institution. He said he had witnessed such changes by already having visited NATO headquarters in the midst of transformation and had held substantive discussions with NATO ambassadors and military leaders about cooperation. Such developments required that the Warsaw Pact define strictly a "defensive alliance being in tune with the UN Charter, not as an instrument for influencing the political and economic system and order of the contracting states." Consequently, Skubiszewski portrayed the proper role of the Pact as "functioning to correspond to international law. It should serve disarmament and cannot impede the unity of the continent." Moreover, he depicted a Warsaw Pact that should "convert its military-political character into a consultative one," primarily because Warsaw had already "departed from the military structure fixed on offensive operational directions." Significantly, Skubiszewski underlined this meant that "the Polish Army will be used exclusively on Polish territory in defense of our state against the alien aggressor—our army has not and will not have other external tasks." Furthermore, Poland no longer believed a joint Warsaw Pact commander-in-chief remained necessary, but instead that the other Warsaw Pact states would need to have their own military leaders serve in the highest command positions, if the Pact transformed itself in the coming years. Effectively sounding its death knell, Skubiszewski called the decayed CMEA "a relic of the past era and adapting to the new goals and needs will be very difficult for regional economic ties do not need the CMEA." In conclusion, Skubiszewski clearly articulated that Poland intended to continue charting its independent foreign policy, but "despite freedom in determining our system and the directions of foreign policy we cannot feel free from potential threats, both political and economic ones." Therefore, he understood that Poland must "seek guarantees of our independence in a broader system of European security and in structures of multilateral and integrating cooperation. We will co-found one. . . . We have carried out far-reaching changes over the past seven months, while maintaining significant stability. We will not depart from this road."[44]

Moscow's commitment to the Polish "2 Plus 4" participation, however, gave Warsaw the impetus to pressure Bonn, both on border guarantees and on gaining a seat at the "2 Plus 4" talks. Moscow obliged that spring and supported Warsaw's request to participate in the "2 Plus 4" talks, but Skubiszewski's first involvement didn't occur until that July. Since Poland employed these tactics during the spring and the Warsaw Pact summit didn't occur until June, Warsaw's maneuvering to obtain Moscow's backing toward Germany also led to the trade-off of not moving as quickly as Budapest and Prague to abrogate Warsaw Pact treaty commitments. Furthermore, Skubiszewski discerned that the planned fall CSCE summit envisioned a major arms control accord that enshrined an unequal bloc-to-bloc European security system, but he also knew Poland needed to maintain short-term linkage to the crumbling Warsaw Pact in order not to antagonize Soviet hard-liners. Hence, this strategy slowed Skubiszewski's efforts to develop linkages too closely to NATO, as NATO began to open up to non-NATO Central-East European nations. Taken together, Skubiszewski confronted these multiple security concerns and determined that, along with gambits between Bonn and Moscow to guarantee Poland's western border, Poland also required synchronizing its ties immediately with Budapest and Prague on the future of the Warsaw Pact.[45]

Putting Negotiation Theory into Practice behind the Scenes

Poland and its Central European counterparts attempted to synchronize their Warsaw Pact strategy, both before and during the Moscow-hosted Warsaw Pact Political Consultative Committee Summit. Analysis of the Central European strategy that uses international negotiation theory illustrates how their bargaining positions succeeded. The concept of "power" between smaller, ostensibly weaker states and larger, stronger states helps to explain why certain negotiating "behavior" leads to particular "outcomes," particularly when middle and smaller powers cooperate and bridge differences. This international negotiation theory takes on important meaning with the analysis below of the asymmetrical Triangle–Soviet negotiations and the beginning of the Warsaw Pact's true demise.[46]

Consistent with the theory of asymmetrical negotiation, the nascent regional cooperative security process first tested by post–Communist policymakers at the 7 June 1990 Warsaw Pact summit demonstrated that seemingly weaker states may exert greater negotiating strength over more powerful states. This thesis points to the importance of the "process of negotiation," not simply "aggregate" and "absolute" power, or power for power's sake. Without threatening the stronger power, particularly when weaker states together still cannot threaten the stronger power by balancing, such states which bandwagon together for "profit," finding ways to bridge their differences may disabuse the stronger power of its notion of dominance via compromise. Asymmetrical negotiation theory shows that weak states possess power relative to stronger states when the former influence facets like the "moral obligation" of the latter to negotiate specific points, the agenda of the talks, and the "agreement" phase—"power" over whether to approve or reject actual agreement. These aspects of asymmetrical negotiation theory contribute to a better understanding of the power of different types of states, how they find other-help options together when unable to fend for themselves, and symbolized the Triangle's efforts toward Moscow. Therefore, these trilateral approaches gave the weaker Triangle some upper-hand options during the June 1990 Warsaw Pact summit and during the subsequent eighteen months, too.[47]

Before the June summit, Skubiszewski deemed it best to work within the Pact's framework, first to discredit the military structures and then to dissolve the political structures, because Poland still needed to secure its western border in a treaty with Germany. To accomplish this objective, Skubiszewski believed it necessary to obtain Hungarian and Czech support to eliminate the Soviet military and political control of the Pact without allowing Moscow to exploit any differences among the three states. The Polish rationale focused on making the pact meaningless without its military control mechanisms and without its ability to use its operational structure against the West and NATO. In order to succeed, Poland needed to persuade Hungary and the CSFR to forge a unified approach toward Moscow that kept the Pact alive politically, but undermined its military raison d'être. Although considerably weaker at the outset of negotiations to transform the Warsaw Pact, the Triangle states used such procedural negotiation devices as time, assertive behavior, and tougher bargaining positions to reverse Moscow's initial positions. This strategy achieved a better outcome than anticipated. Whether this depicted an other-help strategy trilaterally in which bridging took priority over balancing or bandwagoning in nonalliance circumstances merits the following analysis.

Before the leaders arrived for the June summit, the three Central European ministerial staffs coordinated to try to change the negotiation's "atmospherics" vis-à-vis the stronger Soviets and other, less reform-minded Pact delegations. During the negotiations, Warsaw and the other Triangle foreign policy–makers countered Soviet demands by inducing Moscow negotiators to accept "trade-offs" by the close of the negotiations.[48] As a result, Warsaw and its Triangle counterparts gained more than originally stipulated by Moscow by persuading the USSR to agree to begin dismantling the Warsaw Pact militarily, instead of restructuring it as Moscow preferred. How did Poland and its Central European counterparts attain such a far-reaching result?

A behind-the-scenes description provided by Grzegorz Kostrzewa-Zorbas contributes to a much better understanding of the overall synchronization strategy throughout the summit.[49] On 1 June, an electrifying, late-afternoon cable arrived at the *MSZ* directly from President Havel. This last-minute initiative came as a "total surprise," with the proposal to draft the dismantling of the Warsaw Pact and, in turn, to use the 7 June Moscow summit to launch the dismantling process. In order to draft a declaration by the time the summit convened, the *MSZ* needed to navigate among some very difficult bureaucratic and domestic political realities. Recall that Jaruzelski occupied the presidency, the Communists enjoyed a majority in Sejm, and the mixed post-Communist government cabinet, including the vice premier and interior minister, General Czeslaw Kiszchak, and the defense minister, General Florian Siwicki. Apparently, much of this drama stemmed from improvised policymaking.

Havel drafted the formal Czechoslovak position in the Prague Castle late on Friday by himself. He appears to have sent it out personally without coordinating with his own foreign ministry. Cables went to Warsaw and Budapest on 1

June and Skubiszewski sent Kostrzewa-Zorbas to Moscow on 3 June to start staff-level coordination. The Central European negotiating teams began quite easily to coordinate since all three post-Communist delegations comprised mainly former underground activists. On 4 June, the experts began to coordinate and quickly accepted the Czechoslovak line. The Poles also used the time from 4 to 6 June to gain Czechoslovak and Hungarian support for Poland's larger regional security concerns, particularly on German unification, to buttress Warsaw's policy of a "2 Plus 4 plus Poland" negotiation format. From the other non-Soviet Warsaw Pact members, whose post-Communist leaderships coalesced much slower than in the Triangle states, the Triangle states encountered neither support for Soviet Pact tactics nor rejection of the Triangle negotiating strategy. The support from Prague and Budapest staff-level negotiators during those important presummit days significantly helped to bring all three states closer in the coming months on other security issues, too.

On 5 June, vice foreign and defense ministers joined the working-level groups and by 6 June, the full delegations began the last deliberations before drafting the summit's declaration. Prior to his departure from Warsaw on 6 June, Mazowiecki disclosed that "we are in favor of a fundamental reform of the Pact and gradual progress toward collective European security, but this cannot happen overnight."[50] Once Skubiszewski arrived, he realized that his Central European strategy toward the progressive dismantling of the Warsaw Pact took a new turn as he, Mazowiecki, and Jaruzelski met with President Havel on 7 June to discuss how to coordinate Central European strategy toward Moscow. After this pre-Pact strategy session, Mazowiecki gave a press conference at which he stated that "we met President Havel at his own request to discuss questions of the agenda of today's debates. I think that the Warsaw Treaty should be essentially reformed on the principle of full equal rights of its participants in all areas, both political and military ones. One should at the same time think about a new European security system today."[51] In Moscow on 7 June, Havel also argued publicly to "launch the process of dismantling by drafting a declaration" among Central European delegations to present to Gorbachev.[52] Such calls to change the Pact came on the heels of the statement by newly appointed post-Communist Hungarian foreign minister Geza Jeszenszky regarding potential Hungarian Pact withdrawal.[53]

These events accelerated Skubiszewski's change of course. He modified his position on the Warsaw Pact's transformation, sensing that what initially he thought rash because of the delicate balance between Bonn and Moscow, already appeared overtaken by events. With support from Prague and Budapest for Warsaw's participation in the "2 Plus 4" talks, Skubiszewski quickly understood the importance of the Triangle's bandwagoning toward Moscow to disband the Warsaw Pact. Moreover, Havel's initiative provided increasing momentum to the summit and he divulged "Czechoslovakia has brought to this meeting its own draft of the final declaration that has become a subject of intensive talks." In praise of the Triangle's negotiation strategy, rapidly formulated to move the summit as much on its own terms as possible, the CSFR president underscored that

> various experts have been working throughout the night [6 June] and so far everything indicates that this session could arrive at a consensus, at unity; that it could adopt this declaration and this would be a very important declaration because it would mean a fundamental transformation of the entire Warsaw Pact and its function.[54]

As the talks continued among Warsaw Pact ministers, Gorbachev and his negotiators declared that a new, more loosely configured Warsaw Pact based on a voluntary military bloc of independent states should replace the one previously controlled by Moscow. In his opening luncheon, Gorbachev told the Warsaw Pact leaders he believed the Pact needed reform and, "despite all our differences, we are capable of contrasting views and approaches calmly and constructively; we are demonstrating a commitment to listen and to understand each other, and to find sensible compromises and solutions in line with common interests."[55] In response, Havel spoke on behalf of the non-Soviet Warsaw Pact leaders and proclaimed that "all the signs are that this meeting of ours will be truly historic, because it will give impetus to a large-scale transformation of the Warsaw Pact, a transformation which will reflect the historic, new situation in which our part of Europe now finds itself. I firmly believe that we will reach an agreement today and that this autumn our forum will gather again to turn this radical transformation into a reality."[56] Though the Soviet and Triangle positions remained opposed initially, Moscow's domestic political and economic preoccupation coupled with the Triangle's steadfast and cohesive negotiating stance. This bandwagoning effort strengthened the Triangle's cooperative strategy, one that demonstrated how the Triangle trilaterally bridged differences with Gorbachev's politics and his military's opposition to the Warsaw Pact's potential disbanding.

Gorbachev failed to maintain control of the Warsaw Pact, however. He never envisioned that the Triangle states would actually break with Moscow in such a forum. At one point, the Soviet leader attempted to persuade the non-Soviet Warsaw Pact members by proposing that "Germany should be a member of NATO and the Warsaw Pact simultaneously. . . . In Washington, the existence of the Warsaw Pact is counted upon. What is more, it is considered that its elimination would only complicate the disarmament talks and the realization of an all-European collective security system."[57] The Triangle leaders worked together to obtain a common, more comprehensive strategy to overcome Moscow's arguments. Such an achievement became possible because the Triangle asserted itself during the negotiations when it realized the USSR's growing vulnerability. The Triangle recognized its strengthened posture as a group and together weakened Moscow's bargaining tactics by refusing to participate in any future Pact military bloc, basically fulfilling Skubiszewski's original bridging objective that at least sought to separate the detrimental military stipulations from the temporary political compromises within the Pact.

According to Kostrzewa-Zorbas, the Triangle states employed somewhat different tactics within they unified their respective strategies toward Moscow. Polish negotiators joined Czech and Hungarian counterparts behind the scenes in order to reconcile with the reality that Poland's Communist and post-Communist leaders shared the same podium. Hungary also provided a political buffer by declaring it would be the first Pact member to withdraw from the unified military command and decision-making structure. The Soviets did as much as possible to maintain their positions, but the Triangle leaders moved faster. Though the Czechoslovaks initiated the Warsaw Pact's formal disintegration, Hungary developed the most concrete scenarios about next steps. Antall stated that "the Warsaw Pact is a remnant of European confrontation and has lost its main function. Our nation is initiating negotiations to review the organization of the Warsaw Pact and our membership. It would be desirable from Hungary's point of view to eliminate the military cooperation within the organization by late next year."[58] Once Moscow grasped that the Triangle had engineered a virtual fait accompli and now offered the demise of the Warsaw Pact as the only option, Moscow yielded to salvage some agreement. In effect, the Triangle changed its negotiating tactics in the middle of the negotiations by "toughing" it out and weakening Moscow's negotiating "rate" for a better result.[59]

The summit's outcome resulted in the Triangle changing the momentum of the negotiations on several key issues. First, after much wrangling and tense back-room negotiation, the final declaration supported the Triangle's main security concerns, namely the path leading to the Pact's dismantling, relations with NATO, and German unification.[60] Secondly, during the final phases of the summit, the Central Europeans persuaded the Soviets to consider having the next Warsaw Pact summit represent the formal end of the Pact's military unity. The Central Europeans desired Budapest to host this summit in November 1990 and Moscow agreed. Third, the Central European leaders forged a consensus over the several days in Moscow to back Antall publicly closing the summit with Hungary declaring it expected soon to withdraw from the Warsaw Pact's unified military command structure.[61] Such actions defined the rapid pace of developments as Poland, with the CSFR and Hungary, combined to give Moscow few options. The Moscow summit also spurred the Triangle's synchronization.

For Skubiszewski, the Warsaw Pact declaration signified several distinctive successes. Just after the summit he revealed that Poland had gained agreement from all Warsaw Pact states for Warsaw's participation in the July "2 Plus 4" talks. This public acknowledgment from the Pact states meant that each favored the "general, final, internationally legal regulation of the questions connected with German unification." He also expressed satisfaction over a more synchronized Central European regional cooperation and mentioned that while "today, there is full freedom in the formation of these relations, nonetheless there is a place for far-reaching cooperation." Furthermore, he welcomed the fact that Gorbachev recognized the "considerable room for the coordination of certain activities between the [uncertain] Warsaw Pact and NATO. . . . President Gorbachev said quite a lot about the difficulty created by the possible membership of a united Germany in NATO."[62] To put the Pact in perspective, Skubiszewski declared that "it is going through a crisis. Relations with the Pact—that is, relations between states which are its members, and therefore allies—require restructuring." According to Skubiszewski, "the Pact's military role is declining as a result of the obvious truth that the danger of war in Europe does not at present exist, other than through some tragic mishap or misunderstanding, and this of course has a bearing on the role of the Pact." Even though NATO believed the Pact served as a "reliable partner for talks," Skubiszewski saw the Pact as only "a defensive alliance in accordance with the UN Charter, without any functions of an ideological nature or those influencing the systems of states." Specifically, he underlined that "these are closed issues, and from what President Gorbachev said, it transpires that this unfortunately long period in the pact is fortunately now closed."[63]

Shortly after the summit Skubiszewski also detailed the role Poland and the Central Europeans anticipated playing in post–Cold War European security. Skubiszewski dismissed concerns about the recent American–Soviet summit in Malta by stating that "such fears are a fantasy today because there is no longer any possibility of a new Yalta now that the satellite countries have regained or are regaining their sovereignty. The [U.S.–USSR] summit is a negation of Yalta rather than a repetition of it." More importantly, he declared that "while building a Europe-wide security system, it is important to create ways of preventing disputes and of solving them if preventing them proves unsuccessful. When such mechanisms exist, the role of the superpowers will assume secondary status." Yet, he ensured that the Polish public understood that having U.S. forces withdraw from Europe would signify an even more dramatic geostrategic alteration, one that would lead toward much greater instability. Moreover, Skubiszewski contended that "as long as NATO exists, the United States will continue to play a major role in Europe." Poland needed the Americans in Europe "to stabilize the situation and create the kind of system of security we want." Furthermore, he cautioned that "although the USSR has lost its satellites, it is still a power, even with all its economic, ethnic, and political difficulties." What remained crucial for Skubiszewski, as it did for his Central European counterparts, pointed "to the USSR's military strength; European equilibrium still exists despite all the changes in the Eastern bloc." And, in a telling statement, he underscored that "transferring the military frontier from the Elbe to the Bug Rivers would be of secondary importance, especially because there is for the time being a consensus about Soviet forces remaining in Germany for a few years."[64]

Given Skubiszewski's slow, but consistent development of Polish–NATO relations, his entreaty to maintain American forces in Europe could be understood to mean that Poland wanted to balance against any residual Soviet threat. Warsaw remained very concerned over Moscow's contingencies against its satellite states that seemingly slipped farther away with each Warsaw Pact gathering. Yet, Skubiszewski also realized that Soviet troops on Polish territory still commanded enough residual power to threaten any Polish balancing strategies. Or, for that matter, any bandwagoning attempts since other Western powers might want to counter Soviet power and ignore Warsaw unless it jumped on the bandwagon. The Polish foreign minister thought that by first gaining international legal approval for Poland's western border, advancing Central European cooperation, and then negotiating, like his Central European counterparts, Soviet force withdrawals, Poland did not need to balance America and, by extension, believe NATO balanced against the USSR. Nor did Poland believe that simply jumping on the American, German, or any other Western European nation's bandwagon would Poland solve its problems with Russia. America did need to remain in Europe, according to Skubiszewski, because NATO needed to maintain its value as an institution that prevented its members from fighting, not just as a bulwark against Soviet expansionism. Since Soviet influence in Central and Eastern Europe rapidly declined from 1989 to 1990, Skubiszewski saw that America's importance to Europe resided in its ability to bring nations together, including even a reformed Moscow leadership toward NATO. Skubiszewski recognized before most of his European and North American counterparts that the USSR was also dissolving, as the previous chapter assessed. He surmised that, with Poland's efforts about to begin on the two-track Eastern policy during the summer–fall of 1990, he could devise a bridging strategy to find common ground between Poland and both the Soviet and non-Soviet leaderships. These combined strategies offered Poland a means to become a pivotal middle power between stronger Germany and Russia, even as Poland's military prowess could never take on these two powers; its political savvy could gain new adherents to its cause as a bridge builder in the heart of Europe. For the foreign minister, Poland characterized an increasingly self-assured nation. To achieve genuine political accomplishments that required full sovereignty over foreign policy, Poland needed to develop new linkages bilaterally with its great power neighbors and ensure that it didn't ruin its European reintegration opportunities by becoming belligerent toward any European powers. The NATO June 1990 statements expedited such a Polish strategy as NATO's North Atlantic Council called for new and broad European linkages between East and West.

From 7 to 8 June in Turnberry, Scotland, NATO foreign ministers met and responded affirmatively to the Moscow summit. Their "Message to All European Countries" underscored that "we are encouraged by the positive spirit conveyed in this [Moscow] declaration and in particular by the readiness on the part of the countries issuing it for constructive cooperation."[65] The NATO foreign ministerial communiqué continued, "the visits to NATO by the Soviet, Czechoslovak, and Polish foreign ministers exemplify this broadened dialogue." In conclusion, NATO ministers expounded that "we are prepared to widen and deepen the scope of our cooperation with them [Warsaw Pact states] as they progress, thus contributing to the success of their reform programs."[66] For NATO particularly, this statement began a series of extremely important transitional steps to survive the post–Cold War world. Since the Berlin Wall's fall, the Warsaw Pact's demise, and the USSR's apparent evolution toward a much lesser threat, NATO needed to act or else devolve and disband, as alliance theory usually dictates.[67] Certainly, great debate over NATO's future survival erupted, particularly whether NATO should disband and be replaced by other institutions like the CSCE. Throughout the Cold War, Moscow had always remained keen to see NATO falter and America withdraw from Europe.[68] What quickly followed a month later, however, in terms of NATO and CSCE summits, enabled these European security institutions to transition much more effectively over the coming years. The NATO London Summit declaration particularly gave Poland and its Central European counterparts hope for their future security and stability.

Polish Visions for Central European Security Cooperation

After the early June Warsaw Pact summit and NATO ministerial meeting, the *MSZ* concertedly pursued formalizing the Central European coordination, especially cooperative security efforts. Throughout the summer and fall, the *MSZ* launched important regional cooperative initiatives with both Prague and Budapest, and toward NATO. The first initiative occurred within the context of the 10 July 1990 CSCE summit preparatory meeting in Vienna. Within a week of the Moscow Summit, Warsaw, Prague, and Berlin proposed trilaterally "the institutionalization of the pan-European process to enhance security, develop cooperation, and create a mechanism for regular meetings of leading representatives and experts from the states participating in the Helsinki" procedures. The three states also included in this proposal the establishment of a "Council for Security and Cooperation in Europe" to convene biannually at the level of foreign ministers, a consolidation and compromise by both Warsaw and Prague of the separate but similar initiatives they had promoted during the past six months. By September, in consultation with many other CSCE delegations, Polish and Austrian CSCE ambassadors jointly sponsored the final proposal that culminated the Warsaw–Prague–Berlin summer security endeavor, gained the approval of all CSCE members, and elicited praise from the Austrian ambassador. The ambassador recognized Poland's pivotal role when he described "Poland's special role in preparing the joint initiative of both states."[69]

The 5–6 July 1990 NATO London Summit also played a significant role for Poland and Central Europe. NATO's "London Declaration" gave Skubiszewski and his *MSZ* team increased links to the alliance and Central European counterparts. NATO leaders acknowledged the impact of the Central and Eastern European revolutions on European security and announced that "Europe has entered a new, promising era. Central and Eastern Europe is liberating itself. The Soviet Union has embarked on the long journey toward a free society. . . . They are choosing a Europe whole and free. As a consequence, this

Alliance must and will adapt." To adapt, NATO leaders committed themselves to implement a wholly different concept for NATO security, by "inviting [these states] to come to NATO, not just to visit, but to establish regular diplomatic liaison with NATO," both politically and militarily, "to overcome the legacy of decades of suspicion."[70] NATO's declaration marked a major step for Poland and the Central Europeans toward European reintegration. As Skubiszewski stated several weeks later, "Poland is not going to prolong artificially the Warsaw Treaty's life. It does not form today a plane of cooperation that is needed. We see cooperation on numerous planes, namely trilateral (Poland–CSFR–Hungary) but first of all, pan-European with a stress on extending ties with the European communities." Moreover, he argued that "while still remaining in the Warsaw Treaty, Poland has no political objectives other than those represented by the states belonging to NATO."[71] Additionally, he revealed that "the cooperation in the Czech, Hungarian, and Polish Triangle is getting closer. Soon, important consultations will be held in Warsaw."[72]

Several other Polish *MSZ* representatives also placed Poland and the Triangle's role toward the Warsaw Pact in perspective. Kostrzewa-Zorbas expanded on Skubiszewski's points, stating that the NATO London Summit demonstrated a turning point, not just for Poland but for NATO, too, with its "proposal of a declaration of nonaggression between the NATO and Warsaw Pact countries. . . . Such a declaration would be the cornerstone of the new Europe." European security, he argued, must focus on how NATO provides stability-enhancing measures, as the bipolar world ends and as a "single Europe bereft of divisions" emerges. As a result, he viewed the Warsaw Pact "as a group of states, joined for self-defense, created in accordance with Article 51 of the UN Charter. That is what the Warsaw Pact is, and nothing more. It is not a bloc; there is nothing political about it." In anticipation of the Pact's potential disbanding after the planned November Pact summit, Kostrzewa-Zorbas asserted that

> More and more people are inclined to believe that NATO should act as a stabilizer, offering protection against the dangers that are still occurring—internal dangers in the shape of local conflicts such as the Balkans, where these threats are the most serious, and external dangers, e.g., from the Middle East, where there are a lot of warlike regimes."[73]

This candid assessment presaged the evolution both of Poland toward NATO and of NATO's strategic transformation. By the end of August, Poland's relations with NATO advanced; Skubiszewski assigned Poland's ambassador to Belgium to the new role of diplomatic liaison to NATO in Brussels created by the London Declaration. The dual-hatted ambassador soon said,

> We foresee a gradual withdrawal from the Warsaw Pact's military structures and we can say that there is now a need for change in Poland's bilateral approach to NATO, as there is in the case of the other states in our part of the

continent the new situation has prompted—and this applies to both sides—organizational moves intended to institutionalize contacts.[74]

Finally, in a preview before the NATO secretary general's first visit to Poland in September, the *MSZ* European institutions director, Jerzy Nowak, commented that Warsaw's notions of security appeared "far ahead" of many [Western and Eastern] European states and "we cannot rule out any options, in other words a dissolution of the Warsaw Pact or our departure from it."[75]

The first visit of a NATO secretary general to Poland coincided with the confirmation of Poland's western border in the 12 September treaty on German unification. This underscored a major foreign policy success by Skubiszewski that not only reduced the tensions with Germany one year to the day after he assumed office, but also enabled him to accelerate relations with NATO. During his four-day visit, NATO secretary general Manfred Woerner met with the entire Polish leadership, including Walesa in the latter's home base of Gdansk, and jointly addressed the foreign and defense affairs committees in Parliament. Symbolically, the staunchly conservative former West German defense minister came to Warsaw to deliver the clear message Skubiszewski and many Poles wanted to hear. In his parliamentary address, he declared that "no nation can provide for its security alone or in isolation from its neighbors. Nations seeking total security by their own efforts only create insecurity around them. So we must never renationalize European security." Moreover, he defined "real security" as "achieved only through freedom, prosperity, cooperation and sharing. . . . The Alliance I have the honor to represent is open and ready to share with you the benefits of its community of security and cooperation. . . . Your country is a key partner in the building of a new Europe.[76]

For Skubiszewski's part, he reiterated that Poland, independent of a failing Warsaw Pact, focused primarily on an evolving NATO–Poland relationship. He held the secretary general's trip as "the best possible proof that the Cold War is a thing of the past and that the old confrontation ought to be converted into cooperation."[77] As Skubiszewski and Woerner met, both *MSZ* and NATO staffs "exchanged reports and proposals about NATO's stabilizational role in Europe, agreeing to the political goals of the organization," and establishing a working-level program over the next year at various levels between the Polish Government and NATO.[78] The transformed Cold Warrior Woerner remarked at the conclusion of his visit that "the government of post-Communist Poland, a Poland which is in the front line of profound changes in Central and East Europe, accepts that NATO is a stabilizing element of Europe. It considers it a permanent element in the construction of an all-European structure of security and cooperation. Our views on this issue are identical."[79] Finally, after their Gdansk meeting, Woerner and Walesa gave a press conference at which the Polish *Solidarnosc* leader stated that "the organization [NATO] which you represent has contributed much to Europe and to the world. That sort of achievement is going to be needed today and for a long time still."[80] Hence, Polish political leaders and Skubiszewski considered the secretary general's trip successful as Poland took steps toward closer NATO ties.

These statements appeared indicative of Poland's specialized role as bridge builder between East and West, nonthreatening in its strategy to reintegrate into Europe via structures such as NATO, since NATO also reached out to Moscow. Poland understood that it couldn't provide for only its security. Warsaw could attain security by bridging to other neighboring states, as part of its post-Communist other-help strategy, while building upon these bilateral and trilateral linkages toward NATO's increasingly pan-European cooperative security vision. Decisions on security and stability certainly emanated from Warsaw, but regional stabilization needed to evolve between and among the great powers which continued to dialogue within the corridors of Brussels at NATO's headquarters, its NATO ambassadors and military representatives receiving their guidance from their national capitals. NATO's evolution took many further twists and turns as evidenced by its partnership and cooperation programs that engaged more Central, Eastern, and Southeastern European, and post-Soviet nations enlarging by the late 1990s. Yet, the beginnings of this engagement and enlargement process arguably started out of capitals such as Warsaw, from the first statements by Skubiszewski who called for unified Germany as part of NATO, a call to build bridges when none declared that strategy either "East" or "West."

As Warsaw's ties to NATO advanced, its efforts to disband the Warsaw Pact increased and its synchronization within the Central European Triangle progressed. During September and October, several important senior-level meetings occurred among the Triangle states, with the growing view that all three capitals wanted to disband the Warsaw Pact at the anticipated November 1990 summit. Kostrzewa-Zorbas claimed that Poland and the Triangle states foresaw that "every one of the premises on which this Pact was based no longer exists. . . . This pact is an anachronism. . . . We do not consider the Warsaw Pact to be a political pact, and it does not affect our field of consultation. We desire the liquidation of all military coordinating structures." Moreover, he emphasized that "it is true that a growing number of people view NATO, especially if it is considerably altered, as a factor stabilizing the situation in Europe. . . . Nowadays we must view differently the military alignments formed in previous decades and carry out a fundamental revision of strategic assumptions."[81]

By mid-September the first meeting of the Warsaw Pact Provisional Commission convened and the Triangle capitals circulated a joint draft for changing the Pact into a "purely advisory" body. The Hungarian ambassador represented the three states and described the Triangle's objective to "devote more attention and more energy to the creation of Europe-wide structures" because "the framework of the Warsaw Treaty has been exhausted." In response, the Soviet ambassador depicted the Triangle's assessment as "premature," but affirmed that Moscow intended to "honor the commitments undertaken within the alliance." The meeting ended, however, inconclusively, with the USSR indicating that the upcoming November Budapest summit remained in doubt as a result of the un-expected Triangle initiative.[82] The Soviet reaction only galvanized the Triangle capitals to coordinate more closely, without consulting Moscow, and, led by the Poles, two October meetings occurred at the level of vice ministers of defense and vice ministers of foreign affairs.

At a low-key meeting in Zakopane, Poland, of Triangle vice defense minis-ters, some important interaction at the working level began to occur without Warsaw Pact constraints. The three civilian deputy defense ministers and their general staff counterparts met ostensibly to discuss education, culture, training, and military chaplain work. Polish vice defense minister Bronislaw Ko-morowski, appointed as the second vice minister that spring with Onyszkiewicz, and Brigadier General Krzysztof Owczarek, chief of the Polish Armed Forces Training Department, led the first formal high-level Triangle meeting. None of the participants revealed very much to the press, except for Komorowski, who retorted that "nothing in the military takes place by accident" when asked if it was a coincidence that the Zakopane meeting occurred during the Polish defense minister's trip to Prague. After the meeting, the delegations drove to Warsaw for an unplanned meeting with the Polish defense minister, who had returned that day from Prague, diverging from what one Polish newspaper analyzed as the low-profile intent of the meeting.[83]

When the next Triangle meeting occurred, this time among foreign ministry officials, it set the stage for their leaders to convene informally at the November CSCE summit. On 17 October 1990, Vice Foreign Minister Jerzy Makarczyk met with his Triangle counterparts in Warsaw. The goal focused on creating a consultative committee mechanism at the deputy foreign ministerial level in order "to facilitate the solution of common problems in the region." The vice ministers agreed to establish working groups, not only to prepare what later be-came the Visegrad Declaration, but also to implement regular Triangle meet-ings.[84]

Within a month, Mazowiecki met with Havel and Antall during the Paris-based CSCE summit. They discussed regional cooperation as a means to con-front multilateral problems. Importantly, Mazowiecki related that the three Cen-tral European leaders committed their states to stronger cooperation in the Council of Europe and toward membership in the EC, while underlining that "we will also work together to guarantee the security of our region." To expedite this cooperation, all three leaders assented to hold summits in Visegrad, Hun-gary, and then Krakow, Poland, the objectives "to conclude a joint agreement but also to formulate a system of bilateral treaties strongly linking our coun-tries."[85] For Mazowiecki, however, this Triangle gathering proved to be his final trilateral event, as he lost the presidential election to Walesa shortly after the CSCE summit. Opposition from Moscow also continued to delay the final War-saw Pact summit, at which the Triangle still expected formally to eliminate the Pact, but did not prevent the Triangle from institutionalizing its cooperation at the beginning of 1991.

The Visegrad Triangle Promotes
Cooperative Security

As 1991 began, the three Triangle foreign ministers resolutely solidified their regional cooperation, particularly because of their grave concern over Moscow's conservative turn. Once Soviet foreign minister Shevardnadze resigned in December 1990, warning of the coming dictatorship of the military and security apparatus, the Central European leaderships took even more seriously the necessity to disband the Pact. They remained concerned about their bilateral linkages to a threatening USSR and wanted to begin to consider more seriously how each of the three states necessitated renegotiation of their respective USSR friendship and cooperation treaties. With regard to a strategy for European reintegration, Skubiszewski realized that he needed to navigate, along with his Central European counterparts, the objectives of expanding relations with neighboring states such as the USSR and increasing ties to NATO.

The Polish foreign minister and his Prague and Budapest counterparts determined to steer their respective foreign policies toward both the West and East cautiously and pragmatically. Instead of balancing the West and East against one other, they tried to promote a bridge between Western states and Moscow, primarily through economic incentives for intermediate trade and political declarations of peaceful intentions. Yet, in the wake of Shevardnadze's resignation, Walesa's election, Soviet military violence in Vilnius, and the war in the Persian Gulf, Skubiszewski faced a myriad of uncertainties. He and his Triangle interlocutors still waited for NATO to define its priorities for NATO–Central European relations and responded in ways they thought appropriate to support NATO positions.[86] At the same time, Skubiszewski and the *MSZ* continued the momentum of regional security cooperation, pointing toward the Visegrad Summit, even through the Warsaw Pact summit remained indefinitely postponed.

Both domestic and regional concerns challenged Skubiszewski to weigh issues simultaneously for how best to plan the Visegrad Summit with his Central European colleagues. The Prague leadership became very apprehensive in late December about the potential for increased refugee flows from the growing upheaval in the USSR. As a result, Foreign Minister Dienstbier invited Polish and Hungarian vice foreign ministers for a series of consultations, which ultimately evolved into the first rounds of foreign and defense ministerial meetings, starting in late January.[87] Simultaneously, Walesa's presidential victory disrupted the hitherto smooth regional cooperation because he believed his international reputation held him in much higher esteem than his Central European counterparts. His staff decided to try to postpone the Visegrad Summit indefinitely. Some Polish analysts observed that some of Walesa's pro-Soviet advisors influenced the *Solidarnosc* leader to project submissiveness to Moscow, verging on neutralizing Polish foreign policy—Finlandizing it—rather than promote what synchronized and regional stability-enhancing behavior through Warsaw–Prague–Budapest ties. Skubiszewski remained consistent and practical, attempting to advance linkages to the Central European Triangle. During this period the president's chancellery also tried to postpone indefinitely all of Walesa's foreign trips because of the "tense international situation," particularly given the Soviet killings in Lithuania and the Gulf War. With Prague's anxiety rising, Skubiszewski used the pretext to send Vice Minister Makarczyk, Kostrzewa-Zorbas, and other *MSZ* staff to various consultations abroad and via the CSFR and Hungarian embassies in Warsaw, to maintain planning for the Visegrad Summit.[88] He hoped to convince the president about the Visegrad Summit and soon prevailed, as all three Visegrad foreign ministers and their respective leaders moved toward final planning for mid-February, while the Warsaw Pact summit remained uncertain.

In the aftermath of the Soviet military violence in Vilnius, Skubiszewski also responded to some impulsive moves by CSFR foreign minister Dienstbier regarding the formal disbanding of the Warsaw Pact at the Visegrad Summit. The Polish foreign minister felt that any Warsaw Pact issues needed to remain separate from the Visegrad Summit so that all three states might strengthen their cooperation in order to negotiate more firmly with the Soviets at the Warsaw Pact summit. As he stated to the Polish press on 14 January, "we must deal with the question of the Warsaw Pact without further delay, but separately" from the Visegrad Summit. Moreover, to minimize potential recriminations by Moscow against Poland and the other Central Europeans because of their criticism of the Baltic violence, he explained that "Poland will not link the Lithuanian issue with Polish withdrawal from the Warsaw Pact."[89] Similarly, he indicated that the first foreign ministerial meeting in Budapest, to prepare the Visegrad Summit Declaration, underscored "the issue of dismantling the military structure and through this finally putting an end to the Warsaw Pact [which] is much older than the Lithuanian crisis."[90] Clearly, Skubiszewski attempted to achieve several important objectives at once. He wanted to institutionalize the regional cooperative process, particularly its coordination on security issues; convince Moscow to hold the Warsaw Pact summit; and grapple with the Baltic tragedy with the best diplomacy, given Moscow's increasingly worrisome hard-liners. By not attempting to balance against Moscow, but realizing that an other-help strategy remained his only feasible option, that is, synchronizing cooperative security efforts with Central European counterparts while NATO's great powers dealt with the USSR about NATO's future, Skubiszewski sought to promulgate stability-enhancing measures. Therefore, all three Central European states worked together during January 1991 to commit whatever political and military support was possible to the American-led coalition against Iraq, as war appeared imminent. Notably, the USSR also supported the coalition led by the United States to remove the Iraqi Army from Kuwait.[91]

The first Triangle foreign ministerial meeting convened in Budapest on 24 January to complete the drafting of the Visegrad Declaration and to coordinate positions among the three states before their leaders met several weeks later. As Skubiszewski remarked after this initial meeting, "a declaration is being prepared—the result of rather lengthy work, which is to determine the three states' common aims, aspirations, and interests." Moreover, the Polish foreign minister argued in favor of an "all-European system of democratic relations," not "to reinstate a protective cordon to the west of the USSR," especially not one symbolizing a zone of neutrality.[92] Viewed by some USSR commentators as a "tripartite union" designed to overcome "Moscow's gravitation force," the foreign ministerial gathering did produce a path-breaking joint communiqué that expressed "deep concern" about the January 1991 violence in Lithuania. In it, the ministers stated that "this attempt to reverse the peaceful transition to democracy. . . . threatens stability in Central and Eastern Europe." Above all, Skubiszewski maintained that "cooperation involving Poland, the CSFR, and Hungary is very important. Our countries possess definite potential, they have similar, coincident, and, in a number of matters, identical interests, and they are trying to develop a new regional cooperation in this part of the European continent. It strengthens European cooperation and meets our varied interests."[93]

This strategy carefully undergirded the bridge building and regionally cooperative security initiatives that Warsaw had promoted since the early stages of its post-Communist transition in the fall of 1989. Though the USSR showed many strains of disintegration throughout 1990 and 1991, residual Soviet military power certainly worried Warsaw and the other Triangle capitals. They definitely looked to the Western great powers, particularly via NATO, to move the rapidly changing European security system favorably toward Central and Eastern Europe. Yet, the Central Europeans also understood that European security depended on Moscow's participation in this revolutionary process and that hardline Soviet leaders negated the progressive stances taken by Gorbachev and the emerging non-Soviet Russian and non-Russian republic leaders. Skubiszewski and his *MSZ* staff possessed the important insight from Poland's two-track Eastern policy that reformers existed in Russia and Ukraine who wanted political "bridges" built to the West via Poland. They related this keen understanding to their Western and Eastern counterparts consistently. They worried that, without a transformed NATO, European security and stability threatened to cascade into violence, as witnessed by the violence in Lithuania and growing fissures in what became former Yugoslavia, as the world's attention also turned to the Persian Gulf. Though they didn't promote balancing initiatives against the USSR, the Polish leadership, with Skubiszewski's Polish strategy underlining the benefits of cooperative security, advocated a strong Western pillar to tie Moscow to Europe. The goal remained to avoid isolating Moscow while building a new Europe based on pragmatic ties, not historically confrontational alliances, and especially not competing bilateral and trilateral pacts. The bottom line focused on the Polish strategy to implement its middle power role as a specializing interlocutor and link for great powers because it realized it couldn't defend its own security for very long.

Given these realities, Skubiszewski still did encounter difficult policy disputes domestically. Though Walesa and his advisors agreed to meet in Visegrad several weeks after the Triangle's 24 January foreign ministerial meeting, the Polish leader appeared to bow to some Soviet pressure. Before his departure, he stated that "Poland is interested in the development of relations with the CSFR and Hungary, but it does not want to conclude an organized alliance with them just now." He focused on the "great differences between these countries, particularly in the economic spheres, and only when a certain balance is established can a formal alliance be considered."[94] The Polish president's statements hindered Skubiszewski's strategy, as well, but for different reasons. Skubiszewski never intended the Visegrad cooperation to become an alliance and, though differences remained among the three Central European states, he constantly sought to display unity or purpose and peaceful intent. Whenever possible, he tried to lessen the policy differences publicly and promote the regional cooperative efforts toward East and West.

Walesa's statement at least revealed his turnaround and newfound commitment to hold the Visegrad Summit, a momentum created by the late January Triangle foreign ministerial meeting. These developments finally spurred Gorbachev to realize that Moscow needed to do something to supersede Visegrad and could no longer delay the Warsaw Pact summit; the Soviets would lose the otherwise last semblance of control over their nominal "allies." In a letter dated 12 February and delivered to Warsaw the next day, the day Walesa and the Polish leadership departed for the Visegrad Summit, Gorbachev resorted to a new strategy aimed at reviving Soviet control over the three Central European states bilaterally. Importantly, however, he yielded to the Triangle's near fait accompli to disband the Pact. He wrote that he now expected the dissolution of the Pact's military structures, a defeat as a result of the Triangle initiatives in the Pact's "review" commission during the past several months. At the same time, he declared "it would also require the appropriate response of the NATO member states," a statement almost certainly at odds with the Triangle's position. Moreover, his letter tacitly admitted failure in the Soviet attempt to postpone indefinitely the Pact summit. He yielded by "advising to organize" a late February foreign and defense ministerial meeting, not a summit, to resolve "relevant decisions." Finally, the letter portended a protracted and new political battle between Moscow and the Central European states. Gorbachev underlined that "as regards the future development of relations among the Pact member states, they should in our opinion be quickly switched onto a track of bilateral relations, taking into account, in each individual case, the new internal and international conditions."[95] Although Skubiszewski's strategy originally concentrated on developing bilateral ties to great powers to reduce regional tension and hostility, he also acknowledged that trilateral efforts to pursue multilateral and institutional cooperative security strategies lay at the heart of Poland's stability. Moscow's signaling of tough and hard-line efforts to revert to bilateral security negotiations gave Poland much to consider in the months ahead.

Gorbachev's political and military salvo certainly proved an unexpected development, but failed to disrupt the three Central European leaderships from gathering at the historic town of Visegrad for their summit from 13 to 15 February. Before his departure from Warsaw, President Walesa commented on the acceleration of the Central European cooperation, illustrating important insights for his Visegrad counterparts, Moscow, and Western leaderships. Walesa said, "we are now on our way out of a bloc that was imposed on us. . . . We do not want to act against anyone, as was the norm against us. We must do everything to preserve our freedom, but we should not quarrel with other countries." To eliminate misperceptions by Moscow or Western states about the objectives of Central European regional collaboration, Walesa stressed that "we are not preparing a political pact, but we must guarantee the values that connect us. We will jointly protect these values and will support each other in this endeavor [because] we are closer to each other than to the West." Importantly, he also tried to preempt criticism about what Visegrad represented militarily by declaring that "we should not represent any threat to Germany, the Soviet Union, or to each other. In military terms, we must deploy for defense, rather than offense, not against someone, but to deter, and to preserve our revolutions, our democratic achievements, and our development." He argued, therefore, that, "for this reason, we must think about how to develop our economic, political, and other relations, so we have a faster transition to the level of the Western countries."[96]

Out of the Visegrad Summit came two significant documents, a "Ceremonial Declaration" and a "Summit Declaration." Each crystallized the Triangle's synchronized cooperation. In the "Ceremonial Declaration," Walesa, Havel, and Antall pledged to uphold "the historical traditions connecting us, and in harmony with traditional European values and dominant trends, to do everything in our power for the peace, security and development of our nations."[97] After weeks of coordination, the three leaders also signed the "Summit Declaration," a watershed that formalized their yearlong informal cooperation process. Furthermore, the summit underscored a victory for the *MSZ* because its initiative to include the security dimension of relations became an integral part of the process at Visegrad. The declaration said security "cooperation represents an important step on the path towards all-European integration." Moreover, the three states undertook to "harmonize efforts . . . to establish cooperation and close relations with European institutions and hold consultations on matters relating to their security."[98] To preserve their democratic processes, the Visegrad states used the summit to highlight cross-border political, economic, security, and sociocultural cooperation, reform in the USSR, and Central Europe's reintegration into Europe. For all three states the cooperative Visegrad process allowed them to fortify their positions vis-à-vis Moscow, especially since Soviet military forces remained on their territories and, in Poland's case, Moscow refused to reach a force withdrawal agreement.[99]

The Visegrad leaders also wanted to demonstrate to NATO leaders the stress they placed on their European reintegration. They declared that "in a united Europe, to the construction of which all the three states wish to contribute actively, the universal system of humanist values can be pursued without prejudice to national culture, along with all national characteristics." These words underlined that "we should seek to build a community of people cooperating harmoniously, tolerant of each other and of individual families and local, regional, and ethnic communities, free of hatred, nationalism, xenophobia, and feuds between neighbors."[100] Finally, the Visegrad states agreed that their cooperation now focused on comprehensive consultations at many different governmental and nongovernmental levels, with the objective that "cooperation shall in no way hinder or restrain relations with other countries and shall not be directed against anyone's interests."[101] Therefore, as German unification and Soviet disintegration continued to transform the turbulent European security landscape, the summit resulted in a more formalized consultative process by which Visegrad leaders sought to coordinate more effectively—a cooperative capacity they employed two weeks later during the Warsaw Pact summit.

On 25 February in Budapest, the Warsaw Pact's foreign and defense ministers met to disband the Warsaw Pact's military structures. This momentous event occurred because the Triangle maintained a unified front politically toward Moscow. By dissolving the Pact's military organization, the ministers ended nearly forty years of what the post-Communist states considered "discredited illegal practices" and Soviet authoritarian rule. In determining the requirements for post–Cold War European security, Skubiszewski declared, "the new international structure of our region will be founded on modified bilateral relations, on a new regionalism and on an emerging all-European system." To uphold the fundamental tenets of his overall foreign policy, he stated, "we are ready for cooperation taking account of new circumstances, based on mutual respect and on full compliance with international law." Whereas Skubiszewski wanted a demarcation for how Pact states needed to conduct "businesslike" relations, he also recognized that Soviet strategy sought to regain control. In anticipation of such Soviet moves, he tried to dissuade Moscow from taking such steps and to caution the other states. In his speech, he argued that each Pact member maintained its sovereignty and each needed to respect international law in cooperating with one another. Irrespective of future ties, Skubiszewski said that Poland continued to "respect the interests of others." He cautioned, however, that "we shall demand the same attitude to our own affairs." Lastly, he asserted that "Central Europe cannot become a neutral or buffer zone" and argued that any future bilateral cooperation treaties should be based on "security in the broad sense." For the foreign minister, it remained important to "go beyond the strictly military and defense sphere" so that "economic, social, and ecological security [become] indispensable in order to ensure political stability on the European continent."[102] Though his statement indicated Poland's direction for European security, Skubiszewski and his Visegrad colleagues found it difficult to specify the means by which Central European cooperation needed to evolve. Meanwhile, the pressure from Moscow continued and the issue of renegotiating friendship and cooperation treaties tested the formalized Visegrad consultation.

In the aftermath of the Visegrad Summit and Warsaw Pact ministerial meeting, Central Europeans strove to clarify how they foresaw the Visegrad security process functioning, particularly in response to crises affecting their states, either separately or collectively. Antall tried to clarify any misperceptions that the Triangle represented an integrated alliance. He stressed that the primary purpose of the Visegrad "Declaration of Cooperation" focused on facilitating the Triangle members' "association status" with the EC and that Europe need not see the Visegrad consultative process as a "new organization."[103] By comparison, Havel offered a more concerted view toward security cooperation when he revealed that if Central Europe faced an "external threat," its leaders believed trilateral consultation included "mutual assistance or something similar" to each other. Moreover, he reconciled himself to the reality that NATO first needed to decide "whether to accept us [and] the process of joining NATO would take several years." As a result, Havel saw Visegrad consultation as the best means by which to cooperate in crisis.[104] In Poland's case, Skubiszewski defined the Triangle not as a "military alliance," but as a mechanism for "loose cooperation." To lessen apprehension by Moscow, he anticipated increased "stability" and "security" in Central Europe, but also maintained that Visegrad states required bilateral military agreements to cooperate and promote transparency the way Western states function democratically.[105]

Skubiszewski raised the issue of military cooperation as a lever for European militaries to cooperate. His rationale focused on the need for Central European militaries, like any democratizing and Western European militaries, to defend against new threats from states not involved in international arms control regimes such as the CFE Treaty.[106]

Negotiating Security Treaties from Positions of Strength

With the formal synchronization of the Visegrad cooperative security process in early 1991, the three Central European states increased their coordination on a unified bridging strategy toward Moscow. Their main concern stemmed from the protracted and controversial negotiations of the new bilateral friendship and cooperation treaties sought by the USSR as the CMEA and Warsaw Pact formally dissolved.[107] Between winter 1990 and fall 1991, each Triangle nation negotiated tenaciously against the consistent pressuring by Soviet hard-liners. Moscow's negotiators wanted to maintain specific control mechanisms over their soon-to-be-former Warsaw Pact satellites. The Soviets attempted political maneuvers to coerce each Visegrad state separately. Importantly, the contentious bargaining between Warsaw and Moscow to obtain an equitable friendship treaty not only demonstrated that the Visegrad cooperative security process functioned effectively, but also provided another pertinent example of asymmetrical negotiation theory. Though Triangle states negotiated separately with Moscow, Poland formulated its strategy trilaterally in intervals between each respective negotiation's stages.[108]

The steps taken during the respective negotiation processes underline a series of moves and countermoves that resulted in another unconventional, if unanticipated, outcome in the quickly disintegrating Cold War context. The importance of similar histories of Soviet intervention or the threat of Soviet military intervention in each Visegrad state—Hungary in 1956, Czechoslovakia in 1968, and Poland in 1980–1981—contributed to the "bonding" process and "motivational orientations" among post-Communist Triangle negotiators.[109] The personal characteristics of grit, determination, cohesiveness, regional focus, and independent-mindedness manifested the dichotomy between Central Europe and the USSR.[110] Certainly, the objectives by the post-Communist Triangle states to reintegrate into Europe and to attain membership eventually in European institutions placed them in an awkward position vis-à-vis the USSR. Indeed, Moscow determined to obtain new treaties, especially to include security clauses to limit the sovereignty of each Triangle state. Yet, initial hard-line Soviet demands to control negotiation terms only served to stiffen Triangle determination to reverse the Soviet tactics.

Until the August 1991 aborted Soviet coup d'état, the Soviet Ministry of Foreign Affairs, Central Committee, and General Staff insisted on security clauses to negotiate new and individual friendship and cooperation treaties with Warsaw, Prague, and Budapest. Even after the dissolution of the Warsaw Pact and CMEA in 1991, Soviet Central Committee International Relations Department chief Valentin Falin and his hard-line staff maintained primacy over the foreign ministry in handling relations with Central and Eastern Europe.[111] Falin's staff wrote a significant document on Soviet strategy toward Central and Eastern Europe in January 1991. The document actually appeared in the Central Committee's unclassified journal in March 1991. Though Deputy Foreign Minister Iulii Kvitsinskii disagreed with the Falin strategy of prohibiting the Visegrad states from establishing relations with alliances Moscow viewed as hostile, he nevertheless played a key role in implementing the hard-line policy.[112] As the Central Europeans attested, the "Falin–Kvitsinskii Doctrine" of "Finlandization" replaced the void left by the rescinded "Brezhnev Doctrine."[113] In the document, the hard-liners lashed out at those Central and East European leaderships who conceivably threatened "the military security of the USSR" through their contacts and increasing ties to Western organizations and governments.[114]

The document also elaborated several objectives that seriously threatened the sovereignty and independence of Central and Eastern Europe. According to the Polish *MSZ* negotiating team,[115] Moscow expected Central and Eastern European states "not to join alliances that might jeopardize the security of the other party." This warning implied that "the other party" delineated "acceptable" and "unacceptable alliances." Furthermore, the Soviet document declared that Warsaw Pact states must "not embark on similarly 'unacceptable' military and intelligence[116] cooperation with third parties." Additionally, Moscow required the Warsaw Pact states "not to invite foreign armed forces to deploy on their territory (presumably, Soviet forces were not entirely foreign), and particularly to use for such a purpose the bases left or expected to be left by the Soviet Army." Moreover, the "Falin-Kvitsinskii line necessitated the guarantee of free transit through territory according to the other side's [Moscow's] needs— freedom of military transit was not excluded." Finally, Soviet hard-liners underlined the need "to reinvigorate scientific cooperation" to reduce any dependence on Western technology. Not only did these security clauses nullify European reintegration by Central and East Europe, but the Soviet demands also bound Poland on Soviet force withdrawals, an extremely controversial matter in Warsaw when this document surfaced.[117]

Even though Polish negotiators received their first drafts of the hard-line treaty from Soviet negotiators only in early 1991, the Triangle's close coordination had allowed the Poles in December 1990 to obtain a copy from the Hungarians, who were the first to acquire the Soviet document. By the time the Visegrad Summit convened, Skubiszewski and the *MSZ* already grasped the extent of the Soviet strategy to renegotiate the 1965 bilateral treaty. In his speech to the Polish Sejm on 14 February 1991, the foreign minister outlined his strategy, declaring that Moscow recognized the need to devise a treaty that reflected the "present-day realities," one that necessitated the "regulation of our cooperation and good-neighborly relations in a comprehensive manner." However, he argued that "membership in an organized Europe and at the same time maintenance of links with the East stand for the role Poland is to play for the reason of her geostrategic and geopolitical position. . . . Poland should do more as a link between the USSR and Western Europe."[118] Thus, Skubiszewski's bridging strategy depended not on submitting to Moscow's goal of limiting Triangle reintegration into Europe, but on still serving as a bridge for Moscow to Europe.

Just after the respective treaty renegotiations began between Moscow and each Triangle capital in March, Skubiszewski again spoke to the Sejm and divulged that "the three state's policies on security are coordinated on an ongoing basis." He also praised the regional cooperative achievement in the dissolution of the Warsaw Pact and elaborated on the importance of cooperation on the "views and experiences pertaining to the withdrawal of Soviet forces, an issue on which Poland finds itself in a different, more difficult position than Hungary and Czechoslovakia." Specifically, Skubiszewski detailed the withdrawal problems which Budapest and Prague helped Warsaw to reduce via Triangle coordination. He disclosed that all three states had compared and contrasted "assessments regarding the value of the assets left behind by the Soviet Army, the question of outstanding financial settlements, and the issue of compensation for environmental damage." Particularly important for Warsaw remained Prague's support not to permit Soviet transits from Eastern Germany, unless synchronized with Polish negotiators. Unlike German negotiators, who dealt exclusively with Moscow until the late August Soviet plot, Poland and the CSFR maintained withdrawal coordination. Above all, Skubiszewski held that "the consultations that the three states hold on the clauses concerning security in the accords that each of the states will conclude with the Soviet Union are a matter of fundamental importance."[119] Such consultation reinforced Poland's confidence in the difficult and protracted treaty deliberations that lasted from spring to summer 1991.

From March 1991 to December 1991, Moscow and the Visegrad Triangle states debated their respective drafts of the new Soviet-initiated bilateral friendship and cooperation treaties, particularly the disputed security clauses. Each draft contained identical demands based on what one Polish negotiator described as "post–Warsaw Pact principles of relationships obliging the parties of each intended treaty" to conform.[120] As the negotiations continued into the summer of 1991, however, the Triangle negotiators placed the onus on Soviet negotiators to extract steeper concessions. By adopting a similar tough line and challenging the Soviet position, like the strategy implemented during the Warsaw Pact negotiations, the Triangle negotiators constructed common solutions in response to these common problems. It followed, therefore, that throughout each of the three negotiations with Moscow, Warsaw's senior and mid-level officials ensured that periodic Triangle consultations occurred to compare positions, strategies, and difficulties, in order to develop common approaches for the next respective set of treaty negotiations. Consultations focused on comparing preliminary texts and coordinating similar drafts among the three capitals before one Triangle member would return to negotiate with the Soviets.[121] In this manner, the Triangle again showed how its multilateral, regional cooperation bolstered the leverage each state used during the bilateral talks with Soviet counterparts. Ultimately, the Triangle determined the negotiation terms of trade and rejected the security clauses as an infringement on sovereignty.[122]

Bilateral negotiations coordinated among the Visegrad members to yield a common strategy during negotiations resulted in several friendship and cooperation agreements with Moscow after the August coup, making obsolete the ones with the USSR government. Antagonism and toughness shaped Triangle strategy toward Moscow, together and in coordination between individual negotiating sessions. In the end, the best trade-off became the Triangle's willingness and flexibility to give Moscow its three new friendship and cooperation security treaties, but on the Triangle's terms.[123] The Triangle states gained a more "valued position" after "Soviet" Moscow, weakened by the internal demise of the Soviet Union in the fall of 1991, gave up its originally belligerent stipulations in order to obtain individual treaties.[124] Finally, these agreements exemplified to many Western European and North American policymakers that the Visegrad regional collaboration meant more than overseeing the demise of the Warsaw Pact.[125] It testified to the Triangle's substantive foundation and constructive role in European security. More importantly, the period from 1990 to 1991 demonstrated that Poland's determination to develop the Visegrad regional cooperative security process set a good foundation for reintegration into Europe.

Polish Strategy for European Reintegration

In coordinating key aspects of its national security strategy with Hungary and the CSFR toward the USSR, Poland believed that it also aided ties to European institutions. Characterized by Skubiszewski's step-by-step strategy that prioritized regional cooperation over "go it alone" policymaking, Poland formulated with Visegrad colleagues its increased efforts on European reintegration.[126] Poland acknowledged that it needed other help in developing its European integration strategy. Thus, in serving as a middle power bridge rather than as a barrier, Poland, along with its smaller power Visegrad counterparts, projected a much better prospect of gaining support by European, American, and Russian great powers. By late 1991, Russian reformers indicated their strong promotion of European integration, too, at least in the early post-Communist Russian transition.

The *MSZ*'s December 1990 initiative to forge a Central European cooperative security consultative process and to strengthen it in the February 1991 Visegrad Declaration provided the basis for Skubiszewski's European Directorate to draft a March 1991 memorandum on Poland's regional security strategy. The *MSZ*'s analysis provided a framework to facilitate European reintegration without threatening Moscow and offered the vision of long-term NATO membership with short-term close NATO ties beyond liaison missions.[127] Certainly, during the winter and spring of 1991 the *MSZ* understood that NATO membership remained a long-term goal since the key NATO great powers remained focused on the U.S.-led coalition in the Gulf War and were concerned about the conservative turn in the USSR. Consequently, NATO members remained averse to further NATO enlargement, except in the unique case of the GDR's integration into the alliance. In frustration, however, the *MSZ*'s memorandum also underscored the necessity to avoid Soviet "Finlandization" during the renegotiation of the bilateral security treaties by establishing NATO-Central European "treaties of democracy." This bold initiative focused on creating explicit arrangements for Central European linkages to NATO based on NATO's institutional principles of like-minded democratic and free market systems, enshrined in the 1949 Washington treaty. Well ahead of nearly all initiatives from senior NATO staff and individual NATO member capitals, the *MSZ* provided specific ways for Warsaw, Prague, and Budapest to integrate into NATO, especially as Polish politicians began public debates on NATO's merits.[128]

The first public debates on NATO membership by Polish politicians emanated from the call by Jaroslaw Kaczynski at the First National Congress of the Center Alliance. This staunchly center-right party increasingly criticized Skubiszewski's foreign policy for not moving quickly enough to advocate

NATO membership and a more concerted Eastern policy toward the emerging non-Soviet republic leaderships. At the congress, Kaczynski declared that "in connection with the need to establish a new system of security in Central Europe, which cannot be done without NATO, we must attach particular importance to our relations with the U.S." For these prominent national security and foreign policy specialists in the Center Alliance's congress the impetus given to the NATO debate provided the foundation for their strong NATO advocates like Kaczynski, Najder, and Jan Parys to advocate from senior policy positions in what became Jan Olszewski's government in late 1991.[129]

Skubiszewski's regional cooperative security strategy between East and West, however, sought continually to buttress Poland's role, particularly within the Triangle framework, as a bridge for cooperation and integration, not to balance to disrupt Soviet and Central–East European ties to Western institutions. From the winter to the summer of 1991, he articulated the important argument "based on the assumption that NATO, as the pillar of European security cannot remain indifferent to security in Central and Eastern Europe."[130] Finally, by June 1991, Skubiszewski's reiteration of this theme began to resonate as NATO foreign ministers pledged to link NATO's "own security inseparably to that of all other states in Europe." The NATO declaration from Copenhagen, Denmark, added "the consolidation and preservation throughout the continent of democratic societies and their freedom from any form of coercion or intimidation are therefore of direct and material concern to us, as they are to all other CSCE states under the commitments of the Helsinki Final Act and Charter of Paris."[131] Though the NATO declaration remained vague about specific measures to consolidate and preserve security of nonmember states, the Visegrad states welcomed the decision to oppose coercion and intimidation, at least as NATO members defined it in principle. Given how far NATO came institutionally to support closer and more concerted linkages to Poland and other former Warsaw Pact nations, this NATO declaration marked a key point in the membership debate for former NATO enemies.

At the same time, though, some Soviet security specialists cautiously and surprisingly supported the evolving Triangle cooperation, while others expressed age-old fears and concerns about Western intentions. One prominent Soviet journalist and informal Gorbachev advisor on national security, Aleksandr Bovin, believed that Triangle cooperation enhanced security and stability in terms of increased commercial, technological, ecological, agricultural, and cultural ties.[132] Another long-time Soviet political analyst and important Gorbachev foreign policy advisor, Nikolai Shishlin, dismissed any concern over a possible threat to the USSR and stated that "the Prague-Budapest-Warsaw Triangle presents no danger whatsoever, especially from the point of view of security policy for the Soviet Union." Further, he said some Soviet policymakers remain "contaminated by imperial thinking [and] continue to consider Eastern Europe as their own sphere of interest, without even thinking through as to what the real interest in this region is for the Soviet Union."[133] Other Soviet views also underlined the need to overcome "the bloc mentality so deeply ingrained in our consciousness that we sometimes keep faith with it even when we want to say the opposite." Yet, other Soviet analysts opposed Triangle efforts to increase ties to NATO, fearing that such a strategy ultimately allowed for the possibility of NATO to survive, especially if the alliance integrated former Warsaw Pact members.[134]

Although security specialists from both the USSR and Triangle states generally insisted that regional security could not occur in a post–Cold War and post–Warsaw Pact security "vacuum," several Soviet experts advocated views ranging from no new NATO or EC membership for former Warsaw Pact states to the abolition of NATO. One Soviet view advocated the "preservation of the consultative structure" based on the Warsaw Pact's old mechanism for exchanges of information in lieu of the "dash toward Europe" and establishment of new security ties.[135] This argument assumed that political, economic, and ethnic instability in the Triangle states precluded membership in NATO and the EC.[136] To a certain extent, this Soviet reasoning, albeit soon overtaken by the USSR's collapse, recognized some of the historical problems and enmities stirring beneath the surface in the Triangle and regionally. The arguments revolved around some very serious regional tensions, such as the possible breakdown between the Czech lands and Slovakia, and rising concerns over an economically strained Polish economy. Poland appeared caught between a stabilizing, powerful unified Germany and emerging Baltic states, while instability grew in restive Russia, Belorussia, and Ukraine. Moreover, civil war in Yugoslavia and unrest in Romania bordering an anxious Hungary made southeast Europe even more destabilizing to European security. These regional security pitfalls only led to more instability, argued these Soviet assessments. Another Soviet commentator expressed concern that the Triangle's "orientation" toward Western Europe and its democratic societies pushed it into NATO, directly threatening the USSR's Central European borders.[137] Such analysis represented Soviet Communist Party hard-line thinking, anathema to the Central European states for its imposed "loyalty" and "protection" by the Warsaw Pact and the USSR, particularly Soviet troops remaining on Poland's territory after forty-five years.

Yet, the Triangle's stance to reintegrate into Europe and to uphold the NATO London and Copenhagen Declarations caused other Soviet commentators to contend that NATO and CSCE must change even more dramatically. Reactions from Moscow to the changes in NATO's political and military policies favored USSR participation in a future European security architecture that deemphasized NATO and promoted CSCE.[138] For one of the most prominent Soviet and international security experts, Sergei Karaganov, the CSCE defined the only European structure to serve as an umbrella organization for the United States, the USSR, and other European states.[139] He stressed that the CSCE also signified a mechanism for combining discussions on political, economic, ethnic, and environmental issues. Instead of joining the current structure of NATO, Karaganov enunciated the official Soviet "vision" to divert Triangle members from their NATO focus. He wanted to forge what Moscow envisaged as a "collective security agreement" founded on "complementing the Helsinki Final Act." Taken within the "security" context that Karaganov promoted, that is, diluting NATO's raison d'être for collective defense, the CSCE defined a collective European security mechanism in which individual states or groups of countries might seek "security guarantees" and "legal help." According to this strategy, Europe needed to avoid a new "iron curtain" by "the gradual expansion of West European security structures into Central and Eastern Europe," in which the CSCE absorbed NATO and effectively attenuated its collective defense requirements.[140] In response, the Visegrad states steadfastly rejected the notion that NATO required its post–Cold War mission to exclude collective defense because "collective security" failed to guarantee individual nation-state security. Without collective defense against unconventional threats beyond the Cold War, Central Europeans felt that Europe might descend into competitive counterbalancing nations, again.

Indeed, in contrast to his statements in early 1991, Polish president Walesa, when first traveling to NATO headquarters on 3 July 1991, echoed the revisions Skubiszewski and the *MSZ* staff made to his important speech. Behind the scenes, though, Skubiszewski needed to maneuver with Walesa's pro-Soviet advisors to ensure the *MSZ*'s language made it into the speech.[141] The Polish president underscored NATO "as the main pillar of the European security system." Furthermore, the *MSZ* ensured Walesa's speech contained the phrase that Poland wanted NATO "preserved" and that Warsaw "shares the credo and also shares the political goals of the Alliance." Given the increasingly conservative turn in Moscow and its arguments against NATO's role in post–Cold War European security, the *MSZ* also got Walesa's staff to accept the language that "the security of the Central European region" remained "indivisible." Moreover, the *MSZ* recommendations included the passage "that is why at Visegrad we stressed cooperation among Poland, Czechoslovakia, and Hungary as the basis of security (and other goals) in the region. . . . But, without a secure Poland and a secure Central Europe, there can be no secure, stable Europe." Finally, consistent with Skubiszewski's determination for step-by-step European reintegration, the *MSZ* succeeded in getting Walesa's staff to incorporate the statement that "our goal is integration with Europe. An essential element of this effort is cooperation and ties with NATO."[142] Clearly, disputes continued within Poland's highest political circles over whether NATO remained the preeminent institution for ensuring Central Europe's security.

Despite their efforts to become more closely tied to European security institutions during the summer of 1991, Triangle policymakers and security specialists still feared being caught in a "no-man's-land" or "security vacuum," or being seen merely as "buffer states." They remained concerned not only about abandonment by the West amid the chaos of the disintegrating USSR and its increasingly ominous hard-liner resurgence in Moscow, but also isolated economically from the growing power of unified Germany. Participation in the

CSCE failed to provide the kind of comprehensive security sought by the Triangle, although it facilitated, to an extent, working together in order to strengthen the political, economic, and security (arms control) capabilities of the Triangle. Of necessity, however, the Triangle states still looked to NATO as the oldest and most reliable European security institution. It is important to highlight that from 28 to 30 June 1991, Skubiszewski hosted a consultative meeting in Krakow, in cooperation with the Polish Jagiellonian Foundation, to promote political, economic, cultural, security, and defense issues in support of the Visegrad regional cooperative process. Many officials from the ministries of foreign affairs, defense, finance, and economics participated. Ostensibly, the consultation's purpose concentrated on co-opting the pessimists who disagreed with Poland's approach to the Triangle's regional cooperation, while also strengthening intergovernmental coordination on policies toward the Triangle. As a result, Triangle foreign and defense ministers maintained their consultations and tried to expedite their respective European reintegration efforts.[143]

In addition to Skubiszewski's efforts to promote regional security cooperation and improve cooperation with Moscow and NATO, Lech Kaczynski, appointed by Walesa in the late spring of 1991 as his minister of state for national security, reasoned that only NATO gave Central Europe the confidence of future stability.[144] He stated in early June 1991 that "it is obvious Poland will not raise the NATO membership question at the immediate time." Yet, he still challenged NATO to broaden itself so that a "more relaxed associate membership" status for Poland and other Central European states might exist. For Kaczynski "the danger of instability increased daily to Poland's east with the potential for mass migration of refugees, delays in Soviet force withdrawals from Poland, and even the possibility that Soviet intervention could occur to defend what is viewed as Soviet strategic interests, however defined." Moreover, Walesa's key national security advisor said "Russia is currently unpredictable. El'tsin's victory as Russian president also raises the question of the potential for him to take power over the entire USSR, or what becomes of the future USSR." These possibilities for El'tsin's rule of the Russian Federation, Kaczynski believed, "reinforces democratic values throughout the USSR, but a El'tsin ruling the entire country causes some fears," mainly because "Poland would then be uncertain about any course the USSR would follow."[145] Therefore, such Polish national security beliefs only fed Triangle state apprehension as the Soviet Union disintegrated.

The failed August Soviet coup d'état confirmed the Triangle's concerns, but the key Triangle ministers and their staffs utilized their regional cooperative consultation mechanism to coordinate during their first crisis and to build the basis for a more concerted effort to reintegrate into Europe. During the emergency in Moscow, the Triangle's deputy foreign ministers and senior military officials met in Warsaw for unscheduled crisis coordination on joint measures to take in case the Soviet rebellion succeeded. Even more importantly, as Polish vice foreign minister Jerzy Makarczyk stated, the emergency consultation focused on establishing a "permanent trilateral consultative group" that "served the process of further integration of Europe," especially integration based on a stable USSR. The deputy ministers also released a joint statement advocating "a full integration with Western European political and economic structures and creation of equal security and respect for human rights for all Europeans." For his part, Walesa stated that "we will defend our achievements, independently of whether the Soviet Union is led by Gorbachev, or by another team, but our actions will have less chance for success without the help of Europe." Additionally, Walesa emphasized that "we will not be able to resolve the crisis in our own reform programs without support from Europe, without association with the EC."[146] Given Walesa's statement on 20 August, coupled with El'tsin's defeat of the Soviet hard-line plot by 21 August, the Triangle meeting ended, but the planning for the next Triangle summit began immediately. This series of crisis steps underscores that important Polish policymakers believed in bridging rather than balancing against threats. They understood they couldn't guarantee their own security, that any self-help policies would be futile in response to the Moscow turbulence, and that they needed Triangle political support. As they stated consistently at the highest levels, even if disputes proceeded over whether or when they might join NATO, Warsaw always signaled its determination not to isolate Moscow, not to balance NATO against Moscow. Poland believed in El'tsin's reformist leadership, especially after the coup failed, and believed a post-Soviet, postimperial Russia could contribute to European security, too.

The Krakow Summit:
Institutionalized Security Cooperation

Planned for Krakow on 5–6 October 1991, the Triangle summit intended to formalize the tenets of the Visegrad Declaration and to extend relations with NATO. On 2 October, however, the surprise statement by U.S. secretary of state James Baker and German foreign minister Hans-Dietrich Genscher provided more momentum to the Triangle's summit preparation by calling for a "Euro-Atlantic pact from Vladivostok to Vancouver."[147] The Baker–Genscher statement contributed to the impetus for the final planning of NATO's projected November summit and gave the Krakow Summit an important baseline from which to work. At Krakow the Visegrad foreign ministers stated that "the ideas in the proposal fully corresponded to their ideas for further development of cooperation between the Alliance and Czechoslovakia, Poland, and Hungary."[148] In a Polish interview shortly before the summit's start, Walesa declared that "we must assimilate knowledge more quickly and cooperate with each other better." Warning about the disintegration of both the USSR and Yugoslavia, particularly the dangers of extreme nationalism and attendant ethnic violence, the Polish president stressed that "a new NATO strategy is required, especially toward our countries. This will consolidate the European nature of our partnership [because] in today's Europe, security cannot be based on bilateral or trilateral guarantees. Today, security must be collective."[149]

After the summit's first day, Skubiszewski stated "each one of the three countries is interested in having closer relations with NATO and in building in Europe cooperative security—that is, security which assumes cooperation in the greatest number of areas."[150] In the wake of the foiled coup and the impending end of the USSR, the Krakow Summit brought together concerned Central European leaders, intent on demonstrating their solidarity and far-sighted goals for European reintegration that wouldn't threaten a post-Soviet Russia. Additionally, the Krakow Summit evinced the culmination of cooperation as the declaration set forth "the principal task of full-range integration into the European political, economic and juridical, as well as security system." What set this summit apart from the other Triangle declarations or statements during the previous eighteen months stemmed from the explicit and concerted objectives for European security. These signified the goal to gain EC associate membership, to extend NATO ties and institutional linkages, to expand nascent West European Union relations, and to strengthen the CSCE process. In Krakow, all three Triangle leaders also resolutely condemned the civil war in Yugoslavia and stated that "the crisis may be solved only by involvement of the international community." More importantly, the Triangle leaders stated their intention to contribute to any international peacekeeping operation undertaken. With regard to the disintegration of the USSR, the Triangle pledged that, "while integrating into European structures," their member states intended to champion a "more active common policy towards states and nations of this neighborly territory." Further, they determined to solidify "the ideals of freedom, democracy, human rights, and principles of market economy." Lastly, in attempting to "pay special attention to those parts of the continent which have been excluded so far from the process of European integration," the Triangle leaders "attached fundamental importance to safeguarding a lasting security on the continent." For signatories, this section of their declaration meant "that the Triangle states regard Europe as a single and indivisible territory where the security of each of the countries is indissolubly connected with the security of others and each of them will have equal conditions for preserving its own security."[151] Clearly, since the first Triangle summit in Bratislava, the Triangle states had focused more concertedly on their common security and stability, including the bridging strategy to encourage nonthreatening linkages to the post-Soviet states.

In the postsummit press conferences, Polish policymakers reinforced the their cooperative strategy toward East and West, and NATO's importance to European security and stability. Walesa asserted that "we want to gain common security, but everyone is aware, of course, that NATO is going through organizational changes because there is a different political situation in Europe and in the world." He concluded by saying that, through debate, the Triangle states believed their unified positions produced better results toward NATO and "assured" greater security for each state. To Skubiszewski, the Krakow Summit and the Baker–Genscher statement captured the essence of Poland's consistent and long-term strategy, in tandem with the Triangle, toward NATO. He foresaw the linkages "deepening and being enriched," but cautioned that NATO needed to institutionalize its ties to the former Warsaw Pact nations and urged that "we constantly move forward within the scope of these contacts."[152]

The Krakow Summit consolidated the Triangle's objectives for membership in the evolving European security architecture, objectives that remained constant for the rest of Skubiszewski's time as foreign minister. Continued use of a step-by-step NATO and regional cooperative integration strategy undergirded Skubiszewski's overriding international security objectives. As previous chapters demonstrated, Skubiszewski vied at times with senior Polish officials from 1992 to 1993 over differing strategies for Poland to gain NATO membership, but the Polish leadership never veered from its goal of membership. Even with the formal dissolution of the USSR in December 1991 and the reduction of the threat from the East, Polish national security policy and defense strategy upheld the fundamental tenets of NATO integration via Central European regional cooperation and democratization.[153] Indeed, Warsaw and its Central European Triangle counterparts provided one of the main influences during the early post–Cold War years in Europe to persuade NATO members to transform its institution, render membership criteria, and, ultimately, just a few years after Skubiszewski's *MSZ* tenure, issue invitations for the Triangle to join.[154] As a result of their short-term cooperative security arrangement in the heart of historically unstable Central Europe, the Triangle states played an important role in affecting NATO members to begin changing NATO gradually at the 7–8 November 1991 NATO Rome Summit.

The NATO Rome Declaration attested to the alliance's commitment to strengthen ties to the new democracies in Central and Eastern Europe and to those in the Commonwealth of Independent States. Its recommendations focused on "formalizing" ties between NATO members and the new democracies by integrating the "liaison" states into selected ambassadorial, ministerial, and working-level meetings. Participation in some of NATO's political, military, economic, and scientific committee meetings marked an advance for all of these non-NATO states into the new North Atlantic Cooperation Council (NACC). NATO intended this discussion mechanism to allow for the sharing of allied "experience" and "expertise" on "defense planning, democratic concepts of civilian-military relations, civil-military coordination of air traffic management, and defense conversion to civilian purposes."[155] Yet, for the Triangle states, this NATO initiative signified an extension of discussion mechanisms, but not specific political consultation and military cooperation. For the Triangle, key concerns concentrated on reducing tensions and flash points for conflict found mostly in non-NATO states.

Though Poland and the Triangle wanted greater integration initiatives by NATO beyond simply a more intensive discussion format, the Triangle states also realized they each must implement significant political, economic, and military reforms to prove their contributions to a changing NATO. Coupled with the NATO summit, the EC reached out to the Triangle states by offering agreements on association in December 1991. The EC's move signified the first preparatory step on the long road to membership.[156] Such institutional integrative steps represented small victories for Poland and the Triangle, but fell short of the commitments the Triangle believed necessary to solidify their post-Communist transformations. Although Skubiszewski remained frustrated by the response of the two European institutions, he realized that only a consistent and gradualist policy guaranteed long-term integration.[157]

Over the final eighteen months of his *MSZ* leadership Skubiszewski continued to advocate growing NATO ties via Triangle regional cooperation, even as domestic political divisions increased within the CSFR. He believed that the West needed to bestow a special status on the Triangle states for their promotion of regional stability and democratization. Undoubtedly, Skubiszewski realized that consensus to enlarge NATO remained a distant prospect. Yet, he constantly propounded throughout 1992 and 1993 that, under his leadership, Poland's road to NATO had started in 1990 and Warsaw's "policy of specific steps linking us with NATO to our strategic objective in the security sphere now to join NATO remains a goal that will not be easy to attain." For the foreign minister, "this was a policy not of words, not of pious wishes [but one] that requires small, gradual steps, one step at a time, whereby each step must be successful." Furthermore, he considered this strategy successful when Poland and the Visegrad Triangle moved "step by step, from one stage to the next; from the elimination of different elements of the Alliance's indifference toward our region to convincing it of the need for its protective influence in our part of Europe." He maintained that, within the framework of the Visegrad Triangle, Poland's priority remained "to fulfill all the conditions and requirements necessary for us to achieve as close links as possible with NATO." Jointly to coordinate policy and participate internationally, Skubiszewski argued that, with the Triangle, "we are making use of all the possibilities of cooperation that exist not just [as] something that involves the NACC; it also involves joint NATO activity with Hungary and the CSFR." Above all, he believed that "regular political consultations and better coordination of views on major issues make it easier for all three states to become involved in the processes of broadly conceived West European and North Atlantic integration."[158] Consistent with this strategy, prior to the first NACC defense ministerial meeting on 1 April 1992, Triangle ministers met to coordinate their NACC positions.[159] This NATO gathering, however, preceded the Triangle's final summit in May amid worsening political tensions in the CSFR.

Though the Triangle leaders proclaimed as "the most successful" their fourth summit on 6 May 1992 in Prague, the growing tensions and eventual disintegration of the CSFR several months later significantly weakened the Visegrad process by early 1993. At Prague, the original Visegrad leaders used their summit to reinforce their determination for membership in NATO and the EC. To underscore their regional cooperation as a "stabilizing force" in the heart of Europe, the three leaders held that they provided "a new framework for Central European relations based on common traditions and characteristics, similar efforts at establishing democracy and a market economy, and their mutual desire for full participation in European integration." They argued that they raised possibilities for NATO membership through their willingness to commit Triangle peacekeeping forces to NATO's increasingly important supporting role under CSCE- or UN-authorized peacekeeping operations. In terms of their push toward the EC, the summit communiqué stressed, coming within six months of their first EC breakthrough on signing the three respective EC association treaties, that the Triangle now wanted to use the EC agreements "to prepare for full membership in the European Union." To achieve membership, the Triangle statement underlined the need for European parliaments from EC member states to speed ratification of the Triangle's association agreements.[160] Notwithstanding the summit's strong communiqué, after the June 1992 Czech and Slovak elections the new Prague leadership under Premier Vaclav Klaus disagreed with the commitment to institutionalize Triangle cooperation and the new Slovak government under former Communist Vladimir Meciar also distanced itself from the Triangle.

With gradual progress toward closer EC and NATO linkages throughout 1992, the Czech leadership still criticized the Visegrad coordination. Czech premier Klaus led the criticism, saying, among other things, that the Triangle represented an "artificial" process and a danger toward becoming a bureaucratic institution.[161] Warsaw and Budapest rebutted Klaus's contentions, underlining the importance of regional cooperation and emphasizing that West European opinion believed in regional cooperation as the means for integration.[162] Eventually, though, even Klaus admitted that the Visegrad consultative mechanism provided advantages to his European integration strategy. Given that European reintegration for these former Communist countries meant overcoming so many historical drawbacks, Klaus acknowledged that "Central European cooperation has been assuming special importance. Coexistence means to have common problems and to solve them by joint effort."[163] To reinforce Poland's Visegrad cooperative security strategy, Skubiszewski, while in Prague, stated that "regional cooperation is important and beneficial and it will not prevent anyone from joining West European structures. [Visegrad] is a group of countries linked by their proximity to each other and by their common interests, history, and traditions."[164] Yet, even the common bonds bringing the Triangle and the Central European region more closely together couldn't accelerate either EC or NATO membership decisions.

Though the new post-CSFR Visegrad "Group" faltered during 1993, regional cooperative security process already laid the foundation for EU (transformed from the EC in late 1992) and NATO integration coordination, even as membership failed to materialize. These regional cooperative efforts continued after Skubiszewski's terms in office, expanding beyond the Visegrad framework, as well. In linking high-level officials in a Polish–West European regional consultative framework, Skubiszewski also bequeathed to his successors another regional bridge-building process, accelerated in the 1990s with Poland, Germany, France, and, periodically, Great Britain.[165] These two regional cooperative security efforts enabled Poland to demonstrate its serious intent to rejoin Europe via the primary security institutions trying to fill the void in Europe's constant post-1989 flux. For middle power Poland and its smaller power Visegrad counterparts, other-help solutions to their security voids became their best options. They well understood from historical happenstance that, too often, self-help options ended in conflict and the need to bridge to post–Cold War great powers if they were to survive regional anarchy.

During 1993, NATO nations finally began in earnest to address the serious alliance enlargement questions avoided since Central and East Europe's 1989 revolutions. The issue of whether or not to enlarge NATO to include former Warsaw Pact enemies set off major alliance debates and disputes. Like the arguments leading up to the July 1990 NATO London Summit regarding whether NATO would "go out of area or go out of business," the disputes breaking out publicly concerning enlargement threatened NATO's very integrity and even post–Cold War transition. Even though several additional trips to NATO headquarters before he left government yielded greater NATO verbal commitments to Poland's future membership, Skubiszewski still came away without any alliance consensus on the specific criteria and timeline for such a membership decision.[166] By the late spring and early summer, Skubiszewski saw that the new U.S. administration under President Bill Clinton and some West European leaders started to talk publicly about NATO enlargement, providing Poland and the other Visegrad states with optimism about joining the alliance.[167] By the time of Poland's September 1993 elections, in which the *Solidarnosc*-led government finally lost, Skubiszewski left office as NATO leaders debated whether to expand or initiate more extensive political and military links to non-NATO NACC members.[168] Such decisions to postpone enlargement and initiate the regionally integrative NATO–Partnership for Peace process occurred nearly six months after Skubiszewski left office. But Skubiszewski's successors possessed a solid strategy from which to lobby NATO more pragmatically.

What Skubiszewski also left for his successors to advance concerned the fruition of building upon Poland's middle power bilateral links to great power neighbors to achieve European reintegration. He enshrined this strategy when he delivered an important and lesser-known speech at the Sorbonne in Paris during his last year in office. By that time, Poland looked toward NATO and the EU to institutionalize its other-help security enhancement, but Warsaw's confidence in reintegrating into Europe stemmed from the key Polish–German relationship built several years earlier. Skubiszewski spoke about how the Franco–German post–World War II reconciliation provided a regionally cooperative model for Poland and Central Europe. Just as the Polish–German post–Cold War rapprochement followed the Franco–German reconciliation, and reduced regional threats and increased regional integration, so, too, could the Franco–German model serve as the Visegrad Triangle's baseline for European reintegration.[169] But these regionally cooperative bilateral and trilateral models did not remain limited to Central and Western Europe for Skubiszewski.

The Polish foreign minister likened these bridge-building block bilateral linkages to the East, as well. He truly believed that, though Moscow remained capable of imposing its will on Poland through a variety of political, economic, or military means, Warsaw could not counterbalance this residual power. By establishing the first formal relationships to Russia and Ukraine of any nation globally, Poland tried to provide a bridge between them and the West. Just as Warsaw solidified its bilateral ties with Germany and modeled it after the Franco–German reconciliation, so, too, did it begin similar efforts with both the Ukrainian middle power and the Russian great power. This strategy might be seen as trying to ward off any Moscow threat, but as argued above, Poland simultaneously expanded its bilateral ties with western and eastern neighbors. Warsaw implemented these bilateral reconciliation pieces to its overall strategy while also helping to create the Central European cooperative process that enunciated to post-Soviet states a bridge-building model for regional Western orientation and integration. Even though Poland wanted American troops to stay in Germany to ensure NATO survived and Russia limited in its residual power pressuring on Central Europe, Poland also wanted new options to survive Europe's perennial anarchy. Skubiszewski realized that America would not remain in Europe indefinitely and that NATO might not last forever. That is why he determined from the start that new bilateral ties must first be put in place— West and East. Only then could Poland really fulfill its European reintegration strategy—and do so with others and not only on its own.

Understandably, the upheaval in the East and enlargement delay in the West made Polish policymakers uneasy. As analyzed in the previous chapter, Warsaw believed that when Russian president El'tsin declared in Warsaw that he didn't oppose Poland's desire to become a NATO member, NATO would react favorably. Since this statement caused such a backlash in Russia, amid the mounting problems for the Russian president before the October 1993 parliamentary confrontation, El'tsin retracted his agreement with Walesa and NATO leaders decided not to offer invitations at their January 1994 summit.[170] Unlike Poland's eastern or western neighbors, Skubiszewski captured Poland's sentiments when he stated that "Russia is a power that is going to have good cooperation with NATO, while Poland's presence in the Alliance would have a good influence on Russia's security."[171] Perhaps Skubiszewski best summarized Poland's regional cooperative and bridging policy toward NATO just after the Polish elections brought the first non-*Solidarnosc* party to power. He assessed that "Poland and the Visegrad Group [developed] a new concept accentuating that the security of Central European democracies and their striving for integration into West European and Atlantic structures cannot be viewed as a threat to the interests of a non-imperial Russia."[172]

Regional Cooperation to Bridge
East and West

Skubiszewski's rationale for reinforcing Poland's sovereignty and solidifying regional stability lay in establishing two main other-help goals. He recognized Poland's regional limitations and the necessity for its security and stability to bridge cooperatively to key neighboring powers. As a result, he and his innovative *MSZ* staff helped Poland to survive regional anarchy, build new and significant bilateral and trilateral linkages with all neighboring states, and reduce historic security dilemmas. Many of these achievements emanated from the Central European regional cooperative security triangle that Warsaw aided in creating with Prague and Budapest. In utilizing cooperation rather than historic confrontation Poland achieved its regional security and stability-enhancing objectives more effectively between East and West. The *MSZ*'s initiative to create the Triangle's security process enabled unified political consultation and coordination more effectively to negotiate with Moscow, while also increasing ties to NATO and the EU. From 1989 to 1993, the Warsaw–Prague–Budapest Triangle strengthened Poland's capability to bargain with Moscow on several important national security issues. During his four terms as foreign minister, Skubiszewski prioritized the development and employment of the Triangle's consultative and negotiating processes. This led to the Warsaw Pact's dissolution, equitable bilateral treaties with Moscow, and initial NATO and EU links, especially better U.S. and European ties to Central Europe via NATO.

The benefits and drawbacks of balancing, bandwagoning, and bridging alignment also entered into Skubiszewski's strategy when considering crucial elements in international negotiation theory and why bridging best fulfilled Poland's objectives. Using international negotiation theory, this chapter explained how Poland and the Triangle bargained from weaker postures individually vis-à-vis Moscow, but together designed political stances to present Moscow with unexpected options and often winning strategies. Consequently, Skubiszewski and his Prague and Budapest counterparts attained major national security goals via the Visegrad negotiation framework. For all three foreign ministers, their trilateral policies illustrated bridging alignment toward Moscow. These three evolving democracies demonstrated that they wanted to reintegrate into Europe without threatening Moscow's security. In fact, they argued that, as a group of stable and independent states, the Triangle provided a democratizing Russia a bridge to a more stable Europe, as the Triangle integrated into such democratic and transforming institutions as NATO and the EU.

Though Skubiszewski failed to attain the objective of integrating Poland into NATO while serving as foreign minister, he left the important legacy of domestic consensus on regional cooperation and European reintegration in foreign policy. After Skubiszewski's departure, all the major Polish political parties agreed on the requirement for Poland's NATO membership by the mid- to late

1990s. By building a methodical, painstaking, and pragmatic strategy focused on regional Central European security cooperation and step-by-step NATO and EU integration, Skubiszewski had an impact on Poland that regionally endured as Poland, the Czech Republic, and Hungary integrated into NATO in 1999 and the EU in the early twenty-first century.

For Skubiszewski the overriding purpose of regional security concentrated on fostering cooperation with all of Poland's neighbors, especially to its east via bilateral and trilateral processes. Even as such a strategy began to overcome tense or even violent history, Skubiszewski demonstrated most importantly a regional cooperative integration policy founded upon international law to re-integrate into the European community of democracies, instead of threatening bravado and empty political gestures. Bridging with Triangle Communist-era underground activists–cum–post-Communist foreign policy–makers marked Poland's diplomacy toward a weakened Moscow. Yet, the Triangle concertedly negotiated with a post–Soviet Russia to try to reinforce efforts at Russian reform, democratization, and European cooperation. The Polish foreign minister promoted this policy to solidify Poland's sovereignty and to eliminate the historic geopolitical warlike intentions of Poland, the Triangle members, and their stronger great power neighbors. This bridging behavior thus provided a model for how a post-Communist, post–Cold War European state contributed to European security and stability. Via its practical and nonconfrontational strategy of cooperation and integration—relying on neighboring states—middle power Poland cooperated with smaller neighboring powers to strengthen its other-help options to survive, stabilize, prosper, and reintegrate into Europe.

Notes

1. "Polska a bezpieczenstwo Europejskie—przemowienie Ministra Spraw Zagranicznych RP Krzysztofa Skubiszewskiego, do Zgromadzenia a Polnocno-atlantyckiego" [Poland and European Security, Address by the Polish Foreign Minister Krzysztof Skubiszewski to the North Atlantic Assembly] (London, 29 November 1990), *Zbior Dokumentow*, no. 4 (1991): 10–12, 15.

2. For an in-depth analysis of the implications of the CSFR's split by 1993, see Jeffrey A. Simon, "Czechoslovakia's Velvet Divorce: Visegrad Cohesion and European Fault Lines," Institute for National Strategic Studies, National Defense University, McNair Paper 23, October 1993.

3. Paul Schroeder, "Historical Reality vs. Neo-realist Theory," *International Security*, vol. 19, no. 1 (summer 1994): 108–148.

4. This chapter utilizes I. William Zartman and Maureen Berman, *The Practical Negotiator* (New Haven, Conn.: Yale University Press, 1982); William M. Habeeb, *Power and Tactics in International Negotiation: How Weak Nations Bargain with Strong Nations* (Baltimore: The Johns Hopkins University Press, 1988); and Terrence Hopmann, *The Negotiation Process and the Resolution of International Conflicts*, (Columbia: University of South Carolina Press, 1998).

5. Habeeb, *Power and Tactics in International Negotiation*, 130, 134.

6. This chapter analyzes specific pre-1989 roots for Poland's policies toward Central European regional cooperation.

7. Edited by Kostrzewa-Zorbas, *Nowa Koalicja* allowed Czech and Hungarian intellectual dissidents and underground activists to publish foreign policy issues aimed specifically to influence democratic and free market change throughout Central, Northeastern, Eastern, and Southeastern Europe, including the Baltic states, Belorussia, Ukraine, and Russia, as distinct from the USSR. Kostrzewa-Zorbas focused specific journal issues on important Czech and Hungarian topics. See "Bedziemy mogli stworzyc realny potencjal: C rozmow z Czeskimi dzialaczami niezaleznymi, 1984–1986" [We Will Be Able to Create a Real Potential: Talks with Czech Independent Social Workers (signatories to Charter 77, 1984-1986), *Nowa Koalicja*, no. 3 (1987): 16–20; and Ivan Baba, "Jedna partia plus druga—rowna sie: ile?" [One Party Plus Another Party Makes How Many?], *Nowa Koalicja*, no. 8 (1989): 20–23. Note that Baba wrote his piece in March 1989, as the first free elections in Central–East Europe approached in Poland.

8. Some of the key parts of that motto underlined that "there are many peoples in Europe dominated by Soviet imperialism and the totalitarian system. . . . Every nation was fighting separately, alone and single-handedly. Cooperation could bring enormous chance and hope . . . to recapture independence and sovereignty, and execute the right of self-determination, once endorsed by the UN, and, thus, create in Europe order and balance based on justice." See Marcin Mieguszowiecki [Grzegorz Kostrzewa-Zorbas] and Adam Realista, "Wspolnota Losow i Celow" [Common Destinies and Goals], *Nowa Koalicja*, no. 1 (1985): 1–2.

9. "Czech, Polish Dissidents Hold Border Meeting," AFP (Paris), 2016 GMT, 26 June 1989, *FBIS-EEU*, 27 June 1989, 49; W.A.I., "Poland-Czechoslovakia: Meeting with the Opposition," *Gazeta Wyborcza*, 24 July 1989, *FBIS-EEU*, 28 July 1989, 30; A.J., "A Response to 'Few Sentences,'" *Gazeta Wyborcza*, 24 July 1989, *FBIS-EEU*, 28 July 1989, 30–31.

10. Jiri Dienstbier, "We Are Watching Poland," *Gazeta Wyborcza*, 24 July 1989, *FBIS-EEU*, 27 July 1989, 23–24.

11. Vaclav Havel, "Open Letter," *Gazeta Wyborcza*, 12 September 1989, *FBIS-EEU*, 25 September 1989, 34; and "Mazowiecki Replies to CSSR Dissident Letter," Warsaw Domestic Service, 1300 GMT, 3 October 1989, 41. Note that the Carnogursky case soon dissipated as Communist control over Czechoslovakia disintegrated. The Slovak dissident, as Havel predicted, soon rose to prominence in Slovakia, becoming one of the first post-Communist prime ministers.

12. "Oswiadczenie Sejmu PRL w zwiazku z 21 rocznica interwencji wojsk ukladu warszawskiego w Czechoslowackiej Republice Socjalistycznej" [Statement of the Sejm of the PPR on the 21st Anniversary of the Warsaw Pact Armed Forces' Intervention in the Czechoslovak Socialist Republic] (17 September 1989), *Zbior Dokumentow*, no. 3 (1990): 11.

13. "Speech by Premier-Designate Tadeusz Mazowiecki at the Sejm Session in Warsaw," Warsaw Television Service, 1011 GMT, 24 August 1989, *FBIS-EEU*, 25 August 1989, 31; "Expose sejmowe premiera PRL Tadeusza Mazowieckiego/fragmenty dotyczace pomocy zagranicznej i stosunkow miedzynarodowych" [Sejm Exposé by the Polish Prime Minister Tadeusz Mazowiecki/Excerpts Concerning Foreign Aid and International Relations] (Warsaw, 12 September 1989), *Zbior Dokumentow*, no. 3 (1990): 24–25.

14. "Expose sejmowe premiera PRL Tadeusza Mazowieckiego," 26.

15. Roman Prister, "Exclusive Interview with Polish Foreign Minister Professor Krzysztof Skubiszewski: Without a Trace of Dependence," *Ha'aretz* (Tel Aviv), 19 October 1989, *FBIS-EEU*, 26 October 1989, 57; and Thomas S. Szayna, *Polish Foreign Policy under a Non-Communist Government: Prospects and Problems* (Santa Monica, Calif: RAND, 1990), 23.

16. "Shevardnadze's Interview for PAP: Abridged," PAP, 2154 GMT, 25 October 1989, *FBIS-EEU*, 26 October 1989, 55.

17. Adam Michnik, "Interview with Eduard Shevardnadze, Soviet Minister of Foreign Affairs: Why Has Our Relationship to Other Nations Changed?—Because Our Relationship to Our Own People Has Changed," *Gazeta Wyborcza*, 27–29 October 1989, *FBIS-EEU*, 31 October 1989, 41.

18. "Komunikat z posiedzenia komitetu ministrow spraw zagranicznych panstwstron Ukladu Warszawskiego" [Communiqué from the Session of the Committee of the Ministers for Foreign Affairs of the States Parties to the Warsaw Pact], *Zbior Dokumentow*, no. 4 (1990): 260.

19. Lucian Meysels, "We Were Also Divided: Interview with Polish Foreign Minister Krzysztof Skubiszewski," *Wochenpresse* (Vienna), 10 November 1989, *FBIS-EEU*, 14 November 1989, 61.

20. Wojciech Zielinski, "Foreign Policy without Ideology: Interview with Krzysztof Skubiszewski, Polish Minister of Foreign Affairs," *Rzeczpospolita*, 16 November 1989, *FBIS-EEU*, 24 November 1989, 61.

21. "Komunikat prasowy o spotkaniu przywodcow panstw-stron Ukladu Warszawskiego" [Press Communiqué Following the Moscow Meeting of Leaders of the States-Parties to the Warsaw Pact] (Moscow, 4 December 1989), *Zbior Dokumentow*, no. 4 (1990): 255.

22. "Skubiszewski, Mazowiecki Remarks," PAP, 2233 GMT, 4 December 1989, *FBIS-EEU*, 5 December 1989, 61. See also "Poland's Mazowiecki," PAP, 2139 GMT, 4 December 1989, *FBIS-EEU*, 7 December 1989, 6.

23. Piet de Moor, "For Us the Border Question No Longer Exists: Interview with Foreign Minister Krzysztof Skubiszewski," *De Volkskrant* (Amsterdam), 9 December 1989, *FBIS-EEU*, 20 December 1989, 56; "Mazowiecki Wants Warsaw Pact Changed," Kyodo (Tokyo), 7 January 1990, 1232 GMT, *FBIS-EEU*, 9 January 1990, 9.

24. "A Long Way Off: Deputies' and Senators' Statements to PAP," *Sztandar Mlodych*, 4 January 1990, *FBIS-EEU*, 10 January 1990, 67; Adam Michnik, untitled commentary, *Gazeta Wyborcza*, 5 January 1990, *FBIS-EEU*, 12 January 1990, 45; Zdzislaw Najder, "An East European Alliance," *Rzeczpospolita*, 16 January 1990, *FBIS-EEU*, 23 January 1990, 48–50; and Bronislaw Geremek, "The Polish Variant," *Rzeczpospolita*, 17 January 1990, *FBIS-EEU*, 31 January 1990, 49. See also Zdzislaw Najder, *Jaka Polska: Co i komu doradzalem* [What Kind of Poland: What and To Whom I Advised] (Warsaw: Editions Spotkania, 1993), 43–47.

25. See "Report on Speech by Polish Premier Mazowiecki at the 45th CMEA Session in Sofia on 9 January," *Rzeczpospolita*, 10 January 1990, *FBIS-EEU*, 16 January 1990, 2; Katarzyna Kolodziejczyk, "Two Trends—The 45th Session of the CMEA: Interview with Premier Tadeusz Mazowiecki," *Rzeczpospolita*, 12 January 1990, *FBIS-EEU*, 25 January 1990, 1; "CSSR-Polish Officials Meet, Discuss Cooperation; Mazowiecki Receives Klaus," PAP, 2052 GMT, 3 January 1990, *FBIS-EEU*, 11 January 1990, 58; and "CSSR's Klaus on CMEA Breakup, Withdrawal," CTK (Prague), 1301 GMT, 4 January 1990, *FBIS-EEU*, 5 January 1990, 1.

26. Piotr S. Wandycz, *Czechoslovak-Polish Confederation and the Great Powers, 1940–43* (Bloomington: Indiana University Press, 1956).

27. "Skubiszewski on Confederation," Warsaw Domestic Service, 11 January 1990, 0730 GMT, *FBIS-EEU*, 11 January 1990, 60; M.K., "Question of the Day: Reply by Minister of Foreign Affairs Krzysztof Skubiszewski," *Zycie Warszawy*, 11 January 1990, *FBIS-EEU*, 22 January 1990, 74; Piotr Wywicz, "CSSR's Dienstbier Holds News Conference," *Rzeczpospolita*, 12 January 1990, *FBIS-EEU*, 22 January 1990, 75; and "[Dienstbier] Gives News Conference," Prague Domestic Service, 2000 GMT, 11 January 1990, *FBIS-EEU*, 16 January 1990, 77.

28. Kolodziejczyk, "Two Trends—The 45th Session of the CMEA," 1.

29. Najder, "An East European Alliance," 50.

30. "Speech by Premier Tadeusz Mazowiecki at Sejm Session in Warsaw," Warsaw Domestic Service, 0822 GMT, 18 January 1990, *FBIS-EEU*, 19 January 1990, 57. See also Ronald D. Asmus and Thomas S. Szayna, with Barbara Kliszewski, *Polish National Security Thinking in a Changing Europe: A Conference Report* (Santa Monica, Calif: RAND/UCLA, 1991), 30–33. Mazowiecki's initiative reaped some dividends when the CSCE summit's Charter of Paris in November 1990 approved the establishment of the CSCE Office of Free Elections in Warsaw. Although different than Mazowiecki's original vision for a European Council, the CSCE also took steps to institutionalize security cooperation by creating a secretariat in Vienna, the CSCE headquarters, and a Center for Conflict Prevention in Prague, but within the limits of its operational capabilities and its significant budget constraints. "Polityka zagraniczna Rzeczypospolitej Polskiej w roku 1991—Expose sejmowe Ministra Spraw Zagranicznych RP Krzysztofa Skubiszewskiego" [The Foreign Policy of the Republic of Poland in 1991—Sejm Exposé of the Polish Foreign Minister Krzysztof Skubiszewski] (Warsaw, 27 June 1991), *Zbior Dokumentow*, no. 1 (1992): 46–50.

31. "Mazowiecki Meets Leaders," PAP, 2207 GMT, 22 January 1990, *FBIS-EEU*, 23 January 1990, 19–20; "Mazowiecki Interviewed on Return from CSSR," Warsaw Domestic Service, 2300 GMT, 22 January 1990, *FBIS-EEU*, 23 January 1990, 45.

32. "Further on Mazowiecki Talks [with Havel]," CTK, 1815 GMT, 25 January 1990, *FBIS-EEU*, 30 January 1990, 60. Both Kostrzewa-Zorbas and Ananicz emphasized to me in Warsaw on 12 June 1991 the tremendous impact Havel had made on the Polish leadership, the Parliament, and the population with his speech, and how it galvanized the Central European regional cooperation.

33. "Havel Addresses Sejm," Prague Domestic Service, 1930 GMT, 25 January 1990, *FBIS-EEU*, 30 January 1990, 62–63. See also "Havel Advises 'Synchronized' Return to Europe," CTK, 1546 GMT, 27 January 1990, *FBIS-EEU*, 6 February 1990, 14; Matthew Rhodes, "The Idea of Central Europe and Visegrad Cooperation," *International Politics*, vol. 35, no. 2 (June 1998): 173–175.

34. Katarzyna Kolodziejczyk, "Three Directions: Skubiszewski Outlines Foreign Policy Goals," *Rzeczpospolita*, 10–11 February 1990, *FBIS-EEU*, 13 February 1990, 50–51.

35. Bohuslav Borovicka, "Businesslike and Open Negotiations," *Rude Pravo* (Prague), 19 March 1990, *FBIS-EEU*, 22 March 1990, 1; Angela E. Stent, *Russia and Germany Reborn: Unification, the Soviet Collapse, and the New Europe* (Princeton, N.J.: Princeton University Press, 1999). Stent cites Horst Teltschik, German chancellor Helmut Kohl's national security advisor and a trained Sovietologist, from Horst Teltschik, *329 Tage* [329 Days] (Berlin: Siedler Verlag, 1991), 201. She concludes, based on Teltschik's insights, that after Shevardnadze's speech against united Germany in NATO at this War-

saw Pact meeting, the Soviet foreign minister then "thanked them [Polish, CSFR, Hungarian foreign ministers] privately for their speeches, explaining that he and Gorbachev were under growing pressure from the military at home and welcomed the support by Warsaw Pact colleagues for Germany's NATO membership."

36. See Robert Mroziewicz, coordinator, "Zespol Badan Europy Wschodniej: Konfederacja Europy Srodkowej?" [Eastern European Research Establishment: Central European Confederation?], MSZ memorandum (internal), 31 March 1990, Warsaw, 1–3.

37. For background on the summit, see also Rudolf L. Tokes, "From Visegrad to Krakow: Cooperation, Competition, and Coexistence in Central Europe," *Problems of Communism*, vol. 40, no. 6 (November–December 1991): 103–104; and Joshua Spero, "The Budapest–Prague–Warsaw Triangle: Central European Security after the Visegrad Summit," *European Security*, vol. 1, no. 1 (spring 1992): 60–61.

38. Hungary's crucial role in Central European regional cooperation quickly changed once Antall's leadership took charge. Note that during the Bratislava Summit, Budapest representatives spent their time focused more on the Hungarian minority problems in Slovakia than on broader Central European cooperation.

39. "PAP Summarizes Bratislava Summit," PAP, 2115 GMT, 9 April 1990, *FBIS-EEU*, 10 April 1990, 12.

40. "PAP Summarizes Bratislava Summit," 12. See also Evelyn Forro, "Hungarian-CSFR Nationalities Statement Adopted," Budapest Domestic Service, 1600 GMT, 9 April 1990, *FBIS-EEU*, 10 April 1990, 7–8; and Armin Wolf, "'Conflict,' 'Frictions' between Prague, Budapest," Vienna Domestic Service, 0500 GMT, 10 April 1990, *FBIS-EEU*, 10 April 1990, 13–14.

41. "Statement by Premier Tadeusz Mazowiecki for Polish Television in Bratislava," Warsaw Television Service, 1730 GMT, 9 April 1990, *FBIS-EEU*, 10 April 1990, 6–7. See also "PAP Summarizes Bratislava Summit," 12.

42. "Bratislava Summit News Conference," Prague Domestic Service, 9 April 1990, *FBIS-EEU*, 12 April 1990, 9–10.

43. "Sejmowe expose Ministra Spraw Zagranicznych RP Krzysztofa Skubiszewskiego" [Sejm Exposé by Minister of Foreign Affairs of the Republic of Poland, Krzysztof Skubiszewski] (Warsaw, 26 April 1990), *Zbior Dokumentow*, no. 2 (1991): 11, 14–15, 21.

44. "Sejmowe expose Ministra Spraw Zagranicznych RP Krzysztofa Skubiszewskiego," no. 2 (1991): 23–24, 28–29.

45. Maria Skolarczyk, "Lack of a Security System," *Rzeczpospolita*, 15 May 1990, *FBIS-EEU*, 22 May 1990, 33–34. In their respective interviews with me, the following Polish experts also recounted Skubiszewski's multitiered strategy to reconcile Poland's security concerns toward Bonn and Moscow: Artur Hajnicz and Tadeusz Chabiera, members of the Senate's Center of International Studies, on 10 June 1994 in Warsaw, and Janusz Onyszkiewicz, member of parliament at the time of the interview, on 10 June 1994 in Warsaw. In his experiences as a newly appointed civilian vice defense minister in March 1990, Onyszkiewicz recounted the overwhelming difficulty he faced in dealing with Moscow, not only on sensitive issues such as asserting Poland's independent positions on the Warsaw Pact and Soviet force withdrawals from Poland, but also due to the fact that he was a civilian in a military world:

"I accompanied General Jaruzelski to Moscow in May 1990 to be introduced to the Soviet military leadership, but they didn't respond. They refused to meet with a *Solidarnosc* representative, let alone a civilian playing a leading role in the Polish Ministry of National Defense. Our delegation traveled to Lvov and Kiev, all the time waiting to meet with our Soviet counterparts. When we saw General Secretary Mikhail Gorbachev in Moscow, he called Defense Minister Dmitrii Yazov, who not only showed up immediately, but also called out all of the top brass to the meeting. It was quite surreal to be the only civilian and former dissident in the room with all of these military adversaries. However, I indicated to Yazov that Soviet force withdrawals from Poland were inevitable. Yazov agreed that it would be done in the future. He understood the implications, particularly with ongoing force withdrawal negotiations in Hungary and the CSFR, but he said force withdrawals from Poland would be slow.

"With the German unification process, Poland also needed to secure its borders through treaty guarantees and adapt to policies at that time which would be considered within the 2 Plus 4 negotiations. It was of utmost importance for us to win a consensus from the four big powers and not worsen relations with the USSR. The Western powers were cautious and noncommittal, while we convinced the USSR to play a supportive role. This was helped because we knew not to raise the issue of Soviet troop withdrawals from Poland at that time officially. In Hungary and the CSFR, something totally different was occurring: Soviet troops had not been stationed in those countries in World War II as in Poland. Soviet troops were also stationed in Germany and would need to withdraw by transport across Poland. Thus, we didn't push as hard as Hungary and the CSFR, and we didn't push the Warsaw Pact either. We wanted to have a flexible formula and we wanted it to work. We Poles suggested, within the Warsaw Pact's guidelines, that maybe the Poles should be leading. Our strategy was based on the fact that we couldn't be accused of undermining the Warsaw Pact if we played by its charter."

46. Habeeb, *Power and Tactics*, 145; and Hopmann, *The Negotiation Process and the Resolution of International Conflicts*, 115.

47. Habeeb, *Power and Tactics*, 8–9; and I. William Zartman, "Negotiating from Asymmetry," *Negotiation Journal*, no. 1 (February 1985): 121–138. See also Schroeder, "Historical Reality vs. Neo-realist Theory" and Randall L. Schweller, *Deadly Imbalances: Tripolarity and Hitler's Strategy of World Conquest* (New York: Columbia University Press, 1998).

48. For insight into the negotiation process and tactics used to achieve victorious outcomes, see I. William Zartman, "In Search of Common Elements in the Analysis of the Negotiation Process," *Negotiation Journal* (January 1988): 4; Glen Snyder and Paul Diesing, *Conflict among Nations* (Princeton, N.J.: Princeton University Press, 1977), 118–124; and I. William Zartman and Maureen Berman, *The Practical Negotiator* (New Haven, Conn.: Yale University Press, 1982), 147–198.

49. Interview I conducted with Kostrzewa-Zorbas, who joined the *MSZ* as Skubiszewski's deputy director of the *MSZ*'s Department of Europe on 1 June 1990. The interview occurred on March 25, 1993 in Washington, D.C.

50. "Jaruzelski, Mazowiecki Arrive," Warsaw Television Service, 1730 GMT, 6 June 1990, *FBIS-EEU*, 8 June 1990, 4.

51. Jerzy Malczyk, "Mazowiecki Meets Jaruzelski, Havel," PAP, 1325 GMT, 7 June 1990, *FBIS-EEU*, 8 June 1990, 7; and "Mazowiecki Meets De Maisiere, Havel," Warsaw Domestic Service, 1309 GMT, 7 June 1990, *FBIS-EEU*, 8 June 1990, 7.

52. "CSFR Brings Draft Declaration," Czech State Television (CTK), 1201 GMT, 7 June 1990, *FBIS-EEU*, 8 June 1990, 7.

53. "[Hungarian Minister of Foreign Affairs Geza Jeszenszky] to Discuss Withdrawal in Moscow," Budapest Domestic Service, May 28, 1990, *FBIS-EEU*, May 31, 1990, 32.

54. "Havel on CSFR 'Draft' Declaration," Prague Domestic Service, 1000 GMT, 7 June 1990, *FBIS-SOV*, 8 June 1990, 12; and "CSFR Brings 'Draft' Declaration," CTK, 1201 GMT, 7 June 1990, *FBIS-EEU*, 8 June 1990, 7.

55. "Gorbachev, Havel Speak at Luncheon," Moscow TASS International Service, 1858 GMT, 7 June 1990, *FBIS-SOV*, 8 June 1990, 4.

56. "Gorbachev, Havel Speak at Luncheon," 4.

57. "Gorbachev Addresses Meeting," Budapest Domestic Service, 1000 GMT, 7 June 1990, 8.

58. "Hungary's Antall Addresses Meeting," MTI (Budapest), 1520 GMT, 7 June 1990, *FBIS-SOV*, 8 June 1990, 10; "Antall Proposes 'Winding up' Pact," Budapest Domestic Service, 1400 GMT, 7 June 1990, *FBIS-SOV*, 8 June 1990, 10.

59. I. William Zartman, "The Structure of Negotiation," in *International Negotiation: Analysis, Approaches, Issues*, ed. Viktor Kremeniuk (San Francisco: Jossey-Bass, 1991), 69.

60. "Deklaracja panstw-stron ukladu warszawskiego przyjeta na naradzie doradczego komitetu politycznego" [Declaration of the States-Parties to the Warsaw Treaty Adopted at the Session of the Political Consultative Committee] (Moscow, 7 June 1990), *Zbior Dokumentow*, no. 2 (1991): 137–138.

61. "Hungary Not to Participate in Pact Exercises," *MTI*, June 8, 1990, *FBIS-EEU*, June 8, 1990, 53; and "Pact Demilitarization to Begin 1 January 1991," Budapest Domestic Service, 1600 GMT, 7 June 1990, *FBIS-EEU*, 8 June 1990, 1.

62. Andrzej Siewienecki, "Poland's Skubiszewski Comments," Warsaw Domestic Service, 1021 GMT, 7 June 1990, *FBIS-EEU*, 8 June 1990, 13.

63. "Skubiszewski: Pact in 'Crisis,'" Warsaw Television Service, 1730 GMT, 7 June 1990, *FBIS-EEU*, 8 June 1990, 37; "Skubiszewski on Gorbachev Address," PAP, 1816 GMT, 7 June 1990, *FBIS-EEU*, 8 June 1990, 37; and "Mazowiecki, Skubiszewski, Jaruzelski Remarks," PAP, 0035 GMT, 8 June 1990, *FBIS-EEU*, 8 June 1990, 38.

64. "Nobody Wants Any Spheres of Influence Today: Statement by Foreign Minister Krzysztof Skubiszewski," *Tygodnik Powszechny* (Warsaw), 10 June 1990, *FBIS-EEU*, 13 June 1990, 47.

65. "Poslanie ministrow spraw zagranicznych panstw NATO do wszystkich krajow Europejskich" [Message of the NATO Foreign Ministers to All the European Countries] (Turnberry, Scotland, 7–8 June 1990), *Zbior Dokumentow*, no. 2 (1991): 141.

66. "Komunikat koncowy spotkania ministerialnego Rady Polnocno-atlantyckiej" [Final Communiqué of the North Atlantic Council Ministerial Meeting] (Turnberry, 7-8 June 1990), *Zbior Dokumentow*, no. 2 (1991): 142, 146.

68. For example, Steven M. Walt, *The Origin of Alliances* (Ithaca, N.Y.: Cornell University Press, 1987), 19–48.

69. For some of the more prominent arguments for and against NATO's future, especially compared to the CSCE, during the upheaval between the Berlin Wall's fall and the USSR's demise, see the following. Stephen J. Flanagan, "NATO and Central and Eastern Europe: From Liaison to Security Partnership," *Washington Quarterly*, vol. 15, no. 2 (spring 1992), 141–151; Beverly Crawford, ed., *The Future of European Security* (Berkeley: University of California at Berkeley, Center for German and European Studies, 1992); Charles L. Glaser, "Why NATO Is Still Best: Future Security Arrangements for Europe," *International Security*, vol. 18, no. 1 (summer 1993), 5–50; Gunther Hellmann and Reinhard Wolf, "Neorealism, Neoliberal Institutionalism, and the Future of NATO," *Security Studies*, 3 (autumn 1993): 3–43; Robert O Keohane, Joseph S. Nye, and Stanley Hoffman, eds., *After the Cold War: International Institutions and State Strategies*

in Europe, 1989–1991. (Cambridge, Mass.: Harvard University Press, 1993); Charles L. Barry, ed., *The Search for Peace in Europe: Perspectives from NATO and Eastern Europe* (Washington, D.C.: National Defense University Press, 1993); and Sean M. Lynn-Jones and Steven E. Miller, *The Cold War and After: Prospects for Peace,* exp. ed. (Cambridge, Mass.: MIT Press, 1997).

69. See "Initiative to Institutionalize CSCE Process," ADN (East Berlin) International Service, 1021 GMT, 15 June 1990, *FBIS-EEU,* 22 June 1990, 1; "CSFR, GDR, Poland Present Vienna Proposals," Prague Domestic Service, 1300 GMT, 11 July 1990, *FBIS-EEU,* 16 July 1990, 2; "Tripartite Security Proposal Presented," CTK Report, "In Favor of Establishing Pan-European Institutions," *Hospodarske Noviny* (Prague), 12 July 1990, *FBIS-EEU,* 16 July 1990, 2; Andrzej Rayzacher, PAP, "Joint Initiative with Austria on CSCE Process," 13 September 1990, *FBIS-EEU,* 17 September 1990, 31. Note that, given their concerns over economic dependency on Moscow, the Hungarians disagreed about how to institutionalize such mechanisms and were reluctant to initiate, as opposed to support, as a CSCE member, this particular proposal. Polish and Hungarian foreign ministry officials expressed these concerns to me at a NATO–Central European conference in Oslo, Norway, from 4 to 6 February 1991, sponsored by the Norwegian Institute for Defense Studies and NATO headquarters, and during talks in Warsaw on 11 June 1991 and in Budapest on 14 June 1991.

70. See North Atlantic Council, "London Declaration on a Transformed North Atlantic Alliance," 5–6 July 1990, NATO Information Service, Brussels, 7, 9.

71. "We Are Revising the Warsaw Treaty: Interview with Polish Minister of Foreign Affairs, Krzysztof Skubiszewski," *Gazeta Wyborcza,* 26 July 1990, *FBIS-EEU,* 27 July 1990, 20.

72. "Skubiszewski Reviews Polish Foreign Policy," Warsaw Domestic Service, 2100 GMT, 1 September 1990, *FBIS-EEU,* 4 September 1990, 30.

73. Michal Ksiezarczyk, "Otwartosc wobec wschodu" [Openness Toward the East— interview with Grzegorz Kostrzewa-Zorbas, Deputy Director of the European Department, *MSZ*], *Zycie Warszawy,* 18–19 August 1990, 1, 4.

74. Zygmunt Slomkowski, "Closer to NATO: Interview with Ambassador to Belgium Tadeusz Olechowski," *Trybuna,* 29 August 1990, *FBIS-EEU,* 5 September 1990 34 and Maria Wagrowska, "From Confrontation to Cooperation" *Rzeczpospolita,* 17 August 1990, *FBIS-EEU,* 22 August 1990, 22.

75. Jerzy Rajch, "The Road to Security: Interview with Jerzy Nowak, Director of the Department of European Institutions, *MSZ,*" *Zolnierz Rzeczypospolitej,* 12 September 1990, *FBIS-EEU,* 20 September 1990, 25.

76. "Ku nowej Europie—wystapienie sekretarza generalnego NATO Manfreda Woernera (wygloszone na spotkaniu polaczonych Komisji Spraw Zagranicznych i Obrony Sejmu i Senatu RP)" [Towards a New Europe—Address by the Secretary General of NATO, Mr. Manfred Woerner (delivered before the Joint Foreign Affairs and Defense Committees of the Sejm and the Senate of the Republic of Poland] (Warsaw, 13 September 1990), *Zbior Dokumentow,* no. 3 (1991): 116, 119, 125; and Manfred Woerner, "NATO, Polska, Europa" [NATO, Poland, Europe], *Polska w Europie,* (January 1991), 3–18.

77. "Skubiszewski, NATO's Woerner Hold News Briefing," Warsaw Television Service, 1730 GMT, 14 September 1990, FBIS-EEU, 18 September 1990, 36. See also Marek Jurkowski, "M. Woerner has Left Poland," *Zolnierz Rzeczypospolitej,* 17 September 1990, *FBIS-EEU,* 21 September 1991, 24

78. "NATO's Woerner Meets Leaders, Addresses Sejm," PAP, 2355 GMT, 13 September 1990, *FBIS-EEU*, 14 September 1990, 35. See also Jan Rylukowski, "New Challenges, Old Answers—A Repertoire of Polish Foreign Policy," *Tygodnik Solidarnosc*, 14 September 1990, *FBIS-EEU*, 21 September 1990, 25–27.

79. Ewa Boniecka, "The Facts Have Surpassed the Imagination: Interview with Manfred Woerner, NATO Secretary General," *Zycie Warszawy*, 15–16 September 1990, *FBIS-EEU*, 20 September 1990, 25–26.

80. "NATO Secretary General Woerner Continues Visit; Meets Walesa in Gdansk," Warsaw Domestic Service, 1700 GMT, 15 September 1990, *FBIS-EEU*, 19 September 1990, 54.

81. Jerzy Rajch, "The Twilight of the Blocs: Interview with Grzegorz Kostrzewa-Zorbas, Deputy Director of the Europe Department, Ministry of Foreign Affairs," *Zolnierz Rzeczypospolitej*, 6 September 1990, *JPRS-EER*, 16 October 1990, 8–9.

82. "Warsaw Treaty in for Changes," BTA (Sofia), 1536 GMT, 18 September 1990, *FBIS-EEU*, 24 September 1990, 1; "Pact Meeting Discusses 'Radical Transformation,'" Budapest Domestic Service, 2000 GMT, 19 September 1990, *FBIS-EEU* 20 September 1990, 1; "'Novel Cooperation' at Pact Meeting," MTI, 0655 GMT, 20 September 1990, *FBIS-EEU*, 24 September 1990, 1.

83. Miroslaw Cielemecki, "Maneuvers at the Foot of Mt. Giewont," *Przeglad Tygodniowy* (Warsaw), no. 40 (7 October 1990), *JPRS-EER*, 4 December 1990, 23–24.

84. "Hungary, Poland, CSFR Form Consultative Committee," Budapest Domestic Service, 0530 GMT, 18 October 1990, *FBIS-EEU*, 22 October 1990, 1. This background was also provided in interviews that I conducted with Grzegorz Kostrzewa-Zorbas and Andrzej Ananicz, deputy director for Central Europe, *MSZ*, in Warsaw on 12 June 1991 and with Ivan Baba, director of policy planning, Hungarian Ministry of Foreign Affairs, Budapest on 18 June 1991.

85. "Mazowiecki Conducts Talks with CSFR's Havel," PAP, 1642 GMT, 20 November 1990, *FBIS-EEU*, 21 November 1990, 30; "Mazowiecki, Skubiszewski Meet Foreign Counterparts," PAP, 1926 GMT, 20 November 1990, *FBIS-EEU*, 21 November 1990, 30; and "Speech by Prime Minister Tadeusz Mazowiecki to Sejm on Paris CSCE Session," Warsaw Domestic Service, 1508 GMT, 22 November 1990, *FBIS-EEU*, 23 November 1990, 26–27.

86. See Skubiszewski's speech to the NATO North Atlantic Assembly, the parliamentary wing of NATO, a meeting at which Poland and the other Central and Eastern European states became associate members. "Polska a bezpieczenstwo Europejskie—przemowienie Ministra Spraw Zagranicznych RP Krzysztofa Skubiszewskiego, do Zgromadzenia a Polnocnoatlantyckiego" [Poland and European Security—Address by the Polish Foreign Minister Krzysztof Skubiszewski to the North Atlantic Assembly] (London, 29 November 1990), *Zbior Dokumentow*, no. 4 (1991): 10–12. See also Istvan Kulcsar, "5 Nations Become North Atlantic Assembly Members," Budapest Domestic Service, 1700 GMT, 29 November 1990, *FBIS-EEU*, 30 November 1990, 1.

87. Background detailed during my interviews with Kostrzewa-Zorbas and Ananicz in Warsaw on 12 June 1991.

88. Jaroslaw Kurski, *Lech Walesa: Democrat or Dictator?* (Boulder, Colo.: Westview, 1993), 14–17, 109, 120; Grzegorz Kostrzewa-Zorbas, "Imperium kontratakuje" [The Empire Strikes Back], in *Lewy Czerwcowy* [Blow from the Left], eds., Jacek Kurski and Piotr Semka (Warsaw: Editions Spotkania, 1992), 178–179; and Najder, *Jaka Polska*, 196–206. For the presidential chancellery statement, see "President Walesa's Foreign

Trips Postponed,' Warsaw Domestic Service, 1310 GMT, 17 January 1991, *FBIS-EEU*, 18 January 1991, 30.

89. "Skubiszewski Clarifies Proposed Pact Session," PAP, 2250 GMT, 14 January 1991, *FBIS-EEU*, 17 January 1991, 29 and "Skubiszewski Rejects Lithuanian-Pact Linkages," CTK, 1141 GMT, 15 January 1991, 17 January 1991, *FBIS-EEU*, 17 January 1991, 1.

90. Kazimierz Woycicki, "The Continuity of Polish Efforts in a Turbulent World: Interview with Foreign Affairs Minister Krzysztof Skubiszewski," *Zycie Warszawy*, 17 January 1991, *FBIS-EEU*, 23 January 1991, 22.

91. "Oswiadczenie ministra spraw zagranicznych RP Krzysztofa Skubiszew-skiego w zwiazku z rozpoczeciem dzialan zbrojnych na froncie iracko-kuweickim" [Statement by the Polish Foreign Minister Krzysztof Skubiszewski on the Launching of Military Action on the Iraqi-Kuwaiti Front] (Warsaw, 17 January 1991), *Zbior Dokumentow*, no. 1 (1992): 17–18; "'Minifleet' to Arrive in Gulf 22–23 January," PAP, 1530 GMT, 14 January 1991, *FBIS-EEU*, 17 January 1991, 26.

92. Ewa Boniecka, "Poland Plus Two," *Zycie Warszawy*, 26–27 January 1991, *FBIS-EEU*, 31 January 1991, 34–35; Spero, "The Budapest-Prague-Warsaw Triangle," 62.

93. F. Luk'ianov, "Reshaetsia sud'ba Varshavskogo Dogovora" [The Fate of the Warsaw Pact is Being Decided], *Izvestiia* (Moscow), 24 January 1991, 1; Valentin Sharov, "Viewpoint: Troika in Central Europe," *Pravda* (Moscow), 25 January 1991, *FBIS-SOV*, 29 January 1991, 25–26; and Tokes, "From Visegrad to Krakow," 104–109.

94. "Walesa Cited on Relations with CSFR, Hungary," Prague Domestic Service, 1730 GMT, 11 February 1991, *FBIS-EEU*, 12 February 1991, 36.

95. "List Prezydenta ZSRR Michaila Gorbaczowa do Prezydenta RP Lecha Walesy dotyczacy likwidacji struktur wojskowych ukladu warszawskiego" [Letter from Mikhail Gorbachev President of the USSR to Lech Walesa President of the RP Concerning Liquidation of the Warsaw Treaty Military Structures] (12 February 1991, Delivered in Warsaw on 13 February 1991), *Zbior Dokumentow*, no. 1 (1992): 213–214.

96. Miklos Ritecz, "Walesa: Let There Be an Opening," *Nepszabadsag*, (Budapest), 13 February 1991, *FBIS-EEU*, 19 February 1991, 2–3; "Walesa to Attend Cooperation Summit in Visegrad; Views European Cooperation," Prague Federal 1 Television Network, 1830 GMT, 12 February 1991, *FBIS-EEU*, 14 February 1991, 30; and "[Walesa] Interviewed Prior to Meeting," CTK, 2114 GMT, 12 February 1991, *FBIS-EEU*, 14 February 1991, 30.

97. "Ceremonial Declaration," MTI, 15 February 1991, *FBIS-EEU*, 19 February 1991, 5.

98. Kostrzewa-Zorbas provided this important insight to me about Poland's initiative to create a formalized cooperative security process among the Visegrad states when they both participated in the first NATO–Central European workshop from 4 to 6 February 1991 in Oslo, Norway, just one week before the Visegrad Summit. See "Deklaracja o wspolpracy Rzeczypospolitej Polskiej Czeskiej i Slowackiej Republiki Federacyjnej i Republiki Wegierskiej w dazeniu do integracji Europejskiej" [Declaration of the Republic of Poland, the Czech and Slovak Federal Republic and the Republic of Hungary on Cooperation in Pursuit of European Integration] (Visegrad, 15 February 1991), *Zbior Dokumentow*, no. 1 (1992): 236–237; and "Declaration Accepted at the Tri-partite Summit in Visegrad," MTI, 15 February 1991, *FBIS-EEU*. 19 February 1991, 4.

99. Kostrzewa-Zorbas, "The Russian Troop Withdrawal from Poland," 117–118.

100. "Deklaracja o wspolpracy Rzeczypospolitej Polskiej Czeskiej i Slowackiej Republiki Federacyjnej i Republiki Wegierskiej," 236.

101. "Deklaracja o wspolpracy Rzeczypospolitej Polskiej Czeskiej i Slowackiej Republiki Federacyjnej i Republiki Wegierskiej," 238; Tokes, "From Visegrad to Krakow," 111–112; and Spero, "The Budapest-Prague-Warsaw Triangle," 63–64.

102. "Przemowienie ministra spraw zagranicznych RP Krzysztofa Skubiszewskiego na posiedzeniu doradczego komitetu politycznego ukladu warszawskiego" [Address by the Polish Foreign Minister Krzysztof Skubiszewski at the Session of the Political Consultative Committee of the Warsaw Treaty] (Budapest, 25 February 1991), *Zbior Dokumentow*, no. 1 (1992): 217–220. See also "Protokol o uchyleniu porozumien wojskowych zawartych w ramach Ukladu Warszawskiego oraz o rozwiazaniu jego organow i struktur wojskowych" [Protocol on the Waiver of the Military Agreements Concluded in the Framework of the Warsaw Pact and on the Dissolution of its Organs and Military Structures] (Budapest, 25 February 1991), *Zbior Dokumentow*, no. 1 (1992): 221–224.

103. Istvan Kulcsar, "Antall Summarizes Summit," Budapest Domestic Service, 15 February 1991, *FBIS-EEU*, 19 February 1991, 11.

104. "Havel on Regional Foreign Policy," MTV Television Network (Budapest), 2010 GMT, 15 February 1991, *FBIS-EEU*, 19 February 1991, 11–12.

105. See "Skubiszewski on Cooperation with Hungary, CSFR," PAP, 17 April 1991, *FBIS-EEU*, 18 April 1991, 29; and "Skubiszewski on Cooperation with Prague, Budapest," *Rzeczpospolita*, 18 April 1991, *FBIS-EEU*, 23 April 1991, 32.

106. Indeed, shortly after the Visegrad Summit, Poland signed bilateral military agreements with both Central European counterparts. See Wieslaw Rasala, "A Working Visit by the CSFR Defense Minister," *Polska Zbrojna*, 28 February 1991, *FBIS-EEU*, 5 March 1991, 26; F.E.D., "Polish-Hungarian Military Accord," *Gazeta Wyborcza*, 21 March 1991, *FBIS-EEU*, 27 March 1991, 26.

107. "Protokol o rozwiazaniu Rady Wzajemnej Pomocy Gospodarczej" [Protocol on the Disbandment of the Council for Mutual Economic Assistance] (Budapest, 28 June 1991), *Zbior Dokumentow*, no. 1 (1992): 232–233; "Protocol o prekrashchenii deistviia Dogovora o druzhbe, sortudnichestva i vzaimnoi pomoshchi, podpisannogo v Varshava 4 Maia 1955 goda, i Protokola o prodlenii sroka ego deistviia, podpisannogo 26 Aprelia 1985 goda, v Varshave" [Protocol Ending the Validity of the Treaty of Friendship, Cooperation, and Mutual Assistance Signed in Warsaw, 14 May 1955 and of the Protocol Extending its Validity Signed in Warsaw, 26 April 1985], *Izvestiia*, 3 July 1991, 5. For an excellent overview of the history of the Warsaw Pact, including very important and recent revelations from German documents about the Pact's demise, see Frank Umbach, "Die Evolution des Warschauer Paktes als aussen—und militarpolitisches Instrument sowjetischer Sicherheitspolitik 1955–1991" [The Evolution of the Warsaw Pact Externally—The Military-Political Instrument of Soviet Security 1955–1991] (Ph.D. dissertation, 1995, University of Bonn).

108. Zartman, "In Search of Common Elements in the Analysis of the Negotiation Process," 7–8; Daniel Druckman, "Stages, Turning Points and Crises," *Journal of Conflict Resolution*, no. 30 (1986): 327–360; and Joshua B. Spero, "Evolving Security in Central Europe," *Military Review*, vol. 74, no. 2 (February 1994): 56–63.

109. See Jeffrey Rubin and Bert Brown, *The Social Psychology of Bargaining and Negotiation* (New York: Academic, 1975)

110. Some of the fundamental aspects of contemporary negotiating behavior originated in Francois De Callieres, *On the Manner of Negotiating With Princes* (Notre Dame, Ind.: University of Notre Dame Press, 1963) and in F. De Felice, "Negotiations, or the

Art of Negotiating," in *The 50% Solution*, ed. I. William Zartman (New York: Anchor, 1976), 45.

111. For important analysis of the battle over policies toward Central and Eastern Europe between the Soviet Communist Party Central Committee's international department and the foreign ministry, see Suzanne Crow, "International Department and Foreign Ministry Disagree on Eastern Europe," *Report on the USSR*, Radio Liberty, vol. 226, no. 91 (13 June 1991): 4–8.

112. See Iulii Kvitsinskii, "Vostochnaya Evropa: Chto gryadet s peremenani" [Eastern Europe: What is Coming from the Changes], *Pravda*, 18 March 1991, 1.

113. See Kostrzewa-Zorbas, "The Russian Troop Withdrawal from Poland," 120.

114. "O razvitii obstanovski v Vostochnoi Evrope i nashei politike v etom regione" [On the Development of the Situation in Eastern Europe and Our Policy toward that Region], *Izvestiia TsK KPSS* (Moscow), no. 3 (1991): 3-6.

115. The following Polish *MSZ* accounts come from the chief negotiator, Grzegorz Kostrzewa-Zorbas, who led Warsaw in tough head-to-head talks and who coordinated closely with his Czechoslovak and Hungarian counterparts to challenge Soviet hardliners. He resigned from his negotiation posts for both the friendship and force withdrawal treaties in July 1991, on account mainly of his frustration with Poland's acquiescence to Moscow hard-liners. Insights provided by Kostrzewa-Zorbas to me in Oslo on 5 February 1991 and in Washington, D.C., on 25 March 1993. See also Kostrzewa-Zorbas, "The Russian Troop Withdrawal from Poland," 120–121; and Kostrzewa-Zorbas, "Imperium kontratakuje," 177–178.

116. Kostrzewa-Zorbas told me in Washington, D.C., on 25 March 1993 that, in December 1990 "a restriction on intelligence cooperation appeared only in the earliest draft, addressed to Hungary. Budapest's reaction was so strongly negative that Moscow erased that fragment from all the later drafts." Hungarian official Ivan Baba, chief of policy planning in the Ministry of Foreign Affairs, also confirmed this Soviet strategy to me on 18 June 1991 in Budapest.

117. Suzanne Crow, "Negotiating New Treaties with Eastern Europe," *Report on the USSR*, Radio Liberty, vol. 252, no. 91 (8 July 1991): 3–6; and Michael Stuermer, "Vistula, Moldau, Danube: How the Soviet Union Is Seeking a New Concept of Eastern Europe," *Frankfurter Allgemeine*, 7 June 1991, *FBIS-SOV*, 25 June 1991, 18–19.

118. "Problemy polityki zagranicznej u progu roku 1991—wystapienie ministra spraw zagranicznych RP Krzysztofa Skubiszewskiego w sejmie" [Foreign Policy Issues at the Start of 1991—Address by Polish Foreign Minister Krzysztof Skubiszewski in Sejm] (14 February 1991), *Zbior Dokumentow*, no. 1 (1992): 33–34.

119. "Report on Speech by Foreign Minister Krzysztof Skubiszewski during a Meeting of Sejm Foreign Affairs Commission," *Rzeczpospolita*, 18 April 1991, *FBIS-EEU*, 23 April 1991, 32. See also Miklos Ritecz, "Wedged between Two Powers: Interview with Foreign Minister Krzysztof Skubiszewski," *Nepszabadsag*, 6 June 1991, *FBIS-EEU*, 11 June 1991, 31–32; and "Polityka Zagraniczna Rzeczypospolitej Polskiej w roku 1991—Expose Sejmowe Ministra Spraw Zagranicznych RP Krzysztofa Skubiszewskiego" [The Foreign Policy of the Republic of Poland in 1991—Sejm Exposé of the Polish Foreign Minister Krzysztof Skubiszewski] (Warsaw, 27 June 1991), *Zbior Dokumentow*, no. 1 (1992): 53, 58.

120. Quote from Kostrzewa-Zorbas during interview with me in Washington, D.C., on 25 March 1993. See also J.B., "We Are Still Neighbors," *Zycie Warszawy*, 13-14 July 1991, *FBIS-SOV*, 16 July 1991, 39–40; and "Report on [Falin] Visit [to Warsaw]," TASS International Service, 1417 GMT, 14 July 1991, *FBIS-SOV*, 16 July 1991, 40.

121. Interview I conducted with Kostrzewa-Zorbas in Washington on March 25, 1993. See also Grzegorz Lubczyk, "Closer rather than Further: Interview with Jerzy Sulek, Chief of the European Department, Ministry of Foreign Affairs," *Zycie Warszawy*, 17 July 1991, *FBIS-EEU*, 22 July 1991, 22–23; and Ewa Boniecka, "We Are Helping Europe Unite: Interview with Polish Foreign Minister Krzysztof Skubiszewski," *Zycie Warszawy*, 24 July 1991, *FBIS-EEU*, 30 July 1991, 31.

122. "Breakthrough in Polish-Soviet Relations," PAP, 2314 GMT, 7 October 1991, *FBIS-EEU*, 8 October 1991, 28.

123. "Makarczyk Hails 'Splendid Treaty' with Russia," Radio Warszawa Network, 11 December 1991, *FBIS-EEU*, 12 December 1991, 23; "Polish Vice Foreign Minister Holds Talks; Treaty Seen as 'Model," PAP, 1904 GMT, 10 December 1991, *FBIS-SOV*, 11 December 1991, 9; "Antall, Jeszenszky Return from Moscow, Kiev Tour: Antall Notes Prospects for Ties," MTV Television Network, 7 December 1991, *FBIS-EEU*, 9 December 1991, 19; and "Dienstbier, [Soviet Foreign Minister] Pankin Sign Cooperation Treaty," *Ceskoslovenky Rozhlas*, 3 October 1991, *FBIS-EEU*, 4 October 1991, 7.

124. For winning techniques in final negotiating stages, see George Homans, *Social Behavior* (New York: Harcourt Brace, 1961), 61; and Zartman and Berman, *The Practical Negotiator*, 191–202.

125. Joshua B. Spero, "Central European Security," in *The Future of European Security: The Pursuit of Peace in an Era of Revolutionary Change*, ed. J. Philip Rogers. (New York: St. Martin's, 1993), 141–151; Alfred Reisch, "Central and Eastern Europe's Quest for NATO Membership," *RL/RFE Weekly Report* (9 July 1993): 33–47; Jeffrey Simon, "Does Eastern Europe Belong in NATO?" *Orbis* (winter 1993): 21–35; and Tokes, "From Visegrad to Krakow," 110–114.

126. "Foreign Policy Outlined Further," PAP, 2045 GMT, 12 March 1991, *FBIS-EEU*, 13 March 1991, 38. Among the top issues for 1991, Skubiszewski prioritized "closer Visegrad regional cooperation" and "more intensive cooperation with security organizations such as NATO."

127. The following analysis comes from the *MSZ* memorandum written by Grzegorz Kostrzewa-Zorbas, "System Bezpieczenstwa Miedzynarodowego: Dla Polski i Europy Srodkowej na lata dziewiecdziesiate" [The International Security System: For Poland and Central Europe in the 1990s] (Warsaw, 16 March 1991), 1–9. It is very important to note that Kostrzewa-Zorbas, even before he entered Skubiszewski's *MSZ* in June 1990 and a year before the Warsaw Pact disbanded, discussed the innovative concept of "observer NATO status" with both Phillip Petersen and me on 21 March 1990 in the Pentagon. According to Kostrzewa-Zorbas, "observer status in NATO for all the member states of the Warsaw Pact would ease 90 per cent of the expected security tensions in Central and Eastern Europe." Kostrzewa-Zorbas integrated this notion into his *MSZ* memorandum for Skubiszewski's NATO policies. See also Petersen, "The Challenge to Soviet Strategic Deployment," 330.

128. Najder, *Jaka Polska*, 210–215.

129. "Center Alliance Congress Proceedings Reported," PAP, 2124 GMT, 2 March 1991, *FBIS-EEU*, 8 March 1991, 39. Note that Kostrzewa-Zorbas also spoke at the national congress as a guest expert on foreign affairs and discussed the importance of NATO membership. Kostrzewa-Zorbas told me in Washington on 17 March 1998 that his speech to the Center Alliance's congress seven years earlier might have "pushed the envelope on Poland's future NATO membership, realistically or not." Even so, Kostrzewa-Zorbas believed he played a catalytic role in the important "Polish national debate on NATO membership itself."

130. See, for example, Ryszard Malik, "We Are Opening Up to the West, but Not Closing to the East: Interview with Foreign Minister Krzysztof Skubiszewski," *Rzeczpospolita*, 26 March 1991, *FBIS-EEU*, 3 April 1991, 25; Ritecz, "Wedged between Two Powers: Interview with Foreign Minister Krzysztof Skubiszewski," 31–32; and "Polska a bezpieczenstwo Europejskie—przemowienie Ministra Spraw Zagranicznych RP Krzysztofa Skubiszewskiego, do Zgromadzenia Polnocnoatlantyckiego" [Poland and European Security—Address by the Polish Foreign Minister Krzysztof Skubiszewski to the North Atlantic Assembly] (London, 29 November 1990), *Zbior Dokumentow*, no. 4 (1991): 10–11.

131. Statement issued by the North Atlantic Council Meeting in Ministerial Session in Copenhagen, 6–7 June 1991. At a press conference afterwards, U.S. secretary of state James Baker stated that "we believe that the principles we have announced will make it clear to the Soviets and to the Central and Eastern Europeans that NATO is serious about reaching out to former adversaries to build an atmosphere of trust and cooperation across Europe." See Press Conference by Secretary of State James A. Baker III at the Conclusion of the Ministerial Meeting of the North Atlantic Council, Bella Conference Center, 7 June 1991.

132. Aleksandr Bovin, "Mnenie politicheskogo obozrevatelia: Voennoe sotrudnichestvo prekrashchaetsia" [Political Observer opinion: Military Cooperation Ending], *Izvestiia*, 28 February 1991, 6.

133. Gabor Izbeki, "Political Scientist Who Works in the CPSU Central Committee," Budapest Domestic Service, 24 March 1991, *FBIS-SOV*, 25 March 1991, 22–23.

134. Valentin Sharov, "Tochka Zrenie: 'Troika' v Tsentre Evropy" [Viewpoint: 'Troika' in Central Europe], *Pravda*, 25 January 1991, 4; and F. Luk'ianov, "'Troistvennyi Soiuz' v Vostochnoi Evrope?" ['Triple Alliance' in Central Europe?], *Izvestiia*, 16 February 1991, 1.

135. A. Iazkova, "Two Days without Allies; No War So Far," *Komsomol'skaia Pravda* (Moscow), 2 April 1991, *FBIS-SOV*, 9 April 1991, 4.

136. Iazkova, "Two Days without Allies"; and S. Egorov, "Pol'sha: V Poiskakh Novoi Kontseptsii Oborony" [Poland: Looking for a New Defense Concept], *Krasnaya Zvezda*, 9 May 1991, 2.

137. L. Kliusa, "Polputi Eshche Vperedi" [Halfway Point Still Ahead], *Krasnaya Zvezda*, 27 March 1991, 5.

138. V. Peresada, "Flagi v Rotterdame: V NATO-svoia Perestroika" [Flags in Rotterdam: NATO's Own Perestroika], *Pravda*, 29 May 1991, 4; and Vikentii Matveev, "Mnenie politicheskogo obozrevatelia: Perestroika v NATO" [Political Observer's Opinion: Perestroika in NATO], *Izvestiia*, 11 June 1991, 4.

139. Karaganov belonged to the Institute for Europe and often made statements on behalf of the Soviet leadership. Interview by Philip Petersen and me with Karaganov in Moscow on 21 March 1990.

140. Csilla Medgyesi, "Europe Needs Collective Security: Interview with Sergei Karaganov, Deputy Director of the USSR Institute of Europe," *Magyar Hirlap* (Budapest), 15 June 1991, *FBIS-SOV*, 19 June 1991, 15.

141. The language quoted in Walesa's 3 July 1991 speech at NATO headquarters reflects the changes made by the *MSZ* and approved by Skubiszewski for inclusion in Walesa's final draft. The revisions come from the 27 June 1991 *MSZ* draft I obtained, which show all of the *MSZ* revisions accepted by Walesa's staff.

142. In addition to the text of the Polish president's speech, see "Poland's Walesa Speaks at NATO Headquarters: Alters Speech on USSR," PAP, 2152 GMT, 3 July 1991,

FBIS-WEU, 5 July 1991, 2; and Valerii Peresada, "Dogonit li Pol'sha 'Briussel'skii Ekspress?'" [Will Poland Catch up with the 'Brussels Express?'], *Pravda*, 8 July 1991, 3.

143. "Kolodziejczyk Meets Hungarian, Czech [Defense] Ministers," PAP, 1651 GMT, 2 August 1991, *FBIS-EEU*, 5 August 1991, 28; and "[Polish Defense] Minister Discusses Regional Security, Technology," MTI, 1622 GMT, 25 September 1991, *FBIS-EEU*, 26 September 1991, 20–21. Both Najder and Kostrzewa-Zorbas, who participated in the Krakow consultative meeting, told me in Warsaw on 11 June 1991 about their hopes for the meeting. Najder also recounts his satisfaction with the success of the event in Najder, *Jaka Polska*, 244.

144. The minister of state for national security, a close colleague of Kostrzewa-Zorbas from their Gdansk *Solidarnosc* days when Kaczynski advised labor leader Walesa, advocated the tenets of Kostrzewa-Zorbas's March 1991 NATO memorandum, as analyzed above.

145. Zbigniew Lentowicz, "An Emergence from 'No Man's Land' into the West,'" *Rzeczpospolita*, 23 May 1991, *FBIS-EEU*, 30 May 1991, 16; and Krzysztof Skubiszewski, "Future Architecture of European Security," in *Jane's NATO Handbook, 1991–1992*, ed. Bruce George (Coulsdon, U.K.: Jane's Information Group, 1991), 391–393. In an interview by me with Lech Kaczynski and Grzegorz Kostrzewa-Zorbas in Warsaw on 11 June 1991, Kaczynski related many of these points about Poland's national security concerns.

146. For descriptions of the Triangle's emergency meeting in Warsaw and the post-Soviet rebellion analysis, see, inter alia, "Polish, Hungarian, and Czech Ministers Meet," *DPA Communiqué* (Warsaw), 20 August 1991, 1; "Walesa Discusses Soviet Situation with World Leaders; Bush Calls Walesa," PAP, 0036 GMT, 20 August 1991, *FBIS-EEU*, 21 August 1991, 20; "Mitterrand, Delors Calls," PAP, 2102 GMT, 20 August 1991, *FBIS-EEU*, 21 August 1991, 20; Peter Michielsen, "Interview with Polish Foreign Minister Krzysztof Skubiszewski," *NRC Handelsblad*, 4 September 1991, *FBIS-EEU*, 11 September 1991, 21; Mary Battiata, "3 E. European Nations Discuss Soviet Crisis," *Washington Post*, 22 August 1991, A27; and Maria Wagrowska, "State of Alert Called Off: Interview with Defense Minister Piotr Kolodziejczyk," *Rzeczpospolita*, 11 September 1991, *FBIS-EEU*, 17 September 1991, 23-25.

147. Joint Statement by Secretary of State James A. Baker III and Hans-Dietrich Genscher, minister of foreign affairs for the Federal Republic of Germany, U.S. Department of State, Washington, D.C., 2 October 1991.

148. "Declaration Issued," PAP, 1720 GMT, 6 October 1991, *FBIS-EEU*, 8 October 1991, 5; "Baker's NATO Plan Welcomed," MTI, 1931 GMT, 5 October 1991, *FBIS-EEU*, 8 October 1991, 7; "Ministers Welcome Euro-Atlantic Pact Idea," Cekoslovensky Rozhlas Radio Network, 1500 GMT, 6 October 1991, *FBIS-EEU*, 8 October 1991, 8.

149. Robert Walenciak, "Poland and the Triad: Interview with President Lech Walesa," *Sztandar Mlodych* (Warsaw), 4–6 October 1991, *FBIS-EEU*, 10 October 1991, 18–19; and "Walesa on Joint Activity with CSFR, Hungary," Radio Warszawa Network, 0700 GMT, 4 October 1991, *FBIS-EEU*, 4 October 1991, 24.

150. "Interview with Polish Foreign Minister Krzysztof Skubiszewski after a Tripartite Meeting between Delegations from Poland, Czechoslovakia, and Hungary in Krakow," Radio Warszawa Network, 1800 GMT, 5 October 1991, *FBIS-EEU*, 8 October 1991, 2.

151. MSZ, "The Krakow Declaration," 6 October 1991, Krakow, Poland, 1–4; Timothy Thomas, "The Significance of the Cracow Summit," *European Security*, vol. 1, no. 1

(spring 1992): 101–108; Spero, "The Budapest-Prague-Warsaw Triangle," 70–72; and Tokes, "From Visegrad to Krakow," 110–114.

152. Both Walesa and Skubiszewski quoted in "Leaders Hold News Conference," Radio Warszawa Network, 1818 GMT, 6 October 1991, *FBIS-EEU*, 8 October 1991, 5-6. See also *Report on the State of National Security: External Aspects*, ed. Henryk Szlajfer (Warsaw: Polish Institute of International Affairs, 1993); and Latawski, "The Polish Road to NATO," 69–88.

153. "Kierunki polityki zagranicznej: Doroczne exposé wygloszone w Sejmie RP" [Directions of Foreign Policy: Annual Report Delivered in the Polish Sejm] (27 June 1991), in Kryzsztof Skubiszewski, *Polityka zagraniczna i odzyskanie niepodlegnosci: przemówienia, oswiadczenia, wywiady 1989–1993* [Foreign Policy and Regaining Independence: Addresses, Declaration, Interviews, 1989–1993] (Warsaw: Wydawa Interpress, 1997), 143–160.

154. Though this book only analyzes Polish foreign policy until late 1993 in its case studies of the Skubiszewski era and does not examine the evolution of NATO in great depth, particularly its substantial post–Cold War transformation after 1993, it is important to note that NATO arguably failed to define the framework for NATO enlargement in the post–Cold War era until late 1995, with the release of its *Study on NATO Enlargement*. Furthermore, NATO only issued invitations to the Triangle states in 1997 and integrated them into NATO's political and military structures in March 1999, the first invitations offered in the post–Cold War period excluding the absorption of the GDR into unified Germany in 1990. For important and detailed analyses of Poland's foreign and defense policy efforts to integrate into NATO in the period from 1994 to 1999, see, among others, Andrzej Ananicz, Przemyslaw Grudzinski, Andrzej Olechowski, Janusz Onyszkiewicz, Krzysztof Skubiszewski, and Henryk Szlajfer, *Poland-NATO: Report of the Discussions at the Euro-Atlantic Association and the Stefan Batory Foundation* (Warsaw: Center for International Relations, 1995); Andrew A. Michta, "Safeguarding the Third Republic: Security Policy and Military Reform," in *Polish Foreign Policy Reconsidered: Challenges of Independence*, eds. Ilya Prizel and Andrew A. Michta (Houndmills, U.K.: Macmillan, 1995), 73–94; Jeffrey Simon, *NATO Enlargement and Central Europe: A Study in Civil-Military Relations* (Washington, D.C.: National Defense University Press, 1996); Joshua B. Spero, "Poland's Perennial Crossroads: Between East and West?" in *The Future of East-Central Europe*, eds. Andrzej Dumala and Ziemowit Jacek Pietras (Lublin, Poland: Maria Curie-Sklodowska University Press, 1996), 273–291; Daniel N. Nelson and Thomas S. Szayna, "New NATO, New Problems: NATO's Metamorphosis and Its New Members," *Problems of Post-Communism*, vol. 45, no. 4 (July–August 1998), 32–43; and *America's New Allies: Poland, Hungary, and the Czech Republic in NATO*, ed. Andrew A. Michta (Seattle: University of Washington Press, 2000).

155. North Atlantic Council, "The Rome Declaration on Peace and Cooperation," 7–8 November 1991, NATO Press Service, Brussels.

156. Note that this book does not analyze Polish–EC relations in great depth because other Polish ministries primarily covered the strategies and negotiations with the EC than the *MSZ*. "Polska w Radzie Europy: Przemowienie wygloszone podczas uroczystosci przystapienia Polski do Rady Europy" [Poland and the European Union: Speech Delivered during the Important Meeting between Poland and the European Union] (Strasburg, 26 November 1991), in Kryzsztof Skubiszewski, *Polityka zagraniczna i odzyskanie niepodlegnosci: przemówienia, oswiadczenia, wywiady 1989–1993* [Foreign Policy and Regaining Independence: Addresses, Declaration, Interviews, 1989–1993] (Warsaw: Wydawa Interpress, 1997), 185–186; Jacek Safuta, "Poland-CSFR-Hungary Discuss

Future Cooperation," PAP, 2320 GMT, 16 December 1991, *FBIS-EEU*, 17 December 1991, 2; and "Skubiszewski Urges Continued Reforms," Warsaw TVP Television Network, 1830 GMT, 16 December 1991, *FBIS-EEU*, 17 December 1991, 31.

157. See, for example, Petr Janyska, "We Have to Keep Together: Interview with Foreign Minister Krzysztof Skubiszewski," *Respekt* (Prague), no. 5 (3–9 February 1992), *FBIS-EEU*, 7 February 1992, 17–19; Vinton, "Domestic Politics and Foreign Policy," 54–56; and Jan B. de Weydenthal, "Poland's Security Policy," *RFE/RL Research Report*, vol. 2, no. 14 (2 April 1993): 31–33.

158. Andrzejewski, "Leopards on the Vistula: Interview with Polish Foreign Minister Krzysztof Skubiszewski," *Wprost* (Poznan), 8 March 1992, *FBIS-EEU*, 17 March 1992, 11; "Address by Polish Foreign Minister Krzysztof Skubiszewski at Sejm Session," Warsaw TVP Television Network, 0733 GMT, 8 May 1992, *FBIS-EEU*, 12 May 1992, 17, 19; and Lech Lewandowski, "Reforms and the Interests of a Law-Governed State: Interview with Foreign Minister Krzysztof Skubiszewski," *Polska Zbrojna*, 19–21 June 1992, *FBIS-EEU*, 30 June 1992, 24.

159. "Visegrad Triangle Defense Meeting in Budapest: Antall Meets Ministers," Kossuth Radio Network, 6 March 1992, *FBIS-EEU*, 9 March 1992, 2–3; "NATO, CIS, Ex-Warsaw Pact Nations Hold Talks; Dobrovsky: 'Exceeded Expectations,'" CSTK, 1 April 1992, *FBIS-EEU*, 2 April 1992, 2.

160. "[Visegrad Triangle] Joint Communiqué Adopted," MTI, 6 May 1992, *FBIS-EEU*, 7 May 1992, 3.

161. "Klaus Calls Visegrad Grouping 'Artificial,'" CTK, 11 January 1993, *FBIS-EEU*, 13 January 1993, 7; and "Czech Premier Klaus' 'Aversion' to Visegrad Noted," *Gazeta Wyborcza*, 11 January 1993, *FBIS-EEU*, 14 January 1993, 30. For important analyses of the difficulties arising from the CSFR's breakup and its impact on broad regional cooperation and Central European–NATO relations, particularly assessment of the period after that covered by this book, see, inter alia, Simon, "Czechoslovakia's Velvet Divorce," 11–26; Cottey, *East-Central Europe after the Cold War*, 131–148; and Rhodes, "The Idea of Central Europe and Visegrad Cooperation," 179–183.

162. Maria Wagrowska, "Visegrad Is Still Relevant: Interview with Defense Minister Onyszkiewicz," *Rzeczpospolita*, 29 January 1993, *FBIS-EEU*, 4 February 1993, 26; Jozsef Martin, "The Strategic Goal of the Hungarian Government Is to Develop the Best Relations with Neighboring Countries: Interview with Foreign Minister Jeszsenszky," *Magyar Nemzet* (Budapest), 6 February 1993, *FBIS-EEU*, 10 February 1993, 15; Jan Zizka, "It Is Not True That Visegrad Was the West's Initiative: Interview with Foreign Minister Jeszsenszky," *Rude Pravo*, 1 March 1993, *FBIS-EEU*, 9 March 1993, 4; and "Walesa Sees Regional Cooperation as 'Protection,'" CTK, 2 March 1993, *FBIS-EEU*, 5 March 1993, 4. It remains important to understand that Triangle ministers continued to coordinate and meet, even after the Czech reluctance to advance the Visegrad cooperation. "Visegrad Troika Ministers Discuss CSFR Split," Kossuth Radio Network, 25 September 1992, *FBIS-EEU*, 28 September 1992, 7; "Visegrad Countries to Cooperate in Military Production," CSTK, 20 November 1992, *FBIS-EEU*, 24 November 1992, 19; and "Visegrad Three Chiefs of Staff Meet," *RFE/RL Military and Security Notes*, Issue no. 48 (24 November 1992): 11.

163. "Klaus Says Economic Reforms Vital for Region," CTK, 18 January 1993, *FBIS-EEU*, 19 January 1993, 23. For insights on the Visegrad Group's economic progress and military consultations, see Karoly Okoliczanyi, "The Visegrad Triangle's Free-Trade Zone," *RFE/RL Research Report*, vol. 2, no. 3 (15 January 1993): 19–22; "Visegrad Defense Ministers Discuss NATO Ties," CTK, 29 March 1993, *FBIS-EEU*, 29

March 1993, 5; Jan B. de Weydenthal, "The EC and Central Europe: A Difficult Relationship," *RFE/RL*, vol. 2, no. 21 (21 May 1993): 7–9; and Milada Anna Vachudova, "The Visegrad Four: No Alternative to Cooperation?," *RFE/RL Research Report*, no. 34 (27 August 1993): 33–47.

164. Pavol Minarik, "There Should Not Be Various Security Zones in Europe: Interview with Foreign Minister Krzysztof Skubiszewski," *Rude Pravo* (Prague), 9 June 1993, *FBIS-EEU*, 16 June 1993, 21.

165. "Oczekiwania Polski wobec Wspolnoty Europejskiej i NATO: Wypowiedz podczas dyskusji Okraglego Stolu zudzialem Ministrow Spraw Zagranicznych Francji, Niemiec, Polski i Wielkiej Brytanii" [Poland's Expectations for the European Community and NATO: Declaration during Round Table Discussions with French, German, Polish, and British Foreign Ministers Participating] (Bonn, Germany, 10 September 1993), in Kryzsztof Skubiszewski, *Polityka zagraniczna i odzyskanie niepodleglosci: przemówienia, oswiadczenia, wywiady 1989–1993* [Foreign Policy and Regaining Independence: Addresses, Declaration, Interviews, 1989–1993] (Warsaw: Wydawa Interpress, 1997), 357–358.

166. "Skubiszewski, NATO Secretary General Meet," PAP, 1447 GMT, 9 March 1993, *FBIS-EEU*, 10 March 1993, 32; Malgorzata Alterman, "On the Threshold of the Pact: Interview with NATO Secretary General Manfred Woerner," *Gazeta Wyborcza*, 17 March 1993, *FBIS-EEU*, 24 March 1993, 27.

167. See, among others, "Ruehe Favors Extension of NATO into Eastern Europe," DPA (Hamburg), 31 March 1993, *FBIS-WEU*, 31 March 1993, 19; "Ruehe Open for New NATO Members," *Frankfurter Allgemeine*, 22 May 1993, *FBIS-WEU*, 24 May 1993, 22–23; and "Press Conference of Secretary of Defense Les Aspin and Minister of Defense Volker Ruehe," Inauguration of the George C. Marshall Center for European Security, Garmisch-Partenkirchen, Germany, 5 June 1993, 2.

168. This book does not account for NATO initiatives toward non-NATO states in-depth after Skubiszewski's terms in office, such as NATO's January 1994 summit announcement of the Partnership for Peace process, but the concluding chapter does assess the implications for Skubiszewski's legacy within the context for Poland's integration into NATO by March 1999 and for Poland's middle power role in coalition building for the twenty-first century. For important background that recounts critical NATO turning points, especially after 1993, see Spero and Umbach, *NATO's Security Challenge to the East and the American-German Geo-Strategic Partnership in Europe*; Catherine M. Kelleher, *The Future of European Security* (Washington, D.C.: Brookings Institution, 1995), 78–135; Sean Kay, *NATO and the Future of European Security* (Lanham, Md.: Rowman & Littlefield, 1998), 89–122; and David S. Yost, *NATO Transformed: The Alliance's New Roles in International Security* (Washington, D.C.: U.S. Institute of Peace Press, 1998).

169. "Wspolpraca Francusko-Niemiecka—Model dla Polski i Europy Srodkowej?" [Franco-German Collaboration—Model for Poland and Central Europe?], in Kryzsztof Skubiszewski, *Polityka zagraniczna i odzyskanie niepodleglosci: przemówienia, oswiadczenia, wywiady 1989–1993* [Foreign Policy and Regaining Independence: Addresses, Declaration, Interviews, 1989–1993] (Warsaw: Wydawa Interpress, 1997), 293–297.

170. "Walesa, El'tsin News Conference," Warsaw TVP Television First Program Network, 0901 GMT, 25 August 1993, *FBIS-EEU*, 26 August 1993, 12; "Skubiszewski on Talks with Russian Foreign Minister," Radio Warszawa Network, 1700 GMT, 25 August 1993, *FBIS-EEU*, 26 August 1993, 13; "[Russian] Envoy: Russian View of

NATO Membership 'Misunderstood,'" PAP, 2027 GMT, 15 September 1993, *FBIS-EEU*, 16 September 1993, 20; "El'tsin's Secret Letter on NATO Expansion," *Mlada Fronta Dnes* (Prague), 2 December 1993, *FBIS-SOV*, 3 December 1993, 6; Prochazkova and J. Stetina, "Interview with El'tsin Foreign Policy Advisor, Dmitrii Rurikov: You No Longer Need to Be Afraid of US," *Lidove Noviny* (Prague), 15 December 1993, *FBIS-SOV*, 20 December 1993, 49.

171. Skubiszewski quoted in "Havel Meets with Walesa during Visit," PAP, 2118 GMT, 21 October 1993, *FBIS-EEU*, 22 October 1993, 17.

172. Krzysztof Skubiszewski, "The Imperative of Continuity," *Rzeczpospolita*, 29 September 1993, *FBIS-EEU*, 30 September 1993, 28.

Conclusion

Why Middle Powers Matter

Did post-Communist middle power Poland matter to its great power neighbors geopolitically from 1989 to 1993? Indeed, this book contends that Polish foreign minister Krzysztof Skubiszewski and his dynamic *MSZ* European Department staff devised, crafted, and promulgated an other-help alignment strategy that mattered toward Warsaw's transitioning post–Cold War neighbors. When faced with a range of potentially threatening developments by Poland's larger, rapidly changing neighbors, particularly between Germany and Russia, Skubiszewski's other-help alignment epitomized mainly a "bridging" strategy. This strategy of building bilaterally linked ties among and between great, middle, and smaller powers increased Poland's security and decreased its historic security dilemma. Skubiszewski recognized throughout his academic career during the Communist era and his four successive terms as the longest lasting post-Communist minister that Poland's options remained limited geopolitically. The security threats stemmed mainly from the great powers Germany and Russia. To reintegrate into Europe, Skubiszewski publicly pronounced from September 1989 that Poland needed to crystallize its policy of *racja stanu*—its *raison d'état* or "interest of the state." By regaining this key objective of full sovereignty over foreign policy, Skubiszewski demonstrated Poland's *racja stanu* by redefining and, as assessed in this book's case studies, also defining new bilateral and trilateral linkages to all neighbors.[1] This signified Poland's grappling with historical turning points very rapidly regarding German unification, Soviet disintegration, and European security upheaval. By seeking cooperation to reduce perceived and real regional threats, Skubiszewski attempted to gain the reward of European reintegration. Thus, he chose to encourage and shape, rather than prevent, the development of beneficial state-to-state linkages with all neighbors.[2] What he

achieved abroad also resulted in a great impact on foreign policy consensus domestically:

> Membership in an organized Europe and at the same time maintenance of links
> with the East stand for the role Poland is to play for the reason of her geo-
> strategic and geopolitical position. To date, this position has been harmful to
> us, now we want to turn it to our advantage and to the advantage of Europe.[3]

> We must develop our relations with Germany and the USSR [sic] in a way that
> is different from the way we developed them between the two world wars. Dur-
> ing the thirties, Poland's foreign policy was characterized by the fact that we
> kept an equal distance from Berlin and Moscow. Now, I have a different con-
> cept. . . . In the era of pan-European cooperation, this previously disadvanta-
> geous situation can be turned into something beneficial.[4]

To achieve these long-term goals, Skubiszewski forged Polish foreign policy to enable the country to become a pivotal middle power in the heart of unstable and uncertain early post–Cold War Europe.[5] He carved out an important
niche for Warsaw between West and East to specialize in the role of bridge
builder, not regional disrupter. Each of this book's case studies underlined important alignment strategies that Poland employed as a middle power seeking to
survive in other-help anarchy. Certainly, Skubiszewski maintained that middle
power Poland didn't possess the capability to develop such a regional strategy
on its own amid stronger, rapidly transformed, and potentially aggressive and
hostile great powers. Consequently, Skubiszewski, his *MSZ* European strategists, and the Polish leadership, during four years of constant negotiating and
compromising, methodically implemented a foreign policy characterized by
practical and limited ways to reintegrate into Europe. To a great extent, Poland
achieved these goals without antagonizing regional great, middle, and smaller
powers. On the whole, such a long-term strategy inherently projected a purpose-
ful set of notions that placed Poland in a specialized middle power role to help
countries communicate and cooperate, rather than construct counteralliances.[6]

In a word, realizing that pivotal middle power Poland needed to promote an
other-help approach, Warsaw relied on the "well-being of others," not just depending on itself to achieve its security most effectively.[7] Skubiszewski rendered regional, "multidirectional," and stability-enhancing linkages as his priority. First, German strategy adhered to what his advisor Artur Hajnicz described
as the "with-with" effort, not an alignment pitting Poland "against" Bonn/Berlin,
but rather a way to reconcile and obtain a legally bound western border and support for European institutional reintegration.[8] Secondly, Poland's "two-track"
Eastern policy, emanating primarily from the arguments by Grzegorz Kostrzewa-Zorbas, established vital linkages to Communist and post-Communist
leaders as the USSR dissolved. Given Poland's transition toward a democracy-
based system, Warsaw pulled post-Soviet states toward the West in their foreign
policy decision making, as much as they deemed appropriate. All of Poland's
eastern neighbors supported democracy building during the early Cold War

years, but some like Belarus, Ukraine, and, to an extent, Russia, regressed periodically in their democratic reform implementation. Finally, the Visegrad Triangle process enabled Poland to capitalize on its bilateral linkages to great, middle, and smaller powers between West and East in bridging to countries and institutions nonprovocatively. By using an asymmetrical negotiating strategy, Poland attained such goals as disbanding the Warsaw Pact and instituting equitable and new bilateral security treaties, respectively negotiated between each Visegrad nation and Russia. These achievements allowed Poland to synchronize Triangle strategies toward NATO and the EU for eventual European reintegration. All told, "this multi-directional network of connections was to become a *sui generis* bridge prior to the period when it would become possible to expand Western security institutions into Central Europe."[9]

Skubiszewski consistently chose nonthreatening alignment with Poland's neighbors, not only because of the security and stability realized, but also as a result of the distributive gains to all regional states involved. As argued and analyzed earlier, Skubiszewski's foreign policies toward Germany, the USSR and post-Soviet successor states, and the Visegrad Central European Triangle portrayed predominantly bridging alignment. Bridge building began to overcome historic regional security dilemmas rather than balancing states against one another, bandwagoning with some states against others, or threatening states directly to achieve Polish national security objectives. Yet, instances of balancing alignment or fleeting periods of balancing and bandwagoning policies occurred during the Skubiszewski era, albeit rarely. The instance when Skubiszewski tried to balance Germany and Russia against each other transpired while he failed to convince Bonn to confirm the Polish–German border. Skubiszewski attempted to balance Moscow against Bonn by using Soviet forces in Poland as a diplomatic bargaining chip to gain concessions. After he encountered steadfast German opposition, Skubiszewski quickly abandoned the stratagem of maintaining Soviet troops in Poland, but not without repercussions. He only realized his mistake after Bonn rejected Warsaw's balancing strategy, when Moscow took advantage of Warsaw's delay in starting Soviet force withdrawal negotiations. More often other Polish politicians, including President Lech Walesa and his chancellery, tried unsuccessfully to balance and bandwagon simultaneously. One example of the Polish president's simultaneous bandwagoning and balancing notions concerned the fleeting concept of a preparatory stage to future NATO membership by creating a Baltic–to–Black Sea alliance of states, the NATO-II, that would have excluded Russia. In response, the Polish foreign minister quietly opposed this concept as it isolated a weakened Russia and failed to impress the stronger NATO alliance. Soon, Walesa abandoned his security concept.

For Skubiszewski, the priority remained to promulgate consistently a cooperative set of policies toward all neighboring states and institutions. He always based this priority on Poland's European reintegration and outreach to Russia, a democratizing Russia, even though some pro-Western Russian politicians sometimes viewed antagonistically Poland's attempts to cooperate with NATO.

Given the inconsistent Russian reactions to Polish cooperative strategy toward NATO, Skubiszewski argued continuously for building bridges to Russia and for upholding the merits of integration into democratic European institutions such as NATO. Specifically, he asserted that NATO should promote defensive military doctrine and cooperative security in post–Cold War Europe. Poland maintained this foreign policy position even when NATO nations hesitated to invite Poland to become a NATO member out of fear of angering Russia. Skubiszewski never wavered on the Polish policy of trying to tie Russia to Western security structures, even when both the USSR and Russia, respectively, experienced serious upheaval in late 1991 and late 1993. Consequently, Poland endeavored to promote a policy based on European democratization and integration, trying to support not only those of its neighbors who mattered for regional security, but also those who implemented stability-enhancing policies. Subsequently, Skubiszewski left a strong legacy both regionally and domestically through Poland's foreign policy. The foreign ministers who followed Skubiszewski continued to broaden and expand the bridges he built with all neighbors, reaching beyond the region to solidify bonds across the Atlantic to America. Today, as Poland attempts to promote regional security and stability—for example, in post–Saddam Hussein Iraq—the legacy of Skubiszewski's bridging alignment strategy plays a fundamental role.

Building Domestic Foreign Policy Consensus as a Legacy

Because he remained politically neutral and brought an internationally recognized legal scholar's background to his ministerial responsibilities, Skubiszewski personified a pragmatic post-Communist foreign policy practitioner. Each premier and president supported him as foreign minister and never threatened to force him to resign. His four-year set of terms exemplified Poland's distinct, relatively consistent, and nonprovocative foreign policy. Though he often reacted to the monumental international security changes in Central Europe, Skubiszewski always stuck to his original intent to gain full sovereignty in foreign policy–making and establish new cooperative ties with all the states bordering Poland.

Without fanfare during these four years, he methodically navigated post-Communist Polish foreign policy through periodic domestic upheaval. At times, President Walesa's mercurial policies or Premier Jan Olszewski's governmental stalemate with the president's chancellery, and maintained his foreign policy tenets caused Skubiszewski to sidetrack his methodical approach. Notwithstanding such temporary sidetracking, Skubiszewski brought some bright non-Communist *Solidarnosc* activists to the *MSZ* who contributed significantly toward his innovative and practical policymaking. The *Solidarnosc* policies differed markedly from the Communist-era bureaucrats and interwar strategists.

Together, Skubiszewski and his new *MSZ* team actualized Poland's policies to deal with the security dilemma between larger, historically hegemonic Germany and Russia. From 1989 to 1991, they needed to formulate policies different from Poland's interwar and post–World War II eras to grapple with German unification and Soviet disintegration, the latter resulting by the end of 1991 in four new eastern bordering states. During this geopolitical transformation and its aftermath over Skubiszewski's latter two years, the Polish foreign minister and his team laid the foundation for Poland's future NATO membership by 1999 and its close links to the EU, with an expectation for membership in 2004. Throughout his *MSZ* leadership, Skubiszewski continually garnered the support from the majority of the Polish political leadership and the population, guiding both meticulously with step-by-step strategies toward West and East. Thus, as one political commentator depicted less than a year after Skubiszewski's departure:

> The interesting thing is that Polish foreign policy became and consistently remained popular with society. Skubiszewski's personal popularity probably resulted from making everyone feel like he's everyone's uncle. He also didn't engage in the kind of infighting we always had. By and large, there seems to have been a consensus that this was the kind of foreign policy we needed. It was extremely difficult for Polish post-Communist society to whip up public discontent about foreign policy. Yet, we are still speaking about our very painful struggle over the past and the tradition of using history as a subsidiary to politics.[10]

Given the Cold War's systemic disintegration, Skubiszewski might easily have perceived threats regionally to Poland's national security and acted belligerently. Instead he sought opportunities, at almost every turn, to promote a constructive foreign policy for nascent democratic Poland to create new relationships with its neighbors and to build links impossible in previous decades, particularly with great powers Germany and Russia and middle power Ukraine. Illustratively, this book revealed that Poland dealt pragmatically and cooperatively with its historic security dilemma between its greater, middle, and smaller power neighbors. Indeed, the book demonstrated that, during the four *Solidarnosc*-led governments in which he served, Skubiszewski primarily aligned Poland with stronger neighboring states to create opportunities and gain rewards rather than playing states against one another or threatening them. He also steered Poland away from the historical instances of trying to dominate weaker neighbors. By not looking to balance against or bandwagon toward the stronger or weaker neighboring states to play them off of each other, Skubiszewski built, sustained, and bestowed to his successors long-term bridges. To this day, this bridge building serves as a firm reminder of stability and security without which this region might have again gone to war. Therefore, the book offers a model of how a post-Communist European state tried to overcome its centuries-old security dilemma. Poland achieved this significant goal without promoting predatory alignment, while also securing its sovereignty after historic partition or satellitedom. This bridging strategy enabled Poland to obtain state treaties with all its neighbors to solidify long-term linkages. Such developments proved vital time and again to ensure that even when bilateral relations worsened, as with Belarus or Russia and even with Ukraine or Germany, Poland had already established the foundation from which to reduce historic security dilemmas.

Toward the Future
in Central-East Europe—and Beyond?

European middle power politics arises from different kinds of alignment in anarchy and such states seek other world help to survive, let alone persist. Few works apply case studies comparing post–Cold War Polish–German ties in the early 1990s[11] with Polish–Ukrainian ties at the end of the 1990s,[12] and their impact on Russia. Little analysis exists about the effect of extensive post–Cold War civil–military cooperation on German, Polish, and Ukrainian territory under the auspices of NATO's Partnership for Peace (PfP) process.[13] This political-military cooperation led to joint military units, duties together in NATO-led Balkan and Afghanistan operations, and coordinating counterterrorist strategy.[14] These successes brought broader economic ties, as indicated by Poland and Ukraine's quest for EU membership. Finally, no analyses extend self-help international relations theory to test empirical implications for this kind of regional security cooperation.

Skubiszewski forged a long-term vision for Poland's middle power position in Europe's rapidly changing security system by bridging to the East, based on Poland's solid Western foundation. Poland's objectives toward Germany signified a relatively consistent effort to reduce Poland's security dilemma between a unifying Germany and disintegrating USSR. Poland sought to increase its non-confrontational security ties with post–Cold War unified Germany amid great anarchy, factoring in post-Communist Ukrainian and Russian intentions. Skubiszewski greatly expanded the foundation for Polish–German relations, broadening the 1970 Polish–German normalization treaty and formulating a national consensus to bridge toward the West via Bonn/Berlin.[15] The Polish–German reconciliation also empowered Poland to bridge more effectively to the East.

Given Poland's long struggles over the borderlands with Russia during the previous several centuries, Skubiszewski's post-Communist Eastern policy manifested a departure from past imperial stances. The new Eastern policy planks set down by Skubiszewski's leadership provided Poland with the foundation for expanding democracy, not enlarging territory. By upholding territorial inviolability for all the state treaties he signed or negotiated with his Eastern counterparts, Skubiszewski defined for his successors and their post-Soviet interlocutors the key tenet for regional stability. His middle power strategy attempted to assure Poland's Eastern neighbors of Warsaw's sincerity on democratization and European reintegration. To attest to the principles based on sovereignty and cooperation, Skubiszewski's successors sought to expand Poland's Eastern relationships within the state treaty frameworks settled between 1990 and 1993. This consistency allowed Warsaw to broaden its nonthreatening foreign policy practices in the mid- to late 1990s. Buoyed by the benefits of NATO membership and closer EU links by the end of the twentieth century, Poland increased its outreach and cooperative programs with the eastern neighbors to the greatest extent possible. Warsaw's objectives remain to assist these states in becoming part of Europe peacefully and democratically. To avoid European isolation of these post-Soviet successor states, Poland continually tried to cooperate with these four eastern neighbors. At the turn of the twentieth century, Warsaw believes it offers one of the best bridges to European integration for its eastern neighbors, whether they take advantage of the opportunities or not. This Polish determination remains one of Skubiszewski's most enduring legacies.

Importantly, when the Ukrainian independence movement coalesced in late 1989 and began to separate from Moscow as the USSR disintegrated, Poland became the key state.[16] A decade after it regained independence from nearly seventy-five years under Soviet rule, Ukraine faces uncertainty about its stability.[17] As a result, Warsaw confronts the challenge in the twenty-first century of either maintaining its decade-old cooperative bridge with Kiev and Moscow extending to the West or devising different external alignments.[18]

Like Polish–German relations, Polish–Ukrainian ties during the 1990s redefined Central-East European security and affected Europe broadly.[19] First, stable, NATO-member Poland expects EU membership, but also strained Polish–Ukrainian ties due to EU border restrictions. Secondly, Poland worries about Ukrainian dependence on a potentially neoimperial Russia, particularly as the result of Ukraine's rampant corruption and ill-devised reforms. Much Western assistance disappeared, like it did in Russia, without strengthening Ukraine democratically and economically.[20] As a role model for European integration, however, Poland reassures an uncertain Ukraine grappling with internal and external threats to nascent democracy.[21] Thus, tracing Polish–Ukrainian alignment explains how bridging more than other forms of alignment succeeded, to a great extent, in conflict-ridden Central-East Europe and how it paralleled Poland's strategy with Germany.

The critical linkages established by Poland and Germany gave Warsaw an alignment paradigm to pursue with Kiev, a relationship some argue the most important in Europe and Eurasia. They contend that an independent Ukraine keeps Russia from becoming neoimperialistic and solidifies regional democratization.[22] Most assessments of Polish–Ukrainian ties praise NATO-member Poland's efforts in the mid- to late 1990s to reinforce Ukraine's sovereign foreign policy.[23] Akin to West German NATO membership in the mid-1950s that set the stage for integration into the European Economic Community, Poland's accession into NATO established the foundation for Warsaw's EU integration.[24] Ukrainian independence in 1990 and increasing consolidation over sovereign foreign policy by the late 1990s[25] enabled Kiev to seek closer NATO and EU ties.[26] Ukraine's membership in key European security institutions remains distant, due to residual security concerns from Moscow and stringent reform requirements from Brussels.[27] Consequently, Polish–Ukrainian regional security renders a key cooperative political, economic, and military bridging paradigm for Kiev's European linkages. When bolstered by U.S. and European leaders without provoking Russia, Polish–Ukrainian bridging contributes cooperatively, but how can Ukraine achieve regional alignment separately from Russia?

Political–Military Factors in Polish–Ukrainian Relations

Polish–Ukrainian political–military ties represent the magnitude of change in European security since the Cold War ended. In September 1994 the first NATO PfP military exercise, Cooperative Bridge, witnessed Poland, Ukraine, and Germany cooperating regionally and multilaterally with ten other NATO and former Warsaw Pact states, including America. Notably, Cooperative Bridge occurred on Polish territory at the former Soviet Drawsko training facility. Beyond the importance of advancing Polish–Ukrainian military relations in this peacekeeping exercise, German troops reentered Polish territory for the first time since World War II—this time peacefully.[28] Not only did German troops come in peace to exercise, they joined those troops of other nations, including Poland's neighboring states of Lithuania, Ukraine, the Czech Republic, and Slovakia.[29] Most importantly, American troops greatly assisted the execution of the event and played a fundamental role in bringing together the troops from these states.

As the NATO PfP process became an institutionalized mechanism in post–Cold War European security, several more developments occurred that underscored importance of the Polish–German and Polish–Ukrainian linkages. The second example involved Poles and Germans, along with the Danes, each of whom increased links to help reintegrate Poland into Europe by establishing a trilateral corps-level joint military headquarters based in Szczecin, Poland.[30] This early 1990s evolution marked the beginning of the annual NATO PfP exercise cycle and led to significant cooperative security achievements throughout the decade of the 1990s and will continue into the twenty-first century—as long as NATO continues to exist. One of those integration-oriented advances centered on the creation of the Polish–Ukrainian peace operations battalion, an enabler for expanding long-term NATO political and military linkages. Secure in its NATO membership by the late 1990s, Poland backed Ukraine to maintain NATO–Ukraine relations. Warsaw persuaded Kiev to continue Western-oriented national security objectives and remain steadfast during the NATO-led 1999 Kosovo bombing campaign. Even if the Ukrainian side fails to meet some of the battalion's standards today, the majority of its complex missions focus on civil affairs requirements—crucial to rebuilding and stabilization.[31] These ties have become essential to advance the Polish–Ukrainian relationship, particularly given that a large Ukrainian military contingent began serving under Polish command in Iraq, starting in the summer of 2003.[32] These examples show how far-reaching Poland's bilateral links were and underline significant facets to Poland's prelude to NATO membership and then entry in March 1999. NATO membership demonstrated a major achievement, only ten years after Poland's peaceful democratic revolution and aided by Bonn's political and military sponsorship.

The commanders, officers, and soldiers, like thousands of others in the Polish and Ukrainian military and foreign policy apparatus during the 1990s, forged integral political–military linkages. The serious cooperative capabilities attained in planning at NATO strategic and regional-level command headquarters, and operationally in Bosnia, Kosovo, Afghanistan, and Iraq, reduced regional tensions and the security dilemma's severity. Poland's pivotal bridging role reinforced Ukrainian security. Political–military ties allowed the cooperative framework to enhance Ukraine's stability nonprovocatively via the multilateral NATO–Ukraine and broader PfP processes. Like the Polish–Ukrainian PfP regional political–military cooperation, Poland also greatly utilized its regional middle power role to reach out to Russia. Poland always offered Russia the chance to participate in military exercises on Polish territory and sought to send troops to any Russian-sponsored military exercises on Russian territory. Moreover, Poland strongly supported the NATO–Russia Cooperation Council, created in 1997, even raising in NATO PfP forums the initial idea for the council. Arguably, Poland tried to show that an evolving relationship with NATO would not threaten Russian security if Russia cooperated closely with NATO. As a result, Poland tried to reconcile whatever historical animosities it had with Russia, as a means to solidify a long-term practical and peaceful good-neighborly set of links and a cooperative security dialogue that remained open to closer Russia–NATO ties. Poland recognized that Russia might see Polish NATO membership as threatening and Poland tried to reduce those concerns with cross-border cooperation, transparent political–military planning, military exercises, and cooperative efforts in Bosnia, Kosovo, and Afghanistan. Hence, like the Polish–German reconciliation model, Polish–Ukrainian political–military ties and Polish outreach to Russia politically and militarily decreased some serious Polish–Russian, Ukrainian–Russian, and Polish–Ukrainian concerns and illustrated significant growth in cross-border cooperation.[33] This NATO and PfP strategy intensified by political–military events on Polish, Ukrainian, and Russian territory, and in North America and Eurasia, also enhanced Poland–Ukrainian economic ties in tandem with Russian interests.[34]

Political–Economic Factors in Polish–Ukrainian Relations

Given this stability-enhancing cooperation, the 1997 Joint Polish-Ukrainian Presidential Declaration marked a major turning point.[35] The formal recognition of World War II and postwar ethnonationalist violence, expulsion, and death committed by both nations against each other stressed the need for reconciliation. Not only did both states want to overcome harsh histories of ethnic conflict, but also "strengthen security and stability in East-Central Europe."[36] This declaration completed yet another bilateral stage as part of Poland's regional stability-enhancing middle power role toward middle power Ukraine, and great powers Russia and Germany. Indeed, Poland and Ukraine bridged cooperatively toward both West and East when Warsaw could have abandoned Kiev to gain NATO and EU membership. Instead, Poland assisted Ukraine even when confronted by stringent membership stipulations.[37]

EU membership requirements challenge cross-border Polish–Ukrainian ties in several ways. First, EU parameters dictate a partial closing of Poland's large, significant Ukrainian border. This cross-border trade remains crucial for millions of Poles and Ukrainians.[38] EU members argue, however, that, upon assumption of EU membership, Poland must conduct all commerce with non-EU members like Ukraine according to strict border-crossing standards. Secondly, the EU demands that Ukraine seriously implement long-delayed economic reforms to meet the criteria enunciated in the 1998 EU–Ukraine agreement. Only then will the EU negotiate seriously.[39]

To compound these difficulties, Ukrainian–Russian disputes arose in the late 1990s over several key geoeconomic issues that affected Poland's regional bridging strategy between Germany and Russia. First, uncertainty resulting from Ukrainian domestic political crises weakened Kiev's leadership and increased dependence on Russia. Second, Russian neoimperial moves in Ukraine reconsolidated former Soviet economic sectors—steel plants, oil refineries, electric power grids, and banks—and threatened Kiev's sovereignty in foreign policy. Third, EU requests for doubling Russian gas and oil exports over twenty years strengthened Moscow's pipeline strategy toward Kiev and Warsaw because German, French, and Italian investment greatly dictates gas and oil flow via the pipelines traversing Ukraine and Poland. Faced with Ukraine's alleged siphoning of gas and oil from the Russian Druhzba pipeline to Europe across Ukraine and Slovakia, Russia raised several important complaints. Moscow accused Kiev of increasing regional tensions by siphoning and reselling key Russian commodities, some 90 percent flowing from Russia through Ukraine to Europe. As a result, Russia periodically shut down the pipeline to prevent Ukraine's supposed siphoning, but caused more economic tension between the two states. Consequently, Russia wanted to extend its Yamal–Belarus–Poland pipeline through Slovakia to Germany, circumventing Ukraine. This pipeline epitomizes geoeconomic dilemmas for Poland and Ukraine by potentially decreasing Druzhba transport and increasing Yamal–EU–German trade.[40]

These geostrategic issues continually caused serious problems between Ukraine and Russia that Poland tried to resolve. Poland politically walked a fine line between negotiating for Ukraine to participate in Russian Yamal initiatives and appeasing Russia and the EU despite their energy deals continually excluding Warsaw. Yet, Poland determined to preserve Ukrainian sovereignty without alienating either the EU or Russia. Warsaw faced both strict EU membership requirements on the Polish–Ukrainian border and demands for Russian energy. Conceivably, Russian and EU strategies could have isolated Ukraine, placing Poland in a catch-22 situation. The challenge to choose between EU membership and Ukrainian sovereignty has greatly strained Poland since Warsaw remains dependent on Russian gas and oil exports.[41]

Poland's cooperative bridging with Ukraine during the 1990s to uphold Ukrainian sovereignty also centered on moving Ukraine toward the West and establishing a political–economic bridge to Russia. Warsaw refused to balance Moscow and Kiev to reintegrate into Europe. Warsaw argued that Kiev's sovereignty remained more important for European security than some economic losses. By pulling Kiev and Moscow toward the West, Warsaw sought to reduce the security dilemma by neither aligning with Ukraine or Russia, nor favoring one state over the other. Moreover, Poland and Ukraine avoided balancing in tandem against the EU or Russia. To a great extent, Warsaw and Kiev tried to construct economic, political, and military linkages between Russia and EU and NATO states. Yet, Polish and Ukrainian dependence on Russian energy finally convinced them to try to obtain some type of alternative oil and gas supplies. Despite such geoeconomic policies, Ukraine's economic dependence on Russia continues as Russian political, economic, and military demands grow. Such Russian policies to reintegrate Ukraine into the Russian fold, with American and European acquiescence, portends negative consequences for democratized Poland, as Warsaw may fail to maintain an open border and freer market with Ukraine. The best option for Poland's specialized role between great powers focuses on providing regional stability, expanding geostrategic cooperation, enabling increased coalition building, and reducing any Russian neoimperialist maneuvers. At its worst, Polish bridging strategy capitulates in the face of binding EU membership and energy requirements. Compounding this dilemma, Russian geoeconomic compulsion potentially succeeds when tacitly empowered by American national security interests that look beyond Ukraine's possible loss of sovereignty.[42]

Even with these regional geostrategic tensions and conceivable pitfalls, progress occurred during in the early years of the new century. Polish and Ukrainian tenacity appeared to prevail, at least in the short term, when favorable Russian and European energy deals emerged—resolving issues that had been intractable in the late 1990s.[43] Importantly, some Russian opinion publicly supported Poland's middle power reform "model" for its cooperative post-Communist European re-integration strategy. One prominent Russian strategist declared, "Polish politicians now look upon their former communist-camp comrades through the eyes of prosperous Europeans—rationally and without emotion."[44]

A Middle Power Model

As America and Russia, and other great powers, attempt to combat nonstate-actor threats, middle power enhancement of historically unstable regions becomes ever more important. A post-9/11 era coalition against terrorism stems from multilateral cooperation among great and smaller powers. Such cooperation may better be advanced if great powers depend on stable middle powers, contributing regionally and internationally. Such cooperation greatly reduces security dilemmas. Democratized middle powers like Poland model middle power politics to decrease destabilizing threats—bridging through other-help means to survive regional and global anarchy. This alignment characterizes middle power bridge building in a productive and specializing role between great powers, but one reliant for its security and stability on other powers, without other options or having only a few good choices within the extant international system.[45]

Several conclusions arise from this book's analysis for European security and middle power politics. In terms of the post–Cold War Polish–German and Polish–Ukrainian relationships a middle power cooperation paradigm emerges. Like the Franco–German post–World War II reconciliation, Germany and Poland reconciled after the Cold War. Today, Poland and Ukraine have overcome many centuries-old animosities. Poland still seeks to help Ukraine increase its security and stability without threatening Russia. Whether Ukraine and Russia can reconcile, and Ukraine maintain its sovereign foreign policy to integrate with a nonimperial Russia into Europe, underlines a critical security problem. Poland appears to have done what it can to bridge Kiev and Moscow to Europe. By buttressing post-Soviet democratization and European integration, Poland seeks security defensively and nonthreateningly. Its balance of interests between great powers and efforts to reduce security dilemmas underscore Poland's central European role.[46]

Polish strategy toward Germany and Ukraine provides the foundation to examine other case studies of cooperative middle power alignment. This book described the merits of post–Cold War bridging more than hiding, bandwagoning, or balancing against states to advance, but not through regionally traditional aggrandizement of territory. Furthermore, the book delineated how security shapes integration-focused policies, avoids disintegration tendencies amid great systemic change, reduces hostile alignment, diminishes regional tension, and decreases aggression. Empirical analysis illustrates that a new security dilemma may arise, however. If Ukraine fails to become an advanced democracy like Poland, and if Russian democratization falters, Russia may look to regain primacy over Ukraine. Russia may not only threaten to make Ukraine more politically dependent on Russia, but also negate the Polish–Ukrainian "bridge" by pursuing more EU deals for natural gas and oil, excluding Kiev and Warsaw.

Though such trends seem unlikely, given the global fight against terrorism, one cannot discount potential unforeseen developments.

This book also attempted to advance understanding of a new middle power politics approach that revealed how post-Communist middle powers implemented far-reaching and different alignment. Once Polish underground activists turned democratically elected policymakers, they transformed Poland regionally by creating political, economic, and security bridges from the post–Cold War systemic anarchy. Their efforts reduced and altered historic security dilemmas when Poland sought to exist differently in an other-help world because it could not guarantee its own security via self-help strategies. Without promoting predatory or aggressive alignment against other states, and without hiding from its regional middle power role, Poland contributed to European security by bridging with great powers, whenever possible. First, the book asserted that middle powers that promote cooperative political, economic and security bridges matter to great power–dominated regional security. These regional bridges benefit great powers by tying democratizing and nonthreatening behavior to increased cooperative security. Secondly, the book studied how middle powers like Poland overcame hostile alignment and moved beyond centuries-old territorial disputes, to learn better how Poland constructed new linkages to Germany, Russia, and Ukraine primarily, but also toward Lithuania, the Visegrad Triangle, and Belarus. Sometimes this strategy succeeded and at other times has fallen short since Polish foreign minister Krzysztof Skubiszewski left office in 1993.

Had post-Communist Poland chosen to balance Germany and Russia during the 1990s or bandwagon extensively with one of them against the other, different security outcomes likely would have occurred. NATO and EU members, given their initial hesitancy to respond to Poland's predominantly cooperative policies, likely would have delayed or even failed to extend membership to former Warsaw Pact enemies. At the outset of the post-Communist revolutions in 1989, Poland's foreign policy–makers led their emerging counterparts in Central-East Europe and the deteriorating Soviet republics by creating a regional cooperative security model. This strategy focused on pragmatic European reintegration between and among great as well as middle and smaller power neighbors. Ethnically torn, post-Communist Balkan states now seem to follow a similar path. However, unlike Poland's promotion of cooperative security and regional bridging, in the early to mid-1990s Southeast European states like Albania, Croatia, and Romania initially demonstrated the futility of balancing or aggression. When these states tried to balance neighbors against one another or antagonize neighbors by forcing concessions—inciting border disputes, drawing larger powers into Balkan conflicts, or hindering ethnic minorities—NATO and the EU delayed cooperation and membership. In Croatia's case, NATO rejected entreaties to join the NATO PfP process for most of the 1990s and allowed Croatia to accede to the PfP Protocol only when it held its first free and fair elections. For Romania, NATO and EU accession evolved once reformers changed their economic structures accordingly and implemented regional cooperation. And after its near total financial meltdown in the late 1990s, Albania needed to rebuild its infrastructure to support regional stability, particularly in the 1999 Kosovo war's aftermath.[47] Given Serbian democratization since 2000, Belgrade's development of cooperative security appears to dovetail with Croatia's European reintegration. Perhaps the Polish model between great powers also provides a baseline for other pivotal European middle powers or other middle powers globally.[48] In such an uncertain world of nation-state and nonstate-actor power plays, where terrorists often throw powerful states off kilter, cooperative middle powers can undergird larger powers to stabilize regions and counter such nonstate-actor threats.

Lasting Bridges?

As this book argued, middle power Poland contributed to Central-East Europe's regional stability with its bridging alignment strategy during the post–Cold War era.[49] In the post-9/11 world, middle powers like Poland may still contribute to regional stability between and among great powers, but certain trends may be emerging to undo such gains. In trying to read the tealeaves, we should look at how such trends might reverse the security and stability gained in Central-East Europe. One of the most worrisome trends concern the transatlantic strains in the aftermath of the U.S.-led war against Iraq in 2003. For middle power Poland, such strains portend fissures between the great powers who opposed the war—France, Germany, and Russia—and America. Both America and some of its European allies appear to be moving toward a possible disjuncture over the so-called old Europe (Western) and the new Europe (Central-East), as coined by U.S. secretary of defense Donald Rumsfeld. If such a geostrategic fault line continues enlarging across the Atlantic as a result of this antagonistic framework, Europe may witness the rapid decline, if not demise, of the very core political, economic, and military institutions both sides of the Atlantic built after World War II. Such fissures, if not alleviated, could revive historic security dilemmas that Poland helped to reduce less than a decade ago.

Since 9/11 and especially after the Iraq war, middle power Poland has become an even closer ally to America, the unipolar power. This development put America's West European allies on notice. President George W. Bush's European strategy that rewards friends and seeks to punish those opposing it in Iraq poses great risks. Consequently, this strategy could backfire and the likely loser would primarily be Poland, along with the other members of the "new Europe" that America courted as among its closest allies in the war against Iraq. Ironically, what today stands as a shining moment for Poland might ultimately harm its vital role as a bridge builder between an increasingly independent Germany and a struggling Russia. America's strategy, therefore, could unravel one of the stabilizing bridges between East and West: that of the German–Polish reconciliation, codified in 1999 by NATO's enlargement. Failure by the United States and its allies to solidify greater mutual trust and find compromise on respective aims for transatlantic security may ultimately marginalize Poland from key European security developments, aggravate transatlantic tensions, and disrupt post–Cold War regional stability.

Given these trends, we also need to consider that critical European political and economic power shifts already presage a growing tectonic shift away from America's geostrategic goals to counter global terrorism and expand democracy. Evidence of this schism is mounting: Polish–German rancor over Germany's refusal to send troops from its German–Polish–Danish Corps to the Polish-led multinational division command in Iraq; Polish–French tensions over Poland's special U.S. relationship; perceptions of the United States splintering the EU; discord over the rapid reaction force structures in NATO and the EU; residual U.S.–German hostility as U.S. troops redeploy from Germany to Poland, Bulgaria, and Romania, while virtually ignoring Germany's command role in Afghanistan; and American hollowing out of NATO institutionally, using it only when deemed necessary to serve U.S. interests. These trends jeopardize already worsening inter-European regional relationships. One repercussion concerns Germany struggling once again to find its most comfortable zone of strategic engagement with its neighbors, putting undue pressure on the disunited European side of the transatlantic relationship.[50]

This very disturbing reality would possibly leave a united Germany at the heart of Europe with a decreasing interest in maintaining the institutional status quo. Since Washington's strategy focuses on moving U.S. troops out of Germany, managing the question of "Germany" will very likely emerge as the key foreign policy problem for its neighbors. If America becomes unreliable as far as managing the rise of German power in the heart of Europe, then the EU will inevitably emerge as a functional alternative to U.S. power symbolized in NATO. If, however, such trends occur before the EU becomes truly equipped for shouldering such responsibility, Europe hazards disintegrating into a new period of dangerous geopolitical competition.

How then can European integration reinvigorate the transatlantic link and reinforce an American bridge between the "old" and "new" Europe? America could reinforce long-term European stability by promoting the EU as a partner or even as a healthy competitor instead of trying to divide Europe by unduly elevating individual countries (such as Poland) while holding Germany and France at arm's length. More equitable responsibility sharing between America and Europe would strengthen ties between NATO and the EU, while reinvigorating the transatlantic relationship. The further weakening of this relationship will only enable exploitation by antagonistic states and allow hostile global nonstate actors to decouple America from its long-standing European allies. Rather, America and Europe need to revive allied bonds by making the dominant European security institutions relevant in the fight against global terrorism and the proliferation of weapons of mass destruction, let alone in the quest to spread democracy.

"Old" and "new" Europe, and Washington, must invest in key security institutions like NATO and the EU to keep them relevant. By creating NATO–EU joint counterterrorism planning for military and civilian police operations, transatlantic allies, via NATO and the EU, would better anticipate, coordinate, and synchronize how to reestablish basic government functions. Public order and safety should always define the top priority in multilateral operations, as crucially evidenced by missions in Kosovo, Afghanistan, Iraq, and likely in any kind of "road map" solution to the Israeli–Palestinian disputed territories or in places like the Republic of Congo. Such joint NATO–EU planning could economize effective postwar peace-support operations in Afghanistan and Iraq, while better preparing the EU to lead in the Balkans and on the African Continent. By focusing on harmonizing American and European responses to terrorist threats, NATO can revive as a premier European security institution. A further means to reinvigorate transatlantic links may also arise from the recent NATO military command restructuring that America wants implemented as lessons churn out from the conflicts in Afghanistan and Iraq. In exploring in the NATO–Russia Council the foundation for tying future NATO military headquarters in "new" East Europe to out-of-Europe missions, the United States and its NATO allies should seriously consider devising a NATO–Russia contingency planning cell to grapple much more effectively with rapid response operations. Based in several locations, including Russia and inclusive of NATO, EU, and non-NATO PfP and NATO Mediterranean Dialogue nations, a NATO–Russia contingency planning cell could very effectively coincide with NATO–EU planning.[51]

Given NATO–EU tensions over competitive rapid reaction frameworks and doubt over the uncertainty in Iraq, America, NATO allies, PfP partners, and EU nations must prioritize NATO–EU relations together. Otherwise, "new" Europe will continue to buckle under U.S. pressure to prioritize national missile defense over rapid response capabilities and divest from more critical and stabilizing NATO peace-support operations and EU civil–military police missions. As a result, NATO will not be able to survive, let alone evolve.

To avoid increasing transatlantic tensions, "new" Europe needs to reach a balanced and productive set of transatlantic and European preferences. America's vital interests need to uphold stable and integrated Europe in which "new" European allies feel welcome and NATO enlargement contributes to European security. Promoting a division between Poland and Germany (whether unwittingly or purposefully) goes against everyone's long-term security interests, only serving America's desire to cherry-pick coalitions for America's global policies. To a key nation like Poland, success as a bridge builder must also be measured in terms of how it helps Washington to better understand the need for multilateralism, spurring Europe and America to invest in multilateral security cooperation.[52] Paradoxically, post-9/11 U.S. deployments in Central Asia and the Caucasus forced Russia to reassess its force projection strategy, while many European NATO or EU nations did not. If Europeans want to play a significant role in international coalitions, they must seriously restructure their forces for global missions, undergird U.S.-led operations, or lead such operations themselves. Lessons from Africa, Afghanistan, and NATO-led Balkan operations demonstrate the necessity for both "old" and "new" European militaries to modernize, reform rapid collective defense commitments and determine how to build less expensive NATO Rapid Reaction/Response Forces.

For a key country like Poland, success as a bridge builder must also be measured in terms of how it helps Washington better understand the need to advance unifying multilateral strategies, giving all of Europe and the United States an interest in investing in multilateral security cooperation. However, only if Poland and other "new European" countries equally prioritize their relationships with Germany, France, and other "old" European nations will true security gains result in advancing everyone's shared interest in a Europe whole and free.

Notes

1. "Racja Stanu Rzeczypolpolitej Polskiej" [The Republic of Poland's Racja Stanu] (Warsaw, 21 January 1993) in Kryzsztof Skubiszewski, *Polityka zagraniczna i odzyskanie niepodlegnosci: Przemówienia, oswiadczenia, wywiady 1989–1993* [Foreign Policy and Regaining Independence: Addresses, Declaration, Interviews, 1989–1993] (Warsaw: Wydawa Interpress, 1997), 299–303.

2. Roman Kuzniar, ed., *Poland's Security Policy, 1989–2000* (Warsaw: Scholar Publishing House, 2001).

3. "Problemy polityki zagranicznej u progu roku 1991—Wystapienie ministra spraw zagranicznych RP Krzysztofa Skubiszewskiego w Sejmie" [Foreign Policy of the Republic of Poland in 1991—Address by the Polish Foreign Minister Krzysztof Skubiszewski in the Sejm] (Warsaw, 14 February 1991), *Zbior Dokumentow*, no. 1 (1992): 34.

4. Miklos Ritecz, "Wedged between Two Powers: Interview with Foreign Minister Krzysztof Skubiszewski," *Nepszabadsag* (Budapest), 6 June 1991, *FBIS-EEU*, 11 June 1991, 31.

5. Janusz Reiter "New Map of World: Does Russia's Return to Europe Bode Ill for Poland?" *Rzeczpospolita*, 31 January 2002, www.rp.pl/gazeta/wydanie_020131/publicystyka/publicystyka_a_1.html (accessed 8 February 2002).

6. Paul Schroeder, "Historical Reality vs. Neo-realist Theory," *International Security*, vol. 19, no. 1 (summer 1994): 108–148.

7. Jonathan Mercer, "Anarchy and Identity," *International Organization*, vol. 49, no. 2 (spring 1995): 233–236; and Colin Elman and Miriam Fendius Elman, "Correspondence—History vs. Neo-realism: A Second Look," *International Security*, vol. 20, no. 1 (summer 1995): 182–195, especially 188.

8. Randall L. Schweller, *Deadly Imbalances: Tripolarity and Hitler's Strategy of World Conquest* (New York: Columbia University Press, 1998).

9. Roman Kuzniar, "Security Policy in Polish Foreign Policy," in Kuzniar, ed., *Poland's Security Policy, 1989–2000*, 56.

10. Interview I conducted with the deputy editor-in-chief of *Gazeta Wyborcza*, Konstanty Gebert, in Warsaw on 6 June 1994. See also Jan B. de Weydenthal, "Poland on Its Own: The Conduct of Foreign Policy," *RFE/RL Research Report*, vol. 2, no. 2 (8 January 1993): 1–4.

11. Ilya Prizel and Andrew A. Michta, eds., *Polish Foreign Policy Reconsidered: Challenges of Independence* (London: Macmillan, 1995); Ilya Prizel, *National Identity and Foreign Policy: Nationalism and Leadership in Poland, Russia, and Ukraine* (Cam-

bridge: Cambridge University Press, 1998), 112–124; and Elizabeth Pond, *The Rebirth of Europe* (Washington, D.C.: Brookings Institution Press, 1999).

12. Ian Brzezinski, "Polish-Ukrainian Relations: Europe's Neglected Strategic Axis," *Survival*, vol. 35, no. 3 (autumn 1993): 26–37; Stephen R. Burant, "International Relations in a Regional Context: Poland and Its Eastern Neighbors—Lithuania, Belarus, Ukraine," *Europe-Asia Studies*, vol. 45, no. 3 (1993): 395–418; Sherman W. Garnett, *Keystone in the Arch: Ukraine in the Emerging Security Environment of Central and Eastern Europe* (Washington: Carnegie Endowment Press, 1995), 85–91; and Roman Wolczuk, "Ukrainian-Polish Relations between 1991–1998: From the Declarative to the Substantive," *European Security*, vol. 9, no. 1 (spring 2000): 127–156.

13. Joshua B. Spero, "Paths to Peace for NATO's Partnerships in Eurasia," in *Limiting Institutions: The Challenge of Eurasian Security Governance*, eds. James Sperling, Sean Kay, and S. Victor Papacosma (Manchester, U.K.: Manchester University Press, 2003), 166–184.

14. F. Stephen Larrabee, "Ukraine's Place in European and Regional Security," in *Ukraine in the World*, ed. Lubomyr A. Hajda (Cambridge, Mass.: Harvard University Press, 1998), 249–270; and Martha Brill Olcott, Anders Aslund, and Sherman Garnett, eds., *Getting It Wrong: Regional Cooperation and the Commonwealth of Independent States* (Washington, D.C.: Carnegie Endowment Press, 1999), 204–208.

15. Prizel, *National Identity and Foreign Policy*, 112–124; and Arthur Rachwald, "Looking West," in *Polish Foreign Policy Reconsidered: Challenges of Independence*, eds. Ilya Prizel and Andrew A. Michta (Houndmills, U.K.: Macmillan, 1995), 134–136.

16. Piotr Chmura, "Ukraine in 1988: Beginning the Road toward Independence?" *Nowa Koalicja*, no. 7 (1989): 12–18; Prizel, *National Identity and Foreign Policy*, 359–362; and Burant, "International Relations in a Regional Context," 413.

17. Roman Solchanyk, "As Kiev Goes, So Goes the East," *Wall Street Journal Europe*, 30 March 2001; and Jennifer D. P. Moroney and Taras Kuzio, eds., *Ukraine's Foreign and Security Policy: Theoretical and Comparative Perspectives* (Westport, Conn.: Greenwood/Praeger, 2002).

18. Katarzyna Nazarewicz, "Interview with Foreign Minister Krzysztof Skubiszewski: Politics Does Not Have to Clash with Morality," *Zycie Warszawy*, 15 June 1993, *FBIS-EEU*, 30 June 1993, 25.

19. "Declaration on Principles and Directions of Development of Polish-Ukrainian Relations," *Zbior Dokumentow*, no. 4 (1991): 25–30; and "Treaty between Polish Republic and Ukraine on Good Neighborliness, Friendly Relations, and Cooperation," in Hajda, *Ukraine in the World*, 304–312.

20. Janine Wedel, *Collision and Collusion: The Strange Case of Western Aid to Eastern Europe* (New York: Palgrave, 2001).

21. Taras Kuzio, "'Pro-Ukrainian' or 'Pro-Kuchma?' Ukraine's Foreign Policy in Crisis," *RFE/RL Newsline* (26 April 2002): 3–8.

22. See, among others, Zbigniew Brzezinski, "Ukraine's Critical Role in the Post-Soviet Space," *Ukraine in the World*, 3–8; Stephen R. Burant, "Ukraine and East Central Europe," *Ukraine in the World*, 45–78; and Larrabee, "Ukraine's Place in European and Regional Security," *Ukraine in the World*, 257–263.

23. Margarita Mercedes Balmaceda, "Two's Company, Three's a Crowd: The Role of Central Europe in Ukrainian Security," *East European Quarterly*, vol. 32, no. 3 (fall 1998): 345–348; and Prizel, *National Identity and Foreign Policy*, 137–145, 388–396.

24. John Reed, "Poland's Pro-US policy May Not Be to All EU Liking," *Financial Times*, 15 March 2001, www.ft.com/europe (accessed 1 June 2001).

25. "Treaty on Friendship, Cooperation, and Partnership between Ukraine and the Russian Federation," in *Ukraine in the World*, 319–329.

26. Fraser Cameron, "Relations between the European Union and Ukraine," in *Ukraine and Its Western Neighbors,* eds. James Clem and Nancy Popson (Washington, D.C.: Woodrow International Center for Scholars, November 2000), 93–106.

27. Askold Krushelnycky, "Why Did Kiev Choose to Seek NATO Membership?" *RFE/RL Poland, Belarus, and Ukraine Report*, vol. 4, no. 22 (4 June 2002): 15–18.

28. *Report to Congress on Implementation of the Partnership for Peace Initiative* (Washington, D.C.: U.S. Department of State, 1998), 7–8.

29. The Russians sent exercise observers, but not a platoon, like the other PfP states. Note that, within one year, the NATO–PfP process expanded its military exercising scale dramatically to conduct, inter alia, a corps-level command post exercise that witnessed twenty-five NATO, former Warsaw Pact, and historically neutral European states participating on military posts and in selected preparatory events in six different countries over an eighteen-month period. See *Report to Congress on Implementation of the Partnership for Peace Initiative* (Washington, D.C.: U.S. Department of State, 1994), 7–8; and *United States Security Strategy for Europe and NATO* (Washington: Department of Defense, 1995), 10–12. I worked in the European and NATO Division of the Joint Chiefs of Staff's Directorate for Strategic Plans and Policy from 1994 to 2000, directed the U.S. Joint Staff positions on NATO's PfP policies, as part of my responsibilities to develop and implement the larger U.S. national security and military strategy of enlargement and engagement.

30. See *Partnership for Peace* (Washington, D.C.: U.S. Department of Defense, 1996), 15–17; and *Report to Congress on Implementation of the Partnership for Peace Initiative* (Washington, D.C.: U.S. Department of State, 1998), 18–19.

31. See the NATO Kosovo Operations web site: www.kforonline.com/ kfor/mnb_east.htm (accessed 1 June 2001).

32. "Plans for NATO Support to Poland's Iraq Mission Finalized," NATO Headquarters, www.nato.int/docu/update/2003/06june/e0630b.htm. (accessed 30 October 2003) and "Poland Assumes Command in Iraq with NATO Support," NATO Headquarters, 4 September 2003, www.paginedidifesa.it/2003/nato_030904.html (accessed 30 October 2003). The Polish command of the Multinational Division (MND) Central South in Iraq exemplified the remarkable evolution of Poland and the other new and future NATO members and long-term PfP nations working in the MND. It demonstrated the rapid progress in Poland's leadership role in NATO and globally. In early June 2003, NATO's North Atlantic Council approved giving military support to Poland and its sector by "providing intelligence, logistics expertise, movement co-ordination, force generation and secure communications support." This support, coupled with troop contingents provided by Bulgaria, Hungary, the Czech Republic, Latvia, Lithuania, Kazakhstan, Romania, Slovakia, and Ukraine, shows that new NATO members and PfP-partner nations are making sizable contributions to postwar Iraq. These multinational deployments have an impact on shaping NATO's future, particularly in terms of Poland's abilities to take command and the lessons learned about transferring knowledge from Central-Eastern Europe to Western Europe. For NATO, it illustrates how the alliance's planning, training and implementation abilities are still relevant, despite the transatlantic rift caused by the American-led invasion of Iraq in March 2003.

33. Joshua B. Spero, "Looking beyond NATO and EU Enlargement: Northeastern Europe and Russian Security Dynamics," in *The Translatlantic Relationship: Problems and Prospects*, ed. Sabina A.-M. Auger (Washington, D.C.: Woodrow Wilson Interna-

tional Center for Scholars/East European Studies, West European Studies, Stanley Foundation, March 2003), 104–111; and Celeste A. Wallander, "Institutional Assets and Adaptability: NATO after the Cold War," *International Organization*, vol. 54, no. 4 (autumn 2000): 705–735.

34. Robert Cottrell and Charles Clover, "Ukraine Welcomes Closer Ties with Russia: Moves to Support Reintegration of the Two Economies Are Growing," *Financial Times*, (1 June 2001): 4.

35. This section draws on analysis from Joshua B. Spero, "The Polish-Ukrainian Inter-State Model for Cooperation and Integration: Regional Relations in a Theoretical Context" in *Ukraine's Foreign and Security Policy: Theoretical and Comparative Perspectives*, eds. Jennifer D. P. Moroney and Taras Kuzio (Westport, Conn.: Greenwood/Praeger, 2002), 155–178; and Spero, "Looking beyond NATO and EU Enlargement."

36. "Joint Declaration of the Presidents of the Polish Republic and Ukraine on Understanding and Unity," 317.

37. "Brussels Urges Warsaw to Step Up EU-Oriented Effort," *RFE/RL Poland, Belarus, and Ukraine Report*, vol. 3, no. 44 (20 November 2001): 4–5.

38. Jan Maksymiuk, "Warsaw Obliges Itself to Build EU's 'Berlin Wall,'" *RFE/RL Poland, Belarus, and Ukraine Report*, vol. 4, no. 29 (6 August 2002): 7–8.

39. Cameron, "Relations between the European Union and Ukraine," 88–91; and Vera Rich, "Traffic Across Poland's Eastern Frontiers Drops Due to New Visa Regime," *RFE/RL Poland, Belarus, and Ukraine Report*, vol. 5, no. 37 (7 October 2003) www.rferl.org/pbureport/2003/10/37-071003.html (accessed 6 January 2004).

40. Amy Myers Jaffe and Robert A. Manning, "Russia, Energy and the West," *Survival*, vol. 43, no. 2 (summer 2001): 133–152; and Vera Rich, "Which Way Will Oil Flow through Odesa-Brody Pipeline?" *RFE/RL Poland, Belarus, and Ukraine Report*, vol. 5, no. 45 (2 December 2003), www.rferl.org/pbureport/2003/12/45-021203.html (accessed 6 January 2004).

41. Michael Lelyveld, Russia Seeks Large Stake in Ukrainian Gas Pipeline," *RFE/RL Poland, Belarus, and Ukraine Report*, vol. 4, no. 26 (2 July 2002): 3–4.

42. "U.S. National Security Adviser Presses Kuchma over Journalist's Murder, Reforms," *Agence Press France* (25 July 2001), 2; Sujata Rao, "Russian Gazprom Extends Kremlin reach in EU, Asia," *Reuters* (26 October 2001): 1; Roman Kupchinsky, "The Finlandization of Ukraine," parts 1–2, vol. 5, no. 36 (30 September 2003) www.rferl.org/pbureport/2003/09/36-300903.html (accessed 6 January 2004); and vol. 5, no. 37 (7 October 2003), www.rferl.org/pbureport/2003/10/37-071003.html (accessed 6 January 2004).

43. "Kiev Counts on 10-Year Gas-Transit Deal with Moscow," *RFE/RL Poland, Belarus, and Ukraine Report*, vol. 14, no. 15 (16 April 2002): 6–7; Michael Lelyveld, "Poland's Gas Deal with Norway Offers Relief to Ukraine," *RFE/RL Poland, Belarus, and Ukraine Report*, vol. 3, no. 33 (4 September 2001): 2–3.

44. Andrei Piontkovski, "Different Directions for Poland, Russian Progressive Sees Poles Confident as a Part of Europe," *Russia Journal* (14–20 April 2001): 12–14.

45. Schroeder, "Historical Reality vs. Neo-realist Theory"; and Mercer, "Anarchy and Identity."

46. Schweller, *Deadly Imbalances*, 191–192; Glaser, "Realists as Optimists," 162–163; and Taliaferro, "Seeking Security under Anarchy," 158–160.

47. Juan J. Linz and Alfred Stepan, *Problems of Democratic Transition and Consolidation: Southern Europe, South America, and Post-Communist Europe* (Baltimore,

Md.: Johns Hopkins University Press, 1996); Karen Dawisha and Bruce Parrott, eds., *Politics, Power, and the Struggle for Democracy in South-East Europe Societies* (Cambridge: Cambridge University Press, 1997); and Vladimir Tismaneanu, *Fantasies of Salvation: Democracy, Nationalism, and Myth in Post-Communist Europe* (Princeton, N.J.: Princeton University Press, 1998).

48. Such examples of middle powers which potentially offer similar types of bridging alignment between and among middle and greater powers to assess might include, in Europe, Turkey, and for states on other continents, South Korea, Indonesia, Kazakhstan, Jordan, Iran, Israel, Pakistan, Botswana, and Ecuador. Note that some of these middle powers border more than one other state because some have bodies of water separating them. The regional cooperation facet remains the most important variable to apply in analysis.

49. This final section draws from and builds on the following: Charles Barry, Sean Kay, and Joshua Spero, "Completing the Transatlantic Bargain: The United States and European Security," *Current History* (March 2001): 129–144; Sean Kay and Joshua Spero, "America's Precarious Transatlantic Bridge," *Defense News* (18 August 2003), 51; Sean Kay, "NATO in Iraq? But Not Yet," *Globe and Mail*, 26 August 2003; Joshua B. Spero, "The Impact on NATO of the Emerging Role of Eastern Europe and the NIS in Iraq," in *East Europe's Emerging Role in the Middle East*, ed. Nida Gelazis (Washington, D.C.: Woodrow Wilson Center for International Scholars, 2004); and Joshua B. Spero, "Beyond Old and New Europe." *Current History* (March 2004): 135–138.

50. "Charlemagne—Of Wars and Weighted Votes: The History and Future of the German-Polish Relationship," *Economist* (3 January 2004), 37.

51. Peter B. Zwack, "A NATO–Russia Contingency Command," *Parameters* (spring 2004): 89–103.

52. Elaine Sciolino, "The Great Divide: The U.S. and Europe Stretch to Close It," *New York Times*, 8 December 2003, A3; and Thomas L. Friedman, "Where U.S. Translates as Freedom," *New York Times*, 28 December 2003, www.nytimes.com/2003/12/28/opinion/28FRIED.html?th (accessed 28 December 2003).

Bibliography

Books

Ananicz, Andrzej, Przemyslaw Grudzinski, Andrzej Olechowski, Janusz Onyszkiewicz, Krzysztof Skubiszewski, and Henryk Szlajfer. *Poland-NATO: Report of the Discussions at the Euro-Atlantic Association and the Stefan Batory Foundation.* Warsaw: Center for International Relations, 1995.

Aron, Raymond. *The Century of Total War.* Garden City, N.Y.: Doubleday & Co, 1954.

Ash, Timothy Garton. *The Magic Lantern: The Revolution of '89 Witnessed in Warsaw, Budapest, Berlin and Prague.* New York: Random House, 1990.

————. *In Europe's Name: Germany and the Divided Continent.* New York: Random House, 1993.

Asmus, Ronald D., and Thomas S. Szayna, with Barbara Kliszewski. *Polish National Security Thinking in a Changing Europe: A Conference Report.* Santa Monica, Calif.: RAND/UCLA Center for Soviet Studies, 1991.

————. *Germany in Transition: National Self-Confidence and International Reticence.* Santa Monica, Calif.: RAND, 1992.

Axelrod, Robert S., and Robert O. Keohane. "Achieving Cooperation under Anarchy: Strategies and Institutions." Pp. 85–115 in *Neorealism and Neoliberalism: The Contemporary Debate*, edited by David A. Baldwin. New York: Columbia University Press, 1995.

————. *The Complexity of Cooperation: Agent-Based Models of Competition and Collaboration.* Princeton, N.J.: Princeton University Press, 1997.

Balcerowicz, Leszek. *Socialism, Capitalism, Transformation.* Budapest: Central European University Press, 1995.

Baranczak, Stanislaw. *Breathing under Water and Other East European Essays.* Cambridge, Mass.: Harvard University Press, 1990.

318   Bibliography

Barcz, Jan and Mieczyslaw Tomal. *Polska-Niemcy: Dobre sasiedztwo i przyjazna wspol-praca* [Poland–Germany: Good-neighborly and friendly cooperation]. Warsaw: Polski Instytut Spraw Miedzynarodowych, 1992.

————. *Udzial Polski w konferencji "2 + 4": Aspekty prawne i proceduralne* [Polish Participation in the "2 + 4" Conference: Legal and Procedural Aspects]. Warsaw: Polski Instytut Spraw Miedzynarodowych, 1994.

Barry, Charles L., ed. *The Search for Peace in Europe: Perspectives from NATO and Eastern Europe*. Washington, D.C.: National Defense University Press, 1993.

Barston, R. P., ed. *The Other Powers: Studies in the Foreign Policies of Small States*. London: Allen & Unwin, 1973.

Bauwens, Wener, Armand Clesse and Olav F. Knudsen, ed. *Small States and the Security Challenge in the New Europe*. London: Brassey's, 1996.

Bernhard, Michael, and Henryk Szlajfer, ed. *From the Polish Underground: Selections from Krytyka, 1978–1993*. University Park: University of Pennsylvania Press, 1995.

Bichniewicz, Michal, and Piotr Rudnicki. *Czas na Zmiany: Z Jaroslawem Kaczynskim rozmawiaja* [Time for Change: Conversations with Jaroslaw Kaczynski]. Warsaw: Editions Spotkania, 1994.

Bochenski, Adolf. *Miedzy Niemcami a Rosja* [Between Germany and Russia]. Warsaw: Polityka, 1937.

Boyer, Mark A. *International Cooperation and Public Goods: Opportunities for the Western Alliance*. Baltimore, Md.: Johns Hopkins University Press, 1993.

Bratkiewicz, Jaroslaw. "Relations with Russia, Ukraine and Belarus," Pp. 129–134 in *Yearbook of Polish Foreign Policy, 1993/1994*, edited by Barbara Wizimirska. Warsaw: Polish Institute of International Affairs, 1994.

Bromke, Adam. *Poland's Politics: Idealism vs. Realism*. Cambridge, Mass.: Harvard University Press, 1967.

Brown, J. F. *Surge to Freedom: The End of Communist Rule in Eastern Europe*. Durham, N.C.: Duke University Press, 1991.

Brown, Michael E., Sean M. Lynn-Jones, and Steven E. Miller, eds. *The Perils of Anarchy: Contemporary Realism and International Security*. Cambridge, Mass.: MIT Press, 1995.

Brzezinski, Zbigniew. *The Soviet Bloc: Unity and Conflict*, rev. and enl. ed. Cambridge, Mass.: Harvard University Press, 1976.

————. *The Grand Failure: The Birth and Death of Communism in the Twentieth Century*. New York: Collier Books, 1989.

Budnikowski, Tomasz, Lech Janicki, Piotr Kalka, Jadwiga Kiwerska, Krzysztof Mali-nowski, and Tadeusz Wroblewski, "Stosunki polsko-niemieckie" [Polish–German Relations]. Pp. 171–186 in *Rocznik Polskiej Polityki Zagranicznej, 1992* [Yearbook of Polish Foreign Policy, 1992], edited by Barbara Wizimirska. Warsaw: Polski Instytut Spraw Miedzynarodowych, 1994.

Bueno de Mesquita, Bruce, and David Lalman, eds. *War and Reason: Domestic and International Imperatives*. New Haven, Conn.: Yale University Press, 1992.

Bull, Hedley. *The Anarchical Society*. New York: Columbia University Press, 1977.

Burg, Steven L. *War or Peace? Nationalism, Democracy, and American Foreign Policy in Post–Communist Europe*. New York: New York University Press, 1996.

Bush, George, and Brent Scowcroft. *A World Transformed*. New York: Vintage, 1998.

Buzan, Barry, Charles Jones, and Richard Little, eds. *The Logic of Anarchy: Neorealism to Structural Realism*. New York: Columbia University Press, 1993.

Cameron, Fraser. "Relations between the European Union and Ukraine." Pp. 93–106 in *Ukraine and Its Western Neighbors*, edited by James Clem and Nancy Popson. Washington, D.C.: Woodrow International Center for Scholars, 2000.

Carter, Ashton B., William J. Perry, and John D. Steinbruner. *A New Concept of Cooperative Security*. Washington, D.C.: Brookings Institution, 1992.

Chase, Robert, Emily Hill, and Paul Kennedy. *The Pivotal States: A New Framework for U.S. Policy in the Developing World*. New York: Norton, 1999.

Chay, John, and Thomas E. Ross, eds. *Buffer States in World Politics*. Boulder, Colo.: Westview, 1986).

Cottey, Andrew. *East-Central Europe after the Cold War: Poland, the Czech Republic, Slovakia and Hungary in Search of Security*. Houndmills, U.K.: Macmillan, 1995.

Cox, Robert. *Production, Power, and World Order*. New York: Columbia University Press, 1987.

Crawford, Beverly, ed. *The Future of European Security*. Berkeley: University of California at Berkeley, Center for German and European Studies, 1992.

D'Abernon, Viscount. *The Eighteenth Decisive Battle of the World: Warsaw, 1920*. London: Hodder and Stoughton, 1931.

Dahrendorf, Ralf. *Reflections on the Revolution in Europe: In a Letter Intended to Have Been Sent to a Gentleman in Warsaw*. New York: Times Books, 1990.

Davies, Norman. *White Eagle, Red Star: The Polish Soviet War, 1919–1920*. New York: St. Martin's, 1972.

———. *God's Playground: A History of Poland*, vols. 1–2. New York: Columbia University Press, 1982.

———. *Heart of Europe: A Short History of Poland*, 2nd ed. Oxford: Oxford University Press, 1986.

Dawisha, Karen. *Eastern Europe, Gorbachev and Reform: The Great Challenge*, 2nd ed. Cambridge: Cambridge University Press, 1990.

Dawisha, Karen, and Bruce Parrott, eds. *The Consolidation of Democracy in East-Central Europe: Authoritarianism and Democratization in Postcommunist Societies*. Cambridge: Cambridge University Press, 1997.

———. *Politics, Power, and the Struggle for Democracy in South–East Europe Societies*. Cambridge: Cambridge University Press, 1997.

De Callieres, François. *On the Manner of Negotiating with Princes*. Notre Dame, Ind.: University of Notre Dame Press, 1963.

De Felice, F. "Negotiations, or the Art of Negotiating." Pp. 44-119 in *The 50% Solution*, edited by I. William Zartman. New York: Anchor Books, 1976.

Deutsch, Karl W., et al. *Political Community and the North Atlantic Area: International Organization in the Light of Historical Experience*. New York: Greenwood Press, 1969.

Dmowski, Roman. *Niemcy, Rosja i kwestja polska* [Germany, Russia and the Polish Question]. Warsaw: Instytut Wydawniczy PAX, 1991.

Doel, Theo van den. *Central Europe: The New Allies? The Road from Visegrad to Brussels*. Boulder, Colo.: Westview Press, 1994.

Duffield, John. *Power Rules: The Evolution of NATO's Conventional Force Posture*. Stanford, Calif.: Stanford University Press, 1995.

Dziewanowski, Kazimierz. *Polityka w Sercu Europy* [Politics in the Heart of Europe]. Warsaw: Oficyna Wydawnicza, 1995.

Dziewanowski, M. K. *Joseph Pilsudski: A European Federalist, 1918–1922*. Stanford, Calif.: Hoover Institution Press, 1969.

————. *Poland in the Twentieth Century.* New York: Columbia University Press, 1977.

Eisenhower, Susan, ed. *NATO at Fifty.* Washington: Center for Political and Strategic Studies, 1999.

Fox, Annette Baker. *The Power of Small States: Diplomacy in World War II.* Chicago: University of Chicago Press, 1959

————. *The Politics of Attraction: Four Middle Powers and the United States.* New York: Columbia University Press, 1977.

Frankel, Benjamin, ed. *Realism: Restatements and Renewal.* Cambridge, Mass.: The MIT Press, 1996.

————, ed. *Roots of Realism.* London: Frank Cass, 1996.

Friedman, Thomas L. *The Lexus and the Olive Tree: Understanding Globalization.* New York: Anchor, 2000.

Garnett, Sherman W. *Keystone in the Arch: Ukraine in the Emerging Security Environment of Central and Eastern Europe.* Washington, D.C.: Carnegie Endowment Press, 1995.

Gati, Charles. *The Bloc That Failed: Soviet–East European Relations in Transition.* Bloomington: Indiana University Press, 1990.

German-Polish Dialogue: Letters of the Polish and German Bishops and International Statements. New York: Atlantic Forum, 1966.

Gilpin, Robert. *War and Change in World Politics.* Cambridge: Cambridge University Press, 1981.

Glaser, Charles L. "Realists as Optimists: Cooperation as Self-Help." Pp. 122--163 in *The Perils of Anarchy: Contemporary Realism and International Security,* edited by Michael E. Brown, Sean M. Lynn-Jones, and Steven E. Miller. Cambridge, Mass.: MIT Press, 1995.

Glenny, Misha. *The Rebirth of History: Eastern Europe in the Age of Democracy.* London: Penguin Books, 1990.

Goetschel, Laurent, ed. *Small States inside and outside the European Union: Interests and Policies.* Dordrecht, Netherlands: Kluwer Academic Press, 1998.

Goldfarb, Jeffrey C. *After the Fall: The Pursuit of Democracy in Central Europe.* New York: Basic Books, 1992.

Goldstein, Judith, and Robert O. Keohane, eds. *Ideas and Foreign Policy: Beliefs, Institutions, and Political Change.* Ithaca, N.Y.: Cornell University Press, 1993.

Golembski, Franciszek, Andrzej Kupich, and Jozef Wiejacz. "Polska w ugrupowaniach regionalnych." [Poland in Regional Groupings]. Pp. 83–89 in *Rocznik Polskiej Polityki Zagranicznej, 1992* [Yearbook in Polish Foreign Policy, 1992] edited by Barbara Wizimirska. Warsaw: Polish Institute of International Affairs, 1994.

Gomulka, Wladislaw. *Przemowienia* [Speeches]. Warsaw: n.p. 1956–1957.

Gorbachev, Mikhail. *Perestroika: New Thinking for Our Country and the World.* New York: Harper & Row, 1987.

Grieco, Joseph M. "Anarchy and the Limits of Cooperation: A Realist Critique of the Newest Liberal Institutionalism." Pp. 116–142 in *Neorealism and Neoliberalism: The Contemporary Debate,* edited by David A. Baldwin. New York: St. Martin's, 1995.

————. "Understanding the Problem of International Cooperation: The Limits of Neoliberal Institutionalism and the Future of Realist Theory." Pp. 301–338 in *Neorealism and Neoliberalism: The Contemporary Debate,* edited by David A. Baldwin. New York: St. Martin's, 1995.

Griffith, William E., ed. *Central and Eastern Europe: The Opening Curtain?* Boulder, Colo.: Westview, 1989.

Grunberg, Karol. *Polskie koncepcje federalistyczne 1864–1918* [The Polish Concept of Federalization] Warsaw: n.p. 1971.

Haas, Peter M., Robert O. Keohane, and Marc A. Levy, eds. *Institutions for the Earth: Sources of Effective International Environmental Protection.* Cambridge, Mass.: MIT Press, 1993.

Habeeb, William M. *Power and Tactics in International Negotiation: How Weak Nations Bargain with Strong Nations.* Baltimore, Md.: Johns Hopkins University Press, 1988.

Hajda, Lubomyr A., ed. *Ukraine in the World: Studies in the International and Security Structure of a Newly Independent State.* Cambridge, Mass.: Harvard University Press, 1998.

Hall, Aleksander. *Zanim bedzie za pozno: przed wyborami prezydenckimi* [Before it's too Late: Before the Presidential Elections]. Gdansk, Poland: Info-Trade, 1994.

Handel, Michael I. *Weak States in the International System,* 2nd ed. London: Cass, 1990.

Herz, John H. *Political Realism and Political Idealism: A Study in Theories and Realities.* Chicago: University of Chicago Press, 1959.

Hey, Jeanne A. K., ed. *Small States in World Politics: Explaining Foreign Policy Behavior.* Boulder, Colo.: Reinner, 2003.

Holsti, Ole R. P., Terrence Hopmann, and John D. Sullivan. *Unity and Disintegration in International Alliances.* New York: John Wiley, 1973.

Homans, George. *Social Behavior.* New York: Harcourt Brace, 1961.

Hopmann, P. Terrence. *The Negotiation Process and the Resolution of International Conflicts.* Columbia: University of South Carolina Press, 1998.

Hough, Jerry. *Russia and the West: Gorbachev and the Politics of Reform,* 2nd ed. New York: Touchstone, 1990.

Huntington, Samuel P. *The Third Wave: Democratization in the Late Twentieth Century.* Norman: University of Oklahoma Press, 1991.

————. *The Clash of Civilizations and the Remaking of World Order.* New York: Simon and Schuster, 1996.

Hyde-Price, Adrian. *The International Politics of East Central Europe.* Manchester, U.K.: Manchester University Press, 1996.

Jelenski, Konstanty A. "Introduction." Pp. 3–24 in *Between East and West: Writings from Kultura,* edited by Robert Kostrzewa. New York: Hill and Wang, 1990.

Jervis, Robert. *Perception and Misperception in International Politics.* Princeton, N.J.: Princeton University Press, 1976.

Joffe, Josef. "'The Revisionists': Germany and Russia in a Post-Bipolar World." Pp. 95–126 in *New Thinking and Old Realities: America, Europe, and Russia,* edited by Michael T. Clark and Simon Serfaty. Washington, D.C.: Seven Locks Press, 1991.

————. "'Bismarck' or 'Britain'? Toward an American Grand Strategy after Bipolarity." Pp. 596–614 in *American Foreign Policy: Theoretical Essays,* 3rd ed., edited by G. John Ikenberry. New York: Addison Wesley Longman, 1999.

Kaczynski, Jaroslaw. "Gdzie tkwil blad?" [Where is the Error?]. Pp. 7–56 in *Lewy Czerwcowy* [Blow from the Left], edited by Jacek Kurski and Piotr Semka. Warsaw: Editions Spotkania, 1993.

Kamieniecki, Witold. *Ponad zgielkiem walk narodowosciowych: Idea jagiellonska* [Above the Noise of the Nationality Struggles: The Jagiellonian Idea]. Warsaw: n.p. 1929.

Kaminski, Antoni, and Jerzy Kozakiewicz. *Polish-Ukrainian Relations, 1992–1996.* Warsaw: Center for International Relations, Institute of Public Affairs, 1997.
Kaminski, Bartlomiej. *The Collapse of State Socialism: The Case of Poland.* Princeton, N.J.: Princeton University Press, 1991.
Kaplan, Lawrence S. *NATO and the United States.* New York: Twayne Publishers, 1994.
Karkoszka, Andrzej, and Pawel Wieczorek. "The New Challenges Facing Poland's Armed Forces." Pp. 93–130 in *Report on the State of National Security: External Aspects,* edited by Henryk Szlajfer and Janusz Prystrom. Warsaw: Polish Institute of International Affairs, 1993.
Karp, Regina Cowen, ed. *Central and Eastern Europe: The Challenge of Transition.* Oxford: Oxford University Press, 1993.
Karpinski, Jakub. *Countdown: The Polish Upheavals of 1956, 1968, 1970, 1976, 1980. . .* New York: Karz-Cohl, 1982.
Karsh, Efraim. *Neutrality and Small States.* London: Routledge, 1988.
Katzenstein, Peter. *Small States in World Markets.* Ithaca, N.Y.: Cornell University Press, 1985.
————, ed. *The Culture of National Security: Norms and Identity in World Politics.* New York: Columbia University Press, 1996.
Kay, Sean. *NATO and the Future of European Security.* Lanham, Md: Rowman & Littlefield, 1998.
Kegley, Charles W., Jr., and Gregory A. Raymond. *When Trust Breaks Down: Alliance Norms and World Politics.* Columbia: University of South Carolina Press, 1990.
————, eds. *Controversies in International Relations Theory: Realism and the Neoliberal challenge.* New York: St. Martin's, 1995.
Kelleher, Catherine M. *The Future of European Security.* Washington, D.C.: Brookings Institution, 1995.
Keohane, Robert O., Joseph S. Nye, and Stanley Hoffman, eds. *After the Cold War: International Institutions and State Strategies in Europe, 1989–1991.* Cambridge, Mass.: Harvard University Press, 1993.
Kipp, Jacob, ed. *Central European Security Concerns: Bridge, Buffer or Barrier?* London: Cass, 1993.
Kissinger, Henry. *Diplomacy.* New York: Simon & Schuster, 1994.
Knorr, Klaus. *The War Potential of Nations.* Princeton, N.J.: Princeton University Press, 1956.
Kolakowski, Leszek. "The Intelligentsia." Pp. 230–268 in *Poland: Genesis of a Revolution,* edited by Abraham Brumberg. New York: Vintage, 1983.
Kosicka-Pajewska, Aleksandra. *Polska miedzy Rosja a Niemcami: koncepcje polityczne Adolfa Bochenskiego* [Poland between Russia and Germany: Political Concepts of Adolf Bochenski]. Poznan, Poland: Oficyna Wydawnicza Book Service, 1992.
Korbel, Josef. *Poland between East and West: Soviet and German Diplomacy toward Poland, 1919–1933.* Princeton, N.J.: Princeton University Press, 1963.
Korbonski, Andrzej. "The Security of East Central Europe and the Visegrad Triangle." Pp. 159–177 in *The Legacy of the Soviet Bloc,* edited by Jane Shapiro Zacek and Ilpyong J. Kim. Gainesville: University of Florida Press, 1997.
Kostrzewa, Robert, ed. *Between East and West: Writings from Kultura.* New York: Hill and Wang, 1990.
Kostrzewa-Zorbas, Grzegorz. "Imperium kontratakuje" [The Empire Strikes Back]. Pp. 147–188 in *Lewy Czerwcowy* (Blow from the Left), edited by Jacek Kurski and Piotr Semka. Warsaw: Editions Spotkania, 1992.

————. "The Russian Troop Withdrawal from Poland." Pp. 113–138 in *The Diplomatic Record, 1992-1993*, edited by Allan E. Goodman. Boulder, Colo.: Westview, 1995.

Koziej, Stanislaw. *Polish Defense Policy*. Warsaw: National Defense Academy, 1992.

Kramer, Mark. "Neorealism, Nuclear Proliferation, and East-Central European Strategies." Pp. 385–463 in *Unipolar Politics: Realism and State Strategies after the Cold War*, edited by Ethan B. Kapstein and Michael Mastanduno. New York: Columbia University Press, 1999.

Kuczynski, Waldemar. *Zwierzenia Zausznika* [Confidence of a Confidante]. Warsaw: Polska Oficyna Wydawnicza, 1992.

Kurski, Jaroslaw. *Lech Walesa: Democrat or Dictator?* Boulder, Colo.: Westview Press, 1993.

Kuzniar, Roman. "Polish Foreign Policy: An Attempt at an Overview." Pp. 9–20 in *Yearbook of Polish Foreign Policy, 1993/1994*, edited by Barbara Wizimirska. Warsaw: Polish Institute of International Affairs, 1994.

————, ed. *Poland's Security Policy, 1989–2000*. Warsaw: Scholar Publishing House, 2001.

Lampe, John R. and Daniel N. Nelson, eds., in collaboration with Roland Schonfeld. *East European Security Reconsidered*. Washington, D.C.: Wilson Center Press, 1993.

Larrabee F. Stephen, ed. *The Two German States and European Security*. New York: St. Martin's, 1989.

————. *East European Security after the Cold War*. Santa Monica, Calif.: RAND National Defense Research Institute, 1993.

————. "Ukraine's Place in European and Regional Security." Pp. 249–270 in *Ukraine in the World: Studies in the International and Security Structure of a Newly Independent State*, edited by Lubomyr A. Hajda. Cambridge, Mass.: Harvard University Press, 1998.

Larson, Deborah Welch. "Bandwagon Images in American Foreign Policy: Myth or Reality?" Pp. 85–111 in *Dominoes and Bandwagons: Strategic Beliefs and Great Power Competition in the Eurasian Rimland*, edited by Robert Jervis and Jack Snyder. Oxford: Oxford University Press, 1991.

Latawski, Paul, ed. *The Reconstruction of Poland, 1914–23*. New York: St. Martin's, 1992.

————. *The Security Road to Europe: The Visegrad Four*. London: Royal United Services for Defence Studies, 1994.

Lebow, Richard Ned, and Thomas Risse-Kappen, eds. *International Relations Theory and the End of the Cold War*. New York: Columbia University Press, 1995.

Lefever, Ernest W., and Robert D. Vander Lugt, eds. *Perestroika: How New Is Gorbachev's New Thinking?* Washington: Ethics and Public and Policy Center, 1989.

Lewis, Flora. *A Case History of Hope: The Story of Poland's Peaceful Revolution*. New York: Doubleday, 1958.

Linz, Juan J., and Alfred Stepan. *Problems of Democratic Transition and Consolidation: Southern Europe, South America, and Post-Communist Europe*. Baltimore, Md.: Johns Hopkins University Press, 1996.

Lipski, Jan Jozef. "Two Fatherlands; Two Patriotisms." Pp. 52–71 in *Between East and West: Writings from Kultura*, edited by Robert Kostrzewa. New York: Hill and Wang, 1990.

Lynn-Jones, Sean M., and Steven E. Miller, eds. *The Cold War and After: Prospects for Peace*, exp. ed. Cambridge, Mass.: MIT Press, 1997.

Mackinder, Halford J. *Democratic Ideals and Reality.* Westport, Conn.: Greenwood, 1962.

Mandelbaum, Michael. *The Dawn of Peace in Europe.* New York: Twentieth Century Fund, 1996.

Mastanduno, Michael. "Preserving the Unipolar Moment: Realist Theories and U.S. Grand Strategy after the Cold War." Pp. 138–181 in *Unipolar Politics: Realism and State Strategies after the Cold War,* edited by Ethan B. Kapstein and Michael Mastanduno. New York: Columbia University Press, 1999.

Mathisen, Trygve. *The Functions of Small States in the Strategies of the Great Powers* Oslo: Bergen Tromso, 1971.

Matraszek, Marek. *Poland: The Politics of Restoration.* London: Alliance, 1994.

McGwire, Michael. *Perestroika and Soviet National Security Policy.* Washington, D.C.: Brookings Institution, 1991.

Mearsheimer, John J. "The False Promise of International Institutions." Pp. 332–376 in *The Perils of Anarchy: Contemporary Realism and International Security,* edited by Michael E. Brown, Sean M. Lynn-Jones, and Steven E. Miller. Cambridge, Mass.: MIT Press, 1995.

————. "Back to the Future: Instability in Europe after the Cold War." Pp. 141–192 in *The Cold War and After: Prospects for Peace,* exp. ed., edited by Sean M. Lynn-Jones and Steven E. Miller. Cambridge, Mass.: MIT Press, 1997.

————. *The Tragedy of Great Power Politics.* New York: Norton, 2001.

Michnik, Adam. *Letters from Prison and Other Essays.* Berkeley: University of California Press, 1987.

————. "Revolt of the Radiators." Pp. 199–205 in *Perestroika: How New Is Gorbachev's New Thinking?* edited by Ernest W. Lefever and Robert D. Vander Lugt. Washington: Ethics and Public and Policy Center, 1989.

————. *The Church and the Left.* translated by David Ost. Chicago: University of Chicago Press, 1993.

Michta, Andrew. *Red Eagle: The Army in Polish Politics, 1944–1988.* Stanford, Calif.: Hoover Institution Press, 1990.

————. *East Central Europe after the Warsaw Pact: Security Dilemmas in the 1990s* New York: Greenwood Press, 1992.

————. "Poland, Czechoslovakia, and Hungary: The Triangle in Search of Europe." Pp. 53–83 in *Post-Communist Eastern Europe: Crisis and Reform,* edited by Andrew A. Michta and Ilya Prizel. New York: St. Martin's, 1993.

————. "Safeguarding the Third Republic: Security Policy and Military Reform." Pp. 73–94 in *Polish Foreign Policy Reconsidered: Challenges of Independence,* edited by Ilya Prizel and Andrew A. Michta. London: Macmillan, 1995.

————. "Democratic Consolidation in Poland after 1989." Pp. 66–108 in *The Consolidation of Democracy in East-Central Europe,* edited by Karen Dawisha and Bruce Parrott. Cambridge: Cambridge University Press, 1997.

————, ed. *America's New Allies: Poland, Hungary, and the Czech Republic in NATO.* Seattle: University of Washington Press, 2000.

Mieroszewski, Juliusz. *Kehrt Deutschland in den Osten zuruck? Polen-Deutschland-Europa* [The German Turn-About in Eastern Restraint? Poland–Germany–Europe]. Berlin: n.p. 1961.

————. *Ewolucjonizm* [Evolutionism]. Paris: Instytut Literacki, 1964.

————. *Polityczne Neurozy* [Political Neuroses]. Paris: Instytut Literacki, 1967.

————. *Modele i Praktyka* [Theory and Practice]. Paris: Instytut Literacki, 1970.

————. "The Political Thoughts of Kultura." Pp. 245–340 in *Kultura Essays*, edited by Leopold Tyrmand. New York: Free Press, 1970.

————. *Materialy do Refleksji i Zadumy* [Materials for Reflection and Musing]. Paris: Instytut Literacki, 1976.

————. "Imperialism: Theirs and Ours." Pp. 39–51 in *Between East and West: Writings from Kultura*, edited by Robert Kostrzewa. New York: Hill and Wang, 1990.

Mojsiewicz, Czeslaw. *Polska i jej nowi sasiedzi (1989–1993)* [Poland and her new neighbors(1989–1993)]. Torun, Poland: Wydawnictwo Adam Marszalek, 1994.

Morgenthau, Hans J. and Kenneth W. Thompson. *Politics among Nations: The Struggle for Power and Peace*, 6th ed. New York: Knopf, 1985.

Moroney, Jennifer D. P., and Taras Kuzio, eds. *Ukraine's Foreign and Security Policy: Theoretical and Comparative Perspectives*. Westport, Conn.: Greenwood/Praeger, 2002.

Muchler, Gunter, and Klaus Hofmann. *Helmut Kohl: Chancellor of German Unity, A Biography*. Bonn, Germany: Press and Information Office of the Federal Government, 1992.

Nagorski, Andrew. *The Birth of Freedom: Shaping Lives and Societies in the New Eastern Europe*. New York: Simon & Schuster, 1993.

Najder, Zdzislaw, ed. *Polskie Porozumienie Niepodleglosciowe: Wybor Tekstow* [Alliance for Polish Independence: Electoral Text]. London: Polonia, 1989.

————. *Jaka Polska: Co i Komu Doradzalem* [What Kind of Poland: What and To Whom I Advised]. Warsaw: Editions Spotkania, 1994.

Nolan, Janne E., ed. *Global Engagement: Cooperation and Security in the 21st Century*. Washington, D.C.: Brookings Institution, 1994.

Nye, Joseph. *The Paradox of American Power: Why the World's Only Superpower Can't Go It Alone*. London: Oxford University Press, 2002.

Olcott, Martha Brill, Anders Aslund, and Sherman Garnett, eds. *Getting It Wrong: Regional Cooperation and the Commonwealth of Independent States*. Washington, D.C.: Carnegie Endowment Press, 1999.

Ostrowski, Zdzislaw. *Pozegnanie z Armia* [Farewell from the Army]. Warsaw: Czytelnik, 1992.

Parrott, Bruce. *Politics and Technology in the Soviet Union*. Cambridge, Mass.: MIT Press, 1983.

Parys, Jan. "Bitwa o wojsko" [The Battle for the Army]. Pp. 71–74 in *Lewy Czerwcowy* [Blow from the Left], edited by Jacek Kurski and Piotr Semka. Warsaw: Editions Spotkania, 1992.

Petersen, Phillip A. "The Challenge to Soviet Strategic Deployment: An Emerging Vision of European Security." Pp. 323–334 in *Jane's NATO Handbook, 1990–1991*, edited by Bruce George. Coulsdon, U.K.: Jane's Information Group, 1990.

Pond, Elizabeth. *The Rebirth of Europe*. Washington, D.C.: Brookings Institution Press, 1999.

Posen, Barry R. *The Sources of Military Doctrine: France, Britain, and Germany between the World Wars*. Ithaca, N.Y.: Cornell University Press, 1984.

Pounds, Norman J. G. *Poland between East and West*. Princeton, N.J.: Van Nostrand, 1964.

Powell, Robert. *In the Shadow of Power: States and Strategies in International Politics*. Princeton, N.J.: Princeton University Press, 1999.

Prizel, Ilya. "Russia and Germany: The Case for a Special Relationship." Pp. 21–52 in *Post-Communist Eastern Europe: Crisis and Reform*, edited by Andrew A. Michta and Ilya Prizel. New York: St. Martin's, 1992.

―――――. "Warsaw's Ostpolitik: A New Encounter with Positivism." Pp. 95–128 in *Polish Foreign Policy Reconsidered: Challenges of Independence*, edited by Ilya Prizel, and Andrew A. Michta. London: Macmillan, 1995.

―――――. *National Identity and Foreign Policy: Nationalism and Leadership in Poland, Russia, and Ukraine*. Cambridge: Cambridge University Press, 1998.

Prizel, Ilya and Andrew Michta, eds. *Polish Foreign Policy Reconsidered: Challenges of Independence*. London: Macmillan, 1995.

"Program Polskiego Porozumienia Niepodleglosciowego w Kraju," [Program of the Alliance for Polish Independence]. Pp. 7–26 in *PPN: Polskie Porozumienie Niepodleglosciowe* [PPN: Alliance for Polish Independence], sponsored by Gustaw, Herling-Grudzinski, Leszek Kolakowski, and Jerzy Lerski. Paris: Instytut Literacki, 1978,

Rachwald, Arthur R. *Poland between the Superpowers: Security vs. Economic Recovery* Boulder, Colo.: Westview, 1983.

―――――. *In Search of Poland: The Superpowers' Response to Solidarity, 1980–1989* Stanford, Calif.: Hoover Institution Press, 1990.

―――――. "Poland Looks West." Pp. 129–155 in *Post-1989 Poland: Challenges of Independence*, edited by Andrew Michta and Ilya Prizel. New York: St. Martin's, 1995.

Raina, Peter. *Political Opposition in Poland, 1954–1977*. London: Poets and Painters, 1978.

Riasanovsky, Nicholas V. *A History of Russia*. 3rd ed. New York: Oxford University Press, 1977.

Rothschild, Joseph. *East Central Europe between the Two World Wars*, vol. 9. Seattle: University of Washington Press, 1974.

Rothstein, Robert L. *Alliances and Small Powers*. New York: Columbia University Press, 1968.

―――――. *The Weak in the World of the Strong*. New York: Columbia University Press, 1977.

Royen, Christoph. "The Visegrad Triangle and the Western CIS: Potential Conflict Constellations." Pp. 75–92 in *East European Security Reconsidered*, edited by John R. Lampe and Daniel N. Nelson, in collaboration with Roland Schonfeld. Washington, D.C.: Wilson Center Press, 1993.

Rubin, Jeffrey, and Bert Brown. *The Social Psychology of Bargaining and Negotiation*. New York: Academic, 1975.

Russett, Bruce. *Grasping the Democratic Peace: Principles for a Post-Cold War World*. Princeton, N.J.: Princeton University Press, 1993.

Sagan, Scott D., and Kenneth N. Waltz. *The Spread of Nuclear Weapons: A Debate*. New York: Norton, 1995.

Schroeder, Paul. *The Transformation of European Politics, 1763–1848*. Oxford: Clarendon Press, 1994.

Schuman, Frederick L. *International Politics: The Destiny of the Western State System* New York: McGraw-Hill, 1969.

Schweigler, Gebhard. "German Questions or The Shrinking of Germany." Pp. 73–105 in *The Two German States and European Security*, edited by F. Stephen Larrabee. N.Y.: St. Martin's, 1989.

Schweller, Randall L. *Deadly Imbalances: Tripolarity and Hitler's Strategy of World Conquest*. New York: Columbia University Press, 1998.

Seton-Watson, Hugh. *Eastern Europe between the Wars, 1918–1941*. Cambridge: Cambridge University Press, 1946.

Simon, Jeffrey, ed. *European Security Policy after the Revolutions of 1989.* Washington, D.C.: National Defense University Press, 1991.

————, ed. *NATO: The Challenge of Change.* Washington, D.C.: National Defense University Press, 1993.

————. *NATO Enlargement and Central Europe: A Study in Civil-Military Relations.* Washington, D.C.: National Defense University Press, 1996.

Simons, Thomas W., Jr. *Eastern Europe in the Postwar World,* 2nd ed. New York: St. Martins, 1993.

Skubiszewski, Krzysztof. *Zachodnia Granica Polski* [Poland's Western Border]. Gdansk: Wydawnictwo Morskie—Instytut Baltycki w Gdansku, 1969.

————. "Future Architecture of European Security" Pp. 391–393 in *Jane's NATO Handbook, 1991–1992,* edited by Bruce George. Coulsdon, U.K.: Jane's Information Group, 1991.

————. "Racja stanu z perspektywy polskiej" [Raison d'état from the Polish Perspective]. Pp. 35–44 in *Rocznik Polskiej Polityki Zagranicznej, 1992* [Yearbook on Polish Foreign Policy, 1992], edited by Barbara Wizimirska. Warsaw: Polski Instytut Spraw Miedzynarodowych, 1994.

————. "Perspectives of Poland's Foreign Policy." Pp. 21–30 in *Yearbook of Polish Foreign Policy, 1993/1994,* English ed., edited by Barbara Wizimirska. Warsaw: Polish Institute of International Affairs, 1994.

————. *Polityka zagraniczna i odzyskanie niepodleglosci: przemówienia, oswiadczenia, wywiady 1989–1993.* [Foreign Policy and Regaining Independence: Addresses, Declaration, Interviews, 1989–1993]. Warsaw: Wydawa Interpress, 1997.

Snyder, Glen, and Paul Diesing. *Conflict among Nations.* Princeton, N.J.: Princeton University Press, 1977.

Snyder, Jack. *Myths of Empire: Domestic Politics and International Ambition.* Ithaca, N.Y.: Cornell University Press, 1991.

Sodaro, Michael J. *Moscow, Germany, and the West from Khrushchev to Gorbachev.* Ithaca, N.Y.: Cornell University Press, 1990.

Spero, Joshua B. "Central European Security." Pp. 42–57 in *The Future of European Security: The Pursuit of Peace in an Era of Revolutionary Change,* edited by J. Philip Rogers. New York: St. Martin's, 1993.

————. "Poland's Perennial Crossroads: Between East and West?" Pp. 273–291 in *The Future of East-Central Europe,* edited by Andrzej Dumala and Ziemowit Jacek Pietras. Lublin, Poland: Maria Curie-Sklodowska University Press, 1996.

————. "The Polish-Ukrainian Inter-State Model for Cooperation and Integration: Regional Relations in a Theoretical Context." Pp. 155–178 in *Ukraine's Foreign and Security Policy: Theoretical and Comparative Perspectives,* edited by Jennifer D. P. Moroney and Taras Kuzio. Westport, Conn.: Greenwood/Praeger, 2002.

————. "Looking beyond NATO and EU Enlargement: Northeastern Europe and Russian Security Dynamics." Pp. 104–111 in *The Translatlantic Relationship: Problems and Prospects,* edited by Sabina A.-M. Auger. Washington, D.C.: Woodrow Wilson International Center for Scholars/East European Studies, West European Studies, Stanley Foundation, 2003.

————. "Paths to Peace for NATO's Partnerships in Eurasia." Pp. 166–184 in *Limiting Institutions: The Challenge of Eurasian Security Governance,* edited by James Sperling, Sean Kay, and S. Victor Papacosma. Manchester: Manchester University Press, 2003.

————, "The Impact on NATO of the Emerging Role of Eastern Europe and the NIS in Iraq." Pp. 8–9, 14 in *East Europe's Emerging Role in the Middle East*, edited by Nida Gelazis. Washington, D.C.: Woodrow Wilson Center for International Scholars, 2004.

Spykman, Nicholas J. *America's Strategy in World Politics*. New York: Harcourt Brace Jovanovich, 1942.

Staar, Richard F. *Poland 1944–1962: The Sovietization of a Captive People*. New Orleans: Louisiana State University Press, 1962.

Stehle, Hansjakob. *The Independent Satellite*. London: Praeger, 1965.

Stein, Arthur A. *Why Nations Cooperate: Circumstance and Choice in International Relations*. Ithaca, N.Y.: Cornell University Press, 1990.

Stent, Angela. *Russia and Germany Reborn: Unification, the Soviet Collapse, and the New Europe*. Princeton, N.J.: Princeton University Press, 1999.

Stokes, Gale. *The Walls Came Tumbling Down: The Collapse of Communism in Eastern Europe*. New York: Oxford University Press, 1993.

Swiatkowski, Lucja Cannon. "Polish Transition Strategy: Successes and Failures." Pp. 142–158 in *The Legacy of the Soviet Bloc*, edited by Jane Shapiro Zacek and Ilpyong J. Kim. Gainesville: University Press of Florida, 1997.

Szabo, Stephen F. "Federal Republic of Germany: The Bundeswehr." Pp. 189–206 in *European Security Policy after the Revolutions in 1989*, edited by Jeffrey Simon. Washington, D.C.: National Defense University Press, 1991.

————. *The Diplomacy of German Unification*. New York: St. Martin's, 1992.

————. "The New Germany and Central European Security." Pp. 35–54 in *East European Security Reconsidered*, edited by John R. Lampe and Daniel N. Nelson. Washington, D.C.: The Woodrow Wilson Center Press, 1993.

Szlajfer, Henryk, and Janusz Prystrom, eds. *Report on the State of National Security: External Aspects*. Warsaw: Polish Institute of International Affairs, 1993.

Szrett, Jozef. "The Valley between the Mountains." Pp. 25–38 in *Between East and West: Writings from Kultura*, edited by Robert Kostrzewa. New York: Hill and Wang, 1990.

Taras, Ray. *Poland: Socialist State, Rebellious Nation*. Boulder, Colo.: Westview, 1986.

Terry, Sarah M. *Poland's Place in Europe: General Sikorski and the Origin of the Oder-Neisse Line, 1939–1943*. Princeton, N.J.: Princeton University Press, 1983.

————. "The Future of Poland: Perestroika or Perpetual Crisis?" Pp. 178–217 in *Central and Eastern Europe: The Opening Curtain*, edited by William E. Griffith Boulder, Colo.: Westview, 1989.

Tismaneanu, Vladimir. *Fantasies of Salvation: Democracy, Nationalism, and Myth in Post-Communist Europe*. Princeton, N.J.: Princeton University Press, 1998.

Toranska, Teresa. *"THEM": Stalin's Polish Puppets*. New York: Harper & Row, 1987.

————. *My* [Us]. Warsaw: Oficyna Wydawnicza MOST, 1994.

Tyrmand, Leopold, ed. *Kultura Essays*. New York: Free Press, 1970.

Ullman, Richard H. *Securing Europe*. Princeton, N.J.: Princeton University Press, 1991.

Van Evera, Stephen. *Causes of War: Power and the Roots of Conflict*. Ithaca, N.Y.: Cornell University Press, 1999.

Vinton, Louisa. "Domestic Politics and Foreign Policy, 1989–1993." Pp. 23–72 in *Polish Foreign Policy Reconsidered: Challenges of Independence*, edited by Ilya Prizel and Andrew A. Michta. Houndmills, U.K.: Macmillan Press, Ltd, 1995.

Vital, David. *The Survival of Small States: Studies in Small Power/Great Power Conflict* London: Oxford University Press, 1971.

Walesa, Lech. *The Struggle and the Triumph: An Autobiography.* New York: Arcade, 1991.

Walt, Steven M. *Origin of Alliances.* Ithaca, N.Y.: Cornell University Press, 1987.

———. "Alliance Formation in Southwest Asia: Balancing and Bandwagoning in Cold War Competition." Pp. 51–84 in *Dominoes and Bandwagons: Strategic Beliefs and Great Power Competition in the Eurasian Rimland,* edited by Robert Jervis and Jack Snyder. Oxford: Oxford University Press, 1991.

———. *Revolution and War.* Ithaca, N.Y.: Cornell University Press, 1996.

Waltz, Kenneth N. *Theory of International Politics,* rev. ed. Reading, Mass.: Addison-Wesley, 1983.

Wandycz, Piotr S. *Czechoslovak-Polish Confederation and the Great Powers, 1940–43.* Bloomington: Indiana University Press, 1956.

———. *Soviet-Polish Relations, 1917–1921.* Cambridge, Mass.: Harvard University Press, 1969.

———. *The Lands of Partitioned Poland, 1795–1918,* vol. 7 Seattle: University of Washington Press, 1974.

———. *The Price of Freedom: A History of East Central Europe from the Middle Ages to the Present.* London: Routledge, 1992.

Wedel, Janine. *Collision and Collusion: The Strange Case of Western Aid to Eastern Europe.* New York: Palgrave, 2001.

Weitz, Richard. "Pursuing Military Security in Eastern Europe." Pp. 342–380 in *After the Cold War: International Institutions and State Strategies in Europe, 1989–1991,* edited by Robert O. Keohane, Joseph S. Nye, and Stanley Hoffman. Cambridge, Mass.: Harvard University Press, 1993.

Wendt, Alexander. *Social Theory of International Politics.* Cambridge: Cambridge University Press, 1999.

Wight, Martin. *Systems of States.* Leicester, U.K.: Leicester University Press, 1977.

Winiewicz, Jozef, ed. *Polish Viewpoint, Disarmament, Denuclearization, European Security Documents, Declarations, Statements.* Warsaw: Polonia, 1967.

Wohlforth, William C. *The Elusive Balance: Power and Perception.* Ithaca, N.Y.: Cornell University Press, 1993.

Yost, David S. *NATO Transformed: The Alliance's New Roles in International Security.* Washington, D.C.: U.S. Institute of Peace Press, 1998.

Z [Martin Malia]. "To the Stalin Mausoleum." Pp. 283–339 in *Eastern Europe . . . Central Europe . . . Europe,* edited by Stephen R. Graubard. Boulder, Colo.: Westview, 1991.

Zartman, I. William, and Maureen Berman. *The Practical Negotiator.* New Haven, Conn.: Yale University Press, 1982.

———. "The Structure of Negotiation." Pp. 65–77 in *International Negotiation: Analysis, Approaches, Issues,* edited by Viktor Kremeniuk. San Francisco: Jossey-Bass, 1991.

Zelikow, Philip, and Condoleezza Rice. *Germany Unified and Europe Transformed: A Study in Statecraft.* Cambridge, Mass.: Harvard University Press, 1997.

Zielke, Krzysztof. "Polityka Wschodnia Rzeczypospolitej Polskiej na Progu Lat Dziewiedziesiatych." [Poland's Eastern Policy on the Threshold of the 1990s]. Pp. 25–43 in *Polityka Wschodnia Rzeczypospolitej Polskiej* [Poland's Eastern Policy], edited by Jadwiga Staniszkis. Warsaw: Instytut Studiow Politycznych Polskiej Akademii Nauk, 1991.

Zimmerman, William. *Soviet Perspectives on International Relations, 1956–1967.* Princeton, N.J.: Princeton University Press, 1973.

Ziolkowski, Janusz. "The Roots, Branches and Blossoms of *Solidarnosc*." Pp. 47–48 in *Spring in Winter: The 1989 Revolutions*, edited by Gwyn Prins. Manchester, U.K.: Manchester University Press, 1990.

Journal Articles and Monographs

Art, Robert J. "Why Western Europe Needs the United States and NATO." *Political Science Quarterly*, vol. 111, no. 1 (1996): 1–39.

Asmus, Ronald D., Richard L. Kugler, and F. Stephen Larrabee. "Building a New NATO." *Foreign Affairs* 4 (September/October 1993): 28–40.

Baba, Ivan. "Jedna partia plus druga—rowna sie: ile?" [One Party Plus Another Party Makes How Many?] *Nowa Koalicja* (August 1989): 20–23.

Balmaceda, Margarita Mercedes. "Two's Company, Three's a Crowd: The Role of Central Europe in Ukrainian Security." *East European Quarterly*, vol. 32, no. 3 (fall 1998): 345–348.

Barry, Charles, Sean Kay, and Joshua Spero. "Completing the Transatlantic Bargain: The United States and European Security." *Current History* (March 2001): 129–144.

"Bedziemy mogli stworzyc realny potencjal: Z rozmow z Czeskimi dzialaczami niezaleznymi, 1984–1986" [We Will Be Able to Create a Real Potential: Talks with Czech Independent Social Workers Signatories to Charter 77, 1984–1986]. *Nowa Koalicja* (March 1987): 16–20.

Blank, Stephen. *Russia and the Baltic: Is There a Threat to European Security?* Carlisle Barracks, Pa.: U.S. Army War College, 1993.

Bobrowski, Ryszard. "Polska Poza Europa?" *Polska w Europie: ZSSR 1990* (May 1990): 35–39.

Bromke, Adam. "Polski 'Ost-Zachod Politik'" [Polish 'East-West Politics']. *Kultura* (November 1973): 52–55.

Brooks, Stephen G., and William C. Wohlforth. "Power, Globalization, and the End of the Cold War: Reevaluating a Landmark Case for Ideas." *International Security*, vol. 25, no. 3 (winter 2000/2001): 3–51.

"Brussels Urges Warsaw to Step Up EU-Oriented Effort." *RFE/RL Poland, Belarus, and Ukraine Report*, vol. 3, no. 44 (20 November 2001).

Brzezinski, Ian. "Polish-Ukrainian Relations: The Geopolitical Dimension." *The National Interest*, no. 27 (spring 1992): 48–52.

Bunce, Valerie. "The Empire Strikes Back: The Transformation of the Eastern Bloc from a Soviet Asset to a Soviet Liability." *International Organization*, vol. 39, no. 1 (winter 1985): 1–46.

Burant, Stephen R. "Polish-Lithuanian Relations." *Problems of Communism* (May–June 1991): 67–84.

Burant, Stephen R., and Voytek Zubek. "Eastern Europe's Old Memories and New Realities: Resurrecting the Polish-Lithuanian Union." *East European Politics and Societies*, vol. 7, no. 2 (spring 1993): 370–393.

————. "International Relations in a Regional Context: Poland and Its Eastern Neighbors—Lithuania, Belarus, Ukraine." *Europe-Asia Studies*, vol. 45, no. 3 (1993): 395–418.

Chmura, Piotr. "Ukraina 1988: Poczatek drogi do niepodlegosci?" [Ukraine in 1988: Beginning the Road toward Independence?] *Nowa Koalicja* (July 1989): 12–18.

Christensen, Thomas J., and Jack Snyder. "Chain Gangs and Passed Bucks: Predicting Alliance Patterns in Multipolarity." *International Organization*, vol. 44, no. 2 (spring 1990): 137–168.

Crow, Suzanne. "International Department and Foreign Ministry Disagree on Eastern Europe." *Report on the USSR*, Radio Liberty, vol. 226, no. 91, (13 June 1991): 4–8.

————. "Negotiating New Treaties with Eastern Europe," *Report on the USSR*, Radio Liberty, vol. 252, no. 91 (8 July 1991): 3–6.

Druckman, Daniel. "Stages, Turning Points and Crises." *Journal of Conflict Resolution* 30 (1986): 327–360.

Duffield, John S. "Political Culture and State Behavior: Why Germany Confounds Neorealism." *International Organization*, vol. 53, no. 4 (autumn 1999): 765–803.

Elman, Colin. "Horses for Courses: Why Not Neorealist Theories of Foreign Policy?" *Security Studies*, no. 6 (1996): 7–53.

Elman, Colin, and Miriam Fendius Elman. "Correspondence—History vs. Neo-realism: A Second Look." *International Security*, vol. 20, no. 1 (summer 1995): 182–195.

Elman, Miriam Fendius. "The Foreign Policies of Small States: Challenging Neorealism in Its Own Backyard." *British Journal of Political Science*, vol. 29, no. 2 (April 1995): 101–119.

Flanagan, Stephen J. "NATO and Central and Eastern Europe: From Liaison to Security Partnership." *The Washington Quarterly*, vol. 15, no. 2 (spring 1992): 141–151.

Glaser, Charles L. "Why NATO Is Still Best: Future Security Arrangements for Europe." *International Security*, vol. 18, no. 1 (summer 1993): 5–50.

Gorski, Krzysztof. *Dwutorowosc Polskiej Polityki Wschodniej w latach 1989-1991* [Polish Two–Track Eastern Policy, 1989–1991]. Master's Thesis, Uniwersytet Warszawski, 1992.

Hajnicz, Artur. "Poland within Its Geopolitical Triangle." *Aussenpolitik* (1/1989): 30–40.

Halecki, Oskar. "Idea jagiellonska [Jagiellonian Idea. *Kwartalnik historyczny*, vol. 51 (1937).

Hall, Aleksander, excerpted from *Polityka Polska*, no. 2/3, in *Stadium Spraw Polskich* (5 July 1984): 25.

Hellmann, Gunther, and Reinhard Wolf. "Neorealism, Neoliberal Institutionalism, and the Future of NATO." *Security Studies* 3 (autumn 1993): 3–43.

Herspring, Dale. "After NATO Expansion: The East European Militaries." *Problems of Post-Communism*, vol. 45, no. 1 (January–February 1998): 10–20.

Hoffman, Gottfried-Karl. "The Munich School of Neorealism in International Politics." Unpublished manuscript, University of Munich, 1985.

Jaffe, Amy Myers, and Robert A. Manning. "Russia, Energy and the West." *Survival*, vol. 43, no. 2 (summer 2001): 133–152.

Jervis, Robert. "Cooperation under the Security Dilemma." *World Politics*, no. 2 (January 1978): 167–214.

Kipp, Jacob. "Vladimir Volfovich Zhirinovskii and the Liberal-Democratic Party: Statism, Nationalism and Imperialism." Foreign Military Studies Office (Fort Leavenworth, Kans.) and Conflict Studies Research Centre (Royal Military Academy Monograph Series, Sandhurst, U.K.), January 1994.

Kostrzewa-Zorbas, Grzegorz. "Security for the East Europeans." *Problems of Communism*, vol. 41, nos. 1–2 (January 1992): 148–149.

Kostrzewa-Zorbas, Grzegorz [Marcin Mieguszowiecki, pseud.], and Adam Realista. "Wspolnota Losow i Celow." [Common Destinies and Goals]. *Nowa Koalicja*, no. 1, (1985): 1–2.

————. "Razem jestesmy silniejsi: O portrzebie koalicji narodow Europy Srodkowo-Wschodniej" [Together We are Stronger: The Need for a Coalition of Eastern European Countries]. *Nowa Koalicja*, no. 1 (1985): 66–72.
————. "Wspolnota Losow i Celow" [Common Destiny and Goals]. *Nowa Koalicja*, no. 1 (1985): 1–2.
Koziej, Stanislaw. "Military Doctrine: A Non-Confrontational Model of Military Doctrine in the Future European Security System." *The Journal of Slavic Military Studies*, no. 4 (December 1993): 515–540.
Krasner, Stephen D. "Approaches to the State: Alternative Conceptions and Historical Dynamics." *Comparative Politics* (January 1984): 223–246.
Krauthammer, Charles. "The Unipolar Moment." *Foreign Affairs*, vol. 70, no. 1 (1990/1991): 23–33.
Krushelnycky, Askold. "Why Did Kyiv Choose to Seek NATO membership?" *RFE/RL Poland, Belarus, and Ukraine Report*, vol. 4, no. 22 (4 June 2002).
Kuklinski, Ryszard J. "Wojna znarodem widziana od srodka" [The War against the Nation Seen from the Inside.] *Kultura*, no. 4, no. 475 (1987): 3–57.
Kupchinsky, Roman. "The Finlandization of Ukraine," Parts I-II, *RFE/RL Poland, Belarus, and Ukraine Report*, vol. 5, no. 36 (30 September 2003) www.rferl.org/pbureport/2003/09/36-300903.html and *RFE/RL Poland, Belarus, and Ukraine Report*, vol. 5, no. 37 (7 October 2003), www.rferl.org/pbureport/2003/10/37-071003.html (accessed 10 January 2004).
————. "Kyiv Counts on 10-Year Gas-Transit Deal with Moscow," *RFE/RL Poland, Belarus, and Ukraine Report*, vol. 14, no. 15 (16 April 2002).
Labs, Eric J. "Do Weak States Bandwagon?" *Security Studies*, vol. 1, no. 3 (spring 1992): 383–416.
Lange, Peer. "Kaliningrad District: Crossroads for Russia's Political Strategy." *Europa Archiv*, no. 10 (25 May 1993), *FBIS-WEU* (27 June 1993): 3–8.
Latawski, Paul. "The Polish Road to NATO: Problems and Prospects," *Polish Quarterly of International Affairs*, no. 3 (summer 1993): 69–88.
Legro, Jeffrey W., and Andrew Moravcsik. "Is Anybody Still a Realist?" *International Security*, vol. 24, no. 2 (fall 1999): 5–55.
Lelyveld, Michael. "Poland's Gas Deal with Norway Offers Relief to Ukraine." *RFE/RL Poland, Belarus, and Ukraine Report*, vol. 3, no. 33 (4 September 2001).
————. "Russia Seeks Large Stake in Ukrainian Gas Pipeline." *RFE/RL Poland, Belarus, and Ukraine Report*, vol. 4, no. 26 (2 July 2002).
Lukacs, John. "Finland Vindicated." *Foreign Affairs*, vol. 71, no. 4 (fall 1992): 50–63.
Mackinder, Halford J. "The Geographical Pivot of History," *Geographical Journal*, vol. 23 (1904): 421–444.
Maksymiuk, Jan. "Warsaw Obliges Itself to Build EU's 'Berlin Wall.'" *RFE/RL Poland, Belarus, and Ukraine Report*, vol. 4, no. 29, (6 August 2002).
Mansfield, Edward D., and Jack Snyder. "Democratization and the Danger of War." *International Security*, vol. 20, no. 1 (summer 1995): 5–38.
McCalla, Robert. "NATO's Persistence after the Cold War." *International Organization*, vol. 50, no. 3 (summer 1996): 445–475.
Mercer, Jonathan. "Anarchy and Identity." *International Organization*, vol. 49, no. 2 (spring 1995): 229–252.
Mieroszewski, Juliusz. "Ksiegi ugody i diaspory Adama Bromke" [Books of Conciliation and the Diaspora of Adam Bromke]. *Kultura* (November 1974): 10–13.
Moravcsik, Andrew. "A Liberal Theory of International Politics." *International Organization*, vol. 51, no. 4 (autumn 1997): 513–553.

Nelson, Daniel N., and Thomas S. Szayna. "New NATO, New Problems: NATO's Metamorphosis and Its New Members." *Problems of Post-Communism*, vol. 45, no. 4 (July–August 1998): 32–43.

Nowakowski, Jerzy Marek. "Nowy zwiazek czy nowa Rosja?" [A New Union or a New Russia?] *Polska w Europie: ZSSR 1990* (May 1990): 11–34.

———. "Polska-Litwa: Zagrozenia i perspektywy." [Poland-Lithuania: Dangers and Perspectives.] *Polska w Europie: ZSSR 1990* (May 1990): 63–72.

———. "Polska pomiedzy wschodem a zachodem: Szansa 'Pomostu' czy historyczne fatum." [Poland between East and West: A Chance of 'Bridge Building' or Historical Fate.] *Polska w Europie* (April 1993): 5–20.

Okoliczanyi, Karoly. "The Visegrad Triangle's Free-Trade Zone." *RFE/RL Research Report*, vol. 2, no. 3 (15 January 1993): 19–22.

Partem, Michael Greenfield. "The Buffer System in International Relations." *Journal of Conflict Resolution*, vol. 27, no. 1 (March 1983): 3–26.

Piontkovski, Andrei. "Different Directions for Poland Russian Progressive Sees Poles Confident as a Part of Europe." *Russia Journal* (14–20 April 2001), JRL, 5202, davidjohnson@erols.com.

Prizel, Ilya, "The First Decade after the Collapse of Communism: Why Did Some Nations Succeed in their Political and Economic Transformations While Others Failed?" *SAIS Review*, vol. 19, no. 2 (summer–fall 1999): 1–15.

Reisch, Alfred A. "Central and Eastern Europe's Quest for NATO Membership." *RL/RFE Weekly Report* (9 July 1993): 33–47.

Rhodes, Matthew. "The Idea of Central Europe and Visegrad Cooperation." *International Politics*, vol. 35, no. 2 (June 1998): 173–175.

Rich, Vera. "Traffic across Poland's Eastern Frontiers Drops Due to New Visa Regime." *RFE/RL Poland, Belarus, and Ukraine Report*, vol. 5, no. 37 (7 October 2003). www.rferl.org/pbureport/2003/10/37-071003.html (accessed 6 January 2004).

———. "Which Way Will Oil Flow through Odessa-Brody Pipeline?" *RFE/RL Poland, Belarus, and Ukraine Report* vol. 5, no. 45 (2 December 2003). www.rferl.org/pbureport/2003/12/45-021203.html (accessed 6 January 2004).

Rurarz, Zdzislaw M. "The Polish-German Border Question." *Global Affairs* (fall 1990): 60–73.

Schroeder, Paul. "Historical Reality vs. Neo-realist Theory," *International Security*, vol. 19, no. 1 (summer 1994): 108–148.

———. "Correspondence—History vs. Neo-realism: A Second Look," *International Security*, vol. 20, no. 1 (summer 1995): 193–195.

Schweller, Randall L. "Bandwagoning for Profit: Bringing the Revisionist State Back In." *International Security*, vol. 19, no. 1 (summer 1994): 72–107.

Schweller, Randall L., and William C. Wohlforth. "Power Test: Evaluating Realism in Response to the End of the Cold War." *Security Studies*, vol. 9, no. 3 (spring 2000): 60–107.

Shumaker, David. "The Origins and Development of Cooperation in Central Europe." *East European Quarterly* (fall 1993): 351–373.

Simon, Jeffrey. "Does Eastern Europe Belong in NATO?" *Orbis* (winter 1993): 21–35.

———. "Czechoslovakia's Velvet Divorce: Visegrad Cohesion and European Fault Lines." Institute for National Strategic Studies, National Defense University, McNair Paper 23 (October 1993).

Skorzynski, Zygmunt. "Konwersatorium i Fundacja 'Polska w Europie'" [The Seminar and Foundation 'Poland in Europe']. *Polska w Europie*, (May 1990): 98–100.

Skubiszewski, Krzysztof. "Inauguracyjne posiedzenie Rady Konsultacyjnej przy Prze-wodniczacym Rady Panstwa" [Inaugural Meeting of the Consultative Council by the Presiding State Council]. *Rada Naradowa* (21 March 1987): 2–3.

—————. "Problemy polskiej emigracji" [Problems of Polish Emigration]. *Rada Na-radowa* (2 July 1988): 4–5.

Snyder, Glenn H. "Alliance, Balance, and Stability." *International Organization*, 45 (winter 1991): 121–142.

Spero, Joshua. "The Budapest-Prague-Warsaw Triangle: Central European Security after the Visegrad Summit." *European Security*, vol. 1, no. 1 (spring 1992): 58–83.

Spero, Joshua, and Frank Umbach. *NATO's Security Challenge to the East and the American-German Geo-Strategic Partnership in Europe.* Bundesinstitut fur ost-wissenschaftliche und internationale Studien, Cologne, Germany (1994).

—————. "Evolving Security in Central Europe." *Military Review*, vol. 74, no. 2 (Feb-ruary 1994): 56–63.

—————. "The International Coalition against Terrorism." *Insight Magazine* (3 Decem-ber 2001): 41–43.

—————. "Beyond Old and New Europe." *Current History* (March 2004): 135–138

Stent, Angela. *The Soviet Union, Eastern and Western Europe before and after German Unification.* The National Council for Soviet and East European Research. (Octo-ber 1990).

Szayna, Thomas S. "Addressing 'Blank Spots' in Polish-Soviet Relations." *Problems of Communism*, vol. 37, no. 6 (November–December 1988): 37–61.

—————. *Polish Foreign Policy under a Non-Communist Government: Prospects and Problems.* (Santa Monica, Calif.: RAND, 1990).

Szukalski, Wieslaw. "Geopolityczne warunki dla realizacji suwerennosci narodow Eu-ropy Wschodniej" [The Geopolitical Stipulation for the Realization of Sover-eignty of the Eastern European Nations]. *Oboz* (November 1987): 47–54.

Talbott, Strobe. "Why NATO Should Grow." *New York Review of Books*, vol. 42, no. 13 (10 August 1995): 22–35.

Thomas, Timothy. "The Significance of the Cracow Summit." *European Security*, vol. 1, no. 1 (spring 1992): 101–108.

Tokes, Rudolf L. "From Visegrad to Krakow: Cooperation, Competition, and Coexis-tence in Central Europe." *Problems of Communism*, vol. 40, no. 6 (November–December 1991): 100–114.

Umbach, Frank. "Die Evolution des Warschauer Paktes als aussen—und militarpolitische Instrument sowjetischer Sicherheitspolitik 1955-1991" [The Evolution of the Warsaw PactExternall—The Military–Political Instrument of Soviet Security, 1955–1991]. Ph.D. dissertation, University of Bonn, 1995.

Vachudova, Milada Anna. "The Visegrad Four: No Alternative to Cooperation?" *RFE/RL Research Report*, no. 34 (27 August 1993): 33–47.

Wallander, Celeste A. "Institutional Assets and Adaptability: NATO after the Cold War." *International Organization*, vol. 54, no. 4 (autumn 2000): 705–735.

Walt, Stephen M. "Alliance Formation and the Balance of World Power." *International Security*, vol. 9, no. 4 (spring 1985): 3–43.

—————. "Alliances, Threats, and US Grand Strategy: A Reply to Kaufman and Labs—Balancing vs. Bandwagoning: A Debate." *Security Studies*, vol. 1, no. 3 (spring 1992): 448–482.

Waltz, Kenneth N. "Structural Realism after the Cold War." *International Security*, vol. 25, no. 1 (summer 2000): 5–41.

Wandycz, Piotr. "Poland's Place in Europe in the Concepts of Pilsudski and Dmowski." *East European Politics and Societies* (fall 1990): 451–468.

Weisser, Ulrich. *Toward a New Security Structure in and for Europe: A German Perspective.* Santa Monica, Calif.: RAND, 1990.

Wettig, Gerhard. "German Unification and European Security." *Aussenpolitik* (1/1991): 13–19.

Weydenthal, Jan B. de. "The Visegrad Summit." *Report on Eastern Europe* (1 March 1991): 28.

———. "Polish-Ukrainian Rapprochement." *RFE/RL Research Report* (28 February 1992): 25–27.

———. "Political Problems Affect Security Work in Poland." *RFE/RL Research Report* no. 16 (17 April 1992).

———. "Poland Supports the Triangle as a Means to Reach Other Goals." *RL/RFE Weekly Report* vol. 1, no. 23 (5 June 1992).

———. "Poland and Russia Open a New chapter in Their Relations." *RFE/RL Research Report* no. 25 (19 June 1992).

———. "Poland on Its Own: The Conduct of Foreign Policy." *RL/RFE Research Report* vol. 2, no. 2 (January 1993): 1–4.

———. "Poland's Security Policy." *RL/RFE Research Report* vol. 2, no. 14 (2 April 1993).

———. "The EC and Central Europe: A Difficult Relationship." *RFE/RL* vol. 2, no. 21 (21 May 1993): 7–9.

Woerner, Manfred. "NATO, Polska, Europa." (NATO, Poland, Europe.) *Polska w Europie* (January 1991): 3–18.

Wolczuk, Roman. "Ukrainian-Polish Relations Between 1991–1998: From the Declarative to the Substantive." *European Security*, vol. 9, no. 1 (spring 2000): 127–156.

Zartman, I. William. "Negotiating from Asymmetry." *Negotiation Journal* I (February 1985): 121–138.

———. "In Search of Common Elements in the Analysis of the Negotiation Process." Negotiation *Journal* (January 1988): 1–14.

Zielonka, Jan. "Security in Central Europe: Sources of Instability in Hungary, Poland and the Czech and Slovak Republics with recommendations for Western policy." *Adelphi Paper* 272 (autumn 1992).

Zubek, Voytek. "Walesa's Leadership and Poland's Transition." *Problems of Communism*, nos. 1-2 (January–April 1991): 69–83.

Interviews

Ananicz, Andrzej, Deputy Director, Soviet Section, *MSZ*; Under Secretary of State, Chancellery, Office of the President, Warsaw, 9 June 1991; Warsaw, 10 June 1994.

Baba, Ivan, Director of Policy Planning, Hungarian Ministry of Foreign Affairs, Budapest, 18 June 1991.

Chabiera, Tadeusz, member of the Senate Center of International Studies; member of the National Security Bureau, Warsaw, 9 June 1991; Warsaw, 10 June 1994.

Czaputowicz, Jacek, member of the Policy Planning Staff, Ministry of Foreign Affairs, Warsaw, 8 June 1994.

Dziewanowski, Kazimierz, Ambassador to the United States and Op-Ed writer, *Rzeczpospolita*, Warsaw, 13 June 1994.

Gebert, Konstanty, Deputy Director, *Gazeta Wyborcza*, Warsaw, 6 June 1994.

Hajnicz, Artur, Analyst, Senate Center of International Studies and German specialist to Skubiszewski, Warsaw, 9 June 1991; Warsaw, 10 June 1994.

Handzlik, Mariusz, former advisor to Prime Minister Suchocka; member of staff to prime minister; and First Secretary and Counselor, Polish Embassy in Washington, D.C., Warsaw and Lublin, 12–15 June 1994; Washington, D.C., numerous conversations, September 1994–April 2000.

Kaczynski, Lech, Minister of State for National Security, Warsaw, 11 June 1991.

Kaminski, Andrzej, Director, Polish Institute of International Affairs (*MSZ*), Warsaw, 10 January 1992; Washington, D.C., 15 April 1993; Warsaw, 13 June 1994.

Karkoszka, Andrzej, Director of Plans, Ministry of Defense and Deputy Minister of Defense, Washington, 10 March 1995; Warsaw, 10 September 1997.

Kostrzewa-Zorbas, Grzegorz, Deputy Director, *MSZ* Department of Europe; Chief Negotiator, Soviet Troop Withdrawal Negotiations; Chief Negotiator, Polish–Soviet Bilateral Treaty Negotiations; and Director of Policy Planning, Ministry of Defense, Warsaw, 30 August 1990; Oslo, Norway, 4–6 February 1991; Washington, D.C., on 20 March 1991; Warsaw, 9–11 June 1991; Washington, D.C., 28 August 1992; Washington, D.C., 25 March 1993; Washington, D.C., 15 October 1993; Washington, D.C., 25 March 1997; Washington, D.C., 17 March 1998.

Koziej, Stanislaw, specialist on Polish military doctrine, General Staff Academy; member, National Security Bureau, Ft. Leavenworth, Kansas, 10–15 May 1993; Washington, D.C., 16–17 May 1993; Warsaw, 13 June 1994.

Kurkiewicz, Michal, Policy Planner, Soviet Section, *MSZ*, Washington, D.C., 20 July 1990, and Warsaw, 10 June 1991.

Kuzniar, Roman, staff, Policy Planning, *MSZ*, Warsaw, 9 June 1994.

Lasota, Eligiusz, staff, Senate Center of International Studies, Warsaw, 9 June 1991; Warsaw, 10 June 1994.

Makarczyk, Jerzy, Vice Minister of Foreign Affairs, Washington, D.C., 20 March 1991.

Milewski, Jerzy, Director, National Security Bureau, Washington, D.C., 15 May 1991.

Najder, Zdzislaw, Advisor, Chancellery, Office of President, Warsaw, 12 June 1991.

Nowakowski, Jerzy Marek, staff, Senate Center of International Studies, Warsaw, 9 June 1991; Warsaw, 10 June 1994.

Onyszkiewicz, Janusz, parliamentarian, Warsaw, 10 June 1994.

Parys, Jan, staff, National Security Bureau; Minister of Defense, Washington, D.C., 15 May 1991; Warsaw, 13 January 1992; Washington, D.C., 28 August 1992.

Rokita, Jan Maria, parliamentarian; former advisor to Prime Minister Suchocka, Warsaw, 10 June 1994.

Sikorski, Radek, former Vice Minister of Defense, Washington, D.C., 5 November 1993.

Skorzynski, Zygmunt, staff, Senate Center of International Studies, Warsaw, 9 June 1991; Warsaw, 10 June 1994.

Soloch, Pawel, staff, Policy Planning, *MSZ*, Policy Planning, Ministry of Defense, 12 June 1991.

Suchocka, Hanna, parliamentarian and former Prime Minister, Warsaw, 10 June 1994.

Szczepanski, Petr, Third Secretary, Polish Embassy, Washington; Vice President, Warsaw Water Foundation, numerous conversations, March 1990–March 1991; Warsaw, 10–14 June 1994; Warsaw, 10 February 1997.

Szlajfer, Henryk, Deputy Director, Polish Institute of International Affairs, *MSZ*; Director of Plans and Studies, *MSZ*, Warsaw and Washington, D.C., numerous conversations, October 1990–February 1997.

Towpik, Andrzej, Director, Department of European Institutions, *MSZ*; Ambassador to NATO, Warsaw, 10 June 1991.

Winid, Boguslaw, First Secretary, Polish Embassy Washington, D.C., numerous conversations, 1992–1996.

Wisniewski, Grzegorz, staff, European Department, General Staff; Director, NATO Policy Department, Ministry of Defense; Defense Advisor, Polish Mission, NATO, numerous conversations, January 1992–March 2000.

Wyganowski, Michael, Third Secretary, Polish Embassy in Washington, D.C., numerous conversations, 1993–1997.

Zielke, Krzysztof, former Deputy Director, Policy Planning, Ministry of Defense; staff member, National Security Bureau, Washington, D.C., 15 June 1993; Warsaw, 18 October 1993.

Index

About the Author

Dr. Joshua B. Spero is an assistant professor of political science in the Department of Social Sciences at Fitchburg State College (Fitchburg, Massachusetts). He has also taught at Merrimack College and Dartmouth College, specializing in international politics (European and Eurasian security), national security decisionmaking, U.S. foreign policy, international organization, and comparative politics. Previously, he held policymaking and research positions at the Joint Chiefs of Staff (European and NATO Division, J-5 Directorate for Strategic Plans and Policy); Institute for National Strategic Studies (National Defense University); Office of the Secretary of Defense; and Foreign Military Studies Office. Dr. Spero's publications include numerous articles and book chapters. He consults for various international affairs organizations and is a member of the Council on Foreign Relations; American Political Science Association; International Studies Association; International Institute for Strategic Studies; Women in International Security; and Atlantic Council (Academic Associate). He holds a Ph.D. from the Johns Hopkins University School of Advanced International Studies and, on 12 March 2003, the fourth anniversary of NATO membership for the Republic of Poland, Dr. Spero received the Knight Cross of the Order of Merit from the Polish President.